2 GRO
R.A

2 GROUP R.A.F.

A Complete History, 1936–1945

Michael J. F. Bowyer

FABER AND FABER
London · Boston

First published in 1974
by Faber and Faber Limited
3 Queen Square London WC1
First published in Faber Paperbacks in 1979
Printed in Great Britain by
Robert MacLehose and Company Limited
Printers to the University of Glasgow
All rights reserved

British Library Cataloguing in Publication Data

Bowyer, Michael John Frederick
  2 Group RAF.
  1. World War, 1939–1945—Aerial Operations, British
  2. Great Britain. Royal Air Force. Bomber Command.
  No. 2 (B) Group
  I. Title   II. Two Group RAF
  940.54'21   D786

  ISBN 0–571–11460–1 (pbk)
  ISBN 0–571–09491–0

'But each one, man for man, has won imperishable praise. . . . Take these men for your example. Like them, remember that prosperity can only be for the free; that freedom is the sure possession of those alone who have the courage to defend it.'

From the Funeral Oration of
Pericles (429 B.C.)

Contents

List of Illustrations

Between pages 160 and 161

Between pages 192 and 193

Between pages 224 and 225

Between pages 256 and 257

List of Maps and Charts

Abbreviations and Terms

A.A.S.	Air Armament School
A.A.S.F.	Advanced Air Striking Force
A.O.C.	Air Officer Commanding
A.O.S.	Air Observer School
A.P.	Aiming point
A.P.C.	Armament Practice Camp
A.S.R.	Air-Sea Rescue
B.A.T. Flight	Blind Approach Training Flight
BFA	Category 'B' flying accident
'Bomphoon'	Typhoon fighter fitted out to carry bombs
C.A.S.	Chief of the Air Staff
Circus	An operation strongly escorted by fighters and designed to draw enemy fighters into combat
Close escort	The role of the fighter escort was direct protection of a bomber force. Close escort indicated that the fighter force was in the immediate vicinity of the bombers
Comm. Flt.	Communications-Flight
E-FA	Category E (write-off) as a result of a flying accident
E-FB	Category E (write-off) as a result of battle damage
Escort cover	The role of the escort cover was to cover the bombers and their close escort from fighter attack throughout the *Circus* or *Ramrod* operation
FBO3	Another title for 'EFB', i.e. Category 3 (write-off) as a result of battle damage
F.P.U.	Film Production Unit
Freshman	Short-range operation to introduce bomber crews to bombing operations, usually flown against the Channel ports
FTR	Failed to return
F24 camera	Film camera (as opposed to plate camera), Type 24
Fw 58	Twin-engined enemy training aircraft
Gee/Gee-H	Radio/radar navigational aids
G.O.I.	Group Operations Instruction

G.O.O.	Group Operations Order
G.P. bombs	General purpose bombs
H/F R/T	High frequency radio telephony
High cover/ Top cover	High-level fighter cover to protect bomber and fighter formations from attacks from above
Hs 126	Henschel 126 army co-operation monoplane
I.A.S.	Indicated air speed
I.E.	Initial equipment of a squadron
I.R.	Immediate aircraft reserve held by a squadron
JG	Luftwaffe Jagdgeschwader (fighter squadron)
KG	Kampfgeschwader (bomber squadron)
Mae West	Life jacket
M.C.T.D.	Medium capacity bomb with temporary delay fuse, usually 11 seconds
Me/Bf	Me/Bf 109, Me/Bf 110: German fighters, correctly styled Bf 109, Bf 110
Met. Flt.	Meteorological-Flight
Mk. XIV bomb sight	Auto-stabilised (gyroscopically controlled) bomb sight
M.R.C.P.	Mobile Radar Control Post
M.T.B.	Motor torpedo boat
M.T.U.	Mosquito Training Unit
M.U.	Maintenance Unit
Nav. Flt.	Navigation-Flight
O.A.P.U.	Overseas Air Preparation Unit
Operation Fuller	Operation to prevent the passage of German capital ships through the English Channel
O.T.U.	Operational Training Unit
P.F.F. (8 Group)	Pathfinder Force controlled by No. 8 (Bomber) Group
P.R.U.	Photographic Reconnaissance Unit
R.A.E.	Royal Aircraft Establishment, Farnborough
Ramrod	Bombing operation (fighter escorted) designed primarily to destroy a specified target
Ranger	Fighter/fighter-bomber deep penetration operation during which targets of opportunity were attacked. Similar to an intruder operation, but the latter was directed against a specific target
Rear support	Its role was to provide cover to a fighter and bomber Circus or Ramrod during the final phase of withdrawal to Britain
Rhubarb	Low-level ground attack sortie by fighter aircraft
RIW	Repaired in Works
Rodeo	Code name for a fighter sweep
S.A.P. bomb	Semi-armour-piercing bomb
S.A.S.O.	Senior Air Staff Officer

Satellite station	Airfield close to the main base intended to accommodate detachment of aircraft up to squadron strength in order to afford maximum dispersal, giving good chance of safety in the event of heavy enemy air attack
SCI	Smoke curtain installation—equipment for laying smoke screen, an alternative to dropping smoke bombs
2nd T.A.F.	2nd Tactical Air Force
S.H.Q.	Station Headquarters
S.O.C.	Struck off charge
Squealer	Small enemy ship equipped with radio equipment to report movements of R.A.F. aircraft
Support (forward, rear, area, target)	The term implied maintaining air superiority in a given area at a given time in order to afford freedom of action to an attacking force
Target X/1A/114, etc.	Method of specifically identifying a flying-bomb site
T.A.S.	True air speed
V-1	Jet propelled flying-bomb
R.A.F. V.R.	R.A.F. Volunteer Reserve
Withdrawal cover	Alternative term for rear support; fighter cover given to a withdrawing *Circus* or *Ramrod* operation
W/T	Wireless telegraphy
XV Sqn.	Distinctive manner of titling of No. 15 (Bomber) Squadron

List of Appendices

Origins and Acknowledgements

It was Empire Air Day, 1938, the venue Duxford. Three of the new secret Blenheims raced low across the field. The siren wailed and 19 Squadron pursued them in its aging Gauntlets. In truth they were unable to catch the intruders, but smoke was induced to stream from the Blenheims in mock success.

It was June 1940. Scattered around Wyton on their dispersals were the Blenheims of XV and 40 Squadrons. There was feverish activity around them, then their engines coughed, spewed grey smoke and burst into life. A few moments later in vics of three many were airborne, an impressive but equally pathetic sight. How many, I wondered, would survive the ordeal through which 2 Group was passing?

It was a chilly grey November afternoon in 1942. Within moments the distant roar of aircraft engines resolved itself into a grand armada of Venturas literally at rooftop height. 2 Group was clearly practising for something special.

It was April 1943, when I found myself in the Nissen hut that served as the Officers' Mess among the pines of Methwold. As a young guest of the Mess, I was thrilled to take tea with the crews of 464 and 487 Squadrons. Security was rampant, but the stories that were related to an impressionable teenager for all his short life devoted to the Royal Air Force would remain for ever. The crews were just back from Ostend chemical works, another *Circus* complete, and clearly these men in their uniforms of mixed hue were relieved. There must, I thought, be a grand story to gather from those days, and surely it would one day be told, for I knew then that 2 Group was something special. Closely knit, it had gathered within it a relatively small number of men who were extremely loyal to it; men who, despite the horror through which it had passed, were nevertheless constantly attracted to it at all times.

Thirty years have passed since that April day—and still little has been told of 2 Group's valiant war, although some of its spectacular operations have been widely related. But of the days when its blood more freely flowed little has been heard. Long sensing that here was a gap in published Royal Air Force history I determined that such heroism must be recorded.

One of the most exciting aspects of research for such a work is the meeting it brings with many of those involved in the story. First, however, I turned to the Royal Air Force Air Historical Branch. Here my suggestion for a 2 Group book won ready support from its then head, Mr. Louis Jackets, who at all times took a very great interest in the progress of my lengthy and deep research into the Ministry's archives. Following the retirement of Mr. Jackets, Grp. Capt. E. Haslam became Head of the Branch, and he continued to give me equal encouragement in what has proved to be a massive undertaking. My initial thanks go to them, and also to their ever willing Staff and in particular to Mr. Eric Turner always ready with practical assistance, Mr. Sidney Bostock who brought his special learning to individual aspects of compilation, and to Mr. N. G. Hoskins who helped in particular with the tedious research needed to produce some of the maps. Without the help of all these people, who over many years have aided me, I would never have been able to complete my task.

Shortly after I had begun the work I made contact with Eric Chandler who served for many years in the Group, and from whom I prised some stories of operations he could recall. It was he who introduced me to his friend 'Watty', Wg. Cdr. T. J. Watkins, from whom I was able to obtain the grim tale that opens this book.

Soon I was meeting many whose names I knew well from the war years, people I had always longed to meet but had never expected to. One such, ever ready to help, has been Grp. Capt. J. E. Pelly-Fry, Boston leader on the famous Eindhoven raid.

I shall always cherish the day I spent with Shaw Kennedy. In ailing health, he still made a magnificent effort to tell me of his experiences with the Group. A person of very great charm who was taken from us a few months ago.

From Bill Edrich I heard of his days on 107 Squadron, and clearly the memory of that time was indelible.

Repeatedly I was told 'You must meet Attie.' This I was privileged to do and he gave me very considerable assistance. Wg. Cdr. L. V. E. Atkinson served with great distinction, and was able to paint a vivid account of the terrible days in Malta.

Grp. Capt. K. C. Doran, D.F.C., very kindly wrote for me an account of 2 Group's first bombing raid of the war. For this unique story I am much indebted to him. From Peter Sarll came his recollections of 2 Group during the pre-war days and the fearful weeks of May 1940. The account of operations with the high-flying Fortresses was checked by Sqn. Ldr. P. Sturmey and Wg. Cdr. Robertson.

Many of the 2 Group people I wanted to meet were in lands far away. One such was John Bergrren, a distinguished member of the Mosquito Light Bomber Wing. To my great delight he recorded the story of a Mosquito raid and this forms the content of one chapter. Similarly, Grp. Capt. Edmund Nelson committed his memories to tape and I have used extracts from this recording for my book. Also from Rhodesia came the contributions of Wg. Cdr. Jack Meakin, long a member of the Group.

Eric Chandler very kindly submitted my original draft of the chapter on Malta to the commander there at the time, Air Chief Marshal Sir Hugh Pughe Lloyd, who very kindly read it and very helpfully commented upon it.

George Parry, leader of the 1942 Oslo raid, told his story of that day. Victor Duffill recalled the catastrophic raid on Amsterdam on 3 May 1943, whereupon Grp. Capt. Leonard Trent, V.C., was able to add some material. From Rupert North I heard of his experiences on the same operation, and Reggie Goude told of his memories of the Eindhoven raid. John Hadland talked about his days on the Mitchells and R. Daughton of the time he spent with 21 Squadron.

Thanks are due to the Dean of Ely Cathedral for the assistance he gave in permitting access to the Group roll of honour.

Very kind contributions of material have been made by Bob Kirby who obtained for me the story of R. E. Hunter's 1940 experiences.

At an 88 Squadron reunion to which I was very kindly invited by Frank Coxall I was able to meet John Reeve, a very experienced Boston pilot, and his wartime colleague Freddie Deeks. Both helped me greatly and Freddie Deeks made some major contributions to the book. The late Wg. Cdr. 'Robbie' Robinson invited me along to a 2 Group reunion where I was able to make contact with others who served the formation well, including in particular A. H. Riseley. Leslie Hunt, who had written *A Short History of 2 Group*, very readily made his records and photographs available, and from Air Vice-Marshal 'Digger' Magill I heard of the introduction of the Mitchell. Wg. Cdr. A. F. Carlisle made very helpful suggestions concerning the story of the Eindhoven raid and provided me with some excellent illustrations for the book.

Gerrit Zwanenburg, a fine friend of the Royal Air Force, helped me in many ways, likewise Sqn. Ldr. Tim Mason, Bruce Robertson, B. T. Gibbins, R. H. Finlayson, E. Hine of the Imperial War Museum who helped with photograph selection, the Royal Netherlands Navy, the French Air Force Historical Branch, Alan Wright, Miss Ann C. Tilbury of *Flight International* who also helped with photograph selection, and John Rawlings whose lifelong admiration of the Royal Air Force brought him and me together. From Peter Corbell I was able to obtain much useful material about the training units which formed part of the Group.

The beautifully executed maps are the work of Alfred M. Alderson, and I am extremely grateful to him for his very fine contribution.

Jorgen Helme made some excellent contributions about the air war over Denmark, and his original research provided much new material.

I missed very much the many hours of companionship that were such a part of *Mosquito* where I worked so closely with Martin C. Sharp. I realised as I wrote this volume just how much he taught me when the earlier book was written. He has contributed some photographs to this volume.

When the book was almost complete I turned to a friend of many years' standing, Keith Braybrooke, with a strong interest in the Royal Air Force. Keith meticulously took on the task of reading the book for me and made most valuable comments on the text and later assisted me with proof reading. His contribution was only equalled in such respects by that of my wife who readily took on the chore of typing the manuscript and gave me repeated encouragement when the labour was hard.

Thanks are due to the Controller of HMSO for permission to quote from some Official documents. Opinions expressed are those of the author and some contributors.

M.J.F.B.

Cambridge, May 1972

Prologue
The Ways of War

Watton was a typical pre-war 2 Group airfield. Huge hangars flanked a tarmac apron on the south side. A perimeter track encircled a grass flying field. Metalled runways were non-existent on 2 Group airfields in early days of the war. Well camouflaged, Watton was set close to a sleepy country town in Norfolk.

It was May 1940. The 'phoney war' had vanished, with Hitler's invasion of Norway and the assault on the Low Countries. Holland had fallen and the German mechanical might had thrust into Belgium.

On Watton's dispersals Blenheim bombers of 82 Squadron waited hesitantly for action. Three times they had been hurled into battle to support the British Expeditionary Force. 82 Squadron was experiencing interminable standbys at varying states of readiness. Today was to be different.

For 2 Group there had never been a 'phoney war'. From the start it was action, bitter bloody conflict for a highly spirited, finely disciplined assembly of talented, courageous men. From the first day of war 2 Group's Blenheims reached into enemy air space whilst the rest of Bomber Command was largely held back from such action. The rape of Norway ended that. Now the butchery of Holland and Belgium left none in doubt that the struggle was for mastery of Europe.

2 Group was at this time a bomber force made ready during darkness for the daylight ahead. Work for the ground crews seemed endless as they slaved to prepare the aircraft to face a vicious, efficient foe.

It was still dark on this fateful morning when twelve crews of 82 Squadron tumbled from their bunks for the customary egg and bacon or 'cowboy's breakfast'—you took your limited choice.

At 04.00 hours, with dawn still some time off, they gathered in the crew room by one of the huge hangars. Orders were 'Be ready to take-off within the hour should a target come through.' In command was Wg. Cdr. the Earl of Bandon, a long established and ever revered figure in 2 Group. At the head of the assembly was Sqn. Ldr. 'Paddy' Delap, his strong Irish overtones matched by those of his able commander. With them was as wide an assortment of officers and other ranks as one could imagine, mostly in their early twenties. All were professional Royal Air Force personnel.

The situation on the Continent was alarming for the Germans had made a breakthrough. It seemed that action must come this day.

Perhaps the greatest problem which Group faced at this time was its lack of up-to-date intelligence. Pitted against fast moving mechanised columns it needed precise details of where and when to attack.

As dawn spread over the battlefield on 17 May the picture was confused. Unhindered, Panzer columns were moving fast by night. Sooner than expected the executive order came through: 'You are to attack an enemy column near Gembloux, where the enemy has broken through.' Watton burst into life.

Around twelve serviceable aircraft activity surged. Ground crews checked that all was well, and manhandled 250-lb. bombs. Soon the crew wagon appeared. As pilots, observers and gunners made their way from a simple briefing, routes in mind, there was an air of grim determination tinged with moments of despondency. 'Open up only if the flak is extremely heavy, close ranks rapidly for mutual protection lest enemy fighters appear.'

From the east the sun streamed through the misty dawn. It was to be another fine warm day, the sort of day when, in a peaceful world, it would be good to breathe the daybreak air and enjoy the dawn chorus. But in the clear sky predicted by the station weather man there were terrifying hazards for unescorted Blenheims.

Ground crews greeted their flight crews, trios tumbling from the transport clutching maps and cluttered by flying kit. Minimum checks were carried out before each man positioned himself in the aircraft. At 04.45 hours twenty-four engines burst into life. With minimum fuss ground crews saw their precious charges pass into hands that had spent years learning to cull the best from their machines. A wave, and they were taxiing out, jostling over the bumpy surface, forming into vics of three for take-off. A final burst of power from each engine, a few puffs of blue smoke, a roar and they were rolling. A few moments and all were away.

Quickly they formed into two tight stepped-up boxes of six, then crossed the airfield climbing towards the southern battlefields.

What lay ahead? First a controlled passage to the exit point, a route notified to the defenders. Thirty minutes' flying and both boxes were running up on Tangmere where, with luck, they might find a group of Hurricane fighters which, if all went well, would tag along to give some measure of protection.

For ten minutes they orbited the famous fighter field. No fighters appeared. There had been a mix-up over timing. Rapid consultation resulted in the order to proceed unescorted. At 8,000 feet, they crossed the calm Channel and then the French coast near Le Touquet. A flight of about 110 miles lay ahead. Below passed countless villages with names familiar to the older generation, then they passed close to Lille. The enemy had yet to penetrate north-east France, fighting being heaviest in western Belgium. 82 Squadron was bound for a small town about twelve miles north-west of Namur. Thrusts had already been made towards France, the Germans rushing up anti-aircraft guns to defend such successes.

Shortly before 07.00 hours the enemy was alerted—British bombers were approaching an armoured spearhead on the Gembloux–Namur road. This was a tempting target and guns were already in place to afford protection.

Closely packed, the formation was a few moments from target when all Hell was let loose, a barrage of quite unexpected intensity. There was no choice, the formation had to spread to avoid accurate fire. Within seconds Flg. Off. McConnell's machine was a seething mass of flames falling towards the ground.

Sgt. T. J. Watkins had just passed a cigarette and his matches to his observer, Sgt. Algy Lees, asking him to light up for him, when the anti-aircraft guns opened up. The imprint of those next few minutes would last a lifetime.

'We all jinked and weaved, in that beautiful clear blue sky. As suddenly as it had started the flak ceased and, whilst we were spread, the worst happened. About fifteen 109s ripped into us. My rear gunner, L.A.C. Read, was firing back when his guns stopped—we were on fire, the port engine blazing alongside me. I throttled it back, switched off the fuel supply, pulled the nose up and told the crew to bale out. Sgt. Lees just disappeared through the floor hatch in the nose—then I found the roof escape hatch had jammed. There was a Hell of an explosion, and I was out. I think I must have gone on to my back making a half roll or loop. It was all so quick, the air full of smoke. The helmet R/T fitting must have stuck because I skinned my nose as the helmet tore from my head when I left the seat and fell out.

'Within the formation the Me 109s were having a field day shooting bombers out of the sky. Sgt. Grierson's Blenheim belched flames from its mainplane and two others were falling out of the sky a mass of brilliant yellow and red fire and acrid smoke. In a matter of seconds almost the entire formation was shattered, fluttering to earth in a welter of fragments.

'Finding myself in clear air I pulled my parachute ripcord. On the way down little registered, but my aircraft tore past me and hit the ground beneath my feet. I landed in the middle of the pieces. Meanwhile fighters above had waded in and shot down all but one of our Blenheims. Only Sgt. Morrison was to fly home to tell the tale.

'I searched—there was no sign of Algy Lees or his 'chute, and he was never heard of again. I found L.A.C. Read—he had been shot dead.

'I headed south-west by the sun . . . no cigarettes or matches now, when I desperately needed them. Curse it! Germans were everywhere on the roads so I kept to fields and ditches. With my .38 pistol I soon

captured two soldiers behind a haystack. They turned out to be French
so we teamed up, walked for about three hours, and reached a village.
Soon I was in an ambulance bound for Reims, for I had bumped my
knee which was now swollen like a pumpkin, and I had pieces of
shrapnel in my left shoulder. In a street I spotted Plt. Off. Fordham of
"B" Flight. I left the ambulance quickly and joined him. We made our
way to Epinoy and 105 Squadron with whom, a fortnight later, I was
evacuated through Cherbourg.

'My first daughter was born on this day, 17 May, at about 7.00 a.m.,
the time when I was shot down. My wife had received the usual
"Missing" telegram a mere couple of hours after giving birth—that *was*
rough. But I was able to phone her a fortnight later from Southampton.
I was one of the luckier ones.

'I found on rejoining my squadron at Watton that only one Blenheim
had come back, L8858 "W Willie" badly shot about. Morrison flying it
had spun down, recovered at deck level, and flown home on one . . .
it packed up as he scraped over the hedge on finals. At the end of his
landing run the aircraft fell apart. Jock Morrison all but fainted when
he saw what he had flown home. He was killed soon after in a ferry
unit.'

Sgt. Watkins heard more of the story from Sqn. Ldr. Delap, formation
leader. His aircraft had caught fire. He had all but passed out over the
controls as the aircraft spun down in flames. Sgt. Frankie Wyness was
ready to bale out when he found that Delap had collapsed. He took off
his own chest parachute pack, attached it to his pilot, opened the roof
and threw Delap out. Wyness was then able to escape with the aid of
his pilot's parachute. It was a most courageous deed. Both men
eventually met up again at Watton.

When Morrison had landed the entire station had turned out aghast
at the horrific turn of events. It seemed impossible, eleven crews—
thirty-three close friends—perhaps never to be seen again. Almost a
whole squadron wiped out. Mesmerised, the ground crews made their
stunned way back to the hangars and bore the shock for the rest of
their lives.

82 Squadron wiped out . . . or was it? The Earl of Bandon would have
none of this talk. Disband the squadron? Never! 82 must be reformed,
he argued. In France squadrons in similar plight were being amalgamated
or disbanded—there were precedents. But no, 82 must not die. The
courage of those men must live on in a new '82'. But crews and aircraft
were in short supply. No matter, Bandon was adamant, and '82' was
re-established—and it was not many days before some of the survivors
of the carnage were back once more ready for the fray. On 20 May
No. 82 Squadron resumed operations, a mere three days after the
catastrophe.

Of course, it was a highly disciplined unit—W. Off. Paisley, the
squadron discip officer, saw to that. And when '82' wasn't flying they

were marching, so much so that No. 82 (Bomber) Squadron was otherwise known as 'Paisley's 82nd of Foot'.

. . . .

France had fallen. The odds were too great. Throughout June and July 82 Squadron and others of 2 Group were in the thick of the fighting, pitching attacks deep into the Fatherland. They ignored the inadequacy of their equipment, were ever ready to face the dashing Messerschmitts.

Soon the Battle of Britain was at its height, and on Aalborg aerodrome in north Denmark German aircraft massed for possible raids on England. Luftwaffe activity there did not go unheeded. An attack was planned, only to be called off at the last moment—the weather was bad.

Tuesday, 13 August, dawned bright and clear. Again the crews of 82 Squadron assembled at Watton. A long flight—to Aalborg—was detailed to them, and the pre-flight ritual was repeated. Twelve Blenheims led by Wg. Cdr. E. C. Lart took off for the distant target.

An uneventful crossing followed until Sgt. Baren broke radio silence to say his fuel was running out fast, that he must turn about for base. The remainder pressed on heading for the enemy coast which, it was planned, would be crossed near Ringkobing. Puffy white clouds drifted lazily across the azure sky for, once more, it was a beautiful blue day.

A few moments before 10.00 hours a German observation post at Sondervig reported eleven Blenheims flying north-east across the coast. The Germans were alerted to the presence of raiders. At first there was confusion for another report filtered to Luftwaffe Headquarters referred to a formation of Heinkel bombers proceeding north-east. A quick check revealed this was not so. Feldwebel Tessin, the commander there, consulted his maps. Clearly an enemy raid on Aalborg was developing. Over northern Denmark the air raid sirens moaned as 82 Squadron proceeded unmolested on course. Unbeknown to them the enemy was in wait.

At Aalborg the fighter force and the flak units had been brought to readiness, an ambush was prepared. Just before the Blenheims arrived the 6th Staffel of Jadgeschwader 77 were scrambled, led by Oberleutenant Friedrich. Repeating the tactics of three months before the anti-aircraft gunners took careful aim from a steady supply of information on the high-flying bombers. Suddenly these received a shattering reception. In seconds a Blenheim was hit, the yellow flames from an engine marking its course as it fell away. Momentarily its pilot regained control, the Blenheim did a half roll and fell downwards enveloped in flames, crashing with a violent explosion. High above a white parachute fell slowly bringing a lone survivor.

Watchers witnessed a pathetic spectacle unfold. One saw a burning aircraft break in two. He saw two of the crew fight to get clear, but one parachute became entangled with falling wreckage. The other reached some measure of safety in the low water of Limfjorden. He waded ashore where some of the local people quickly assisted him. For a while he rested, dazed, at the water's edge, stunned by sudden calamity. Moments later he was in German hands.

A young impressionable girl watched the drama unfold. She later told how she had seen five Blenheims shot down, mostly in flames. One crashed about forty yards away in shallow water near the island of Egholm, the crew of three sitting helpless in their wreck. Local people waded out and found one man very seriously wounded, with both arms and legs broken and having terrible facial burns. The other two, badly disfigured, were bleeding profusely. With tender care these strangers were lifted from the aircraft and carried to land. A rescue squad took them by motor launch to Aalborg where they were quickly transferred to hospital.

Those five Blenheims shot down all fell to flak. Despite their reception several crews dropped their bombs within, or close to, the two targets, the main airfield and the seaplane base of Küstenfliegergruppe 706.

Remnants of the two boxes turned north-west for escape. It was now that Messerschmitts motored in for the kill. Their onslaught was relentless and a terrific battle took place between Kaas and Pandrup during which five more Blenheims were shot down. The sky over Kaas seemed full of the roar of engines and the chatter of machine guns as the pitched fight took place at quite a low level. In the streets of the little town people took cover for the bullets were ripping past. They soon met two British airmen who had baled out and were walking along a country lane as if disbelieving all that had happened, smoking cigarettes and talking to those in Pandrup who knew their language.

The final exchange of fire took place about noon. Two remaining Blenheims were both making their way along the coast towards Thorop Strand and escape. One, particularly pestered by fighters and already badly damaged, flew in from the sea towards V. Thorup at rooftop height. The whole town shook from the booming as it rushed to and fro in a desperate effort to escape. Odds were too great, it flopped in a field just east of Vust near a main road. Two of the crew were badly wounded, one with a fractured skull and the other, the navigator, with serious skin lesions. Both were taken to the County Hospital in Fjerritslev and miraculously recovered after treatment. Astonishingly the third crew member was uninjured and, after burning all the papers, stayed by his aircraft until the Germans arrived.

What to 82 was a second shattering blow was to the enemy a great success. Unteroffizier Menge was credited with shooting down three Blenheims. Personnel of Flafwache 8 at Sondervig, and the commander of the guns, Hauptmann Wilhelm Letz of 15./Lg-Nachr-Regiment 11, were awarded Iron Crosses of the Second Class.

But even to the enemy the courage of all who had taken part in this grim tragedy was obvious. On 16 August thirteen of the airmen of

82 Squadron were buried with full military honours in the cemetery at Vadum. To this day their graves are tended by those to whom such courageous deeds brought hope in a dim world of despair.

Repeatedly 2 Group lost entire squadrons. For much of the war its losses were excessive since the tasks its crews were called upon to perform were so frequently hazardous. Attacking German columns in France alone, unescorted; streaming smoke in desperately dangerous sorties over the landing forces during the Dieppe raid, fighting the cold in the Flying Fortress miles high over Germany, taking an unarmed Mosquito to Berlin in daylight, or just acting as bait for enemy fighters as so many of 2 Group's crews did: all these tasks called for tremendous courage from some of the most talented of our race. This story is of their part in the campaign for ultimate victory.

Chapter 1
Shadows of Conflict

Small, and highly professional, the Royal Air Force of the 1930s policed an empire. When the need for expansion arose this cadre, owing its origin to far-sighted Lord Trenchard, was made ready to face Hitler and Mussolini.

Plans for vast expansion in terms of men and machines were hurriedly drawn up. Right-wing politicians readily accepted the need for expansion whilst the Left showed a regrettable unreadiness to accept realistic appraisal of a serious situation. Under the third scheme—by which an expanded force was to exist by 1937—there would be seventy bomber squadrons, twice the number of fighter squadrons. It was argued that the ultimate shield rested in a strong bomber force realistically equipped with fast, monoplane, light, medium and heavy bombers operating from new and well-protected bases in eastern England. Basic thinking never altered despite many amendments to the plans.

Policy thus agreed, attention turned to the structure of the air force. Hitherto overall command lay in the hands of the A.O.C., Air Defence of Great Britain. It was now argued that it would be better to have independent commanders of defensive and offensive forces. Each could be divided into Groups within Commands. Each Command would have a specific role. A bomber force commander could judge his response to enemy action, leaving protection of the home base to the fighter commander.

In 1935 it was decided to establish Fighter and Bomber Commands. Even before Headquarters Bomber Command came into being on 14 July 1936, its Groups were forming. Already the Air Staff had agreed that Bomber Command would, if needs be, wage a strategic offensive against Germany. The first Bomber Group to form was No. 2—and it differed from the others in that it was intended as an army support organisation. It never entirely neglected its *raison d'être* from the moment it became the spearhead of Bomber Command until its demise, although frequently it operated outside this intended framework.

No. 2 (Bomber) Group was established at Abingdon on 20 March 1936, under Grp. Capt. L. J. E. Twistleton-Wickham-Fiennes. H.Q. Staff slowly assembled and on 14 July, the day Bomber Command formed, Wg. Cdr. P. H. Cummings was posted in for Air Staff duties.

B

Wg. Cdr. F. H. Lawrence arrived as Senior Personnel Staff Officer and
Flt. Lt. C. V. J. Pratt to attend to armament duties. All were experienced,
long-service officers.

The large bombers of 3 Group were stationed in East Anglia where
suitable hangars to accommodate them existed. Nos. 1 and 2 Groups
had to lodge where best they could, and were placed over a wide area.
It was 1 August before Nos. 21 and 34 Squadrons brought their
combined strength of Hawker Hind biplanes into 2 Group. These were
based at Abbotsinch. Three days later No. 83 Squadron's six Hinds were
transferred to the Group, and also based in Scotland—in this case at
Turnhouse.

On 6 August Grp. Capt. C. H. Blount, O.B.E., M.C., was posted in as
Senior Air Staff Officer. 21 August saw the transfer of Hucknall from
6 Group, with Nos. 98 and 104 Squadrons which vacated their 1 Group
station, Abingdon near Oxford. Air Commodore S. J. Goble was
appointed A.O.C. 2 Group on 1 September. A start had been made.

Danger of major conflict receded after the Abyssinian war. Bomber
squadrons despatched to the Middle East in October 1935 were being
brought home. In August Nos. 35 and 207 Squadrons returned to
England and on 3 September their twenty-four Fairey Gordon day
bombers joined 2 Group, along with six Hinds of 49 Squadron. All were
based at Worthy Down.

Andover entered 2 Group on 6 October, then strength rapidly rose as
Nos. 103 and 107 Squadrons each with six Hinds, and No. 12 with a
dozen, were added. Staff College was also inherited. Now that strength
had expanded Nos. 21 and 34 Squadrons passed to 1 Group. No further
changes came that year.

Used as we are now to highly sophisticated aeroplanes, enveloped in
a world of advanced technology, it comes hard to realise just how
primitive the R.A.F. of the 1930s was by comparison. All the 2 Group
bombers were still biplanes, in the case of the Gordon two-bay biplanes
festooned with wires and struts, defended by a manually trained rear gun
and having another forward firing for ground strafing. Such bombs as
they carried were small, suitable only for counter-insurgency operations,
carried in clutches beneath the wings.

Radio equipment was almost non-existent. In the mid 30s about one
aircraft in eight had a radio, but by the outbreak of war they all had an
H/F R/T set with a range varying from ten to thirty miles for voice
contact, dependent on height and weather and frequently poor in
quality.

There was no real air traffic control as such. It was enough that a
Duty Pilot sent off a signal to a destination station that an aircraft was
on its way; if he thought it unlikely the telegram would reach the airfield
before the aircraft he remained silent on the matter, sometimes he
telephoned. The roster was such that 'duty pilot' came round about once
in six weeks.

Also missing was a station meteorological office and at a time when weather conditions mattered so much. A route or destination forecast was available from the Central Meteorological Office in London— provided sufficient warning was given. Alternatively, pilots flew on a 'hope and see' basis.

During their five-day week, squadrons practised the art of flying. They practised navigation and the arts of bombing and gunnery, in style far removed from the daily occurrences of the 1940s. Formation flying was important, down to heights of 250 feet, and so was economical flight for maximum range at optimum heights for the engines concerned at optimum engine settings. Cross-country flying, requiring careful map reading by the pilot, also featured as 'W S & D'—Wind Speed and Direction finding. It was a process of measuring drift on various courses and calculating the 'W S & D' from data so obtained which were fed into an elementary computer disc strapped to the pilot's knee, or hanging free on the end of a piece of string. 'W S & D' so found were used to calculate courses to fly for the remainder of the flight. In many cases the aircraft would be flying at 85 to 130 m.p.h., not much above the wind speed experienced at height. Thus, pilots would be practising and improving navigation and map reading skill at heights from 250 to about 20,000 feet facing the cold in a thick, lined, leather suit, carrying limited oxygen and facing an instrument panel adorned by a few elementary gadgets.

About once a year squadrons underwent a month's busy training at an Armament Training Camp at Sutton Bridge, North Coates Fitties or West Freugh. There they actually bombed targets using small smoke bombs from high level, low level or in steep and shallow dives. They fired live bullets into targets on the ground or towed behind other aircraft, which provided keen competition.

Back at the home base they practised bombing on the *camera obscura*. This was a little room like a camera set up facing vertically. The bombing aircraft could be seen on a sheet of paper through the camera arrangement, and a flash of light from a magnesium bulb in the aircraft showed when the bomb aimer pressed the bomb release tit. An armourer on the ground then calculated where the bomb would have fallen. The accuracy of the 'W S & D' expertise which preceded the bombing the accuracy of the bomb run and the pilot's flying skill all came into the following criticism.

Wg. Cdr. T. J. Watkins, recently retired from the Royal Air Force, recalls those days thus: 'This training may sound fearsome, but in fact it was a gentlemanly life. Hangar doors were firmly shut on the aircraft by pack-up time, otherwise there were grim looks from "Chiefy" *the* Flight-Sergeant—except of course when we flew by night doing more or less the same sort of things which we did by day. Life was fun, flying was fun, we flew because we loved it. I actually did some of my courting by courtesy of His Majesty's Royal Air Force. In a Hind from Cranfield

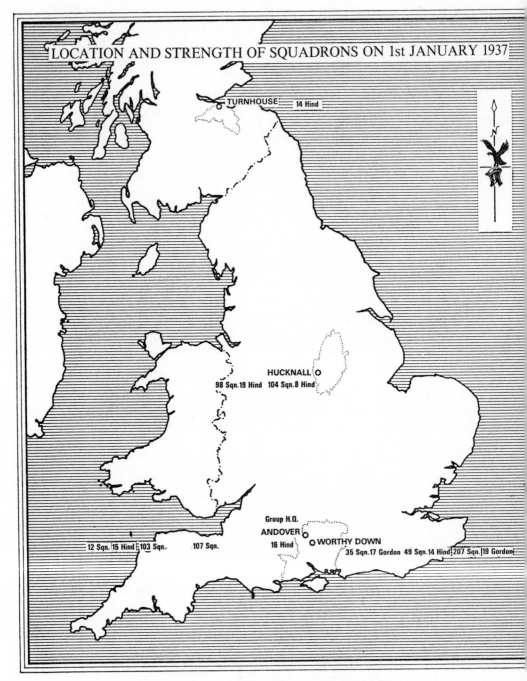

LOCATION AND STRENGTH OF SQUADRONS ON 1st JANUARY 1937

TURNHOUSE   14 Hind

HUCKNALL
98 Sqn.19 Hind   104 Sqn.8 Hind

Group H.Q.
ANDOVER   WORTHY DOWN
16 Hind
12 Sqn. 15 Hind   103 Sqn.   107 Sqn.   35 Sqn.17 Gordon 49 Sqn.14 Hind 207 Sqn. 19 Gordon

MAP 1. *See Appendix 12, page 493 for notes*

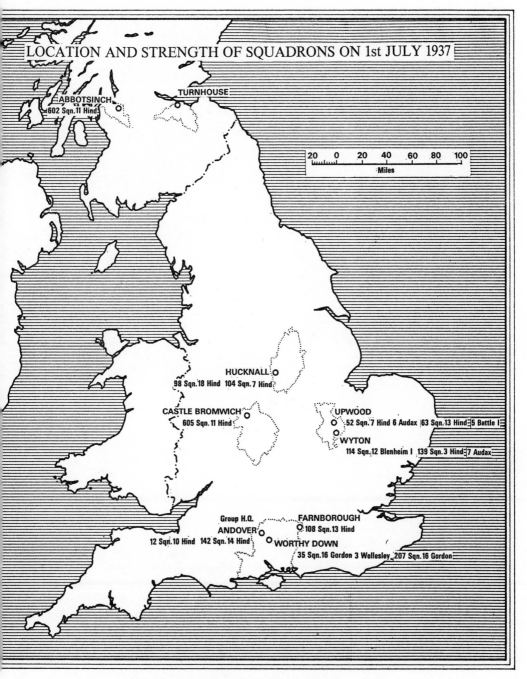

LOCATION AND STRENGTH OF SQUADRONS ON 1st JULY 1937

ABBOTSINCH
602 Sqn. 11 Hind

TURNHOUSE

20 0 20 40 60 80 100
Miles

HUCKNALL
98 Sqn. 18 Hind 104 Sqn. 7 Hind

CASTLE BROMWICH
605 Sqn. 11 Hind

UPWOOD
52 Sqn. 7 Hind 6 Audax | 63 Sqn. 13 Hind 5 Battle I

WYTON
114 Sqn. 12 Blenheim I 139 Sqn. 3 Hind 7 Audax

Group H.Q.
ANDOVER
12 Sqn. 10 Hind 142 Sqn. 14 Hind

FARNBOROUGH
108 Sqn. 13 Hind

WORTHY DOWN
35 Sqn. 16 Gordon 3 Wellesley 207 Sqn. 16 Gordon

MAP 2. *See Appendix 12, pages 493/4 for notes*

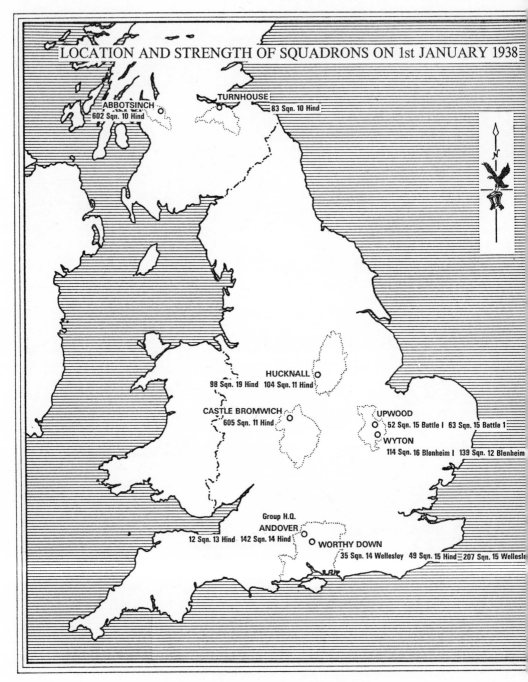

LOCATION AND STRENGTH OF SQUADRONS ON 1st JANUARY 1938

ABBOTSINCH
602 Sqn. 10 Hind

TURNHOUSE
83 Sqn. 10 Hind

HUCKNALL
98 Sqn. 19 Hind   104 Sqn. 11 Hind

CASTLE BROMWICH
605 Sqn. 11 Hind

UPWOOD
52 Sqn. 15 Battle I   63 Sqn. 15 Battle I

WYTON
114 Sqn. 16 Blenheim I   139 Sqn. 12 Blenheim

Group H.Q.
ANDOVER
12 Sqn. 13 Hind   142 Sqn. 14 Hind

WORTHY DOWN
35 Sqn. 14 Wellesley   49 Sqn. 15 Hind   207 Sqn. 15 Wellesley

MAP 3. *See Appendix 12, pages 494/5 for notes*

LOCATION AND STRENGTH OF SQUADRONS ON 28th SEPTEMBER 1938

Mobilised at War Stations.

O ABBOTSINCH
602 Sqn. 14 Hind

20   0   20   40   60   80   100
Miles

201 Bomber Wing
COTTESMORE
35 Sqn. 14 Battle II   98 Sqn. 16 Battle II 1 Hind   207 Sqn. 18 Battle II

CASTLE BROMWICH O
605 Sqn. 18 Hind

Group H.Q.
WYTON
114 Sqn. 23 Blenheim I   139 Sqn. 19 Blenheim I

BASSINGBOURN
104 Sqn. 20 Blenheim I   108 Sqn. 16 Blenheim I

16 Blenheim I   34 Sqn. 16 Blenheim I   57 Sqn. 16 Blenheim I

UPPER HEYFORD O O

CRANFIELD

BICESTER
62 Sqn. 18 Blenheim I   82 Sqn. 23 Blenheim I

90 Sqn. 21 Blenheim I   101 Sqn. 15 Blenheim I

HARWELL O
107 Sqn. 14 Blenheim I

EASTCHURCH
21 Sqn. 16 Blenheim I

MAP 4. *See Appendix 12, page 495 for notes*

I often flew to Castle Bromwich for the weekend. My girl friend—now my wife—was a nurse in Birmingham. The weekend Air Force, the Auxiliaries, would look after my machine and help me to get off again on Monday morning. All very good flying practice because come Hell or highwater weatherwise if I had a date, I got there! And I got back—so as not to jeopardise my chances next time.'

The Hinds and Gordons were already outdated. Their range was limited, their overall performance poor even by contemporary standards. As army co-operation aircraft they were inadequate, but as yet there was nothing with which to replace them. Soon all was to change and in this respect 1937 saw astonishing advances. This was the year of the Vickers Wellesley, the Fairey Battle and—most important—the Bristol Blenheim. Equally important, new airfields came into use. There was participation in the year's Hendon display and the more important annual defence exercise. And training took on a more realistic image.

When the year opened 2 Group was ten squadrons—134 aircraft—strong and based at Andover, Hucknall, Turnhouse and Worthy Down. It was thus widely spread, geographically ill sited. The newest squadron, No. 142, re-formed at Andover on New Year's Day and had twenty Hinds by 20 January. It had recently returned from the Middle East Air Commodore C. H. B. Blount, O.B.E., M.C., became S.A.S.O. the same day, and on the day following Sqn. Ldr. D. A. Boyle took command of 83 Squadron.

Strength further increased with the transfer of No. 605 Squadron, A.A.F., from 6 Group in February. No. 63 Squadron formed at Andover and had on loan seven Hinds from 12 Squadron. No. 107 Squadron moved to Old Sarum and No. 108 became a lodger at Farnborough, both stations situated well for army co-operation. Hawker Audax army co-operation aircraft were introduced in March when 63 Squadron, Upwood, received them since Hinds were in short supply. By the end of March '63' had twelve. With some of 52 Squadron's thirteen Hinds they were employed to search for the Duchess of Bedford missing in the Kettering–St. Neots area after a snowstorm.

Two more squadrons joined the Group in March, Nos. 114 and 139, both flying Hinds. They were based at Wyton, close by Upwood, another 'new' station with a typically chequered start. Wyton stood on the site of a World War One airfield. It opened as a 3 Group base. No. 139 Squadron re-formed there on 3 September 1936, and 114 three months later. Wyton of the 1930s covered a much greater area than the earlier airfield. When 139 formed the only hangar space available was in one of the rickety '14–'18 War wooden sheds. After the doors had been dragged open by tractor it was found impossible to close them for the roof sagged too much. It was necessary to picket the Hinds in the hangar to prevent damage by high winds.

On the south side of the field large 'C' Type hangars were now being built, as at many expansion airfields. The first, No. 1 Hangar, came into use in November 1936. Three others were under way to complete the standard quartet, each intended to accommodate one flight of a pair of two-flight squadrons intended for each bomber base. Squadron accommodation and S.H.Q. were sited in the wooden buildings still partly to be seen on the west side of the aerodrome, until 139 moved into hangar offices on 16 January sharing its accommodation with busy painters and 114 Squadron.

Another difficulty soon manifested itself at Wyton, as indeed at some other new aerodromes. Heavy rain and winter weather rendered the field unserviceable. Drainage problems were apparent. An interesting aspect was that at Wyton one-third of the airfield remained relatively dry, the part which had formed the old flying field. The Station Commander ordered this to be used whilst the remainder was drained. Only a small space was available for taxiing aircraft from tarmac to flying field, and this became a morass. A temporary taxi-track was laid of planks which were frequently moved.

Sqn. Ldr. L. W. Dickens was appointed to command 139 Squadron on 22 January. Almost immediately he was detached to 206 Squadron at Bircham Newton to gain experience on the new Avro Anson, a novelty with its monoplane configuration and retractable undercarriage. Wyton soon buzzed with rumours of what was really afoot.

No. 114 Squadron was also busily preparing itself for the future. By the time of its transfer to 2 Group many pilots had been detached to Bircham Newton to fly Ansons. There was no secret now, both squadrons would soon fly the wonder bomber, the fastest bomber in the world, the Bristol Blenheim.

Its story had already circulated throughout the Air Force. The Bristol Aeroplane Company had designed a high-speed twin-engined monoplane transport for Lord Rothermere. Performance trials at Martlesham impressed the Air Staff tremendously. Then Rothermere generously presented the aeroplane to the nation for more tests, and it became commonly known as the 'Britain First'. Bristol redesigned it as a medium bomber the prototype of which first flew on 25 June 1936. An order for 150, named Bristol Blenheim, had been placed on 22 August 1935. By the end of 1936 no fewer than 1,568 were on order.

There was no aircraft type available upon which to train crews for the new machine, apart from the Anson which little resembled it. This was much slower, less powerful. The Blenheim had landing flaps, the Anson none. Steep angles of approach with power off were already known to cause undershoots with the Blenheim, whereas the Anson's flat guide approach led to overshoots. A long period of float was a feature as the Anson landed and it needed little skill to hold it off, whereas the Blenheim sank fast on finals. Blenheims had variable pitch airscrews, Ansons did not. Retracting the Anson's undercarriage meant so many winds of a handle that it was rarely retracted. The Blenheim's mechanical retraction meant that it was invariably retracted, but not always so

B2

readily lowered. Both were utterly different to the Hind which side-slipped into final approach and stall-landed with the power off, and took a short landing run. With a top speed 100 m.p.h. greater than the Hind the Blenheim weighed more than twice as much, had a third and vital crew member, was quite mighty and outstandingly superior.

With limited training on twin-engined aircraft, 114 Squadron seemed ready for its Blenheims by March. On 10th the first one, K7036, touched down at Wyton. Alas, the pilot braked too hard. The aircraft flipped on to its back and was a total loss. Nevertheless next day six Hinds of the squadron were passed to 44 Squadron which gratefully took them to Andover. Their place was subsequently temporarily taken by six Audaxes from Sealand used whilst initial training took place on Blenheims, five of which (K7035, K7037–40) joined 114 Squadron during March.

Aircraft establishment for 114 Squadron was soon set at sixteen I.E. plus four I.R. aircraft, served by ten officers and 114 men, N.C.O. pilots forming a goodly portion of its strength. The need for an observer introduced a new concept and now a crew working in close co-operation was needed. The third man was the gunner set in a power-operated dorsal turret, an airman receiving a small pittance for flying duties of a very exacting (and in wartime, very dangerous) nature. Complexity of the new aircraft soon made great demands upon the ground staff: maintenance troubles were multiplied and required different skills from those already practised. The engines were now air-cooled radials, the guns different, bombs heavier. The aircraft consumed relatively huge fuel loads and their entire mode of operation was radically different from the Hinds, yet the training programmes were astonishingly simple. During April Audaxes left 114 Squadron passing to No. 105 and out of the Group.

For squadrons re-equipping a new era was born. 'The news broke,' recalls T. J. Watkins. 'We were giving up our beautiful Hinds for short-nosed Blenheims. We flew our Hinds to Bristol, two pilots per Hind. One or two pilots did a quick circuit in Blenheims at Filton sitting alongside the Work's test pilot. No dual. Then we took off in Blenheims and flew in formation back to base. That was the conversion course, that was! We did eventually get the odd dual conversion Blenheim and my log book records that I did 1½ hours flying with a Squadron Leader in three half-hour spasms. God knows what his qualifications were— no more than mine I guessed, except that he was eight years or so older!

'Up to this time we had no navigators/observers. Each pilot picked one of his ground crew, airframe or engine fitter, and trained him in the rudiments of navigation and bomb-aiming. He eventually qualified for an arm badge after gunnery achievements, a brass bullet with wings, a flying bullet. Now with the Blenheim, that high-speed modern monster, we started to have navigators as well. The "flying bullet" chaps were converted to navigators with a little more training, in most cases purely local in the squadron, and emerged as L.A.C.s with a winged "O" on the left breast. By 1939 these chaps wore Corporal's stripes and after war broke out they were often upped to Sergeant. What glory! Parallel with this some wireless operators were trained in gunnery and became W.O.P./A.G.s but remained as A.C.1 or L.A.C. well into the war.'

At Upwood another re-equipment scheme was under way. On 20 May 1937, one of the sleek new Fairey Battle monoplanes (K7559) joined the Upwood circuit. Two days later it was with 63 Squadron and flying frequently during the rest of the month. A machine with very different characteristics to the Hind and Blenheim had joined the Group. Its Merlin engine was a powerful advance over the trusty Kestrel, but the Battle for all its double power weighed much more than a Hind and carried a far greater load. It had a retractable undercarriage, flaps, variable pitch propeller and, like the Blenheim, had an enclosed cockpit—again all new features. Battle delivery was slow but the first machine had dual control which was a great asset for pilot training. But there were already performance deficiencies, manoeuvrability and general performance being poorer than anticipated. During its development the Air Staff expressed disappointment and proceeded with it mainly to retain the labour force at the Fairey and Austin works. Events were to prove early appraisal sadly justified.

June was dominated by training, and execution of plans for the last of the Hendon displays held on 26th. Nos. 52 and 139 Squadrons contributed to the 255-aircraft fly past, and 114 Squadron had five Blenheims attacking a set piece. Upwood's Battle strength meanwhile rose to four aircraft.

Although there were many squadron moves into the Eastern bases at this period, and new units formed, Group strength remained unaltered at fifteen squadrons. On 1 July Bomber Command comprised 58 squadrons—17 in 1 Group, 15 in 3 Group and 11 in No. 4. At Mildenhall 5 Group formed this day.

On 2 July No. 63 Squadron began intensive flight trials with Battles K7562, '63 and '66. Re-arming was elsewhere picking up momentum with the arrival of 139 Squadron's first Blenheim, K7062, on 18 July. At Worthy Down on 30 July No. 35 Squadron began to receive the third new type to enter the Group, the Vickers-Armstrong Wellesley, three of these lanky machines arriving. This strange looking huge-spanned long-range single-engined monoplane of geodetic construction, which handled like a giant sailplane and carried its bomb load in panniers beneath the wings, never became numerous in the Group. It only served two squadrons briefly.

Between 8 and 13 August the annual Home Defence Exercise was held. For the first time 2 Group participated, as part of the Eastland force. The prime purpose was the testing of London's defences. 63's Battles played a small part and the newly acquired Wellesleys managed five raids by day and night including amongst their targets Fighter Command H.Q. at Bentley Priory, the docks at Tilbury and the R.A.F. Depot, Uxbridge. Two days after the exercise ended, a Wellesley Development Flight formed on 35 Squadron, 500 hours' flying being demanded from K7736, '38 and '39.

On 21 August 114 Squadron began temporary detachment at North Coates practice camp. For the first time the Blenheims were away from Wyton. They had been busily exercising their high speed against defending biplane fighters. Spares were short at Wyton, much more so at North Coates, where serviceability was poor. The Blenheims returned home after only forty hours' flying during which there had been little practice, and none for the gunners because the aircraft lacked hydraulically operated turrets.

At the start of September No. 207 Squadron began re-arming with Wellesleys, but it was December before the last Gordon left the Group. By now 63 Squadron had sufficient experience to demonstrate its Battles to the Duke of Aosta, the Egyptian Government, the Belgians and the Chinese Air Force with a view to securing orders for foreign air forces and a means of diverting many Battles presently destined for the R.A.F.

On 19 October it was the turn of the Luftwaffe to see the new British aircraft when Milch, Stumpf, General Major Udet and Staff astonishingly came to Mildenhall to view the latest aircraft and witness a display of air power intended to impress them. What their feelings were on inspecting the latest aircraft may be surmised, but when I saw them in their huge limousines their faces looked grim, their posture most menacing. Battles of 63 Squadron had performed, also Blenheims of 114 Squadron and a Wellesley from No. 35.

Two of the latter's aircraft set out, on 20 October, on what was then considered a long cross-country flight for purposes of range estimation and fuel consumption. Their route was to take them to Sealand–Orfordness–North Coates and back to base. Unfortunately Sgt. Moon flying K7738 crashed at Spilsby, all the occupants being killed. K7551 then replaced '38 in the Development Flight.

Late in October 139 Squadron flew to Aldergrove for armament training, their work being typical of that undertaken at these camps. They flew high-level bombing sorties, dropping live weapons and finding that accuracy was hard to maintain at the high speeds at which the Blenheims flew. The principal fault lay in the pilot's difficulty in carrying out flat turns on to target. Minimum length of the run-in had to be extended and was now set at about eight miles at 200 m.p.h. During high-level practices both the pilot and bomb aimer released weapons, the former by judgement and the latter by using a home-made sight. On low-level attacks the run in was being made at 200 m.p.h. at 250 feet, average bombing error of the fourteen crews being 52 yards. A 'losing height' method also employed meant a run-in at 260 I.A.S. in a thirty-degree dive. At this time tactics were being evolved for all the new aircraft types.

Most of the Group was still flying Hinds but on 9 November No. 52 Squadron began to receive Battles, the second squadron to do so, beginning with K7602. No. 63 Squadron had its full complement of sixteen by the end of the year, by which time Air Commodore C. H. B. Blount had become the new A.O.C.

1938

At the beginning of the year three squadrons were re-arming with Battles and re-equipment indeed pervaded much of the Group. In the Spring more squadrons received Blenheims.

Then followed geographical re-orientation on a grand scale as more squadrons moved on to new airfields situated in East Anglia and the East Midlands. Before the 1930s the only conceivable foe, an unlikely one, had been France. Now there was no question of who the enemy would most likely be.

The new station at Cottesmore, accommodating 35 and 207 Squadrons from Worthy Down, entered the Group on 20 April. Newly built Bassingbourn had opened on 27 March, and Turnhouse passed to 6 Group since it was too far from the likely scene of operations. Although 2 Group made use of Scottish bases when the war came, Turnhouse was still unsuitably located. Andover passed to 1 Group on 15 June, replaced by Cranfield. Upper Heyford figured in the Group's listing during the autumn crisis.

In January there were still only two squadrons of Blenheims, but already much reliance was placed upon the aircraft's high speed. Evidence of this comes, for example, from a report by Plt. Off. C. J. C. Lee of 139 Squadron. During an 11 (Fighter) Group exercise on 18 January his section of Blenheims had three times been intercepted, yet only once could the fighters make a pass—and this out of range of their guns. 'Our speed,' he reported, 'made it impossible for them to come any closer.' He read the facts truly—but the fighters of a passing era were biplanes whose performance did not match that of the coming Hurricane and Spitfire and their contemporary, the Messerschmitt 109. As soon as the R.A.F.'s eight-gun fighters were the mock adversary it was clear that the Blenheim was simply not fast enough.

At Upwood 52 and 63 Squadrons had been busily working up on the Battle. By 1 February they were at set strength, twelve I.E. and four I.R. aircraft. Two had special de-icers fitted for, if they were to operate at a safe height the year round, they must pass ice accretion tests. To gain some idea of the machine's capabilities when fully stretched three Battles, K7562, '63 and '66, were to fly intensive trials with 63 Squadron. Each was to make three flights, each of three hours' duration, on every working day until 21 March. Meanwhile 12 Squadron began to receive Battles starting on 7 February, and 142 Squadron on 4 March.

It was already apparent that, if war came, putting aircraft in hangars overnight as had long been customary, leaving them there at weekends and indeed during the working day, would expose them to a high loss risk in the event of attack. It was decided that they should be dispersed around the airfield perimeters, in some cases in nearby fields, copses and orchards. Even simple dispersal brought difficulties in communications and maintenance problems multiplied when a more elaborate scheme was decided upon. Each airfield was now to have a satellite field from which to operate and to which to disperse its machines and crews, a few miles from the parent station. On 17–18 May 63 Squadron moved to such a satellite base for trials, being accommodated under canvas. This was the first time that a bomber squadron had tried a dispersal system, commonplace during the war. Group's role was such that it needed to be mobile to give the Army support and it was therefore chosen to test the satellite system.

As yet the Battle squadrons had carried no live bombs. During the night of 28–29 June twelve of 63's machines were bombed up in darkness, in itself an unusual and realistic item of training. They took off around 06.16 hours for a mock raid during which they bombed the North Coates range, watched by the A.O.C. and his staff.

The first major exercise using the new aircraft in any strength came on 12–13 July when the entire Group formed part of Eastland's force in preparation for the annual defence exercise. This followed on 5–7 August. Its aims were 'to test the air and ground home defences against air attack, to test the efficiency and organisation of Bomber Command and to afford conditions as realistic as possible for training consistent with safety'. An imaginary balloon barrage was situated around London and the Observer Corps formed part of the defensive force which embraced squadrons of Nos. 3, 5, 11 and 12 Groups. Attackers were drawn from Nos. 1, 2, 4 and 17 Groups. Weather was appalling, so much so that the exercise was literally washed out. This was quite a catastrophe especially as a frightening test of efficiency was all but at hand.

Hardly was the exercise over when war clouds gathered thick and fast. Between 27 September and 8 October a State of Emergency was in force due to the critical Czechoslovakian crisis. All units were ordered to stand by ready to mobilise fully at a moment's notice. War plans split the Group apart, demanding complete reorganisation. In the event of fighting, into 2 Group would come units at Upper Heyford (18, 34 and 57 Squadrons), Bicester (90 and 101 Squadrons), Eastchurch (21 Squadron) and Harwell (107 Squadron), all from 1 Group, whose remaining squadrons would form the Advanced Air Striking Force, which was indeed established on 28 September, the day upon which the two Upwood Battle Squadrons joined 1 Group as training squadrons for the A.A.S.F. Cottesmore's Battle squadrons, Nos. 35, 98 and 207, stood by to form No. 201 Wing and move to Kent, temporarily staying under 2 Group control. Nos. 21 and 107 Squadrons moved to Cottesmore to be ready to replace them. Plans for operational daylight action were deposited in station safes, German airfields being principal targets. The Air Staff feared a knock-out blow on our bomber bases and intended to forestall this. Neville Chamberlain then made his humiliating jaunt to see Hitler and returned with his infamous paper. The danger at least passed, momentarily, and Group ordered normal organisation from 8 October. But nothing would ever be the same again.

Munich left a visible mark on the Blenheims. All aircraft markings except roundels had been obliterated during the crisis. In their place came grey squadron identity letters, and roundels were now of the type applied to night-flying bombers, the alteration demanded by 2 Group on 27 September and not rescinded until the war had begun.

At the height of the Munich crisis when forty-two bomber squadrons were mobilised 2 Group had thirteen Blenheim 1 squadrons, three flying Battle IIs and two auxiliary squadrons with Hinds. Only half the force was ready to fight, and only one biplane remained on first-line strength. Re-equipment was thus no longer the prime task; bringing squadrons to operational efficiency was paramount.

Throughout the crisis, training proceeded apace. On 6 October Bomber Command ordered a massive special exercise. It was to test the refuelling facilities at Watton and West Raynham from which a hefty blow would be mounted against German airfields and the Ruhr power stations under the current war plan. To afford them maximum range the Blenheims would all operate from these two bases whereas the Battles would take part from France. Approximately ninety Blenheims were provided by seven stations for the 24-hour exercise undertaken whilst the Group was still mobilised for war. Aircraft were to take on sufficient fuel for a penetration of Germany. Their flight plans were to take them well out over the North Sea, back to a target in Britain, out to sea again then back to a refuelling base. As well as showing the enemy we were in a serious mood the exercise provided very useful information tying in neatly with another project in hand.

This was range/fuel load trials being undertaken at squadron level. Practice bombing raids were combined with this. Their culmination came on 28 October when a large 2 Group force made a mock low-level raid on Uxbridge. To the end of the year formation exercises were flown, checking fuel consumption and making low-level assaults in which the whole Group was trained. This work continued into 1939, the fateful year.

1939

Apart from exercises and tactical work-out an important event of the first eight months of 1939 was the delivery of the long-nosed' Blenheim IV. Squadron moves continued; with the opening of Watton in March the entire Group was based in East Anglia to take maximum advantage of aircraft duration.

Upper Heyford's two squadrons rejoined 2 Group in January and now frequent flights were being made over the North Sea and some practice gained in mock raids on shipping. On 7 and 9 January three aircraft of 139 Squadron led by Flt. Lt. Scott practised a new rotating vic formation, tried out in the home defence exercise on 10 January. Nos. 1 and 5 Groups joined this, and concentrated attacks were delivered on four areas of eastern England. Six stations despatched aircraft and Nos. 11 and 12 (Fighter) Groups, aided by the Observer Corps and the new radar stations operating in great secrecy, defended the area. The aim of this special exercise was to provide practice for H.Q. staff when bombers were operating through a heavily defended area. Of seventy-eight 2 Group aircraft taking part, only one encountered trouble, a broken fuel pipe. It appeared that low-level raids were able to escape detection: a report stated 'This form of attack is worthy of further investigation', and 2 Group was encouraged to pursue this tactic. A further chance for the radar crews to practise came when 104 Squadron attacked the Bawdsey RDF station.

Another minor home defence exercise took place on 21 February. It was primarily a Fighter Command affair affording a chance to study problems of reinforcing certain Sectors with the full weight of fighters. Enemy bombers were represented by aircraft of 2 and 5 Groups from the same stations that had participated on 10 January. There was some value in it for 2 Group since it showed clearly that converging attacks confused the defenders.

As yet no strategic photographic reconnaissance force existed. 2 Group began to take on this task at about this time. Its Blenheims were now to carry F24 cameras and their crews' hands' held Leicas. 139 Squadron started to specialise in the task.

Battle squadrons were also working out their own new tactics. No. 63 Squadron commenced practising for close-support bombing trials held at Larkhill 15 March. Flights of three aircraft dive-bombed military targets, bombs being released by the pilot. Blenheims of 18 and 57 Squadrons dropped 20 and 40 lb. bombs from containers on to aged tanks, lorries and poles representing troops de-bussing. These trials appear to have been the first in which the monoplane bombers were used in 2 Group's primary role of support for the Army.

Watton, near Thetford, had opened in 6 Group on 4 January 1939. On 22 February 34 Squadron brought its nineteen Blenheims to the station now in 2 Group, followed by No. 21 on 2 March. With them came Peter Sarll who had then served some time with that squadron.

'My earliest recollections of 21 Squadron,' he recalled, 'were at Lympne where I joined it. My first thumbnail memory of names of those days were Pat Murgatroyd, the C.O. (that wonderful, loveable man who taught me what flying really meant in Hawker Hinds), "Paddy" Menaul and Peter Meston, amongst others. I took over as Squadron Adjutant there. We later moved to Eastchurch to re-equip with short-nosed Blenheims and the era of chaos and stupendous bravery began.

'We flew our Hinds to Filton, and picked up short-nosed Blenheims, and, as no one knew how to fly them, this was an amusing epic. We had a card fastened to the control column with instruction Nos. 1, 2, 3, etc. Undercarriage and flaps were being pulled up at odd moments, and it all seemed rather dicey. However, we survived. Skipper Keans was our C.O. and under him we soon picked up expertise and became a very well disciplined day bomber unit. We had tremendous esprit-de-corps, and I think about this time we could hear the trumpets of war and, I am ashamed to say, I was even looking forward to it. I certainly had no love of the Hitler regime and, although totally opposed to politicians, I was nevertheless tremendously loyal at that time to the Air Force and, as always, a great royalist. No-one was going to smash the Monarchy or the Air Force as long as I had anything to do with it.

'We opened Watton where we were joined by 82 Squadron. Having come from Lympne and Eastchurch, this wonderful new station was a great thrill. I think it was about this time that I met the great Paddy Bandon, C.O. of 82 Squadron. He was a fine morale booster—as we were soon to find out—very loyal to the squadron and, in fact, he commanded affection and loyalty from everyone who met him.

'We were City of Norwich Squadron and, as Adjutant under the guidance of our Orderly Room Corporal (Corporal Grayston) who was a great help in administration matters, there was much to do. We were also flying like mad, practising formation work, bombing, navigation, and it seemed to be a world of non-stop work, with some marvellous interludes—parties, etc. Little did we know what was to come.

'But it really wasn't all work and preparation for the storm. One could never forget our Guest Nights before the war. We had incredible characters like Flt. Lt. Sammy Hall, later killed in action, who, I believe, must have been some form of acrobat. Often standing in a group of visitors he would perform his favourite trick of taking a drink and falling backwards straight as a ramrod crashing to the floor to the astonishment of the uninformed and hilarious amusement of the boys. And Coutty (Coutts-Wood), the great little man who looked like Edward G. Robinson, who had a big heart and a tremendous wit, who would go around taking photographs of everyone and everything with his Leica camera. Some of us keen on shooting and riding had great opportunities at Watton, and we also had very pleasant games of tennis with some of the charming young ladies around the district who accompanied us to many of the excellent dances and parties. How different it was all to be so soon.'

All the time operational training was continuing at a great pace, with many flights over the North Sea. On 10 March 139 Squadron led by Sqn. Ldr. Dickens demonstrated low-level bombing for Lord Chatfield who was preparing a report on the Air Force for Parliament. At Bassingbourn 104 Squadron was still carefully measuring fuel consumption on low-level flights.

An entirely new Air Ministry training policy was promulgated on 17 March. 52 and 63 Battle squadrons were now to become non-mobilising training units. The idea was to retain a nucleus of more senior pilots to remain as instructors whilst others were posted to operational units. The place of the latter was to be taken, for three or four months, by R.A.F. Volunteer Reserve pilots and others direct from Service Flying Training Schools. V.R. pilots would then revert to their civilian occupations and rejoin ERFTSs whilst the SFTS men would go to operational units. As 52 and 63 Squadrons were, on paper, part of the A.A.S.F. (to form mainly from 1 Group squadrons) these two units were to remain as mobilising units until May when 1 Group units would be able to form the entire strength of the A.A.S.F. To aid the training programme ten Ansons were allotted to each squadron and an additional ten Battles. The first three Ansons, N5035, '36, '37, arrived at Upwood on 17 March.

Hardly had the change begun to take effect when tension again rose to fever pitch in Central Europe. Upwood, like the other 2 Group stations, was placed on precautionary alert on 24 March. This time the Battles lost their unit markings in favour of squadron identity letters. Serial numbers were painted out on the aircraft and Flights brought up to full establishment. Personnel were recalled from leave. At noon 114 Squadron at Wyton had mustered five serviceable aircraft, seventeen after another 24 hours, twenty-two a day later. It looked as if the balloon would go up so bombs and guns were made ready. No personnel were allowed to travel more than four miles from the stations and officers had to report back every six hours. The crisis was the most serious yet, and this time the aircraft were fuelled and fully armed for daylight raids on enemy airfields. On 28 March the emergency ended and normal leave patterns were resumed, squadrons stood down.

Crisis passed, training resumed more strenuously than ever. Volunteer Reserve pilots arrived on 52 Squadron on 1 April along with some air observers who came to experience modern aircraft before proceeding to squadrons.

It was at this juncture that a new bomber was joining the squadrons. As the Blenheim 1 was entering squadron service in 1937 the Bristol Aeroplane Company were busy designing an interim general-reconnaissance aeroplane based upon the Blenheim to fill the gap between the

Anson and Beaufort and replace the Hector. It had additional wing fuel tanks, but the most striking feature was its lengthened nose. In shape this resembled the Blenheim 1 nose but protruded an extra three feet because it included a position for the navigator/radio operator ahead of, and to the right of, the pilot. This machine first flew on 24 September 1937.

Flight trials showed the windscreen to be too far ahead of the pilot. Re-design followed with the windscreen closer to the pilot and the front part of the nose lowered. The view was still not good enough so a groove was incorporated on the port side, which proved satisfactory. In the summer of 1938 it was decided to introduce the new nose on Blenheims, these aircraft being designated Mk. IV.

L4835, the first Mk. IV, was delivered to the R.A.F. on 19 January 1939. First to be equipped were two army co-operation squadrons, Nos. 53 and 59. L4865 was the first to enter a bomber squadron, No. 90, which received it on 22 March. Thereafter other Blenheim squadrons re-equipped with Mk. IVs in the following order: No. 101 from 5.4.39 (aircraft L4886 initially), No. 114 27.4.39 (N6144), 107 13.7.39 (N6177, 6178, 6180, 6181), 110 26.6.39 (N6199), No. 139 13.7.39 (N6216), No. 82 13.8.39 (P4828) so that by September 1939 seven squadrons in 2 Group had the type of aeroplane that for three years was to fly into action.

In May 1939, Volunteer Reserve pilots began receiving instruction with Nos. 104 and 108 Squadrons, two units for Blenheim crews offering them conversion and advanced pilot training. Each squadron also received a quota of Ansons. Both became Group Training Squadrons on 1 June 1939, and when this began each had 21 Blenheim 1s and ten Ansons.

Low and high level bombing raids were currently being practised by the squadrons. No. 34 selected Kettering for its target on 9 May. A week later it was amongst the Blenheim squadrons making advertisement flights for Empire Air Day, improving its cross-country flying at the same time. For the display there was a crowd of 10,000 at Wyton and at Mildenhall 139 Squadron had two flights attacking motor transport in low-level passes.

Duration of exercise flights was sometimes lengthy, with raids simulating likely operational ranges. No. 110 Squadron joined the Group at Wattisham on 11 May. Six Blenheims covered 635 miles on 6 June and included a mock attack on Sandhurst from 13,000 feet, and 82 Squadron at this time began assisting in the ferrying of Blenheims to the R.A.F. in Egypt.

At Upwood tests were carried out on the likely effect of gas attack. Six Battles of 12 Squadron sprayed the aerodrome and 52 Squadron provided personnel to form the station's ground defence force. Three days later another defence exercise was held at Upwood after all the Battles had been placed at dispersals. Cottesmore-based Battles made two spray attacks on aircraft and camp buildings. Of the twenty-one Battles on the field only one was heavily contaminated, two lightly. The remainder were untouched although the buildings were heavily affected. One Battle was decontaminated by a high-pressure Jenny, an American invention enabling a jet of mixed steam and water to be sprayed over an aircraft. Though effective, it was unsuitable as it needed external supplies of water and was not mobile. The whole exercise was watched by the C.-in-C. Bomber Command and 2 Group Staff. Next day 63 Squadron received news that it was to be enlarged to 24 I.E. plus eight I.R. Battle IIs organised into three flights. Ten Battles were to arrive from 185 Squadron, Thornaby.

Two regional exercises took place between 7 and 9 July and 13 and 15 July. Meanwhile another major exercise was taking place. This was formation flying over France by R.A.F. aircraft showing the flag and getting further long-range flying training over unfamiliar territory. No. 114 Squadron sent ten Blenheims to Le Bourget on the afternoon of 10 July. On the two following days they flew in formation over France. On 13 July five R.A.F. squadrons participated in a 500-aircraft fly-past over the French capital. Paris was glimpsed through the clouds on 18 July when an 800-mile tour of France was made by 114 Squadron. Nine Blenheims of 82 Squadron next day flew the route Beachy Head–Paris–Orleans–Chartres–Rouen–Dieppe–Beachy . . . Beachy, a point the squadrons were to come to know so well in the years ahead. 101 Squadron based at West Raynham had shared in a fly-past on 11 July, its nine aircraft leading nine more from 110 Squadron. They flew the 650-mile course Le Tréport–Orleans–Le Mans–Barfleur–St. Catherine's Point–Tangmere in 3 hours 20 minutes, and once more useful material on range and fuel consumption was obtained. When another exercise was flown over France on 25 July French fighters twice intercepted the bombers as they flew over Paris, Orleans, Chartres and Dieppe.

Battles of 52 Squadron carried out new tactical weapon trials on 1–3 August, dropping 500-lb. smoke curtain bombs. Smoke operations were to figure prominently in operations three years later.

From 5 to 11 August the major annual home defence exercise was held. Battles of 52 Squadron operated as friendly bombers flying out to sea and home again without making raids. 110 Squadron concentrated on low-level attacks, some delivered from only 250 feet at which height they crossed the coast and headed mainly for Birmingham and Coventry. On the afternoon of 6th six of 114 Squadron raided Stoke-on-Trent, next day it was Birmingham and on 8th and 9th they made surprise low-level mock raids on Marham. North Weald was the target the following day and the North of England on the last day of the exercise.

On 13 August No. 82 Squadron received its first Blenheim IV. The squadron was ordered to move to Watton on 22 August, and soon all personnel throughout the Group were recalled from leave as once more the international sky darkened.

This time the clouds of war were even more menacing and Readiness C came into force at 09.15 hours on 24 August. Mobilisation was cancelled at 16.00 hours, but all operational aircraft were to be ready for operations at twelve hours' notice. Flying training was to continue, and personnel were told to hold themselves ready for recall from leave at six hours' notice.

Readiness D came into force on 26th. Aircraft were then dispersed around the perimeters of the airfields and flying was now to be only for essential air tests. Bombs were not yet to be fused but all personnel were to be recalled from leave and all aircraft be serviceable.

The stage was now set for the curtain-rise, but throughout the Group as elsewhere there was the knowledge that the bombing force was far from ready, many techniques still being in the trials stage. There was, too, the nasty realisation that the Blenheim left plenty to be desired. It wasn't 'faster than the fighter', but nothing could now be done to alter this. It was, for the moment, a question of waiting, listening and praying.

Chapter 2
The Call for Courage

Suspense in past days and increased readiness changed to war fever on 1 September 1939, as Germany brushed aside Poland's frontier defences. In late afternoon Readiness D was superseded by Group's order to mobilise. Operational composition was thus:[1]

70 Wing	Upper Heyford	18 and 57 Squadrons.	For Field Force France.

79 Wing	Watton	21 and 82 Squadrons.	
82 Wing	Wyton	114 and 139 Squadrons.	2nd Echelon A.A.S.F.
81 Wing	West Raynham	90 and 101 Squadrons.	
83 Wing	Wattisham	107 and 110 Squadrons.	

At the time of mobilisation Blenheim IVs were with Nos. 82, 90, 101, 107, 110, 114 and 139 Squadrons. Forty-seven Blenheim 1s comprised non-effective strength. Nos. 18, 21 and 57 Squadrons were in the process

---

[1] Aircraft and crew states at 16.30 hours were as follows:

Squadron	Aircraft serviceable	No. of crews
21	20	13
82	14	15
114	14	16
139	14	12
107	18 plus 1 in 12 hours	14
110	7 plus 11 in 12 hours	14
90	5 plus 2 in 12 hours	5
101	16	9
18	18	12
57	17	5

Additionally there were No. 104 and 108 Squadrons at Bassingbourn and 52 and 63 at Upwood, all of which became Group Pool Squadrons passing to 6 Group on 2 September, with 35 and 207 Squadrons also set aside for training like 98 Squadron, Hucknall. Units transferred to 6 Group under the Western Plan to maintain 1 and 2 Groups in the field. A scatter plan came into force on 1st whereby squadrons moved to satellite and other airfields. 24 Battles and five Ansons of 52 Squadron moved to Alconbury, twelve Blenheim IVs and a Mk. 1 of 70 Wing was to become part of the Field Force in France on 6 September, when 104 and 108 Squadrons were to move to Upper Heyford, changed in the event to Bicester.

of receiving IVs. Before aircraft of 90 and 101 Squadrons could take-off with full load engine changes from Mercury VIIIs to XVs were needed. Blenheims of 82, 107, 110 and 139 Squadrons had been fitted with additional fuel tanks, but only about 50% had completely revised fuel systems. No. 114 Squadron, next to reach full operational status, awaited extra fuel tanks, piping and jettison valves. Additionally many aircraft needed boost regulators pre-set to give maximum take-off boost of 9 lb. instead of 5 lb. Facilities for 100-octane fuel were needed, also more oxygen bottles. This meant that only the four aforementioned squadrons were really available for operations, about 40% of the Group when all aircraft were serviceable.

Before mobilisation was ordered Bomber Command instructions for the following operations were despatched to squadrons under sealed covers not to be opened until receipt of executive orders. They detailed (1) an attack on German warships in Wilhelmshaven and the Jade and Schillig Roads, to drive ships out to sea to meet the Royal Navy, (2) attacks on electricity generating stations in the Ruhr, (3) attacks on oil refining and storage plants in the Ruhr. Orders also covered attacks on fleeting targets at sea by three of the squadrons whose aircraft had extra tankage, and for the dropping of propaganda leaflets on bombing missions. One aircraft of 139 Squadron was to stand by at short notice each day ready to make a photo-reconnaissance, carrying a naval observer, of naval ports in north-west Germany.

At 23.15 hours Bomber Command signalled that three 2 Group squadrons should prepare to attack three airfields in north-west Germany, date of attack to be given later. At the same time the full 'scatter' order was given for four wings to despatch 50% of their aircraft to stations other than their bases: 79 Wing Watton; 82 Squadron to Horsham, its satellite. 81 Wing West Raynham; 90 Squadron to Weston-on-the-Green. 82 Wing Wyton; 114 Squadron to Hullavington. 83 Wing Wattisham; 110 Squadron to Ipswich, its satellite station. Throughout 2 September the three squadrons allocated for airfield attacks waited, until stand-down was ordered at 15.20 hours. Their targets were Delmenhorst (107 Squadron), Oldenburg (110 Squadron) and Jever (139 Squadron). Concentrated level raids from 7,000 feet were planned. Orders were precise on one point—if the target could not be seen from or above 7,000 feet the attack was '*not, repeat not, to be made*' —and civilian targets were not to be bombed.

At Wyton the solitary Blenheim waiting to reconnoitre German naval bases stood ready, in the belief that war would be declared at 18.00 hours today. No take-off instruction came and the Blenheim was ordered to be ready again at 06.30 next day. 107, 110 and 139 Squadrons were to come to readiness at 08.00 hours.

Group was now as prepared for war as was possible at this time and phlegmatically accepted the declaration of hostilities at 11.00 hours on 3 September. There was some concern as to whether Italy might

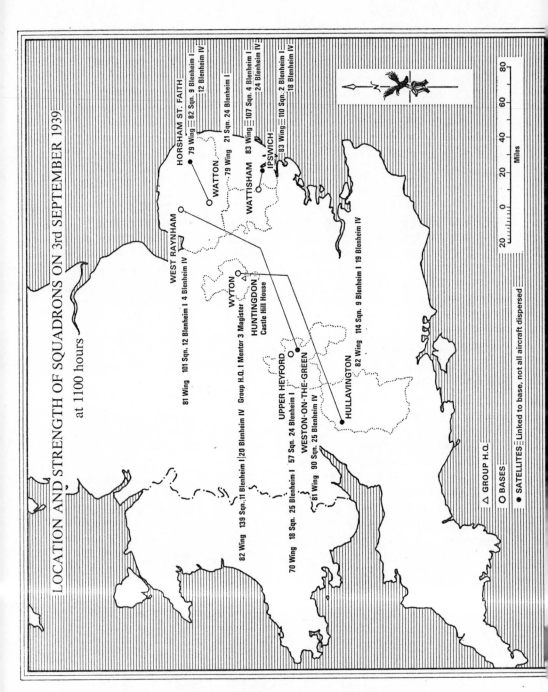

LOCATION AND STRENGTH OF SQUADRONS ON 3rd SEPTEMBER 1939
at 1100 hours

HORSHAM ST. FAITH
79 Wing 82 Sqn. 9 Blenheim I
                  12 Blenheim IV

WATTON

79 Wing 21 Sqn. 24 Blenheim I

WATTISHAM
83 Wing 107 Sqn. 4 Blenheim I
                    24 Blenheim IV

IPSWICH
83 Wing 110 Sqn. 2 Blenheim I
                    18 Blenheim IV

WEST RAYNHAM
81 Wing 101 Sqn. 12 Blenheim I 4 Blenheim IV

WYTON
Group H.Q. 1 Mentor 3 Magister

HUNTINGDON
Castle Hill House

UPPER HEYFORD
82 Wing 139 Sqn. 11 Blenheim I 20 Blenheim IV

WESTON-ON-THE-GREEN
70 Wing 18 Sqn. 25 Blenheim I 57 Sqn. 24 Blenheim IV
81 Wing 90 Sqn. 25 Blenheim IV

HULLAVINGTON
82 Wing 114 Sqn. 9 Blenheim I 19 Blenheim IV

△ GROUP H.Q.
○ BASES
● SATELLITES Linked to base, not all aircraft dispersed

Miles
20 0 20 40 60 80

MAP 5. *See Appendix 12, pages 496/7 for notes*

immediately declare war but at 12.05 Air Ministry confirmed that, as yet, Germany alone was the foe. By then 2 Group had despatched the Royal Air Force's first offensive sortie in the Second World War.[2]

Since 1 September Flg. Off. Andrew McPherson had been waiting at Wyton to fly the reconnaissance over the German Fleet. At 11.01, a minute after the war began on 3 September, he was ordered to take-off at noon and fly to the Wilhelmshaven area and airfields in north-west Germany, carrying Commander Thompson, R.N., and Corporal V. Arrowsmith, in N6215. He took-off at 12.03 and climbed to 21–22,000 feet for the flight. He was in no way intercepted. During the flight units of the German fleet were seen in the Schillig Roads. In misty weather the crew believed they saw three or four capital ships, four or five cruisers and seven destroyers apparently heading north. Sending a radio report was impossible for the W/T set froze at peak height 24,000 feet. Instead the camera whirred. Raid BW 1 landed at Wyton at 16.50 hours bringing 75 photographs of military objectives.

Activity of another sort had been going on at the stations. Soon after war was declared air raid sirens wailed. Personnel were ordered to shelters. At Watton this would have been an uncomfortable business since they were flooded. There was a choice—die under air attack or drown! Everyone decided to risk an attack which never came, for all was false alarm.

In view of imminent operations likely to bring retaliation, further scattering of squadrons had been hastily ordered at 14.15 hours, West Raynham's aircraft going to Brize Norton, 21 Squadron to Sealand and 82 to Netheravon. Then the weather clamped and at 21.40 Wings were told that operations were unlikely on 4 September. Hardly had the telephones been put down when Bomber Command ordered Group to prepare 27 long-range Blenheims for operations against the German Fleet next day. Clarification and urgent planning followed.

At 23.58 hours the order was flashed to Wattisham and Wyton that Nos. 107, 110 and 139 Squadrons were each to have nine aircraft standing by at an hour's notice from 08.00 hours next day, to attack enemy ships that might be passing between Norway and the Shetlands, or sailing through the Straits of Dover. Eight observers from Coastal Command were hastily ordered to report for duty at Wyton and Wattisham. Bomb loads changed, now that plans to attack enemy airfields had been postponed. The latter seems to have been an unfortunate mistake.

Wyton and Wattisham were emphatically told at 01.52 that their task was the destruction of the German Fleet, that there was no alternative target. If enemy ships were not found bombs were to be dropped in the sea. Both Coastal and Bomber Command, not to mention the Royal

---

[2] Protective sorties were started by Coastal Command before the war began.

Navy, urgently wanted further details of position and strength of the German naval force.

A repeat reconnaissance was, therefore, ordered to take-off from Wyton at 08.35. Again it was N6215 that violated German air space attempting to photograph Wilhelmshaven, Cuxhaven and Kiel. Once more Andrew McPherson was the pilot.

Weather for the flight was appalling. It was raining fast with very poor visibility. For an hour McPherson flew blind. At Brunsbuttel and Wilhelmshaven he flew around German warships at about 250 feet without being fired upon. A delayed W/T report was sent from the aircraft but was mainly unintelligible due probably to a faulty Syko transmitter.

It was certain that there was a large warship in the entrance to Wilhelmshaven. Two ships lay off Brunsbuttel. Four destroyers had been seen in the Jade River all of which had sailed by the time the aircraft passed there on return. At 13.35 N6215 landed and amongst its photographs—developed too late for the bombing force to see—was one which showed the cruiser *Leipzig*, and not a supposed battleship, entering Wilhelmshaven.

Quickly Command ordered an attack. Five crews from each of the three squadrons on stand-by were to take-off and attack the warship at the entrance to Wilhelmshaven with the destroyers in the Jade as their secondary target. It was emphasised that no bombs must fall in Bauhafen, and that greatest care must be taken to avoid civilian targets and merchant ships despite expected bad weather. All attacks were to be low-level, each aircraft dropping two 500-lb. 11 sec. delay bombs. Stations were advised that if a warship was attacked from ahead anti-aircraft fire would be less likely to be met than if attack was from astern although no one really had the knowledge upon which to base realistic briefing. Final orders were passed to Wyton at 14.23 and to Wattisham at 14.28.

Five Blenheims of 139 Squadron left Wyton at 15.32 hours. At 15.56 five of 110 Squadron's Blenheims took-off followed by five of 107 Squadron at 16.00 hours. The first R.A.F. bombing raid of the war had been launched. Weather en route was extremely bad, heavy rain and low clouds making visibility very poor. Owing to insufficiently allowing for wind speed 139 Squadron flying ahead sighted the Frisians near Norderney. They turned off seaward then flew to Wilhelmshaven Bay from a northerly direction, passing between Schillig Point and the island in the mouth of the Bay. Then they flew in mist along the western shore. The formation separated into two and a three all flying line astern about ¼ mile off shore at 200–300 feet, passing the entrance to Wilhelmshaven Harbour in heavy rain. Flt. Lt. Scott, the leader, felt certain he would have seen a ship if there was one, but none was seen. He turned the formation out past Schillig Point after completing a circuit of the Bay. They appear to have mistaken the Ems Estuary for Wilhelmshaven Bay.

The pair flying separately jettisoned their bombs in the sea from a low level. From one machine the bombs were seen to ricochet before exploding; the other's load sank without exploding although they were fused. This later led to consideration of lowest bombing heights.

Wattisham's two squadrons were being led by Flt. Lt. Kenneth Doran who recently recalled the memorable operation in the following words:

'One of the strangest things about the start of the war for operational squadrons of No. 2 Group was the sudden transition from peace to war. One day practice bombs were being dropped on ranges and the next live bombs were being dropped on the German Navy. Mess life and social activities were little changed and married families had not been evacuated. The loss of an aircraft and crew became an immediate personal tragedy to the wives and families who expected their husbands to return for tea as usual.

'At the time of the Munich crisis in September 1938, 2 Group squadrons had been at four hours readiness to carry out low level daylight attacks against power stations in the Ruhr; from the target maps issued it was apparent that the power stations were strongly defended with anti-aircraft guns and ringed with fighter stations. It was therefore with something like relief that we learned that we were to attack units of the German Fleet on 4 September 1939.

'Our previous training had included simulated low level attacks against shipping and in favourable circumstances we had shown that it was possible for three aircraft to attack from three different directions, thus diluting the A-A fire, and drop their bombs within the eleven seconds delay of the bombs' fusing. We could now see how the simulated attacks worked with live bombs against a defended target.

'When it was reported that units of the German Fleet were in the Schillig Roads the original plan at Wattisham was to employ a wing formation of 24 Blenheims from 107 and 110 Squadrons. Owing to the forecast weather conditions this was abandoned. Instead it was decided that five aircraft from "A" Flight 110 Squadron and five from 107 Squadron were the maximum which could be operated. The weather forecast for the North Sea and target area was heavy rain with cloud extending from just above sea level to 17,000 feet.

'After a short briefing by the Station Commander, Wg. Cdr. Oswald Gayford, "A" Flight 110 Squadron took off first in "V" formation. A Coastal Command navigator, Flg. Off. Henderson, was attached to the leading aircraft more for ship recognition than navigation as my usual navigator Sgt. Pennington was fully experienced in low level navigation in Blenheims. The flight plan was to make a landfall at Heligoland and then alter course direct to the Schillig Roads. This, it was hoped, would lessen the chances of alerting the defences along the coast of the mainland and also conceal our final objective from any enemy plotting organisation: at that time it was not known whether or not the Germans had any Radar system. In fact the existence of our own

Radar system, then called R. D/F, was little known even to the R.A.F. pilots.

'As we crossed the coast over the North Sea the weather deteriorated rapidly as forecast. It was obviously useless flying in or above cloud as we could never hope to make a descent through cloud to one or two hundred feet and then find our target. We therefore flew under the cloud base in visual contact with the sea, from sea level to 100 feet, frequently in heavy rain. In these conditions we were very gratified to make our landfall at Heligoland as planned. Still in formation we altered course for the Schillig Roads.

'On crossing the German coast the cloud base lifted to four or five hundred feet and the visibility improved; on the left along the shore of the estuary there was a low level balloon barrage, straight ahead a large cargo ship, and just beyond lay the *Admiral Scheer*. Numbers 4 and 5 of the formation (Flg. Off. Emden and Sgt. Abbot) had been ordered to break formation and attack as a pair following the leading three aircraft. Numbers 2 and 3 (Plt. Off. Lings and Sgt. Hanne) were now told to open out into line abreast and attack from port and starboard as planned. The attack was carried out in a slight dive from three hundred to one hundred feet at maximum boost. To get into the right position a slight turn to starboard was necessary and this meant that the leader and No. 2 were over the *Scheer* almost simultaneously with No. 2 slightly ahead. No. 3 on the outside of the turn decided he could not get over the target within 11 seconds, the time of the delay fuse of the bombs, and dropped his bombs on a nearby ship's tender.

'The element of surprise was obviously complete as no shot was fired until we had dropped our bombs. After that everything opened up, both from *Scheer* and the shore. We turned to port to miss the balloon barrage, and took violent evasive action, changing height and direction, until we reached cloud cover. At least two bombs were seen to hit the *Admiral Scheer* amidships followed by two red flashes: we had survived a low level attack at 100 feet in daylight against a German pocket battleship lying alongside a strongly defended area of the German coast.

'After the attack each aircraft returned independently. By now the weather had improved and near Borkum I saw a Dornier flying boat at 6,000 feet and after making two front gun attacks against it finally turned for home when fighters were seen taking off from Borkum.'

107 Squadron following 110 fared far worse since the enemy was alerted. They also arrived late, due to the weather. Of the five sent only Flg. Off. Stevens returned to report that they separated, owing to bad weather north of Borkum, into three and two of which he was the last in the formation. He closed on his leader and they turned south for the Schillig Roads. Weather worsened and the leader climbed into cloud. Stevens kept well below cloud, flying very low to the Jade Roads. A little further on he saw his leader above him and again they remained

in company for a few minutes until the leader entered cloud again and disappeared. Four aircraft then went in from very low level; one was blown up by its bombs. Stevens flew around the Bay seeing only a destroyer. This he did not attack for he was still hoping to see his main target. He eventually returned with his bombs on, landing at Sutton Bridge because it was getting dark. Nothing was heard from the others. Thus ended the first R.A.F. bombing raid of the war.

Next day McPherson set off to collect evidence of the success of the attacks. Fog and mist prevented him from seeing anything.

What had been achieved? Three bombs are known to have hit the *Scheer*. One Blenheim brought down by flak crashed into the bows of the cruiser *Emden* seriously damaging it. It was a courageous raid which achieved little. Sixteen men and five aircraft were lost. (See Appendix No. 6.)

After the operations had been discussed it was agreed that three aircraft would only by chance be over target at the same time, and that it would be better for attacks to be made by pairs. That there had been an element of surprise was certain from ships' crews being about the decks; nevertheless some must have been near the guns for these to open fire so soon. Ideally torpedo bombers should have made the attacks, and to have a chance of bombs staying aboard it was considered that attacks should be made along the line of the ship. The leader would have liked alternative targets available if weather was bad, but political considerations prevented this.

It was obvious that the raid had achieved little, for the enemy was able to put to sea. It was decided to attack again. 82 Squadron flew to Wyton from Netheravon, to join 139 Squadron for a raid on the 6th. Throughout that day both squadrons stood by but at 18.00 hours the operation was abruptly cancelled.

Daily standbys followed. Retaliation for the raid already made was nervously expected. Danger of machine-gun fire on dispersed aircraft was the subject of a reminder to all squadrons on 7th and 90 and 101 Squadrons were told to scatter quickly for increased safety to Weston-on-the-Green and Brize Norton respectively.

From an operational point of view the Scatter Scheme brought problems. Before operations aircraft needed to return to forward stations to arm, for the crews to be briefed. For security reasons they flew in a stream to bases and scatter stations. Fearing the enemy might discover the scatter plan it was decided to change the scheme. On 15th squadrons moved as follows: 114 to Wyton, 21 to Watton, 107 to Benson, 90 to Upwood, 139 to Alconbury, 82 to Netheravon, 110 to Wattisham, 101 to West Raynham; amended on 17th to 21 to Netheravon and 114 to Alconbury.

Armour plating was now being fitted on the bulkhead behind the pilot and behind the radio set, three aircraft per section being modified and the work completed 15 September.

From 11th to 16th 2 Group stood by. The Royal Navy was minelaying three hours daily in the Straits of Dover, with which duty the German Navy might interfere. Each day two Blenheim squadrons and one of 3 Group Wellingtons stood at 45 minutes' readiness, but no call came. For the last three days of the task 54 Blenheims daily stood by, nine from each of 90, 101, 21, 82, 107 and 110 Squadrons. On 15th there were 117 Blenheim IVs serviceable in the Group, and now the squadrons stood by ready to attack enemy warships at sea. None were reported before the next round of employment.

The value of photo-reconnaissance was realised but there were no aircraft capable of carrying out the task effectively. Cameras were barely suitable, supporting organisation non-existent. Understandably the French were eager for early information on any Wehrmacht build-up in the west. It was therefore decided to reconnoitre western Germany to obtain a picture of normal movement so that future traffic density could be compared with what was now found. 2 Group was called upon to photograph the railway routes around Bremen, Osnabruck, Munster, Wunsdorf, Minden, Bielefeld and Hamm, and on the Hanover–Hamm autobahn. Strip pictures for not less than thirty miles were required. Group's tasks now were therefore (*a*) operations against the German Navy, (*b*) photo-reconnaissance of communications, (*c*) photo-reconnaissance of German airfields yet to be more explicitly ordered.

Photographic reconnaissance of enemy communications began on 20th. Two crews from 139 Squadron were despatched at midday but the area to be reconnoitred was cloud-clad. One aircraft was fired upon over Emden and soon after attacked by three Bf 109s. It escaped into cloud. Off Borkum a battleship, three cruisers and six destroyers steaming east with fifteen minesweepers behind them were seen. Next day it was the turn of 110 Squadron to operate. Sqn. Ldr. J. S. Sabine flew N6242 to Osnabruck and Plt. Off. R. J. Hill N6212 to Hanover. On reaching his target area Sabine flew along the Osnabruck–Dalmen railway line at only 200 feet securing forty obliques. Hill was fired at near Solingen but not hit, then he was briefly engaged by a Bf 109. Two more came in to attack and the air gunner claimed one having held his fire until it was at eighty yards. The Blenheim then raced into protective cloud.

On 25 September line overlaps were ordered of the Bielefeld–Hamm line, the Kamen–Holten autobahn and inland waterway Iken–Hirrten–Hamborn. Nose-sited F24 cameras with 8-inch lenses were for use above 4,000 feet and German Contaxes below. Photographs were secured in generally fine weather from 20,000 feet; some balloons were seen; but there was industrial haze and smoke over the Ruhr.

Flying P4857 was No. 107s new tenacious and outstanding commander, one day to command the Group, Basil Embry. At 19,000 feet near Leer he was intercepted by two Me 109s, so he dived into clouds at 6,000 feet. Putting the nose down had marred his gunner's view and bullets hit the aircraft, striking the fuel tank, the tail and the turret.

If other people weren't in the firing line 2 Group clearly was—right from the start.

Next day a new demand was forthcoming. Three aircraft were to discover the location and strength of the Luftwaffe on 28 airfields in west and north-west Germany beginning on 27 September. Three crews of 82 Squadron and two of 21 set forth. Flg. Off. Hall flying between 2,500 and 7,000 feet managed some obliques of the Fassburg and Hamburg areas. Plt. Off. Fordham of 82 obtained some good pictures but near Wunsdorf was forced to fly low by flak and passed between two He 111s on landing approach to the airfield! The air gunner gave them a burst for good measure. The third aircraft was at 20,000 feet in the Koln–Butzweiler area when oxygen failed. Flg. Off. Coutts-Wood and his crew lost their way on turning southabouts and were lucky to reach Auxerre to refuel. Sqn. Ldr. Gibson of 21 Squadron took only one shot before his camera failed. He encountered heavy flak at 20,000 feet over Krefeld. But from operations on 27th Wg. Cdr. Cameron and Flg. Off. D. A. Strachen of 110 Squadron both failed to return. Wg. Cdr. Cameron, the C.O. of 110 Squadron, was carrying out a reconnaissance of Kiel at 12,000 feet on the day Hitler was there to present the first Iron Cross to a U-boat commander. He was attacked by a swarm of 109s, shot down and given a military funeral by the Germans.

Sixteen out of 28 airfields listed were photographed, many line overlaps taken, Emden and Hamburg were photographed. No unusual activity was seen on airfields, but at Langenhagen 28 He 111s were lined up on the tarmac and twenty aircraft at Detmold. At Marienfeld there were 36. Only Fassberg airfield seemed successfully camouflaged and the absence of dispersal was everywhere apparent. The earlier projected attacks would probably have been very effective. Three aircraft of 139 Squadron completed the reconnaissance on 1 October. N6231 flown by Flg. Off. Maclaclan failed to return, and N6223 was engaged by three Bf 109s and later fired upon by naval ships but reached base.

Icing up of guns and cameras was a considerable nuisance so 79 and 82 Wings flew trials with Ever-hot bags on guns. Even at $-40°$ C and at 28,000 feet the guns remained serviceable—to everyone's surprise.

The Blenheim force was currently divided into four parts. There still were many Blenheim Is on the squadrons but few were Immediate Equipment and none were used operationally. Mk. IVs existed in three forms according to fuel tankage. These were: Range State I 900–500 miles with 280 gal. fuel and plus 5 lb. boost. Range State II 1,200–750 miles with 380 gal. fuel and 5 lb. boost. Range State III 1,500–920 miles with 468 gal. fuel and 9 lb. boost. On 17 September aircraft in each state were I: 67, II: 40, III: 21. By 5 October the totals were, I: 26, II: 67 and III: 15. Those in state II could attain the range of III if cameras but no bombs were carried. All Wings had aircraft fitted with long-range tanks and 9 lb. boost by 7 October.

On 6 October trials orientated towards likely future operations were started. 2 Group was still an army-support Group, and now 79 and 82 Wings were instructed to discover the best method of attacking mechanised columns and personnel on roads by stick bombing using 20-lb. bombs. It was found necessary to attack from 1,500–2,000 feet to ensure that bombs burst on impact with grassland, which limited accuracy. Thereafter practice operations were undertaken against army columns when convenient to both participants.

Attacks on enemy shipping were no longer part of 2 Group's war. New employment seemed possible for a conference at Group H.Q. on 8 October discussed once more the possibility of attacks on German power stations. Such plans had long been under consideration at H.Q. Bomber Command, but before much progress could be made photo-reconnaissance cover of potential targets was needed. On 10 October Command ordered such flights over the Ruhr to take place.

The first wartime upheaval of the Group was now about to take place, or so it seemed. It had been decided to re-arm some of the Fairey Battle squadrons of A.A.S.F. in France with Blenheim IVs. 114 and 139 Squadrons were to transfer to A.A.S.F. on 25 October. Two Battle squadrons were to convert at Wyton in six weeks allowing the next two then to come.

Three of 114's aircraft were detached to Villeneuve on 12 October to make the squadron's first operational flights. Next day two took-off to reconnoitre the Ruhr and ascertain details of its balloon barrage in preparation for the power station attacks. N6232 was engaged by flak between Trier and Lince. East of Cologne it was attacked by a Bf 109 and by another at 16,000 feet near Koblenz. It survived and came home with photographs of a bridge near Dortmund, a factory near Eitorf and an airfield near Akkerbath. N6160 failed to return and probably fell to enemy fighters.

A.A.S.F. was currently thinking of special operations to destroy pontoon bridges, railways, roads, barracks and airfields. It would operate over a 30–40 mile wide front with a 2 Group element penetrating deeper after similar targets. The plan was to hold back for this concerted operation. Daylight was already too short for aircraft operating from Britain to make two raids in a day, even if they refuelled in France. Two squadrons could be sent to France to attack fleeting targets in a 3–4 day stay, but administrative difficulties were seen. It was at this time agreed that when enemy troop columns were attacked this should be with 250 and 20 lb. bombs—and only after the enemy had begun an invasion.

There was constant fear of enemy build-up in the west. Indeed on 18 October a signal from Command suggested the enemy might attack France through Belgium that day. 2 Group signalled it would take four hours to prepare aircraft for reply.

It was clear that Blenheim defensive armament was insufficient. The C.-in-C. ordered on 13 October that the possibility of fitting a gun or

1. Hawker Hind of 82 Squadron, of the type used by 2 Group squadrons
2. Fairey Gordon K2763 which served with 207 Squadron 19 September 1935 to 21 September 1937

3. Blenheim I K7037 joined 114 Squadron 17.3.37 and crashed 10.5.38 when her starboard engine failed just after take-off from Wyton

4. Blenheim K7035, the first to join a squadron, after arrival on 114 Squadron 1.3.37. She returned to Bristol Aircraft 25.10.37 and became 1327M in March 1939

5. Blenheim I L1298: BZ-A of 107 Squadron in use 29.8.38–15.8.39 leads two Fairey Battles

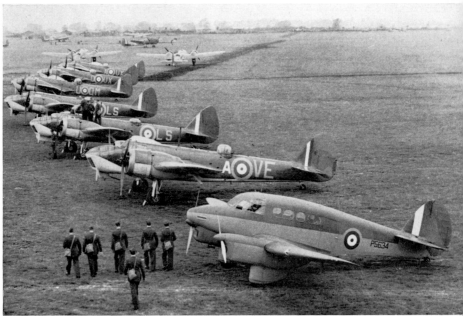

6. Blenheim I K7060 was delivered to 139 Squadron 16.7.37 and was struck off charge 22.2.38 becoming 1043M

7. Blenheim IVs at Wyton, August 1940. VE-A: R3741 has gun mountings at the rear of nacelles, T1957: LS a lengthy gun tray beneath the nose. Note the assortment of marking styles

guns to fire down, and to the rear, be investigated urgently. Suddenly intelligence came through that an enemy attack on this country would take place on 16th, by which time all squadrons must scatter as before and be ready to return to bases to retaliate, but the envisaged raids never materialised.

Already 107 Squadron had worked on extra defensive armament on the Blenheim. The drive of Basil Embry was now part of life at Wattisham where he soon had a machine fitted with three fixed guns firing aft, two in the upper nacelles and one under the extreme rear fuselage, all fired by cable. Few pilots thought that fixed backward-firing guns were of the slightest use. These installations were inspected on 16 October by representatives from R.A.E. and Bomber Command who considered the fitting satisfactory, but not fully to meet the need. Units were invited to suggest alternative mountings. Group, however, was practically satisfied, and requested that all I.E. aircraft be fitted with such armament.

Events had so far largely dictated the operations pattern, but a change was now to come with the issue of No. 2 Group Operations Order No. 7 on 19 October. It was a plan for the immediate reduction and disruption of the German armaments industry by dislocating power supplies from electricity generating stations and gas producing plants. All home-based Bomber Groups were involved in the elaborate scheme. Electricity plants were to be attacked initially. Low-level or shallow-dive precision attacks were to be made with 500-lb. 11 sec. delay bombs. A two-pronged attack was envisaged, squadrons operating from England using a northerly route and those from France flying south of neutral territory. Watton's squadrons were to fly from Bethienville, Wyton's from Auberive. Wattisham's would fly from home via Condé where they would refuel.

Apart from their industrial value electricity plants were considered ideal for attack being conspicuous and vulnerable. Turbines and boilers should easily explode, and control rooms would make excellent targets, it was argued. These would be small and difficult to hit. Transformers were known to be protected by blast-proof walls.

Coking and gas plants were equally vulnerable. Coke ovens, coal service bunkers and quenching towers were easy to identify. Parts of the plants were known to be built in straight lines and tall chimneys marked this. Cylindrical towers indicated by-product plants, highly inflammable targets. There was even the prospect of back fires and oven explosions. The order of priority in these attacks was: (1) principal electricity generating stations and transformer stations, (2) two aqueducts over the Dortmund–Ems Canal six miles north-east of Munster carrying fuel supplies, and (3) central coking plants then other coking plants.

Final run-in to the attacks was planned to be from the east for a fast get-away. 2 Group's aircraft were thought capable of flying easily between the barrage balloon cables, but the larger bombers might find

c

this difficult—hence the recent reconnaissance flights over the Ruhr to investigate the barrage.

The plan to attack these targets remained in hand for many months and from time to time was amended in the light of new information. It was never carried out as intended; had it been it seems likely that the losses on these daylight sorties among relatively slow bombers would have been fearful. Months later some listed targets were raided, in daylight and by 2 Group. Night attacks also took place later in the war, but German power stations were surprisingly largely left alone. They would have made ideal targets for dusk attacks by Mosquitoes, but they did not figure high on the priority lists when Mosquito bombers were active.

On 23 October 139 Squadron was warned of a move to France which was soon cancelled. Instead their aircraft became bogged at permanent standings and had to be dug out. All roadways around Wyton were deep in mud. Transport became impossible, permanent standings useless. Tarmac roads would have been more economical for the aircraft were soon muddy inside and out. At this time new radios were being fitted and trials of 20-lb. bombs were under way at Wyton.

For reasons of safety it was now decided that Group H.Q. should move fully into Castle Hill House, Huntingdon, which was done in the last week of October.

Continued intelligence reports of Luftwaffe concentrations in north-west Germany were being received. There were stories, too, of the assembly of an expedition force of twenty to thirty 2,000-ton merchant vessels being prepared in estuaries of German rivers. It was believed there were small steamers and flat-bottomed barges in the mouth of the Ems. Accordingly 82 Wing was detailed to reconnoitre airfields and estuaries in north-west Germany on 30 October. Six Blenheims of 139 Squadron were despatched and encountered bad weather. N6227: M was chased into cloud by six fighters. Flg. Off. Pepper in N6236: G was successful, but his aircraft, attacked by fighters, also encountered flak which badly wounded his gunner. Sgt. Price in N6224: F was hit by flak and its radio mast was broken. The air gunner in his machine was injured in the thigh and rib. McPherson flying N6219 was also fired upon.

Not only was the Blenheim under-armed, it was too slow. Ultimate endurance with useful load was explored on 21 October when a 110 Squadron machine flew for $6\frac{1}{4}$ hours, then had only twenty gallons of fuel left. On 27 October 82 Wing was instructed to send a Blenheim to Heston so that rough finish could be improved by filling cracks and polishing. This, it was thought, might add as much as 20 m.p.h. to top speed.

Wg. Cdr. Odbert and Sqn. Ldr. Walker visited Wattisham to discuss the armament position. Odbert suggested that the forward-firing Browning in the wing be removed and used as one of the rear-firing guns provided that other extra guns could become available. It was agreed that six additional Vickers gas-operated guns were required per squadron so that when special missions were undertaken a third rearward gun could be fixed. Wattisham workshops manufactured a large-capacity 2 × 100 rounds magazine for a tail gun which was to be strapped under the extreme rear fuselage. Odbert revealed at Wattisham that there was a proposal to fit twin guns in the Blenheim turret. This would unfortunately involve loss of the secondary traverse. Such restriction in the field of fire was at present unacceptable to Group, particularly as loss of area of fire occurred close to the fin and tailplane where many attacks would take place. Armament changes were thus still undecided.

On 8 September Flt. Lt. Kenneth Doran was summoned to H.Q. Bomber Command to give a first-hand account to H.M. King George VI of the attack on the *Scheer*. The King, as a pilot, was most interested, asking many questions.

2 November was a red-letter day for the Group. H.M. King George VI, Air Chief Marshal Sir Cyril Newall, Ludlow Hewitt and the Group Commander, Air Vice-Marshal C. T. Maclean, visited Wyton to award the Distinguished Flying Cross to Kenneth Doran for his part on the first bombing raid of the war, and to Andrew McPherson. Showing great interest the King saw a bombing-up demonstration, inspected N6236 damaged in action on 30 October and saw reconnaissance photographs.

One of the more startling defence schemes of the early months of the war concerned the use of aerial mines. On 3 November Wg. Cdr. Embry went to a conference at University College, Exeter, to discuss their use sown from Blenheims against enemy fighters. The experimental Fairey P.4/34 had been flying into dummy minefields sown by a Harrow, cord having been tied to the dummies. Basically the idea had been to develop defensive mines. One Blenheim of 107 Squadron was now required at Exeter for trials extending the scheme as a means of bomber defence. Hampdens would also carry mines as defensive weapons. Like so many revolutionary ideas this became stillborn, but it was an interesting one.

On 27 October the 139 Squadron Blenheim sent to Heston for streamlining returned to Wyton for testing. At 10,000 feet the full throttle 5 lb. boost speed increase was 13 m.p.h., giving a top speed of 277 as opposed to 264. Perspex bulges had been fitted to the sides of the canopy. These did not reduce top speed and they popularly improved the view aft. Later they became a standard feature. Startling was the colour of the aircraft's underside, for it was the first to wear what was then called 'light sea green' to render it less visible on day raids. This was one of a series of Camotint greenish-blue shades developed by Titanine for high-altitude reconnaissance aircraft. A report on this feature said 'For daylight flying this colour has much to recommend it.' It was February 1940 before its use was common, by which time it was known as 'duck-egg green'. To 'streamline' a Blenheim took 150 man-hours which would have called for considerable effort by a squadron, or civilians working under contract. Eventually it was decided that certain squadrons should have on charge a few polished aircraft wearing the new paint scheme for special reconnaissance duties.

Armament remained under review. On 7 November the Air Ministry ordered that twenty-four Blenheims should be fitted with a backward-firing Browning gun in each nacelle. Four aircraft per squadron were therefore to get them soon. The Bristol Aeroplane Company were currently experimenting with a backward-firing periscopically aimed free gun in a specially constructed blister placed where the forward escape hatch was situated.

No. 139 Squadron came off operations on 17 November. All its aircraft returned to Wyton from Alconbury for 'streamlining' and application of light green under-surfaces. 114 Squadron became non-operational on 23 November for its aircraft to be 'streamlined and re-doped'. All were to have a new smooth finish paint devised by Titanine to replace the rough dope hitherto used. Blenheim undersides wore now, to quote the official records, a shade known as 'Light Sea Green to render them invisible at great height'.

Both squadrons were ordered to proceed to France, leaving 2 Group on 22 November and replacing Nos. 15 and 40 Squadrons. Materials for preparations and painting were in very short supply but by 27 November 139's aircraft were all complete and next day the squadron began its six-day move to the Continent. Soon Short Scyllas, DH 86s, H.P. 42s and Ensigns were moving the squadron. 114 Squadron began its move on 9 December. 2 Group had lost two of its foremost squadrons.

Operations at this time were few. The only special call for photo-reconnaissance came at the end of October. There were many standbys for possible attacks on enemy warships, but none materialised into operations. On 11 November three Blenheims of 114 Squadron went on a photo-reconnaissance of Heligoland to observe any moving warships. They flew over the sea in fine weather and, to approach unseen, came down to 100 feet near the target under a 6,000-feet cloud base. Suddenly there was a blinding flash and N6150 and N6145 disappeared. They had collided. On 25 November four crews of 107 Squadron urgently reconnoitred positioning of warships at Heligoland, Wilhelmshaven, Cuxhaven and Brunsbuttel. Weather was bad and the crews had to fly low over strong defences. None was hit, and all but Brunsbuttel were reconnoitred showing little movement.

An order of 8 December fundamentally affected Group activities. It was to alternate with 3 and 5 Groups as Daily Duty Coastal Group from 15 December having four flights of six aircraft at two hours' readiness. Not only would standbys continue, Group would take its turn making wide North Sea sweeps, useful for training and offering a possible chance to sink warships, large or small, that might enter the North Sea.

In December planned swapping of 114 and 139 Squadrons with XV and 40 took place. The latter units equipped with Blenheim IVs at Wyton but were non-operational for many weeks. On 20 December orders came that no more Fairey Battle squadrons were to be re-equipped. Group composition was then stabilised for six months.

A few more reconnaissance flights were flown in 1939. Two on 24 December by 82 Squadron were made to ascertain whether any Deutschland class ships were in port. Weather was often very bad, sometimes good, and clearer instructions were needed on how and when to proceed. It was decided that such flights would now only take place at high altitudes, and on days when there was possible cloud cover. On 27 December in extremes of cold and heavy flak two Blenheims flew high over Wilhelmshaven. One was forced into the sea off Wangerooge, the other came back with good photos.

Before the year ended a clarification of North Sea sweep policy was laid down. If by 10.00 hours Coastal Command reported no targets the A.O.C. could send out a sweep offering training to squadrons.

Distributions of all bomber aircraft was now categorised as follows: (1) concentrated as normally in peacetime, (2) dispersed; all squadrons at parent stations with serviceable I.E. aircraft at dispersal points, (3) scattered; one squadron dispersed at parent station and one at a satellite or other airfield, (4) withdrawn; all squadrons on airfields west of a line Wyton–York. These rulings remained in force for many months, numbers 2–3 throughout the war.

The New Year began inauspiciously. Three sections from 107 Squadron, each aircraft carrying two 500-lb. S.A.P. bombs, were away at 11.05 hours on 1 January on a North Sea sweep, each section flying a parallel course sixteen miles apart looking for warships. Weather was good and the sea was clear of enemy shipping.

On the morrow two of 107's polished aircraft reconnoitred Sylt, Amrum and Wilhelmshaven looking for ships, balloons, aircraft. Sgt. Harry Walman took N6190 to Wilhelmshaven managing three oblique shots of Heligoland from his Leica at 19,000 feet. No ships were seen there but in Wilhelmshaven's yard *Tirpitz* was photographed, with a large warship nearby. Five good obliques were obtained from 22,000 feet using an eight-inch lens, showing a *Leipzig* class ship listing to port. Twenty miles off Vlieland three fighters were distantly seen, lost to sight when the Blenheim dived to sea level.

North Sea sweeps were the main occupation of the Group. Useful points about such operations were therefore summarised. One of the lessons of disastrous 3 Group day raids was the vulnerability of stragglers. Sweeps gave useful formation flying practice, but the enemy was aware of them and could be expected to react if necessary. Therefore routes and approaches needed to vary. Chances of attacking enemy ships seemed likely to increase. A lesson from the first raid of the war was that all aircraft should not attack from different directions. Four

250-lb. bombs made a better load than two 500-pounders, if the distributor was used.

The operation of 10 January proved the most eventful so far. Four sections left Watton to fly a north-east/south-west sweep over the North Sea. About 45 minutes later nine Blenheims of 82 Squadron took off to be in position to attack any reported vessels, standard procedure. Four sections of 110 Squadron were soon leaving Wattisham. At about 55° 30′ N 05° 10′ E the 110 Squadron formation led by Kenneth Doran sighted five Messerschmitt 110s. The Blenheims were at 5,000 feet in close squadron vic, maintained throughout the subsequent engagement, as the Me 110s approached from above and out of the sun. Immediately the Blenheims dived to sea level maintaining 240 m.p.h. I.A.S. Quarter attacks came singly, the fighters using two cannon and two machine guns then breaking away into a stall turn at about 2,000–2,500 feet for another attack. In the second attack an enemy aircraft flew between the leading section and No. 3 before breaking away, and rear gunners whose shooting was skilfully co-ordinated by Plt. Off. Searle, gunnery leader, saw their tracer enter the fighter. The action lasted for 25 minutes during which Sgt. Pennington, navigator in the lead aircraft, coolly occupied himself by sending coded Syko messages to base. One Bf 110 was seen to crash into the sea, and after about twelve minutes two broke away to the south-east. A badly damaged 110 landed in Denmark. The other two made about nine attacks before running out of ammunition.

Early in the engagement L4859, No. 3 of the third section flown by Sgt. Hanne, lost speed and it was believed he had an engine put out of action. Hanne fell some 400 yards behind, becoming one of the stragglers about whom warning had been issued. L4859 was soon finished off by fighters and exploded on impact with the sea.

Compared with the Blenheim the Bf 110 appeared appreciably faster— 80 to 100 m.p.h.—and more manoeuvrable in this first combat with Blenheims. Outer aircraft had been the main targets and N6203 flown by Plt. Off. Pemberton, damaged by cannon shot and having twenty-three holes from machine guns, force-landed at Manby. Three other aircraft were damaged but there were no crew injuries. N6213 (Plt. Off. Arderne) had its starboard tyre punctured, and its port undercarriage sheared on landing. Doran was awarded a bar to his D.F.C., and as a result of the action awards totalled two D.F.C.s and seven D.F.M.s.

At a Group Station Commanders' meeting on 18 January the engagement—the largest for 2 Group so far—was discussed. There was full agreement that by descending to sea level the correct thing was done, but that if engaged at some height it would be best to stay there and fight it out.

Another important point for discussion was the relative merits of four or six aircraft boxes. Wg. Cdr. Embry maintained that a box of six was no more tiring to fly than squadron vic formation, and more manoeuvrable. It was adopted and used for many years, indeed throughout the war for medium-level attacks. Its main disadvantage was, however, that at low level it was impracticable since No. 6 was flying much lower than the leader.

Grp. Capt. Vincent pointed out the value of changing formation and frontage as an attack developed, by manoeuvring one or two sections in relation to the leading section. For example, if attacked from astern or beam No. 2 Section would slide below so that all guns could bear. Against this it was argued that there might not be time, and that a high standard of flying was called for; without it there would be stragglers. A critic of box section pointed out that the top section could offer no help if the attack was from under the tail of the lower section. By general agreement Wattisham and Raynham squadrons were to continue trials with formations.

On one point feeling was unanimous—the Blenheim remained under-defended even with nacelle and under-tail guns. Twin guns were desperately needed in the turret. Basil Embry described his twin-gun turret, which was inspected by Air Ministry officials on 23 January. Initially Blenheims had a B.I. Mk. I or II turret with a single Lewis gun. Then came the Mk. III with a Vickers K, in use at this time and for many months following. Now the modification existed whereby two Vickers K guns were installed in a Mk. IIIA turret. Ultimately, when supplies permitted, the Blenheim IV had the Mk. IV turret with twin Browning guns with higher rate of fire and continuous belt feed replacing the rotary magazine. This was many months away.

As well as extra guns there was a need for a mirror to give the pilot a view aft, additional to the side blisters now fitted. It was considered that there was an urgent need to provide the observer with a machine gun (fitted later in the noses of some Blenheims particularly for shipping strikes) on a gimbal mounting. Another improvement to aircraft was the fitting of self-sealing petrol tanks only about eight sets of which became available weekly, and which were still being fitted only on inner tanks.

At February's conference the A.O.C. revealed revised orders for large-scale raids on German power plants, to be issued next day, calling for groups of six aircraft (sixty-six in all) to attack eleven primary targets. Tactics for such an operation were discussed—in pairs, singly, in threes, use of cloud cover, etc. What was best? Salvo, or distributed load? Low level was preferred, but shallow dive was possible. At this stage this elaborate, frightening operation was still very much 'on'.

It was at this meeting that the A.O.C. stressed the importance of cloud flying. Perhaps he had a premonition, although for the present it meant often dashing into cloud safety. He said: 'If our crews can fly accurately in cloud they increase their own efficiency as a striking force, and own security.'

Grp. Capt. Vincent raised another important point, that of fighter escort hitherto somewhat overlooked. He suggested that Beaufighters should mingle with the Blenheims, but the A.O.C. said that there was no chance of getting any yet. Currently there was authority for only four Blenheims per squadron with extra guns fitted.

Ever ingenious, Wg. Cdr. Embry suggested filling fuel tanks with nitrogen as petrol was consumed. Test with incendiary bullets showed no fire if nitrogen was present. His interesting proposal was passed to Bomber Command.

Operational sorties were flown on ten days in February, and hindered by heavy snow at bases. On 14 February 21 Squadron carried out a reconnaissance of Borkum. A second machine, L8745 flown by Plt. Off. Stapleton, left at 15.00 hours. It was soon recalled but failed to receive the signal, its aerials having gone in heavy icing. Return was made in darkness. Sgt. Wetton contacted Heston radio but sent the wrong verification and was unacceptable. Too late Bomber Command realised who was calling. At 19.30 hours with fuel running short, and no idea of his position, the pilot ordered the crew out. Then he saw Very lights being fired from an airfield, landed and found it was Tangmere. The reconnaissance was repeated by 21 Squadron next day and severe icing was again met. Sgt. G. H. Tice in L9759 tried next and was shot down by Bf 109s off Heligoland. Photo-reconnaissances were flown by P4925 and N6185 to Cuxhaven, Brunsbuttel, Heligoland and Wilhelmshaven. Next day Sqn. Ldr. Doran flew an armed reconnaissance to the same area with orders to attack shipping thought to be possibly carrying troops for an attack on Norway. Ships flying neutral flags could only be attacked if they opened fire first. A suspected troopship flying a Norwegian flag was intercepted but refused to fire at Doran despite his several low passes. Five 109s intercepted him on the way home and later an armour-piercing bullet was removed from one of the Blenheim's fuel tanks—which proved to Doran quite conclusively that self-sealing tanks were essential.

A British submarine had been sunk off Heligoland and on 28th two crews of 82 Squadron tried to see if the enemy was salvaging it. Royal Navy requirements now were (1) sightings of large warships, (2) salvage on three submarines lost near Heligoland, (3) activity around Wilhelmshaven, (4) Schillig Roads, (5) Hamburg Docks, (6) Kiel Dock, (7) booms and harbour defences.

On 15 February twelve Blenheim crews began the ferrying of a dozen Blenheim Is to the brave Finnish Air Force. Crews were transferred to reserve, wearing civilian clothes for the trip which started from Bicester. Such was the plight of the Finns fighting the Russians that it was decided to send them more Blenheims—IVs this time. On 9 March volunteers were called for, four from 104 Squadron and recently arrived crews on operational units except XV and 40 Squadrons. Fifty crews were needed from 2 and 6 Groups to ferry the machines, and perhaps fly them operationally in Finland. Ten crews were needed to ferry aircraft and another forty to ferry them and fight in them. Eight of the Blenheims came from XV and 40 Squadrons. The scheme for fighting fell through but 24 Blenheims were eventually delivered to Finland before its collapse.

Operational effort in March was almost trebled. North Sea sweeps continued, and reconnaissances were made to fix positions of flak ships off the enemy coast. Searches for signs of the salvage of the British submarines *Starfish* and *Undine* continued but nothing was seen. On 4 March six Blenheims of 107 Squadron stood by for strike and reconnaissance duties. Two captained by Flg. Off. P. E. Warne and Sgt. R. S. Cunningham left Wattisham to reconnoitre flak ships and possible submarine salvage. Cunningham descended below cloud over the Schillig Roads and saw a U-boat sailing northwards on the surface. He dived N6183 to about 1,000 feet and dropped his four 250-pounders in a stick across it observing a bomb strike aft of the conning tower. A cloud of black-grey smoke belched forth and the submarine was surrounded by a mass of seething foam. Soon a wreck marker was in place and the U-boat was possibly sunk. Flt. Lt. H. F. Thompson returned to search for wreckage.

Sqn. Ldr. M. V. Delap of 82 Squadron flying P4852 was off Borkum on 11 March. He descended to 4,000 feet to look for barrage balloons above the cloud tops. He came down to 1,000 feet and was amazed to see a submarine upon which he quickly dropped four bombs. Two direct hits were observed and soon only a large oil patch marked the submarine's grave. Exploding bombs twisted the airframe and Delap had great difficulty in controlling the aircraft which persisted in flying in circles!

Next day Sqn. Ldr. Sutcliffe in P6910 at last found ships trying to salvage one of the British submarines and attacked them. On 16th nine 21 Squadron aircraft set out to attack flak ships. Four were engaged by heavy fire. Bf 109s fired at P6954 putting a bullet in the cockpit without causing injury. The port carburettor of L8738 was damaged. Flt. Lt. Petley of 21 Squadron flying with five of 82 Squadron on 19th flew a reconnaissance and attacked flak ships north of the Frisians. Three Bf 109s intercepted them but these they soon eluded as the bombers entered sea fog. A few minutes later a Bf 110 was avoided, again by flying into fog. 21, 82, 107 and 110 Squadrons all attacked flak ships during the month on a number of occasions without any satisfactory results.

On 27 March eight of 82 Squadron and seven of 107 took off mid-morning to attack the German Fleet after reports that large ships were at sea. Two of 107 Squadron were meanwhile making a reconnaissance of Hornum and Lyst following recent night bombing of Sylt. The 107 bombing force found enemy destroyers a few miles off Borkum and their bombs fell close to the ships. A cruiser and four destroyers were then seen a few miles away. Several attacks were made on flak ships and larger vessels were shadowed for about fifteen minutes. The photo-graphing of Hornum was meanwhile under way. Here Flg. Off. J. D. Murphy was subjected to anti-aircraft fire. Nevertheless he obtained good photos. Enemy fighters also came after him, but he escaped into cloud. Blenheim L8747 with him was last seen entering cloud with fighters on its tail. It was soon shot down. On seventeen days in March the squadrons operated.

Despite being more concerned with operations—especially the attacks on flak ships—107 Squadron detached four aircraft to A.F.D.E. Northolt on 23 March for special trials. One machine at last had a gun blister placed under the nose on the observer's escape hatch, a feature to become common on Blenheims within a few weeks.

Suddenly the entire pattern of 2 Group employment received its first big jolt, when the enemy invaded Scandinavia, bringing to an end the first phase of wartime operations.

Chapter 3
Scandinavian Interlude

At the start of April intelligence sources were again reporting German shipping massing in North German ports. Then some put to sea. Nine Blenheims of 82 Squadron left Bodney on 1 April to attack unidentified enemy ships off Denmark. Weather was unsuitable and the force returned without attacking, except for one section which came across four flak ships paired and some two miles apart. An attack was delivered and P8867 (Flg. Off. Harries) was shot down after bombing.

On 3 April 21 Squadron stood by to attack German submarines leaving by the exits in their mined area, but clouds were too low for operations to take place. Had they been flown it is just possible that crews might have come across even more rewarding targets for, this day, the first German supply ships sailed for the invasion of Norway, into the mist and safety.

Next day 82 Squadron was again busy. P6895 carrying Flg. Off. Hunt, Sgt. Crawley and L.A.C. Thripp left at 04.16 to attack the afore-mentioned submarines near Cuxhaven. Cloud was encountered and nothing seen, so the aircraft turned about. Over the sea their starboard engine momentarily failed at low level. The pilot inadvertently turned off the petrol cocks and lost control of his aircraft which struck the sea, ripping off its tail wheel and bending the tips of the starboard airscrew. He then climbed to 10,000 feet and luckily made base.

Meanwhile P4898 searched for submarines off Wilhelmshaven. Landfall was made at Spiekeroog at only 250 feet and the aircraft flew on to the Schillig Roads over which it spent 25 minutes in the face of intense accurate flak, then reached Wilhelmshaven. Two large warships were facing north in the roads, but no submarines were seen. In the afternoon the squadron sent two sections to attack these capital ships. Weather was poor and after a search the first section returned without sighting them. The second section pulled ahead but severe icing caused Sgt. Morrison to turn about. The other two proceeded east of Heligoland where at 17.15 they found a destroyer of the *Maas* class. Three minutes later two large warships were attacked, the nearest bomb falling forty yards away. They then made a fast get-away towards Heligoland.

With such targets available 21 Squadron next day despatched three sections to Wilhelmshaven. Rain and poor visibility were encountered and eight turned back. Bad weather had again protected the capital ships.

Next morning 21 Squadron sent two machines on an anti-submarine patrol in the same area. One crashed as soon as it was airborne, all being killed. The other turned about in a cloudless sky. This was unfortunate, for had it continued it would have found a large concentration of shipping in Wilhelmshaven Roads and perhaps seen *Scharnhorst, Gneisenau* and *Hipper* which had just put to sea with accompanying destroyers. Word that the force was at sea came from intelligence sources. Although aircraft were prepared none was despatched due to the weather.

Coastal Command searched but its Hudsons were driven off by enemy aircraft. The position of the German ships was known and the order given for 82 and 107 Squadrons to attack. 82 was away first, then Sqn. Ldr. Gibson had radio failure leaving Flt. Lt. Petley to lead. Another machine lost formation leaving only four to attack. This they were unable to do for lack of cloud cover.

Twelve Blenheims of 107 Squadron led by Wg. Cdr. Embry took off at 11.30. It was assumed the ships would be sailing at 15 knots and an estimated position of attack computed. For most of the journey outwards it was fine. Visibility then fell from thirty to five miles near the likely position of the ships, cloud becoming 10/10 at 7,000 feet. Around the estimated point of interception both boxes turned on to course 350 degrees and, after four minutes' flying, found seventeen ships including *Scharnhorst* and *Gneisenau*. In sections of three they attacked from 6,000 feet. Twelve 250-lb. S.A.P. bombs were seen to fall across the battle cruisers, but the nearest bomb was fifteen yards from *Scharnhorst*. When the remainder arrived the enemy was ready, with a hail of flak following the first six as they left. Again bombs missed. Details of the fleet were given by W/T on the homeward journey, but in the heat of battle some ships were wrongly identified. What had been the target was the force partly intended for the seizure of Narvik and Trondheim. A later attack mounted by Wellingtons was unsuccessful.

On 8 April 21 and 82 Squadrons between them despatched eight aircraft to search for ships which 107 Squadron had attacked. Nothing was seen. At last a Sunderland of 204 Squadron found *Scharnhorst* and *Gneisenau*, but *Hipper* and a destroyer screen had by now turned away for the Atlantic. More sorties were sent early on 9th, by which time the ships were in Norwegian waters and beyond the range of East Anglian based Blenheims.

Soon the Germans overran Denmark and were landing by air and sea in Norway. Airfields at Stavanger/Sola and Oslo/Fornebu[1] were quickly

---

[1] Stavanger/Sola, Oslo/Fornebu, Oslo/Kjeller. Method of identifying airfields (and targets) on the Continent. Sola is close to Stavanger, and Fornebu and Kjeller are both close to Oslo. This method will be used throughout. Thus Lille/Nord, Lille/Seclin, Lille/Lomme, etc. Rouen/Sotteville, for instance, refers to the Sotteville district of Rouen.

captured by paratroops and transport-landed troops. Then Oslo/Kjeller fell. In a few hours the Luftwaffe was operating from captured airfields which assumed considerable importance, especially Sola. These were small targets and, as things stood, out of range to all but the Whitleys of 4 Group unsuitable for daylight operations. Standbys continued in case enemy warships came once more into range.

On 13 April No. 2 Group Operations Order 10 was issued: 'It is of utmost importance the enemy activity over Norway and adjacent waters be reduced to a minimum in the immediate future,' it read. 'Heavy bomber Groups will make night attacks on airfields in Norway. Our task is to destroy aircraft and supplies and personnel at Stavanger airfield and seaplane base. 107 Squadron will be under the direct control of 2 Group from 15 April when this order is effective. 107 Squadron is to operate from Lossiemouth up to twelve aircraft daily.' Armed with 250-lb. bombs, attacks were to rely upon cloud cover if possible, otherwise take place in clear weather employing ruses. Even from Scotland attacking Stavanger meant a round trip of over 900 miles.

Hardly had the signal been despatched when a scare arose. Indications implied that the enemy might launch an invasion of Holland and Belgium. Clearly, little of 2 Group could possibly be sent to aid the Norwegian campaign. The invasion never came.

Early on 15th 110 Squadron despatched two reconnaissance sorties to the Heligoland area to see if the enemy ships had returned—they hadn't. L8752 encountered heavy fire when it attacked a patrol ship, and was shot down. Soon after Kenneth Doran brought his aircraft home with hits in the wings and tailplane, an order was received for 110 Squadron also to join 107 at Lossiemouth for attacks on Norway. Three Rapides and an Ensign arrived to carry the squadron north.

The previous day 107 had flown to Scotland with the help of a Bombay transport. On arrival the Blenheims were quickly dispersed and immediately prepared for operations. Ground crews had a difficult task for there was a boisterous wind and driving sleet—it was still very much winter in Scotland. All the 250-pounders had to be manhandled since bomb trolleys were still on a train making the long journey from Stowmarket. Nevertheless twelve aircraft were standing by at dawn for Stavanger, a very good effort. Each carrying four bombs, they set off for the long sea crossing at 10.30 led by Embry. Heavy rain and sleet were encountered en route and a heavy snowstorm near the target. Two seaplanes were destroyed.

Obviously the weather and the long journeys were going to pose problems. On 16 April only one of six machines that set out reached Stavanger. There was severe icing over the North Sea and one machine iced up going out of control at 14,000 feet. It spun to within 600 feet of the sea before recovery was made. Another flew so low that it hit the sea in a blinding snowstorm severely damaging its tail.

At 11.30 the airborne machines received a warning that a He 111 was in the vicinity of base. Wg. Cdr. Embry immediately took off to intercept the raider but did not find it. What a fine example he always set!

Attempts to bomb Stavanger were left largely to 107 who tried again on 17th with a dozen aircraft, the day when Air Vice-Marshal James Robb became A.O.C. Seventy miles from the Norwegian coast at 10,000 feet they observed He 111s attacking a cruiser and four destroyers. Embry wheeled the formation to give the impression his bombers were fighters. The Heinkels fled into cloud. Course was resumed for Stavanger. Once there the formation split, one box bombing from 18,000 feet and the other sweeping in at a little above 1,000 feet. Guns and fighters engaged them and two Blenheims curled away smoking after lengthy engagements. Hits were claimed on runways and dispersals.

When the weather was not too bad it was often too good. When 107 next tried, it came across dangerous, cloudless skies. Twice on 21st 110 Squadron despatched sorties, all abortive due to clear weather. Raids were next preluded by a met. reconnaissance, the first being flown on 22nd by Doran in a clear sky. To combat these conditions six of 107 Squadron left at 01.20 hours to attempt a night raid on 24th. Fires were seen after low passes but night fighters interfered and Plt. Off. J. D. Murphy failed to return.

A weather reconnaissance on 25th showed Stavanger clear, then came news of a shipping concentration at Ulsik in Granvins Fiord. Six crews of 110 Squadron set off. Flg. Off. G. M. Wright attacked a ship but his number two was shot down after failing to reach the target. Two enemy fighters were forced down, after engaging Plt. Off. R. J. Hill a hundred miles out to sea. Three of the other Blenheims attacked ships without success.

Stavanger was next raided on 30th, by six Blenheims of 110 Squadron led by Sqn. Ldr. Doran in L9242. It was a late afternoon attack and, after the bombing, Bf 109s attacked and caught a formation of subs. From the operation Flt. Sgt. Abbott and the famed Kenneth Doran, leader of 2 Group's first wartime raid, were missing. Ironically this was 110's last operation of the campaign for on 1st May it was ordered back to Wattisham where its fifteen remaining aircraft arrived next day.

107 Squadron continued the struggle, twice on 1 May achieving excellent results in perfect weather. Direct hits were scored on the airfield and aircraft. On 2nd good results were again obtained, but the value of these attacks was now in doubt and 107 was told to take its seventeen aircraft back to Wattisham on 3 May. Fear of an attack on Germany's western front was increasing and 2 Group needed its whole strength to face it.

In the course of twenty raids 113 sorties had been despatched and seven crews were now missing. They had done their best under difficult conditions. So far the sea had been 2 Group's backdrop to most operations. Soon it was to be very different.

Chapter 4

Assault on France

Prologue

An attack on France and the Low Countries was long expected, and during the winter of 1939–40 the enemy steadily built up his land forces in the west. Our troops forming the British Expeditionary Force prepared extensive defences along the border with Belgium for it was believed that no German attack was likely against the strong Maginot line. The French Staff considered a thrust through the Ardennes impossible for this was a region where armoured fighting vehicles would find it extremely difficult to operate. Therefore, it was thought likely attack would probably come through Belgium, in the so-called Northern Zone.

The implications of this reasoning were discussed at Bomber Command in October 1939. On 21 October H.Q. Bomber Command shrewdly commented in a letter to 2 Group: 'It is not certain a large bomber force will be economically effective against an advancing army with anti-aircraft and fighter defences. The scale of effort will depend on the gravity of the situation. Battles and Blenheims will normally be employed against columns of troops, AFVs and motorised columns at the head of advancing armies.' Heavy bombers would operate against strategic targets.

Two contingency plans worked out for the B.E.F. related to attack through Belgium. Our troops would move rapidly to take up positions along the River Dyle. This meant an advance of about sixty miles with the Belgians on the left flank and the French on the right, with the B.E.F. flanking Louvain and the French holding the line south from Wavre. The alternative was to hold the line of the Scheldt, known to the British as the River Escaut, much further north-west and allowing little defence in depth.

On 25 October highly detailed notes were issued to bomber stations listing a host of possible targets to be studied in likely areas of enemy advance in Holland and Belgium. There the matter rested for three months, punctuated by an alert in November when intelligence sources indicated a possible enemy attack which never materialised.

The original intention was that 2 Group would move to France as the

Second Echelon of the A.A.S.F. Although the French were keen to have as many British aircraft on their territory as possible to repel the invader, they had not prepared sufficient airfields in time and 2 Group therefore remained at its peacetime stations in East Anglia, poised for operations against Germany. In the event this proved unfortunate. Although the Blenheim medium bombers could still attack German targets from their distant eastern bases, their primary task in the event of an invasion was to assist the A.A.S.F. support the B.E.F. in the defence of France. There was not unanimous agreement on the role for 2 Group, however, and some voiced the opinion that it would be unwise to employ the Blenheim force in this manner. Airfield building went slowly ahead in France, hindered by a hard winter, and some attempt was made to form mobile squadrons for the Continent but none was ready before the spring.

Intelligence sources rightly indicated a possible German attack early in January, and 2 Group issued an Operations Instruction on 14 January to cover the attack expected on 17th. It re-emphasised October's main points. Orders were now given that bomb loads on the Blenheims would be two 250-pounders and twenty 40-pound anti-personnel bombs. They should be dropped in sticks, but precise manner of attack was left to captains. A limiting factor was the safe height to avoid bomb blast— 1,000 feet for the 250-lb. bombs and 700 feet for the 40-pounders. Attacks above 1,000 feet were, however, considered unlikely to be accurate. Whether the bombs were large enough to cause much damage against all except troops was then not questioned. Nos. 21, 82, 107 and 110 Squadrons were told that they would very likely be moved to France as earlier envisaged, forming an advanced echelon to operate for two or three days at high pressure to halt the invasion. The A.A.S.F., which had been under Bomber Command, was now placed under the control of the Air Officer Commanding-in-Chief, Air Marshal Barratt, at whose disposal 2 Group would be placed in the event of the invasion which did not materialise.

Fear of a blitzkrieg on the West increased as weeks passed, better weather came and the enemy gathered strength. In conference with Group leaders on 8 February the A.O.C., Air Vice-Marshal C. T. Maclean, reiterated that Group's task would be to delay any advance. Practice attacks were to be made on troops and convoys in Britain. 'Most opposition,' he said, 'will come from fighters, and the German policy, if attacked, will probably be to keep troops on the move.' The representative from Wattisham thought pairs of aircraft most likely to be successful—lone aircraft if the weather was bad. Wg. Cdr. Foster from Wattisham accurately forecast that targets would be hard to find, and pilots would need to rely on observers for navigation.

A thrust would most likely take place along one of three routes— astride the River Waal to the River Eisel, through Roermond or north of the Waal through Hengelo and Emmerich.

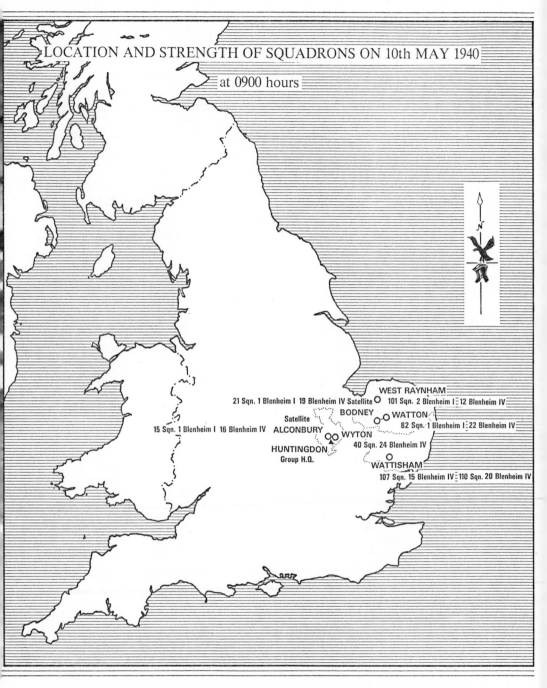

LOCATION AND STRENGTH OF SQUADRONS ON 10th MAY 1940

at 0900 hours

WEST RAYNHAM
21 Sqn. 1 Blenheim I 19 Blenheim IV Satellite ○ 101 Sqn. 2 Blenheim I⁼ 12 Blenheim IV⁼

BODNEY WATTON
Satellite ○○○ 82 Sqn. 1 Blenheim I⁼ 22 Blenheim IV⁼
15 Sqn. 1 Blenheim I 16 Blenheim IV ALCONBURY ○○ WYTON
HUNTINGDON 40 Sqn. 24 Blenheim IV
Group H.Q.
○
WATTISHAM
107 Sqn. 15 Blenheim IV⁼ 110 Sqn. 20 Blenheim IV

MAP 6

On 29 February instructions were given that the squadrons at Watton and Wattisham would initially attack enemy movements on these routes, aiming at the heads of columns at defiles to cause congestion. There was no mention then of possible use of airborne troops by the enemy, which was to alter the pattern envisaged for the invasion of Holland.

Here plans again rested covering three contingencies: an attack on Holland, an attack through Belgium to France and a direct onslaught on France with simultaneous thrusts into the Low Countries.

On 10 May 1940, No. 2 Group Operations Instruction No. 31 reached the stations reiterating the possibility of simultaneous routes of attack. 'The probable role of the squadrons,' it read, 'will be, during the very early stages after the violation of Holland, to reconnoitre to locate the advance of the enemy columns, and to attack columns of AFVs and mechanised columns at the head of the advancing armies.' Nos. 21, 40 and 82 Squadrons—one from each base—were told they might have to operate from France.

Ironically, even before the plans were received at Group stations, the enemy attacked Holland and Belgium using a spearhead of airborne forces as in Norway. These landed on Dutch airfields and also at the Eban fortress in Belgium, whilst land forces hurried into Holland, Belgium and Luxembourg. The assault was on a much larger scale than anticipated, covering a larger area and using unexpected tactics. Confused reports were all that existed during the morning but by midday it was clear that action must be taken—and quickly. The enemy was advancing fast. 2 Group was now placed at the disposal of the A.O.C., A.A.S.F., who could call upon it to give tactical support to the B.E.F.

Reaction

Operations by 2 Group that followed in support of the British Army fell into five phases prior to withdrawal of British troops from Dunkirk. On 10 May raids were made on Dutch airfields in a fruitless attempt to destroy those footholds. Then followed desperate attempts to halt the enemy advance at Maastricht by destroying bridges over the River Meuse. When the enemy crossed that river near Sedan, 2 Group joined the A.A.S.F. in a vain attempt to destroy multiple bridges, facing tremendous anti-aircraft barrage and suffering great loss.

Failing to stop the advance, squadrons of the Group concentrated in attacking roads along which the enemy advanced, and attempted to destroy tanks, motor vehicles and troops. Villages were bombed to slow the enemy, houses were felled to block roads. Bridges, cross-roads, troop concentrations, railway lines—all were attacked, with armoured fighting vehicles prime targets for level raids.

Heavy loss sustained by 82 Squadron on 17 May prompted a consideration to change to night attacks only once tried. Using limited equipment such raids could achieve virtually nothing. In any case 2 Group was not trained for night operations.

It was then decided to continue day raids using cloud cover with fighter escort or support over the target area. Fighters of 11 Group or the A.A.S.F. either gave reasonably close escort or patrolled the area of attack. The former was the better but difficult to arrange. The latter indicated to the enemy where attack would come, attracted his fighters and led troops to disperse quickly. Rather primitive attempts to provide fighter escort quickly revealed need for careful briefing and accurate timing at the rendezvous if the fighters' limited endurance was not to be wasted. They gave emphasis to the need to maintain good formation—and there were complaints on this score. There had been some bad station keeping and, if opened up, bomber formations were easy prey to fighters. But open they had to, in avoiding flak. Bombing on section leader's order or his release was usual, but low-level attack, shallow-dive, line-astern attacks, all were employed.

Most serious of all, there was constantly a lamentable lack of precise target information. Briefing was indeed brief, crews being given lists of roads on which their targets might be found. Group was largely dependent on information relayed from France, often outdated by the time the Blenheims reached their targets. To improve matters Group despatched on its own initiative low-level reconnaissance flights to gather up-to-date information, but this rarely solved a basic problem.

When Allied armour attempted a counter-attack near Arras on 21 May the squadrons gave it their support, but little could be achieved by a handful of Blenheims and a mutilated force of A.A.S.F. Battles. Operations to delay the advance on Boulogne followed. Then the Group flew many sorties harassing the route to Calais, making a particular point of bombing pontoon bridges over marshy ground leading towards Dunkirk.

As the British Expeditionary Force struggled towards Dunkirk 2 Group joined the clearly desperate battle with a vengeance, making very determined attempts to delay the enemy, particularly after it had been decided to take troops from Dunkirk beach. Group then waged an intensive campaign against German troops, armour, supplies, rail links, bridges and transport. As the final and most difficult part of withdrawal took place in the early hours of 3 June, Blenheims patrolled over enemy guns to prevent them firing at shipping and troops embarking.

Such were the phases. The campaign was harsh and bloody. It took a tremendous toll of the Group over an area where British lives had, a little over two decades ago, been laid down in profusion. Place names familiar to the older generation were soon figuring in the new battle orders. It seemed the old story over again.

Response

10 May. Throughout the morning when the blitzkrieg opened, and whilst the A.A.S.F.'s Fairey Battles awaited French permission to attack, reports on the extent of the enemy assault filtered into 2 Group Headquarters. All squadrons were put at immediate readiness. The seriousness of the situation in Holland was soon apparent. Sqn. Ldr. Paddon and Flg. Off. Burns of 40 Squadron left Wyton at 09.05 hours on a fact-finding reconnaissance of the Hague area, in accordance with 2 Group Instruction No. 24. Paddon found many enemy aircraft in the area and drove off a marauding Ju 88. His damaged engine burst into flames as he touched down at base. He was luckier than Burns and crew who did not return, bringing 2 Group its first loss in the campaign.

At midday the decision was made to attack Ju 52 transports and troops on two Dutch aerodromes, rather than follow up plans to attack troop columns the positions of which could not be accurately ascertained. First away was XV Squadron, Wyton, despatching nine Blenheims at 14.15 hours with Sqn. Ldr. H. Y. Lawrence, Flt. Lt. Webster and Flt. Lt. P. G. Chapman as section leaders. All were briefed to bomb Waalhaven. It was held by paratroops, a state of affairs which must be deleted. The Blenheims swept in at 3,000 feet to make shallow dives, and claimed hits on a dozen aircraft. Hangars, too, were bombed and seven Ju 52s left blazing. Three sticks of bombs fell upon a line of anti-aircraft guns already deployed and in action, testimony to German thoroughness. Flg. Off. D. Jones had his port wing holed by flak which missed a fuel tank by inches. Other aircraft were damaged, but all returned.

Sqn. Ldr. G. W. C. Gleed later led a dozen Blenheims of 40 Squadron to bomb Ypenburg. Shallow dive attacks were made, craters soon pitting the airfield. A hangar was left blazing. Cost? Two crews missing.

Finally came twelve of 110 Squadron, Wattisham, led by Sqn. Ldr. Sabine and escorted by six Blenheim 1F Fighters of 600 Squadron, all bent on destroying Ju 52 transports on the beach eight miles north of The Hague. From above the shore six of the bombers dived into a low-level attack. Then the fighters raked the beach, followed by the remainder of the bombers. One transport was lifted off the ground by blast and started to burn.

An evening reconnaissance by L8739 and L8742 of 21 Squadron was ordered to obtain photographs of the Nijmegen–Rhein–Munster–Verhlk area, to gather details of the German land advance and allow planning of tomorrow's operations. The advance was found to be rapid and the fluid situation made targeting unpredictable much ahead.

11 May. Immediately the enemy attacked on 10 May the British Expeditionary Force began to enact Plan D. By 11 May it was in position along the River Dyle in Belgium. Movement had been unimpeded since the Wehrmacht preferred to fight our Army in a region of shallow defence instead of on a fortified border.

The northern front line was now established along the banks of the Meuse and Dyle, between which was a strip of country around Gembloux defended by the French but without any natural defensive features. Therein lay a weakness that was to cost the Allies dear.

Throughout the morning reports reached 2 Group that strong enemy columns were passing through Maastricht towards our troops. Another unexpected thrust was developing through the Ardennes. It was decided to attempt to halt enemy movement through Maastricht. Telephoned orders decreed that Watton and Wattisham were each to send a squadron to bomb the column at suitable defiles, particularly at the bridges over the Maas and Maas Canal in, and west, of Maastricht. If no movement was visible, squadrons were to follow the road to lessen the effect of any flak defences. Success would give the British troops longer to dig in along the Dyle.

Twelve crews of 21 Squadron had been at readiness since 04.30. They had an interminable wait and eventually eleven took off at 15.10 hours. Such long waits, so tiring and trying, were to be a memorable feature of the campaign but were inevitable when intelligence was poor.

They reached the main bridge at Maastricht, but only damaged it. 'We all went in,' recalls Peter Sarll, 'led by Scottie Pryde who chose to circle a bit before leading us in, with the result that when we did start running in we were in the middle of the biggest barrage I could possibly imagine. I do not know to this day how some of us ever got through it for there didn't seem an inch of sky that was not covered with flak. I don't remember how many we lost then, the awful moments I do remember were going back into the villages of Watton where the young wives were waiting for their husbands who had not returned, and never would.'

Official records indicate that only one Blenheim returned unscathed. One plummeted flaming, another fell in Belgium after shooting down a Bf 109. Two of the crew became prisoners and one died from wounds. No. 110 Squadron, alerted for operations all day, eventually did not operate. Instead, Wg. Cdr. Foster tried out a Blenheim with a blister gun turret but this would give little comfort, it was plain to see.

12 May. To halt the enemy advance the bridges at Maastricht *had* to be destroyed. Already the Germans were pouring over them and had seized others over the Albert Canal by airborne assault. The task was urgent. At 08.10 hours twelve crews of 107 Squadron led by Wg. Cdr. B. E. Embry left for the first attack of the day. Fifteen miles from the target the flak began increasing in intensity to form a fearful barrage. Nevertheless they pressed on and again a bridge was damaged. Eleven aircraft were hit by flak and Plt. Off. Thornton shot down. It then became impossible to hold formation. Once this was broken waiting Bf 109s pounced. Flg. Off. Rotherham was engaged but shook off his pursuers to set down his damaged aircraft and wounded observer in Belgium. A few moments later he was astonished to find himself standing before none other than Admiral of the Fleet Sir Roger Keyes and H.M. King Leopold of the Belgians!

Before the remainder of the force could close for protection fighters claimed aircraft captained by Flg. Off. H. E. Edwards and Plt. Off. O. H. Keedwell. The remainder closed up to fight their way out. A twenty-minute battle for survival followed probably costing the enemy two fighters. It left part of a squadron of battered Blenheims to stagger home with battle-shaken crews.

Rightly the enemy assessed this was but the beginning of the day's assault on Maastricht, and waited fully alerted for the next wave of Blenheims. Twelve crews of XV Squadron had come to stand by at Alconbury at 05.30 hours. They were briefed to bring down houses thereby blocking roads through Maastricht, and destroy bridges across the Albert Canal. Sections led by Sqn. Ldr. Glenn, Flg. Off. A. E. Oakley, Sqn. Ldr. Lawrence and Flt. Lt. Webster were over target at 09.15 beneath the protection of a squadron of circling Hurricanes which had the effect of warning the enemy of impending action. As XV Squadron ran in the guns opened up again forcing the squadron to break formation, to the delight of the Messerschmitts which in a swarm dealt with the Hurricanes and the Blenheims. From the ensuing carnage emerged six badly shot-up Blenheims which, three hours after take-off, entered the Wyton circuit fortunately carrying few wounded. The remainder—half the force—had been shot out of the sky. This was a staggering blow, and for all 2 Group its portent was grim.

Of the 36 men who had set off eighteen were missing. Only two of the remaining aircraft could be made serviceable, and XV Squadron was virtually wiped out. Flg. Off. Eames was rushed to Ely hospital with terrible facial injuries caused when an explosive shell burst in the cockpit between the seat and rudder bar. Flt. Lt. Webster had a bullet in each foot. Enemy fighters had holed the hydraulic system of L8800, Plt. Off. Robinson's machine, which nevertheless soldiered on to become a veteran of 32 sorties and eventually crashed when setting off for the Essen 1,000-bomber raid in 1942. But for the Blenheim squadrons the day was far from ended.

Next it was 110 Squadron's turn. Eleven crews managed hits on a bridge. Flak damaged all but three of the Blenheims, and two were shot down, one by fighters which forced it down in Belgium after it had accounted for a Messerschmitt. Cost so far? Eleven Blenheims shot down and XV Squadron almost wiped out.

Since 07.30 hours No. 82 Squadron had been standing by awaiting its turn with trepidation. After a day-long wait it was ordered to take-off at 19.30 hours, nine crews being sent to crater a road on the embankment along the Albert Canal north of Hasselt. A successful raid was carried out and all the aircraft returned.

In the afternoon A.A.S.F. Battles courageously attempted to bring down two bridges, but fighters and flak cut their success. During the evening it was 21 Squadron's turn. This time the target was a road in Tongres which nine Blenheims bombed from 7,000 feet at 20.40 hours. Flt. Lt. Watson, a section leader, was hit and L8739's rear fuselage shattered and fell away. Luckily there was some cloud about, and the remainder were circling Wyton soon after 23.00 hours. It had been a long, cruel, devastating day.

13 May. There were no operations that day. The weather was not good. Heavy losses the previous day called for a temporary halt and assessment of the general situation.

Whilst the crews rested news came through that during the night German forces had forded the Meuse in rubber boats near Houx establishing small bridgeheads at Dinant and Sedan. French forces, weak in this area where they had considered an attack unlikely, had fallen back. It was a severe setback. A most important natural barrier to the Germans had been breached. A serious situation rapidly developed. In the afternoon Stukas mercilessly attacked the French whilst the Wehrmacht consolidated its positions.

14 May. In the morning the A.A.S.F. attacked the Meuse crossing point at Sedan. Then the French implored the British to join in a much heavier attack for the enemy was now across the river on a fifteen-mile front. It was made later that afternoon, and at terrible cost. Forty A.A.S.F. bombers were lost out of 71 despatched. They had been engaged by a swarm of Messerschmitts and destroyed.

The day's effort by 2 Group began when six crews of 82 Squadron tried to block the road east of Breda, cut the railway leading to Tilburg and thereby assist the French Seventh Army. Heavy flak upset their aim but there were bursts on a cross-roads and houses were felled.

All day long the squadrons were at standby, alone with their thoughts, awaiting the call. It came late afternoon following the A.A.S.F.'s disaster.

Fearful of what would befall, 28 crews drawn from Nos. 21, 107 and 110 Squadrons gallantly set forth with strong fighter cover to the frightening Sedan area. Many in the formation had flown together for years. One was amongst good friends—but for how long? At high levels fighters defended the German troops. Against low-level attack quick firing anti-aircraft guns and machine guns were deployed. British fighters—when they were used—were insufficient in strength to remove the Messerschmitts, consequently the Blenheims had to attack at low level trusting to such speed and surprise as they could muster. Their speed was too slow, the surprise rarely achieved. Their losses were consistently high.

Six of 107 Squadron roared in to attack advancing troops near Sedan. The barrage was tremendous and at the count five Blenheims had been hit but somehow survived. In went 110 Squadron and as soon as the flak had forced them apart the fighters rushed in—five out of the twelve Blenheims were soon destroyed.

The last to attack was 21 Squadron whose target lay in a wood a quarter of a mile west of Givons. This was an episode which Flg. Off. Sarll was to recall with horror all his life.

'My memory is first of an amazing collection of aircraft. There seemed to be tremendous dog fights going on between biplanes and monoplanes, and I had a weird thought that I had flown amongst Richthofen's Circus of the 1914–18 War! After we dropped our bombs where we were supposed to we came haring back at plus nine boost, and I think I was Flt. Lt. Petley's No. 2 and "Blankie" Blanckensee his No. 3. I formed up fairly quickly and "Blankie" was trailing behind. There was a bit of cloud cover above, and we were suddenly pounced upon by 109s. "Petters", for some reason unknown, did not take cover but "Blankie" did. He then must have seen "Gilly" (Flt. Lt. R. G. M. Gilmore) go down, and I lost a very good friend; I can only assume that he decided to keep to the golden rule of formation which is, at all costs, after attack rejoin and close up to maintain fire power (which at this time piteously consisted of one effective gun in the turret of each aircraft), and attempted to rejoin us. The odds were very much against him, but he persisted—a courageous young man. Unfortunately he, too, was shot down before he could reach us. Petters and I were alone.

'He must have been hit because he went lower and lower and then disappeared. (He eventually returned to England having forced landed.)

'By this time Lightfoot, my gunner, had received an explosive bullet in his shoulder. We had lost our hydraulic system and, as far as I could make out, had only about 1½ engines. Lightfoot's condition kept my mind so occupied that I carried on. By this time the German fighters had either run out of ammo or decided they had had enough victory and gone home. How I returned to base I shall never know, but with a 109 to Lightfoot's credit, a very bad landing to mine, we made it—to the green fields of Norfolk again.

'On landing I stupidly forgot to jettison the underneath front gun, one of the bits of devilment thought up by Basil Embry; these guns were fired by the observer looking into a mirror, and must have been a very nasty shock to the Messerschmitt boys when they first encountered them. By this time, with the pressure caused by Basil Embry, an armament king and by that time the day bomber pilot of fame, some Blenheims were bristling with guns. I am certain that it was Jock Gibson or Coutts Wood (Coutty) who thought of throwing out empty beer bottles which screamed as they fell to the ground, and I like to think

I had something to do with the idea of firing smoke puffs from a Very pistol. Whether either of these frivolities had any effect on German troops or Luftwaffe we will never know.

'I do not think anyone who did not experience what we were called upon to perform this day could ever visualise the tremendous courage of our people, so many of whom died. We were three to a crew, twelve crews to a squadron, and our lives depended upon one another. We reached out to one another for strength and support; when one was low we tried to boost him up. I remember seeing many of them vomiting before getting into the aircraft—a sure sign of physical and mental exhaustion. There was, too, the toll of the standbys, at 30 minutes readiness in the aircraft, taxiing to take-off, and then being recalled because the square that was chalked on the observer's map was the position of our own troops; and so back to dispersal, switch-off and then that awful waiting again.

'Having a second tour on Lancasters and experiencing the smoothness of the higher organisation and its tremendous efficiency, I used to look back on the old Blenheim days and wonder how any of us survived. At times we came back to a half-empty mess and had the awful business of having to collect our friend's belongings, and yet, with people around like Paddy Bandon, we could not be low for very long. Paddy to us *was* 2 Group and everything that it now stood for, and I do not think he will ever have any idea of the strength of his personality at that time. And, my goodness, we needed someone like him!'

By the end of this day, when many long friendships were brutally smashed, a new threat had occurred. French troops heavily engaged in the Gembloux gap had been forced to withdraw. The thrust here was rapidly appearing more serious than the crossing of the Meuse. To maintain the line the B.E.F. had withdrawn to west of the Dyle destroying bridges across it. Despite vicious attack the British line had held, the B.E.F. had been unyielding—unlike the French Army.

15 May. XV Squadron trickled back into action contributing three crews to Wyton's twelve-aircraft force sent to the Dinant–Celles road. By using high-level attacks at 10,000 feet, and shallow dives from 5,000 feet, it was hoped to confuse the defenders. Houses near Dinant bridges were set ablaze, but most bombs fell half a mile away on the river bank, for heavy opposition upset the aim, and cost the life of Wg. Cdr. E. C. Barlow. Over the Belgian coast on the way home Plt. Off. Harrison lost the propeller from his starboard engine, and force-landed in Belgium. His observer Sgt. Stamford was taken to hospital but Harrison and L.A.C. Moorhouse examined the wreckage of their aircraft. The accumulator leads had been shot away and no bombs released. Miraculously the load—and crew—had survived a bumpy landing. Two other aircraft in the raid were shot down.

Later Wg. Cdr. the Earl of Bandon flying P4848: UX-K led twelve

Blenheims of 82 Squadron to Montherme, between Mézières and Fumé, where the enemy was concentrated. Over the target the Blenheims broke into line astern for bombing, so that the flak could not concentrate on one aircraft for long. Bombs fell on roads and a square, then a Henschel Hs 126 tried to interfere. No match for a Blenheim, it soon fled. A Bf 109 fired—and retired with shots in its wings put there by Cpl. Harris. An escort of French Hawk 75 fighters had reduced the success of the interceptors.

16 May. Hectic battle, high attrition and the sheer effort demanded had been wearing for men and machinery. No operations were flown. On the ground the situation was worsening. Around Gembloux, with no natural barrier, the German Army was successfully breaking through the gap whilst the B.E.F. was hammered around Louvain. Late in the day the Wehrmacht was advancing at Gembloux on a three-mile front. In the Sedan area the advance was even more rapid. To maintain a line the B.E.F. had to withdraw. Over the next three days it fell back to the banks of the River Escaut. In the south strong defences were organised around Arras. Operations absolutely had to be resumed next day, and at daybreak.

17 May. At dawn twelve crews of 82 Squadron set off for the Gembloux gap. The guns and fighters butchered them and only one returned from one of the most disastrous episodes of 2 Group's war, recorded in the opening of this book.

One reaction to losses was a resort to night attacks, where success could be but slight. As an alternative the Group Commander decided upon raids with cloud or fighter cover. The latter was easy to recommend, difficult to implement.

18 May. On this crucial day of the campaign it seemed prudent to order no more operations. Throughout 17 May the Wehrmacht flooded through the Gembloux gap and swarmed forward at Sedan. Things were so bad that the five remaining operational 2 Group squadrons simply had to be hurled into action. From Wyton XV Squadron sent six Blenheims to attack columns approaching Le Cateaux and destroy a bridge there. Fighters and flak intruded upon the bombers and soon destroyed half the force. Sqn. Ldr. Lawrence and Flt. Lt. Chapman were missing. In enforcing heavy losses, the enemy was killing off many squadron and flight commanders and experienced personnel.

En route XV Squadron had landed at Abbeville intending to pick up an escort which they were directed to meet at Douai. None arrived. After bombing, they were told, land at Poix, re-arm and repeat the operation. When they did so, two of the remaining three aircraft were too shot up to fly again.

One was P6913, Flg. Off. L. H. Trent's machine damaged by flak and shot up by a 109. Seeing that two or three days would be needed to repair it the crew settled for a respite in France. Soon they were in Poix enjoying omelettes and copious liquid. Around 20.00 hours they were shaken from their pleasure by a commotion in the street. Greatly agitated, a French motor cyclist proclaimed that the Germans were right behind him. An urgent conference agreed priorities of action.

Loath to be deprived of liquid entertainment and cognisant that the wine cellar would soon be German property, they took advantage of the confusion by visiting the vault where Sutcliffe, the w. op./air gunner, filled his parachute bag with bottles of Cointreau and Benedictine. Very contented the crew piled into the civilian confusion, drew their pistols, then commandeered a Citroen whose unwilling driver took them back to the airfield.

Trent had resolved to attempt a flight home. Whilst the engines were being started the decidedly giggly navigator and gunner tried to load the loot. The navigator threw up the parachute bag, which Sutcliffe promptly missed. It crashed to the ground. Horrified silence ensued until examination revealed only one broken bottle of Cointreau.

Despite the large hole in P6913's wing Trent took-off and was soon facing German fire. Very soon they were sobered with the realisation they were an unscheduled flight. They were also quite lost in the darkness. Suddenly French guns opened up too. Sutcliffe quickly contacted home base, arranging to call for a fix when he was nearer. Knowing he had crossed the French coast Trent turned north and aimed for the Norfolk coast intending a landfall there rather than arouse the suspicions of 'trigger happy' gunners around the Thames Estuary.

When Sutcliffe tried for a fix he had no success. Astonishingly, Wyton had closed for the night. By turning left, they knew, they would soon be over England, albeit in complete darkness in a damaged aircraft. Suddenly an airfield displayed lights. There they promptly landed discovering themselves at Martlesham in Suffolk.

Earlier that day 21 Squadron had also flown to Poix. When no fighters showed up the squadron wisely flew home. No. 40 Squadron was luckier. It operated from Abbeville to bomb troops near Landacres, meeting little opposition. When 107 Squadron followed, it reached Poix only to be told paratroops had landed close by and, like 110 Squadron which soon arrived, had to make a hasty retreat. Using advanced airfields, an attractive idea permitting fast turn-round and more sorties, produced nasty problems.

19 May. Serious 2 Group losses had alarmed the Air Staff. They considered that future Blenheim attacks should be by night. Then Air Marshal Barratt of the A.A.S.F. called for help. Day raids would continue—with fighter escort.

There were no operations. This afforded the crews the chance for rest or a hasty trip to London, or Norwich, on 'black market' petrol. But it was impossible for any to overlook the ordeal through which all were now passing. How many would survive the morrow? Make hay today. Peter Sarll recalls those fearsome days: 'It's strange how many memories still seem so vivid. There was the crofter's cottage used as Bodney's NAAFI, where we could buy cups of tea and bits and pieces. It always appeared to me that at any moment the building would tumble down, just like our lives. I felt if this old wreck could keep standing, offering comfort and cheer, then somehow I might keep going.

'Then there was the Club at Watton where we used to meet, run by some charming people. I can't remember how or why they started it, but we used to go there to meet the young wives and always have good times in spite of the weight that bore down upon us as we lost our friends. "Trickie" Gibbs was always in great demand with his baritone voice and his guitar. "Trickie" he had been since the day he picked the lock on the room of our C.O., Skipper Keenes. "Trickie" defeated the Yale lock without a key and henceforth acquired his nickname.

'We had weird and wonderful superstitions. I had a racing plate, a jay's wing, a blue and white scarf and a hunting horn. Others had their girls' or wives' silk stockings, various rabbits' feet, etc. Unless we had our own bits of witchery we did not want to take off. It was always a question of "Have you got your rabbit's foot?", or what have you, before we took the bus to Bodney. Another thing I always looked for was the sight of a magpie. If I saw one before an operation I felt all right, and as far as I can remember the only time I did not see one was on that awful trip to Sedan.

'There was a dog—I think it was an alsatian—who remained at the end of the take-off area for his master who never returned. No amount of coaxing or food could save it from self-destruction.

'Every day before dawn we used to be driven in an old bus from Watton to Bodney. Our briefing was pathetic compared with that of later days. It was not the fault of our commanders, they just did not have the information to hand. Our job was to search for enemy columns which often entailed flying low in order to find out who we were about to attack. Once we nearly machine-gunned a column of refugees. We were being asked to harass fast-moving enemy columns by front gunning, bombing and rear gunning. With much false information flowing back to this country it's a wonder we found anything, and is a marvel 2 Group achieved so much.

'On looking back I feel sure that I, for one, lacked the stability and leadership necessary for the tremendous task, possibly because of the very tender age of most of us, although many great "big" men did emerge from those young hearts—and fast. Every man I met at that time was a hero and although I think most of us were very frightened, very few ever showed it. To give some idea of the toll of the fighting at this time, I think that after three weeks there were only four surviving crews

of 21 Squadron and two of 82 with, I think, about three replacements
during a period of about twenty-four operations.

'These were bad days, but they were not without their moments of
humour, as when the first WAAFs arrived. Our Station Commander,
unfortunately not a very popular man, put barbed wire around their
quarters. We had an Adjutant called Peirce-Jervis who was in some way
connected with theatricals. He arranged a wonderful party where we
had Douglas Byng, Tom Webster, Alice Delysia and some other famous
people, who gave us a wonderful concert. There the story was told of
the encounter between the WAAF officer and our Station Commander.
Referring to that wire fence she told him that "her girls had got it here"
(tapping her head). The Station Commander replied "I don't care where
your girls have got it, my boys will find it." And the barbed wire
remained.'

20 May. The enemy was pouring through the two gaps. If he could not
be halted, the Belgian Army in the north and the B.E.F. in the centre
would have to retreat towards the Somme or the sea. The advance was
exceedingly alarming, for enemy AFVs were wheeling north behind the
River Somme to surround the Belgians and the B.E.F. The latter was
now strung along the Escaut with a salient at Arras. French troops held
the line Douai–Valenciennes–Condé–River Sensée–Maulde. But in the
confused flux it was difficult for the bombers to identify any target. Try
as they might the French could not close the Gembloux gap. Their
reaction was too slow and insufficient in strength. Crossing of the Escaut
came after enemy AFVs had swept round from Péronne to reach Amiens
and Abbeville. The B.E.F. was soon to be encircled.

During the day 71 sorties were despatched, the greatest number yet in
the campaign. Troops near Vis were bombed by Nos. 21 and 107
Squadrons escorted by three Hurricane squadrons which remained a
thousand feet above and a mile behind throughout the operation.

At midday a special effort was mounted by 2 Group against columns
in the Arras–Cambrai–Péronne area. It was three hours after target
selection that the Blenheims arrived—too late to be effective.

At tea-time 21 Squadron joined 107 and met their Hurricane escort
over Hawkinge. They headed for the Arras–Bapaume area attempting to
delay forces heading for Arras, started fires, and all returned. Fighters
had apparently encouraged the enemy to stay away. The Air Staff, on
hearing that the fighters had not destroyed one Messerschmitt, considered
this was a waste of fighter effort. Their opinion was that even if the
entire air force was thrown into the battle supporting the army the effect
would only be temporary. They decided, once more, that the Blenheims
should operate by night, in conditions of moonlight.

It was up to 40, 82 and 110 Squadrons to try out the new tactics. Each
station was to despatch six aircraft flying independently and operating
over a period of ninety minutes to bomb any sign of movement, using

flares if needed. 82 Squadron, just about recovered from decimation, and led by the Earl of Bandon, was first away. Its bombs were aimed from 2,000 feet at the Halleebeek road near Pepingen. Others fell in Gammerages. But already flak and searchlights were busy. 40 Squadron flying its 157th to 162nd sorties searched for AFVs in the Audenarde–Grammont area seeing little and aiming at roads, railways and a column near Nederorakl. The third wave, 110 Squadron operating from Wattisham between 01.30 and 03.00 hours, attacked indistinguishable targets west of Brussels. It was clear that these attacks were quite fruitless, although they might have some effect on someone's morale. The C.-in-C. A.A.S.F. promptly demanded a resumption of day bombing, for he considered that effective help to the B.E.F. was impossible to give at night.

Also realising day operations must be resumed, H.Q. 2 Group issued a four-point directive to stations. It stressed the importance of position keeping by each section of three aircraft, for stragglers ruined the effectiveness of mutual protective fire. 'It must be impressed upon all pilots,' the letter read, 'that security rests upon mutual support.' Two aircraft in each section were now to carry cameras, to avoid losing possible useful information. Bombs were to be fused just after crossing the British coast to reduce wastage.

21 May. By the end of the previous day the spearhead of the Panzer Divisions had made astonishing progress, reaching Abbeville, Amiens, Arras and Hesdin. In the afternoon of 21st a limited British counter-attack opened at Arras which, for a time, cut German communications and delayed full encirclement of the B.E.F. Meanwhile 2 Group made four raids upon enemy columns between Arras and the coast. Whereas the Wehrmacht and the Luftwaffe were operating as a team, chaos reigned on the British side. Other than limited information from its reconnaissance flights, 2 Group relied upon target information from the War Office which was usually out of date by the time of attack. Now that the A.A.S.F. had been forced to retreat from the B.E.F. 2 Group came under direct Air Ministry control.

At 07.30 Plt. Off. Bell and Sgt. Tonks of 40 Squadron flying N3552 and P4927 respectively were despatched to reconnoitre the Audenarde and Amiens area and gather up-to-date target information. They were ordered to land at Merville just behind the front line for interrogation. On arrival they found the airfield deserted, so returned hastily to Wyton. But already three of their squadron and six of XV Squadron had hurriedly left to bomb vehicles near Montreuil. They aimed to halt columns heading for Boulogne. Twelve Blenheims of 107 Squadron escorted by two squadrons of Hurricanes attacked columns in the Etaples–Abbeville area. Direct hits were scored on vehicles passing through the village of Auixy-le-Château. Moderate flak hit a few aircraft, but none was lost.

In the late afternoon nine aircraft of 21 Squadron set out with a section from 82 Squadron to meet twelve of 107 Squadron being flown by the same crews who had already operated that day. The 24 Blenheims then set course for enemy tanks on the Boulogne–Etampes–Hesdin–Montreuil road network. A section of 21 Squadron claimed direct hits on tanks three miles north of Etampes. Others bombed troops on the road west of Hesdin, where they encountered flak. The three of 82 Squadron made dive-bombing attacks on motor transport and AFVs at Capelle and at Marcouille, near Hesdin. 107 Squadron found the roads packed with refugees which made attack there impossible.

One of XV Squadron's section leaders flying R3706 on the Montreuil attack was Flt. Lt. Webster, who was shot down. R. E. Hunter, air gunner in the aircraft, vividly remembers the raid: 'We were leading and flying really low—literally climbing over hedges and passing between trees, with Nos. 2 and 3 slightly opened out picking their own way, a most exhilarating sight. Ahead of us and running directly across our flight path was a road crammed with AFVs upon whom we unloaded our 250-pounders before they saw us coming. As we raced towards them I remember seeing our No. 2 come to at least line abreast, and converging as though trying to beat us to the same bone. At the same time we spotted a similar convoy on a parallel road to the first, a few fields further on, so we continued straight on intending to let them have our 40-lb. anti-personnel bombs. Whereas the first lot seemed to be taken completely by surprise the second were wide awake and gave us a right old pasting as we went in. It was a very hectic and noisy few seconds with one particularly large bang right under my seat accompanied by a very strong smell of hot angry cordite. I don't remember seeing our No. 2 and No. 3 after the first attack and I wasn't much interested in looking for them after the second, because amongst other things I had spotted the familiar fuel streamer from the port wing and announced over the inter-comm "They have holed the B—— tank again", to which an apparently unperturbed Webster replied "Don't think so, old boy, I think the port engine is on fire." I took a quick look round and, sure enough, the centre section was full of smoke haze. Not for the last time did I then query to myself the wisdom of flying with a panic proof pilot as I listened to a matter-of-fact Webster discussing with the observer "Hoppy" Hopwood whether to take her up high and bale out, whether he could possibly get home or whether it would perhaps be better to put down in France. What I didn't know at that time was that he was winding the wheel from side to side to demonstrate to Hopwood that his aileron control had been shot away. All that concerned me was that he should go up or down quickly and never mind about getting her home.

'First things first was my motto, and the first thing was to get out of that aeroplane. I knew at that moment that I wouldn't mind a tiny bit making my first parachute jump—dicey though it was reckoned to be from a Blenheim. Anyway, Webster elected to put down ("wheels up").

Slowly we came lower and lower—too slowly for me. I couldn't understand why he seemed to be holding off wasting miles and miles of lovely flat French countryside. Afterwards he explained that when a wing dropped a bit he just had to wait for it to come up again, until, when everything was just the way he wanted it, he pushed the nose down into a field of reddish French soil between Etampes and Boulogne. We made a perfect belly landing slithering to a stop in a smother of red dust. With fire on my mind this rosy hue did nothing to soothe me and I was out of that aircraft like a scalded cat. When I took a sensible look round I had to admit that the fire was not a raging inferno—yet—but the port motor was burning nice and steadily as Webster lingered, with his bottom being warmed by the flames, to enquire solicitously after the general health and well-being of his observer. Meanwhile, I had noticed one of our 40-pounders jammed under the tail wheel with others dotted about along the track we had cut, and which I thought were additional reasons for leaving the area fast. We eventually left the aircraft for the nearby road after Webster had satisfied himself that it was burning well enough to be of no use to Jerry. We were still in earshot when things started exploding. Arriving on the road we were faced with the silly situation of packed refugees going in opposite directions, one lot heading for Boulogne and claiming the Germans would already be in Etampes, the others claiming the same the other way round. We decided for Boulogne and walked for I am not sure how long or how far. I recall us investigating the chances of finding a serviceable aeroplane, or a lift, from some French airfield en route, but there was nothing but wrecks and an odd apologetic and slightly agitated French officer just waiting apparently to hand over his airfield. At some stage my left ankle became very painful to walk with and a quick examination showed that something had sliced a neat cut through my flying boot, across the ankle bone, leaving its small scar to this day but without damaging the bone. The underside of my left thigh was stinging and smarting. Although my Sidcot flying suit was shredded in this area my flesh was only peppered with surface scratches. I attributed this to the big bang under my seat and imagine it was caused by bits of the aircraft as much as anything else.

'After a while we managed a lift to Boulogne in an Army ambulance, spending one night pulled off the road. We made Boulogne latish the next day spending that night in a hospital, dossing down somewhere or other. We learned that "the last hospital ship" from Boulogne would be leaving next day. Early in the morning we wended our way to the harbour noticing that every street and side street was packed nose to tail both sides with army ambulances and lorries in apparently new condition, and wondered if they would be destroyed or fall into Jerry's hands.

'Arriving at the dock I nearly had a further heart attack when on enquiring of an Army officer, who appeared to be directing operations

8. A Blenheim IV being rearmed with 250 lb. bombs. Note the mascot on the cowling!

9. Blenheims of 40 Squadron at Wyton in early August 1940. T1849: BL-L was with 114 Squadron 18.11.40–22.7.41, and later 5 A.O.S. and 12 (P) AFU. T1830: BL-Z joined 40 Squadron 8.7.40 and 114 Squadron 8.11.40–22.7.41. Used by 527 Squadron, written off 25.10.44. T1848 passed from 40 Squadron to 105 Squadron 25.11.40–30.3.41, 614 Squadron 1.8.41–29.11.41 and later to 1 A.A.S. T1858 was lost on 114 Squadron 13.1.41.

10. A view across Aalborg looking towards the north-west. The airfield is in the centre and the Island of Egholm may be seen on the left

11. Smoke rises after the bombing of Aalborg on 13 August 1940

12. One of 82 Squadron's Blenheims shot down during the Aalborg raid of 13 August 1940

13. Bleeheim IV WV-M: V6227 flown by Wg. Cdr. Tony Partridge running in leading the attack on Rotterdam on 16 July 1941. The docks are on the skyline

14. No. 21 Squadron (YH-P: V5595 nearest) runs in low towards Rotterdam on the raid of 16.7.41

15. Knapsack power station under attack

at the gang-plank, of our chances of going aboard he gave a very abrupt and determined "No" and ended with "go and find a rifle and fire a shot for Boulogne". I was even more sure I had picked the wrong pilot when Webster appeared to accept this as a perfectly reasonable suggestion. Before I could get my heart going again and enough breath to interject a few suggestions into the discussion Webster had quietly got it across to the Army that we were operating from England. He allowed us to go aboard for a nervous but uneventful crossing to Dover.'

Operations had meanwhile continued unabated.

22 May. The Wehrmacht thrust towards Boulogne continued. Fifty-eight Blenheim sorties were directed against this and the advance on the Somme.

A courageous early reconnaissance was made by Flt. Lt. Pleasance of 107 Squadron. Wg. Cdr. Embry led an afternoon attack on troops closing in on Boulogne, blasting vehicles in the fields. Plt. Off. Miller, an engine and the hydraulic system damaged, tried to nurse P4925 home. About seven miles from the English coast his second engine failed forcing him to ditch. After about $1\frac{1}{2}$ hours a patrol vessel picked up the crew. 107 Squadron mounted a second raid on the same target area and as if this were not enough Wg. Cdr. Embry led a third with 110 Squadron, making a dual attack on German H.Q. at Ribeaucourt. Darkness and fog at Wattisham caused them to land at Manston.

Other squadrons had also been busy, XV repeating attacks of yesterday, 21 and 82 making a low-level evening raid on the Saumur–Montreuil road and 40 Squadron attacking an armoured column sallying north from Abbeville. All day Wattisham's squadrons had been at standby. They operated twice and every aircraft encountered flak. Sqn. Ldr. G. F. Hall leading in L8761 was shot down, and Flg. Off. G. O. Lings put N6207 down on her belly, for her undercarriage had been shot away.

Nine days of concentrated effort and a night had wrought the loss of 44 Blenheims and 108 men had died. Many others were wounded and plenty of Blenheims really beyond the state of repair were patched up through the almost ceaseless efforts of the ground crews. Such aircraft were soon hurled back into battle.

23 May. The previous day at 09.00 hours Group had 73 aircraft serviceable; now the number had fallen to 60. The B.E.F. had retreated leaving the Belgians on the north of the Lys, from Menin to Courtrai and the Escaut. The Arras salient collapsed during the night. It was still hoped that the French could close the gap, a vain hope for today they announced it was impossible. They had barely tried. It was difficult to get information from France but when it did reach Group it was that the enemy had crossed a vital canal from St. Omer to Aire.

Twenty-four Blenheims tried to bomb southern exits from Arras. Of

D

these, twelve, including 107 Squadron, circled Hawkinge for twenty minutes before formating with nine Hurricanes of 32 Squadron. Bad weather was encountered breaking the formations which mostly unloaded their bombs on the Bois de Boulogne. 82 Squadron dive-bombed tanks in the Fort Crèche meeting fire from Allied ships for their trouble. Escorting Hurricanes warded off a serious fighter interception by about thirty Bf 109s and 110s and claimed three 109s.

24 May. Now the enemy was in a strong position to seize Calais. 2 Group was four times ordered to bomb columns moving towards the Aa Canal. As Flg. Off. Henderson of XV Squadron was landing, his port engine cut, the Blenheim spinning in; there were no survivors. 21 Squadron, following a long standby, was away mid morning, attacking stationary vehicles between St. Inglevert and Calais. L.A.C. Lang, air gunner in L8743, had a lucky escape when his aircraft survived a direct hit in the after bomb compartment—just after the load had been dropped. 82 Squadron was with them, and 110 made a morning raid in the same area.

An enemy column near Arras was 40 Squadron's intended target. In bad weather they had taken second choice, the Bois de Boulogne. Flak was heavy and P4909 flown by Wg. Cdr. Llewellyn was shot down and he was killed. Flg. Off. Jackoby's machine L8834 was also shot down.

During the evening a second raid was mounted on Calais approaches by 21 and 82 Squadrons. It was almost dusk as they arrived and 200 reported tanks had merged with the countryside. Twelve crews of 107 Squadron, Hurricane-escorted, went for roads and bridges at Marck. Despite the flak they all survived, but the escort was heavily engaged by 109s. It was so dark when 40 Squadron arrived for its share of the operation that it chose a secondary target, AFVs running up on Calais from the west.

25 May. The Wehrmacht was trying to cross the Lys and pontoon bridges were bombed. Belgian troops were forced back to the Gheluwe–Zonnebeke line, leaving a dangerous gap gallantly plugged by the B.E.F. by an evening race to the scene. Calais was under bombardment all day. Because of very close fighting by the brave defenders 2 Group could no longer give them support. Boulogne was taken by the Germans, and Calais fell on the morrow.

An early morning reconnaissance by 110 Squadron to the Channel ports discovered the current state of fighting. It was followed by a 24-Blenheim raid, twelve of 107, and six each from XV and 40 Squadrons escorted by two Hurricane Squadrons. 107 Squadron damaged a Lys bridge, 40 Squadron bombed about thirty vehicles in the Rety–Guines–Fiennes triangle. 21 Squadron also aimed to destroy other pontoon bridges.

Photographs taken were quickly examined, revealing that when hits were scored on bridges this seriously interrupted enemy progress. A rapid order of the day was issued. This read: 'It must be impressed upon leaders that risks must be taken in this emergency to find the really important targets, then attack them. It must now be accepted that the day has passed when attacks can be launched at definite targets as a result of previous reconnaissance. This is due to the rapidity of movement of enemy forces. In view of the critical situation of the B.E.F. it is essential that all attacks are pressed home with vigour.'

With the enemy closing in on the B.E.F. causing a very serious situation, the position was summarised at 20.00 hours with a view to planning the next day's action. An attack on the junction of the B.E.F. and Belgian forces had come and 2 Group's afternoon effort had been concentrated upon it. This attack was expected to develop northwards. An afternoon attack in the Béthune–Hazebrouck direction had made fast progress. Enemy forces previously held at Gravelines had now crossed the river and a new threat was developing, against Dunkirk. Advanced elements of the British Armoured Division across the Somme the night before were trying to move northwards, and a fresh attack east of Amiens was making progress. Everywhere the situation looked bad, very bad.

The tasks for the 26th therefore seemed to be: (1) a morning attack against the Menin–Coutrai route or the Hazebrouck–Béthune road, and (2) maintaining air superiority over the Calais–Dunkirk area to try to prevent capture of the former, which looked difficult.

26 May. Of the 127-mile perimeter of the pocket in which the B.E.F. was contained, the Belgians held about 30 miles. They were running short of food and ammunition. German troops everywhere vastly outnumbered the Allies. All hope of closing the gap from the Somme to French forces had vanished and, in depth, the B.E.F. was defending its last port—Dunkirk.

Sections from Watton and Wyton set off early to bomb troops believed to be crossing the Lys between Menin and Courtrai. Intelligence reports suggested fighters would be defending the area, so 32 Squadron went along with the Blenheims. No Messerschmitts showed up, and 40 Squadron bombed roads and houses at Harlebeke assisted by 82 Squadron, leaving 21 to bomb bridges in the area. Later 82 Squadron repeated the attack, two sections shallow-diving from 6,000 to 2,000 feet.

Four sections of 107 Squadron and two from 110 flew an afternoon armed reconnaissance in the St. Pol area, escorted by three squadrons of Hurricanes from Manston. Ju 52s were believed to be delivering petrol for Panzer formations. None being seen, armoured vehicles in the Forêt de Hesdin felt the weight of the bombs. Flak was intense and eleven of 107's aircraft were hit.

By late afternoon the plight of the B.E.F. was disastrous. With the net around it closing, 'Operation Dynamo', the evacuation of the troops from Dunkirk, was ordered at 18.57 hours. At this time the fear that tanks and tracked vehicles might become bogged worried the enemy who, whilst hammering at the B.E.F.s perimeter, increased his assault on the French to the south.

27 May. Early that day Group flashed its orders to the stations thus: 'To Watton: AFVs have been seen outside a square of houses at Belle where an enemy H.Q. seems to be established. Two sections using cloud cover are to attack the houses. To Wyton: An armed reconnaissance is ordered to be made by two sections against forces advancing through the forest of Clairmarais. To Wattisham: An M.T. column and AFVs passing through St. Omer on the road to Arques is to be destroyed.' These operations were undertaken by Nos. XV, 40, 21 and 107 Squadrons.

Quickly re-armed they were off again, 40 Squadron bringing down houses to block a road at Belle. 82 Squadron fired warehouses in Blendecques holding supplies and bombed AFVs near Arques.

Late in the afternoon attacks were resumed with 110 Squadron hammering troops around St. Omer. At 18.10 hours a dozen Blenheims of 107 Squadron followed suit and, led by Wg. Cdr. Embry, met heavy flak. Shortly after bombing the leader's aircraft was hit and he soon lost control of it. His gunner lay dead in the turret but the navigator managed to bale out followed by Wg. Cdr. Embry. His loss, the loss of one of the great figures of Bomber Command, was a shattering blow to his beloved squadron.

The story of his escape, an amazing escape, is told in his own words in his book *Mission Completed* (Hutchinson). It was one of the most incredible of the war, adventure closing adventure. Possibly one of the most astonishing moments he had was when he came face to face with the village of Embry in Northern France! He had a tortuous journey south and at one time took refuge in a manure heap before eventually reaching Marseilles. Thence he crossed the Pyrenees and went to Madrid and finally came home via Gibraltar. It was 2 August when he stepped ashore at Plymouth. At once he headed for his old station.

He was by all accounts a tremendously efficient person, with complete devotion to the winning of the war. To all he was revered and now, some thirty years on, one cannot be long in the company of any who served on 2 Group without some mention of Basil Embry. His contribution to the Group's effort in the early months of war was tenacious, his leadership of 2 Group during the invasion of France has become legendary.

The story of his arrival back at Wattisham is often told. A large crowd gathered at the local railway station, headed by Wattisham's Station Commander. The train pulled in, and a grand welcome was about to burst. But where was this wonderful figure? Craftily he had descended on the track side of the train carefully making an unseen exit. Soon he had borrowed the Station Commander's car. A grand welcome poured upon him at Wattisham whilst the Station Commander and entourage were left behind playing trains, to the delight of many and doubtless Wg. Cdr. Embry.

He was pronounced unfit for flying for two months and found himself out of his beloved 2 Group—if only for the time being. None who knew him reckoned he would be away for long, but it was to be three years before he returned. It was then as the A.O.C. of 2 Group.

28 May. Throughout the day troops were snatched from Dunkirk in boats great and small in the greatest evacuation of all time. On three sides the Germans closed in, 2 Group doing all it could to delay their advance. Enemy reinforcements at Ouest-Mont were bombed by XV Squadron, and 40 Squadron had some success attacking troops advancing from St. Omer. But for the most part luck was out since the weather was very bad. No. 21 Squadron had to attack the Clairmarais forest in driving rain from a mere 600 feet, which cost them L8744. Attacks were also delivered on the B.E.F.'s perimeter by Nos. 82, 107 and 110 Squadrons.

29 May. All effort was being directed to holding a zone along the coast around Dunkirk. The weather continued bad, helping and hindering the British. Lorries at Cokelacre were bombed by 40 Squadron which, when it returned, had to make dispersed landings some as much as seventy miles from base. 107 Squadron now under Wg. Cdr. L. R. Stokes made an afternoon foray to the Dixemude–Thourout area bombing AFVs at Ichteghem. 110 Squadron followed with a raid on the Forêt-d'Eperlecques. Bad weather gave useful cloud cover but demanded very low attacks such as 21 and 82 Squadrons delivered on Dixemude.

30 May. By midday the British troops were well in the Dunkirk pocket and the evacuation was in full swing. Attacks on their perimeter were continued, particularly in the Dixemude–Furnes–Ypres–Thourout region, 67 sorties being mounted by the six squadrons. Cloud was very low, although this lifted over the western sector. Three of 82's aircraft flying low were damaged by light flak. In the evening 40 Squadron bombed pontoon bridges over the Nieuport canal.

31 May. The evacuation from Dunkirk reached its climax. 2 Group's effort, by far its greatest of the campaign, was particularly directed against troops massing for an all-out attack on Dunkirk. It was halted largely by 2 Group's grand effort and the B.E.F. held its five-mile-wide strip along the shore.

First into action was 21 Squadron whose attack on pontoons near Nieuport was barely successful. Later in the morning 107 Squadron set off to bomb mechanised transport at Oostvleteken. Flak was intense, then some 109s dived into attack. One was promptly shot down and another turned away hit by lucky shots from a Blenheim's nose blister gun. Such success was considered remote. With the Blenheims were the Hurricanes of 145 Squadron a section of which also engaged the Messerschmitts. Flt. Lt. R. G. Dutton destroyed one and shared another with Plt. Off. M. A. Newling.

At 18.30 hours 24 crews from Wattisham's two squadrons set off for the bridges at Nieuport from where, a short time before, the enemy had launched an all-out attack on Dunkirk. Dust and smoke billowed from the target area. When it cleared the defenders could see that the enemy attack had been halted, in full view of them. It was indeed a fine tonic.

The entire day's effort had been directed with varying success on Nieuport which all six squadrons attacked, but the evening attack was the most successful and a fitting climax.

1 June. The beach head had shrunk considerably there being few troops available to hold it. Two crews of 82 Squadron reconnoitred the Ternuezen area to assess build-up, but it was slight. They reported a destroyer off Zeebrugge and saw some barges at sea, an ominous sign for the future. Three other squadrons kept up harassment of enemy troops on the perimeter, and XV Squadron went to the village of Honshoote where large numbers of troops and much war material had gathered. East of Dunkirk 110 Squadron made further attacks, all the effort being directed to delaying the advance into Dunkirk.

2 June. 107 and 110 Squadrons concentrated their attacks upon heavy guns now in action against our shipping off Gravelines. So intense was the reception that three of 107's aircraft crash-landed at base. Enemy shelling was now seriously interfering with the closing stages of the evacuation, the most difficult part.

3 June. The final phase of the withdrawal came in the morning, and 2 Group's role was of paramount importance. Sections from Watton were ordered to patrol, each for fifteen minutes, and for a total of ninety minutes, over known gun batteries, in order to silence them by bombing on gun flashes. Zero hour for 82 Squadron was 04.30. Instructions were not to release bombs in one stick, and to be prepared to machine-gun the enemy even from low level. Strong fighter cover from first light allowed the Blenheims to operate singly, but smoke and haze hindered their success. But it aided the last remnants of the B.E.F. that were taken from Dunkirk with some success. A disastrous stage in the war had ended which had cost 2 Group dear.

The Reckoning

Once B.E.F. evacuation was complete, 2 Group rested briefly. Relentless courage and great stamina had been demanded of all. Few of the aircrews who stood by for operations on 10 May were still alive. Yet 2 Group's extreme sacrifice had little effect on the final depressing outcome of the campaign.

An average of 69 aircraft was daily available for operations. Sorties totalling 954 had been flown, an average of 38, in the last 25 days. Aircraft and crews had taken a tremendous hammering and the sortie totals do not really reflect the effort extended. Aircraft had to be repaired, crews had to be rested and were often wearied even by the long standbys. Replacement crews were thrown into battle with little operational training. And the greatest difficulty faced was lack of precise information on enemy positions. Frequently it meant long delays before sorties were despatched.

Air Vice-Marshal James Robb, who took command of 2 Group on 17 April, reported fully on the French campaign so far. 'The number of sorties made appears formidable but many were from 2 to $2\frac{1}{2}$ hours duration, and in the Dunkirk operations they were of 2 hours. In view of our fighter operations at Dunkirk crews could have maintained an effort of two sorties per day. Indeed, they would have preferred this to the lengthy standby periods. A difficulty was the absence of information until mid-morning, which precluded keeping up the pressure of the attack. Consequently turn round for each squadron to make two sorties per day would have meant a rush for re-arming.' Nevertheless this was often achieved and as a result ground crews were literally working until they dropped exhausted, to keep the Blenheims flying.

Casualties had been grievous. They were summarised as follows:

	Missing	Killed	Wounded/injured
Officers	33	2	10
N.C.O./Airmen Pilots, Observers	49	2	13
Air gunners	39	3	14
	121	7	37

Finally the mortality rate was shown to be 26 for officers, 57 for N.C.O.s and 35 for airmen, and shows the considerable contribution by non-commissioned ranks. Fortunately a number of aircraft came down in friendly territory and aircrew quite often made astonishing journeys back to their squadrons.

The net result was a serious shortage of gunners. Whereas pilots and observers could be stood down for a period, the ever present shortage of gunners meant these could not. It came hard on these men, Leading Aircraftmen mostly receiving a few extra pence for the grave risks they took. Many a time a Blenheim returned with a dead gunner aboard the removal of whom was a horrifying experience for anyone. Despite the appalling losses morale remained high and the A.O.C. reported that 'there came a steady hardening of the determination to kill every German regardless of cost.'

Aircraft losses were partly attributable to bad formation keeping. It was clear that more practice was needed, but operational squadrons were too busy to train new pilots. The reserve squadron, No. 101 at West Raynham, was ever active but their opinion was that crews should have been better trained before they arrived for operational conversion. 'Many of the younger pilots,' reported Robb, 'break formation for no reason and do not appear to realise the full extent of their crime.'

Some squadrons broke formation over target for individual attacks and were easy to pick off before re-grouping. A section leader would precisely know his position. His followers might not and some bombs had drifted on to Allied positions. Other squadrons, with high standards of formation keeping, quickly bunched after attacks, 'a most inspiring sight'.

Recent operations offered a chance for full appraisal of the Blenheim. When fighters attacked a close box of them they invariably flew around looking for weak positions. Fighters facing two tight boxes of six rarely pressed their attacks. But James Robb considered it 'unwise to use Blenheims without cloud cover' if there was danger of fighter attack. 'Therefore fighter escort must be provided. 11 Group escort has worked admirably.' Already the need for good rendezvous was obvious, and never easy to achieve. Without an escort operations faced great hazards, as on 17 May, if flak split the formation.

It was obvious that photographs of attacks were invaluable. They showed, as well as results, telltale shadows and the enemy army under camouflage. As yet there were too few trained intelligence staff on the stations to obtain maximum value from photographs.

Fifty-six Blenheims failed to return from operations in this period. Another ten had to be written off, but serviceability was kept surprisingly high. Many aircraft were grounded for the repair of the many tears in their skinning, repair to which was a lengthy tedious task. Replacement aircraft trickled into squadrons at first, but soon the speed picked up. Later aircraft were better equipped before they reached the squadrons and in higher modification states.

Testimony to the Blenheim's strength, to the skill and courage of the crews, was included in the A.O.C.'s report: 'The punishment the Blenheim can take and continue to fly has caused much surprise.' One aircraft taking avoiding action in the St. Pol area hit the ground with a wing tip. It was removed for a foot or so, and another foot of wing was bent upwards, but the aircraft returned safely to Wyton. Another was hit by a shell which removed at least a square yard of the top of the wing. Another flew into a power cable across the Somme, which struck the blister gun position and removed two feet of the wing leading edge back to the main spar. Both aircraft returned. Others were so badly holed it is amazing they did not break up in the air. One aircraft in particular was hit so often on the armour that its play-off had almost severed the rear part of the fuselage.

In his overall summary of the operations James Robb concluded: 'It is doubtful if this Group is obtaining an adequate return for its efforts. On several occasions we have destroyed a few lorries and tanks, but the actual hold-up of the enemy has been negligible, despite the cost. Many crews have expressed this opinion not in any spirit of criticism, but of the helplessness at being unable to accomplish more in stopping the enemy. The way to obtain best results has received much consideration, but I suggest air action against roads must not rely on damage to roads but upon stopping and dislocating traffic on them. For that purpose the most suitable targets would be bottlenecks and defiles and other natural targets formed by towns or bridges. The attack on vehicles forward of the enemy railhead is, in my opinion, hardly worth the effort involved.' The policy he suggested, of attacks on communications well behind the front line, was to be a vital feature of 2 Group's contribution after the 1944 invasion.

The fighting in France was far from over, and there were still British troops fighting there who were to the west of the thrust the enemy made when pocketing the main part of the B.E.F. It was now 2 Group's task to give these forces some support.

Fight to the End

Once most of the B.E.F. was home urgent consultations took place on how 2 Group might now be employed. It was ordered, on 3 June, to institute a campaign of cloud-cover attacks on Germany thereby enticing enemy fighters back to the home land. But before these began the bad situation in France led to 5 June's order to defer these plans. Now 2 Group was to give support to the remaining 140,000 British troops in France. It was clear that the forces engaged on raids had been too small. In this second phase the number of aircraft used frequently increased to four boxes of six.

5 June. British soldiers now held a line to the west of the Somme, where the 51st Highland Division was installed. On 4 June it attempted to attack the enemy between St. Valery and Abbeville, fought well, but was rather let down by the French who, since 25 May, had been talking of an armistice.

Operations were resumed when Nos. 107 and 110 Squadrons sent 24 aircraft to raid Albert, attacking supply columns. For the next eight days every squadron fought again at fever pitch.

6 June. The tenacity of the Highlanders delayed the Wehrmacht. To the south the French were retreating fast. Enemy thrusts were again likely to pocket the remnants of the Allies along the coast.

Road and rail targets around Abbeville and St. Valery were bombed by XV Squadron in company with 21 and a fighter escort. Targets included four rail bridges over the River Somme, bombed in an attempt to hold up supplies well behind the fighting in the manner Robb had proposed.

7 June. Now the army was defending along the line of the River Bresle, but it was soon outflanked by a thrust between Formerie and Grandvilliers.

Five squadrons today operated against the enemy's rear. After an early reconnaissance by two crews 21 Squadron attacked armour around Airaines. Three low-flying Blenheims of 107 Squadron sought information on Somme crossings and roads in the Abbeville–Montreuil–Hesdin areas. Wg. Cdr. Stokes flew R3740 at only 100 feet, despite ground fire. Three 109s attacked him for fifteen minutes during which his gunner shot down one from only 50 feet. The second machine took a look at the Abbeville–Montreuil road, the third never returned.

An afternoon attack by six crews of XV Squadron and twelve each from 107 and 110—the largest force yet despatched—was made on western and eastern exits from Airaines. Fighter-escorted, the Blenheims met flak but all returned.

8 June. Enemy thrusts towards Rouen were encircling our forces and in the evening retreat from the Bresle began. Three sections of 21 Squadron were away at 10.00 hours after a five-hour standby. They formed up with 82 Squadron over Watton, picked up the fighters over Hornchurch, then bombed armour at Noroy. Nos. XV and 40 Squadrons sent eighteen aircraft to bomb vehicles and troops near Poix. Meanwhile another eighteen Blenheims of 107 and 110 Squadrons were bombing AFVs near Amiens. Raids were mounted by XV and 82 Squadrons on the Bois Watti and Abbeville respectively. All these targets were well behind the front line.

9 June. Rouen fell and our forces were cut off north of the Seine, no bridges being left for them. Then the enemy turned north to cut off Le Havre. On the Bresle front two British Corps were falling back leaving the Border Regiment and the Sherwood Foresters to hold it, which they did with utmost gallantry for six more days. It was 13 June before 2 Corps yielded, when fighting north of the Seine stopped.

Squadrons were alerted early for more attacks well behind the front. Twelve crews of 107 and six of 110 Squadrons left at 10.45 hours, met fighters over North Weald and bombed AFVs in the Forêt de Boray near Poix. Ten 109s came up but declined to interfere. Three of 107's aircraft were hit by flak, two crashing with engines afire. Nine crews of 21 Squadron, and six of 82, made a late afternoon attack on villages and troops in the Poux–Grandvilliers–Formerie area. Fifteen crews from Wyton made a follow-up raid.

10 June. With Le Havre cut off the 51st Division made for St. Valery-en-Caux to be taken off by the Navy.

At dawn 107 and 110 Squadrons returned to the area of the last evening's bombing. At lunch-time 21 and 82 Squadrons teamed up with Wyton's Squadrons making a 33-aircraft force to bomb Boos, Boissemont and Romilly. Railways at Fleury were hit and collapsing houses blocked the main road.

11 June. The Germans began attacking St. Valery on all sides. Night evacuation had been postponed due to sea fog. Watton and Wyton squadrons combined to bomb La Mare. Enemy concentrations in the Boissemont–St. Clair–Vernon–Venables area were bombed. No. XV Squadron had to fly through a heavy patch of cloud in which Plt. Off. Werner increased speed, overtaking his leader Flg. Off. R. B. G. E. Clark. Werner turned L9024 left hitting Clark and losing a wing. Clark flew on despite the damage and with skill kept L9245 on an even keel. Soon his starboard engine began to fall to pieces, the observer and gunner being ordered out. Then the machine plunged to earth; Clark had given his life for his colleagues. 21 Squadron's second section was destroyed by enemy fighters, another aircraft badly shot up abandoned the operation and a further machine made a belly landing at Watton.

During the morning 107 and 110 Squadrons raided columns in Rouen, losing an aircraft set on fire over the target.

12 June. The 51st Division pleaded for naval cover and to be taken off, but the French in St. Valery gave in and even hoisted a white flag over the British Headquarters. It was promptly hauled down. In a hopeless position, for it could not hold out till nightfall, the 51st reluctantly ceased fire.

It was cloudy today, but 40 Squadron tried to attack guns pounding St. Valery's beaches although cloud interfered. One aircraft was shot down. Deeper operations continued with XV Squadron bombing MT at Le Bourget and 107 and 110 raiding a wood at La Mare near Rouen. Later, 21 and 82 Squadrons bombed troops and AFVs between Berniers and Tosny.

13 June. With the Marne and Seine crossed, and the B.E.F. all but out of the fight, Nos. 21 and 82 Squadrons went after tanks in the Forêt de Gayont S.E. of Paris, losing five of their number. Wg. Cdr. Stokes led six of 107 and twelve of 110 Squadrons raiding Seine crossings at Vernon. Bf 110s intercepted and shot down R3616. XV and 40 Squadrons also attacked Seine crossings in the Louviers area, bombing tanks at Bizy.

14 June. Now the Germans were entering Paris and 2 Group was giving support to the French forces. During the morning Seine crossings and the Louviers area were again bombed, but bad weather interfered with these efforts by the Wattisham squadrons. Nos. XV and 40 Squadrons operated in the same area later, and cost 40 Squadron Sqn. Ldr. Gleed who had been in the fight throughout the campaign. Largely thwarted earlier by bad weather a dozen Blenheims left Wattisham at 17.30 hours joining others from Watton. Over Hawkinge they met an escort of 24 Hurricanes and went to a new type of target, the airfield at Merville where about forty Ju 88s and six Bf 109s were positioned. This was the first attack in a new phase, and it brought to an end 2 Group's participation in the French campaign.

Summing-Up

Again the Group Commander reported on the campaign. He commented: 'This period was generally more effective than the earlier one, due particularly to the experience gained up to Dunkirk. In clear weather it is best to operate as a formation with fighter cover. Up to three aircraft can operate under cloud cover to search roads, railways and rivers.'

Target distances limited sorties to one aircraft per day. Theoretically, this was partly due to the need for fighter cover. Thirty Blenheims were lost and six more badly damaged, hydraulic systems being put out of action. Due to wheels-up landings Bristol Aircraft had been asked to apply modifications allowing manual lowering of undercarriages. Meanwhile Group devised a primitive system.

Some squadrons still split at the target, bombed, then came home singly giving the fighters an impossible task. Those that maintained formation usually returned safely. Experience suggested that the best way to avoid flak damage was for Nos. 2 and 3 in a box to be about fifty yards behind the leader, with the leader of the following section a further 100 yards behind and 200 feet higher.

Fifteen escort missions were flown by 11 Group, but good liaison between fighters and bombers was needed. The best plan was for rendezvous to be over the fighter base. B.A.F.F. provided some standing patrols over target areas and sometimes met the bombers at the French coast. Most lost bombers still fell to fighters of which six were claimed destroyed. Despite an escort, losses on 11 June were heavy, the bomber formation splitting and complicating the escort's task.

Over the period 487 sorties were flown and 166 tons of bombs dropped (82×250 lb., $3,170 \times 40$ lb., 264×20 lb., and $8,800 \times 4$ lb. incendiaries). Bombing accuracy improved since targets were more suitable.

Aircrews losses at the time were summarised as follows:

	Officers	Airmen/pilots	Air gunners	Total
Missing	16	20	20	56
Killed	1	2	2	5
Wounded	2	3	3	8

Post-war research indicates that 13 officers, 34 N.C.O.s and 2 airmen were killed. This brought the total killed during the whole campaign to 39 officers, 91 N.C.O.s and 37 airmen, equivalent to the loss of four squadrons.

On 22 June the French accepted the armistice terms. Agreement brought to an end a period of bitter, terribly costly fighting. The loss of aircraft was more than the equivalent usually available for a day's operations. In terms of manpower the loss of dedicated men was much greater. The task now was to re-orientate effort and gather a force of crews of equal calibre.

Chapter 5
Hide and Seek

Germany's western advance completely upset the strategic pattern, but some contingency plans existed to answer it. Bomber Command reacted fast and on 4 June—two weeks before France fell—a Directive reached James Robb. Part of Plan W.A.8, it stated:

'The general trend of the air operations in the past few weeks has caused the enemy to position a very large number of his fighter aircraft over the Western Front, particularly in the Low Countries where he is in an advantageous position to attempt some degree of local air superiority. It is desirable that we should make every endeavour to cause the enemy to withdraw a proportion of his fighter aircraft from this area with a view to redressing the balance in our favour. Therefore it has been decided that, when suitable weather conditions exist which would give adequate security through cloud cover over areas of operation, Blenheim aircraft should be employed in the general role of delivering sporadic attacks on various objectives.

'From 5 June A.O.C. 2 Group is to employ, at his discretion and dependence upon favourable weather conditions, up to eight sections (i.e. 24 aircraft) on this task daily.'

This instruction changed the whole nature of 2 Group operations for nine months and, in amended form, was its principal manner of employment for years ahead. It was to act intentionally as bait for fighters . . . hardly enjoyable entertainment.

Straightaway the A.O.C. issued 2 Group Operations Order No. 11, adding 'It is essential that the destructive efforts of our night bombing operations over Germany should be continued throughout daylight by sporadic attacks on the same objectives. *The intention is to make attacks only when cloud cover gives adequate security*.

'Targets allocated to stations are as follows:
Wyton: Oil refineries at Hamburg, Gelsenkirchen, Sterkrade, Holten, Wanne Eickel, Kamen, Dortmund, Emmerich.
Watton: Oil refineries at Hanover, Bremen, Ostermoor, Salzbergen, Homberg, Dusseldorf, Monheim, Reisholtz.
Wattisham: Oil refineries at Hamburg; marshalling yards at Osnabruck, Hamm, Soest, Schwerte and Wanne Eickel.
'Stations are to take turns for this task every third day beginning

5 June with Watton, then Wattisham and Wyton in that order. Duty Station is to detail eight sections on the day and they may be despatched without further reference to this Headquarters. *If there is no cloud cover the mission must be abandoned.*

'The targets are allocated partly on a geographical basis in order that the demand for fighter protection is widespread and numerous, and disperses fighter defence. It is essential attacks are made throughout the day and widely separated in space. Monotony of method of attack and getaway must be avoided. It is essential the targets are hit; avoid promiscuous bomb dropping.'

The order came when the battle for France was at its height. Desperate cries for help still came and delayed the introduction of the order. It was a glorious summer. Days when cloud cover obliged were to be few. In any case it was a forlorn hope that the enemy fighter force could be tied down by such mild operations. Nevertheless they continued daily into the late autumn, indeed were being erratically flown until March 1941, and called for much courage. The full extent of the 1940 catastrophe was to make great demands upon 2 Group and seriously interfere with the plan.

Watton came to readiness at dawn on 5 June. The Station Commander detailed four sections of 21 Squadron to attack north-west Germany, but the weather forecast was for clear skies and from the start the operation was abortive.

Once France had fallen, a new danger was only too apparent as the Luftwaffe hurried into newly won bases. Something had quickly to be done to interfere. Group Order 11 was again thwarted since the Blenheim squadrons were now ordered to bomb French airfields. Many dates have been propounded for the start of the Battle of Britain and it is reasonable to consider these raids as its true beginning. They started on 19 June when Nos. XV, 18 and 82 Squadrons raided Boos, opening a campaign against airfields which ran almost to the end of the war. More Blenheims later bombed Amiens/Glisy scoring hits on hangars. Fears of an intruder response were rife when XV Squadron landed at Alconbury in moonlight. No. 18 Squadron was diverted to Redhill.

Next day No. 107 Squadron made another raid on Boos. These operations required a fighter escort and Hurricanes of Nos. 145 and 601 Squadrons watched over the bombers. Dutch airfields were beyond the range of the fighter escort and when No. 21 Squadron set off alone for Schiphol, already a bomber base, it soon found a cloudless sky and returned. Merville was bombed by the Wattisham squadrons on 22nd.

There was concern as to what was happening on the French coast. Nos. XV and 40 Squadrons, covered by four fighter squadrons, were sent to find out. They split into sections covering the area from St. Valery to Rue. Their photographs revealed that the enemy was positioning long-range guns in an attempt to close the Channel to our shipping and

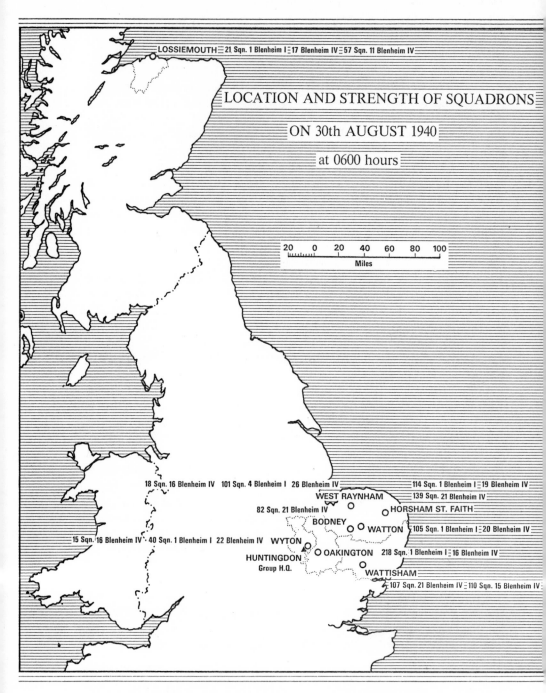

LOSSIEMOUTH ≡ 21 Sqn. 1 Blenheim I ≡ 17 Blenheim IV ≡ 57 Sqn. 11 Blenheim IV ≡

LOCATION AND STRENGTH OF SQUADRONS

ON 30th AUGUST 1940

at 0600 hours

```
20    0    20    40    60    80   100
|__|__|__|  |____|____|____|____|
              Miles
```

18 Sqn. 16 Blenheim IV   101 Sqn. 4 Blenheim I   26 Blenheim IV ≡   114 Sqn. 1 Blenheim I ≡ 19 Blenheim IV ≡
                         WEST RAYNHAM   139 Sqn. 21 Blenheim IV ≡
           82 Sqn. 21 Blenheim IV   ○   ○ HORSHAM ST. FAITH ≡
                                  BODNEY   ○ ○ WATTON   ≡ 105 Sqn. 1 Blenheim I ≡ 20 Blenheim IV ≡
15 Sqn. 16 Blenheim IV · 40 Sqn. 1 Blenheim I   22 Blenheim IV   WYTON ○
                                                 ○ OAKINGTON   218 Sqn. 1 Blenheim I ≡ 16 Blenheim IV ≡
                            HUNTINGDON
                            Group H.Q.   ○ WATTISHAM ≡
                                                    ≡ 107 Sqn. 21 Blenheim IV ≡ 110 Sqn. 15 Blenheim IV ≡

MAP 7. *See Appendix 12, pages 497/8 for notes*

perhaps support an invasion force. Further reconnaissance sorties followed.

Airfield attacks were resumed by 82 Squadron which, led by Sqn. Ldr. Chester, made a successful surprise assault on Abbeville. When 107 Squadron attacked Merville the defenders were ready and intense flak claimed three Blenheims. Another, badly battered, dragged itself into Manston. Escorted, No. 110 Squadron started fires at Vignacourt refuelling station. Over Le Touquet enemy fighters swarmed in to attack but all the bombers returned. Nevertheless it was obvious such missions could be very costly.

It was 21 June when 82 Squadron eventually opened the cloud-cover offensive. Ten crews left early to attack Bremen, Hanover and the Ruhr but there was little cloud and only three proceeded. Sqn. Ldr. Hunt tried for Bremen's oil refinery and Sqn. Ldr. Sutcliffe, unsure of the Ruhr balloon barrage, bombed Hamstede aerodrome. Sgt. Watkins, recovered from his French ordeal, attacked Schiphol. No. XV Squadron operated unsuccessfully next day, then it was 107's turn. Wg. Cdr. E. C. Lart bombed a viaduct near Munster and clouds of smoke and steam arose from Hamm after Plt. Off. T. S. Warren had bombed. If the primary target was not attacked it was usual to bomb an airfield. Daylight operations by Blenheims offered a fair chance of hitting the target, but the load carried was too small to be effective on these lone, hazardous sorties. Out of 82 despatched in June only 22 were at all effective, and two aircraft were lost. The following tabulation details the employment of the squadrons since the fall of France:

Sqn.	Effective/despatched sorties to airfields	Lost	Effective/despatched sorties G.O.O. 11	Lost
XV	12/12	—	2/9	—
21	3/12	—	—	—
40	14/16	—	—	—
82	20/20	—	11/24	—
107	25/38	3	6/16	2
110	24/30	—	3/33	—
Totals	98/128	3	22/82	2

N.B. 40 Sqn. concentrated on photo-reconnaissance sorties over France and Holland making 12/20 effective sorties and losing an aircraft.

With the war at a perilous stage Operations Orders came fast. Instruction No. 37 of June 1940 emphasised Britain's plight:

'Now the enemy occupies the western seaboard of Europe, the threat of invasion is very real. If it comes it will be by air and sea preceded by attacks on communications, airfields and naval bases. 2 Group is to be reinforced, at a time to be decided later, by aircraft operating from these stations: Bassingbourn—24 Hawker Audax and up to 18 Ansons; Cottesmore—24 Audax and up to 18 Ansons; Upwood—16 Blenheims and up to 18 Ansons; Wyton—15 Blenheims. In the event of a landing the Commander's authority is to have control of 50% of the available effort of the affiliated stations. This call takes authority over all other tasks.'

Group-to-Army links were established, for 2 Group retained its army co-operation role. These were: Scottish Command/Lossiemouth, Northern Command/Watton, Eastern Command 11 and 12 Corps/ Wyton, Eastern Command 2 Corps/Horsham, Eastern Command Reserve/Oakington, Western Command/Raynham, Southern Command/ Wattisham.

Counter-invasion directions were concise: 'All aircraft not under army control are to attack enemy convoys at sea. If a landing is effected the main body of the convoys at sea may be attacked at places where the landing has been made, depending on the situation at the time. Enemy forces caught at sea, and craft containing landing parties, are to be primary targets irrespective of enemy warships in the vicinity. If a landing has been effected and it is decided to attack beaches, enemy craft lying off the beaches and stores on them are to be primary targets.' Thus the somewhat impotent response to invasion was set.

A more immediate threat was obviously the bombing of Britain which quickly materialised at night. Operations Instruction 38 of 3 July came as no surprise; it was to extend the campaign against captured airfields.

'The enemy are using airfields and landing grounds in France, Belgium and Holland. . . . The intention is to destroy as many aircraft as possible on the ground thus forcing the enemy to withdraw. Airfields are to be attacked by sections escorted by fighters, or sections or individual aircraft using cloud cover when definite information is received from fighter reconnaissance.'

The region for attack was divided into eleven areas.[1] Watton took A and G, Wattisham B and H, Wyton C and I, Raynham D and J, Horsham E and F with K as reserve. Again they were widely dispersed to cause the enemy maximum disturbance.

Coastal Command had already discovered barges assembling for the expected invasion and Operations Order 12 of 9 July read: 'Barges and other shipping are reported concentrating in waterways in Holland and north Belgium. Attacks on these are to be given high priority. Reconnaissance is being undertaken by Blenheims of Coastal Command, and 2 Group aircraft on missions to Germany. Most profitable areas for attack are likely to be: two canals running east from Zwolle, canal and

---

[1] The areas were A: Haarlem–Apeldoorn–Hamstede; B: Hamstede–Hoogstraten–Brussels–Hoogstraten; C: Hoogstraten–Vervier–Liège–Brussels–Hoogstraten; D: Coast-west of Nieuport to Mons–Bapaume–Ronesar; E: Ronesar–Brussels–Hoouu–Marienburg–Bapaume–Ronesar; F: North bank of estuary at Le Touquet–Bapaume–St. Just–Dieppe; G: Bapaume–Maruenburg–Vaerly–St. Just–Bapaume; H: Huie–Vervier–Verdun–Passevon–Bessancy–Marienburg–Huie; I: Dieppe–St.Just–Pacy–Le Havre–Dieppe; J: St. Just–Vaerly–Epinay–St. Just; K: reserve.

river running south from Zwolle to the Rhine, the area in the vicinity of Rotterdam and around Antwerp, Ostend and Dunkirk.

'Despatch individual aircraft in numbers to use cloud cover. The station to attack ships is to provide one aircraft daily for a meteorological reconnaissance. Subject to cloud cover the eastern limit of the area is to be the Hook of Holland to Den Helder. Aircraft are to do reconnaissances from varying periods sunrise to 09.00 hours. If the weather is found not to be cloudy a code word is to be passed to the stations.' This was a much needed innovation and usefully cut wasted effort.

Rapidly the invasion forces assembled. Growing fears occasioned a special signal from the A.O.C. 'You must bear in mind that your forces may have to play a most important part in repelling an invasion of this country, and you should be prepared at short notice to divert your squadrons to the attack of the invading enemy force at points of departure and subsequently at sea, and points of landing in this country. To meet the threat of invasion twelve aircraft are to stand by (at each station) every morning at 20 minutes notice from twilight to sunrise.' Daily standbys continued in squadron rotation into the winter.

From Lossiemouth Nos. 21 and 57 Squadrons were operating as a strike force ready to repel invasion forces from Norway. They stood available to bomb assembling forces and airfields. Thirdly they were to integrate their effort with a Bomber Command Directive of 6 July. It called for double the existing effort under G.O.O.11. Even larger numbers could be employed if Command sanctioned it. Blenheims were generally to operate singly over a wide area and might be ordered to attack targets chosen by Command.

Lossiemouth's squadrons had a secondary role, attacking enemy warships at sea, and a small force stood by daily to attack any landing made in darkness. Orders read: 'Crews may sleep in their own quarters, carry on normal work and recreation, but the Station Commander is to devise means of quickly summoning them to their aircraft if required.' Briefing would be simple, e.g. 'Go and attack an enemy convoy of barges and light craft attacking Aberdeen.'

Target listing under G.O.O.11 was now revised as follows: (1) aluminium plants at Cologne, Lunne, Ludwigshafen and Grevenbroich; (2) airframe assembly plants at Wismar, Lutzkendorf, Bremen, Dieschausen, Gotha and Kassel; (3) oil targets at Bremen, Hamburg, Hanover, Ostermoor, Gelsenkirchen, Monheim, Reisholtz, Schulau, Castrop Rauxel and Bottrop—all to interfere with the German air offensive; and (4) shipping including Hamburg docks where *Bismarck* lay, *Deutschland* and other large ships in Kiel, Bremen docks, Wilhelmshaven and Brunsbuttel.

Busiest days in July were 3rd, 6th and 8th. On 3rd R3767 of 15 Squadron flown by Plt. Off. Thompson photographed *Scharnhorst* from 8,000 feet using two F24 cameras and a Leica. Wyton's squadrons attempted to bomb Evere and 82 Squadron had six aircraft making cloud-cover raids on French airfields. Bombs from nine aircraft of 107 Squadron fell on railways at Hamm, Hamborn, Wismar, Osnabruck and Leunan. Four sections went after barges on the River Lek and bombed Schiphol too. And, for the future, No. 139 Squadron stood by for the first time. Next day Sgt. Bagguley of XV Squadron took R3770 to oil refineries south of Zwolle and Plt. Off. Lane bombed Schiphol. He met fifteen enemy fighters and in the ensuing engagement his rear gunner, Sgt. T. J. Maloney, was killed. Rear gunners were exceedingly vulnerable in the Blenheims.

Recently reformed in 2 Group after its mauling in France, No. 18 Squadron resumed operations on 4 July with sorties to Germany from which L8866 was missing. Since the start of hostilities No. 101 Squadron, West Raynham, had served as the Group Training Squadron supplying crews operationally trained on Blenheims. Nos. 13 and 17 Operational Training Units opened in April 1940, and had now taken on 101's role releasing the squadron for operations. These started on 4 July when three crews set off under G.O.O.11. Only Flg. Off. Messervy delivered an attack, on a pipeline by the Kiel Canal.

From Lossiemouth 21 Squadron was flying to a given point in the North Sea, then making parallel sweeps forty miles south. Excitement arose when a submarine was sighted . . . it was British. Mock attacks on the beaches were made and once, following a rapid reaction, a Blenheim racing off turned sharply, scraped its wing along the airfield yet miraculously survived.

Five squadrons operated on 6 July. The early morning weather flight by R3905 of XV Squadron revealed clear skies and 18 Squadron's morning operations were over France. Later, 82 Squadron bombed barges at Zwolle and 110, finding clear skies, attacked barges near Katwyke instead of penetrating into Germany. R3673 was reconnoitring airfields when five Bf 109s intercepted her, damaging the hydraulic system. Shots pierced the inner fuel tanks and instrument panel. Flg. Off. Turner shook off the foe after Flt. Sgt. Ravenhill had claimed a fighter. Uninjured, the crew managed a wheels-up landing.

At Honington No. 105 Squadron had been working up since its battered remains had reached the station in the early hours of 13 June. They moved to Watton on 10 July but had no parachutes, few maps and only three gunners. Yet all were rarin' to go.

Operations continued at a rapid pace but mostly the clouds were absent. One of the few shipping strikes of the period other than against barges was mounted on 8 July. Twelve crews of 107 Squadron led by Wg. Cdr. L. R. Stokes attacked ships in a fiord at Aalborg in Denmark. Bombs fell close to three ships, another received a direct hit and the slight flak missed the formation. No. 110 Squadron was also out this day and one of 139 Squadron was intercepted over the Channel. A section of its port wing was blown off and cannon fire damaged the hydraulic system causing a crash landing at Shoreham.

An attack on Stavanger/Sola in Norway was ordered for 21 Squadron on 9 July. Six crews with six of 57 Squadron bombed the airfield as anti-aircraft guns and a pack of fighters engaged the Blenheims. Soon they had shot down four of 21 Squadron and two of 57. Wg. Cdr. L. C. Bennett escaped into cloud but a message came saying he was in the sea. Plt. Off. Rogers' aircraft returned looking like a colander, and he landed with both tyres burst, and observer and gunner wounded. Yet, with typical 2 Group spirit, 21 Squadron set of for Stavanger next day to avenge the loss, only to encounter unfavourable weather.

Next it was the turn of 107 Squadron to face shattering casualties. On 10 July six crews left to bomb the satellite airfield near Amiens. Flak broke up the formation and the inevitable consequences followed. Only Flt. Lt. Pleasance and crew returned. Eleven aircraft had been lost in a few hours.

To cut losses and expand the period of operations some night attacks were introduced. On 17–18 July Sqn. Ldr. Webster of XV Squadron took-off to raid Caen airfield and in so doing made the first night intruder raid by 2 Group. He set a precedent that thousands were to follow. But it was never easy at night and on this occasion the weather was against him. Another crew bombed Morlaix, but from 10,000 feet and too high for successful intruding. Further night operations were made on 21–22 July when 107 Squadron bombed Caen, Morlaix and Querqueville. Next night 107 attacked Creil starting a fire visible forty miles away. 110 Squadron was also out.

Day raids continued in plenty. On 23 July Sgt. Garvy in L9413 tried to bomb St. Omer but a shell burst under the aircraft and the maps blew away. A side window and the floor door blew in, the radio was out of action and the elevators seriously damaged. Moments later the Blenheim was spinning down but a miraculous recovery came at under 1,000 feet.

The Blenheim had sufficient range to reach quite deeply into Germany and within a matter of days the first night bombing there by 2 Group was ordered. The sphere of operations for XV Squadron was thereby extended to airfields around Wilhelmshaven, three crews raiding Elde and others Paarg.

Losses during July amounted to 31 aircraft. Additionally three more aircraft were written off due to battle damage and four in flying accidents. Casualties included three Wing Commanders killed, fifteen other officers and forty Sergeants killed. Fortunately 2 Group was at the peak of its 1940 strength comprising eleven squadrons and having about 180 aircraft available for operations daily.

By August invasion dominated all thinking, the air battles overhead being seen by many as its prelude. A new plan to expand Group was worked upon and promulgated as 'Banquet 22 Group' on 22 August. By this, Blenheims of the training Group would operate from 2 Group stations supplementing the somewhat meagre reinforcement plan already in force. 'Attacks will be pressed home,' ran the order, 'regardless of cost. Each crew should aim to hit one vessel with one bomb, and machine-gun the enemy whenever possible. Squadrons equipped with gas spray are to be ready to operate with this at the shortest possible notice, but it will only be used as a retaliatory measure.'

As the entire Group uneasily stood by to defend its homeland every day at dawn readiness, its offensive operations continued unabated, cloud-cover operations being daily preceded by the 'met. recce' flight. From mid August night operations were regularly flown by six squadrons against airfields as 2 Group's contribution to the winning of the Battle of Britain after dusk. By day G.O.O.11 raids continued interspersed by those on airfields. The pattern of employment by squadrons in August was as follows:

Day raids on airfields by Nos. XV, 105, 107, 110, 114, 139, 218 Sqns.
Night raids on airfields by Nos. XV (from 12 Aug.), 18 (from 14 Aug.), 40 (from 12 Aug.), 101 (from 14 Aug.), 107 (from 8 Aug.), 110 (from 17 Aug.) Sqn., ranging from Brest to Schiphol.
Long-range guns in Pas de Calais by Nos. 18 and 101 Sqns.
G.O.O.11 raids by Nos. 82, 101, 107, 110, 114 and 139 Sqns.
North Sea Sweeps by Nos. 21 and 57 Sqns.

Throughout the month there were many engagements with fighters, and always the risk of meeting a gigantic formation of enemy aircraft. The most disastrous operation came on 13 August when 82 Squadron was again wiped out. A break from the usual routine was tried on 7 August when twelve crews of 82 Squadron attempted a raid from 20,000 feet on Hamstede. There was too much cloud, and it was when a repeat of this tactic was made that 82 Squadron suffered so badly. Any advantages in high-level operations were nullified by enemy radar getting advance warning of such raids.

After its intensive training 105 Squadron was ready for operations, and the first three sorties were flown on 8th. Their first effective sortie came on 10th when Flg. Off. Murray made two low runs over Schiphol. Guns fired accurately damaging his tail unit. Although L9339 made home, it was beyond unit capacity to repair.

Attacks on airfields were widespread and valiantly pressed home, by day and night. On 11th, for instance, 107 Squadron despatched sorties to Brest, Dinard, Waalhaven and Guernsey/Le Bourg. No. 218 Squadron became operational on 19 August when T1996 took-off for Vlissingen and T1990 for De Kooy.

There were few enemy raids on 2 Group's airfields during the Battle of Britain: they were too far north for escorted formations to attack them. One sortie was directed against Watton on 21 August. A Do 17Z completed half a circuit before dropping twenty bombs on an east-west pass causing neither damage nor casualties. The line of craters 300 yards from the hangars was soon filled. Fighters claimed the raider. The first station to suffer from bombing had been West Raynham where a raider sneaked in at dawn on 10 July. Light bombs fell on No. 1 hangar destroying a Gladiator and three Ansons.

The Battle of Britain was at its height in the closing weeks of August. Beneath, the Blenheims of 2 Group were standing by each day to thwart an invasion, were doing their best to disrupt the activity on the multitude of enemy airfields, sink the barges and penetrate into Germany on the few days when cloud permitted. This was their contribution to that great victory, and it cost the Group this month thirteen officers and 47 N.C.O.s. Twenty-eight Blenheims were shot down, eight damaged beyond repair, and two destroyed in accidents.

Chapter 6
Our Fate in the Balance

As September dawned the fate of freedom hung in the balance. Fighter Command was certainly doing well, and 2 Group's attacks on airfields seemed worth while. Invasion fear reached fever pitch, German long-range guns were hurling shells on to the south coast and the Luftwaffe was relentlessly hammering Britain. It seemed to make sense to continue cloud-cover operations, and the need to sink the barges was becoming paramount. Therefore there was no let-up in the tempo of operations, as can be seen from this outline of operations for the night of 31 August/1 September and the following day:

Horsham: 31.8.40 12 acft G.O.O.11 (cancelled, no cloud cover seen by met. recce acft of 139 and 114 Sqns.); 1.9.40 12 ordered for G.O.I.38 (cancelled).

Wattisham: 31.8.40 6 of 107 Sqn. bombed Emden; 1.9.40 6 acft invasion Battle Sections; 1.9.40 2 acft G.O.I.38 (cancelled).

Watton: 31.8.40 12 of 82 Sqn. at invasion Battle Sections. 31.8.40 12 acft G.O.I.40 (cancelled); 1.9.40 6 acft 105 Sqn. and 5 of 82 Sqn. G.O.O.11.

West Raynham: 31.8.40 6 of 101 Sqn. night operations; 1.9.40 6 acft invasion Battle Sections; 1.9.40 5 acft of 18 Sqn. night operations.

Wyton: 31.8.40 3 each of XV and 40 Sqns. night operations; 1.9.40 3 of each Sqn. for night operations.

From Lossiemouth in September each of the squadrons flew a daily six-aircraft sweep. Total sorties planned: 123, flown: 52.

Ultimately, September proved to be the busiest month until 1944. A very wide range of targets was attacked this month and on 5–6 September Wyton's two squadrons started the intensive night campaign against barges in the Channel ports. Nightly raids on Boulogne, Calais, Dunkirk, Antwerp, Ostend and Flushing took place in which much of the Command was employed. Assorted tactics were used—high-level bombing, glide approaches and low-level raids. Frequently violent explosions followed, and there were many fires. When daylight attacks on these targets were attempted they proved costly, as on 8 September when three crews of 82 Squadron were ordered to reconnoitre Dutch harbours. Only Wg. Cdr. Macdonald came home, bombing Dunkirk on the way.

On the previous day the Luftwaffe opened its merciless bombing campaign on London. Soon after, Alert No. 1 'Invasion imminent' was flashed to all units in Britain. The day passed without any sign of the invaders. Then, shortly before dawn, Invasion Alert No. 2 was given by Command. Every serviceable Blenheim was bombed up, but again nothing happened. At each station six crews stood by all day—but still the enemy did not come. At each dawn the crews felt the call must surely be given.

Nightly runs across the Channel were not without their moments of despair. Plt. Off. N. Bicknell and crew of 101 Squadron were experienced, and set off on 9 September to bomb barges at Antwerp. Over the North Sea their port engine coughed then stopped. They pressed on, and reaching the Dutch coast decided to bomb Hamstede. On one engine they attacked from 5,000 feet. Coming home the aircraft began to lose height and speed then was ditched far from land. Luckily it came down near a trawler, but the sea was very rough. Bicknell and Sgt. Gingell climbed out through broken perspex and hurried to the trapped, injured gunner. They fought in vain to free him before the aircraft sank. Half an hour later they were rescued, a pilot with head wounds and an unconscious observer. For their courage they were awarded a bravely won D.F.C. and D.F.M.

The persistence with which heavy guns on Cap Gris Nez hurled their shells into Dover and Folkestone demanded a response which 2 Group frequently delivered, but it was the invasion barges that attracted almost the whole of Bomber Command by mid September. Within a fortnight 12% of the accumulation had been destroyed and the invasion build-up greatly hampered. On 11 September the enemy postponed his landing from 21 to 24 September. Feeling that the assault must soon come Grp. Capt. H. P. Lloyd, S.A.S.O. at 2 Group, lectured 218 Squadron at Oakington on 13th, his words chosen with skill and care. He predicted that if Hitler did not order the invasion by the end of the month it would not come this year. It could therefore be expected any day, and enemy preparations were being constantly watched. He stressed the need for high morale and discipline, essential to halt an enemy landing. Next day across the Channel invasion plans were discussed. Admiral Raeder considered the air superiority needed for the operation was not achieved—and he knew that many of the ships and barges were being sunk. Hitler held to hope and ordered a further review on 17th.

In the far north Nos. 21 and 57 Squadrons were ever alert and on 14th had a short glimpse of a U-boat. They managed only one bomb near the prey before it disappeared. Their sweeps continued into October, some excitement being occasioned when Wg. Cdr. Delap came across an inverted floating Do 18 flying-boat. Earlier Sgt. Davis had engaged one and soon after found a merchant ship with blazing bridge. The full story was never unravelled.

Meanwhile from France Goering had launched the greatest operation of the Battle of Britain, on 15 September on what is now revered as Battle of Britain Day. So much activity by Fighter Command and its foe limited 2 Group's operations which may be summarised as follows:

Night of 14–15 September

2 crews of 82 Sqn.: heavy guns at Haringzelle and Framzelle
2 crews 105 Sqn.: heavy guns at Haringzelle
1 crew 105 Sqn.: heavy guns at Framzelle
4 crews 40 Sqn.: barges at Ostend—many fires
3/5 crews 101 Sqn.: barges at Dunkirk
3/5 crews 107 Sqn.: barges at Calais.

Daylight hours 15 September

Attacks planned on Zeebrugge, Antwerp, Flushing, Calais, Ostend, Dunkirk—all cancelled. 105 and 139 Squadrons to send one aircraft to each target—operations abandoned, no cloud cover.

Night of 15–16 September

6 crews 139 Sqn.: heavy guns at Framzelles
11/12 crews 110 Sqn.: barges at Dunkirk, Flushing also bombed
2 crews 82 Sqn.: heavy guns on Cap Gris Nez
3 crews 105 Sqn.: three gun sites on Cap Gris Nez
10/12 crews XV Sqn.: barges at Ostend—many fires
11/12 crews 18 Sqn.: barges in Dunkirk—excellent attack.

Fighter Command's resounding success on 15 September, and the continuing success against shipping and barges in the invasion ports, were sufficient for Hitler to postpone the invasion indefinitely. Soon almost the entire weight of the Luftwaffe's bombing offensive was switched to night operations. In answer to this came Operations Instruction 41. Both Wattisham squadrons were to operate from half-waxing to half-waning moon, dropping 250-lb. and 40-lb. bombs on airfields, with docks and heavy guns in a three-mile coastal belt as alternative targets. Airfield attacks were now ordered to be from 1,000 feet or less using flarepaths as the guide. The Blenheims were to make as much nuisance of themselves as possible, and the first intruder sorties were born some months before Fighter Command hit the headlines with such operations.

Nightly attacks by nine aircraft were also ordered on the continental rail network upon which the Germans placed much reliance. It was hoped that accumulative pressure would prove embarrassing. As crews at Wyton, Raynham and Watton reached the required standard of night flying they were to be employed on this duty. Only massive later raids, radar-directed, had much effect upon the railway system. 2 Group was at this time too hopeful.

A third aspect of current operations was described in Instruction 13. Against waterways, Horsham and Oakington were to despatch sorties relying on cloud cover. They were also to make day raids upon airfields.

At Bomber Command there was always the wish to use the Group as part of the strategic force. Under a revision of Operations Order 11 dated 16 September, Horsham and Oakington were to follow up night attacks with day cloud-cover sorties embracing damage assessment flights. Since 23 July the Group had been making photo-reconnaissance sorties to attempt to discover results of bombing and in September and November follow-up orders to this were given by Command, to continue until the P.R.U.s were ready.

Twenty-one oil targets were listed as priority 1 under the new daylight bombing order. Within priority 2 were the liner *Europa* at Bremen, docks and shipping at Bremerhaven, Emden, Hamburg and Wilhelms-haven, and the vast Krupp works at Essen. With hindsight it would seem that these targets were ill suited to the Blenheims which might have proved of much more use carrying out night-long intruder patrols over enemy airfields as did Mosquitoes in later years.

Much of the Group was now staffed by aircrew from the pre-war Volunteer Reserve. Some of these joined the squadrons after the fall of France with very little operational training. They learnt fast, boys becoming men in a few hours.

An unusual event happened at Oakington on 19 September. The 6th Royal Sussex Regiment was staging an airfield defence exercise with Bren-gun carriers when six Blenheims made a mock attack. Three made a tree-top approach, broke and landed unseen. Once they were down the troops harassed them hurling 'bombs', in reality bags of stinking fish manure. The other three aircraft meanwhile landed and their crews rushed to seize the operations room. It was grand fun for all and followed by an inquest.

Half an hour later someone perchance gazed from a window. He could hardly believe his eyes—approaching was . . . a Ju 88. Its flaps were out, port engine dead and to his astonishment the port under-carriage leg came down. A real enemy bomber was landing! It touched down, the leg gave way and it slithered to a halt, a timely arrival.

Within seconds Bren-gun carriers were roaring across the field; an officer and three others soon became prisoners. The machine, a Ju 88D reconnaissance aircraft, was of considerable interest. Its cameras were removed and one at least was later fitted in a reconnaissance Spitfire. As far as could be ascertained the '88 had met some fighters two of which wheeled overhead as it landed.

Six crews of 114 Squadron standing by for attacks on shipping concentrations on 24 September were suddenly told that R-boats were minesweeping nine miles west of Dover. With six of 139 Squadron they were ordered off, with fighter cover, for what was clearly a dangerous mission. They met light flak and scored no hits on the fast-moving foe. After bombing, 139 Squadron tangled with 109s and Plt. Off. Hunt in R3698 shot one down with his wing gun. Flg. Off. Turnbull's machine was badly damaged and had to be set down at Manston. T1794 fell to flak and of Sqn. Ldr. M. F. Hendry and crew no trace was found.

During September 509 sorties had been flown. Nineteen aircraft were missing and six written off due to battle damage.

The pattern for operations in October was as follows:

Operations under G.O.O.11: Nos. 40, 82, 101, 105, 107, 139 Sqns.

Against Channel Ports: Nos. 18, 40, 82, 101, 105, 110, 114, 139, 218 Sqns.

Night raids on airfields: Nos. 82, 107, 110, 114, 218 Sqns.

Night raids on Western Germany: Nos. 18, 40, 82, 101, 105, 107, 110 Sqns.

Operations against oil targets: Nos. 82, 105, 110, 114 Sqns.

Operations against guns in Pas de Calais: Nos. 101, 105, 110 Sqns.

Anti-shipping operations: Nos. 114, 139 Sqns.

North Sea Sweeps: Nos. 21 and 57 Sqns.

Daylight armed reconnaissance sorties: Nos. 114, 218 Sqns.

Roving commission operations: Nos. 114 and 218 Sqns.

The last were an interesting feature of October. On 3 October Sgt. Morley and crew took N6183 towards Reisholtz, but being short of cloud they found about fifty barges on the Maas at Heausten and bombed the warehouse where they were being unloaded. Next day Sqn. Ldr. Ault was briefed to bomb Bremen. It was cloudless so he decided to try for Soesterburg airfield; again there was no cloud. Subsequently he reconnoitred Schellingwoulde seaplane station. Flak was fierce so he tried for Ijmuiden where his bombs eventually were placed close to a large black liner. Sgt. Adams had meanwhile persistently attempted to bomb Rotterdam. Finally he crept in from the River Ijssel flying very low to attack the docks.

When Plt. Off. Dawson took L9303 on an early sortie he was intercepted by a dozen 109s. One was shot down before the rest were shaken off. That day 114 Squadron made two shipping raids getting hits on the stern of a coaster.

Operation *Lucid* aiding the Navy took place on 3–4 October. Barges in Calais were attacked using fire-ships whilst destroyers bombarded the harbour. The Navy faced three difficulties: taking the fire-ships into the docks, close-range guns and heavy guns on Gris Nez. Fifteen Wellingtons of 3 Group attacked Calais and Boulogne providing a diversion whilst the fire-ships were taken in. Six aircraft each from Wattisham, Wyton and Raynham bombed Framzelle and Haringzelle gun sites, and others bombed Ostend, again as diversions.

On 9 October clouds hung low over the Low Countries when Plt. Off. Cross was heading for Gelsenkirchen. He came down to 300 feet to check his position in Holland, when suddenly the cloud base fell to 100 feet. After turning about he came across some twenty 109s on Weiringermeer landing ground. He immediately put on plus 9 lb. boost and flew at about twenty feet dodging to avoid houses and a windmill.

Then the cloud rose and, rather than waste his sortie, he headed for Bergen aerodrome—only to find the clouds too low. It was an eventful abortive sortie.

Rarely did the crews encounter enemy aircraft other than Bf 109s, but 9 October brought an exception. Flt. Lt. Shaw of 218 Squadron set out for Homberg. Bad weather led to his looking for an alternative. He found three ships in the Maas, attacked and fled at sea level. He had fired the fixed gun but it stopped after about thirty rounds. He remarked, 'Now is the time when we will meet an enemy aircraft!' Within seconds an He 111 hove into view. He pulled 9 lb. boost and hared after it with the enemy flying flat out. Soon he was abreast and the gunner, Sgt. Gill, opened fire. The Heinkel turned to port and Gill fired again only to have a gun stoppage. Now the crew had only their blister gun to fire with and Sgt. Wynne had the chance he had been waiting for. Shaw turned sharply and Wynne fired—he too had a stoppage. After a fifteen-minute combat in a welter of chagrin the fight had to be abandoned. Damage to P6960? One shot through the rudder's tip.

Another operation with the Navy, *Medium*, came on 10 October with shipping in the Bassins Charles X and Napoleon III at Cherbourg as targets for the heavy guns of H.M.S. *Revenge*. Wellingtons of 3 Group lit the target area, the sea and the coastline. Two Group's contribution was eleven Blenheims to bomb the defending guns and the shipping. A previous warning note was heeded—shells from *Revenge* would reach 5,000 feet during trajectory.

On 17 October an order was given whereby one crew from each of three squadrons, captained by either Plt. Off. Dawson or Plt. Off. Hartland of 114 Squadron, Plt. Off. Turnbull or Plt. Off. Dundee of 139 Squadron and Flt. Lt. Shaw or Plt. Off. Mitchell or Sgt. Morley of 218 Squadron, was to be given a free hand attacking any target in Germany or Occupied Territory under cloud cover whether or not their station was operating. The judgement for the operation was theirs, and these flights preluded the exciting Mosquito *Ranger* flights of later years.

On 21 October Flt. Lt. Shaw flew 218 Squadron's first roving commission. In murky weather he headed for Dunkirk. He lost sight of the harbour and then spied a supply convoy fourteen ships strong, led by a larger one and with three E-boats escorting. He ran in from behind them and was challenged by an unsure enemy firing star cartridges. Sgt. Wynne then released the bombs crying 'I've hit it, I've hit it.' He was amazed to see a ship almost capsize, with deck awash and mast bases in the water. Quickly the convoy scattered and E-boats raced around for survivors.

Cloud-cover operations under G.O.O.11 continued, likewise the North Sea patrols from Lossiemouth. These were uneventful until 26 October. At 18.30 hours six Blenheims of 21 Squadron were waiting to take-off for night flying training when three He 111s roared in below 100 feet to attack the airfield. One bomb fell squarely on T2233, damaged two other Blenheims beyond repair and severely damaged a third. The defending gunners were quick off the mark and one of the raiders burst into flames on the airfield. Four members of the squadron were injured as a result of the raid.

Night raids on enemy airfields were now a common task, but more and more frequently the 2 Group squadrons were participating in the night bombing offensive against Germany itself. Crews on these raids not only faced the foe, they had to measure up to the increasing cold, the weather and the dark. Little wonder, then, that target identification with primitive equipment was difficult. Once located targets were frequently strongly defended by guns and searchlights. Returning, too, had its problems as the crews often groped their ways to bases. On 28 October for instance, one crew ended their sortie in a field at Harlaxton whilst Plt. Off. I. Prosser and crew perished in a crash near Bircham Newton. Sqn. Ldr. Grenham and crew were missing; it was a costly night for one squadron.

Roving commission flights continued throughout October, but an even more exciting highlight came to Sqn. Ldr. Little of 40 Squadron who encountered a Ju 88 during his training flight near Ely. Luckily he was armed. The enemy bomber was soon shot down and its crew taken prisoner.

By the start of November operations were mostly by night due to the inclement weather. Invasion seemed most unlikely and so Nos. 21 and 57 Squadrons flew their last patrols on 29 October and 1 November respectively. No. 21 returned to Watton but 57 Squadron was posted to Wyton. With the enemy night blitz on Britain at its height the Air Staff wished to respond as heavily as possible with night raids on Germany and so, on 1 November, Nos. XV and 40 Squadrons were transferred to 3 Group and soon equipped with Wellingtons and followed by 57 Squadron on 12 November. Wyton left 2 Group never to return. From this station some of the most memorable of 2 Group's operations had been flown. Therefore let us pause with the story and look back upon Wyton in 1940 seen through the eyes of G. Hindley.

'The station master during the time I was there, March to August 1940, was "Pussy Foster" later the R.A.F. commander in Austria. I was one of those classified u/t aircrew, the lowest form of life. Being all aircrew volunteers we turned to with a will, expecting at any moment to start training in the odd phoney war.

'We cleaned lavatories, did guards. As a teenager I was soon blooded by scrubbing out the mortuary, a rather messy variation being hosing the blood from the cramped gunner's turret in the Blenheims. We did a lot of coal heaving—I held a record of 57 bags filled in 57 minutes. Most popular was the delivery to Group H.Q. where we were entertained by the novel and newly arrived WAAFS.

'My other job was helping in stores in charge of an old Chiefy who delighted in making coarse comments to the WAAFS as he passed them intimate garments, including their "blackouts". I think there were only six WAAFS then, and they arrived in their own sports cars. Soon all was to change abruptly.

'One occasion stands out. At night the Duty Officer was inspecting our spotless buttons with a strong torch while an intruding Jerry shot over us, at roof top height, and continued—to bomb Henlow's flare path.

' "Pussy" Foster was well liked but meticulous and likely to creep round corners in his staff car without lights. Woe betide anyone who failed to halt him and check his papers. Stories about spies abounded. It was said they were entering the camp, not difficult from the two main roads.

'The food was good within the limits of communal catering. One point that made a deep impression on me was that the wireless operator/gunners were still not Sergeants even during the hard fighting over France. It seemed tough on these men that they should join the long food queues still wearing their flying boots and straight back from gruelling ops.

'The squadrons here were Nos. XV and 40 later joined by the battered remnants of 57 Squadron just before Dunkirk. I seem to remember we had some short-nosed Blenheims still. What a magnificent machine the Blenheim was. Often they came home with three or more cylinders shot away, jagged ends flying in all directions. One day when I was on guard duty one of the squadrons came home escorting their Wingco who had one engine blazing.

'Rumours poured forth as the position in France worsened, especially when some of 57's aircraft arrived carrying up to seven passengers. We fitted out sleeping accommodation for them—three wooden planks each on two low wooden tripods. Some had kit, some had nothing—and they were feeling pretty sore. Things were clearly desperate. After our day's work we dug slit trenches and manned them, fully clothed, so that for six weeks except for the moments stolen for a bath we never had our clothes off. Most of us were falling asleep on our feet from sheer over-work. The S.W.O. complete with D.C.M. won in the First World War ordered us to "shoot anything that moves"—comic in view of our being placed between two main roads.

'And what of those summer months? Since there was now only one trained armourer we remaining twelve u/t aircrew became armourers the hard way. There were two fusing sheds and we split into three parties. We dropped the delicate fulminate pistols into the fuses, screwed them into the bombs, lifted the bombs on to the trolleys and the third party bombed up. We took turns at these jobs from dawn till dusk when we resumed our vigils in the trenches, fortunately in magnificent weather. Our biggest bombs were 250 pounders each of which had to be hand-winched by a low-gear crank into the bays. We found the quickest way was for two of us, one on each end, to lift it bodily and above our heads on to the slips. Two-and-a-half hundredweight lifted accurately to that height was no mean feat. We developed this technique to such a pitch that the pilots could be away again after only a cup of tea. Sometimes, however, they were too tired even to leave their seats. Those men flew until they just didn't come back. In years to come I repeatedly reflected upon their gallantry.'

6. Knapsack power station under attack
7. Knapsack power station under attack

18. Battle damage to N6207: VE-G from fighter attack. Served 110 Squadron from 7.7.39 until damaged beyond repair 22.5.40. Fought until flak damage destroyed her landing gear and Flg. Off. G. O. Lings crash-landed

19. Damage to engine nacelle and wing tip of V6445: UX-E of 82 Squadron, the result of bird collision. See Eric Chandler's account for the raid on Cologne carried out in this aircraft. V6445 joined 82 Squadron 26.4.41, was written off due to battle damage 20.8.41

20. At Watton in the winter of 1939–40. From left to right: Sqn. Ldr. Sutcliffe, D.F.C., Wg. Cdr. The Earl of Bandon, D.S.O., Flt. Lt. McConnell, Plt. Off. Fordham, Sqn. Ldr. 'Sammy' Hall

21. Pilots of 82 Squadron early 1940. From left to right: Miles Delap, Ken Toft, 'Attie' Atkinson, Richardson, Joe Hunt, John Blake, John Harris and Charlie Breese

22. During the Dieppe raid of August 1942 Air Vice-Marshal Alan Lees (*right*) talking to Wg. Cdr. J. E. Pelly-Fry (*centre*) and Sqn. Ldr. Griffiths

23. Blenheims of 82 Squadron attacking shipping off Scheveningen in August 1941

24. A Blenheim pulls away after bombing a ship off Heligoland on 2.8.41

Chapter 7
By Night and Day

During the winter of 1940–41 the emphasis was on night bombing of German targets and airfields in the Occupied Countries. Group strength was again reduced by the loss of 218 Squadron the day before the latter had planned to celebrate Guy Fawkes Night over enemy territory. It was at this time, too, that the enemy made a number of appearances over 2 Group's bases.

Early on 1 November a Dornier crept low over Wattisham placing its bombs on three barrack blocks and married quarters. Some of the airmen were still abed and one concrete floor crashed on those sleeping on a ground floor. Ten men were crushed and nineteen injured.

On 3 November the enemy came again, a Do 17 and two Ju 88s flying very low at dusk. Several large bombs crashed into a hangar which immediately burst into flames. At once Flt. Lt. G. Parry gathered a team who rushed into the burning mess to drag out blazing aircraft and make some attempt to douse the flames. This they did successfully. Next day a marauding Heinkel came out of the clouds to repeat the dose, but his bombs fell wide.

No. 107 Squadron was stung to anger by the cheek of the foe. On 5 November it held its celebrations at nine enemy airfields. At Ghent Sgt. Ralston received a green to land, had the flare-path lit and promptly bombed it. Flt. Lt. Warren found a bomber landing at Le Culot and peppered it. Sqn. Ldr. Hull's gunner fired at another going into Amiens and everyone felt a little more easy.

The night of 11/12 November was typically eventful for 82 Squadron. It despatched twelve Blenheims to Hamm, Soest, Osnabruck and Le Havre. Weather was very bad and only secondary targets were bombed, including Duisburg's docks and the railway at Dortmund. Plt. Off. Black lost control of L9389 over the sea due to icing, and jettisoned his bombs. One aircraft had trouble and more bombs fell in the sea. Sgts. Waples and Metcalfe both had to put down at sea due to fuel shortage, the former ten miles from a destroyer off Harwich, the second off Flamborough Head. In Waples's aircraft the gunner was killed; in the other the pilot and observer escaped injured but the gunner was last seen clinging to the tail of T2280.

At 14.30 hours on 14 November, crews of Nos. 101, 105 and 110

Squadrons were briefed for the following night's aerodrome attacks. Across the Channel many of their enemies were being briefed too for the most notorious attack on a British provincial city, Coventry. Hitherto the main night target had been London; this time it was to be different and to change the course of the war.

The first of twenty Blenheim crews detailed for the night's operations took-off at 18.00 hours from Wattisham and a few moments later the spearhead of the Coventry raid crossed our coast at Lyme Bay. Eleven of 110 Squadron made for the beacon at Cambrai whilst others attacked Beauvais, home of K.G.76, and Lille where K.G.53 was partly based. Airfields at Etaples, Knocke, Rennes and Amiens/Glisy were in the event bombed, none of them perchance involved in the enemy's night operations. Sgt. Costello-Bowen in T1931 attacked three airfields and engaged a He 111. Otherwise there was little to show for the night's effort.

Usually operations against aerodromes were aimed at preventing bombers landing. Advance information came from intelligence sources on the afternoon of 15 November indicating the enemy night effort would be waged from airfields around Antwerp, and Brussels, from Le Culot and St. Trond. Maximum effort was ordered. Nine crews of 105 Squadron were eventually briefed but bad weather cut the effort to five. Hingene, Evere, Duerne and Vucht were all hit, then Plt. Off. Murray lined up to strafe Dieghem. Three other crews watched as he sped in with T1890's guns blazing, only to be met by intensive ground fire which pulverised the Blenheim into a horribly blazing mess.

Wanne Eickel's oil refinery attracted some of the night raiders. On 24th 101 Squadron was thus engaged when a frightening disaster befell Sgt. Edmond in N6236. Lock nut and spider on the reduction gear of the starboard engine became loose and the gear casing was churned away. Then the propeller fell away over the sea. Edmond made Raynham only to crash in the circuit. He and his observer were injured and the gunner had a fractured skull.

Raids on Western Germany and airfields formed the backbone of the offensive now, and were usually made at night. On 27 November No. 105 Squadron despatched eight crews to Cologne and a *freshman* flight to Boulogne. Six claimed to bomb Cologne, then the weather deteriorated. One crew, after getting permission to land at Swanton Morley, flew off low towards the beacon. A moment later their aircraft came down at Foxley Wood and all perished. Costello-Bowen above dense cloud was unable to find his base and decided to seek a cloud gap. By then he was near Liverpool, some two hundred miles from base. He milled around desperately calling for help until his fuel was exhausted, then the crew baled out near Manchester.

The perils of night raids in Blenheims were considerable. A typical operation of those days has been recalled by Eric Chandler, then a wireless operator/air gunner on 107 Squadron:

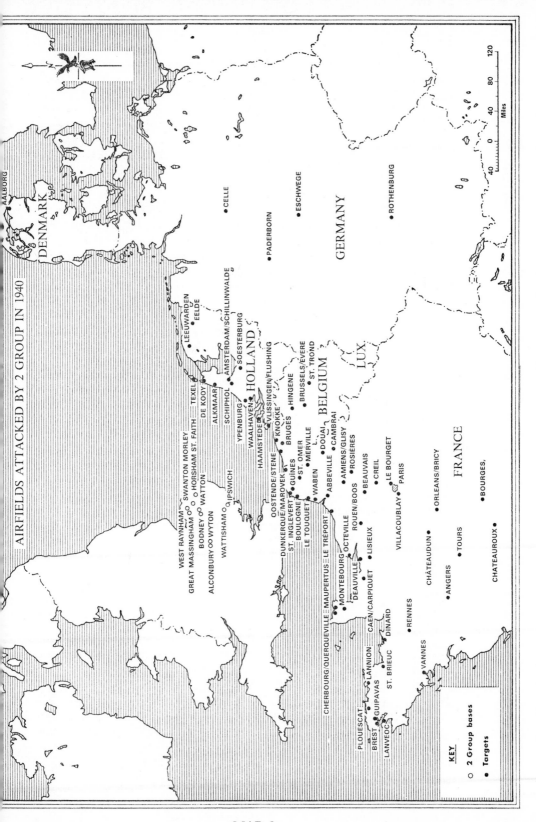

AIRFIELDS ATTACKED BY 2 GROUP IN 1940

KEY

○ 2 Group bases
● Targets

DENMARK

AALBORG

LEEUWARDEN
EELDE
AMSTERDAM/SCHILLINWALDE
SOESTERBURG
SCHIPHOL
HOLLAND

CELLE

PADERBORN
ESCHWEGE
GERMANY
ROTHENBURG

WEST RAYNHAM
SWANTON MORLEY
GREAT MASSINGHAM ○○ ○ HORSHAM ST. FAITH TEXEL
BODNEY ○○ WATTON
ALCONBURY ○○ WYTON DE KOOY
WATTISHAM ○ IPSWICH ALKMAAR
YPENBURG
WAALHAVEN
HAAMSTEDE
VLISSINGEN/FLUSHING
OOSTENDE/STENE KNOKKE
DUNKERQUE/MAROVEK BRUGES HINGENE
ST. INGLEVERT GUINES ST. OMER BRUSSELS/EVERE
BOULOGNE MERVILLE ST. TROND
LE TOUQUET WABEN DOUAI
LE TRÉPORT ABBEVILLE CAMBRAI
CHERBOURG/QUERQUEVILLE MAUPERTUS AMIENS/GLISY
MONTEBOURG OCTEVILLE ROUEN/BOOS ROSIÈRES
DEAUVILLE LISIEUX BEAUVAIS
CAEN/CARPIQUET CREIL
DINARD VILLACOUBLAY LE BOURGET
PARIS

BELGIUM
LUX

RENNES
VANNES
PLOUESCAT
BREST GUIPAVAS
LANNION
LANVEOC ST. BRIEUC

CHÂTEAUDUN
ANGERS TOURS
ORLEANS/BRICY
BOURGES,
CHATEAUROUX
FRANCE

Miles
40 0 40 80 120

MAP 8

'It was a bitterly cold night. I left the Sergeants' Mess at Wattisham and walked along the deserted dark road past S.H.Q. and on to No. 3 Hangar. It was dry with a clear sky, but snow was not far away. The weather had been more or less like this for the whole month. We had been operating on many nights and now it was 21 November. My crew and I were on Battle Order yet again. Our last trip had really scared us when our aircraft iced up over Amiens and began to fall from the sky. We only managed to shake off the ice when almost at ground level, and had hedge hopped all the way home.

'This morning, since it was now 02.00 hours, 107 Squadron were off again on a night intruder to put enemy airfields out of action and make life as difficult as possible for returning bombers.

'Most of the crews were present when I entered the crew room. Despite the hour Oswald Gayford, the Station Commander benign and florid, was there to wish us luck and impress upon us that as long as the weather in the full moon period held, and present channels of information remained open, we must operate at maximum strength.

'Our briefing was simple. We were to fly to a point near Lille and Arras until we received further information by W/T to attack one of the aerodromes in use in that area. Each of the squadron crews had a beat and a list of possible targets.

'The cold may not sound one of the worst dangers we early night bomber boys had to face, but in many ways it was. It is cold of a different kind to that experienced on the ground. It seems to bite into you and attacked your will power making you physically and mentally incapable of doing anything except going to sleep. The half-open turret in which the gunner sat was the coldest place in the aircraft and 65 degrees of frost was quite normal. Later, electrically heated suits were produced for the w.op./air gunner.

'Having put on as much clothing as possible and still able to walk, I now added inner and outer flying suits and three pairs of gloves—silk, woollen, leather. I collected my gas-operated Vickers machine-gun, plodded out to the waiting lorry and was driven to our faithful "L Leather".

'At dispersal we were met by an almost frozen ground crew who helped us into the aircraft with all our war gear, and then waited patiently whilst I struggled to fix the machine-gun on to its mounting. Soon we were taxiing out to the first gooseneck flare. We at once received a "green", throttles were opened, and we were away. A watery haze spread over the countryside. We circled Stowmarket and, dead on time, set course for Orfordness. Like a great stripe of silver paper the North Sea hove into view. It looked cold, unfriendly, and I always had the feeling that once you started to fly over it you cut the last link with everything that meant safety and warmth.

'We crossed the French coast just north of Dunkirk. As usual we saw from time to time "lights" which we felt sure were enemy fighters; they always turned out to be stars although one passed overhead ... we hoped he hadn't seen us. At the coast we met the usual unfriendly welcome from shore batteries. A lot of little flickering lights appeared to be going on and off on the ground. Then you noticed dirty black clouds suddenly appearing all around you and if you were too close you felt the aircraft being thrown about as if it was on a rough sea, and sometimes you could smell cordite.

'We started to lose height rapidly and arrived slap over Lille at 200 feet, where everything came to life. It was just like 5 November—streams of pretty coloured lights—red, yellow, white weaving their way up towards us. It was fascinating but deadly at that height. We hastily fired off what we had been told was the colour of the day, a red and yellow Very light. It worked. Everything at once stopped. They thought we were one of their aircraft returning from a raid. We turned towards Arras hoping we would soon receive instructions. A few moments later the expected call came and I ducked down to try to write the message on my log strapped to my right leg. "Proceed to Cambrai, drome operating now."

'Course changed and we soon saw a line of flashing lights at the beacon and a line of lights on the aerodrome. They were busy tonight. Suddenly all the lights except those at the beacon went out. Within seconds the morse started clicking through my earphones: "Turn away from Cambrai, air raid alarm sounded there." Annoyed, we dived down on the beacon and I gave it a long burst as we flashed by. It went out and I kidded myself I had hit it—more likely they switched it off!

'Fifteen minutes later we decided that we were not where we were supposed to be, and it started to snow. We dropped a flare which lit a town. The next minute the flak opened up. There seemed to be more than we had encountered before, a very pretty sight crawling gracefully towards us, and getting faster and faster as it came, until it went by with a loud whistling hiss and roar to explode a few hundred yards further on. It made a peculiar noise when it did this, a sort of "bob bok", each shell having a different colour. Usually they were in the same colour order—green, white, red. We dived away as fast as we could deciding that the wind met. had given us must be wrong, as usual, for that town looked like St. Quentin which meant we were way south of our intended track.

'All at once a broad searchlight beam got on to us. We were completely blinded, then more swept across the sky to join the first. I started firing down a beam as our observer again fired the colours of the day. Out went the searchlights and the flak stopped. We set course again for Arras. Soon a radio message ordered us to proceed to Lille/Ronchin airfield.

'Once again we found a flare path lit as we approached. Better still, we saw two enemy bombers already on the circuit, their nav. lights on. A third was on his landing approach. We put on our navigation lights and joined the circuit. We decided to follow the machine ahead on his run in, and try to shoot him down once he had lowered his undercarriage and flaps. All went according to plan. Our victim received a green light and started his approach. We followed trying to close on to him. But alas! We still had our lights on and the flare party on the ground spotted this and assumed that two of their aircraft were trying to land at the same time. They fired a red warning light. Our victim was then aware of the danger, putting his lights out just as we opened fire with our fixed gun. Almost at the same time the ground lights went off. We then hopefully released our bombs and climbed away fast. It then appeared that enemy aircraft left in the circuit declared war on each other as their tracer bullets flew.

'Now that the excitement was over we felt colder than ever and wanted to sleep. At 15,000 feet we received an impressive send off from the Calais batteries which we overflew having been blown off intended track.

'After retuning my receiver to base I could hear Wattisham answering other aircraft and giving them homing bearings. We crossed our coast at Felixstowe where we received a warm reception from guns of the Royal Navy; our fault, we should have come in over Orfordness. Everywhere looked unreal for there had been a heavy snowfall. We were the last to land, and had been airborne four hours forty minutes. With eggs and bacon and de-briefing a typical intruder mission of this winter had ended.

'Things were primitive equipment-wise in those days. The only aids we had were battery run 1082–83 radios. If the aerial iced up we could only receive. German ground stations started calling us up when we first transmitted for home bearings. They would do their best to imitate our bases, giving bearings which would take you back into enemy territory where you would be forced down when short of fuel.

'The Darkie system had not then been thought up and it was very easy to get lost over England in bad weather. At this time there were few active airfields in Norfolk or Suffolk. Our aircraft, incidentally, were not painted black. We retained normal day time camouflage colouring.'

Occasionally a special night raid was ordered as on 15 November. Intelligence came to hand that the Luftwaffe planned a follow-up to the Coventry raid, a concentrated attack on a south-east town, probably Harwich or Ipswich. It was believed the entire German bomber force would be employed, making attacks on three consecutive nights. As a reprisal the whole of Bomber Command was to attack a German town the same night for morale and propaganda purposes under Operation *Coldwater*. The task for 2 Group was to bomb airfields to prevent enemy bombers from taking-off. Each station was to have nine aircraft available at from fifteen to twenty minutes' notice to cover listed airfields from an hour before twilight to one hour before dawn. The Luftwaffe did not mount its expected raid but the 2 Group maximum effort went forward as planned.

On the night of 3–4 December No. 82 Squadron operated against Essen. Only Sqn. Ldr. Macmichael claimed to attack the primary and on return he found weather over base atrocious. He climbed to 6,000 feet so that his crew could land safely the only way—they all baled out of T1813. Messervy brought his bombs back and as he came in for a landing at Mildenhall he and his crew had a merciful escape for they had grazed a tall chimney. Plt. Off. Black, finding bad weather, circled base until daybreak when he landed. Sgt. Cartwright crashed at Manston where he and the crew were killed. Sgt. Smith, short of petrol, force-landed skilfully in a field at Messing near Colchester. Plt. Off. McCartney and crew were killed when N3578 crashed near Southend. Sgt. Butcher was heard for a time sending SOS's but gradually the signals faded. Notification later came that N3594 had come down, the crew becoming prisoners. Only four crews made safe landings—and only one at base.

Early on 10 December four crews of 105 Squadron set off to bomb the Focke-Wulf factory at Bremen where Condor bombers which were pestering our shipping were built. Despite the clouds, fires were believed started at the works then R3707 was shadowed by a night-fighter which closed to 150 yards. Sgt. Foster quickly identified it and sent it off in a shower of sparks. Soon after, Sqn. Ldr. Key and crew saw a burst of flame on the ground—it seems likely Foster's 'possible' could at least be a 'probable'.

There were many now in the Government eager to retaliate against German cities for heavy night raids on British cities. Raids in moderate strength against prescribed targets in large population centres had been carried out in November. On 12 December the War Cabinet discussed a large-scale raid, finally deciding upon a mass attack on a German city 'to cause the maximum possible destruction' after the manner of the German raids.

On 16 December 2 Group's Ops 356 were ordered to be scrapped and replaced by Operation *Abigail Rachel*. All available squadrons in Bomber Command were to take part including those of the re-formed 1 Group which had risen from the ashes of the A.A.S.F. 'It is probable that over 200 aircraft will operate,' the order ran. No. 3 Group was to make the initial fire-raising attack using a minimum of eight Wellingtons dropping 4-lb. and 250-lb. LC incendiaries. Unlike the massive attacks of later years this was to be spread over several hours, ending as late as possible whilst allowing return in darkness. The weather on 16–17 December was forecast as likely to deteriorate; consequently the force was cut to 134 aircraft including nine of 2 Group drawn from 101 and 114 Squadrons. One hundred and two claimed to bomb Mannheim and 85 fires were caused. Ten aircraft were lost and all nine from 2 Group suffered damage. Of the two sent by 114 Squadron one had engine trouble soon after take-off, jettisoned its load and crash-landed near Horsham St. Faith. The other could not locate its target and eventually landed at Boscombe Down. 101 Squadron fared very badly. One of its aircraft came down near St. Quentin, another crashed at Fairlight, near Hastings. Three others were lost of which one made a wheels-up landing near Plympton, Devon, one came down near Brixham, and Flt. Lt. Graham managed a safe landing on unlit Christchurch airfield. Only Wg. Cdr. Sinclair landed at base.

Such night raids on Germany had begun on 16 November when 110 Squadron attempted a raid on Altona gasworks, and by the end of 1940 they had been carried out on eighteen nights.

Fighter Command Operational Instruction No. 56 of 12 December 1940 commented: 'Enemy night bombers are operating against this country from airfields in France, Belgium and Holland. Blenheims of 2 Group have been carrying out attacks against these aerodromes which have undoubtedly hampered the enemy's night operations.' Under the instruction Blenheim fighters of No. 23 Squadron were to begin Operation *Intruder* from half-waxing to half-waning moon, or on any opportune occasion. Close co-operation with 2 Group was to be maintained. It had been found that active airfields could rarely be spotted from over 2,000 feet although many dummy airfields could be seen from as high as 8,000 feet. Three target areas were allotted to 23 Squadron and were not to be simultaneously attacked by 2 Group, with whom liaison was to be close. No. 23 Squadron began operations on 21 December.

Intruder 'security patrols' by 2 Group continued, and a revised pattern was ordered in 2 Group Operations Instruction No. 41 of 30 December 1940. The radio counter-measures station at Cheadle would obtain information on enemy operations, usually from the German W/T messages passing after bombing. Information from Fighter Command sometimes revealed the target prior to attack. The usual method now of controlling the Blenheim intruders was to despatch them when estimated time of return of the enemy bombers to base was known; alternatively the Blenheims patrolled beat lines as before, receiving the latest information on activity by W/T when in flight.

Between 22 January and 10 February no night bomber raids were flown by 2 Group, by which time they were covered by Operations Instruction No. 43 of 25 January. It explained that most targets for the night offensive against Germany now lay beyond the Blenheim's range. Furthermore operations should now be carried out on only or about ten days per month when it was moonlight—and then only if the weather was suitable. It was therefore important that all available aircraft should take part in the few ordered night operations. Priorities for attack were now as follows: (1) oil targets, (2) industrial targets, (3) marshalling yards, (4) airfields. The Group was still expected to be ready to repel invasion should it come in the next few months and orders of 27 January 1941 outlined action to be taken. Nos. 1 and 2 Groups would combine with 70 Group, 21 of its Blenheims reinforcing the defenders under *Plan Banquet 70 Group* to destroy the enemy as he attempted to land; and would use gas spray only in retaliation.

On 10–11 February 221 bombers took-off on the largest raid yet, with Hanover and its U-boat component factories as the target. Forty Blenheims set off between 20.59 and 23.00 hours for the night's operations. Of these, six of 18 Squadron, seven of 21, four of 105, six of 107 and six of 110 Squadrons claimed to bomb Hanover adding to fires started. Others attacked airfields, four from 101 Squadron with one of 105 and one of 110 bombed Rotterdam, and one of 21 Squadron was missing. Load for each aircraft was two 250-lb. GP and 120 4-lb. incendiaries. Flt. Lt. Simmons, D.F.C. flying R3871 of 107 Squadron became completely lost when his W/T failed. After 6½ hours' flying he had to force-land. Enemy intruders were active that night and over the English coast Sqn. Ldr. Sabine was attacked and followed home to Bodney during a 1½ hour engagement. Eventually he was forced to crash-land his aircraft at base. As Sgt. Chattaway circled Bodney an intruder was awaiting him. It engaged Z5877 and Chattaway crashed in flames. He was killed and Plt. Off. Cherval, seriously wounded, died next day. The gunner, Sgt. Burch, was wounded in the leg by a bullet.

On four more nights in February, 2 Group participated in Main Force raids, major ones taking place on 15th when 26/35[1] aircraft from Nos. 18, 101, 105 and 107 Squadrons attacked the oil refinery at Homberg, and on 26th when 12/16 despatched attacked Cologne. Such raids could be attempted safely only when it was moonlight.

Night raids increased and on 28 February/1 March 23/32 Blenheims despatched bombed Wilhelmshaven. Naval ports were now the main night targets as a result of heavy shipping losses. A special directive of 6 March ordered this. On 12th 28 Blenheims formed part of the force of 82 bombers sent to Bremen; next night it was Hamburg and on 18th 2 Group made its biggest contribution in this phase of activity with Wilhelmshaven as target. It was 02.41 when the first of 23 Blenheims from Nos. 21, 105 and 110 Squadrons took-off to attack. Alternative targets which some bombed were the harbour at Bremerhaven and oil tanks at Rotterdam. Late that day the biggest raid of the series followed, again directed at Wilhelmshaven. During that night 51 Blenheims were despatched of which 31 claimed to bomb the main target. By the light of fires and flares a dark-brown pall of smoke, visible many miles away, was seen to rise from the town. Attacks were delivered by some aircraft on Ostend, Rotterdam, Waalhaven, De Kooy, barges in the Maas, searchlights at Enkhuisen and Emden. Although night-fighters were active only one aircraft was lost. The last aircraft landed back at 04.00 hours. Before the month ended raids had been mounted on Brest, Dusseldorf, Hamburg, Lorient and Hanover.

By the end of March almost the whole of 2 Group was engaged upon

---

[1] 26 out of 35 aircraft despatched claimed to attack.

two new ventures later described. It fell to 105 Squadron to close this phase of activity with night raids on Cologne, Bremerhaven on 7–8 April, and a nuisance raid on Brest on 11 April. Gone now was Operations Order No. 11 which had been the centre of so much activity for little reward and considerable cost; invasion seemed unlikely, Fighter Command was taking over increasingly the night intruder role and night bombing by Blenheims was simply not on. By now other employment for 2 Group had been decided upon.

Chapter 8
Sink Those Ships

Fear of invasion had abated, night attacks on airfields had brought limited results, daylight operations by lone aircraft were bringing little reward. The offensive against oil targets could not yet cripple the foe, since lack of precise navigation aids made the task impossible. Upon what, then, might the bulk of 2 Group, the Cinderella of Bomber Command, be most effectively employed?

Increasingly worried about mounting shipping losses, and constantly apprehensive lest capital ships should harass our convoys, the Admiralty pressed its worries upon the War Cabinet. Bomber Command should concentrate its effort against naval bases, the lair of the U-boats, and indeed against U-boats themselves. Against the latter it could do little, but if Coastal Command could be concentrated for operations over the Atlantic and freed from unprofitable North Sea patrols . . . Here was an acceptable idea.

Accordingly No. 114 Squadron was taken off Operation *Circus* (see Chapter 9), detached to Coastal Command and moved to Thornaby. It was to search the North Sea for enemy vessels.

Churchill's ear was ever tuned to the claims of the Sea Lords. He was convinced that the greatest threat to Britain's survival now was the assault on Atlantic shipping. On 6 March he issued a Directive—the Battle of the Atlantic was to have full priority, and Bomber Command was to concentrate on naval targets. Coupled with this was the belief that a sea blockade of Germany could be effective. What part could 2 Group play in this campaign?

Orders were given to halt the movement of all coastal shipping between the Brittany peninsula and Germany. Any ship that put to sea into these waters was to be sunk. The A.O.C. 2 Group, Air Vice-Marshal Stevenson, was ordered to see that this was done, and it was done irrespective of the cost which proved considerable. He was undoubtedly placed in a difficult position by his superiors to produce results. In the final reckoning success was far less than was supposed at the time. Whenever those who carried out shipping sorties were to speak of them it would always be with vivid, fearful memories. France had been bad; far worse was now to hand.

At Huntingdon the planning of an intensive campaign forged ahead, and on 25 March Operations Order 20 reached the stations. In it Air Vice-Marshal Stevenson pointed out that enemy ships were carrying iron ore—dug in Sweden—from Norwegian ports to Hamburg; oil was being shipped from Spain past Ushant to France and Germany. Perhaps most important of all, convoys from Hamburg were carrying almost all the stores needed by the occupation forces in Holland, Belgium and France. These convoys in particular offered tempting targets, but their ships would have to be sunk close inshore in the face of murderous fire from accompanying flak ships, shore batteries and defending fighters.

Most profitable lanes for air attack would be in the free bombing areas which were divided into six 'beats'. To ensure the sinking of a ship the maximum number of aircraft available would need to be detailed and make a concentrated assault. Targets were small, difficult to attack. Surprise was essential and could only be achieved by hazardous low flying over the sea where visibility would often be poor and a split-second error would bring instant disaster. It was the only way, though, to evade radar detection and fighter interception. For safety's sake crews were in their beat area—alone or in small packs—for only a few minutes, often as little as three.

In cold front conditions when visibility would be good they were ordered to fly in pairs, threes or more, to ensure that when a ship was sighted it could be heavily and promptly attacked. In warm front conditions the force would spread out, reconnoitring the area for longer. Decision on basic tactics would be Group's. For warm front conditions aircraft allotment was as follows: Beat A: 6, B: 4, C: 5, D: 6, E: 5, F: 6. Squadron commanders would increase allotment number to one flight if needed, allotment being based on a twenty-mile interval between aircraft except on Beat D where it was ten miles. On Beat E it could be reinforced by one aircraft at the Ems Estuary. On Beat F the two centre aircraft could be reinforced by one. As can be seen, the weather played an important part in planning and in cold front conditions each beat was divided into three parts with Headquarters ordering the strength of the strike force.

The Blenheim formation would fly extremely low at the start of the beat, aircraft at specified distance apart line abreast. Start line for each beat was about thirty miles from the coast. On arrival the aircraft would fly at right angles towards the coast from the start line, turn 90 degrees to port still in line abreast when the leader would be three miles from the shoreline, then fly three minutes thus placed before turning for home. In Beat area D they usually turned about immediately three miles from the coast. Any ship that saw them would surely report them, and so the order was to sink the first ship sighted, and indeed any ship in the beat area—and promptly.

If there was no cloud cover the attack would be delivered from a very low level to outwit the early warning radar network, fifty feet being the maximum suggested altitude. Many flew lower. If there was cloud about then use could be made of this for a tactically good approach. Over Beats B and D where fighter activity could usually be expected, Fighter Command was called upon to supply advance warning data from its intelligence system. Operations could thereby be ordered so as to avoid fighter standing patrols, unless there was cloud cover or a layer of strato-cumulus cloud. Fighter cover was only possible up to forty miles from Britain, generally insufficient range. Bomb load for the shipping strikes was set at four 250-lb. bombs.

Under the initial order Nos. 21, 82 and 139 Squadrons were placed in the anti-shipping role. Watton was to operate one squadron per day, 139 Squadron on alternate days. Each squadron would stand down for only one day in eight. Thus the campaign was to be intensive and soon gathered momentum.

It will be recalled that 114 Squadron had already taken up an anti-shipping role. It was ordered to make anti-shipping attacks instead of merely patrols, but in fact it contented itself with reconnaissance flights, once raiding Sola airfield, a base for Fw 200 convoy raiders. No. 107 Squadron began a new task on 5 March from Lossiemouth, sweeping the North Sea one hundred miles off Norway until a week later when 'stand patrols' close to Norwegian shores began.

The first action came when Flt. Lt. Simmons on the Southern Stand was attacked by a Bf 109 which he evaded in darkness near Kristiansand. On a second patrol the same day four aircraft patrolled over the Skaggerak. Hickingbotham attacked five motor vessels in Farsund Fiord, Ralston bombed searchlights on Haland Island, Bristow the airfield at Sandhes. Next day Sgt. Dornay attacked a ship at Kristiansand and as a diversion for a Beaufort raid 107 Squadron attacked shipping, the harbour and searchlights at Hungersund.

2 Group's shipping campaign got fully under way when on 12 March five aircraft of 139 Squadron patrolled Beat A, scoring near misses on two 500-tonners. On 14th 139 Squadron on Beat B had a near miss on an 800-tonner—ships were difficult targets. Operations off the French coast were begun, by 82 Squadron, on 15 March. When attacking four ships on 20th, R3604 and its crew were lost. Meanwhile 139 Squadron's operations were stepped up to become daily.

Off Norway 107 Squadron was busy. On 22 March they scored the first big success by sinking a 2,000-ton ship. As dawn was breaking, Wg. Cdr. Cameron reached the Norwegian coast where the previous day Sqn. Ldr. Biggs had reported a large motor vessel which he had machine-gunned after dropping his bombs on the docks at Egersund. Cameron found the prey, dived Z5795 from 800 feet, and scored three bomb hits on the vessel which was totally destroyed. On 23rd 82 Squadron attacked five ships off the Ems Estuary and a destroyer which they may have damaged. A fishing boat was sunk by 82 Squadron next day—and their first loss off Norway occurred, L9389. No. 21 Squadron flew their first anti-shipping sorties on 26 March, patrolling three miles off shore

between Texel and Ijmuiden. Sqn. Ldr. L. V. E. Atkinson, a legendary
figure to the whole of 2 Group, and flying V5580, attacked a small
fishing vessel. Plt. Off. Marshall tried to sink a coaster and Sgt. Leavers
a small steam trawler and fishing boat. Although flak, fighters and flying
low over the sea were all hazards there was also the risk of bird strike.
On this operation a seagull burst through the perspex of Sgt. Freir's
aircraft hitting him in the face and forcing him to turn about.

No. 21 Squadron was in action on 29 March when Wg. Cdr. Bartlett
in L9029 attacked a 5,000-ton tanker off Flushing. It was surrounded by
six flak ships and as he ran in their fire was murderous. Hits were
received in the cockpit and the port engine was damaged. A busy day
was 31 March when 82 Squadron attacked six ships off Le Havre.
Wg. Cdr. Elworthy and Sgt. Smith each managed to leave a 3,000-ton
tanker ablaze in the most effective operation yet. Later that day the
squadron was up again patrolling off the Dutch coast where Sgt. Haynes
scored hits on a ship in convoy. But by now an extension of these
low-level operations had been ordered.

There were many military targets a few miles inland from the enemy
coast, but they lay in the most heavily defended zones. To attack them
at low level was suicidal, as was fully realised by those who had to carry
out the orders. But was it understood by those who gave the orders?
They doubted it. 'To cause alarm, and to embarrass the enemy air defence system', attacks were ordered in the hope that they would disperse
fighters and flak. Such raids were known as Fringe Attacks and during
them transport columns, vehicles, troops, huts, gun and searchlight
emplacements would be attacked. Nos. 21, 82 and 139 Squadrons were
ordered to extend their current tasks and eleven beat areas were listed.

Eight crews of 21 Squadron led by Sqn. Ldr. Atkinson left Watton at
midday on 31 March to attack ships off the Dutch Frisians and open the
campaign against Fringe targets, a most successful operation. Two
destroyers were found. One, bombed from fifty feet, was damaged.
Direct hits were scored on her stern. She slewed round, listed to port
and a black column of smoke belched forth. Then 'Attie' turned the
formation in over the islands off the Dutch coast and flew over them.
Fringe attacks had started. 'It was about 2 p.m. and on Ameland we
came across what was, I suppose, an after lunch parade. I yelled to my
gunner and we sprayed the lot of them. They were soon all over the
place. Then we sighted a fellow on a gun emplacement, said "good
afternoon" to which he replied, and went on our way.' Flt. Lt. Partridge
bombed and shot up guns west of Hollum on Ameland, and Sqn. Ldr.
Cooper attacked a large hut and troops at Bisterand on Terschelling.
Plt. Off. Marshall machine-gunned three pillboxes and a gun in
Dienshollum, Wg. Cdr. Bartlett attacked a radio station at Hoorn. But
these low-level sorties attracted fire from all manner of light guns and at
the rallying point Sgt. P. A. Adams and crew and Plt. Off. D. A. Rogers
and crew were missing. It was as expected.

By April the enemy had considerably reduced his fighter force in north-west Europe for operations in the Balkans. To entice him to bring them back daylight operations were stepped up, particularly against shipping. Nineteen sorties were flown on 2 April, nine ships being attacked. Sqn. Ldr. Cooper, Scott and Leavers on a Fringe beat attacked Ijmuiden power station from low level on 6th whilst others went after a large beached ship. No. 21 Squadron extended its sphere of operations to Denmark on 8th attacking three ships near the enemy coast and bombing a bridge being built near Ringkobing.

On 7th No. 18 Squadron opened its campaign against shipping despatching ten aircraft and attacking two trawlers. Three days later 21 Squadron came face to face with a crowd of Messerschmitts which opened fire with cannon forcing the Blenheims homewards. Three crews of the squadron were bound for Flushing docks on 12th. Two Bf 109s caught them and in the ensuing fight a Blenheim gunner was killed.

Between the start of the intensive shipping raids on 12 March and 12 April 315 sorties had been flown, over a front of 1,200 miles. Enemy reaction was such that it was clear he realised the danger to him inherent in the campaign. Of 355 ships sighted near the enemy coast 121 had been attacked. Six were claimed to have been sunk, eight including a destroyer damaged and 89 lightly damaged. It was too soon to draw conclusions but on 8 April the first enemy standing patrols had been spotted between Cherbourg and Holland and off Denmark.

The results of a month of raids were considered highly satisfactory, although nine Blenheims had been shot down. Operations Order 27 of 12 April therefore was issued expanding the campaign to stretch from Bordeaux (when previously Lorient had been set as the limit) to Norway. Coastal regions were now divided into 19 beats starting thirty miles out to sea and again running parallel to the shore. Nos. 105 and 110 Squadrons were brought on to the operation.

Sqn. Ldr. David Bennett was currently serving with 105 Squadron. 'It was not really a surprise,' he recalls, 'when the change of Bomber Command policy to employ Blenheims in a low level role came into being, with feverish activity on the East Anglian bombing ranges by Blenheims practising low level, low level and more low level bombing and air firing. At the same time our Blenheims were re-camouflaged from earth brown and green upper surfaces and night black beneath, to dark green and grey with duck egg blue undersurfaces, which was a very effective toning over water. One Spitfire pilot once stated that Blenheims on low-level strikes were hard to pick out from above. In some cases they could only be found by their slipstream wake on the sea's surface. That may sound like a line, but with the adage, the lower the better on shipping strikes, a wake would be left.

'A typical low level Fringe strike was that we carried out on 15 April, when we were briefed to attack a convoy of ships off Borkum. Six aircraft were detailed to seek out this convoy and carry this through at dusk in order that there was some element of surprise. Briefing on this occasion particularly stressed this point. All six aircraft which I led in Blenheim IV L8788 were away on time and after passing over the coast at our normal exit and entry point, Gt. Yarmouth, headed out over the North Sea in loose pairs to a position from which to run in to Borkum. All aircraft attacked individually but in the dusk, a tricky light for judging distance at all times, it was difficult to assess results, and ship bombing with 250-lb. bombs was a very flukey operation at 50 feet.'

Most of the bombs fell on the town with Sqn. Ldr. Bennett and Wg. Cdr. Christian bombing the barracks. Sqn. Ldr. Dunlevie, however, managed a hit on a 4,000-ton freighter aft of its funnel a mile to sea. Everyone went in at roof-top height, Sgt. Sarjeant getting hits on the railway station, with two 500-pounders.

'The flak from E-boats was intense, and the tracer hose pipe effect all the more like a Brock's firework display in dusk conditions. We all returned safely in very poor weather conditions. I had to land at Bassingbourn's satellite, Steeple Morden, and was very nearly shot at by the local A.A. battery, in spite of firing the correct two-star Very of the period. I found out that they had been subjected to an intruder attack the night before by a Junkers 88 and I was lucky since they were trigger happy.'

Mid April was one of the busiest periods for the Group. On 15th alone five raids comprising 24 sorties were despatched, and four ships were attacked two of which sank. 107 Squadron still active off Norway managed to straddle a submarine off Prestkjac on 16th. During mid morning eight Blenheims of 110 Squadron set off from Wattisham, one crashing immediately after take-off. They bombed Heligoland from roof-top height and two managed hits on a trawler.

No. 105 Squadron on Beat 16 operating from St. Eval found a 5,000-ton motor vessel upon which Flt. Lt. Booth scored a hit. Four others on Beat 17 ran into 109s which shot down Sgt. I. G. Sarjeant and crew who perished, and attacked Sgt. Piers for twenty minutes. His aircraft crashed at St. Eval. Three crews of 107 Squadron were on a stand off Norway and coming across a convoy of 25 ships claimed to sink one.

On 18th 21 Squadron led by Wg. Cdr. L. V. E. Atkinson set off on a low-level raid on shipping off Heligoland. He was now most experienced at shipping attacks—and he was quite dissatisfied by the tactics Group specified. He says: 'I disagreed with Stevenson and those at Group over the method of attack they ordered, which was broadside on. I wouldn't make beam attacks because (*a*) the enemy could easily see you coming, and (*b*) you faced all the fire power from the ships. I reckoned that with a Blenheim and its almost total lack of fire power the whole chance of success depended upon surprise. How could it be achieved? In my opinion the only way was low level, really low level right down to the wave tops, and to attack the ship from astern. I worked on the theory, laugh as one may, that a seaman always looks where he is going and not where he's been. If the Blenheims made broadside attacks they would be under maximum fire both before and after the attack.

'There was, today, this big convoy of 12–14 ships in three lines. I took the middle one of the back three. We could see them when some way off. I was right on them before they saw us, as the sailors manning the tripod gun were leaning over the side and forward. This method therefore successfully achieved more surprise. At the last moment we altered position for a quarter attack. We normally flew into attack in a vic and final orders were flashed by lamp. We made our escape between the lines of ships very low indeed, so that if they fired they would hit each other. It was most important to maintain strict discipline. We had to plan for two or three forms of precise attack as you were not always told the strength or pattern of the convoy.

'We aimed our bombs at just below the waterline. On this attack the flak was still very intense and by the time the third ship was being attacked the gunners had woken. Plt. Off. Marshall's aircraft was soon ablaze and Sgt. Dunning was shot into the sea.'

Already the enemy was sailing by night and Group ordered some night operations while the moon was high. Just before dawn on 17th 110 Squadron went after three ships off Terneuzen and operated again the following night in the same area and off Breskens; but daylight raids, for all their horror, were likely to be far more profitable.

Three crews of 18 Squadron led by Sqn. Ldr. Lindsay found a 7,000-ton motor vessel with destroyer escort on 19 April, and roared into the attack at fifty feet. Bombs were hurled into the freighter's side and she was soon listing 35 degrees. The destroyer put up an intense flak screen, but Lindsay's gunner raked the ailing ship. Z5802 then flew on to Ijmuiden where the crew were delighted to find a ship on the horizon was sinking. Then three 3,000-tonners were spotted near Den Helder. Flak hit Z5802 as she raced in, her two 500-pounders falling wide. No. 101 Squadron began shipping operations the same day in Beat area 10. Several ships were found and Sgt. Deane flying N6141 selected a 5,000-tonner. Three of his bombs hit her, she burst into flames and was left stern down.

For 18 Squadron 25 April was a busy day. The crew of R3741 on Fringe Beat 7 came across a large ship of over 7,000 tons. From 100 feet hits were scored on a forehatch resulting in a terrific explosion, the flash rising to the height of the aircraft. After this broadside assault Flt. Lt. Jenkins nipped in to drop 40-pounders on an escort vessel. Sgt. Wood and crew on their first operation, and flying L9192, scored a hit on the stern of a motor vessel.

Six crews of 21 Squadron were despatched to shipping and Fringe targets near Schiemonikoog and Vlieland on 26 April. A convoy of three 4,000-tonners including eight smaller ships and three flak ships was spotted. As Wg. Cdr. G. A. Bartlett turned on to his run the firing began. Within moments his aircraft, V6338, was down followed soon after by Sgt. C. F. Spouge in V5822. All the crews were killed. One of the large ships was damaged and three other crews tried unsuccessfully to sink flak ships.

The same day, thirteen Blenheims of 82 Squadron swept the sea off southern Norway, Sgts. Ford and Harrison and Plt. Off. White attacking three cargo ships. Other crews went for Fringe targets including a radio station. As Plt. Off. Tallis beat up an airfield west of Sand he noticed five Bf 110s lining up for take-off and another airborne. Roaring low over the field he surrounded a 110, in the act of taking-off, with bombs and machine-gun fire. It burst into flames and others were damaged. Tallis then went to the aid of Sgt. Inman and between them they had a sixteen-minute running fight with three Bf 110s, and survived.

Meanwhile a new development had taken place. On 24 April a Flight of 101 Squadron moved into Manston, an 11 Group station, on detachment. Thus was inaugurated the infamous *Channel Stop* affair. They had arrived to open an intensive campaign to close the Straits of Dover to enemy shipping during daylight, leaving it to the Royal Navy's M.T.B.s to continue the task at night. The Blenheims were to have fighter protection but at the start nothing could stop the tremendous fire power of the flak ships which protected every enemy merchantman in the area. Of the first flight of three Blenheims, which opened the new phase of operations by attacking trawlers off Calais on 28 April, one fell to flak. Escorting Spitfires of 74 Squadron drove off a snooping Bf 109. Next day another trio from 101 Squadron operated against two 1,500-ton ships off Nieuport. One Blenheim was shot up, its navigator having a wounded arm. Escorting Hurricanes and Spitfires drove off three 109s. Two section operations followed, Plt. Off. Brown claiming to sink a 2,000-ton ship off Ostend on 2 May, the first success of the new phase of operations. A small convoy off Boulogne was attacked on 3 May. 101 Squadron was usually running in at fifty feet, probably too high for safety, and on this occasion two veteran Blenheims, T1825 'Y' and T2234 'H', were shot down. On 6 May a ship was reported off Gravelines in the early afternoon. Three Blenheims were despatched, with an escort of eleven Spitfire IIs of 74 Squadron. No ship was seen, instead Messerschmitts were in waiting. A pitched battle followed and one Blenheim was badly damaged. On 9 May 101 Squadron withdrew to Raynham, and *Channel Stop* temporarily halted.

The main anti-shipping campaign remained under way at a fast pace. On 29 April, fifteen Blenheims of 82 Squadron made another of their sweeps off Norway. Bombs from Sgt. Inman's machine resulted in black smoke curling up from a large freighter. Others raced in to attack and Flt. Lt. R. E. Tallis and Plt. Off. D. White were both seen to have been shot down. On the last day of April, 21 Squadron searched for shipping between The Hague and Flushing. Three crews found a convoy of no less than eight flak ships escorting a tanker. Overhead Bf 110s were giving escort. Undaunted the Blenheims soared in for attack and Sgt. Denning was shot down. Another Blenheim badly shot up on the bomb run was then intercepted by the 110s, but escaped.

Every day from 1 to 10 May shipping operations were flown. Periodically crews participated in high level *Circus* operations, 'a piece of cake compared with those low level strikes'. Antwerp and Rotterdam docks were raided by small forces, a convoy heading for La Pallice was attacked—and losses mounted. With the arrival of the moon period, night attacks were resumed and by day on 6 May 110 Squadron found a convoy of five ships, three destroyers and two large corvettes. Such was their fire power that they were engaging the Blenheims at three miles' range. 110 Squadron tried an attack but was beaten off.

A tempting idea was the blocking of the Kiel Canal. In daylight this would be extremely hazardous since the Canal banks were lined with guns. The initial attempt was made by 110 Squadron on the night of 8–9 May, and was unsuccessful. Other crews active that night included four of 21 Squadron briefed to bomb the liner *Europa* in Bremerhaven.

The third month of shipping operations had a grand start with five squadrons in one day despatching 41 sorties. Thirteen aircraft of 82 Squadron made an early flight to Portreath from where eight later set out for St. Nazaire, where one crew managed hits on a 2,000-ton ship. Defences were strong and alert and, even before he bombed, Plt. Off. Chadwick lost all his bomb controls. With hydraulics out of action he limped home to a crash landing with the bomb load still aboard . . . and the load fused. In another machine the observer was killed by a cannon shell and Flg. Off. Duggen-Smith, after bombing, was wounded in the foot. His observer had serious face and body injuries. Sqn. Ldr. Joe Hunt attacked a 3,000-tonner. At the rallying point it was soon clear that some crews had not survived the attack, that Wg. Cdr. King and Sgt. Miller and their crews had fallen.

There was no point in denying that heavy losses throughout the squadrons were taxing morale which remained surprisingly high. These gallant men covered up their feelings to the best of their ability, and they were led by splendid squadron commanders. During the fight over France when losses were high intensity of operations gave little time for reflection and to consider the many faces missing from the Mess. But now crews were coming home and having time to think. Many questioned the value of the operations they were despatched upon and some felt that the demands upon them were excessive. Whereas the Army and Navy went into action for days or weeks at a time, Bomber Command returned to England after each foray. Crews could quickly turn from fearful battle to a peaceful homecoming in an unreal situation where, one minute, comrades were being shot to pieces, and moments later all was excessive calm. A trip to Norwich would bring them into the civilian world so removed from that of minutes before. Little wonder there were wild parties, moments of deep depression, seconds of elation.

But morale never cracked. Again, during the fight for France many participants were older Regular servicemen, whereas now many were inexperienced wartime volunteers most of them exceedingly young. Faces were coming and going so quickly that they belonged to almost unknown beings.

Losses seemed most poignant when a known and admired, indeed loved, squadron commander failed to return. One such was Wg. Cdr. Arnold L. Christian highly regarded by his men.

'After a long spell as an instructor at 13 O.T.U.,' recalls Sqn. Ldr. David Bennett, 'I had amassed over 350 hours on Blenheims before being posted to No. 105 Squadron at Swanton Morley as a Flight Commander in the Acting (and fortunately paid) rank of Squadron Leader, for my first tour of operations.

'My squadron commander was Arnold Christian who had, as a Squadron Leader, been my Flight Commander in the Dual Conversion Flight of 13 O.T.U. which also boasted the then Sqn. Ldr. (and now Marshal of the Royal Air Force) "Sam" Elworthy as O.C. Flying, for which he was awarded the A.F.C. for his work on Blenheim night flying techniques in particular.

'Arnold Christian, an A.1 Category C.F.S. Instructor, could fly a Blenheim better than most, and inspired us all with his skill and leadership. He was a relative of the Fletcher Christian of "Mutiny on the *Bounty*" fame, and Captain Bligh's confrontation with Christian is well known. Like his ancestor, our squadron commander was a stubborn never-say-die character with inborn leadership of a somewhat rebellious nature, traits possessed by so many 2 Group squadron commanders.

'He had been responsible for our rapid conversion from night bombing to daylight low-level operations in April, 1941. Training was intense and I remember carrying out four sorties in a day dropping 32 practice bombs in the Wash as Christian encouraged us to fly accurately over the sea at fifty feet and lower.

' "The lower the better," were his words, and "effective jinking manoeuvres near the deck can get you out of trouble in the target area." He was right. A Blenheim could be thrown around and his example inspired us all.

'Arnold's sense of fun and his good dry humour, added to his superb airmanship, made 105 a good squadron. It was a bitter blow to us all when, on 8 May 1941, following a shipping strike on Stavanger, his Blenheim was seen to be hit by flak in the port engine. He headed for the coast but no more was heard of him or his crew. Their names, like many more from 2 Group lost over the North Sea, are honoured on the walls of the R.A.F. Memorial on Cooper's Hill, Runnymede.

'He was greatly mourned by 105 Squadron and ultimately succeeded by Wg. Cdr. Hughie Edwards who later won the V.C., an audacious, pugnacious Australian whose sheer determination carried him through.'

Such leaders and their brave crews received scant recognition for their efforts. This was in direct contrast to the limelight the fighter leaders always had. Yet 2 Group felt it was the only offensive force really achieving results at this period of the war—and hardly a word of praise ever appeared. Barely a day passed without a shipping beat and vacant seats after. 'We are sure we sank her, a 2,000-tonner. . . . I attacked the docks at Rotterdam . . . we completed Beat 8 but saw no shipping. . . . I found the convoy off Borkum and left a 2,500-ton ship burning . . . we were with 18 Squadron off Norderney when a swarm of 109s came in and we lost two aircraft. . . . 82 Sqn. made this sea sweep near Heligoland and Harrison got hits on a trawler, then fighters came in and attacked Sqn. Ldr. Carr's section. Three Blenheims were shot down in flames and L-Love landed shot up at Horsham.' The blood bath continued throughout May.

Sqn. Ldr. Edmund Nelson had joined 139 (Jamaica) Squadron. He recalls: 'I found on arriving that the Wing Commander had recently been posted missing on operations so I was promoted Acting Wg. Cdr. and given command of the squadron. Losses had been high and I found that most of my aircrew had little more experience than myself. As far as Blenheims were concerned this amounted to little more than the O.T.U. course at Upwood. A Sgt. Pilot was the only one about to finish his tour of operations, and from him I obtained most of my knowledge about what the squadron was doing. I decided that the first large scale raid under my command should be led by him, with me flying as his No. 2.

'The squadron had been briefed for a low level raid on Lannion airfield, a fringe target in Brittany. This was a station where bombers were lined up for an attack on the British Fleet then chasing the *Scharnhorst*. We took off at dawn and flew just above the wave tops. As we approached the enemy coast my experience as an army co-operation pilot told me we were off course. However, I followed my leader and we went in and turned left with the idea of attacking the target on the way out. Much to my surprise in front of me was an airfield and we bombed a number of aircraft there. Black puffs of smoke soon appeared and tracer from fighters. As we left the target I could hear bursting bombs. But I remained convinced that we had not attacked the correct target and this later proved to be the case. We had been about half a mile off course and had bombed Morlaix. Lannion was later attacked successfully.'

By the end of May 77 ships totalling 220,000 tons had been claimed as successfully attacked with a further 18 (41,000 tons) probably hit and 54 (52,000 tons) variously damaged. There can be no doubt that these figures were considerably inflated.

On 2 June stations were informed that Fringe targets in Germany were now to be attacked with the aircraft hugging ground contours. The idea was to encourage the enemy to withhold fighters from other theatres. This was an unrealised hope, although a few fighter engagements took place.

On 2 June another raid on the Kiel Canal area was attempted, and in daylight, this time very effectively by 105 Squadron. Nine Blenheims led by Sqn. Ldr. Booth crept in under cloud cover and using a variety of approaches. Seven attacked ships ranging from 1,000 to 5,000 tons, also villages and the Friedrichskoog naval barracks north-west of Kiel. All returned safely. Booth opened the raid from 12,000 feet bombing a 3,000-tonner and getting his tail unit damaged by flak. Plt. Off. Clayton delivered a beam attack on a ship in the River Eider and Plt. Off. Walsher scored a hit on a ship in the Canal, causing it to slew round and strike the bank. He then audaciously attacked a 3,000-tonner from its bow. Sgt. Seals went after a large ship in a convoy three miles from Brunsbuttel, Sgt. Bruce bombed a 6,000-ton motor vessel east of Rensburg and Plt. Off. Broadley a collier in the Canal at Boorgstedt. An intelligence report of 12 June revealed that the Canal was closed still, blocked by two sunken ships.

The operation had been part of a three-pronged attack on north-west Germany with 107 Squadron operating against towns between the Ems and Elbe whilst 110 Squadron headed for the liner *Europa* berthed at Bremerhaven. Theirs was an afternoon raid thwarted by lack of cloud cover.

4 June was a busy day, low-level attacks on Dutch airfields being made by Nos. 18, 107 and 139 Squadrons. No. 21 had six crews on Beat 3, Sqn. Ldr. Tony Partridge and Sgt. Chambers scoring four hits amidships on a very large ship which was claimed a total loss.

On 6 June Winston Churchill visited 2 Group. He had instituted the anti-shipping campaign, and went to West Raynham with the A.O.C. to hear first hand of its progress and drama. His visit revealed a new line of thinking; for on the airfield for all to see was the new B-17 Flying Fortress, and also a Douglas Boston bomber. Was this, many asked, to be the long overdue Blenheim replacement? Churchill addressed the crews, praising their immense courage during recent weeks.

Sqn. Ldr. Peter Simmons flew two tours each of 25 sorties on Blenheims, completing his second tour on 7 June. He was one of those 2 Group people admired by many, and it was he who was chosen to pioneer the introduction of the Mosquito. Tragic indeed it was when, having survived the war, he was killed flying a Turkish Air Force Mosquito. With him in a formation of nine Blenheims of 107 Squadron was another well-known 2 Group figure, in his cricket career known to millions. He was Bill Edrich on one of his first operations with the Group, and he remembers it clearly.

'I was No. 3 to Simmons, Sgt. Walker was his No. 2, I was very green. We flew very low over the sea the three vics making their own way to the Beat area. We had received a naval report of a supply convoy sailing from Hamburg to Rotterdam. Its progress along the coast had been timed and off Ijmuiden was the ideal point for attack. We had planned to separate at the Beat entry point forming two wide pincers in order to find the convoy.

'Low over the water we could see a thick layer ahead. Pete Simmons flew in but the other formations turned back. Ours was the only vic to go on. I was scared—I had only a blurred outline of Peter's aircraft. Sometimes I lost him, and all below a hundred feet. Sgt. H. F. Fordham had crashed into the sea without trace. I came out of a cloud and then I saw them and ships ahead, two big ships. Pete took the south one, I took the further, and we both attacked. I aimed our bombs like torpedoes. There was a lot of flak but I didn't realise we'd been hit. I made a wide circuit attempting to avoid flak ships.

'I re-entered cloud following Pete Simmons. Then I lost contact with my wireless operator/air gunner and was worried. The observer found he was all right, by which time we were in the mist again and at 300 feet. The gunner had seen the bombs fall with only two flashes in front of the ship, so two bombs must have hit it.

'I pushed and pulled the controls then the engines cut for a second as we flew along as if on a switchback. Flak had hit the tail, indeed the entire tail was shot to ribbons. I didn't realise it then. When we looked back we could see two ships burning. Simmons was awarded a bar to his D.F.C.

'Once home I changed out of flying kit removing my old short sleeved M.C.C. Touring sweater which I always wore as a lucky mascot. Battle for the day wasn't finished though. Colonel Birkbeck, squire of Massingham, had repeatedly arranged cricket matches between us and his local team. Each time something had come up and we had to cancel them. The postponed match took place this afternoon. I scored 88 runs in half an hour. I hit a ball for six towards some trees and someone cried "He's hit it into Suffolk!" I did the only thing I could, ran myself out.'

In Brest harbour the cruiser *Prinz Eugen* lay, a tempting target but in an almost impenetrable situation. Three crews of 107 Squadron headed by Sqn. Ldr. 'Zeke' Murray, a New Zealander, with Plt. Off. Edrich and Sgt. Charney flew to Portreath with a load of two 500-pounders apiece and each carrying two ground crew members. Portreath's runway ended at a cliff top—with such loads as the Blenheims carried it was a hazardous touch-down. Ten-tenths cloud was needed to cover the attack on the harbour; nevertheless the raid was to be at low level to defeat the radar. With sufficient cloud cover individual attacks might just be possible but the weather was now unsuitable. Overnight accommodation was in tents—and it was a rainy night. They took with them a mobile telephone in order to contact Group H.Q. Some snags occurred and it was some time before they contacted the A.O.C. He was not amused and quickly retorted 'Why haven't you gone?' Outside the rain was falling in torrents but when an improvement came Murray and Edrich took off. They pressed on but, as so often when cloud cover was required, the cloud ran out just short of France. This was yet another of those abandoned operations which were often far from uneventful—

but who can say what the outcome would have been if the crews had proceeded?

On 14 June 105 Squadron tried for the *Hipper*, but once more cloud ran out. There was no cloud next day when 107 had a go, by which time plans were advancing for *Sunrise*, the major Bomber Command day raid on Brest.

On 12 June stations were informed that shipping attacks in the Straits of Dover by Blenheims were currently considered impracticable because of the large number of shore batteries which now protected ships always sailing close inshore. Squadrons in rotation would later send three Blenheims to Manston for *Channel Stop* operations, and they would operate under special fighter support.

An increasing number of trawlers seen recently were carrying an assortment of radio aerials. Shipping attacks were now seriously worrying the enemy. He felt he could reduce them if he had advanced warning of the approach of bombers. Now he was carefully siting radio-equipped trawlers to spread the alarm. So far it had been the practice to ignore small ships well out to sea during shipping raids but it was realised that these, using short-wave transmitters which did not require elaborate aerials, were being used for warning purposes. Blenheim interceptions had increased lately and were sometimes being made fifty to sixty miles out to sea, obviously as a result of the activities of small ships. It was decided to operate against these 'squealers', then retire before enemy fighters could intercept. Not only would these ships be attacked; any ships found in the free bombing area, irrespective of nationality, were ordered to be sunk. Little flak came from the squealers as yet, so precise attacks with 4 × 250 S.A.P. bombs were ordered in two beat areas.

Off the Frisians on 16 June three crews of 21 Squadron sank a squealer. One of the three attackers, Sgt. Leavers, had gone in so low that V6034-D hit the ship's mast—a not unusual event particularly if an aircraft was damaged by flak—and cartwheeled into the sea.

Meanwhile the round of daily raids continued. Wg. Cdr. Edwards led 105 Squadron into action on 15th on Beat 10. He made a bow attack on a 4,000-tonner and saw an explosion in its bows, debris thrown high and a column of black smoke. It was a profitable operation for, soon after, Sgt. Jackson made a beam attack on a large ship. Sqn. Ldr. D. E. Bennett, Sgt. D. O. Beacham and Flg. Off. P. H. Watts turned to port at the end of the run, then they saw, in line astern, ten E-boats. The leader recognised them for what they were—heavily armed. Two other crews thinking they were small motor ships turned in to attack. As Sgt. Beacham (killed a few days later) turned away he saw two columns of smoke with flames at their bases. Watts then went in, his bombs shooting under the leading vessel. As he roared over the ships he was hit by flak in the starboard fuel tank which immediately erupted in flames which engulfed the aircraft. Watts kept it under control for a few moments then it touched the water, rose, turned right over and dived in.

Soon the whole pattern of the war changed for, on 22 June, Germany attacked Russia. Hitler's armies advanced rapidly and the War Cabinet immediately met to discuss how Britain might aid the Russians. Active operations over the Eastern Front were impossible; instead it was decided to mount a campaign to force the enemy to keep a large fighter force to repel daylight raids on Germany. On the day of the German invasion Bomber Command was ordered to react and 2 Group advised its stations rather by chance that Operation *Manicure*, the attack on German transport targets, was under way, and, more important, the long-planned raid on the huge Fortuna I and II power stations near Cologne with the Goldenburg plant as a secondary target. Such deep penetrations were considered as feasible only by night—but the nights were very short. The moon would be high in a few days' time. Nevertheless no final decision on the time of attack was made although shipping operations were accordingly cut.

Soon after the Russian invasion Winston Churchill visited 2 Group again. At Swanton Morley he addressed representative crews from all the squadrons in a large draughty hangar. In a grey suit and holding a cigar—unlit, the crews noticed, for even he was not risking anything— he mounted a fitter's stand serving as rostrum. He harangued the assembly. Their anti-shipping campaign which he referred to as 'the charge of the Light Brigade' had been magnificent, and he knew they had suffered grievously. Then he revealed the new strategy. 2 Group was to spearhead the initial aid to the Russians. It was to make penetrations deeply into Europe by daylight to force the Germans to pull back their fighters. Churchill's oratory was impelling as ever: in the words of one present, 'He made you feel you were part of it.'

On 5 July 139 Squadron had a running fight with five Bf 110s and escaped. Work was still shipping operations daily with a steady attrition rate. On 7th 105 Squadron made a midday attack against a convoy of eight ships between Ijmuiden and the Hague and were joined in the target area by six of 139 Squadron. Sgt. Farrow scored two hits on the stern of a 4,000-ton ship, but his aircraft was badly shot up necessitating a belly landing. Plt. Off. Bradley left another ship on fire, likewise Sgt. Bruce. Buckley went in so low that he hit the water, jettisoned his load and crash-landed at base. Sqn. Ldr. A. A. Scott was last seen on his run-in, and two aircraft of 139 Squadron were also shot down, making it a costly operation.

Between 5 and 12 July 23 anti-shipping operations were flown, by which time Operation *Gudgeon 1* had been mounted when, on 10 July, two low-flying formations each of twelve Blenheims raided Cherbourg and Le Havre docks. In the latter cranes and a tanker were hit, two large fires spewing volumes of smoke. The pilots had to watch for a hill beyond the town. One crew, thrown off the bomb run by flak, craftily shot their load into a railway tunnel. This was direct disobedience since they had been ordered to avoid essentially civilian targets. Whether a tunnel was such was debatable—but the pilot was court-martialled. In making its attack 226 Squadron flew so low that the fighter pilots of 10 Group later said 'Christ, we've never seen anything like it. But don't fly so low, as the wake from your aircraft is so easily picked up by fighters overhead'—and they were not joking. The formation had flown so low that many propeller tips had been bent on touching the sea.

Wg. Cdr. E. Nelson led a second raid on Le Havre in V6249 on 14 July. 'This target,' he was told at the briefing, 'was very important. We were to attack shipping and the harbour installations at low level. We took off very early and set course for the south coast where we found other aircraft and a fighter escort. In order to avoid detection we flew at sea level and approached the coast of France. As we did so I saw a very large ship steaming on my starboard side and I was very tempted to ignore my briefing and attack it. My orders were to bomb Le Havre and we went in, turned to port, came towards France and arrived at the docks only to find very little shipping there. We bombed and did considerable damage to port installations. Enemy fighters attacked us and we lost R3704 and V6253. Another Blenheim crash landed at Shoreham. On return to base the aircrews were elated, as often, and relieved that it was all over. Their feeling was that at this time 2 Group were the only part of Bomber Command finding their targets and successfully attacking them.'

How successful they were may never be known. Between 1 April and 30 June over a thousand sorties had been despatched, 297 aircraft had delivered attacks and 36 had been lost.

There was at this time some disagreement as to the areas in which Bomber Command and Coastal Command should be attacking shipping. On 15 July it was agreed that 2 Group should operate between Cherbourg and Texel leaving the remaining areas to Coastal Command, but, soon after, 2 Group's territory was extended eastwards to Wilhelmshaven. To increase the effectiveness of *Channel Stop* two Blenheim squadrons were now to be placed at Manston, these new arrangements being effective from 18 July.

On 16 July 2 Group attacked the huge docks at Rotterdam. This turned out to be one of the Group's most memorable raids of the period. The prize target was the Rotterdamse Lloyd liner *Baloeran*, a 17,000-tonner. She had been requisitioned by the Germans on 31 May 1941, was rebuilt for use as a hospital ship, and renamed *Strassburg*. Despite being damaged she put to sea on 31 July for a safer haven.

This operation was an attempt under Operations Order 47 to increase the effectiveness of the shipping campaign since many ships sailed to or from Rotterdam whose installations were important too. A heavy raid was considered likely to split the fighter defences and relieve some pressure on Russia, although it turned out to be a forlorn hope. On the chosen day there was a very considerable tonnage of shipping in the harbour and this, coupled with the Le Havre and Cherbourg attacks, might deprive the enemy of ships and dislocate three main docks.

The plan was that two boxes each of six aircraft would operate from Watton, one from Wattisham, two from Horsham and one from Swanton Morley with 12 Group cover. Each aircraft would take four 250-lb. S.A.P. bombs and attack from very low level in two waves from the south-west, Wg. Cdr. P. F. Webster leading the first and Wg. Cdr. A. Partridge the second.

By all accounts it was a gripping experience to have taken part. 'The first I saw of Rotterdam was a sky-line of high cranes over the docks,' recalled one participant. 'Climbing as high as the cranes were fat columns of black smoke marking targets already successfully bombed.

'I was in the second formation to attack. I had watched the leading squadrons cross the Dutch coast only a few feet above the sandy beaches, where people waved us on, and I wondered if they had noticed us unconsciously giving them a V-for-Victory as we roared across in vic. There was the astonishing flatness that I had expected and only occasionally could I feel our aircraft lifted to avoid windmills, farm-houses and villages; but most of all I was fascinated to find that country Dutchmen really did wear baggy trousers and vivid blue shirts. Cows galloped nervously as we hedge-hopped over the fields. Nearly everyone gave us some sort of cheery gesture; but I noticed one man, evidently terrified, was crouching against a telegraph pole. We flew so low that some of us brought back evidence. One pilot was to cut through a crane cable. He got a dent in his aircraft, and some red dust which he said he'd scraped from a chimney. The same intrepid fellow had evidently indulged in premature harvesting for he returned with a small sheaf of corn wedged in a niche in the wing leading edge!'

The lead squadron went in at fifty feet and almost immediately Tony Partridge was hit by flak which brought V6267 down on Noordersingel. 'N-Nuts' bombed the 5,000-ton *Hermod* causing a tremendous explosion and a spectacular fire. Within seconds flames were belching from another ship hit by Plt. Off. Walkden's bombs. Sgt. Jefferson went for a ship in Berth 28. Sgt. R. J. B. Roost's aircraft was hit by flak, he regained control but crashed near Delft. He and his crew died in hospital.

Hot on 18 Squadron's tail was No. 21 whose main aim was for the *Baloeran*. They hit five other ships too and a factory. With its cable cutters one aircraft sliced through a hawser on a 70-ton crane.

Murderous was the flak now being hurled up. Flt. Lt. Broadley of 105 Squadron reached the docks and aimed for a large ship being completed, Sgt. Bruce bombed a large ship and a string of barges, but the three crews who tried for the *Baloeran* all missed. Miraculously all of the squadron survived.

Sgt. Gibbs of 139 Squadron raced in guns blazing and claimed hits on a cargo boat which erupted into fragments as he roared away. V6266 went in higher to confuse the defenders, her bombs finding a 4,000-tonner. After V6322 had bombed there was another huge explosion—one of the Blenheims had crashed into Waalhaven. 226 Squadron fired an 1,800-ton vessel, started blazes in Dock 13 and in withdrawal shot up barracks at The Hague for good measure.

Once clear of the inferno the aircraft re-bunched—only four were missing out of the 36 sent.[1] In the words of the German report on the raid, 'considerable damage, material as well as personal, was done'. Only 107 Squadron had been left out of the show—it was sedately carrying out an army co-operation exercise.

Safely home, the crews had a host of stories to tell, of the exhilaration of the low-level flight, of Sqn. Ldr. Kercher's courageous attack which earned him a D.S.O. Kennedy related how he saw a large ship ahead and 'at the last moment I saw that it was a Red Cross ship. I avoided it and bombed a 7,000-ton ship alongside when flying my pet aeroplane V6510 named "Jane", after my wife. I remember flying over countless glass houses and en route we flew under a Do 17 Flying Pencil. I was tempted to pull up and have a squirt—I'll swear he never even saw us.'

Another crew member recalled: 'We bombed Rotterdam at 4.55 p.m. As we flashed across the docks our observer picked out a ship with bulky black hull and one funnel. We nipped across the last building and from mast height let fall our load. She was a medium sized ship— I should think about 4,000 tons. I could feel the bomb doors spring too, then we were suddenly away over the town. In ship bombing of this kind you often couldn't see the results, but I had a clear view this time. There was a terrific explosion and instantaneous flames and smoke. I saw lots of these explosions but this was easily the biggest. To the left I could see ships and buildings burning after the first wave had done its stuff. On the way out white tracer whipped under us above which smoke could be seen springing up from ships our force was bombing. It had been a great day. Out to sea a 105 Squadron Blenheim was circling smoke markers over which we all regained formation beneath the Spitfires of 12 Group.

'Soon after the raid a Dutchman escaped to England with news of its effect. The *Baloeran* had been damaged also the *Oranje Fontain*. A 10,000-ton ship had been hit and the M.V. *Frauenfels* slightly damaged. One bomb which penetrated her ricochetted from the deck and left the

---

[1] Aircraft used were: *18 Squadron:* V6267: M (crashed at Delft), V6361: N, V6038: H, Z7489: T, V6437: C, Z7496: W, V6497: U, V6197: D (FTR: Wg. Cdr. T. N. Partridge). *21 Squadron:* V5580: X (Wg. Cdr. Webster), V6240: B (crashed in Waalhaven), Z7520: R, V6321: Z, V6252: U, Z7435: S, V5595: P, V6337: T, V6361: F, Z7437: L, Z7438: D, V6360: K. *105 Squadron:* Z7486, V6453, V6455, V6373: O, V6399: T, L9379: Y, V6039. *139 Squadron:* Z7431, V6266: S, V6322, Z7362 (crashed in Waalhaven). *226 Squadron:* Z7305 (aborted, Z7271: K), V6515: K, V6510: A, Z7312: N, Z7280: M.

ship through its other side then exploded. A tanker was burnt out after her cargo had exploded, and several iron ore carrying ships were also hit. Twenty-two ships had been damaged. The population gave a warm welcome to the shot down crews who survived—until the Germans sent armoured cars to the scene which opened fire to disperse the crowds.'

Relatively few ships were sailing through the Straits of Dover now. When they did, attacks upon them were exceedingly costly. Nevertheless it was decided through Group Operations Order 49 of 17 July to order operations to continue. 'Denial of these waters would be a blow to the enemy's transport system,' the order commented, and now two squadrons would be on *Channel Stop*. Control remained with 2 Group, exercised by the Bomber Controller in 11 Group. From dawn to one hour before dusk Blenheims would be at readiness, two sections now to get away within thirty minutes, with Spitfires of 222 Squadron at standby too.

A few days later new tactics were ordered. The escort would now ideally be six cannon-armed Hurricane IICs and six twelve-gun Hurricane IIBs. When the Blenheims were about twenty miles from the target the cannon-armed Hurricanes were to draw ahead to engage flak ships from 1,000 feet. Although this might spoil surprise it would cut back the enemy fire.

These terribly costly operations are vividly remembered by Wg. Cdr. L. V. E. Atkinson, D.S.O., D.F.C., thus: '*Channel Stop* had started in April. The basis of it was that we had a squadron of Blenheims at Manston and by the time I was there a squadron of Hurricanes to act as front gun attack, with always a wing of Spitfires available as escort. The Hurricane and Blenheim crews lived at Manston. Average life of a Blenheim squadron there was about two weeks by which time it was depleted to such an extent that it had to be withdrawn and replaced. A similar thing happened, to a lesser degree, to the Hurricane squadrons. The first of these involved was 242 Squadron commanded by Sqn. Ldr. Whitney Straight. These chaps lived together and fought together. The Directive was "No ship is to pass between Cherbourg and Ostend" without us attacking it in daylight—there was no point in night attacks and in any case the Navy was busy then. We used as our eyes, No. 91 Squadron based at Hawkinge. We used to call them Jim Crows. They went out in Spitfires flying up and down the route to see if anyone was coming out of the ports. The ships used to do the port run at night, and the object of the exercise was to catch ships leaving port a bit early or not having made it in time. Consequently attacks were nearly always at dawn or dusk, and very seldom in the middle of the day.

'Three Blenheims would go out with about a dozen Hurricanes and a Wing of Spitfires, a wonderful sight over Manston. You'd see the boys taking off and as they came back over the airfield the Hurricanes would be to either side of the bombers, and outside this the squadron of Spitfires. They used to come over Manston at nought feet and, with a "whoosh", they'd soon be down over the sea. Thirty or forty minutes later they'd be back—one Blenheim and ten or so Hurricanes.

'As the Blenheims went in the Hurricanes pulled away and climbed over the top, diving and making front gun attack to keep the enemy heads down. The most they had to face was, I think, 19 flak ships. There were also the shore guns and the fighters. You hadn't a hope in Hell as you tossed your bombs at the ships.

'I well remember Sqn. Ldr. Harris, the Canadian commanding 88 Squadron, coming home showing his hat shot to ribbons. He crash landed on Manston, the only one in his formation to get back. Although the casualty rate was tremendous, the morale was never higher. They were in a forbidden area, but the locals could see all that was going on and you couldn't buy yourself a drink or anything after a raid if they were around. The local police turned a blind eye at closing time and the pubs would still be serving at 2 and 3 o'clock in the morning.

'I was at this time Bomber Controller at 11 Group, the person responsible for despatching these squadrons. On occasions when one attended the squadron briefs of these crews you were looking at two crews out of three who would not get back. How did you feel? It is impossible to express it, but then this was true of all the raids 2 Group was doing. On *Channel Stop* you knew that they were going to get it— no "ifs" and "buts"; and there was nothing you could do about it. Did it stop the passage of ships? It certainly made life difficult for them, but for their forces this was their life blood and they were always going to try to run the gauntlet. In theory they could move only by night but in practice tides, etc., forced them to sometimes move in daylight. Sometimes ships were hit, sometimes slowed down. There were some tremendous battles over the Channel.'

On 18 July, for instance, three Blenheims of 21 Squadron led by Sqn. Ldr. Hogg left Manston to attack a 6,000-ton ship in the Channel. Despite escorting fighters' fire the flak ships brought down a Blenheim.

Off the Dutch coast attacks continued unabated. Eight motor ships escorted by six flak ships were sighted off The Hague by 105 Squadron on 19th. After Smithers had attacked the leading ship it burnt fiercely. Flt. Lt. Broadley left another smoking amidships and a third was left burning by Sgt. Jackson. Sgt. Farrow's four bombs hit a 4,000-tonner which exploded, but moments later his crippled Blenheim plunged into the sea. Taylor then had a go at the same ship and suffered a similar fate.

Both 18 and 139 Squadrons presently had detachments at Manston and they went into action on 20th, successfully attacking a 7,000-tonner creeping close inshore between Le Touquet and Berck. Sqn. Ldr. Hughes of 18 Squadron led the attack but went in so low that he hit the masts of the ship and crashed into the sea. The last bomb from the second attack careered into the ship amidships and as the third machine pulled away the ship was on fire. A Bf 109 attacked the Blenheims and was driven off smoking. V6266 of 139 Squadron then had a go and caused a tremendous explosion from the vessel's stern, Z7499 tried but was shot down. Bombs from the third aircraft missed.

On 23rd there were three operations. No. 18 Squadron was detailed to join 139 Squadron seeking an enemy convoy off Holland but nothing was seen. Just as Sqn. Ldr. Roe was turning the formation for home Bf 110s of 5/ZG76 appeared and for fifteen minutes there was a tough fight. All the Blenheims were damaged, two were shot down and two crew members seriously wounded. No. 21 Squadron fared far more grievously. Escorted by fighters, six crews set off from Manston to attack a 4,000-ton tanker escorted by four flak ships off Ostend. Flak was murderous. Almost immediately Sqn. Ldr. C. Rogers was shot down, three more aircraft fell to enemy fire—and the tanker escaped.

Very extensive operations were planned for 30 July. Twelve crews of 18 and 82 Squadrons were detailed to attack either shipping in the Kiel Canal or nearby towns and villages. Some distraction was caused by ten crews of 114 Squadron, six of 226 Squadron and twelve of 139 Squadron which roamed between the Ems and Weser attacking any worthwhile targets. Three more of 226 Squadron were to silence any 'squealers' found ahead of the forces. Orders were to use what cloud was available, and to operate early in the day. In view of suspected squealers 114 Squadron was later told to operate four of its aircraft on the northern part of Squealer Beat 4.

No. 18 Squadron headed for the Kiel Canal area as ordered. Some miles away cloud cover began to run out and the first vic saw enemy fighters. They decided to turn about, but the remainder pressed on. Sgt. Kew and crew did not return. Another crew had mechanical trouble and turned back, which left one machine to make the most of its chance by attacking a ship in convoy off Heligoland. 82 Squadron also turned back from the primary, then found a convoy on the way home. It left three ships seriously damaged but lost two crews. This was 82's last shipping raid over Europe for many weeks, much of its strength being in Malta.

Shipping raids were of course not the Group's entire employment, for over forty *Circus* operations had been attempted, and these were demanding an increasing amount of effort. Group strength was reduced also by squadrons participating in Malta operations.

In the first six days of August nine operations were flown against shipping, then the squadrons were taken off operations for intensive training for the Cologne raid described in Chapter 7. August 10 found 226 Squadron on *Channel Stop* at Manston. At 11.15 hours came a report of a 2,000-ton ship with two flak ships as escort nearing Calais. At 11.50 three Blenheims led by Sqn. Ldr. M. W. Waddington took-off with a fighter escort. Half an hour later one Blenheim circled base. Messerschmitts and flak ships had formed a crescent on the northern side of the target through which the bombers had to pass. Waddington led the attack at fifty feet and, facing the full concentration of flak, dropped his bombs short. Hit, he stalled and V5854 fell into the sea. Sgt. Osborne in Z7280 was running up on his target when a Bf 109 swooped upon him and he was shot down in flames three miles north of Port Philippe. Sgt. Chippendale nevertheless courageously ran the gauntlet scoring two hits amidships on the vessel which soon was burning. His ordeal had been so fearful that he and his crew were soon taken off operations. But for 226 Squadron the battle was not over and three more crews were soon off to attack the same ship now reported off Gravelines. They never found it.

Shaw Kennedy was with 226 Squadron at this time. 'We had only limited training, using 11-lb. bombs on a wreck in the Wash. 226 Squadron employed line abreast broadside attack. We would race in taking up and down violent evasive action and following a zig-zag course on the run in, to ruin the gunner's aim. Convoys often hugged the coast for cover from shore guns. We were in no way bunched for the attack, and took what came ... you couldn't afford to be greedy or choosey. Discipline was tough, anyone not keeping to the plan losing all privileges for a week—if he survived. To fly low effectively we had to accustom our eyes, descent being slowly made to very low level. The leader would concentrate on watching for any high object on fringe operations and the wing man kept an eye on station keeping. There was always the risk of exploding bombs destroying the aircraft—this happened to Wg. Cdr. Pepper when he bombed an ammunition ship. Casualties were frightful, particularly under inexperienced squadron commanders. Everything really depended upon the skill of the leader, and morale was kept or lost according to his personality. Some of our crews came from other Commands, from overseas, and some would listen to the stories of operations from the experienced few. Others wouldn't and didn't last long. Keeping your tactics up to date was important too.'

One of the ever-present hazards was colliding with the mast of a ship, as Plt. Off. Johnston did on 20 August when attacking a 'squealer'. He was lucky for, although he tore the outer five feet from his starboard wing, he was able to nurse Z7348: MQ-Q back to North Coates.

There were fewer squadrons available for operations by late August, by which time long-range Spitfires based at Coltishall and Ibsley were providing escort. On 26 August 226 Squadron led by Sqn. Ldr. J. S. Kennedy went to Beats 9 and 10 with Spitfire escort. A convoy was located near Ijmuiden, and they swung in to attack. Kennedy flying V6511: B left a 4,000-tonner burning and Sgt. Connell added bombs to an already crippled 7,000-tonner. Z7305 was hit by navy flak and, with an engine blazing, soon crashed into the sea.

After a break of a few days 21 Squadron was detached to Lossiemouth to resume the campaign off Norway. On 8 September 12 Blenheims of 88 and 114 Squadrons rendezvoused with fighters over Ibsley. Spitfires of 234 Squadron gave close escort with 501 Squadron to port and the

25. V6041: GB-J, a Blenheim IV of 105 Squadron during the 1941 detachment to Luqa, Malta. Note modified gun mounting under the nose

26. 107 Squadron's Boston IIIs at Great Massingham on 8.4.42. From right to left: A: AL280, R: W8373, K: AL290, D: W8387, B: AL284, C: W8355, Q: AL744, S: AL296, O: Z2179 and M: AL288

27. Three Boston IIIs photographed in November 1941, in the hands of 226 Squadron and flown by Flg. Off. A. F. Carlisle, Sgt. Abott and Sgt. Smart

28. Flt. Lt. A. F. Carlisle flying Boston III OM-F: AL702 Squadron. The embellishment on the nose is Churchill's V-for-Victory sign

29. Crews of 88 Squadron before a sortie during the Dieppe raid. Aircraft shown are lettered C, R, U, B, J

30. Another view of Bostons at Ford during the Dieppe raid. Engines are running before take-off on operations

31. Boston IIIA BZ267: RH-N of 88 Squadron fitted with SCI for training during 1943. Served with 88 Squadron from 18.2.43 and in the hands of Flt. Sgt. Davies was shot down during a sortie to Langerbrugge power station on 12.7.43

rear. Alongside these were Spitfires of 118 Squadron and Whirlwinds of 263. When they reached the target area off Guernsey they found two small convoys of tugs towing barges. The Whirlwinds this time swept in to soften up the main body of ships, then the Blenheims went in very successfully. Meanwhile our fighters engaged some Bf 109Fs, but there were neither claims nor losses.

Still the shipping attacks went on and the losses abounded. On 17 September, during a *Channel Stop* operation, three crews of 88 Squadron tried for a 5,000-ton ship but it reached port before they could attack. Early next day they tried again. The tanker was off Blankenburg surrounded by flak ships and a destroyer. Six Spitfires of 91 Squadron escorted the Blenheims whilst 41 Squadron wheeled overhead giving top cover. Sqn. Ldr. Gillan led a dozen Hurricanes of 615 Squadron making up the anti-flak force which drew ahead in classic style to engage the defenders. 88 Squadron followed them in and without loss placed their bombs so well that the stern was blown off the ship. As they turned for home about 20 Bf 109s jumped them, 41 Squadron having lost formation and 615 having expended most of its ammunition, but de la Bouchere in Z3749 destroyed a 109 and damaged another. The enemy fighters seized upon the Blenheims and shot down two. One Blenheim gunner continued the fight until his aircraft hit the water, and a second 109 was thereby shot down. Miraculously Sqn. Ldr. Charles Harris escaped, to make his memorable belly landing (already mentioned) at Manston. His observer, Flt. Sgt. B. C. Woolridge, died in hospital and the crews captained by Plt. Off. T. E. Cooper (flying Z7488: F) and Flg. Off. B. E. Hislop (in V6380) were lost. In the mêlée Plt. Off. Hamilton of 615 Squadron in BD875 was also shot down and Plt. Off. Mills in BD787 baled out, his aircraft being short of fuel, but was luckily picked up by a Dover launch.

Twenty-two Blenheims of 18, 139 and 226 Squadrons operated in Beat 10 on 20th. A motor ship found by 18 Squadron and a tanker were seriously damaged, but Sgt. J. M. Nickelson, his starboard engine blazing, was brought down in the sea and the crew killed. Off the Hook 226 Squadron found fourteen ships flying protective balloons. Undaunted the squadron went in firing four ships and leaving one with a broken back. After Flt. Lt. Namias attacked he was forced to belly flop in the sea. A quarter of a mile from his target his starboard engine had been hit, but he had pressed on. Flt. Lt. Wheeler's aircraft, Z7283: G, was also hit in an engine. Twice he bounced on the water but managed to get home. Sgt. Colmer's Blenheim was blown up by bursting bombs.

By now there was a tailing off in the number of shipping raids as *Circus* and Malta demands increased. It was 11 October before any shipping raids were flown that month. Next day a dozen aircraft of 82 Squadron searched for shipping between Ijmuiden and Scheveningen. About eight miles from the coast one box found a convoy of seven ships with three flak ships. Sqn. Ldr. Meakin in V6226: D scored a direct hit

F

on a 5,000-ton tanker and when T1828: V pulled away a large freighter was on fire. As V5824 ran in it was hit by fire from Flak Ship 1107 and flopped into the sea. Z-Zebra was last seen in the sea by the convoy. L9303 lost an airscrew but she staggered home to Horsham.

For operations in Beats 7, 8 and 9 it was now usual to have fighter escorts from Coltishall or other 12 Group stations, but the fighters were operating at the limit of their duration. On 27 October six crews of 114 Squadron with a fighter escort set off in three sections to patrol two parts of Beat 9. Those on the northern fringe found a southbound convoy of four ships escorted by four flak ships. A 3,000-tonner was attacked, then Messerschmitts of 2/JG 53 arrived and shot down a Blenheim just after it had completed its bomb run. Another attempting to bomb was shot down. Both Blenheims had been disabled by flak and were then pounced upon by Lt. Dinger and Uffz. Museter.

Ironically the last shots fired against the Blenheims in the anti-shipping campaign were not from the enemy, but from the trigger-happy Royal Navy some fifteen miles out from Yarmouth. 2 Group was ever bitter about this which, to a varying extent, took place almost throughout the war and particularly during the French campaign and the shipping raids. On this last occasion the matelots taking no chances managed to get a cannon shell into a Blenheim, holing the elevators and slicing some control cables. To all intents and purposes the shipping raids ended on 31 October although one attack followed on a squealer.

For months there had been wrangling in high places as to whether the Group should entirely change its face and equip with Hurricane fighter-bombers. Finally the C.A.S. decreed that these should go to Fighter Command's 607 Squadron which on 9 October took over *Channel Stop*. 2 Group was finally relieved of its shipping commitment on 25 November.

Earlier that month Admiral Raeder reported to Hitler: 'The decided enemy air superiority in the West has made the sea transport situation and the mounting threat to our defence forces more acute. Utmost demands are made on matériel and personnel of our inadequate escort forces; the physical and nervous strain of the men is very great. By using all available forces it has been possible to escort convoys and keep the routes open. . . . The only way to rectify the position at sea is to reinforce the fighter units, an urgently needed step.' Thus it seems that at the height of possible success the campaign ended as far as 2 Group was concerned. It was now up to Coastal Command and Fighter Command.

A combination of factors halted the shipping raids. But the main reason was the appalling casualty rate and its accumulative effect on the crews. Unlike many others, 2 Group's squadrons could at least see the results of their raids—but they also saw their comrades perish, and experienced operations demanding utmost courage. By comparison with others 2 Group was small in number, and losses were intimately felt. The effect upon morale when a squadron commander was lost— and this quite often happened—was considerable for, if one of experience failed to return, what chance did the inexperienced have? Shipping raids snatched from the Group, indeed the whole Air Force, many whose contribution in war and now in peace would surely have been very considerable.

Let it not be thought that at any time 2 Group failed in the demands put upon it, for it fought in a manner unexcelled in our long history. Even in utmost distress it was quick to seize upon a spark of humour if this were possible. Wg. Cdr. Atkinson, 'Attie' to all of 2 Group, keeps within his diary of those days a poignant postcard written by a friend in a prison camp. It reads:

'I'm sorry I failed to return on 26th June, but a destroyer picked me off going in to attack and a merchantman got my second engine. This left me no alternative but to fall in the drink about three miles from the convoy. At 3 o'clock we saw you looking for us but the aircraft turned north about ten miles away. We'd lost rockets. My crew are well. Felton received a nasty cut over right eye but is now well. Thompson O.K. My regards to all the boys on behalf of the crew. . . . Hoping to see you soon.

Harrison Broadley.'

Just how much shipping was destroyed in these operations may never be known. Captain S. W. Roskill in *The War at Sea* (HMSO) states 'substantial claims to have sunk or damaged enemy shipping had, for some months, been made by the aircrews employed on this work, but it became gradually clear that to make correct estimates was extremely difficult, and that the claims bore little relation to the true results obtained.' An Air Ministry Anti-Shipping Operation Assessment Committee scaled down claims by half and post-war analysis revealed even this figure as seeming too high. In the autumn of 1941 an Admiralty Committee estimated that between March and September 1941 101 ships (328,000 tons) were sunk or seriously damaged and another seventy slightly damaged. When the German records for the same period were examined they showed a loss of 29 ships (29,836 tons) with 21 (43,715) seriously damaged.

What can be confirmed is the appalling loss rate. During August 1941, of 77 aircraft which attacked ships, 23 were lost; at 30% clearly a prohibitive rate. Out of 480 sorties flown by the Blenheims in the same month, 36 never returned. Additionally there were the aircraft damaged so badly that they never flew again. But the loss was most grievous in men. Coupled with the losses being sustained in Malta it was for 2 Group a terrifying period, a very demanding and expensive war.

Chapter 9
Setting the Trend

'Intention: To harass the enemy on the ground by bombing Forêt de Guines and destroy enemy aircraft in the air, or, should insufficient or no enemy aircraft be seen, to ground strafe St. Ingelvert aerodrome.' An entirely new and lasting phase of the air war was to begin: Operation *Circus* was on.

With the Battle of Britain won and the invasion off, a daylight offensive over France, using fighter-escorted bombers primarily to entice German fighters to battle and prevent the Luftwaffe from renewing daylight attacks on Britain, was decided upon.

There were basic snags to overcome. British fighters had limited duration, and were specialised defensive machines. The Luftwaffe would be fighting over home territory and thereby lose fewer pilots than the R.A.F. Little damage could be done by a dozen Blenheims bombing from 12,000 feet or so. Enemy fighter reaction might be slight, but predicted flak from well-defended targets like Calais and Boulogne directed against large, steady formations could bring trouble. Yet against all this an offensive had much to commend it, bringing a renewed spirit to forces involved when they most desperately needed it. The offensive planned to begin in late December started in 10 January 1941, the first day of suitable weather.

At noon six Blenheims of 114 Squadron, Wg. Cdr. Elsmie leading, climbed away from the famous fighter field at Hornchurch. About the same time 103 fighters of nine squadrons became airborne. They milled around Southend until rendezvous was complete. All had been carefully planned.

At 10,000–11,000 feet 24 Hurricanes of 242 and 249 Squadrons flew ahead to attack St. Inglevert airfield giving forward support. At 12,000 feet was the box of six Blenheims whose close escort was provided by Hurricanes of 56 Squadron. To prevent enemy fighters diving upon the bombers there were three squadrons of Spitfires giving top cover, Nos. 41, 64 and 611 stepped up and back from 13,000 feet to 15,000 feet. This was the largest formation of fighters and bombers yet assembled for a wartime R.A.F. operation. Withdrawal cover was afforded by Spitfires of Nos. 74, 92 and 66 Squadrons patrolling Cap Gris Nez.

Once position jockeying was complete the formation flew towards

Calais and, close to the coast, turned to make landfall at Gravelines. Blenheims and close escort dived to 6,800 feet, the bombing height. Sixteen 250-pounders and 48 40-lb. incendiaries fell in a wood camouflaging an ammunition dump. Two fires were started. Then the bombers turned for home on what for them was a rather uneventful operation. No fighters challenged them.

The fighter pilots had a far more exciting time. After the bombing 611 Squadron flew north. Sqn. Ldr. Bitmead dived from 15,000 feet to ground level to shoot up a gun position in sand dunes north of Wissant village and troops in the streets. 'B' Flight meanwhile kept top cover. To the target and on return there was heavy flak, particularly between Calais, Gravelines and Sangatte. In the target area more guns were firing, fortunately inaccurately. Four Bf 109s were seen at 20,000 feet some way off, obviously observing the unexpected activity, but there were no engagements.

Both 242 and 249 Squadrons led respectively by Douglas Bader in V6913 and Victor Beamish in V7000 found little activity on the snow-clad roads and airfields of France. Sgt. Maciejowski of 249, separated from his squadron, saw five Hs 126s lining the edge of Guines-la-Place airfield. He opened fire from about 300 feet without seeing the result. Then he saw two Bf 109s at the same height as himself, climbed to 1,000 feet and attacked the nearest. It turned steeply, dived towards the ground and crashed in a belt of trees. The first enemy fighter destroyed on a *Circus* had fallen to V6615. During the engagement Maciejowski discovered his throttle was jammed fully open and was compelled to return to England at full bore. He landed at Hornchurch in the only possible manner—by switching off his ignition!

The remainder of 249 Squadron encountered heavy fire from four patrol boats anchored about three miles off Calais. Beamish dived and machine-gunned them. Plt. Off. W. M. McConell was attacked by a yellow-nosed Messerschmitt, wounded and forced to bale out of P3579. His aircraft crashed on the cliffs of Dover and he was admitted to St. Margaret's Hospital with a broken leg and splinter wounds. Victor Beamish had turned back to assist him, and shot the 109 into the sea.

Squadrons participating were congratulated (see Appendix 6). From A.O.C. 11 Group came the signal 'Please convey to 114 Squadron that the Prime Minister and C.-in-C. Fighter Command wish to congratulate all concerned in the very satisfactory operation over France. I look forward to further operations of this kind.'

Not for three weeks was there another *Circus*. Winter weather was not conducive to elaborate operations. Lessons from the first needed to be digested. It was debatable whether fighters should leave their charge to engage in ground strike activities, and planning the fighter support needed careful consideration.

A tempting alteration would be to increase the size of the bomber force, reasonably safe under strong escort. One of the aims of the

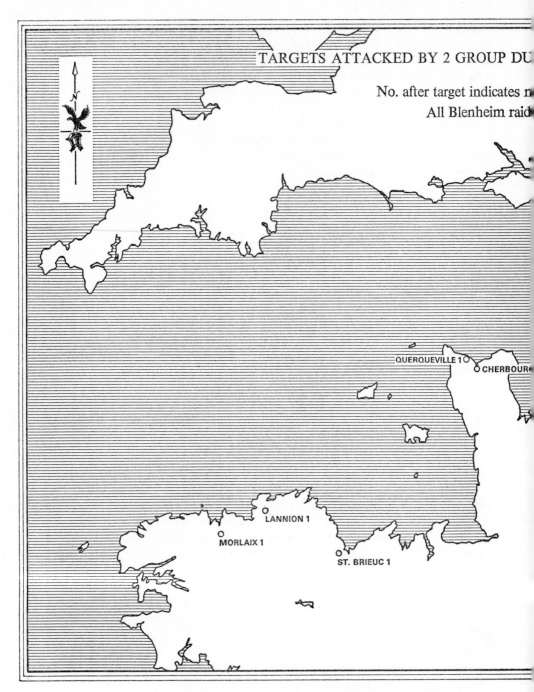

TARGETS ATTACKED BY 2 GROUP DU

No. after target indicates n

All Blenheim raid

QUERQUEVILLE 1

CHERBOUR

LANNION 1

MORLAIX 1

ST. BRIEUC 1

MAP 9. *See Appendix 12, pages 498–500 for notes*

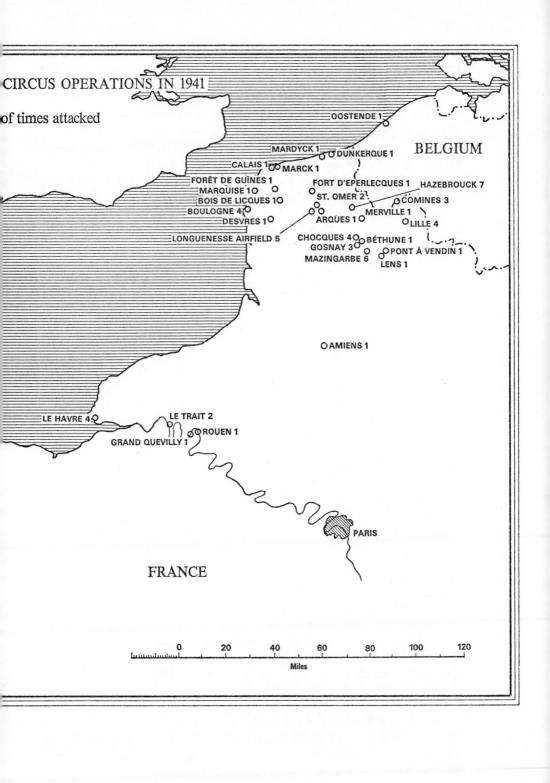

CIRCUS OPERATIONS IN 1941

of times attacked

OOSTENDE 1

BELGIUM

MARDYCK 1
DUNKERQUE 1
CALAIS 1 MARCK 1
FORÊT DE GUÎNES 1   FORT D'EPERLECQUES 1   HAZEBROUCK 7
MARQUISE 1   ST. OMER 2
BOIS DE LICQUES 1   CÔMINES 3
BOULOGNE 4   MERVILLE 1
DESVRES 1   ARQUES 1   LILLE 4
LONGUENESSE AIRFIELD 5   CHOCQUES 4 BÉTHUNE 1
                        GOSNAY 3   PONT À VENDIN 1
                        MAZINGARBE 6   LENS 1

AMIENS 1

LE HAVRE 4
                LE TRAIT 2
                    ROUEN 1
GRAND QUEVILLY 1

PARIS

FRANCE

0   20   40   60   80   100   120

Miles

Circuses was to prevent enemy use of Channel ports in preparing an invasion and for his coastal supply convoys, whilst putting him on the defensive. The A.O.C. 2 Group considered that as many boxes of six aircraft as crew situations permitted should be operated.

Accordingly both Nos. 114 and 139 Squadrons were told on 25 January that under Operations Order No. 19 their role would remain threefold— (1) fighter escorted short-range daylight operations, (2) harassing fringe targets or shipping off the enemy coast and (3) night attacks on oil targets if the weather was satisfactory for concentrated attacks. To ensure the first aim was effective, bombers must cause enough damage to make it impossible to ignore them. Fighters must operate at 20,000–30,000 feet to a co-ordinated time-table . . . and bombers must agree tactical requirements of fighters, especially attack at 17,000 feet or higher if practical, and make only one run. Approach and withdrawal were to be agreed with the Close Escort Wing Leader. Targets were to be invasion ports, airfields, camps, dumps in range of fighter cover. Rendezvous with close escort was set at 15,000 feet over a fighter airfield. Withdrawal would be at the bombing leader's discretion, by a gradual turn to the point of crossing the French coast. Speed and method needed to be regulated, there must be no straggling. Our coast was to be re-crossed at one of the three A.S.R. boat rendezvous points— Dunkirk–N. Foreland; Calais–Dover; Boulogne–Dungeness.

The second *Circus* took place on 2 February. Six Blenheims of 139 Squadron led by Wg. Cdr. Kyle flew to Northolt to meet their close escort, Hurricanes of 601 Squadron. Then they bombed Nos. 3, 4 and 7 docks at Boulogne. One shell burst near the cockpit of a Blenheim, flak in the area being accurate. On return formations of enemy fighters were seen but did not interfere, so Flt. Lt. Whitney Straight of 601 in Hurricane R4112 broke formation and shot down a yellow-nosed Messerschmitt.

On 5 February the bomber force was doubled. Six Blenheims of 114 Squadron tagged on behind six of 139 Squadron over Horsham and flew to Northolt to meet the close escort. Over Rye Hurricanes of Nos. 1, 615 and 302 Squadrons took up stations, also Spitfires of Nos. 65 and 610 Squadrons giving forward support. Ten minutes later a three-squadron Spitfire Wing set out to provide withdrawal cover. The ground around St. Omer was snow-clad and the target was so difficult to see that three runs had to be made before the 250-lb. and 40-lb. bombs were dropped from 7,000 feet, this giving the defenders ample time to react. Such repeated runs though rarely made were undesirable. Enemy fighters rose to the bait but none pierced the screen defending the Blenheims. 610 Squadron stayed with the bombers and this cost them four aircraft.

About ten miles into France 65 Squadron went after some 109s, three of which fastened their attention on to Plt. Off. Hill shooting him down. Flt. Lt. B. F. 'Paddy' Finucane in P7694 then destroyed the enemy leader who crashed in a wood, but a second Spitfire P7733 was lost.

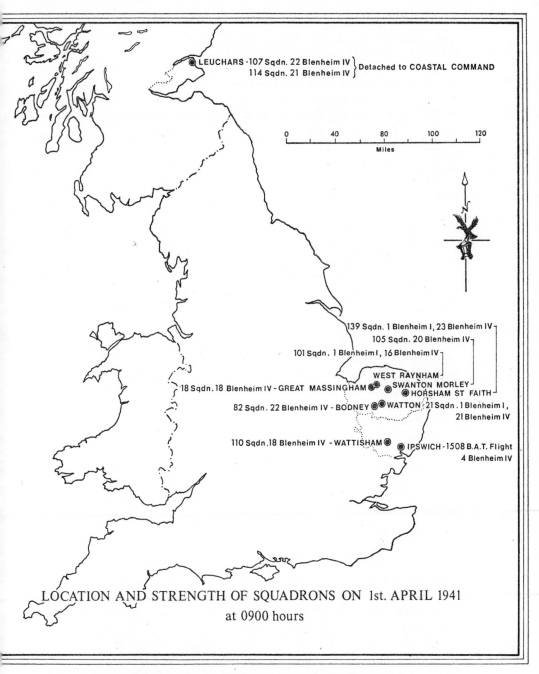

LEUCHARS -107 Sqdn. 22 Blenheim IV
114 Sqdn. 21 Blenheim IV } Detached to COASTAL COMMAND

0   40   80   100   120
Miles

139 Sqdn. 1 Blenheim I, 23 Blenheim IV ⌐
105 Sqdn. 20 Blenheim IV ⌐
101 Sqdn. 1 Blenheim I, 16 Blenheim IV ⌐
WEST RAYNHAM ⌐
18 Sqdn. 18 Blenheim IV - GREAT MASSINGHAM
SWANTON MORLEY
HORSHAM ST FAITH
82 Sqdn. 22 Blenheim IV - BODNEY
WATTON - 21 Sqdn . 1 Blenheim I,
21 Blenheim IV
110 Sqdn. 18 Blenheim IV - WATTISHAM
IPSWICH - 1508 B.A.T. Flight
4 Blenheim IV

LOCATION AND STRENGTH OF SQUADRONS ON 1st. APRIL 1941
at 0900 hours

MAP 10. *See Appendix 12, pages 501/2 for notes*

Messerschmitts bounced 615 Squadron and Sgt. Jenkins was shot down. Two others from the squadron collided over Dover. Nine fighters had been lost, but the bombers returned safely.

Circus 4 came on 10 February. Fighters met 139 Squadron[1] over North Weald, 56 Squadron giving close escort at 10,000 feet, 17 and 249 Squadrons at 15,000 feet and Hurricanes of 303 Squadron above and behind. Other fighters flew ahead to clear the target area. Forward support was an established part of such operations. The main formation crossed in west of Dunkirk, turned left to make a wide inland sweep, then as a surprise bombed Dunkirk docks on the way out. Nos. 1, 605 and 615 Squadrons swept in behind to give withdrawal cover. The plan had worked well, for flak opened up late and twenty Bf 110s vectored to the target area arrived too late to defend it and too late for the Hurricanes to deal with them. 249 Squadron engaged about a dozen 109s claiming two for the loss of one. For the effort involved enemy losses were still very slight.

Two *Circuses* were flown in March but there was no enemy reaction. Hoped-for response was not arising, and new employment for the Group—the shipping offensive—drastically cut the number of *Circuses*, only two being flown in April. Different squadrons were now on the offensive, and on 17th a dozen Blenheims of 101 and six of 18 Squadrons attacked Cherbourg. 101 was ordered to lead the bombers forming up over East Anglia and meet six fighter squadrons over Tangmere at 4,000 feet. For the first time three bomber boxes were employed on a *Circus*, bombs being released, as customary, on the leader's signal. Despite the increased bait, enemy fighters still did not react.

To maintain Group's daylight offensive 'B' Flight of 61 Squadron flying Handley Page Hampdens was detached to 2 Group on 13 April and moved into Watton and Bodney. It was to fly unescorted cloud-cover operations over north-west Germany under Group Operations Order No. 24. Rarely did cloud permit the Hampdens to proceed and they had to be content with aiming bombs on De Kooy, Ijmuiden and Cherbourg. So little was being achieved that on 30 April they returned to 5 Group (see Appendix 3).

Much of May's effort was again expended on anti-shipping operations. Only two *Circuses* were flown, one abortive and one to Gosnay oil refining plant. It was an elaborate operation. Kenley Wing comprising Nos. 1, 258 and 302 Squadrons escorted the eighteen Blenheims whilst Diversionary Wing offensive patrols were flown by Nos. 56 and 242 Squadrons over St. Omer with 609 Squadron affording withdrawal cover, and by Nos. 303 and 306 Squadrons over Berck-sur-Mer with 145 Squadron covering their withdrawal. A *High Sphere* (high altitude patrol) operation was placed between the target and the French coast by 92 Squadron whilst rear support Wings patrolled the French coast

---

[1] Blenheims: T2320: G, V5498: A, V5460: J, T1799: S, L9386: T, L9307: H.

and the Dover Straits (Nos. 54, 603 and 611 Squadrons) and in the Canterbury–Dover area (a 12 Group Wing comprising Nos. 19, 266 and 310 Squadrons) for there was a hunch that the enemy might spring an intruder raid upon our landing fighter squadrons. This did not happen, but the bomber escort engaged Bf 109s claiming four. A Blenheim and six fighters were lost.

Early in June, after three weeks of bad weather, *Circus* operations took on new life. St. Omer/Longuenesse was bombed before low cloud and rain halted the second *Circus* planned for the day.

The Air Staff still cherished the idea of heavy bombers attacking Germany in daylight. Halifaxes and Stirlings considered well enough armed to defend themselves against fighters were now to hand. 2 Group's contribution to the new plan was to cause enemy fighters to be held in the Pas de Calais thereby helping pave the way for day raids on Germany. Co-ordinated *Circuses* were to take place with 11 Group support. *Circus 12* on 14 June to St. Omer was the first in the new series and sixteen *Circuses* were attempted that month.

The basic formation used was the close box of six Blenheims comprising two sections in vic flying high/low to provide maximum fire power if attacked. Initially the bombers had operated in boxes stepped down to the rear. This was an unwieldy formation and flak casualties could be quite heavy since even a near miss was effective. Fighters found it difficult to escort and often were dropping back. Bomber boxes were now to be at slightly differing levels with fighters on their flanks and in echelon aft. More flew well behind giving rear cover, whilst above flew the fighter escort cover, and above this top cover for the whole operation to prevent the Messerschmitts bouncing the so-called 'beehive'. Up to 24 Blenheims would now be operated at about 12,000–14,000 feet, too high for light flak to reach them and below the effective level of heavy guns.

Close escort was being afforded by Nos. 56, 242 and 306 Squadrons on 17 June. Enemy fighter reaction was quicker than hitherto probably because the large British force was easily detected by radar defences. Northolt and North Weald squadrons fought off every attack on the bombers but lost three of their number mainly because the high cover squadrons had been briefed to fly too high to effectively safeguard the escort wing. The operation was a comparatively deep one, and it cost us nine fighter pilots.

There were presently three types of *Circus*—as operation orders promulgated. The pure *Circus* aimed at forcing the enemy to fight under conditions tactically favourable to our fighters, which meant employing a large fighter force operating mainly around 20,000–30,000 feet. A *Blot* operation was an attack with fighter escort on a Fringe target without cloud cover. Group decided whether such attacks were to be very low—as low as 50 feet—or at medium heights. In any case visual contact had to be maintained between bombers and fighters, and cloud

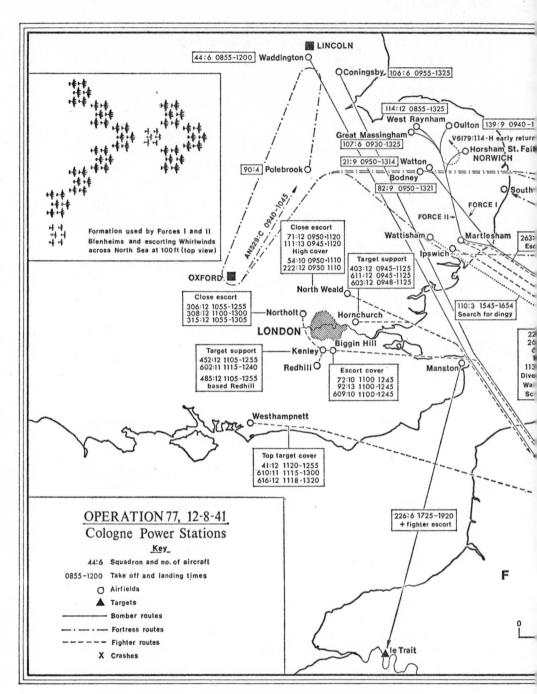

LINCOLN

44:6 0855-1200 | Waddington

Coningsby | 106:6 0955-1325

114:12 0855-1325
West Raynham
Oulton | 139:9 0940-1

V6179:114-H early returr

Great Massingham
107:6 0930-1325

Horsham St. Fait
NORWICH

90:4 | Polebrook

21:9 0950-1314 | Watton
Bodney
82:9 0950-1321

South

FORCE I

FORCE II

Wattisham
Martlesham | 263:
Esc

Ipswich

AN529:C 0940-1045

OXFORD

Close escort
71:12 0950-1120
111:13 0945-1120
High cover
54:10 0950-1110
222:12 0950 1110

Target support
403:12 0945-1125
611:12 0945-1125
603:12 0948-1125

110:3 1545-1654
Search for dingy

North Weald

Close escort
306:12 1055-1255
308:12 1100-1300
315:12 1055-1305

Northolt
Hornchurch

LONDON

Biggin Hill

22
26
6

113
Dive
Wa
Sc

Kenley

Target support
452:12 1105-1255
602:11 1115-1240
485:12 1105-1255
based Redhill

Redhill

Escort cover
72:10 1100 1245
92:13 1100-1245
609:10 1100-1245

Manston

Westhampnett

Top target cover
41:12 1120-1255
610:11 1115-1300
616:12 1118-1320

226:6 1725-1920
+ fighter escort

F

OPERATION 77, 12-8-41
Cologne Power Stations
Key

44:6   Squadron and no. of aircraft
0855-1200   Take off and landing times
O   Airfields
▲   Targets
——————   Bomber routes
—·—·—·—   Fortress routes
- - - - -   Fighter routes
X   Crashes

0

le Trait

MAP 11. *See Appendix 12, pages 502/3 for notes*

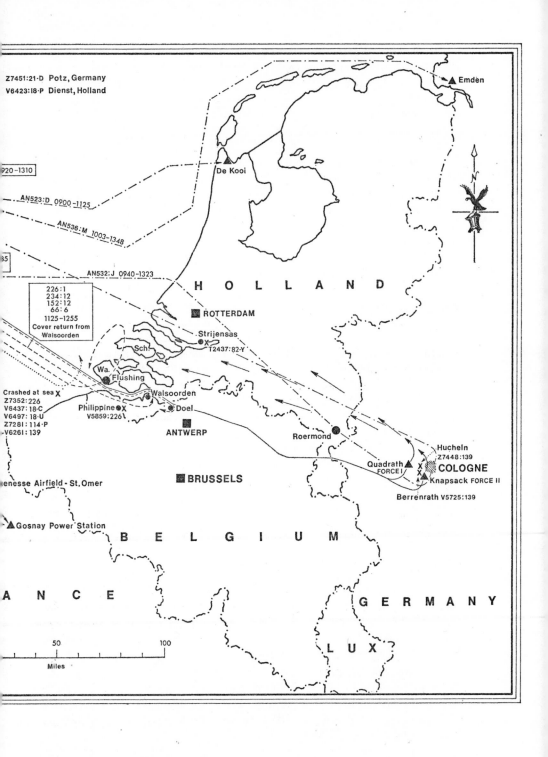

Z7451:21-D Potz, Germany
V6423:18-P Dienst, Holland

▲ Emden

De Kooi

920–1310

AN523:D 0900–1125

AN536:M 1003–1348

85

AN532:J 0940–1323

H O L L A N D

226:1
234:12
152:12
66:6
1125–1255
Cover return from
Walsoorden

■ ROTTERDAM

Sch.

Strijensas
X
T2437:82-Y

Wa.
● Flushing

Crashed at sea X
Z7352:226
V6437:18-C
V6497:18-U
Z7281:114-P
V6261:139

● Walsoorden

Philippine ● X
V5859:226

● Doel

■ ANTWERP

Roermond ●

Hucheln
Z7448:139

Quadrath
FORCE I
X
X
Berrenrath V5725:139

COLOGNE
▲ Knapsack FORCE II

■ BRUSSELS

enesse Airfield - St. Omer

▲ Gosnay Power Station

B E L G I U M

G E R M A N Y

A N C E

L U X

50   100

Miles

must not exceed 3/10. In low attacks fighters would approach the target stepped up slightly from 5,000 feet, circle the target either left or right and keep out of the way of flak. High cover at 12,000–14,000 feet would be given. Bombers would usually withdraw at sea level with fighters giving them top cover until all had left the target area. In medium-level attacks close escort was at 5,000 feet, above and behind the bombers, and again stayed until they were clear of the target. The fighters did not leave the bombers unless actually attacked. High cover was 3,000 feet above, the escort maintaining this position over the whole formation and fighting only if forced to do so.

A mixed operation was the *Circus Blot*. This embraced a small bomber force with fighter protection intending to attack a target within close distance of enemy aircraft likely to be engaging a main *Circus* or *Blot*. It was a diversion, as on 23 June when 107 Squadron attacked Mardyck airfield whilst the main *Circus* was directed against Chocques chemical factory. For the *Circus* one section of bombers would be escorted by fighters. Rendezvous would be over a fighter airfield while the *Blot* operation would pick up two squadrons of fighters over a fighter field, then fly to the target at 180 m.p.h., I.A.S. Both fighter squadrons would be within sight of the bombers. This second operation took place about ten minutes after the main *Circus*. An outline of these orders had been passed to Station Commanders on 22 April 1941.

Operation 520 alias Operation *Derby*, the *Blot* on Le Havre of 19 June, to which Nos. 18, 21, 105, 107 and 139 Squadrons each contributed six aircraft, was to be a major attack. It called for 36 aircraft (see Appendix 6) all positioned at selected airfields by noon on the day. Nos. 21 and 110 Squadrons from Watton, Wg. Cdr. P. F. Webster leading, with each aircraft carrying two 500 S.A.P. bombs, were to deliver a low attack whilst the remainder of the force operated from Swanton Morley. All took off at 16.00 hours. The high-levellers climbed to 5,000 feet leaving the others at 1,500 feet. They flew to Tangmere intent upon meeting their fighter escort, the high-level group twice orbiting at 12,000 feet awaiting the four fighter squadrons. It was very hazy with huge cumulus clouds towering over much of eastern and southern England. Soon it was clear that the fighters could not rendezvous and 24 keyed-up, but nevertheless disappointed, crews had to turn about. Included in these was the low-level formation whose leader considered it unwise to proceed because of sea fog. Nos. 107 and 105 Squadrons escorted by Nos. 145, 303, 610 and 616 Squadrons pressed on led by Wg. Cdr. H. I. Edwards, attacking Le Havre from the west and taking the defences by surprise. Five of 105 Squadron managed hits south of the dry dock, on the central mole and Bassin de Marée and on oil tanks north-east of the dry dock. 107's bombs straddled the Bassin Pétrole leaving a large pall of white smoke.

Airfields at St. Omer/Longuenesse, Desvres and Mardyck; Hazebrouck Chocques chemical works, Comines power station, the Fives-Lille steel works and Pont à Vendin power station—all were targets for June *Circuses*. Seven Blenheims of 18 Squadron were among the 24 that raided Chocques on 17th dropping bombs on the south-west corner of the target causing fires with incendiaries. There was heavy flak on the way home, from Boulogne, Marquise and Ambleteuse. One of the yellow-nosed Messerschmitts which persistently attacked the Blenheims almost to the British coast was shot down by a Hurricane. 56 Squadron giving close escort was repeatedly attacked and lost four pilots. Two Blenheims of 18 Squadron were shot up and Flg. Off. Duffill, six times attacked by a 109F, belly-landed at Horsham.

A new policy first employed on 20 June and periodically repeated was the operation of a *Circus* in waves. Later in the war sometimes operations were flown in which different squadrons attacked several targets almost simultaneously to confuse the defences. Six crews of 21 Squadron made a morning raid on Desvres airfield with three fighter squadrons forming the close escort. In the afternoon the attack was repeated by 110 Squadron.

Generally speaking the Luftwaffe still failed to rise and intercept the bombers although this was not so on 23 June when Chocques was the target. Included in the escort were the Hurricanes of No. 71 (Eagle) Squadron, American-manned, making their first bomber escort. Intense flak for once broke up the formation from 107 Squadron, then just inland about twenty Bf 109s dived upon the bombers. Their close-support fighters were quite unable to drive off the enemy and the bombers had a four-minute running fight. Sgt. Fairbanks and Flg. Off. Redfearn-Smith were shot down and two more Blenheims limped to Manston badly shot up. Ballands flying Z6271 came down at Dover.

A new squadron now entered the Group, No. 226. Since its mauling in France in 1940 it had been stationed in Northern Ireland where, using Fairey Battles, it performed three tasks. One was the flying of anti-submarine patrols over the Irish Sea. It was also on standby against a possible invasion of Ireland. But, perhaps more important, it was engaged in very low flying at 50 feet or so to give troops some idea of how to react to very low attack. Its training now stood it in good stead.

Late in 1940 226 Squadron received some Blenheim 1s for twin conversion and in January 1941 the first ex-French Douglas Bostons arrived, their instruments metrically calibrated. Accustomed to the Battle the pilot's initial impression was of a terrifying landing speed and a hair-raising route on approach to Sydenham often over gantries in Belfast shipyards. AE472, AW401 and AW472 were in use, but Bostons were in short supply and, being unsuitable for operations, were soon withdrawn for conversion to night-fighters. Back came the Battles, nightly dispersed to Long Kesh to avoid the Belfast blitzes which nevertheless caught a few of them.

On 26 May 1941, 226 moved to Wattisham where conversion to the Blenheim IV, already started, continued until operations against 'squealers' began. On 28 June six aircraft of the squadron raided Comines power station. No. 303 Polish Squadron was giving high-escort cover when numerous Bf 109s appeared over the target. Plt. Off. Dreckr was attacked and became detached. He then shot down two attackers before being shot down into the sea. He was picked up unhurt. No bombers were lost.

226 then stood down for a rest. Shaw Kennedy was alone in the mess at Wattisham when he was told to gather a crew of Sergeants—Hicks and Moss volunteered—and fly to Watton to make up 21 Squadron's strength for something special. On arrival he asked Wg. Cdr. Webster, C.O. of 21 Squadron, what was afoot. 'Briefing is at 01.30, you'll find out then, old boy,' he replied. Kennedy recalls that in no time the batman was at the door with a 'Wake up, sir.' Soon it was bacon and eggs then briefing for selected crews.

Grp. Capt. Sinclair opened it: 'Gentlemen, tonight—and at this very moment—we are bombing Bremen.[2] We want to prove to the Germans we can bomb them 24 hours a day, and you, Gentlemen, will attack in daylight soon after the heavies have left. No excuses will be tolerated, you MUST get to the target.'

Kennedy looked at Hicks. His distinctive Adam's apple seemed drooping to his stomach—and talking of stomachs the plan unfolded was enough to make anyone's frightfully uneasy. Bremen, and in DAYLIGHT! Kennedy had earlier noticed the telltale strings from base to the target and the photograph of Bremen but dismissed the likelihood of any such foolhardy idea. 'My blood went cold as I realised what it was,' he recalled. 'My hopes were that they would be cleaning their anti-aircraft guns after the night raid—and that the balloons would be down.' He had little confidence in the plan. At the briefing there were also five crews from 21 Squadron and nine of 105. Some slight measure of protection was planned to come from an attack by 107 Squadron on Westerland airfield—little comfort.

'No minor unserviceability would be tolerated' . . . but when Kennedy climbed into his aircraft he found the intercom was unserviceable. He climbed into the reserve machine, but the engine would not start. Back to Z7438. He would have to go without the intercom working. He had been wishing his mother might come and lead him away by the hand from the danger ahead, as she had in his childhood. But no, he had to face it.

Soon after the formation left the coast it descended to fifty feet, even

[2] The force of 76 aircraft of which 52 attacked Bremen—35 Wellingtons and 17 Whitleys—included three Wellington 1cs of 2 Group's 101 Squadron, R1801, R1780, R1781. This unit operated Wellingtons at night from West Raynham until it was transferred to 3 Group on 7.7.41. 105 Squadron also received a few Wellingtons possibly in error but never operated them. See also Appendix 3.

below, skimming the wave tops. Then trouble came. It entered sea fog and the crews found themselves flying at around 100–200 feet on instruments only. Kennedy remembered the order—'You MUST get to the target.' The fog remained for about 45 minutes and flying through it so low was a terrifying experience. Indeed, in a long distinguished operational career he came to rate the experience one of the most frightening he knew.

Suddenly the mist disappeared. Kennedy emerged and not another aircraft was to be seen, but not for long. He soon came across another whose pilot removed his oxygen mask revealing he was Tony Partridge. Soon they were joined by two more. In a few moments the weather again became bad, and they were all juggling with death at 0 feet in and out of the mist. Try as they might they could not find Bremen.

Only one did so, Sgt. Giblin flying V6388: YH-R who quite un-expectedly came upon the target and quickly bombed a building and timber yard north of the Hotz und Faverickshavn containing two tall chimneys. He had attacked in very poor visibility from fifty feet flying between those chimneys. Debris was thrown into the air before two Bf 109s engaged the Blenheim which escaped into cloud. Off Terschelling Giblin was intercepted by three 109s which assaulted him for ten minutes. His gunner claimed hits on all three, large chunks being blown off the wing of one. R-Roger made a belly landing at Marham.

Kennedy and the other four aircraft were still searching for the target when they came upon the marshalling yard at Oldenburg, full of rail waggons probably stopped there because of the Bremen night raid. They made independent attacks, bombing and strafing the yards. After Kennedy had attacked he found the others had gone into the mist. It was customary for the crews to wear tin hats at this time. He took his off and threw it at his navigator—there was no intercom—requesting a course for home. Soon a Ju 88 was after them but, bless the mist, they lost it. All this time they had no contact with the gunner, so Hicks passed a note to Moss asking him to radio for a QDM to get them to base.

After they landed they spoke to Moss. He had been quite convinced they had turned for home in the mist and whilst Kennedy had been seeking the target Moss, over Germany, was calling for QDMs and giving their position away all the time! They had used up a lot of fuel and the ground crew on looking at the aircraft exclaimed, 'Christ, there's hardly any petrol in anything!' Had they continued their course there is little doubt they would have flown along the Channel and been forced to ditch.

What of the others? The formation from 105 Squadron led by Hughie Edwards had decided to turn about when mist was persistently encountered, and try for other targets. Sqn. Ldr. Scott flew to Terschelling and bombed its radio station. Sqn. Ldr. Booth found a convoy N.W. of Norderney and attacked a 5,000-tonner. Smoke and flames were seen by Flg. Off. Lambert, who attacked and sank a 3,000-tonner. Thus the operation was not entirely fruitless.

107 Squadron flying the diversion made a wrong landfall encountering heavy flak. Target was quickly changed to a railway line and power station east of Rantum, but most bombs fell in the sea. Bf 109s intercepted, two Blenheims being lost and three badly shot up. Sgts. Chown and Drysdale were missing.

Origin of the intended Bremen raid had lain in a Group order of 27 June. The offensive against Russia emphasised the need to hit the enemy hard whilst his hands were full in the east, and operations over France continued. Originally eighteen Blenheims operating from West Raynham and Swanton Morley were to attack Bremen on the morning of Saturday 28 June at about 07.00 hours. To exhaust enemy fighters a heavy night attack on the city would prelude the raid, and even if cloud cover was inadequate the daylight operation would proceed. It was to be concentrated in a maximum of ten minutes, aiming point being between the railway station and the docks.

Operation *Wreckage*, as it was called, was unsuccessful on 30 June. Therefore it was decided to repeat it on 4 July, a day long to be remembered in 2 Group. At 05.21 nine crews of 105 Squadron took-off, led by Wg. Cdr. Hughie Edwards. They joined six of 107 Squadron. Of these three aircraft soon dropped out. Sqn. Ldr. Murray's guns were unsynchronised. Flt. Lt. Jones fell ill and Flg. Off. Charney could not keep up with the formation.

The remainder flew at sea level and, turning in from a point off Heligoland, successfully attacked the docks, railways, factories, a timber yard and Bremen town. Sgt. Mackillop and crew perished bravely when their Blenheim, hit by flak, crashed into a factory and blew up. Flg. Off. Lambert's aircraft hit by flak was last seen heading inland on fire. Two others were also lost. Utmost gallantry was shown by the entire force as, at roof-top height, they penetrated the heavily defended city. Particularly did the leader exhibit great courage. Subsequently he was awarded the Victoria Cross. His citation read thus: 'Wing Commander Hughie Idwal Edwards, D.F.C., although handicapped by physical disability resulting from a flying accident, has repeatedly displayed gallantry of the highest order in pressing home bombing attacks from very low heights against strongly defended objectives.

'He led an important attack on the port of Bremen, one of the most heavily defended towns in Germany. This attack had to be made in daylight and there were no clouds to afford concealment. During the approach to the enemy coast several ships were sighted, and Wg. Cdr. Edwards knew that his aircraft would be reported and that the defences would be in a state of readiness.

'Undaunted by this misfortune he brought his formation fifty miles overland to the target, flying at a height of a little more than fifty feet, passing through a formidable balloon barrage.

'On reaching Bremen he was met by a hail of fire, all his aircraft being hit and four of them destroyed. Nevertheless he made a most successful attack, and then with the greatest skill and coolness withdrew the remaining aircraft without further loss.

'Throughout the execution of this operation, which he had planned personally with full knowledge of the risks entailed, Wg. Cdr. Edwards displayed the highest possible standard of gallantry and determination.'

To reach his target Edwards flew beneath high-tension cables and zigzagged between the barrage-balloon wires to place his bombs on a factory. Pieces of it were hurled to 700 feet. One of the Blenheims in the formation returned festooned with telegraph wires. Every gun at Bremen seemed to fire at the raiders, and Sgt. Jackson had to make a belly landing.

226 Squadron was also airborne on 4 July whilst the Bremen raid took place. Five crews led by Wg. Cdr. Hurst set off for Norderney to create a fighter diversion. Hurst attacked as detailed, but light flak hit him on pulling up. Kennedy raced in attacking the gun that had fired. It was too late. Hurst's aircraft blew into smithereens. Gun emplacements on the shore and wooden buildings on the dunes were shot up, but no fighters appeared.

The Bremen raid occasioned a signal from the C.-in-C. Bomber Command: 'Your attack this morning had been a great contribution to the day offensive now being fought. It will remain an outstanding example of dash and initiative. I send you and your captains and crews my warmest congratulations and the admiration of the Command.'

Sir Charles Portal, then C.A.S., was also prompted to offer congratulations: 'Convey to the units concerned my warmest congratulations on the splendid operation today. I'm sure that all squadrons realise that besides encouraging the Russians, every daylight attack rubs into the Germans the superiority of our units. You are doing great work.'

Such attacks by small forces might be compared to Commando raids. What the enemy could not know was whether large forces might also be employed. They therefore tied up his defences and created some sense of nervousness along his shores.

Later in the day 226 Squadron with eleven fighter squadrons flew *Circus 32*, one of five flown in the first four days of July by Nos. 18, 21 and 226 Squadrons. The most eventful of these was that of 2 July when 226 suffered badly. With 21 Squadron it set out for Lille power station, could not locate it and so bombed Lille marshalling yards and Merville aerodrome getting direct hits on a hangar and airfield buildings. Stung to reply, along came some 109s which waded into the raiders. The gunner of Z7310 claimed two fighters and Z7305 also of 226 Squadron another. Four of our fighters were lost.

'There had been complications on this raid from the start,' recalled Grp. Capt. Kennedy. 'I was No. 3 to the leader, Wg. Cdr. Butler, and

I wasn't the best formation flier then. We attacked the railway junction at Lille. I think the fighter controller had boobed because we sailed on without top fighter cover. So, before the target, and over it and on the way out, we were under continual attack. We could even see 109s hurtling between the boxes of bombers. A 109 came in and because of our loose formation, picked off V6365. A Spit. then got him. Sgt. Henshell was wounded, a bullet passing through his neck. His navigator requested a course to Manston and started to fly the aircraft. I could see something was wrong as Z7310 danced up and down in unskilled hands. Henshell was helping between bouts of unconsciousness. At one time the aircraft fell behind and the gunner shot down a 109. They reached Manston but only one flap would come down and the aircraft nearly cartwheeled on landing. Henshell was awarded an immediate D.F.M. After recovery he joined 90 Squadron but was killed. For myself I could really see the value of formation flying—I became the best formation flier!'

Then followed raids bearing resemblance to anti-shipping operations, and which are mentioned in Chapter 8. One was a diversion to an attack by Halifaxes on Kiel in support of the intended daylight offensive by heavies against Germany.

The existing situation at sea made it imperative that *Scharnhorst* and *Gneisenau* be kept immobilised at Brest. Satisfactory attacks at night were rarely possible: searchlights and smoke screens made it difficult to identify the ships; therefore it had been decided in June to mount a large-scale daylight raid relying on precision bombing by about 120 aircraft.

Five Spitfire squadrons with long-range tanks fitted so that they could operate in the Brest area were ready by 15 July. Within fifty miles it was believed that there were thirty enemy fighters—109s, 110s, Ju 88s based at Brest/Guipavas, Lanvioc and Morlaix. About 60 Bf 109s were dispersed in the Cherbourg Peninsula and Channel Islands. If the attack could be concentrated it seemed feasible that enemy fighters would be overcome, especially if brought into conflict with the Spitfires, which would be picked up by enemy RDF whose range at 5,000 feet would be 100 miles. At Zero Hour 2 Group Fortresses would deliver a high-level raid, the timing of which needed to be exact. 2 Group Blenheims were to make three *Circus* diversion raids on Cherbourg.

The plan for G.O.O. 52 Operation *Sunrise* was outlined as follows: 120 Wellingtons and all available Manchesters, Stirlings, Halifaxes, Fortresses and Blenheims were to take part. In Phase A there would be a light initial very high-level attack by unescorted Fortresses of 90 Squadron. This alarm raid, it was hoped, would cause the enemy to despatch any fighters at immediate readiness. Phase B of fifteen minutes later was for eighteen Hampdens of 44, 106 and 144 Squadrons escorted by three long-range Spitfire squadrons to ensure that the enemy committed all remaining fighters in an attempt to intercept the raid, whose escorting Spitfires would dispose of the enemy. Unescorted, the main attack would then develop as the enemy aircraft were refuelling, and before reinforcements could arrive from the Cherbourg area. Two squadrons of long-range fighters were to give withdrawal cover over the target area to mop up any German fighters present.

Meanwhile all available 2 Group Blenheims with 11 Group escort would make raids on Cherbourg discouraging enemy fighters from flying to Brest. The first *Circus* was timed for Zero plus ten minutes, the second for Zero plus thirty and the third for Zero plus 75. Fortresses would open the raid attacking at 25,000 feet, or higher, the Blenheims on the diversion from 12,000 feet. The Boeings would withdraw at 20,000 feet minimum to seventy miles from the enemy coast. It was a complex pattern, intended for the first suitable day after 23 July 1941.

As the orders for *Sunrise* were being finally formulated the situation suddenly changed. Late on 21 July *Scharnhorst* sailed from Brest and, following sea trials, put in to La Pallice. *Sunrise* was therefore deprived of a major objective—had there been a leakage of plans?

It was decided to strike fast and on the afternoon of 23 July six Stirlings (three each of 7 and XV Squadrons) took-off for La Rochelle. N6029 did not leave Wyton's circuit for her undercarriage would not retract. Sgt. Jones in LS-F: W7428 attacked Fromentine instead. R-Robert N6038, 15 Squadron's other aircraft, found La Pallice but was set upon by fighters and, badly damaged, had to be ditched fifty miles off Milford Haven. The three crews from 7 Squadron were more fortunate. Flg. Off. D. K. Witt's aircraft bombed the target area dropping three 2,000-lb. A.P. bombs about 100 yards from the battle cruiser before he was attacked by three 109s and dived to sea level to escape. Only one bomb fell from N6037, on to the stern of the ship. Two 109s dived upon the Stirling out of the sun but both were shot down by the rear gunner and were seen in the sea. N6035's load hit an outer jetty, and this aircraft was damaged by flak and fighters. For both squadrons it brought an end to their present phase of day raids.

Battle Order for the 2 Group Blenheim Squadrons on 24 July, the day chosen for the operation, was as follows: Horsham: twelve aircraft at standby, Polebrook: three aircraft at standby, Swanton Morley: 88 Squadron stood down, 105 Squadron ready to leave for Portreath and the Mediterranean, West Raynham: twelve of 114 Squadron and six of 107 Squadron at standby, Wattisham: six aircraft at standby with the remainder on army co-operation exercises, Watton: 21 Squadron on *Channel Stop* and 82 Squadron stood down.

There was feverish activity on many bomber stations as crews were briefed, aircraft loaded and the fuel pumped aboard for the long daylight run. But already the operation had suffered some reeling blows. Ever troublesome, the Avro Manchesters had to be withdrawn at the last moment leaving it to the Hampdens to mount 5 Group's contribution. The removal of *Scharnhorst* to La Pallice brought about another major change. Unescorted, fifteen Halifaxes were to attack her while the Brest raid took place. Wellingtons of Nos. 1 and 3 Groups in vics of three would provide the main part of the force with the diversions going ahead as planned.

At 11.00 hours the engines of three Fortresses burst into life. *Sunrise* was on. Between 11.20 and 11.30 they took-off, and above other stations elements of fifteen other squadrons were forming up. Halifaxes of 35 and 76 Squadron meanwhile left Stanton Harcourt for their lonely, dangerous mission.

The Fortresses made a steady battle climb into the stratosphere and it fell to Wg. Cdr. MacDougall and Sqn. Ldr. Maclaren to open the attack at 14.06 hours, bombing from 30,000 feet in perfect weather with C-Charlie 2,000 feet above them. Despite the claimed accuracy of the Sperry bombsight their loads missed, falling instead on the torpedo station, on the west side of the Rade Abrie quay and the outer corner of the dry dock. Two Bf 109s were seen climbing towards the bombers followed by a further three, but soon all were diverted to easier, more tempting targets. The Hampdens were on the run-in.

Ninety Hampdens and Wellingtons attacked as planned, meeting fierce opposition as a result of which a Hampden and eight Wellingtons were shot down. Twelve enemy fighters were claimed, and seven hits on the *Gneisenau*, *Prinz Eugen* and a large tanker, other bombs falling in the dock area and on barracks. Of the fifteen Halifaxes which were despatched to La Pallice fourteen bombed, five were shot down and nine were damaged, five seriously. Five hits were claimed on *Scharnhorst* which sailed in the evening for Brest with 3,000 tons of water in her.

Circus operations by 2 Group's Blenheims went as planned. First, nine crews of 139 Squadron and three from 18 attacked the whale oil ship *Ole Wegger* in dry dock at Cherbourg. Bombs, however, fell in the south-east part of the town and in the dock area where a warehouse burst into flames. Then came 107 and 226 Squadrons whose bombs fell on Dock 4 causing oily smoke to curl to 1,000 feet. The third diversion by 114 Squadron started more dock fires. The principal reason for these raids had not been achieved since enemy fighters were not attracted to them and the *Ole Wegger* remained untouched. Flak had been intense, 114 Squadron led by Wg. Cdr. Hull facing a veritable barrage which damaged V5875's fin and elevator, and the wings of L8751 and V6391. L9382 flew home with hits in ten places. The day's operations, the largest so far undertaken that year in daylight, also embraced fighter operations over north-east France.

Between mid June and the end of July over 300 bomber sorties had been despatched on *Circuses* and fourteen aircraft lost. They called for considerable fighter effort amounting to over 8,000 sorties and brought the loss of 123 aircraft.[3] *Circuses* were resumed but soon 2 Group's energy was being put into large-scale low-level flying practice for one of the most spectacular operations it ever mounted.

'Operation 77' was special, answering several principal requirements of the current bombing programme. It was to be a deep penetration into Germany to worthwhile targets. It was intended to rouse German fighters and, more important, encourage the enemy to recall others from the Russian front to prevent further incursions.

Objectives for attack had certainly to be worth while. They were indeed, being the power station at Knapsack with the largest steam generators in Europe—output 600,000 kilowatts—and the generating station at Quadrath, output 200,000 kilowatts. Both were near Cologne. Great reliance was placed upon both for German factories. Their destruction would have a serious effect upon the enemy's war machine. Power stations remained, as ever, tempting targets.

Three boxes of six Blenheims each, from Horsham, Watton and West Raynham—54 Blenheims in all—with four Fortresses from Polebrook, were to comprise the force. Westland Whirlwind fighters were to escort the bombers as far as possible—to Doel, ten miles north-west of Antwerp. Three squadrons of long-range Spitfires would cover the bombers' withdrawal from the Dutch coast. Hampdens of 5 Group escorted by fighters of Nos. 11 and 12 Groups would operate diversions.

The Blenheim force was divided into two. Three boxes of six aircraft drawn from Nos. 21 and 82 Squadrons comprised Force 1 which was to bomb Quadrath. Drawn from Nos. 18, 107, 114 and 139 Squadrons Force 2 was to attack Knapsack. Zero Hour for the bombing was finally set as 12.30 hours on 12 August. Wg. Cdr. Kercher was to lead Force 1, Wg. Cdr. Nichol Force 2.

Sixty-seven minutes before Zero a Fortress would bomb De Kooy. At Zero minus sixty, Hampdens would fly a diversion *Circus* over the

---

[3] No. 11 Group Operations Record Book (Appendices) summarises claims and losses from 10 January 1941 to 14 July 1941 in the following tabulation. Claims to enemy fighters are very inflated, but the heavy losses incurred by the fighter forces are clear:

Notes on Circuses	Participants	Enemy casualties			British losses	
		destroyed	probable	damaged	pilots	aircraft
No. 1–11	11 Group	11	12	11	23	31
10.1.41 to	12 Group	—	—	—	1	1
21.5.41	Bombers	1	—	—	1	1
No. 12–32	11 Group	205	81	86	51	65
14.6.41 to	12 Group	5	3	9	4	7
4.7.41	Bombers	4	—	—	7	8
No. 33–48	11 Group	80	33	52	43	55
5.7.41 to	12 Group	4	1	—	1	2
14.7.41	Bombers	1	—	1	2	2
Grand totals		311	130	159	133	172

Pas de Calais, tempting bait. Diversion 3 was a high-level attack by a
Fortress on Emden. Two others providing diversion 4 would bomb
Cologne at Zero Hour. Diversion 5 would be by 226 Squadron, and it
was hoped that 5 Group's Hampdens would fly another *Circus* as the
Blenheims were withdrawing.

Take-off for the Blenheims was set at between 08.55 and 09.30 hours.
Force 1 would cross the coast one mile north-west of Orfordness at
100 feet. No. 2 Force was to rendezvous, then fly to Martlesham from
where the Whirlwinds would then take-off. The second force would then
cross the coast at Orfordness again at 100 feet. Accurate timing was
essential since both forces were to meet at the coast at Zero minus 82.
No. 1 Force would fly in wide vees, No. 2 with its leader ahead of
Box 4 had Nos. 1, 2, 3 on his right and 5 and 6 to his left. Individual
boxes were ordered to maintain close cohesion, but the entire formation
would be well spread but keeping up with the leaders. There would then
be strong fire power for fighters to face and they, it was hoped, would
anyway be attracted to the diversions.

About three miles from the Dutch coast the Whirlwinds were to climb
to deal with any enemy fighters and initially give the Blenheims top
cover as they sped inland. For the latter it was to be low level all the way
at about 180 I.A.S. After attacking, the bombers were ordered to spread
out to obtain dispersal effect from expected fierce defences, but as far as
possible maintain box formation for maximum protection. They could,
of course, use their guns against any worthwhile target in Germany,
and each would have been carrying two 500-lb. G.P. 11 sec. delay
bombs.

Three squadrons of Spitfires—Nos. 66, 152 and 234—amounting to
30 aircraft were to be in position over Walsoorden at maximum
endurance from Zero plus 35 minutes to cover the return. All Blenheims
should be clear of the enemy coast by Zero plus 50 minutes. Fighter
Command was to arrange for a large fighter force to be over Flushing
from Zero plus 41 to afford further cover.

As well as flying a later *Circus* to Le Trait, No. 226 Squadron was to
provide two Blenheims acting as navigating leaders for the long-range
Spitfires and the other fighter force, one operating from Martlesham
the other from Ipswich. Both Blenheims were shot down.

Such was the outline of the exciting operation, and it was carried out
largely as planned, slightly delayed by the weather.

Force 1 left Watton after an elaborate briefing by Wg. Cdr. Kercher
at 09.50, Nos. 21 and 82 Squadrons each despatching nine aircraft. On
the way to the target flak was variously encountered and T2437 of
82 Squadron crashed in flames close to Strijdens, near Moerdyck bridge,
and the crew was killed. The remaining seventeen attacked Quadrath
leaving black and white smoke and seeing debris rise. Some of the
bombs burst among the chimneys. 21 Squadron reported that the centre
of the power station was set on fire.

It was a memorable operation, and to Eric Chandler, a wireless operator/air gunner of 82 Squadron, quite unforgettable:

'At a steady 20 m.p.h. we proceeded along the deserted Bodney–Watton road in "The Green Goddess". We were the flying crews of No. 82 Squadron, and "The Green Goddess", an old 1930 single-decker bus, was the official transport of the aircrews. The road was deserted because, firstly, it was 06.15 hours, and secondly, it was 12 August 1941.

'For well over a week we had been waiting for this day. Today was the day for "the operation of the war". It had to be undertaken at all costs, or so we were told. The phrase "at all costs" was being used by everyone and had almost become a theme song. So far we had been told the target was a power house producing 600,000 kilowatts, and that by putting it out of action we would be doing far more harm to the German War Machine than many heavy raids of the night bombers gutting factories. The Prime Minister was, as always, to follow the operation with keen interest. We seemed to know it all—except where the target was; most of us thought it must be somewhere outside Paris, and that seemed a Hell of a way to go, in daylight, in a Blenheim.

'Jock, our navigator, like myself, had already done a tour of ops. in 1940 and now we were half-way through a second tour and had, in fact, only just returned to Bodney after flying out to and operating from Malta.

' "The Green Goddess" entered the gates of R.A.F. Watton and proceeded to No. 2 Hangar. The whole station seemed alive with people we had never seen before. The main crew room which had been given over to us had a blackboard set up with a map and coloured pins etc. etc. We looked at it in utter disbelief—the target was Cologne in what then seemed the heart of Germany, precisely a place called Quadrath.

'From then on it seemed a mad rush, as always, just before take-off. We were given such information as the time of rendezvous with other squadrons, time check with T.I.M., the times we must be at certain places coming home if we were to expect any help from our fighters. We were told that Bomber Command would carry out daylight diversions to draw off fighters. Our own fighters would meet us on the enemy coast and bring us safely back across the sea—one snag, they could only wait three minutes for us because of their limited fuel. This small point didn't seem to worry anyone because mostly they thought, as I did, that we should be very lucky if we reached the target; the chances of returning seemed very remote.

'In an open lorry we drove out to the aircraft then climbed aboard. The ground crew was even more helpful than usual. Engine start, cockpit drill carried out, we started to taxi out and the ground crew wished us luck with the traditional thumbs up sign. We took off in formation of threes. As usual I watched our number two and three as we all raced across the grass and into the air, just to see they didn't get too close for comfort. We set course at once, having no spare fuel to play with, and commenced hedge-hopping our way to the coast. In a flash we seemed to be going out over the sands and down to the water. For a moment it seemed we must all go in the water, we were so low. Blenheims were everywhere. A great armada, fifty-four of them all hell bent, on the lowest low-level attack in the war so far.

'The sea looked very cold, grey and choppy, but somehow much more friendly than the thought of the three hundred odd miles of enemy territory which we would have to cross at a speed only half as fast as that of the average German fighter.

'In next to no time we seemed to be turning into the estuary of the Scheldt, dashing over the sand dunes and climbing up over trees and walls, but having to look up to the church spire on our right and the windmill tops to our left. So far the only signs of human life I had seen were two men in a fishing boat who looked up, in amazement, or fear, as we roared over them. Not a shot had been fired by the coastal defences. Now we started flying past workers in the fields, nearly all of whom waved to us. On we rushed, all the time telling our pilot what a good job he was doing, and sincerely hoping that he could keep it up since one slip at that height and we would have had it.

'The workers in the fields were not now all waving to us, a sure sign that we were rapidly approaching the frontier. Then there was no waving—the Germans didn't wave, they ran in all directions. This was the first deep daylight penetration of the Fatherland, and they weren't taking any chances. There was no motor transport on any of the roads, in fact the only transport I had seen was several people on cycles. Such animals as horses and cows either heard or sensed us before we arrived, and were already scattering by the time we passed over them.

'Still no sign of the Luftwaffe; it appeared that the stories we had been told of the many diversions arranged by the tactical planning boys at Group were having their effect. "Seven minutes to target," Jock's voice, calm as always, and at the same time following aircraft pulling up and turning away to the other power plant. I was able to pick out various landmarks which we had been told to look for, and knew that despite all the weaving about to miss built-up areas, etc., we were now dead on track.

'"Target to starboard"—Jock's voice sounded excited now. Yes, I could see the chimneys of the power station almost coming up out of the ground. All aircraft banked and turned into the attack. We seemed to have missed the turn, throttled back and then banked around to follow well in the rear of all the other aircraft.

'We appeared to be climbing a hill and, as we reached the top, I could see distant spires of Cologne Cathedral. Up again and over the high-tension cables of the Brauweiler Grid system, and over fat condensers we had been told not to try and bomb. Line up now, and with twelve chimneys line up with the aircraft ahead. It seemed to be disappearing into a cloud of smoke. "Bombs gone." One could almost feel the bombs banging open the spring-loaded doors as they left the aircraft.

'We were through the smoke and jets of flak came at us from either side, in bright red streams that seemed they must hit us. It was every man for himself now. Get away from the place and form up again as soon as possible was the order. We were climbing to about 800 feet as the first two Messerschmitts that must have been circling above us came in to attack. We were on our own now as the pilot had, in the excitement of his first attack, forgotten to pull his Plus 9 lb. boost lever which would give us that extra speed which we badly needed. I opened up at a fighter well before he came in range, and to my relief and surprise he almost at once dived away—I can only think he must have been a learner!

'The bombs were now exploding, and must have been fairly rocking the plant, as I could see what appeared to be debris just hanging in the sky. Meanwhile whole sections of buildings seemed to be climbing slowly to meet over what had been a power station with turbines setting up 3,000 revolutions a minute. It was disappointing to find much later that the damage caused was far less than we thought.

'We dived into a gravel pit, up and over slag heaps, derricks, small work buildings to finally catch up with the rest of the formation.

'As we crossed the Dutch border we ran into a storm which made it almost impossible to see through the rain. Next moment we were over a town, or rather, going through it. We were so low that it seemed we must poke a wing into someone's bedroom window. Over a railway station, up the main road, and over a 'drome where enemy planes were taxiing out to take off. We all gave them a nice, long burst of fire to put them off the idea for as long as possible. Open country again, and the feeling we might get home after all.

'Suddenly, up ahead, I could see a lot of dots in the sky, and knew that at last the Messerschmitts had found us, and in force. It appeared they were merely waiting to dive down and cut off our line of retreat. Then we were out over the water again, with heavy naval guns firing at us from either side, and behind. Red flames everywhere, and columns of water sprouting around the aircraft. Down after us came the fighters. I drew a bead on one rapidly approaching from port, but before I could fire he was wagging his wings as if to say "Don't shoot, I'm friend, not foe." I had never been so pleased to see a Spit. in all my life. I take my hat off to them for coming down and joining us in that inferno, even though it was their presence overhead that had allowed all the coastal defences to get ready for our arrival on the scene.

'We were almost out of range of the guns when something hit the aircraft. Three times we felt the jolt. We then noticed that the starboard engine seemed to have lost a lot of power. We started to climb and reform, whilst the fighter boys came in close, giving the thumbs-up sign.

'We made it back to Watton, but as soon as we touched down the starboard engine stopped. It was packed with what looked like little roast chickens but were, of course, the remains of a flock of sea gulls we had run into. It was 13.15 hours.

'Back at No. 2 Hangar we were almost dragged off the lorry and hurtled into de-briefing. The reason was that the Press had managed to get on to the operation and wanted stories and photos. We were far too tired to care, and only interested in getting aboard "The Green Goddess" and reaching the Mess at Bodney. Just as I was leaving I saw that they had cornered Bill Edrich but felt he was well used to dealing with them. Sure enough the papers were full of it next day with lines like: "Once again England puts its faith in Bill Edrich, who in the past led them to victory on the cricket field, and leads them again in the all-out fight for freedom."

'In all, Group lost twelve aircraft in this effort, and we considered this pretty good in view of the fact that between 12 March and 14 July we had lost sixty-eight Blenheims on low-level attacks. It was hazardous enough to fly low without the enemy to contend with.'

The attack had been highly successful and ferocious. 107 Squadron reported hits between rows of chimneys and clouds of heavy, black smoke. So intense was the flak that every machine in the squadron was hit, although all returned. 139 Squadron reported a large flash at the target which glowed red and was well alight. Bombs from one aircraft burst at the foot of a row of chimneys. At the target V5725 was hit in the wing and turned away to crash. Another lagged on return and was not seen again, and a third crashed in the sea.

No. 18 Squadron claimed bursts near the eastern chimneys. The power house was enveloped in light-brown smoke, and steam obscured the bomb bursts. There were four fires as the squadron swept over the power plant, machine guns blazing. Before the attack they had lost V6437 when it hit high-tension wires which cut the tail from the aircraft. The leader, in V6497, was not seen after the attack and V6423 disappeared without trace. Coming out from the coast one aircraft inconclusively engaged a Ju 88. 114 Squadron placed its bombs between rows of chimneys, and scored hits on coolers. Steam, fires and smoke followed and debris was thrown high. Two Bf 109s attacked the squadron near Flushing, but all survived. Z7281 however was lost to flak.

What of the fighters? The Whirlwinds of 263 Squadron had positioned themselves with six aircraft between the two large formations and six up-sun of them on the outward sea-level run. The Dutch coast was crossed at 10.43 and the fighters climbed to 1,000 feet weaving above the bombers. At 10.52 at the limit of their range they turned for home four miles N.E. of Antwerp following the course of the Scheldt, six very low and six at 500 feet. Near Walcheren they saw six barges, almost certainly flak barges, and beat them up sinking two. Flt. Lt. Pough in P7041 attacked another off Walcheren. On the way out Flg. Off. Steen had seen some soldiers run out of a house with rifles, and marked the spot on his map saying to himself, 'I'll deal with you later when I've more time.' On the return he and Sgt. King searched diligently for the spot, but were unable to find it. On landing Sgt. Jowatt's machine P6999 was found to have been hit towards the tail by an explosive shell, and two others had machine-gun holes in them from the flak between Vlisingland and Neuzen.

Squadrons that met the bombers had a hectic running battle with the enemy. Very busily engaged was 19 Squadron which left Ipswich at 11.30 flying low with 66 above. At the head of them all was one of 226 Squadron's Blenheims. They patrolled the Walcheren area in fours soon after noon. Several 109s appeared and the chase was on at low level in and out of cloud. Plt. Off. Cox of 19 Squadron in P8241 claimed a 109 as a probable before he was attacked by two more. The first dived on him and he tried to get on the second one's tail giving it two 2-second bursts from 150 yards. Glycol spurted then the 109 dived vertically. Cox came out of cloud at 500 feet without seeing the 109 again. Sqn. Ldr. Wilson gave a squirt at a fighter, chased it into cloud, and managed a 3-second inconclusive burst.

No. 234 Squadron saw a navigating Blenheim (Z7352 Flt. Lt. Young) shot down and a Spitfire of 152 Squadron spiral into the sea hit by fire from a flak group. Their leader damaged a Ju 88 night-fighter and Plt. Off. Masters a 109E.

Claims and counter-claims during the fighting make assessment of the true picture difficult. Oblt. Eichhoff of II/J.G.26 shot down a Blenheim in the sea at 12.00 hours, at the same time as Uffz. Zick of I/JG1 claimed one. Marineflak claimed another, and Flakgr. Rotterdam one. A Spitfire was shot down by a 109F. Twenty-five miles west of West Capelle fighters destroyed a Blenheim over the sea and another off Zouteland around noon. 18, 21 and 139 Squadrons each lost a machine in the sea.

Bomber diversions were despatched as planned. The first 90 Squadron Fortress left at 09.00. Sgt. Wood had low power and aborted leaving three to attack De Kooy, Cologne and Emden as planned. Plt. Off. Sturmey claimed a hit on De Kooy aerodrome, Plt. Off. Taylor dropped bombs on Emden and Plt. Off. Wayman—finding Cologne cloud-clad—bombed on dead reckoning.

The other 2 Group raid of the day was by 226 Squadron, mounted from Manston. Le Trait was the target and four bombed it getting hits on a ship and the slipway.

(Forces involved in the day's operations are listed in Appendix 6. See also Map 11.)

Two days after the Cologne raid *Circuses* were resumed with raids on Boulogne, Lille and Marquise shell factory. On 18th two were directed against Gosnay and Hazebrouck. It was during the former that, on the way, a box containing a metal leg for Wg. Cdr. Douglas Bader was dropped from R3843: F of 18 Squadron crewed by Sgt. Nickelson, Sgt. Meadows and Sgt. Pearson. All of the aircraft of 18 Squadron on the raid were seriously damaged by flak on the run-in and it was too cloudy to bomb Gosnay power station. Ten Bf 109s were claimed by fighters of the fifteen supporting fighter squadrons—Nos. 41, 72, 92, 306, 308, 315, 403, 452, 485, 602, 603, 609, 610, 611 and 616 all of which were frequently engaged on *Circuses*—for the loss of four pilots.

Anti-shipping operations were still busily occupying the Group but by the end of August nine more bombing raids were carried out.

The last but one shipping operation of the month was mounted the evening of 28th. It was another large assault on Rotterdam, Operation 523. Watton, Wattisham and Swanton Morley each despatched six aircraft in boxes of six flying low level astern. They picked up an escort of two long-range Spitfire Squadrons Nos. 19 and 152 from Coltishall, flew to four miles south of Oostvoorm then turned to a point five miles south of Waalhaven. Here the three boxes turned simultaneously to port so that they swept across the docks at roof-top height line abreast, with the leading box then on the east side and the rear to the west. Their targets were the largest ships seen. As the boxes turned the fighters climbed to 1,500 feet to give top cover. After the attack the bombers regrouped and crossed the enemy coast midway between the Hook and The Hague and received extra fighter cover, twelve Spitfires of 266 Squadron.

It was a costly operation. 21 Squadron scored hits on a 3,000-tonner, a 2,000-tonner and the dock buildings but lost 4 Blenheims. Three crews of 110 Squadron with two of 226 attacked from twenty feet. Sgt. Jenkins scored a hit on a red ship of about 8,000 tons leaving it blazing. Wg. Cdr. Cree's machine was hit several times, and he saw another Blenheim fly so low it crashed into a warehouse in the north-west corner of Masshaven starting a large fire. 226 Squadron had a bad start since F Freddy had crashed on take-off. Its other two crews pressed home their attack but Z7289: R was too low and it crashed into the docks. Flt. Lt. Namias in Z7292: J bounced a bomb from the dockside under the stern of a 10,000-ton ship which blew up. 88 Squadron making its first attack on Rotterdam lost two aircraft, but V6032 attacked a 5,000-tonner. V6445 attacked and missed a 4,000-ton ship and was then intercepted by three Bf 109s of 6/JG53 which severely damaged it. Twelve Blenheims were missing, two of 21 Squadron claimed by Lt. Müller of 6/JG53, which unit also claimed two Spitfires.

Another busy day was 31 August. Operations began when six crews of 110 Squadron set off for distant Lannion airfield. Hits were scored on the runway, one aircraft having a lucky escape when it was struck by a bomb from another Blenheim. This was a special form of *Circus* operation known by 10 Group as *Gudgeon 4*. It was flown from Portreath, five Spitfire squadrons participating. Top withdrawal cover was given by Whirlwinds of 263 Squadron at 11,000 feet and Spitfires of 130 Squadron at 14,000 feet and 313 Squadron at 25,000 feet. Whirlwinds infrequently participated in such raids. Next, six Blenheims of 21 and

82 Squadrons aiming for St. Omer airfield had to settle for the railway near Audricq. Nearly an hour later a further twelve crews from 18 and 114 Squadrons found Lille/Sequedin also cloud-clad and bombed a nearby railway. In the late afternoon 139 Squadron operated from Manston against Le Trait shipyards, getting hits on sheds and ships.

Radar in the Pas de Calais was by now much improved. German fighters were often in position very high over St. Omer, Lille etc., waiting to ambush the *Circuses* whilst making sure they had height and sun advantages. With endurance superiority over our Spitfires the Bf 109s were in a strong position to challenge the offenders. To achieve greater tactical advantage the Jadgeschwader moved around on bases in the Lille, Amiens, Abbeville, Bruges and St. Omer areas.

Between 14 June and 3 September Fighter Command claimed 437 German fighters destroyed and 182 probables, lost 194 pilots and covered about 520 bomber sorties. Ten bombers had been lost to flak, four to fighters. These claims were inflated and post-war research revealed 128 German fighters destroyed and 76 damaged over France and the Low Countries—and not all during *Circuses*.

To Air Vice-Marshal T. L. Mallory the small Blenheim bomb load seemed quite insufficient. He wanted to see the Stirling and Hampden used more often, but on such occasions enemy fighters had merely pecked at our fighters. His contention had been that 5% of heavy bomber sorties should be on *Circuses*. Against this the 2 Group commander expressed preference for free-gun fighters considering that fixed-gun escorts were at a disadvantage when intercepted. The Chief of Air Staff, Air Chief Marshal Portal, did not agree. He felt that heavier fighters would be at a performance disadvantage. One thing was obvious, there must soon be a Blenheim replacement. In the meantime *Circuses* continued to the accepted pattern.

Sixteen day raids were despatched against land targets during September. The first effective one took place on 4th when 18 Squadron bombed the ammonia plant at Mazingarbe. Flak and fighters penetrated to the bombers shooting down Sgt. Adams and crew in Z7296: P, but six hits were claimed on the factory. Later that day six crews of 114 Squadron with a Spitfire and Whirlwind escort went after a whale oil ship at Cherbourg. It shifted before they arrived leaving them the docks to bomb. The Whirlwinds took up position astern in lines of fours 250 yards to each side of the bombers and 500 feet above. Just as the bombers were attacking Flg. Off. Steen saw a 109F dive upon them, quickly gave it a burst and watched it fall away. More 109s then tried for the bombers and the Whirlwinds drove them off losing Sgt. Buckwell (in P7042) who came down in the sea five miles from Cherbourg. The withdrawal force, Nos. 118, 234, 501 and the Exeter Polish Squadrons, then brought them safely home.

The main operation on 18th was by ten aircraft of 139 Squadron despatched to the Grand Quevilly power station near Rouen which received three hits. Fire was exchanged with fighters and V6257 was hit. After the bombing 452 Squadron engaged 109s shooting down two 109Fs and two 109Es but lost four of its own aircraft. Flak was usually met, its accuracy varying. The batteries at Le Havre and Gravelines were reckoned by 2 Group crews to be the most dangerous. On one sortie Shaw Kennedy kept back one bomb for the Gravelines shooters. All the squadron knew what was afoot and when his bomb scored a direct hit on the gun position, and the battery stopped firing, a surge of glee ran through the formation!

To add to the defender's confusion a few *Circuses* were now being flown as divided efforts. The 100th, flown on 20th, was in three parts. Targets were set in Rouen and Hazebrouck, while Hampdens of 5 Group bombed Mazingarbe. Next day 452 Squadron was part of the force ordered to cover *Circus 101*. It missed the bombers, then proceeded to Desfres where in a fight Sqn. Ldr. Finucane flying AB852 laid claim to two 109s.

Circus 103 was flown in two parts on 27th; one force comprising twelve Blenheims of 114 Squadron bombed Mazingarbe, and the Hornchurch Wing gave close support to 110 and 226 Squadrons bombing Amiens. Enemy fighters were engaged and two shot down by 54 Squadron, one of them by Flt. Lt. Charles in P8797. He then turned on another radial-engined aircraft which he could not identify for sure. Afterwards he filed a report which intelligence officers were quick to seize upon. He had encountered a Fw 190 radial-engined fighter, the introduction of which was to completely alter the pattern of fighting by day over France. Several of these fighters had been mis-reported over France during September as Bloch 151s, but for some time their existence in the fight was discounted. During the same operation Z5005 of 402 Squadron had been shot down but two other Hurricane pilots, Sqn. Ldr. Corbett in BD765 and Sgt. Macluski in Z3237, shared a 109. Hornchurch Wing had provided close cover, Biggin Hill Wing high cover. Between them the fighters, five of which were lost, claimed seven of the enemy, but none of them the stranger.

Autumn weather was closing in. Unless visibility was good, and clouds were few, *Circuses* were impossible to mount. There were eight in October. The largest was a very successful attack by 24 aircraft on Boulogne on 12th. Next day during a *Circus* to Arques, camera-gun shots of a Fw 190 were obtained by a Spitfire of 129 Squadron, proof that it was in action. Two days later Le Havre was bombed and hits scored on 10,000- and 12,000-ton ships. The formation started its bomb run from eight miles out. Wg. Cdr. Butler led, to the consternation of the formation, at a constant speed and height in a clear blue sky. 'Any minute now,' thought the crews—and sure enough the heavy flak was deadly accurate. Two of Butler's box were shot out of the sky, Plt. Off. Hudson's aircraft being finished off by fighters which swarmed in. Acting as high cover, 118 Squadron detached three aircraft to the

2. The Philips factory at Eindhoven under attack, as seen from a Ventura of
21 Squadron

33. Incendiaries from Venturas burst on the Philips works on 6.12.42

34. Part of the main plant at Philips severely damaged as a result of the raid on 6.12.42

To our valiant allied "intruder"
Wing Commander J. Pelly Fry,
at the occasion of his first
postwar reconnaissance to
Eindhoven, after his wartime bombing mission.
No hard feelings!
6.12.'42 - 24.9.'53

35. Grp. Capt. J. E. Pelly-Fry, Boston leader on the Philips raid, talks to Mr. Otten, Chairman of Philips, some years after the war. 'No hard feelings!' 24.9.53

36. A Boeing Fortress 1 of 90 Squadron about to take-off from Polebrook

37. Fortress 1 AN532: WP-J of 90 Squadron which made 9 sorties during its operational career with 2 Group

bombers' aid and destroyed two Bf 109Fs and damaged one. No. 129 Squadron flying with the Middle Wallop Wing destroyed two more. Some of the aircraft in Kennedy's box were turned on to their sides by flak. All were hit. Kennedy's aircraft, V6510, collected 34 flak holes and he never flew her again. After bombing, the Blenheims scampered home at deck level. The lesson harshly taught was 'develop careful approach. techniques'.

Only two *Circuses* were mounted in November, against Lannion and the railway at Lille. With the Boston becoming available it had been decided to withdraw the Blenheim from *Circuses*. The year's 110 *Circuses* were reviewed and seven main conclusions drawn. The day-fighter was still superior to the bomber, although the untried Mosquito was about to join the Group. A self-defending bomber formation could not protect itself effectively. Fighter escort operations were very complex to mount, current fighters lacking endurance. Day bomber operations called for special training and equipment. British resources were insufficient for the mounting of heavy and effective day and night campaigns—and night bombing was very inaccurate. Operation *Circus* had not enticed the Luftwaffe on terms favourable to us.

One aspect of operations needed more than a glance. On 27 November No. 607 Squadron went into action flying Hurricane fighter-bombers to attack a convoy off St. Valery. They sank a motor vessel and two escorts and the Spitfire escort destroyed two Bf 109s. It could therefore be seen that a fighter-bomber, cheaper and safer to operate, could achieve what a medium bomber had hitherto been called upon to do. Upon reflection the day's operations—costly even so for, in a second operation, three Hurribombers were lost—sounded the knell for the medium bomber, although this was some time away. The Hurribomber, originally intended to drop bombs on enemy bombers, had proven so effective during trials that the two squadrons, Nos. 402 and 607, took over 2 Group's *Roadstead* shipping commitment in the Ostend–Dieppe area in October.

One more special operation remained to be flown in 1941. A Commando raid, Operation *Archery*, in which all three Services participated, was planned for late December. Hitler currently feared an invasion of Norway to halt iron-ore supplies from Sweden. A raid on the Norwegian islands would worry and mislead the Germans whilst boosting Norwegian morale. The Army and Navy would be in Norwegian waters for about seven hours, the length of daylight in the latitude chosen. Vaagsö, an island off the Norwegian coast between Bergen and Trondheim, was the chosen target, and a diversion against Vestfiord was planned.

Intelligence estimates gave enemy strength in the area as 23 bombers and 22 Bf 109s. Most were at Stavanger, but there were others at Herdla, near Trondheim, and at Voss. If fighter reinforcements went to Vaagsö they would need to come from at least one of these two bases, probably

G

Herdla. Four Beaufighters flying from Sumburgh would provide the only cover for the Vaagsö party.

The job for 2 Group was to bomb Herdla, Stavanger/Sola and perhaps coastal targets and shipping and thereby ground or draw off enemy fighters. Herdla on a small rocky island had only wooden runways—highly vulnerable. As the naval party was going ashore at Vaagsö/Mallo some cover might be given from smoke bombs. The operation was set for 26 December, proximity of Christmas improving the surprise.

A slight delay occurred and the raid took place on 27 December. Thirteen Blenheims of 114 Squadron led by Wg. Cdr. Jenkins left Lossiemouth for this, the first Army-Navy-Air Force combined assault. Just before Herdla was reached two Bf 109s shadowed the Blenheims, but made no attack. The bombers roared in very low, getting hits on the runways and dispersals in a wood. They scored a direct hit on a taxiing 109 and faced inaccurate heavy flak and tracer fire. As they ran over the field Sgt. Wood in H: Z7500 careered into V6227: Z flown by Sgt. Fisher. Both aircraft crashed into the water.

No. 110 Squadron's diversion attack on shipping between Obrestad and Flekke Fiord was more costly. Six crews operated from Lossiemouth and found, off Egero, a single ship upon which they claimed hits. One aircraft caught in slipstream hit the water but miraculously survived. They then came across a convoy but Bf 109s were by then ready to pounce. Guns on the ships destroyed a Blenheim and fighters another. A further machine was lost without trace.

Thus ended the main battles of 1941. Soon there would be important advances in tactics and equipment, for 1942 would bring major changes to revitalise 2 Group's war. But before proceeding to these changes the story of the high fliers in 2 Group needs to be told.

Chapter 10
Cloud, Cold and Contrails

On Easter Monday, 1941, a new shape appeared over Britain. It was a Boeing Flying Fortress. In the hands of Major Walsh, U.S.A.A.C., it flew from America to Ayr in record time, 8 hours 26 minutes. On 30 April Walsh brought AN521 into Watton, and a new phase in the air war was born.

The Fortress, with its turbo-supercharged engines for high flying, was conceived around American needs for a long-range bomber for Pacific operations. The prototype flew in July 1935. Thirty-eight B-17C Fortresses followed, differing from earlier aircraft in their armament. Twenty of these were offered to the British Purchasing Commission, quickly snapped up and refurbished. At first the Americans suggested they be used for training until superior versions were available, but they soon became anxious to obtain experience of Fortress operations over Europe. A number of Americans came to Watton for first-hand knowledge of Fortress operations.

British interest centred on the use of the Fortress as a very high-flying bomber bringing a new tactical slant to our offensive. Although lacking power-operated turrets it seemed fairly well defended with one or two .30 in. nose guns, five .50 in. guns (two in waist positions, two in a ventral cupola and one in the dorsal position). On official tests it reached 325 m.p.h. at 28,000–30,000 feet and cruised at 230 m.p.h. at 30,000 feet where it should be immune to enemy fighters. It is said that 90 Squadron later pushed the machine to 352 m.p.h. T.A.S. at 34,000 feet. Radius of action, with four 1,100-lb. demolition bombs, was about 450 miles. Unfortunately only American bombs could be carried.

A few local flights presaged the reformation of 90 Squadron on 7 May in 2 Group under Wg. Cdr. J. MacDougall. The intention had first been to re-arm 21 Squadron with Fortresses, but this meant taking a front-line squadron off operations when it was sorely needed. Hence the 'new' squadron formed to use them.

Fortresses were far more complicated than other 2 Group types. Their problems were not initially realised and solving was made difficult by the small number received. With built-in ash trays, carpeted floors, padded walls and fitted Thermos flasks in typical American style, they were soon known as 'Gentlemen's aircraft'.

Before 90 Squadron officially formed Fortress AN521 was flying, with Plt. Off. Roake at the controls. On 5 May the first crew was posted in from Marham. These men had been hand-picked for they needed to be exceptionally fit for high altitude operations. Age limit was set at 24 years but this was not adhered to. All needed to be experienced, and each had to pass a four-hour oxygen test at a simulated 35,000 feet.

AN521 went to Burtonwood for modifications on 7 May and AN534 arrived giving the squadron its first machine. Next day MacDougall undertook conversion training. The following day saw the arrival of crews from a variety of Bomber Command squadrons, and they were briefed.

They were told that the Fortresses would rely on speed and height to avoid trouble. Enemy fighters would be at a disadvantage and less manoeuvrable at high altitudes. Crew would number seven—two pilots, an observer/navigator, radio operator, radio operator/air gunner and two more gunners. They would wear electrically heated clothing, put on in two stages to avoid sweating as the aircraft climbed, to counter the extreme cold which would be as low as $-50°$ Centigrade. Ample spare oxygen bottles would be carried, but crews might be affected by the strain of high-level operations leading to exaggerated hope—even despair. For this reason they would fly only twice a week, a select band in short supply.

Shortage of ground crews was chronic—indeed there were at this time none with B-17 experience. It was clear that it would be advisable to give the Fortress squadron their own airfield—but where? Circuits were flown from Massingham, but it was not ideal.

AN529 arrived on 11 May and now 90 Squadron had two aircraft. Next day the squadron was told to operate from Bodney whilst keeping crews at Watton. Both Fortresses flew in but the airfield surface undulated too much for such large aircraft. The Wing Commander went to Huntingdon to report on it. Circuits followed at Bodney all next day with Capt. Connally, U.S.A.A.C., converting pilots. The A.O.C. and Grp. Capt. Elworthy arrived at Watton to inspect the aircraft, then a conference decided they should be moved to Massingham, not entirely suitable. With them when they moved on 15 May went Franklyn Joseph, an expert on the specially accurate Sperry 01 bombsight with which the aircraft were equipped. Boeing representatives also went along, among them the engineer Crawford.

King George VI and his family were particularly interested when they looked over a Fortress at Abingdon on 23 May, by which time the squadron was making dummy bombing runs to see for itself just how good this bombsight was that could supposedly 'place a bomb in a pickle barrel' from some staggering height. On 25 May squadron strength comprised AN521, 523, 527, 529 and 534. Four crews had converted by 26th.

A new airfield was now complete at Polebrook, near Peterborough.

Wg. Cdr. MacDougall took a look at it from the air. The five Americans with the squadron were meanwhile giving great help at Massingham, and at Raynham where the Fortresses went for overhaul.

4 June was one of the first hot days of the year. In brilliant sunshine MacDougall took a Fortress to 38,000 feet, which he reached in forty minutes. He was then still climbing at 500 f.p.m. But the crew were feeling the effects of the extreme altitude, and some of the equipment was clearly imperfect. A conference at Farnborough followed where the radio gear, intercom and oxygen equipment came under scrutiny.

On 6 June Winston Churchill came to see things for himself, with Sir Richard Peirse, Sholto Douglas, the A.O.C. 2 Group and General Royce of the U.S.A.A.C. Walsh and Connally gave a flying demonstration, but the Americans urged caution when the question of flying the aircraft operationally was mooted. The British, with years of wartime flying behind them, considered themselves better able to judge this aspect, and felt that operations were now feasible.

Height tests, dummy bombing runs and air firing against a drogue towed over the Wash by the squadron's Blenheim were now taking place. When the weather allowed, Fortresses climbed to around 32,000 feet giving crews a taste of things to come and showing up faults in equipment. Oil leaks were already a nuisance and were to continue to be. On 21 June practice bombing began on Watton's range, Stanford Warren.

At 14.30 hours on the afternoon on 22 June Flg. Off. Hawley and crew set off in AN521 on a height test. They headed north and soon telltale white contrails streamed behind each engine. It was a stormy afternoon and at 18.00 hours news broke that the aircraft had crashed near Catterick Bridge. What had happened was later related by Flt. Lt. Steward, A.F.C., a Farnborough medical officer who was the only survivor of the accident. At 33,000 feet the Fortress entered cumulus cloud encountering heavy ice accretion and hailstones of exceptional size. Some, large as golf balls, entered the aircraft through the open side gun ports. The pilot lost control, the machine went into a dive, turned into a spin then hurtled down in a terminal velocity dive. At 25,000 feet the port wing was wrenched off, then the fuselage broke in two. Excessive G pinned the crew down, although one of the two medical officers aboard was hurled out. He lacked sufficient oxygen even to pull his ripcord. The tail unit fell slower than the rest, but the gunners were overcome by lack of oxygen. Steward forced himself from the wreckage at 12,000 feet and lived to tell the tale.

Already it was abundantly clear Fortress operations would bring serious problems. Apart from satisfactory supply of oxygen for long periods which, it was surmised, brought physiological problems anyway, there was the intense cold, increased in its effects by having open gun ports. Additionally there was decompression sickness, or bends, bringing a variety of painful symptoms. For these two reasons two doctors from the Institute of Aviation Medicine frequently flew with the crews noting the effects of altitude, checking oxygen equipment and masks, seeing the effects of the low temperatures.

On 23 June orders came for two Fortresses, AN519 and '526, to go to Burtonwood for a new modification. Long-range tanks were fitted and the two machines returned to Massingham. Two crews were then briefed to take Sir Stafford Cripps and party to Archangel to discuss British aid to Russia. This, on the face of it, seems an amazing idea, for the discomfort of the passengers would have been exceptional. Mercifully for all concerned the intention was dropped as suddenly as it had arisen.

A final squadron move was decided upon—Polebrook had the ideal surface and facilities for the squadron and presented it with a runway superior to the grass fields so far used. Thus, between 27 and 29 June, the squadron moved yet again.

Smaller bombing targets were now in use and at Ashton Range a pyramid target twenty yards square and thirty feet high was set up for practice with the Mk. 01 Sperry sight. Bombing errors were averaging 150 yards from 10,000 feet. But even at this relatively low altitude there were few days when practice could be undertaken due to clouds.

Late on 3 July AN528 was destroyed by fire, only five days after her arrival on 90 Squadron. Operations near, the machine had been earmarked for use when engine troubles occurred. Late working by the ground crew rectified them and at 23.15 hours the offending engine was run for a final test. It burst into flames and soon the aircraft was gutted leaving only the tail intact.

In better weather more height tests took place. On one bombing practice the error was cut to 95 yards. A height of 34,200 feet had been reached after $1\frac{1}{2}$ hours and all the guns fired satisfactorily at 32,000 feet, where gunners reported easy handling. On 6 July the bombing error fell to 78 yards in a drop from 20,000 feet. All was set for operations to begin.

Throughout 7 July three aircraft (AN519, 526, 529) were prepared and crews fitted out with their special clothing. At 13.00 hours on 8 July briefing began. The chosen target was the centre of the submarine building dock at Wilhelmshaven. Three aircraft in open formation were to bomb from 27,000 feet then climb to 31,000–32,000 feet for their getaway.

Engines burst into life around 15.00 hours. The chosen machines rolled, Wg. Cdr. MacDougall leading in AN526 taking with him Sgt. Wood, Flg. Off. Skelton, Flg. Off. Barnes, Sgt. Imrie, Sgt. Danby and Sgt. Clifford. Next away was AN519 piloted by Sqn. Ldr. Maclaren whose crew was Plt. Off. Wayman, Plt. Off. Boast, Sgt. Pegg, Sgt. Neal, Sgt. Street and Sgt. Jones. Last to go was Plt. Off. Mathieson in AN529 with Sgt. Sleath, Sgt. Lewis, Sgt. Davies, Sgt. James, Sgt. Wills and Sgt. Allen.

'C' and 'G' reached Wilhelmshaven shortly before 16.50 hours and in the next ten minutes delivered their attacks between 28,000 and 30,000 feet. Four bombs fell from 'G', but 'C' had two hang-ups and tried unsuccessfully to drop them on the Frisians. Hits were recorded 250 yards west of the Bauhafen at Wilhelmshaven and others at 150 yards' interval to the south-east. G's astrodome froze up at 18,000 feet making fire control, if needed, impossible. In any case her guns and mountings were frozen too. It was fortunate that only two Bf 109s were seen after the attack, some 2,000 feet below the raiders and west of Terschelling. Both fighters closed on the starboard beam of 'G' to about 800 yards when one seemed to enter an involuntary spin. The second followed it down and no fire was opened.

Sqn. Ldr. Maclaren encountered engine trouble at 20,000 feet whilst climbing en route as well as having oil leaks from all four engines. At 27,000 feet oil had frozen one inch thick on the tailplane. As oil pressure was falling Maclaren decided to bomb the Frisians instead. He ran up on Norderney at 16.45, but his bombs fell on the sands 500 yards from the town. He then encountered lateral flutter due to oil freezing on the tailplane. It built up to seven inches and caused considerable vibration. All propellers were feathered in turn but they had no effect upon the situation which improved only after the aircraft had descended to 5,000 feet for the journey home.

In the next few days an electromagnetic intercom system came into use for trials, whilst the weather prohibited more sorties. On 14 July crews reported for operations only to find the weather unsuitable. AN530 made a flight to 38,000 feet on 21st testing new oxygen equipment. The squadron accepted a service ceiling of 36,000 feet, but physiological problems meant that this height could rarely be contemplated for operations. There were range limitations too, since much fuel was consumed on the battle climb although climb performance which took the bomber to 30,000 feet in about 45 minutes was good. Some attacks on Berlin from 35,000 feet were planned but never executed. To achieve such range additional fuel tanks were to replace two bombs cutting the offensive load to 2,200 lb.

At 06.30 hours on 23rd July three crews were briefed for operations with Berlin and Kiel as targets, the former being the alternative if fuel state permitted. Macdougall, Mathieson and Maclaren took off at 09.00. Soon they met huge cumulus clouds and thundery conditions. Maclaren turned back sixty miles from the Danish coast unable to keep up. For 58 miles across Denmark the others left contrails and decided it wise to abort. They brought back their bombs which were American and in short supply. Small loads and high flights led to the well-known R.A.F. jingle of later years: 'Forty thousand Fortresses at forty thousand feet, but they only had a teeny-weeny bomb!'

Next day, as related in Chapter 9, there was a large-scale attack on Brest. Three Fortresses opened the operation at 14.08. Hamburg and Emden were set as targets on 26th, but Sgt. Wood returned after encountering thunderstorms over the North Sea. Flt. Lt. Mathieson in

AN530 bombed Emden from 32,000 feet despite severe icing and storm clouds topping 30,000 feet, but had to land, when his engines gave trouble, at Horsham. It had rained all day at Polebrook, an unpleasant reception for the new C.O. of the squadron, Wg. Cdr. P. F. Webster, D.S.O., D.F.C., ex-21 Squadron, who arrived at lunch-time.

The second flying accident befell shortly after 17.00 hours on 28 July. AN534 departed on a high-altitude test and encountered severe turbulence. It crashed at Wilbarston, Northants, after losing the starboard wing when the pilot attempted recovery.

Two aircraft were detailed for operations on 2 August flown by Sqn. Ldr. Mathieson and Plt. Off. Sturmey. The target was Kiel. Due to a misunderstanding Sturmey formated with a training aircraft and, after finding his error, landed. He was later despatched to bomb Emden. Mathieson successfully bombed his primary without interference but as Sturmey approached Emden cloud was encountered so the target was switched to Borkum, bombed through a cloud gap. Twenty miles N.W. of Texel two Bf 109Fs attacked the bomber and although it was hit in several places damage was not serious and the crew were uninjured. Defensive fire was seen to enter the engine of a fighter.

The next operation came on 6th when Mathieson and Sturmey again set off this time to bomb *Scharnhorst* and *Gneisenau* in Brest. Mathieson's bombsight froze over and bombs were jettisoned in the dock area. Sturmey attacked from 32,000 feet placing his load in the Rade Abrie.

On 12th four aircraft were detailed to provide high-altitude diversions to 2 Group's raid on Cologne's power stations. Sturmey dropped his bombs on the airfield at De Kooy, but it was too cloudy to see the results. Sgt. Wood set off to bomb Cologne. Over Oxford he abandoned the mission due to a leaking exhaust pipe which caused a supercharger to fail. Plt. Off. Wayman reached Cologne bombing from 36,000 feet in cloudy conditions. Cloud also upset the aim from Plt. Off. Taylor's aircraft, Emden being his target. Pleased with the Group's effort on the preceding day Sir Richard Peirse and the A.O.C. interviewed crews of the Fortresses and some of the Blenheims which flew to Polebrook.

Effort was spread on 16th with two aircraft taking off for Düsseldorf, two for Brest. Because of the weather the Düsseldorf raids were abandoned, but 'J' and 'D' made Brest. 'J' bombed successfully from 35,000 feet, the only opposition being slight inaccurate flak. 'D' ran in at 32,000 feet, then serious trouble followed. Seven enemy fighters swept in to attack making the highest interception yet known. The dorsal gun was out of action and enemy attacks soon wounded the radio operator. Attacks were persistent and the Fortress was badly shot up. As he unfortunately lost height, Plt. Off. Sturmey took violent evasive action. Attacks continued down to 6,000 feet. Assistance by R.A.F. fighters was impossible for the fight was fought too far out to sea. Due to the damage and the fact that some of the crew were wounded Sturmey decided to land the crippled aircraft at Roborough airfield near

Plymouth. In so doing he overshot and the Fortress burst into flames. Sgts. Needle, Ambrose and Weil were killed in the engagement and Flt. Sgt. Goldsmith was seriously wounded. The engagement showed how vulnerable the aircraft was to fighter attack, and that its high-altitude capability did not give immunity.

Three days later Sgt. Wood and Plt. Off. Weyman flew at 35,000 feet to make the planned attack on Düsseldorf. It was so cold that most of the guns froze up in one aircraft. The other was streaming give-away contrails so again the mission was abandoned. When on 21st another try was made Sqn. Ldr. Mathieson had to abort over Flushing for once more the guns were frozen and contrails appeared. Before August was out four more sorties were attempted, only one successfully when Sgt. Wood bombed Kiel.

Sqn. Ldr. Mathieson took Mr. Vose of the Sperry Company as his bomb aimer on 2 September when Bremen was the target. There was heavy flak and bombs fell wide despite the skill of the expert.

On 5 September four Fortresses were bombed up and proceeded to Kinloss. Sqn. Ldr. Maclaren flying the reserve aircraft took along ground personnel. Next day four crews set out to bomb the *Admiral von Scheer* in Oslo harbour. Because of a troublesome supercharger, as often, one aborted, but the rest arrived over Oslo yet could not locate the ship. Instead they bombed docks and oil tanks from 30,000 feet. Because they had missed the primary target they were told to stand by for further operations, bombs for which had to be brought from Polebrook.

Sqn. Ldr. Mathieson, Flg. Off. Romans, Plt. Off. Sturmey and Sgt. Wood set off for Oslo soon after 09.00 hours on 8 September. This time enemy fighters were alerted in time and the most disastrous of the Fortress operations evolved. At 11.27 two 109s intercepted Flg. Off. Romans at 25,000 feet. His aircraft was soon ablaze and crashed in the Norwegian mountains after shooting down one attacker. Sgt. Wood some four miles behind, seeing interception was inevitable, abandoned his sortie. He jettisoned his load then climbed to 34,000 feet, and encountered serious oxygen troubles. In addition the intercom system was not working well. In the rare atmosphere voice production was bad, the pilot's vocal chords failing to vibrate effectively in the rarefied air. A gunner misunderstood an instruction, disconnected himself from the main oxygen system and began to use his portable bottle. Its supply was soon used and he collapsed. The other gunner who went to his aid failed to plug correctly into his portable supply and soon passed out. Sgt. Wood was unaware of what had happened and flew on for fifteen minutes before, failing to contact his gunners, he asked the radio operator to see if they were all right. When he found out what had happened Wood dived, but at 29,000 feet a Bf 109 came into the attack firing a long burst from fifty yards astern. Both gunners were hit, Sgt. Wilkins soon died of his wounds, and Flt. Sgt. Tates had arm injuries.

A piece of shrapnel fractured the radio operator's oxygen lead and soon he was unconscious. Damage to the glycol system in the cabin caused it to fill with dense white smoke which blinded the crew. They jettisoned the perspex astrodome and fumes poured out probably misleading the fighter pilot into thinking the bomber was ablaze.

Three engines had been damaged, the other put out of action, and aileron controls were shot away. In desperate plight the Fortress began its long flight home, controlled by elevators and rudder. One of the crew walked aft to wind shut the bomb bay doors and soon he passed out when his oxygen supply failed. The second pilot soon connected him to another bottle. But the exertion of the second pilot caused him to collapse and it was some moments before he recovered consciousness. Sgt. Wood nursed the crippled aircraft back to Kinloss by which time most of the crew had recovered and Flt. Sgt. Tates's injured arm could be attended to.

Plt. Off. Sturmey had courageously carried on to the target only to be greeted by 10/10 cloud making bombing impossible. He therefore returned with his load. Of Mathieson nothing was heard after take-off. Whitleys of 19 O.T.U. searched for his machine and next day two Fortresses carried out a sea search covering 3,000 sq. miles, all to no avail. It was a grievous loss to the squadron.

Thereafter came a spell of concentrated fighter affiliation with a Defiant and Spitfire from Castle Kennedy to improve tactics. Bad weather and persistent contrails were now making operations difficult and unlikely, but one special mission was billed. Information was received that a fair of household goods and textiles—particularly from Belgium and Holland—was to be held in Cologne. It was believed the fair would rival that of Leipzig. A large exhibit was placed on the Deutscher Unfer on the Rhine embankment north of the Hohenzollern Bridge. It was further thought that at the opening on 14 September important Nazis would be present. This would be a fine time to attack the exhibition hall making a grand opening—and finale—to the event. All depended on the weather, and because this was a deep penetration the attack must not take place below 32,000 feet. If contrails formed the raid would have to be abandoned and attempted later.

Unfortunately the weather on the 14th was too bad for operations but on 15th AN536 set out. At 32,000 feet trails formed and the sortie had to be halted. Next day Sturmey tried for Cologne, but the operation was ill fated. An engine lost power then a gunner contracted stomach trouble. Operation *Ingo* was abandoned.

Two more sorties were flown by Sturmey, one on 20th when bombs were accurately placed on the target in Emden. On 25th trails formed at 27,000 feet and this final raid was abandoned fifty miles from target.

Training continued for the next five months, but operations were impossible in winter. Detachments were made to Kinloss for possible operations over Norway, but nothing came of these. On 6 December it was finally agreed that the Fortress 1 was useless for day raids over Europe. It was suggested that flame dampers be fitted for night operations. These never materialised.

The idea of raining bombs from the stratosphere on to an unsuspecting enemy still held attraction, so the squadron remained intact. On 27 October a detachment of four Fortresses led by Sqn. Ldr. Maclaren left for the Middle East where better weather suggested the possibility of success. In fact there were other problems to overcome and again it was a dismal story. The idea was not matched by the aircrafts' capabilities and lone high-altitude raiders were soon out of favour.

Something of what the crews of 90 Squadron had undergone in that summer was related on the B.B.C. on 26 September by Flt. Sgt. Mulligan. He had flown with Flg. Off. Sturmey who had received a well-earned D.F.C. Mulligan's story included the following:

'I have flown in the sub-stratosphere in a Fortress over Holland, France, Norway and Germany. If the people on the ground in those countries have seen us at all, we have appeared no more than the tiniest dot in the sky.' (He might have added that the contrails were an awful give-away for a lone aircraft, four broad white stripes in the blue sky having been a source of great interest over many parts of Europe, not least over Britain.)

'On your first ascent you are very much aware of flying in unexplored space, relying completely on oxygen. After a few trips you become accustomed to new colours in the sky. I was in the Fortress which was attacked by seven fighters when we were returning from Brest. Three minutes after our bombs had gone the fire controller called out that there were enemy fighters coming up to us from the starboard quarter, 1,000 feet below. They closed in and there was almost no part of the Fortress which was not hit. Some of my friends in the crew were killed, others wounded. A petrol tank was punctured, bomb doors were thrown open, flaps were put out of action, tail tab shot away, tail wheel stuck half down, brakes not working, only one aileron any good and the rudder almost out of control. The centre of the fuselage had become a tangle of wires and broken cables, square feet of the wings had been shot away, and still the pilot managed to land the Fortress on a strange aerodrome. This is a testimony to the makers in America.

'Fortunately these thrills are rare. Our attack on Emden last week was almost without incident, except, of course, for the dropping of the bombs by the Sperry sight with beautiful accuracy on the target. We lost sight of our aerodrome at 2,000 feet and never saw the ground again until we were off the Dutch islands. Foamy white cloud, like the froth on a huge tankard of beer, stretched all over England and for about thirty miles out to sea. The horizon turned—quite suddenly—from purple to green and from green to yellow. It was hazy but I could see Emden fifty miles away.

'I called out to the pilot "Stand by for bombing, bombsight in detent,

George in. O.K. I've got her." The drill is that I push a lever on my left for the bomb doors to open, and on a dial in my cabin two arms move out like the hands of a clock to show me the position of the bomb doors. I keep my eye down the sighting tube which, incidentally, contains 26 prisms, and with my wrist I work the release. As the cross hairs centred over a shining pinpoint in Emden on which the sun was glinting, the bombs went down. We were still two miles away from Emden when we turned away. Almost a minute later one of the gunners told us through the intercom "There you are, bursts in the centre of the something target," and back we came through those extraordinary tints of the sky.

'During the whole sortie I only had one thrilling moment. I saw a Messerschmitt coming towards us. He seemed an improved type, and I looked again. It was a mosquito which had got stuck on the perspex in the take-off and had frozen stiff. Otherwise it proved an uneventful typical trip in a Fortress, with the temperature at minus 30 degrees below zero Centigrade.'

In November 1941 the use of the Fortress 1 was reviewed. Clearly it was not a stratosphere bomber, and its fighter defences were poor. Before it could fight any engagement waist guns needed to be fitted into position after huge side panels had been removed. This was an almost impossible task for gunners at high altitudes, and the gaping holes made the aircraft bitterly cold inside. Contrailing made lone operations hazardous, and for half the year possible on about only one day per month. With the Wellington VI pressure cabin bomber soon becoming available consideration was given to switching Fortress 1s to night operations. The squadron was therefore passed to 8 Group on 2 January 1942 which was forming to use Liberators for night raids. Night bombing of Germany was not the task of 2 Group, and it was now left to others to make the Fortress work in daylight.

Operations Log 90 Squadron: July–September, 1941

Date	Aircraft	Captain	Time up/down	Target	Remarks
July					
8	AN526: G	W/C MacDougall	1500–1905	Wilhelmshaven	2 bombs dropped
	AN519: H	S/L Maclaren	1500–1835	,,	Att. Norderney, eng. tr.
	AN529: C	P/O Mathieson	1500–1900	,,	Att. target
23	AN530: F	W/C MacDougall	0902–1221	Berlin or Kiel	Returned from Denmark—contrails
	AN529: C	F/L Mathieson	0857–1335	,,	Ditto
	AN523: D	S/L Maclaren	0900–1235	,,	Early return
24	AN530: F	W/C MacDougall	1130–1545	Brest	Op. *Sunrise*,
	AN523: D	S/L Maclaren	1120–1545	Brest	all attacks
	AN529: C	F/L Mathieson	1120–1530	Brest	successful

Date	Aircraft	Captain	Time up/down	Target	Remarks
July					
26	AN529: C	Sgt. Wood	0730–0930	Emden	Aband. Bad weather on route
	AN530: F	S/L Mathieson	1730–1150	Emden	Bombed target
August					
2	AN529: C	S/L Mathieson	1441–1940	Kiel	Bombed primary target
	AN530: F	P/O Sturmey	1438–1515	Kiel	Abandoned, formated wrongly
	AN530: F	P/O Sturmey	1715–2105	Emden	Cloudy, bombed Borkum
6	AN529: C	S/L Mathieson	0638–1041	Brest	Bombs jett. on target
	AN523: D	P/O Sturmey	0640–1105	Brest	Successful
12	AN523: D	P/O Sturmey	0900–1125	De Kooy	Bombed target
	AN529: C	Sgt. Wood	0940–1045	Cologne	Aband. over Oxford, eng. tr.
	AN532: J	P/O Wayman	0940–1323	Cologne	Bombed through cloud
	AN536: M	P/O Taylor	1003–1348	Emden	Ditto
16	AN529: C	Sgt. Wood	1530–1700	Düsseldorf	Aband., weather bad
	AN536: M	P/O Taylor	1530–1645	,,	Ditto
	AN532: J	P/O Wayman	0903–1255	Brest	Successful attack
	AN523: D	P/O Sturmey	0903–1145	Brest	Ditto intercepted
19	AN529: C	Sgt. Wood	0544–0809	Düsseldorf	Guns froze. Aborted
	AN532: J	P/O Wayman	0542–0845	,,	Contrails. Aborted
21	AN536: M	S/L Mathieson	0650–1010	,,	Aband. Flushing. Contrails
	AN532: J	P/O Wayman	0655–1015	,,	Aband. Dordrecht. Supercharger tr.
	AN518: B	Sgt. Wood	0645–0930	Düsseldorf	Contrails. Guns froze
29	AN533: N	Sgt. Wood	—	,,	Aband. take-off
	AN536: M	F/O Wayman	0620–0936	,,	Contrails, eng. tr.
31	AN525: D	S/L Mathieson	1454–1958	Hamburg	Bombed Spikerooge
	AN518: B	Sgt. Wood	1453–2009	Kiel	Successful
	AN532: J	P/O Wayman	1430–2000	Bremen	Supercharger tr.
September					
2	AN533: N	S/L Mathieson	1400–1730	Bremen	Successful
	AN532: J	P/O Sturmey	1400–1710	Hamburg	Aband. Contrails Heligoland
	AN518: B	Sgt. Wood	1330–1500	Duisburg	Aband. Intercomm. tr.

Date	Aircraft	Captain	Time up/down	Target	Remarks
September					
4	AN533: N	F/O Romans	1420–1735	Essen	Aband. Eng. tr. Rotterdam attacked
	AN518: B	Sgt. Wood	1410–1540	Hamburg	Aband. Intercomm. tr.
	AN532: J	P/O Sturmey	1410–1730	Hanover	Aband. Eng. tr.
6	AN533: N	S/L Mathieson	0800–1350	Oslo	Attacked docks & oil installation
	AN525: D	F/O Romans	0800–1330	Oslo	Ditto
	AN532: J	P/O Sturmey	0810–1320	Oslo	Ditto
	AN536: M	Sgt. Wood	0800–0930	Oslo	Aband. Engine trouble
8	AN533: N	S/L Mathieson	0925–FTR	Oslo	Lost without trace
	AN525: D	F/O Romans	0925–FTR	Oslo	Shot down at 11.27
	AN535: O	Sgt. Wood	0915–1415	Oslo	Aband. cloudy, att. by Bf 109
	AN532: J	P/O Sturmey	0910–1335	Oslo	Aband. 11.30 cloudy
15	AN536: M	P/O Sturmey	1305–1600	Cologne	Aband. Contrails
16	AN536: M	P/O Sturmey	1310–1555	Cologne	Aband. Engine trouble
20	AN518: B	P/O Sturmey	1256–1712	Emden	Successful attack
25	AN518: B	P/O Sturmey	1200–1550	Emden	Aband. Contrails

Abbreviations: att. = attacked.   tr. = trouble.
aband. = abandoned.   jett. = jettisoned.

Chapter 11
Mediterranean Crusade

An association between 2 Group and the Middle East commenced in August 1940, when a Horsham crew was instructed to ferry Blenheim T2049 to that war theatre. By the end of the year about forty Blenheims had been delivered in this manner, then such flights stopped.

Shortly after the start of the 1941 anti-shipping campaign it was decided to explore whether 2 Group's detachments could effectively operate from Malta against shipping supplying the Italians in the North African desert. Six crews of 21 Squadron under Sqn. Ldr. L. V. E. Atkinson were selected for the trials. They set off on 26 April for a long tiring flight to Gibraltar, almost the limit of endurance for crew and aircraft. They then faced an equally perilous journey across the Mediterranean to Malta.

Atkinson recalls, 'We flew half a dozen raids prodding this way and that. I sent a signal back that we could operate a squadron or a "squadron plus". The situation in Malta was far from satisfactory, things had been badly neglected for years. For instance, we had to have our aircraft serviced by the Navy. We all arrived home, but one aircraft had been destroyed in an air raid. We were the only crews to fly our Blenheims back. Luck was out for me. I ran out of fuel just after crossing the Cornish coast. My Blenheim ended in a cloud of dust thrown up as we belly landed in a dry field. We managed to get out then the aircraft was put under Army guard. I was not pleased to find the soldiers had stripped it of some of the treasures I had brought home from the East!'

Air Chief Marshal Sir Charles Portal, Chief of Air Staff, sent for Grp. Capt. Hugh Pughe Lloyd, S.A.S.O. at 2 Group. Lloyd had no certain idea of the reason although he had authorised 21 Squadron's detachment to the Middle East. Portal soon explained to Lloyd, long a respected figure in the Group, that he had been chosen to command Malta. 'Your main task is,' he said, 'to sink Axis shipping sailing between Europe and Africa.'

Atkinson's detachment had shown this to be feasible and now a new scheme was inaugurated. Squadrons of 2 Group would, in rotation, equip with tropicalised long-range Blenheims at Watton, fly them to Malta and operate them for about five weeks. The aircraft would then be flown to Africa. Some of the crews might return home, some would stay depending upon requirements.

When Air Commodore Hugh Pughe Lloyd took command in Malta he was shaken to find defences and facilities in a deplorable state. Airfields were far from ready as operational bases, there were no dispersals and equipment problems were immense. He was astonished to find this vital base had been so neglected by the politicians. Before long he had Luqa made ready for the first Blenheim squadron to enter the sunlit region.

Meanwhile Atkinson had been promoted to Wing Commander and now commanded 82 Squadron. He relates how he came back and was promoted, 'then Hugh Pughe Lloyd said he wanted me in Malta. He had sent me out in the first place, called me in the second. I admired him a lot. He did everything for you, backed you, doing all he could to help you.'

The news of the Malta detachment was met with mixed feelings. First there was the task of getting there, crossing Biscay, flying along the enemy coast with no fuel to spare for a pitched battle. Some crews cut the corner over neutral territory. It also did not go unheeded to some that whereas there was usually some cloud cover over the North Sea, and some protection from poor visibility, over the deep blue Mediterranean the sky was usually cloudless . . . ideal conditions for defenders who would easily see you coming.

Before leaving for Portreath 82 Squadron took over 'tropicalised' Blenheims needed for the desert war. The first batch left Watton on 4 June headed by the squadron commander and followed by nine more on 11th. They flew to Gibraltar in widely spaced groups of three, awaited suitable weather, then proceeded to Luqa.

Among those in the second batch was Flt. Lt. Watkins flying Z9545: UX-B also crewed by Sgt. Sargent and Sgt. Chandler. As was often to be the case they had engine trouble and were forced back. Next day they left again heading a group of eleven other Blenheims for a flight lasting over eight hours made possible only by the fitting of a barrel fuel tank over the bomb well amidships. Fuel was hand-pumped into the main tanks when the gauges showed them low. Ground crews wedged themselves into some aircraft for the grim flight. Sgt. Hadland's crew spotted enemy fighters but these were apparently too short of fuel even to take on sitting ducks.

Eventually the crews met at Gibraltar where the racecourse served as an airfield. They were billeted in stables, and refuelled their aircraft from hand-held petrol tins under the eager gaze of Germans on the Spanish edge of the track. On the second leg to Malta the wind was against them. Fuel was flowing alarmingly fast so they decided to turn back. Next day they tried again, half being briefed to fly to Luqa half to Takali. Unfortunately their take-off time was set an hour too late, and the consequences were nearly disastrous.

When Wg. Cdr. Atkinson worked out their likely time of arrival he was extremely worried. He knew that four out of six crews detailed for Luqa had no night-flying experience. In his own words: 'I was petrified! Malta was being bombed more or less three times a day, morning and dusk raids being almost regular. We laid out gooseneck flares to guide the boys in, just as the air raid sirens wailed. Nearly everybody went to ground just as the flare path was being lit and my chaps were coming in. I saw to my horror that one fellow was also running along putting the flare path out, so I ran and started relighting the flares. I then heard our Blenheims overhead, circling and hopefully making landing approaches. I turned round and there was a fellow putting out the flares I had relit! I quickly put a stop to that, as one of the Blenheims did an overshoot. Then I ran along one side of the flares relighting them, with "Doc" Monro attending to the other. This was the sort of problem one was fighting all the time in Malta.'

Seven Martin Maryland reconnaissance aircraft were based on Malta. Their tasks were to watch for enemy shipping, to reconnoitre Naples for signs of sailings or assembling convoys which usually sailed after dark, to look for tankers which usually set out for Libya from Taranto to no set time-table and try to locate ships northward bound. They had their hands full. Convoys from Naples generally followed a westerly route past Sicily, then sailed directly to Africa where they hugged the coastline to Tripoli. If they used an eastern route through the Straits of Messina they sailed along the toe of Italy to the Greek shore, followed it southwards to Navarino then headed for North Africa again hugging that coast or entering Benghazi. At best they would never be nearer than about 140 miles from Malta during which time they were under fighter protection from either Sicily and Pantelleria, from Greece, or were sailing in darkness. The south-bound convoys carried food, ammunition, guns, lorries, tanks and spares. These and the precious oil tankers with vital fuel loads were to become principal targets for the Blenheims, supported by Swordfishes and at night by Wellingtons whose operations began on 24 June.

Malta itself was already in poor state. Its bombing, yet to reach the peak, had been extensive. Crews were subjected to a front-line situation all the time. 'Consider the setting,' recalls Sir Hugh Lloyd, 'where everybody—civilian, soldier, sailor, airman—everybody was united. Morale was tremendously high and our aircraft were left out unguarded on aerodromes every night. How easy for a few folk to have burnt the lot!' Atkinson says, 'I was proud and pleased to fight with them, but I never liked the way some too quickly took to the shelters because this could lead to unnecessary panic that could easily spread. You never knew when the next raid might come. Once I was in the club at Valetta—we were suddenly rolling everywhere, for the whole place was blown up by a bomb.'

All except one of the south-bound convoys in June 1941 were attacked from the air and soon 82 Squadron drew its first blood. On 22nd six crews of 82 Squadron attacked a convoy escorted by destroyers when it was off Lampedusa. A motor vessel of 6,000 tons was severely damaged, but there was strong defending action from ships and fighters. Flying UX-B: Z9545 was Flt. Lt. T. J. Watkins—survivor of the raid of 17 May 1940 on Gembloux—with Sgt. Sargent, and Sgt. Chandler as wireless operator/air gunner. Watkins roared in at low level, dropped his bombs in a close stick on a huge ammunition ship and zoomed away as his bombs exploded. Throughout the attack his machine had been under fire in a clear blue sky, conditions which meant the run-in was extremely dangerous. Flak peppered the Blenheim and Watkins had a leg all but severed. A .50 in. shell also came between his legs near the join as he raced over the ship. He righted the aircraft but was in great distress. Sargent came back to him and took over the controls, although he had never flown a Blenheim before. Meanwhile Chandler was exchanging fire at very close range with a Fiat CR 42 which had closed in for the kill of an almost out of control bomber. The Italian paid for his mistake!

Between bouts of horrific pain Watkins came-to and gave flying instructions to his navigator. Eventually they joined the Luqa circuit. Watkins managed to land the aircraft, then collapsed at the controls. Soon the machine was surrounded by ground personnel and medical men. The senior officer expressed utter astonishment that one so grievously wounded could have brought his crew in. Watkins was immediately awarded the D.S.O., the D.F.M. was given to Sgt. Sargent and Chandler was quite satisfied with an enemy fighter to his credit. Their aircraft was written off.

On 24th Chandler teamed up with Sgt. Knight whose wireless operator/air gunner was ill. Led by Wg. Cdr. Atkinson they bombed what was left of the convoy now in Tripoli harbour, a tremendously exciting low-level operation led by the anti-shipping master.

For Chandler and Sargent there was to be an ironic adventure some three months later. They were among the few 82 Squadron men who managed to get back to England. Flying with Flt. Lt. Bartlett they were on a shipping strike off the Frisians when, once more, their pilot was hit, in the legs and feet. Again Sargent took over the controls. Chandler, soon alarmed at the behaviour of the aircraft, called up his captain—'What the Hell's going on?' It was Sargent who replied 'These bloody pilots can't take it; he's caught a packet.' Once again the two sergeants brought their aircraft home, but this time they landed with a live 250-lb. bomb aboard. Ground staff and medical crews, alerted by Chandler's radio signal for assistance on landing, watched in amazement as the two sergeants jumped out of their aircraft in the middle of the airfield. Dragging their wounded pilot between them, they started running to clear the aircraft before it blew up.

Early in July Wg. Cdr. Atkinson led an attack on a convoy sheltering in Palermo. For sheer cheek and nerve the operation took some beating. The formation flew along the Sicily Channel, abruptly turned, bombed then raced across the island. The enemy was so astonished that he never fired a shot at the bombers. When Intelligence assessed the raid they declared a 10,000-tonner and a 5,000-tonner were burnt out, a 10,000-ton ship had a broken back, three ships were badly damaged and a large ship was being towed back to Naples.

Into July 82 Squadron operated until it was torn asunder by heavy casualties. A few of the personnel returned by an elaborate route which took them home partly by Catalina flying-boat and then on a ship from Gibraltar. The order was that they should stay in the Middle East, but they wanted to keep with 2 Group and their strange journeys home they reckoned were well worth the risks involved. Meanwhile 110 Squadron was making its way to Malta. It was soon in action. A highlight of its operations came on 22 July when it co-operated with Swordfishes attacking a convoy including a 7,000-tonner. Two days later they located ships sheltering at Trapani and claimed to sink two of them.

Next came 105 Squadron which reached Luqa on 28 July. Three days later, led by Wg. Cdr. H. I. Edwards, six crews flew the squadron's first operation. As a four-ship convoy with destroyer escort came into view 200 miles N.E. of Pantelleria a barrage opened up. Fiat CR 42s were above and level with them. The latter latched on to Jackson's aircraft. He shook them off, but the shipping attack was abandoned. Next day three crews attacked two medium-sized ships with a destroyer close to Lampedusa. As they rushed over the harbour spraying the barracks and docks with machine-gun fire, the defenders caught Z9605 and shot it into the sea.

Every day, when at all possible, the Blenheims now were operating. On Malta everyone had to earn a living the hard way and aeroplanes did not do this by sitting on the ground. Therefore, when no shipping was reported, the 2 Group detachments were now thrown into attacks on land targets, initially in North Africa. On 2 August 105 Squadron attacked without loss the barracks near Misurata. Such raids were soon tying down enemy strength away from the front line and the anti-shipping raids demanded further defensive action in strength to defend vital supply links.

A convoy attack on 7 August resulted in only two out of six ships reaching Africa. One tanker was beached on Lampedusa and after a second attack she burnt for eight days. So low were her attackers that the enemy guns fired down upon them. On 15th five crews of 105 Squadron on a sweep between Tripoli and Benghazi found two 4,000-ton tankers escorted by two large schooners. Both tankers were attacked off Buerat. One exploded whilst the other spewed flames and black smoke. Plt. Off. P. H. Standfast's aircraft was hit and exploded. The ever-present hazard of striking a mast claimed another Blenheim and a third was shot down by machine-gun fire. Such attacks were nevertheless frightening the Italian crews who demanded more and more protection for themselves and their ships.

Throughout August 105 Squadron was exceedingly active. Off the Greek coast on 28th, for instance, three hits were scored on two cargo vessels. From one much of the superstructure was blown away. One bomb passed right through the other. Before August ended an ammunition factory at Licata and its power station had been bombed.

By the end of August it was assessed that 58% of all enemy supplies intended for North Africa had been lost at sea. Those that escaped risked being destroyed in nightly attacks on Tripoli by Wellingtons. It was obvious that ship defences had much increased. All ships on the run bristled with anti-aircraft guns. The casualty rate was around a steady 12%; bad for morale, perhaps, although the job was seen to be paying good dividends. Losses were averaging about one crew per day, almost a squadron a week. Replacements were made by holding Blenheims and their crews ferrying through Malta to Egypt and impressing their crews into the squadrons. Casualties were at times frightening, and the chances of surviving a tour increasingly slight. Many of the men were known personally to Hugh Pughe Lloyd, who was in rather a different position from many commanders since he had long been part of 2 Group which was always a small close-knit community.

'I had no peace of mind when they were out,' he wrote. 'I could not stay in my office. And when they returned I was afraid to ask "How did it go?" Those aircrew were the flower of our race: all of them had been given a good education in their youth and they were far above average in intelligence, men who knew what they were doing and why it had to be done, and men who volunteered to be aircrew in preference to many other far less hazardous tasks. Theirs was a calm and conscious courage. To every one of these volunteers the sinking of ships was their crusade, and without any doubt they were Knights of St. John—the modern Crusaders.'

No. 107 Squadron prepared itself for the Malta ordeal late August. Twenty-six crews set forth, and began operating on 15 September. Two days later they delivered a low-level attack on factories at Licata. They had joined 105 Squadron. On 11th 105 Squadron had found a south-bound heavily laden convoy destroyer escorted. Despite a tremendous barrage from the warships three crews pressed home their attack and were rewarded by the sight of dense smoke billowing from the largest ship.

At dawn on 17th three crews made a dawn assault on a large liner in Tripoli. It was a surprise attack during which hits were scored on the ship and a freighter. Two days later Wg. Cdr. Harte and Sqn. Ldr. Warren of newly arrived 107 Squadron searched in vain for the liner. Instead Harte found a stationary destroyer, and a cruiser which he attacked broadside on from ten feet. His bombs rammed home near the funnel and Harte saw black smoke rising when he was ten miles away. The large liner, escorted by six destroyers off Lampedusa, was located on 21st, by Wg. Cdr. Harte and Wg. Cdr. Skivio of 105 Squadron. After finding her they circled out of sight then ran in when it was almost dark. They scored no hits. Skivio's engine was set on fire but he managed to get home safely. Later two more crews had a go at the liner off Kurit Island. This time bombs hit her; steam poured forth and she stopped.

During August attacks began on coastal shipping off Africa and in September on the coastal fringe. Nos. 105 and 107 Squadrons made a sharp raid on the Tripoli–Benghazi road on 22 September. Barracks, dumps and petrol lorries were left burning but during a pass against troops Wg. Cdr. Skivio and Sgt. Williams collided. Williams somehow managed to limp home, but the tail fell from Skivio's aircraft.

Many convoys were being escorted by fighters—often by four Ju 88s when well out to sea. It was bad enough facing the flak, and fighters increased the hazards. On one occasion, when five merchant ships were being escorted by four destroyers and four Ju 88s, six Blenheims came upon the force. Undaunted, they roared in. The first section placed their loads, then came the second led by Wg. Cdr. Pepper. As he raced over the target, 11 sec. delay bombs from the first wave burst and his aircraft disintegrated in a fireball. A second machine close by was severely twisted by blast but limped back to Luqa.

Such had been the success of the operations that in September the enemy ceased sailing his convoys west of Sicily; subsequently shipping took the easterly route tracking along the Balkan coast. Sorties to attack them were long and tiring, and there were even more fighters to face.

A pitched battle took place on 4 October when eight crews of 107 Squadron led by Sqn. Ldr. Barnes attacked the harbour at Zuara. So fierce was the pom-pom fire from three destroyers that the first three Blenheims were beaten off. Four Fiat CR 42s then engaged them. The other five bombers diverted inland to find a worthwhile target. Cr 42s then attacked them shooting down Sgt. Hamlyn's aircraft. The fighters followed the Blenheims fifty miles out to sea making a lengthy engagement.

The first night attack by the Blenheims came on 7–8 October. It demanded courage and skill for it was a moonlight attack from a mere twenty feet on a 2,000-tonner off Tripoli. Two hits were scored followed by explosions and the crew taking to the boats.

On 11th six crews of 107 Squadron on a sweep came across two cargo boats escorted by a corvette and a floatplane in the Gulf of Sirtes. Greenhill ran in for the attack but the large vessel held her fire until he was fifty yards away. His bombs hit the vessel forward but her fire brought him down. Sgt. Broome then attacked leaving the ship burning. Routh went for the smaller ship, set it on fire and then crashed, hit by fire from the larger ship.

In the second half of October, by which time a detachment from

18 Squadron had reached Malta, some '*Circus*-like' operations were mounted. On 17th while 107 Squadron attacked along the Zuara–Sirte road, No. 18 Squadron's six Blenheims with a Hurricane escort bombed Syracuse seaplane base from 12,500 feet. Factories at Licata and Catania and barracks near Homs were also raided, although the main October effort was against Italian army targets in Africa.

On 1 November six Blenheims (three each of 18 and 107 Squadrons) found a 3,000-tonner escorted by a destroyer and three Macchi 202s. No bombs hit the ship but a running battle ensued with the fighters. Levin's aircraft was hit in the cockpit and Sgt. Nolan the observer was injured. A downward-firing gun on the large ship scored two hits on Sgt. Anderson's wing but his gunner scored a probable claim of a fighter.

November's first major success came on 5th when six crews of 18 Squadron attacked two 3,000-ton motor ships destroyer-escorted in the Gulf of Sirtes. One ship was left sinking, but two crews were lost. On 8th six crews of 107 Squadron went after another cargo boat destroyer-escorted. Anderson and Lee approached in formation to attack, but the destroyer opened up on their run-in causing them to take violent evasive action. This opened the way for others to attack, but Hopkinson's aircraft was fired upon, crashed into the ship's mast then blew up. Sgt. Kidby and Crowe together attacked a small vessel but fierce defensive fire hit Crowe's turret. Meanwhile the first two crews made four attempts to attack over a 26-minute period but the destroyer's fire drove them off. Six aircraft of 18 Squadron delivered a follow-up raid and one was lost.

Mellaha airfield was attacked on 12th during a low-level attack led by Wg. Cdr. Dunlevie of 107 Squadron, workshops and hangars being heavily damaged. A mast-high operation off Cape Kiri resulted in direct hits on the bow of a 4,000-tonner and a tremendous explosion. Drums of petrol on her deck erupted into a conflagration from which the smoke column was visible thirty miles away. On 17th six crews of 107 Squadron found three large ships. Sgt. Broome went in first, machine-gun fire from his aircraft evidently hitting the ship's fuel supply since large flames gushed from her. Gillman managed a hit on her bows and he had to bank away very sharply to avoid the blast. When Broome reached home he counted twenty holes in his aircraft.

A steady flow of replacement Blenheims and crews was arriving in Malta bound, in theory, for the Middle East. One such comprised Sgts. Noseda, Deeks and Webber. Their names had been drawn from a hat at Wattisham, three newly trained men with little experience. For a couple of days they flight-tested their tropicalised Blenheim from Watton where Sqn. Ldr. Ian Spencer commanded a special Flight, an offshoot of 82 Squadron formed to control the flow of aircraft to the Mediterranean. Recalling the journey to Malta Freddie Deeks remembers: 'We had a pretty cursory briefing at Portreath and took off for Gibraltar setting course from the Scilly Isles and heading for the N.W. tip of Spain. When we reached it we followed the Spanish coast turning into Gib. at the end! During the trip it was my job to pump the petrol and as we were flying at over 10,000 feet this became tiring, but due to our inexperience it was some time before we thought of using a little of that strange oxygen to help! Every now and again an engine would give a sickening cough and threaten to cut out. This had to be instantly followed by cessation of pumping and much juggling of the throttles. Whether we were doing the right thing or not we didn't know. Over Biscay we had to climb through some cloud and the interior of the aircraft began to ice up. We were so inexperienced that we wondered what was going on.

'Gibraltar's runway was short and because of turbulence from the Rock the approach was invariably dangerous, a pile of wrecks proving the point. At this time *Ark Royal* was being used to ferry Hurricanes to Malta. They would fly off her some distance from the island and be navigated there by a Blenheim en route such as ourselves. We awaited such a task but the ship was torpedoed. We therefore made the journey with two other Blenheims, but as we were too slow they forged ahead and left us to it. Both were shot up by fighters near Pantelleria, and one crashed on Malta.

'We were ostensibly en route for Egypt, and you can imagine our feelings when, on the morning of departure, we were told that we had instead been seconded to 107 Squadron. Malta had an unsavoury reputation and this sentence had a ring of death about it. I thought I would never see England again, but we were lucky and between November and January 1942, completed a tour of operations in which shipping targets played a lesser part than of late. Our morale was much affected by round the clock bombing by the other side. Our situation was rather unusual in that the commanding officer of 107, Wg. Cdr. Dunlevie, was a Canadian whose substantive rank was Flt. Lt. Apart from him and the Adjutant all the crew were Sergeants, but later Sgt. Ivor Broome became a Pilot Officer (he later rose to Air rank) and some officers from 17 O.T.U. joined us. Our mess was on the coast at Marsa and we used to travel daily to the airfield at Luqa. Food, of course, was in very short supply and quite awful. Living conditions under constant attack were quite appalling. At Luqa we hung around the crew room with foreboding, awaiting a sighting by the Maryland crews. If nothing was available we were told to get a "quick meal" at the nearby transit mess, a former hospital and leper colony just down the road and usually crowded with crews en route to Egypt. Invariably the "quick meal" would be interrupted by air raids, and was sometimes followed by an afternoon sortie. On return we had to circle Filfla Island until any raids in progress ended. By then the catering staff had left the mess and it was merely "cha and wads" in the NAAFI. None of these conditions helped morale. Overhead there were repeated air battles, and sometimes Ju 88s would roar over very low despite tremendous barrages. The conditions on Malta were really grim.'

At the end of November the fast 10,000-ton tanker *Reichenfels* was found berthed in Naples. She took on 7,000 tons of fuel, sailed on her maiden voyage and was located by a Maryland. Blenheims of 18 and 107 Squadrons went after her when she was off Tripoli, braving the fire of her destroyer escort, the *Alvisa da Mosto*, and facing four Cant Z 501 floatplanes. After the first attack her crew abandoned her. The same day four Blenheims attacked train ferries at San Giorvani, Italian terminus for the Sicilian ferry. A 2,000-ton ship was also bombed at Messina where a train of 24 petrol tankers was left blazing. In the bad weather of 8 December shipping was raided off Catania and two Blenheims collided; three days later another crew was lost attacking a 5,000-tonner in Argostoli harbour where on 12th six Blenheims of 18 Squadron attacked two large ships and a destroyer for the loss of two of their number.

On 13 December a vic of three Blenheims of 107 Squadron led by Plt. Off. Ivor Broom made a repeat attack on Argostoli. A second vic for this low-level raid was led by Sgt. Crossley on his second detachment to Malta. The first vic flew along a valley to reach the harbour which they found empty. Therefore they turned their attention upon a smaller haven. 'Flak started coming up fairly heavily,' recalls Freddie Deeks. 'To make matters worse we seemed to be in a horseshoe-shaped harbour with hills to climb before we could get out. We were banking, one eye on the flak, the other on the nearby hillside. Eventually on crossing the hills at the closed end we could see the comparative safety of the sea ahead. It seemed like a lifetime poised above the hills before we could descend from the view of the ships. Our sense of safety was short lived, however, for we met following flak from shore batteries.

'Then came a warning call over the R/T, a fighter was sitting on our tail. I immediately flung myself forward to the nose to work the periscopically aimed backward-firing guns—an awkward manoeuvre at the best of times. In Britain the Blenheim had a single backward-firing gun under the nose sighted by the aid of a mirror which meant doing everything in reverse. The tropicalised Blenheims differed in that there was a "box" containing two backward-firing Brownings sighted periscopically. They were virtually useless and it was the practice in Malta to reverse the guns so that they could be fired forward for strafing, without the aid of the sight.

'As soon as I reached the firing seat it collapsed. Ray Noseda, my pilot, thought I'd been hit. On looking through the periscope I eventually saw a Macchi 202 coming up, behind our tail and well down on the sea. I fired a burst and immediately the periscope filled with cordite fumes thus blotting out the view! The rounds were going in the right direction so I just kept my finger on the trigger and hoped for the best. This caused the fighter to break away.

'Sgt. Gracey had attacked the target with Sgt. Crossley, but was not seen afterwards. Sgt. Lee's aircraft was also hit. The sea we had been crossing was a flat turquoise stretch shimmering in a heat haze—almost a travel agent's dream with its fringing white villas and red roofs backed by olive groves. Such conditions always made height judgement difficult and was the possible cause of Sgt. Lee hitting the water. I saw the air gunner's hatch open afterwards and this prompted me to write to the gunner's family in Canada to say they had a good chance of escaping. The crew were indeed taken prisoner and Sgt. Lee eventually became a Squadron Leader and was tragically killed in the early days of helicopter cas-evac flying in Malaya, in 1950. The observer, Sgt. Dicky Haggett, survived and became a doctor.'

Sgt. Crossley was one of the many unsung heroes. On one occasion he brought a Blenheim back from North Africa after it had suffered blast damage from an oil transport fired upon on a desert road. The side of the fuselage was pushed in, the wing panelling blown out and most of the perspex and instruments blown away. Crossley was later killed when attacking a merchant ship. His courage was agreed by all to have been outstanding.

It was now the depth of winter, but there was no let-up in operations. Sgt. Noseda and Plt. Off. Williamson were on a sweep along the African coast when they passed close to Zuara aerodrome from which a fighter took off. Five miles on, attention was drawn to a train including some petrol bowsers. They immediately attacked it when Sgt. Webber cried 'Fighter!' Then the intercom went dead and the crew wondered what was happening. Suddenly a Fiat CR 42 came up alongside and Noseda's Blenheim banked away behind it. Then the fighter latched on to Williamson's aircraft keeping up a continuous attack. After it had given up Williamson called up to say his aircraft had been hit. Indeed it had—twice for, on crossing the coast on the way in, a flock of birds had crashed into the front perspex increasing the drag and slowing the machine. The observer was in a bad state, covered in blood from the birds, and now with a bullet wound in his hand. They managed to get home and years later Williamson was the squadron commander of an Australian Lincoln squadron during the Malayan emergency.

Winter weather converted many Italian airfields into quagmires. Only four were serviceable in Sicily at the start of 1942, and aircraft were concentrated upon them. The best was Castel Vetrano, and on the afternoon of 4 January ten Blenheims left to attack it.

'Between them,' recalls Freddie Deeks, '107 and 18 Squadrons could muster only ten serviceable aeroplanes—six of them from 18 Squadron. Our aircraft was flying No. 2 in a box of four led by a Squadron Leader of 18 Squadron. The raid was planned as a low level attack. We took off in Z7966 at 15.35 hours and crossed the Sicilian coast at 16.58. We then followed a dried up river bed and to attack the aerodrome at 17.03 had to climb up to it. Enemy aircraft on the ground were silhouetted against the skyline. We flew across the airfield in three vics practically line abreast, crossing it from east to west, taking the enemy completely by surprise. Only one machine-gun opened up, when we were half way across. I can still visualise an Italian ground crew servicing an aircraft and looking up in absolute amazement before we dropped our bombs on them.'

The aircraft were lined up wing tip to wing tip. At least thirty were destroyed by fire, and many others seriously damaged. Blue-uniformed men were everywhere and many were shot down. Smoke billowed to 1,000 feet, and after dark Wellingtons resumed the bombardment and fourteen more aircraft were destroyed.

More attacks followed, on shipping, barracks and troops; losses continued unabated as on 14 January when four Blenheims on a sweep from Kerkenna to Tripoli came across a 5,000-ton motor vessel and destroyer escort. Possible hits were claimed but one Blenheim crashed into the ship's mast and two more fell to flak. Fights with CR 42s were increasingly common now.

Kesselring's all-out attack on Malta began in October 1941, and was well under way by January 1942 when 21 Squadron arrived. Blenheims were now being bombed on their wide dispersals at Luqa. Coupled with the high attrition rate in combat this was virtually bringing a 100% loss. Emphasis was now on defending the island and keeping its fighters flying. Nevertheless the 2 Group offensive was maintained for a little longer.

On 4 February six 21 Squadron Blenheims set out to bomb shipping in Palermo. Unfortunately they made a wrong landfall and were flying so low that, as they turned, one aircraft dug a wing deep into the sea and cartwheeled straight in. Because of their error they missed Palermo. Instead they bombed a goods train near Karini. Scoppe rail bridge was also hit. Then the navigation error suddenly brought the formation straight towards cloud-clad hills. Their only hope was that they could pass safely between the mountains—but no, three aircraft smashed into the hillsides.

With so much enemy activity over Malta return to base was an increasingly dangerous risk. When three Blenheims returned from a Buerat sweep on 6 February Me 109s closed on them shooting them into the sea. There were no survivors. On 11th Blenheims were despatched on a shipping strike to the Gulf of Gabes. They unsuccessfully attacked three schooners then, as they reached Malta, 109s were in wait. They pounced and sent a Blenheim spinning into the water.

By the second half of February the Blenheims were back on their beats off the Balkan coast for that route had reopened now that Rommel was in Cyrenaica. Bad weather prevented much success and it was hard to find any ships. The final sorties in the campaign were flown on 22 February during a reconnaissance to Gerba and Kuriat. The end in Malta for 2 Group came with the disbandment of 21 Squadron on 4 March.

What had 2 Group, with its high loss rate, achieved? The passage of shipping to Africa west of Sicily had been halted largely by its efforts. Much shipping on the Africa run during the second half of 1941 had been stopped. By January 1942 Rommel had only three days of supplies left, such had been the success of the combined campaign from Malta—and he was desperate. Nearly all of his oil tankers had been sunk. A large number of Italian servicemen had been tied down in Africa, Sicily and on the ships for purely defensive purposes when these might have been fighting in the desert. But the losses in men and aircraft were telling. What finally halted the campaign was the very heavy enemy onslaught on Malta and its supplies. The Blenheim, too, was outpaced as the fighting over Europe had shown . . . and no replacement type was yet available.

Chapter 12

New Role, New Aircraft, New Year

With the fine weather gone, *Circus* operations halted in November 1941. Group's status was considered at Command. How should it be employed? Were its aircraft suitable for their tasks? Clearly the Blenheim was outdated and vulnerable, at least for daylight raids. It certainly could no longer be expected to wage a very effective offensive when better weather returned. Was there any way in which it could be operated until replacement aircraft were obtained? What types should these be?

A Bomber Command directive was issued in November 1941. It ordered certain squadrons to start intensive night-flying training, and revealed that some would receive the new, untried, revolutionary de Havilland Mosquito. Re-equipment of others with Bostons already under way would continue, such units preparing for the next round of *Circuses*. Group's main role would remain, i.e. bait to entice enemy fighters to battle; none too comfortable, questionably effective.

2 Group operations Order 81 of 27 December 1941 presented new plans to stations. It explained that the enemy long-range bomber force in the West numbered about 300 aircraft, used for mining, shipping attacks and raids on coastal targets. There were about 1,200 aircraft in Germany in units re-equipping after the initial stages of the Russian campaign. It was thought that some of these might move westwards. In the West the enemy consistently homed on to a limited number of airfields, in addition to which there were others used for training purposes. All lay within the Blenheim's operational range.

Present enemy operations rarely brought his aircraft into contact with our night-fighters. German airfields were well dispersed, and runway repair after bombing was rapid so that attacks were unprofitable unless they coincided with landings or take-offs. Therefore it had been decided to again mount intruder operations based on intelligence reports, harassing enemy aircraft landing after operations or making runways useless to cause diversions and perhaps crashes due to fuel shortage. Current intruder work was being undertaken by Havocs of 11 Group, but their limited range precluded them from operating over Holland or south of Paris.

In the early afternoon the monitoring service sometimes detected enemy movement to forward bases for operations. Enemy aircraft usually crossed their coast at between 900 and 1,600 feet at regular places, homing on to W/T beacons. This gave a good opportunity for intruders to use similar heights and crossing points. Enemy aircraft were in the habit of circling their base with navigation lights on and firing the colour of the day. Sometimes they fired an emergency signal and then would be directed to the nearest airfield, if lost, by aid of pointer searchlights. At bomber bases visual Lorenz was often displayed and the runway to which it led usually had a twin flare-path.

With such information in hand a campaign aiding 11 Group was to be waged. Intelligence sources would indicate airfields most likely to be active. From Bodney 82 Squadron was first to launch these raids, having six aircraft at half-hour's readiness from dusk to two hours before dawn during the moon period, ready to attack airfields especially in Holland and south of Paris. A list of twenty bomber bases, six training bases and a dozen night-fighter airfields was passed to stations.

The first operation of the new series, a rather specialised one, took place on 27–28 December. Information suggested that there were about sixty Dornier 217s at Soesterburg in Holland. Blenheims of 82 Squadron would attack them using 250- and 40-lb. bombs. Strictly speaking this was not an intruder raid, for the bombers were ordered not to await activity. If they saw other aircraft they were not to attack unless these had their navigation lights on. Fighter intruders would operate over the night-fighter base at Gilze Rijen. Led by Wg. Cdr. Roe six Blenheims were despatched during the evening of 27th. They found plenty of activity at Soesterburg. 'Y' using its front gun engaged a twin-engined bomber head on, then the rear gunner joined in, damaging it. 'D' found itself followed by an enemy machine, which spoilt its attack. 'H' followed by a Dornier opened fire, then bombed the airfield from 700 feet. Others also bombed, but the results were generally disappointing.

Next night 82 Squadron began intruder operations, making attacks on Eindhoven, Gilze Rijen and Schiphol. By the end of the year a dozen sorties had been flown, nine effectively, then came bad weather. The moon period passed, then '82' resumed intruder operations on 10 January 1942. 110 Squadron entered the arena on 14 January when four aircraft were ordered to attack Leeuwarden. That night diversity again appeared, nine aircraft of 110 and 114 Squadrons being despatched to Rotterdam on *Freshman* bombing operations.

First noteworthy success in the campaign came to 'A' of 82 Squadron whose bombs fell ahead of a landing aircraft, but intruding was not an easy task. Airfields were hard to locate unless they were lit and aircraft frequently returned with their loads. Alternative targets in occupied territory were few. 110 Squadron dropped bombs in the path of a bomber landing at Schiphol on 22nd, but there were few effective night sorties in January out of the 69 flown.

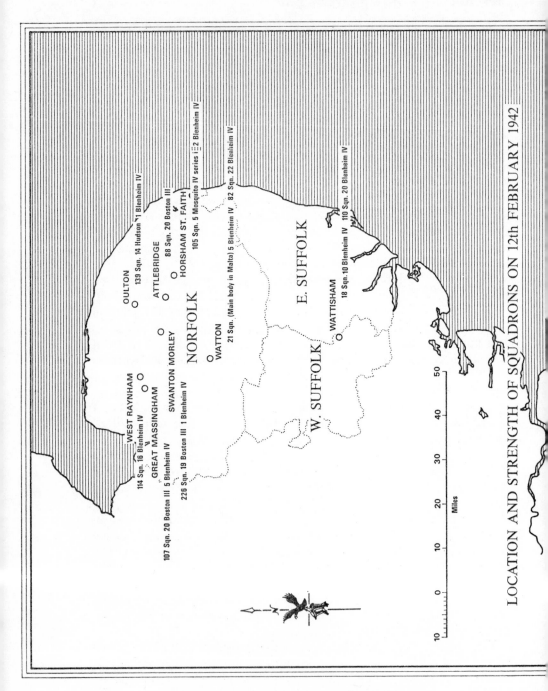

WEST RAYNHAM
114 Sqn. 16 Blenheim IV

GREAT MASSINGHAM
107 Sqn. 20 Boston III 5 Blenheim IV
226 Sqn. 19 Boston III 1 Blenheim IV

OULTON
139 Sqn. 14 Hudson 1 Blenheim IV

ATTLEBRIDGE
88 Sqn. 20 Boston III

SWANTON MORLEY

HORSHAM ST. FAITH
105 Sqn. 5 Mosquito IV series i 2 Blenheim IV

WATTON
21 Sqn. (Main body in Malta) 5 Blenheim IV 82 Sqn. 22 Blenheim IV

NORFOLK

E. SUFFOLK

WATTISHAM
18 Sqn. 10 Blenheim IV 110 Sqn. 20 Blenheim IV

W. SUFFOLK

Miles
10   0   10   20   30   40   50

LOCATION AND STRENGTH OF SQUADRONS ON 12th FEBRUARY 1942

MAP 12. *See Appendix 12, pages 503/4 for notes*

With the shipping campaign over Group's employment was limited and a high-level decision was made that some of its squadrons should be available to reinforce the Air Force in the Far East if needed. Accordingly 139 Squadron stood down for training early in November. On 5 December it moved to Oulton where Lockheed Hudsons were received and a few Boston IIIs flew in, in case there was a change in plan. During January 1942 the Hudsons stood by for possible maritime operations but the situation in Malaya was very bad. After brief leave 139 Squadron left for the Far East where it was so badly mauled that on 30 April its remnants were gathered into 62 Squadron.

Events in the Far East brought serious alarm, and a rapid decision was made to strengthen the bomber element in India. 82 Squadron was taken off operations. Early in March it prepared for the East, its long, meritorious service with 2 Group at an end. Operations also ceased for 110 Squadron, which proceeded on embarkation leave on 24 February and, like 82 Squadron, was soon heading East. This left only 114 Squadron to continue intruder raids, and one squadron could achieve little. The campaign had received an early blow.

Since 1938 Blenheims had formed the backbone of 2 Group. Now radical change was coming as faster, more potent aircraft came into use —the Boston, Mosquito, Ventura and Mitchell. Ideally one type should have replaced the Blenheim, for a multiplicity brought diverse problems and produced spares complications. Each type had particular tactical suitability and welding four into a fighting force was no simple matter. A Blenheim replacement had not been specified until 1940.

First of these to engage in battle was the Douglas Boston, an American machine which gave excellent service almost to the cessation of hostilities. Born as the Blenheim entered production in 1936, its original design weight was 11,850 lb. Therefore, from the start, it was appreciably heavier than the Blenheim. Design maximum speed was set at 280 m.p.h., at 5,000 feet, which placed it in the low attack category. A crew of three was decided upon.

The French Government took an early interest in the prototype, placing orders for its production derivative, the Douglas DB-7. This first flew on 17 August 1939, by which time all-up weight was 14,000 lb. Many DB-7s were delivered to France, and Britain acquired some of these after the French collapse calling them Boston I and II. They had French armament, bombing equipment and metrically calibrated instruments. Thus they were of little use to Britain—their numbers were small, anyway—being seconded for training and trials pending arrival of others to British specification bought by the British Purchasing Commission in 1940.

A Mk. 1, AE458, was delivered to Boscombe Down for appraisal. It was currently undecided in which role the aircraft could perform. Bomber, fighter, reconnaissance? Its radical features included nose-wheel undercarriage, clean aerodynamic form and power twice that of the Blenheim. Simplicity of undercarriage retraction at once appealed; points of note included the unusual dihedral tailplane and air intakes in front of beautifully cowled and faired engine nacelles.

After only a few days it was clear the machine was unsuitable as a fighting vehicle, although there was plenty to commend it basically. The pilot's view forward and to the sides was good, although the noise level for him was high.

Britain acquired examples of the DB-7A first flown in 1940. These had vertical tail surfaces of increased area, longer nacelles and an engine change. They were still unsuitable for the bombing role, being mainly converted into Havoc II night-fighters or intruders.

An order for a variant was placed in the spring of 1940. This, the DB-7B Boston III, was to be identical to the U.S. Army's A-20A apart from the installation of British armament, bombing equipment, radio and oxygen. Nose armament consisted of four fixed .303 in. Browning guns whilst in the rear were twin .303s and a single Vickers .303 on a flexible mounting in the lower station. The bomb bay, extended aft to accommodate British-type chemical and smoke tanks and small bomb carriers, carried two 500-lb. bombs in each of two bomb bays.

Boston IIIs began arriving in Britain in May 1941. Early examples were modified into intruders or night-fighters for Fighter Command. W8286 was delivered to A.F.D.U. Duxford for tactical trials on 27 July 1941, by which time No. 88 Squadron was equipping. W8295 arrived on 88 Squadron on 23 July and W8293 next day. A trickle of Boston IIIs then reached 88 Squadron for training. On 14 October three (W8332, W8337, W8347) arrived at Wattisham for 226 Squadron's conversion.

During November 88 Squadron at Attlebridge began accepting operational aircraft and in December its Blenheims were discarded. Sixteen Bostons left for Long Kesh, Northern Ireland, on 15 January for three weeks' intensive training including low-level army close support work—still 2 Group's allotted role.

Arrival of the Boston at Swanton Morley caused much excitement, and no little concern. Its high landing speed was feared and there was rumour of a high-speed stall. Endurance was limited, it was said, and the lack of a turret caused some worry. Free guns wouldn't afford much protection. A trio broke for landing and the crews watched the first one touch down satisfactorily. It taxied in and stopped. To everyone's astonishment out stepped a gorgeous blonde. 'Hey, how many hours have you done on *that*?' yelled someone wanting rapid acquaintance with both newcomers. 'Oh, it's the first time I've ever flown one,' she replied. Fear evaporated. 'It's got no vices,' the A.T.A. girl tartily added. From then on the Boston was 'in'. Its range was not as good as the Blenheim's, but it was faster and gun worries departed.

It was about this time that another type of aeroplane was unkindly suggested as 2 Group equipment for shipping operations, namely that unhappy aeroplane the Armstrong Whitworth Albemarle. Flt. Lt.

38. Boston III RH-A: W8297 served with 107 Squadron 15.4.42–27.4.42 and 11.6.42–9.7.42, when 226 Squadron received it. Joined 88 Squadron as 'A' 24.9.42. Written off after 120.40 flying hrs. 1.11.42

39. Boston III RH-A: Z2216 which flew more sorties than any other Boston III. Note the flame damper exhausts

40. Boston IIIA RH-A: BZ214 which served briefly with 88 Squadron in July 1943

41. The Boston's shoulder wing and underslung engines, and its very sleek form, are evident in this view of Mk. IIIA ('O'-BZ394 of 342 Squadron) wearing A.E.A.F. stripes

42. Mosquito IV DZ353: GB-E flew 12 sorties with 105 Squadron between 12.10.42 and 31.1.43. Later served with 139 Squadron and lost during a raid on Rennes as AZ: B of 627 Squadron on 8.6.44

43. Short tailed 500 lb. bombs about to be loaded into a Mosquito of 105 Squadron

44. Ground crews of 21 Squadron assemble by a 21 Squadron Ventura at Methwold
45. A Ventura of 487 Squadron races low over Woensdrecht airfield during the Philips raid in December 1942

Kennedy and Flg. Off. Maclachlan were ordered to Boscombe to test it for the Group . . . they condemned it on sight as too large, too slow, too cumbersome. Its turret was far too heavy for the aircraft, its wings were of wood and it seemed to be completely utilitarian in the worst manner, but P1368 had still to be tested. Flight trials were worrying, to say the least, as each day the load was increased and take-off run lengthened considerably. 'I'm going to end up on that hill,' thought Kennedy each time the Albemarle began to roll.

After load trials it was flown to Warboys where all and sundry from Group descended upon it for close inspection. All condemned it—how could anyone have thought 2 Group could operate such an aeroplane! During its flight tests from Warboys P1368 twice force-landed at Raynham. On one occasion six Spitfires formed up to attack the strange being. Maclachlan was subsequently killed during tests which removed any possibility that 2 Group might use the Albemarle.

By now the third Boston squadron, No. 107, was equipping. It received its first aeroplane, Z2200, from 226 Squadron on 1 January 1942. During the next two months 107 Squadron was busy training, especially in low flying. 107 and 226 Squadrons converted in concert using the firing range over Brancaster Bay, where Towing Flight, West Raynham, provided target tugs.

All three squadrons were busy with their training programmes for the spring offensive when sudden alarm burst upon them. Operation *Fuller*, long billed but unexpected, was on. *Scharnhorst* and *Gneisenau* had crept out of Brest to dash through the English Channel. In a matter of moments 2 Group found itself once more hurled into the anti-shipping struggle, this time against its old antagonist, the German Navy.

Air firing practice was under way for 226 Squadron when the news broke. At once all was cancelled. It seemed unbelievable that these huge ships should be making such a daring move and in daylight. When the news reached the squadron that the ships had in fact passed Dover there was stunning astonishment. Action would need to be fast—but how should it be taken? A low-level attack would be the most accurate, but 500-lb. bombs with 11 sec. delay, semi-armour piercing bombs would merely bounce off the ships. Therefore the bombers would need to go in fairly high, yet the weather reports spoke of dense low cloud. The operation was doomed to failure.

Nevertheless, maximum effort and fast reaction were demanded by Group. Six Bostons were hurriedly bombed-up and at 14.25 hours six were away. 107 Squadron was not yet ready to fight, but 88 was and orders were to sink those ships. Four of its Bostons led by the indomitable Wg. Cdr. England set off at 16.03 hours.

The weather was atrocious. None of 88's crews saw the enemy, and all brought their bombs back. Through a cloud gap Flt. Lt. Wheeler of 226 Squadron had a momentary glimpse of them, but the rest drew a blank. Wheeler's aircraft, Z2281, was fired upon by a fighter as he ran up on the convoy, and his starboard wing was damaged by a 20 mm. shell.

Bostons were not 2 Group's only contribution to Operation *Fuller*, Blenheims flew 37 sorties. 110 Squadron was undertaking normal training flights when all crews were suddenly recalled. After rapid briefing thirteen aircraft led by Wg. Cdr. Cree took off at 13.30 hours. Only one crew saw the ships and then it failed to bomb due to low cloud. Of another crew no more was heard. Six aircraft of 114 Squadron left at 14.10, led by Wg. Cdr. Jenkins. Each carried two 500 S.A.P. bombs and four 40-pounders. When at 10,000 feet over the target area, they decided to dive through the clouds, and in so doing became split up. Wg. Cdr. Jenkins immediately saw two large ships in line ahead escorted by smaller ones. He aimed his bombs at a battle-cruiser, but could not see the results because of rain and mist. Sgt. Shackleton also saw them but was unable to attack. During his fifth run his port engine gave trouble forcing him to return. Others saw nothing but Plt. Off. Drysdale was known to have been over the ships. He failed to return.

Next it was the turn of 82 Squadron's dozen crews. They saw nothing, all returning with their bombs. Three more crews of 114 Squadron left at 17.10 and two dropped bombs near the capital ships. Three others of 110 Squadron tried for the grand prize but none located the enemy. It was a demoralising day for all concerned.

Now that the Bostons had been committed to action it was decided that this should continue, for the present with maritime operations. Wg. Cdr. Harris commanding 88 Squadron led four aircraft on the following day to search for possible survivors from the battles of the 12th. On 16 February 88 and 226 Squadrons operated a 'squealer' beat. On 17th they again combined, despatching eight aircraft for an afternoon attack on a convoy of eleven motor vessels reported off Ijmuiden, in the event unlocated.

Practice formation flying for *Circuses* to come was now the main preoccupation of the Boston squadrons. Then on 26 February the first major action came the way of 226 Squadron. Four of its aircraft each with four 500-lb. bombs—double the Blenheim's load—went into action against shipping off the Hook of Holland. G: Z2209 and H: Z2234 bombed a ship of 1,500–2,000 tons whilst X: AL736 attacked two flak ships. As ever the latter's return fire was accurate, the Boston being hit in the starboard engine and its rear gunner wounded. Crippled, it landed at Coltishall.

Although the Blenheim squadrons were committed to night operations they stood by for day raids until the Boston crews were fully prepared. They were to fly just one more. Six aircraft of 114 Squadron, fighter-escorted, took off in the late afternoon of 28 February to attack three U-boats in pens at Ostend. They met their fighter escort over Manston and dropped bombs near the targets and in dockland. Flak was heavy and Sgt. Shackleton had shrapnel lodge in the back strap of his harness.

Other pieces tore into the trousers of Sgt. Kennedy's gunner. There were dogfights for the escort, but all the Blenheims came home.[1]

Training having reached the required standard, and better weather being at hand, Operation *Circus* was resumed on 8 March 1942. Planning was more elaborate now, and for the first time the Douglas Boston offering greater speed and bomb capacity was available. It also packed a useful punch with its four nose guns, which the pilot could use on low-level operations.

At the start of March the Group totalled four operational squadrons, two more with elements detached to Malta and a Mosquito squadron. Establishment on the operational squadrons was sixteen aircraft with four in reserve.

A special raid, Combined Operation No. 352, was billed to open the 1942 day-bombing offensive. It comprised four phases, viz (1) a low-level attack by six Bostons of 88 Squadron and six of 226 Squadron on the Matford Works at Poissy, near Paris, (a deeper penetration than usual), (2) a *Circus* using six aircraft from 88 and 226 Squadrons against Comines power station, cover being provided by fighters of 11 Group, (3) a *Circus* by six crews of 107 Squadron on Abbeville marshalling yards covered by 11 Group and (4) a fighter diversion by squadrons of 10 Group.

For phase I 88 and 226 Squadrons were to fly unobtrusively at below 500 feet from their base at Swanton Morley to Thorney Island on the day of the operation, maintaining radio silence en route. At the agreed zero time they would take-off and head for a point nine miles N.E. of Caen opposite the Orne Estuary, then in sections line astern fly until Zero plus 31 minutes, next setting a dog-legged course for the target, there to arrive at Zero plus 60 and attack the factory from the north-east. This they would leave at 240 I.A.S. turning at 0 plus 83 for Thorney Island meeting their fighter escort for the return journey from the French coast, making the entire flight at very low level.

Meanwhile six Bostons destined for Comines would rendezvous with fighters over Bradwell Bay at Zero Hour at 12,000 feet, fly to five miles west of Dunkirk and attack at 0 plus 31 minutes returning via Mardyck and Manston.

Six of 107 Squadron would meet their fighter escort over Rye at 0 plus 26 minutes, fly to ten miles south of Berck arriving at 0 plus 40, head for Abbeville attacking at 0 plus 46 then fly direct to Dungeness. The amount of detail planning required for such an operation was considerable, but such work was to be repeated many times in 1942. It required excellent co-operation between the fighter and bomber controllers, and good weather.

The three targets had been chosen with deliberation. Twenty lorries a

---

[1] Aircraft used: F: Z7356 Wg. Cdr. Jenkins, Q: Z7700, V: V5456, P: Z7319, H: V6510, K: Z6043.

day were leaving the Matford works for the German Army. At Poissy the target was the main factory block of modern sectionalised construction, sandbagged to prevent each part being damaged. The fireproof roof was made of concrete slabs, but the N.E. and S.W. sides with much glass were more vulnerable.

Comines power station with an output of 170,000 kilowatts fed the industrial areas of Lille and Béthune. It was an important switching station on the French grid system connected to Belgium. It had been hit by Nos. 18, 21, 139 and 226 Squadrons on 28 June 1941, which caused a 50% reduction in the industrial output from the Lille area, but was now fully repaired.

Abbeville marshalling yards were usually full of rolling stock and well away from the populated area. It was known that attacks on shipping, not to mention the Russian campaign, were putting great demands on the rail network and rolling stock.

Wg. Cdr. Harris, C.O. of 88 Squadron, was on leave at this time. Wg. Cdr. England was away and so Wg. Cdr. Butler and Sqn. Ldr. Kennedy were called to Group to hear from A.V.M. Alan Lees about the operation. On the morning of 8 March, after a delay due to bad weather, fourteen Bostons of 88 and 226 Squadrons secretly slipped into Thorney Island, avoiding built-up areas for security reasons during their low transit. As the crews lunched they saw some lovely creatures pass, Windmill girls there for a show later. In the middle of the afternoon they lined the peritrack to wave the Boston crews farewell, with six of 226 Squadron leading the procession. Suddenly the third machine of 88 Squadron accidentally swung off the track, its wheel at once becoming stuck in a mud patch. Immediately brakes squealed in those following. There was a frantic attempt by ground crews to push the aircraft clear, but to no avail. Meanwhile 226 on the runway could hold no longer without sabotaging the entire elaborate operation and at 15.24 they began to roll with two of 88 Squadron tagging on. The remaining four of 88 Squadron made a late take-off and never found the target.

A low-level dash was made across the Channel. As they crossed the enemy shore, soldiers threw themselves to the ground for safety. There was slight upper cloud and visibility was so far moderate, although a gusty wind blew from the south-west. Flg. Off. B. M. Sayers, navigator in the lead aircraft flown by Wg. Cdr. Butler, D.F.C., led the formation on a dog-legged course, turning it repeatedly so that three times they saw fighters wrongly assembled to intercept as a result of receiving a false vector. All went well with 226 Squadron flying at nought feet until, near the target, there was increasing mist. Butler's six roared in at roof-top height and all placed their bombs on the Paris factory encountering only minimal flak.

They were extremely low and it seems feasible that bursting bombs damaged Butler's aircraft, Z2209: G, or else he hit something or was damaged by light flak. He never closed his bomb doors. Radio silence was maintained; then away from the target Butler spotted a clearing near Beauvais, and turned to port towards it with the others following. He was exceedingly low and, before he could reach the field in which he clearly hoped to put down the crippled aircraft, he hit a tree with his port mainplane. 'G George' hurtled across a field, hit the ground, crumpled up and disappeared in a blinding flash. No one, it seemed, could have survived. Saddened, the formation made its way safely back to Thorney. Only two crews of 88 Squadron bombed the target. The remainder, lost, failed to locate it and jettisoned their loads in open country.

For the Comines raid 88 and 226 sent six Bostons, five of which bombed but scored undershoots. Spitfires of the Northolt, North Weald, Hornchurch Wings and a 12 Group Wing gave escort. They shot down a '109 and a '190 but lost three of their number. 107 Squadron closely escorted by the Biggin Hill and Kenley Wings and two squadrons from 10 Group successfully dropped 24 500-pounders on the marshalling yards at Abbeville, bursts being seen in the north and S.E. areas. There was little opposition. This was 107's first operation since re-equipping.

Back in the mess at Swanton Morley that night Chapman, a clairvoyant, was approached for his knowledge of the accident to Butler and crew. He maintained he knew that the air gunner, Robertson, was still alive but seriously ill. None believed this possible. After the war when some of those who took part in the operation visited the graves of Butler and crew they noticed the headstones gave the dates of their deaths as two on March 8—and Robertson on 10th. All were tremendously popular people. Butler was a wonderful pilot and George Sayers a superb navigator, and all were sadly missed.

Air Chief Marshal A. T. Harris, C.-in-C. Bomber Command, signalled those taking part in the day's operation: 'Please give my congratulations to the crews engaged on the highly successful operation which will produce results exceeding those immediately evident. An excellently conceived and executed operation.' Coming, as it did, soon after the massive raid by Bomber Command on the Renault Works at Billancourt, it gave 2 Group the feeling it was contributing to the main offensive. Nevertheless the scale of the operation was such that it could do relatively little to halt production. This came a month later when Bomber Command in strength attacked the Matford Works. (See also Appendix 6.)

Boston operations now got under way in plenty, and soon the fight was furious. On 9 March 107 Squadron flew in a *Circus* to the power station at Gosnay. Fw 190s penetrated the fighter escort and one bomber was shot down. On 13th 88 and 107 Squadrons set off for Hazebrouck marshalling yards and once again the 190s came up to intercept. Grp. Capt. H. V. Beamish was leading the Kenley Wing giving escort cover when a hectic battle opened over St. Inglevert. Sqn. Ldr. B. F. Finucane of 602 Squadron destroyed a '190 and shared another;

Flt. Lt. Bocock claimed two. Another was a probable and two others were damaged, all for the loss of one Spitfire. After bombing, 452 Squadron, part of the forward cover wing, had a fierce fight with '109s and '190s. At one time a section of four were fighting a dozen of the enemy about five miles south of Gravelines. Plt. Off. Sly in AB260 claimed one after a three-second burst.

Number 19 Squadron with 412 and 609 Squadrons forming a 12 Group Wing escorted six Bostons to Abbeville marshalling yards on 24 March. As they were running into the attack about fifty Fw 190s were seen. Repeatedly they tried to dive to attack the bombers but only one was able to reach them, and this did no damage. The following day Le Trait shipyards were 107's target. Bombing, in the face of little opposition, was accurate, hits being scored on the western pier and on a motor vessel in dock. Escorting fighter pilots were most impressed and congratulated the Boston crews after they had landed at Tangmere.

Next day, 24 of 88 and 107 Squadrons were detailed to attack two vessels in Le Havre from 8,000 feet. Direct hits were again scored, the docks straddled, and hits secured on the dock entrance. Just after the bombers had swung on to the bomb run twelve '190s came in for a head-on battle but to little avail, and Finucane of 602 Squadron flying BM124 shot one down. The intense flak damaged Sgt. Barker's aircraft in the starboard wing as a result of which he crashed near Thorney Island. Boston Z2244 broke up in the air after bombing and AL268, damaged, slid to a halt at Manston.

Fighter operations in support of the bombers consisted of forward or target support clearing the way, close escort which sometimes meant that fighters were some way off, cover for the escort, top or high cover, and rear support to bring the bombers home and dispose of any remaining fighters after the escort and others had engaged and perhaps run low on ammunition and fuel. The usefulness of rear support can be seen from the operations of 27 March. Twelve Bostons were returning from Ostend covered by 411 Squadron. A mile from the British coast three '190s dived on the Bostons. 411 swung quickly into action, Plt. Off. Green in Spitfire AA839 shooting one down.

Limited night intruder operations continued, but with only No. 114 Squadron participating. There were thirty sorties—11 were abortive and only 16 attacks were made—and three Blenheims were lost, one to a night fighter pilot, Obfeld Gildner of II/NJG2. Targets were mainly in Holland. Operations were flown entirely at between 1,500 and 2,000 feet with a bombing height set at 1,200, for accuracy, at which height even sound locators could easily track the aircraft. Searchlights were active making attack difficult. They could not be easily evaded at low levels and it was best to drop a flare blotting out the lights. Flak was not serious and two losses were probably due to coastal guns.

Circus operations continued and on 4 April a morning raid on railway sheds at St. Omer was delivered by 88 Squadron. No. 303 Polish

Squadron acting as escort cover was dived upon by two groups of Bf109s and Fw 190s. 316 Squadron swept in to engage and 303 turned to fight, shooting down two '190s. One of the Bostons was badly damaged and, escorted by 303 Squadron, limped back to Manston. Nine crews of 107 Squadron set out for Hazebrouck on 12 April meeting their escort of Debden, Northolt, Tangmere and 10 Group Wings over Beachy Head. Just inside France about thirty German fighters were spotted climbing westwards and soon eight more were parallel with the beehive. After the bombing eight of the foe dived upon 303 Squadron whilst eight more came in from the direction of Boulogne for stern attacks. Wg. Cdr. Rolski leading the Northolt Wing ordered 316 Squadron to wheel and engage. There was a free-for-all during which Flt. Sgt. Popeck claimed a '190 and Flg. Off. Horbaczewski another before he escorted a crippled Boston.

As part of the diversion to the Lancaster raid on Augsburg of 17 April, 88 Squadron flew an extremely effective operation against Grand Quevilly power station near Rouen whilst a further six bombed the nearby shipyards. 107 Squadron aimed for the artificial silk factory at Calais but had to satisfy themselves with hits on nearby railway lines. Several 109Fs reached through to the bombers and Ashman curled away to the sea, Z2255's port engine blazing. Twenty-four Spitfire squadrons participated. The escort wing was provided by Tangmere (41, 129, 340 Squadrons), escort cover by Northolt (303, 316 and 317 Squadrons), high cover by Kenley (457, 485 and 602 Squadrons). A large-scale *Rodeo* over the Pas de Calais was flown by Nos. 72, 124 and 401 Squadrons (Biggin Hill), 411, 609 and 611 Squadrons of 12 Group, Nos. 64, 122 and 313 Squadrons (Hornchurch), Nos. 65, 71 and 111 Squadrons (Debden) and Nos. 121, 222 and 403 Squadrons (North Weald).

All three Boston squadrons operated on 25 April, 88 against Le Havre, 107 on Cherbourg and 226 on Dunkirk. Plt. Off. Pasterfield of 226 Squadron was shot down by two Fw 190s which set his port engine blazing. He ditched in a rough sea and no one was seen to get out. During 107's second raid of the day '190s again intercepted the force, two penetrating to the bombers which had faced heavy flak. Most of the Bostons were damaged and the stern blown off one whose rudder then jammed. Nevertheless it flew home. Debden Wing Spitfires of Nos. 65, 71 and 111 Squadrons giving high cover were engaged by thirty enemy fighters two of which were destroyed. Thirty Boston sorties were flown during the day.

Twelve of 107 Squadron raided Lille/Sequedin power station on 27 April. Fw 190s tackled 316 Squadron flying high cover and a fight developed. Two shot-up Bostons were escorted home to Manston while 452 Squadron damaged two of the enemy. Close escort was being given by Nos. 65, 71 and 111 Squadrons. The bombers had crossed the coast six miles east of Dunkirk and then made a slow right turn to run up on the target. Forty '190s dived out of the sun and were quickly engaged by

71 Squadron. Three penetrated the fighter screen and two of them were driven off by 65 Squadron. The third picked off the last Boston, which fell into the Channel. Flt. Lt. Stillwell of 65 Squadron detached his dinghy and threw it to one of the crew. Apparently he had died for he made no effort to reach it.

Bombs from six Bostons straddled the railway sheds at St. Omer on 28th whilst 317 Squadron took on six '190s above. Flt. Lt. Duryasz saw his go into a spin. Flg. Off. Koc destroyed one and Sgt. Kolczynski another. Next day, when 317 Squadron claimed another '190, 226 Squadron bombed Ostend power station and W/O Keech, hit by flak, landed on the Dunkirk shore. So heavy was the flak at Le Havre on 30th that the squadron could not concentrate on its bombing, and two of its six aircraft had to belly-land at Thorney Island. Fighters so damaged Flt. Lt. Houghton's Boston during 107's raid later that day on Abbeville that it caught fire, and yet it limped home.

During April the Bostons flew 218 high-level sorties under fighter escort, 89% claiming to bomb the target. Attacks were generally flown at 12,000 to 14,000 feet—too high for light flak to reach the bombers and too low for heavy flak. These limits were usually maintained to the end of the war. More enemy fighters than expected were getting through to the bombers. Once they exploited the Boston's blind spot—by attacking from below—fortunately unsuccessfully. More gunners were immediately posted to the squadrons to take station at the under gun hitherto unmanned. Policy was next to man the bottom guns in the last three aircraft in each box of six. When the boxes were closed up there was reasonable defence against stern attacks by cross fire, and two enemy fighters had been destroyed by rear gunners. The camera fitting in the Boston had prevented the belly gun from being installed, and now had to be shifted into the flare chute. 194 Bostons claimed to make attacks during April. Six failed to return, three falling to fighters.

Flak was a menace although often inaccurate. Group decided to issue guidance on its evasion. On all occasions the latter needed to be varied. One day height should be lost after attack, gained on another. Such changes would upset predicted fire more than course changes of even 30 degrees. Turns of up to 20 degrees were possible without putting much strain on formation keeping. More than one turn was suggested, and irregular course changes on to the bomb run which should be out of the sun when practicable. Crossing of the enemy coast was to be at differing heights from the bomb run, which should not exceed thirty seconds. On *Circus* operations the fighter escort had to be fully considered, thus height changes were restricted to 2,000 feet. Pre-arranged heights for rendezvous, coastal crossing and bombing run needed to be accurately adhered to. If a course change of over 20 degrees was made the fighter leader must be warned on VHF. Approach to the run-up should generally be made losing height on a turn out of the sun. Here again the fighters needed to be considered because their fuel supply was limited. It was desirable to cross the sea as low as possible to avoid radar detection. From this it can be seen that the planning of *Circuses* was quite complicated, and at all times represented a compromise.

Evidence suggested that bombing accuracy was none too good. Consequently the Mk. IX bombsights were partly replaced by the superior, gyroscopically controlled Mk. XIV, but the results barely improved. It appeared that 226 Squadron's bombing was marginally better than 88's, and the squadron commanders discussed ideas for improving matters. They tried to shorten the bombing run which was dependent upon the wind. An early run-in with a tail wind was decided upon, short in a head wind. Trouble was being met on the run-up too, the Bostons unsteady and porpoising. Group was informed and it was decided that the bomb doors should be opened well short of the target allowing time for trim adjustment. There was also much trouble from dust entering the aircraft when the doors opened.

Blenheim night intruder raids had continued throughout April. 114 Squadron flew 52 sorties dropping bombs on 39 occasions. Intruding assumed more importance when the Luftwaffe resumed concentrated night operations under the *Baedeker Plan*. Luckily 18 Squadron had completed intruder training by the end of the month, during which it had mounted night raids on the dry dock at Dunkirk and Langerbrugge power station near Ghent. The sorties of 114 Squadron were largely uneventful, but on 14th–15th Sqn. Ldr. Iredale's machine was seriously damaged by flak which holed the starboard wing and a fuel pipe. Nevertheless he bombed a lighting system N.E. of Amsterdam.

May proved disappointing for daylight operations. Heavy cloud over Britain in the second half reduced *Circuses*. Of 25 projected only fifteen were flown. Zeebrugge power station was bombed by 226 Squadron on 5th, and on their second *Circus* that day they headed for another at Sequedin. It was cloud-clad so they turned to the nearby chemical works. The leader's bombs hung up and the remainder thought he had decided not to attack. Top cover was being provided by Nos. 64, 122 and 313 Squadrons led by Wg. Cdr. R. P. Powell supported by Debden and North Weald Wings. Six '109s/'190s sneaked in behind the high cover from Ostend and over Lille another fifteen appeared. During the developing dogfight Flt. Lt. Fredjfar of 313 Squadron destroyed two '190s.

On 7th there came the month's most effective raid when six Bostons of 107 Squadron led by Sqn. Ldr. Forsythe dropped 500-pounders and incendiaries on the coke-oven batteries of the Solway Coking Plant, Zeebrugge. Direct hits were scored on its east end and the lubricating-oil depot. No. 226 Squadron also on the operation had all its machines hit by flak.

Ramrod 33 was flown on 17 May by 226 Squadron, against Boulogne docks. Forty 500-lb. bombs fell on shipping, the quayside, nearby railway station and the south end of the tidal basin. W8368 'K' flown by

H2

Plt. Off. O'Malley was hit in the port engine and he had to belly-land her at Manston. After the bombing fifteen-plus bandits were reported near Le Touquet. Kenley Wing giving top cover was vectored to Marquise, then Guines, where 602 Squadron dived on 10 Fw 190s then itself was bounced by another fifteen. Individual combats followed during which Sqn. Ldr. 'Paddy' Finucane claimed one. Flt. Lt. Major was attacked and crashed into the sea off Cap Gris Nez. Dennehey circled and threw him a dinghy but he could not reach it. By the time a rescue launch was at the spot he had died. Eight fighters were lost during the operation.

Plans for Operation 760 were signalled on 27 May 1942. Clearly it was to be outstanding. They read: 'It has been decided that a bombing attack on an unprecedented scale is to be made on target Dace [i.e. Hamburg] or, in the event of weather being unsuitable for that target, on target Trout [i.e. Cologne]. The decision as to which is being attacked will be passed to station operations rooms by 12.30 on the day of the operation. Aircraft of 2 Group will not take part in the main attack, but with attack squadrons of Army Co-operation Command carry out widespread intruder attacks on enemy night-fighter airfields to prevent interference with the main attack.' These latter came under the control of Station Commanders at their 2 Group advanced bases under what was known as M Plan, scheduled to take place on 28–29 May, or on the first suitable night thereafter up to 31 May–1 June. The force was to 'embrace all available Blenheim crews of Nos. 13, 18, 114 and 614 Squadrons for which competent crews are available'—estimated to be 40–50 crews.

Two Army Co-operation Command squadrons, Nos. 13 and 614, moved from Odiham and Macmerry to Wattisham and Raynham respectively to await orders. Briefing came on 30 May, with Cologne the chosen target. For the Blenheim crews their selected targets were further away than usual. Crews were told not to pass a point off the enemy coast before a given time to ensure they had full cover of darkness, approach to this point being as low as failing light safely permitted. Then they climbed to their bombing heights—an average of 2,000–3,000 feet—and headed towards their targets along flak-free routes. Most airfields could be identified by visual Lorenz and flare-paths. Half the aircraft had two 250-lb. G.P. and sixteen 40-lb. bombs, the remainder two 250-lb. delayed-action bombs and Small Bomb Containers carrying eight 40-lb. bombs and 24 9-lb. anti-personnel bombs. Their splinter effect would, it was calculated, affect morale and disturb operations.

Fifty-three sorties were despatched late on 30 May. (See Appendix 6.) Of these, 34 crews attacked their primaries, a very worthy effort since many were untrained for such operations. Nos. 18 and 114 Squadrons did excellent work at Bonn, St. Trond, Venlo and Juvincourt and there can be little doubt they helped cut Main Force losses. When the attack on Bonn opened lights were on, some aircraft bombing before they were switched off. Only one crew found Vechta, delivering an ineffective attack. That on Twente was none too successful. Six Blenheims claimed to attack St. Trond from a low level, bombs falling on the runway and among buildings. Venlo was bombed but not put out of action.

As the Blenheims struggled home something tremendously exciting was happening at Horsham; it was to revitalise the whole of 2 Group's war. That glittering performer, the Mosquito, was about to bite.

Chapter 13
Mosquito, Performer Supreme

No military aeroplane has proved more versatile than the wooden de Havilland Mosquito. From the start it was an incredible performer and when Geoffrey de Havilland cavorted around the sky in 2 Group's first Mosquito all were astonished. Here was an unarmed bomber relying entirely on speed for safety, schemed at a time when emphasis lay on heavily armed bombers. Its origin and development are fully discussed in *Mosquito* (Faber and Faber) and the reader is invited to consult this volume for details. Suffice to say, the Mosquito went ahead despite official reluctance to believe in it. It was ordered into production as a reconnaissance machine, entering service in July 1941, and beginning operations the following September, twelve months later than it need have done if de Havilland's performance forecasts had been accepted.

What a punch squadrons of Mosquito bombers and fighters could have packed in 1940—when they certainly could, and should, have become available. 2 Group could have been operating them by the height of the Battle of Britain. Now, at the end of May 1942, No. 105 Squadron was ready to take the Mosquito bomber into action, about to test the efficiency of an unarmed high-speed bomber.

Not until July 1941 had it been decided to produce Mosquitoes as bombers, and then the order was for a measly ten converted from P.R. airframes. It was September before the first conversion flew and 15 November when the first reached 105 Squadron. A further sixty bombers—true bombers from the start—had been ordered, but not until February 1942 did they appear on the production line at Hatfield. DK288 became, on 16 May 1942, the first Mk. IV srs. ii (as the production version was known) to reach 105 Squadron. For early operations the squadron had depended upon the P.R.U./Bomber Conversion Type (Mk. IV srs. i).

With only a handful of aircraft—five in January and seven by March—flying was much restricted. Handling qualities and range assessment had to be deduced, tactics needed special attention. By April 105 Squadron had twenty crews but only seven aircraft. There was fear that general morale might suffer if no operations soon took place. The main hold-up concerned the bomb load, which Group insisted should be four 500-

pounders. Fitting them in the Mosquito was at first impossible for the bomb doors would not close on the girth of such bombs. Slight dishing of the doors was one possibility, but de Havilland, enterprising as ever, came up with the solution—shorter tails on the bombs thus allowing four to be carried. Shortened tails were first received in small quantities at the end of April.

Operation 761 was notified by Group on 27 May 1942 to 105 Squadron, now at Horsham St. Faith near Norwich. Here was a Top Secret document detailing the first operation by the new wonder bomber, one which everyone hoped would not turn out like that pre-war bomber 'faster than the fighters', the Blenheim. 105 Squadron was committed to follow the great raid on Cologne.

'Your aim is to continue harassing attacks the following day, and obtain photographic evidence of damage caused by the main attack.' 105 Squadron was told to despatch up to four Mosquitoes each carrying an F24 camera with 20 in. lens and 125 exposure film to use to the maximum extent over the target. The Mosquitoes were to fly there and back by the shortest route which avoided gun and fighter defended areas, and keep out of RDF range if possible. They were to operate singly at irregular intervals, attacks being dictated by cloud state. If the latter favoured cloud-cover attacks these were to be undertaken; alternatively 'the aircraft should operate at or above heights where optimum speed superiority over fighters is obtained'. Load would be four 500-lb. M.C. bombs being specially delivered to Horsham.

'Owing to the outstanding nature of this operation,' read the order, 'special precautions must be taken to safeguard its success. Only the minimum number of persons whose duty makes it essential should be allowed to know any details.' Group was taking no chances.

Eight Mosquitoes were with 105 Squadron when the attack on Cologne took place on 30–31 May. Before Main Force had returned two were being prepared for the operation and at 04.00 hours. Sqn. Ldr. Oakeshott took off in W4072: D on the first sortie, followed 1½ hours later by Plt. Off. Kennard in W4064. Oakeshott flew at 24,000 feet over Cologne, blotted out by smoke rising to 14,000 feet. Photography was impossible but bombs were aimed into the smoke.

Kennard fared badly. Possibly defences were on the alert for reconnaissance aircraft or nuisance raiders, and anti-aircraft fire brought down his aircraft.

At 11.40 Plt. Off. Costello-Bowen took off, Flt. Lt. Houlston following five minutes later. They found smoke still enveloping the smouldering ruins and once more bombs were aimed into it.

All so far had been high-level sorties with limited success, so another was ordered. This time it was flown by Sqn. Ldr. Channer who took off for a low-level reconnaissance. He flew into cloud en route then dived towards the city when sixty miles away. There was still a lot of smoke and again bombs were dropped. More important, the Mosquito returned safely proving that low-level sorties in daylight over Germany by a lone unarmed aircraft were feasible. The Mosquito had made it.

Operation 784 was billed for 1–2 June, being roughly a repeat of the Cologne raid but with, this time, Essen as target. With large forces marshalled Bomber Command had decided to strike again. Once more Blenheims of the inflated four-squadron 2 Group force were to attack airfields at St. Trond, Venlo, Rheine, Juvincourt, Twente, Schiphol, Bonn and Vechta. Allocation of routes and targets was as for the Cologne raid. Of the 23 despatched from Wattisham, 22 claimed to attack despite poor weather. In all, three were lost. For this operation the weather was not so good, there was haze and much cloud.

After the raid 105 Squadron again went into action in a bomber reconnaissance role some eighteen hours after the main attack, to discover what had happened at Essen. The target was seen to have escaped relatively lightly with damage to the railway near the Krupp works and to the residential property in the south and south-east. Nearby Oberhausen, with extensive factories, commercial and residential buildings had, however, suffered severely.

Lone Mosquito high-level raids using cloud protection continued, sixteen sorties being made in June mainly to north-west Germany and all in daylight. Twelve were flown at between 20,000 and 25,000 feet, heights at which the greatest advantage over fighters was held and the Mosquito reached its top speed of about 388 m.p.h. Three missions were primarily photographic flights over Schiphol, Bremen and Hanover. All were completed without loss.

A second Mosquito squadron, No. 139, formed on 8 June at Horsham. There were insufficient aircraft to equip it so it was forced to borrow machines from 105 Squadron even to December. So scarce and valuable were the Mosquitoes that special orders were repeatedly given to take very great care of the aircraft. During June 139 Squadron worked up its crews for an early début. Blenheim Vs were also issued to 139 Squadron and other 2 Group units mainly for training and to prepare them to ultimately form part of the tactical bombing force for the invasion of north-west Africa.

Meanwhile, what of the Bostons? Of 2 Group's 222 daylight sorties in June, 179 were Boston flights. Usually they flew low level to the fighter rendezvous and climbed to bombing height over the sea. Sometimes they continued the climb to the run-in point, on some raids they flew home losing height, and in one instance dived away at 320 I.A.S. losing some 2,000 feet per minute. Dieppe, Morlaix airfield, oil tanks at Bruges, Le Havre power station, Dunkirk, Flushing: all were attacked.

On 10 June 107 Squadron set off for Lannion, only to be recalled. At midday they took-off for another try and dropped 22 500-pounders and 172 40-lb. bombs and met moderate flak. At 6,000 feet about 25 miles from Start Point on return, look-out was relaxed—a fatal move—and a Fw 190 crept to 800 yards unseen. It raked Plt. Off.

Skinner's aircraft, AL715. The tail fell off and the crew were posted missing. Fighters accounted for the intruder.

On 24 June orders were given for Operation *Millennium II* on 25–26 June with Bremen as target. No. 13 Squadron again participated in operations from Wattisham, and 614 from Raynham. These, and Nos. 18 and 114 Squadrons, were to attack airfields. Night intruders of 11 Group were operating too. Coastal Command Beaufighters were to make standing patrols over Stade and Schleswig, and there was another difference too. Boston squadrons were to be engaged.

In Phase 1 Bostons of 88, 107 and 226 Squadrons would make intruder attacks at dusk on selected fighter airfields, joined by four Mosquitoes of 105 and 139 Squadrons, the latter to raid Stade and flying its first sortie. Each of the Boston squadrons was ordered to send nine aircraft, 226 using long-range Bostons for deeper penetration. All attacks were to be as low as possible, made on one pass with guns blazing. If possible, sections were to attack together. The purpose of these raids was to stop enemy fighters from taking off. It was known they were brought to assembly points for night operations and if such were seen they were to have the full weight of attack. Boston crews were ordered to shoot up dispersed aircraft and crews.

Phase II was the Blenheim attack, by Nos. 18, 13, 114 and 614 Squadrons, made during darkness to curtail use of six airfields.

Phase III embraced aircraft sent to gather information about the night's attacks and make harassing attacks on other parts of Germany. Six Mosquitoes were to be available and two of these fly a reconnaissance of Bremen using 36 in. lens cameras. The other four would fly to Essen, Hamburg, Cologne or Kiel and Bremen. Seventy were detailed in all.

The Boston raids proceeded as ordered. 88 Squadron sent nine aircraft in threes to Gilze Rijen, Volkel and Hamstede, and they all attacked their targets. Sgt. Hughes flew across Volkel at 200 feet bombing the runway intersection and perimeter track. Airfield fires could be seen twenty miles away. Sgt. Savage attacked Hamstede from 150 feet. 107 Squadron despatched six Bostons to Leeuwarden and three to Bergen/Alkmaar. It was much darker than expected and four aircraft were unable to locate the airfield. The remainder successfully attacked at 22.30 hours with 11 sec. and 30 min. delay bombs, 500-pounders and incendiaries. Three searchlights were shot out. Flt. Lt. Carlisle was caught by bomb burst and the tail of AL702 was holed. His rear gunner had his guns blown overboard and control of the aircraft was temporarily lost. Light flak prevented Wg. Cdr. Lynn and Plt. Off. Allen from attacking, but Flt. Lt. Maclachlan roared across his target at 75 feet. Plt. Off. Rushden in Z2314 dropped his load from 100 feet near a hangar. Although two aircraft were damaged all returned safely. Two Mosquitoes attacked the airfield at Schleswig, and one Stade.

Long-range aircraft of 226 Squadron went for Jever and Ardorf.

Average fuel load remaining on return was 130 gallons—sufficient for another 260 miles—and all the Bostons landed in darkness.

Blenheims attacked airfields at Venlo, Twente, Elde and Leeuwarden. T2254: A of 13 Squadron was shot down by Oblt. Knacke of III/NJG91.

Additionally three Blenheims of 18 Squadron and eight of 114 Squadron participated in the Main Force attack on Bremen. During June the two Blenheim squadrons of 2 Group managed 171 night sorties delivering 118 attacks. Five Blenheims were lost and one crashed near base.

Four Mosquitoes carried out bomber-photo-reconnaissance/damage assessment operations.

Useful on account of their good medium-level performance, the Typhoon squadrons now ready for action were first employed on a *Circus* operation on 29 June. Six Bostons raided Hazebrouck under close escort of Hornchurch Wing, escort cover from Debden, high cover from Nos. 124, 133 and 401 Squadrons of Biggin Hill and target support from squadrons from Kenley, Northolt and North Weald. The 12 Group Duxford Typhoon Wing gave rear support sweeping the Mardyck–Gravelines area. There was no enemy response. The Typhoon was not ideally suited to such a battle role and its use on these operations was at all times limited, although months later when Mosquitoes made low-level penetrations over northern France they sometimes had a Typhoon escort.

Consideration was given of the accuracy achieved since April by Boston crews. Precision bombing of small targets could be undertaken only by day. Security and defences generally qualified the scale and effort of operations. Normally Bostons attacked in boxes of six, bombs being aimed by the leader of each vic of three. Photographs showed that usually each box laid a bomb pattern fairly narrow but very long, sticks falling at random but in one direction. Average errors of groups of bomb bursts were found to be as follows:

Opposition (mainly flak)	No. of bombs dropped	No. plotted on photographs	No. of groups of bombs plotted	Bomb error in yards		
				Radial	Line	Range
None	155	85	6	200	120	140
Little	191	120	8	400	250	270
Moderate	341	216	15	460	280	290
Heavy	479	269	18	520	230	440
Overall	1166	690	47	440	230	330

It was found that the error doubled when opposition was encountered, but the weight of opposition did not much increase inaccuracy. Neither did the height of attack. Photographs showed that about 10% of bombs dropped hit primary targets and 50% caused damage to factories, warehouses, roads etc. About 90% of bombs dropped on airfields were within their perimeters. Attacks on coastal and shipping targets had been less effective, partly due to strong opposition demanding evasive action. About 46% bombs fell on open ground or in water.

The first three months of action in 1942 were also generally considered. Limited fighter endurance still restricted the radius of operations so that the *Circuses* were over the same areas as in 1941. Most serious was the obvious superiority of the Fw 190 over the Spitfire V, which meant that the campaign was swinging into the enemy's favour. The number of *Circuses* was therefore reduced and in their place 2 Group introduced low-level attack in which it was ultimately to excel. The very existence of the Group was at this time considered and finally it was decided to maintain it for the day when it would afford close support to the Army in the essential invasion of Europe, the testing time for which was almost at hand.

At Charmy Down the Fighter Leader School trained flight commanders and explored tactics. Sqn. Ldr. Pelly-Fry had some experience of Boston operations and Bill Hesketh rang him one day asking him to fly to F.L.S. to talk to the pilots about *Circus* operations. It was here that Pelly-Fry, Dickie England and Sqn. Ldr. Griffiths worked out new tactics for the Bostons. Pelly-Fry had devised a horizontal corkscrew manoeuvre. These skilled pilots worked out an evasive tactic which was to be standard procedure. The leader of the box would porpoise whilst Nos. 2 and 3 did the rotating corkscrew. It needed careful timing but soon it was possible for whole boxes, indeed whole squadrons, to adopt the manoeuvre which completely upset the aim of fighter pilots. On one trial Spitfires tried unsuccessfully to intercept for 32 minutes.

Soon it was standard procedure for a whole Boston squadron to fly to Charmy Down at the end of the F.L.S. monthly course. The Bostons would fly over the Bristol Channel and along would come three dozen Spitfires, a third of them with red tails and red spinners simulating the enemy. The bombers would practise evasion, escort and interception, then the crews would discuss the exercise. The course invariably ended with them all flying to Portreath or Perranporth where the venture would nicely terminate with a spot of bathing and a good soaking in beer!

Some basic points about Boston *Circus* operations were now evident. Below 1,000 feet light flak was very effective, between 9,000 and 12,000 the medium flak was not so good but above 14,000 feet heavy flak came into its own. Therefore operations certainly needed to be flown between about 10,000 and 14,000 feet.

It was essential for fighters to arrive at the rendezvous exactly on time. To Sqn. Ldr. Pelly-Fry this meant plus or minus fifteen seconds, no more or less. Radio silence was essential on the low crossing of the Channel. A waggle on the wings was the sign for the battle climb to begin and throttles to be pushed into boost taking the whole formation to a height agreeable to bombers and fighters. The fighters were often some distance off, looking like a fleet of model aeroplanes. As the beehive climbed the fighters would edge away and two thoughts would be uppermost in the minds of the 2 Group men—'They always shoot at bombers' . . . 'Fighters don't drop bombs!'

July began auspiciously for the Mosquitoes. Six took off at midday to bomb submarine yards at Flensburg. This was their first use in a mass low-level attack. But serious planning failure became evident since, for 190 miles, they were only 25–30 miles off shore. This provided the enemy with a simple interception problem. As they sped along, Bf 109s and Fw 190s were vectored on to three of them and shot one down. Evasive action, controlled by kneeling observers looking aft, consisted of an increase in speed and the usual turn in to meet the attack. Since the Mosquitoes were flying at 320–330 m.p.h. at sea level the number of attacks was few. Soon the Mosquitoes pulling 12½ lb. boost drew away from the fighters. Interception by the enemy was good and well timed. Good visibility had contributed to the fighters' success. Possibly the operation was compromised early, as the Mosquitoes sped over a squealer. One Mosquito seen hit by flak at the target was last seen crossing the enemy coast at reduced speed. The raid cost two fine pilots, Grp. Capt. MacDonald and Sqn. Ldr. Oakeshott. One Mosquito, hit in the fuselage, was chased by fighters. Its superior speed saved it.

Next day new Mosquito employment was promulgated. It was decided that a Mosquito should fly over enemy territory before major operations by heavies, assessing weather conditions which could be radioed in code. 105 Squadron aircraft stood by daily in case of need. Operations were ordered by Command which named the area and height of sortie. A relatively simple code was employed for a weather radio signal, '5/10 cumulus cloud tops 4,000 feet, 10/10 stratus at 10,000 with moderate visibility' becoming 'Yew Hog Cat Nag Bug'.

In the spring of 1942 the 15th Bomb Squadron (Light), U.S.A.A.C., was despatched to Britain, not for bombing but to learn night-fighting techniques. It found the R.A.F. had discarded a plan for airborne searchlights which the Americans had come to study. The 15th Squadron was subsequently attached to No. 226 Squadron to study R.A.F. day-bomber techniques including low-level flying and evasive tactics. Having no aircraft they borrowed 226's for training. By the end of June 1942 they seemed ready to partake in operations. On 25 June 36 U.S.A.A.C. personnel including nine crews reached Swanton Morley on detachment. During the morning of 29th the Americans practised flying and became ready to operate. After lunch four Americans (Capt. Kegelman with Lt. Bell as bombardier, Tech. Sgt. Robert Golay as gunner and Sgt. Cunningham w./op. air-gunner) climbed aboard AL743. Theirs was one of twelve Bostons led by Sqn. Ldr. Kennedy on a *Circus* to Hazebrouck marshalling yards. There was no flak but escorting Spitfires engaged in dogfights. These Americans became the first U.S.A.A.C. members operating as a crew to bomb enemy territory in Europe. A few bursts were recorded on rail lines and sheds at the west of the target, but most were to the south or north of the yards.

Once home it was decided that the Americans should, on American Independence Day, take part in one of the new low-level missions. After the elation of their first operation Kegelman and the others decided they would turn in early to be ready for a dawn call. As they sauntered from the Mess Kegelman called Shaw Kennedy to one side—he had something important to say. 'Shaw, I think you should know something. All this business comes difficult to me. You see, I've a cousin who's German.' Kennedy pointed out that this was a problem he would have to master. A few moments later Lt. Loehrl sidled up to him . . . 'There is something you should know, Shaw, my brother is German, and it troubles me.' Kennedy's silent response was simply 'What on earth have I let myself in for tomorrow?' After some rumination he decided he would tell his crew, he owed it to them.

Take-off began with Sqn. Ldr. J. S. Kennedy in Z2234: X who was leading a raid on De Kooy with Capt. Kegelman in AL750: Z and Lt. Loehrl in AL677: P. Then came Flt. Lt. Yates Earl in AL679: Y with Plt. Off. Henning (Z2213: U) and another American crew piloted by Lt. Lynn in AL741: V. They had Bergen airfield as their target. Next came Flt. Lt. A. B. Wheeler's trio, he in Z2197: H ahead of Plt. Off. Eltringham (W8371: F) and the American Capt. O'Dell (AL746: M) all bound for Hamstede. Finally Z2258 led two other Americans, Capt. Crabtree (AL670: D) and Lt. Hawel (Z2303: J) bound for Valkenburg.

They hugged the waves, and they were all unfortunate. Thirty miles from Holland they flashed over two squealers who without doubt radioed news of their approach. They spread out into line abreast so as to give the coastal gunners the hardest task. Kennedy's trio smashed through the hail of fire to De Kooy only to face more bitter flak. The order was clear: no steep turn after bombing, all turns *must* be flat and very low. Taking evasive action in the murderous hail of fire, Kennedy slightly dropped a wing. He was so low that for five fearful seconds it scraped the ground, dust being hurled to forty feet or more. Loehrl in the heat of battle did the unforgivable. He made a steep banking turn exposing his aircraft to fire. A direct hit from Leichte Flak 4./845 blew the nose away, the aircraft burst into flames and rolled into shallow water near the airfield. Miraculously the bombardier survived as a prisoner.

'Keg' meanwhile was flying very low, so low that one of his propellers touched the ground and was wrenched off. Kennedy made his escape and quickly unloaded his bombs close to a trawler and, experienced, made his getaway. 'Keg' saw him drawing away but misidentified him as an enemy aircraft so kept his distance and was soon far behind in a battered aircraft with his starboard propless engine burning. Over the North Sea he wrestled to control the bomber.

At Bergen all three crews swept in at 08.00. Their mixed loads soon fired a hangar but again the defence was intense, Leichte Flak 3./845 getting hits on Lt. Lynn's machine which fell in pieces four minutes later north of Bergen aan Zee. As the Bostons attacked a Bf 109 of 10./JG 1 scrambled. Uffz. Rathenow was soon on Henning's tail and shot him down at sea west of Den Helder. Only Yates Earl made a getaway.

Hamstede was attacked at 07.59, again at very low level. Bombs fell among the admin. buildings, hangars and dispersed aircraft and a great pall of smoke signalled some success. For good measure Wheeler could not resist gingering up a parade of about 160 Germans in flying kit, with the aid of his front guns. All three who went to Valkenburg met ill luck for the leader opened his doors too late for bombing. The airfield was shot up and an aircraft left burning.

The Bostons trickled into base, but of Kegelman there was no sign. To meet them was a jovial, friendly American little known at that time who said his name was 'Eisenhower'. The crews were bunched around him telling their stories when someone spotted a Boston on finals. It could only be . . . Kegelman. On one engine he made a good landing and sedately taxied the battle-scarred aircraft in. Rejoicing was great as he jumped out and walked across the grass to meet the one-day President. And as he looked back he pointed to the grass sod lodged in his engine cowl. It had been a near thing, and his gallantry won him a D.S.C. and for each of his crew an American D.F.C. There was deep sorrow at the loss of the others. 'Keg' was, indeed, a great Uncle Sam figure.

The squadron licked the wounds until 12 July when Kennedy led six British and six American crews on a *Circus* to Abbeville airfield. The target was half cloud-clad and the mixed loads screamed down from 8,000–8,500 feet, lower than usual, all north of the airfield. Flak hit two aircraft. Fighters were seen but did not intercept. After this the Americans, now blooded, retired to plan their own campaign.

Mosquitoes flew four types of operations in July, the newest high-level sorties at 21,000–22,000 feet against targets mainly in Germany planned to create maximum disturbance. Tracks were dog-legged, heading first for one city for about sixty miles then another, finally turning on to a 20–30 mile run-up to the primary. Twenty-nine such sorties were flown in July, the results of one to Mannheim on 25th apparent from a note in the *Daily Telegraph* for 4 August. It read: 'The raid on Mannheim evidently caught the population unprepared for a warning has since been issued that everyone must go to the shelters when sirens sound and those who suffer from negligence will not be compensated. Many believed the sirens were a test.'

A second low-level Mosquito raid on Flensburg was mounted on 11 July as a diversion to Lancasters raiding Danzig at dusk. This was part of a campaign directed against U-boat building yards. 105 Squadron sent two sections of three to attack submarine-building slips, with airfields or built-up areas in Germany as possible alternatives. This time the Mosquitoes were ordered to retire north of a line 54° 30′ N until past 04° 00′ E. To assist in the Lancaster withdrawal, Blenheims were alerted for operations against airfields, but were not called upon.

It was an eventful operation. The fin of Plt. Off. Laston's Mosquito had two square feet of ply blown away by flak. Sgt. Rowlands flew so low that pieces of a chimney-pot crashed into his lap. His port engine vibrated so badly that he aborted and bombed factories. He brought home the chimney-pot as souvenir of the day. Ralston said that when Rowlands hit the chimney he was looking down on Hughes, leading, who failed to return. Fighters were absent, but the loss rate at this period was 16%, too high for one squadron to bear.

On 16 July orders were issued for the first sorties in a lengthy campaign of low-level attacks by Bostons on power houses, marshalling yards and industrial targets, using cloud cover. Each Boston squadron was ordered to despatch ten aircraft on a day when visibility and cloud cover were good. Each target would be bombed by a pair of Bostons, each squadron attacking five targets. 107 Squadron was to use long-range aircraft borrowed, if necessary, from 226 Squadron. 11 Group would provide cover from the coast home. Success rested upon good map-reading at minimum height at high speed over specially planned routes, using an aeroplane whose fine pilot's view and excellent control response ideally suited it to this new role.

No. 88 Squadron operated on 19 July, but there were rain showers and bird strikes to contend with. Sqn. Ldr. R. D. Griffiths searched in the mist for Comines but after nine minutes decided to attack another power station which hove into view. AL693 and AL692 bombed the power station at Pont à Vendin attacking switch and transformer houses from fifty feet and leaving much smoke. Of two that went to Lille/ Sequedin, one abandoned the operation when birds hit the nose breaking the perspex in the observer's face. The other aborted due to intercom trouble. Z2236 could not find Lille/Lomme so bombed the airfield at Lille/Nord scoring hits on a hangar. Z2231 was shot down in the target area. The observer in AL740 was injured in a bird strike so the crew attacked a factory three miles S.W. of the target in the rain. Z2205 bombed an unknown power station, leaving debris from explosions flying high.

Plt. Off. J. P. L. O'Malley and Plt. Off. V. Faurot set off to attack Mazingarbe power station on 20 July. All their bombs hit a large building, flames and smoke billowing to 2,000 feet in the cloud base. Fighters latched on to them but were evaded in cloud. When their photographs were developed they showed it was Kuhlman's chemical works on the outskirts of Lille that had been hit. Three pairs of Bostons of 226 Squadron set out on 25 July for Pont à Vendin, Mazingarbe and Comines, but all abandoned their attempts.

No. 107 Squadron delivered its raids on 22 July. Sqn. Ldr. Philips and Sgt. Grant attacked from thirty feet getting hits on Langerbrugge. Two others bombed the chemical works at Sluiskil from fifty feet. Incendiaries fell on the roof of the cooling tower, thick brown smoke rising 100 feet. Plt. Off. Rushden in AL266 then machine-gunned a tug towing four barges. Four others abandoned their tasks.

No. 107's low-level operations continued on 25th. Plt. Off. Burghley detailed to raid Sluiskil attacked from a very low level, his load falling across the works which were machine-gunned. He evaded three Bf 109s on the way in. Another was spotted on the way home but he escaped from it. Later that day orders were received to attend an open-air Dutch quisling meeting at Lunteren. There was insufficient cloud cover and 107 and 226 Squadrons had to return from the Dutch coast.

In July, 108 sorties were flown by Blenheim night intruders of 18 and 114 Squadrons in bombing night-fighter stations ahead of Main Force. Of nine aircraft lost three were detailed to attack Vechta. There was one air-to-air combat when a twin-engined aircraft was seen about 1,000 yards away. The Blenheim was between the enemy and the moon, and the German aircraft pressed home three attacks to about fifty yards causing minor damage. On 30–31 July when 18 Squadron despatched five sorties—three to Twente—all were recalled. This was the last time the squadron operated. On 24 August, after some army co-operation work, it stood down to convert on to Blenheim Vs which it later operated overseas.

To increase the effectiveness of night intruders the Bostons were now called upon. On 26–27 July four crews of 107 Squadron were ordered to bomb Leeuwarden after dusk from 2,000–3,000 feet. They crossed the North Sea at low level as darkness was descending, then climbed over the Dutch coast. Visibility was not good but hits were claimed.

Two nights later three Bostons bombed Alkmaar and six others also attacked airfields after dark. Maclachlan was intercepted by a night-fighter but avoided her fire only to be shot at from a coastal convoy's flak ship. No. 88 Squadron had nine aircraft out the same night bombing De Kooy and other airfields from around 1,000 feet.

As explained, *Circuses* for the Bostons were fewer at this time, but a typical operation of the period was mounted by twelve aircraft of 88 Squadron against St. Malo, led by Sqn. Ldr. Griffiths in Z2211, with W8297, Z2285, AL693, AL692, Z2267, AL775, Z2208, Z2292, Z2230, AL740 and Z2216. Fighter cover was given by 10 and 11 Groups. The bombers used Exeter as forward base and the overall escort was given by the Ibsley Wing, three squadrons from Predannack, Portreath Wing, a squadron from Harrowbeer, two squadrons from Bolt Head, the Exeter Wing and three additional squadrons operating from there, 421 Squadron, an 11 Group Wing operating from Ibsley and two 11 Group Wings operating from Tangmere—eight fighter wings of about 100 aircraft.

Ordered route was from Exeter, to rendezvous with the fighters over Bolt Head at below 500 feet, course then being set at sea level at 200 m.p.h. at Zero minus 34 minutes and climbing as fast as possible when thirty miles from France to bomb from 8,000 feet on a N.W./S.E. track. After bombing the Bostons turned left heading for Start Point at 240 m.p.h. and gradually losing height to sea level. Three diversionary sweeps were meanwhile carried out to neutralise enemy fighter opposition between Maupertuis and Morlaix whilst bombing was in progress. Even a relatively straightforward operation needed careful planning and split-second timing to be effective.

Whilst operations were taking place, there were many modification programmes in train. At the suggestion of crews, two side blisters had been added to the Mosquito canopy improving view aft. Now it was suggested that one blister on the top of the canopy on the observer's side would do better. It did not improve the downward view but would be useful at high levels. Nothing came of it, the consensus of opinion being to leave the two side blisters. Hitherto conspicuous sky-coloured spinners were camouflaged ocean grey during July, and the wing leading edge yellow stripes meant to mislead the enemy into believing Mosquito bombers were armed fighters were also removed, like the rear fuselage sky band.

The Mosquitoes were now a going concern, the Bostons busy on daylight raids, the Blenheims all but a memory. Plans were afoot at last for operational army co-operation employment, the main feature of the next round of operations.

Chapter 14
Summer Escapade

Before the Allies could land on the Continent, some large-scale exploration of necessary techniques was required. A Commando raid on the French coast would surely force such a Luftwaffe response as *Circus* operations had never done. It was an attractive idea limited to two periods in the summer of 1942 by tidal states.

An operations order of 29 June covered a 'combined operation' by the Army, Navy and Air Force, on Dieppe. 2 Group was to position 88 and 107 Squadrons at Ford for this, Operation *Rutter*. No. 226 Squadron was to hold its long-range Bostons in readiness at base. Both mobile squadrons were to despatch sixteen aircraft each to Ford holding at readiness. Some *Circus* operations were envisaged for the Group, targets being motor transport and any interfering AFVs. High approach was ordered with a dive to about 5,000 feet for bombing. Rapid take-off might be required, and all available aircraft were to be ready to get away at thirty minutes' notice. The operation was set for 4 July. To speed their response crews were to be briefed well beforehand, final briefing being at squadron dispersals. All preparations made, the operation was suddenly called off due to a chance enemy air raid on some of the assault ships. It was difficult to gather the assault force and keep the plan secret, but a second date was nevertheless chosen.

No. 2 Group Operations Instruction No. 105 was issued on 14 August to cover the revised assault on Dieppe to come in the period 16–20 August. Air forces taking part came under Air Marshal Leigh-Mallory of 11 Group. Nos. 88 and 107 Squadrons would again secretly move to Ford, and 226 Squadron to Thruxton from where it would deliver smoke-laying missions to cover our forces, blinding enemy cliff gunners. Success or failure of the entire operation depended largely upon 226's success in the initial phase, not to mention the withdrawal.

Aircrews of 88 and 107 Squadrons were billeted in a nearby convent school. Moments after they had settled in the building rang to the sound of bells. 'Ring if you require a mistress,' read a notice in each room . . . most people did.

On 14 August 226 Squadron moved to Thruxton to begin intensive work-up with smoke weapons. These consisted of 100-lb. smoke bombs and special Smoke Curtain Installations fitted in the belly of some

Bostons. Four experienced crews, two each from 88 and 107 Squadrons, joined them, the enterprise coming under Wg. Cdr. Surplice who was to lead the first sorties. 226 would have to take-off before first light and operate without fighter escort.

The weather forecast on 17 August seemed set fair with light to moderate south-south-west winds. Visibility was good, likely to fall to 2–5 miles, and haze was expected. On 18th the wind veered to west-south-west and next night it began to rain. By then the assault force comprising thirteen groups of ships and eight destroyers escorted by gunboats had sailed. Three landing zones were prescribed, east, west and centre regions around the harbour, and eight landing points were listed. Before these could be reached two tasks awaited the Bostons.

At 04.16 hours Wg. Cdr. L. A. Lynn and Flt. Lt. R. Maclachlan of 107 Squadron joined four Bostons from 418 and 605 Squadrons in an attempt to silence coastal defence guns as a prelude to the start of the landing at 05.00 hours. Light was poor and results unseen.

A few moments later ten crews of 226 Squadron and two from each of the other Boston squadrons left in darkness to drop smoke bombs to blind two batteries on the eastern cliffs. They reached the *Bismarck* batteries between 05.09 and 05.44 dropping 150 100-lb. smoke bombs from between fifty and seventy feet to the south and rear of the guns. Flying low in face of murderous fire demanded considerable courage and steel nerves. The smoke screen, 800–1,000 yards long, drifted seawards four to five miles increased by volumes of grey smoke from a burning wheatfield. It gave good cover to the invaders. Flak had been intense damaging nine of the twelve returning Bostons. Two crashed at Middle Wallop, one with an injured observer.

Back at Ford the engines of 88 Squadron's aircraft burst into life early and at 04.30 six crews led by Wg. Cdr. England left for a tail-chase operation on guns behind the town. It was cloudy and only three crews claimed to bomb the guns. As Sqn. Ldr. Pelly-Fry flying W8297 was making his run a pale blue searchlight beamed on to him. 'It's one of those new radar-guided jobs,' said Jim Lee. 'It locks on.' Recalling this moment, unusual for a day-bomber crew, James Pelly-Fry says, 'I felt suspended in mid-air, I felt I was in a spider's web. As the beam swept around I saw it coming again and decided to duck and soon escaped. It was still dark as we headed towards the Channel, hurrying back to re-arm. Strings of red beads were streaming from the cliffs, squirting out as it were, and bouncing on the water. But we made our getaway.'

Fire was continuing from the *Hitler* battery so 107 Squadron was ordered to send twelve crews to silence it. A rapid turn round had been made and Lynn was away again at 06.30. A bombing run west to east was made, ground haze bouncing back light from the sun. A few moments too late the target was spotted—and all the bombs were seen to overshoot into some camouflaged houses. Although the flak was intense no aircraft were hit.

A few minutes before 07.00 another six Bostons of 88 Squadron left to bomb the *Rommel* battery, led by Sqn. Ldr. Griffiths. This time the bombs whistled down from 5,000 feet, but again they missed their small target. Suddenly about twenty Fw 190s swooped in from all angles to attack the unescorted Bostons. 'I then felt that all eyes and guns were trained on me,' says one crew member. 'The whole formation was forced to turn and meet them corkscrewing their way down, some to bomb the guns. Their aim was spoilt by the enemy. The second box of three fell back to give freedom of movement to the leader's section, and had to jettison their bombs some of which went down in the target area despite the reception. Our leader dived to sea level and we followed. When we climbed away only one aircraft was undamaged.'

W. Off. C. A. Beach had to ditch S: AL692. Her gunner was rescued. He had been injured by a cannon shell which hit the rear hatch on the port side. Beach had tried to get home, left the formation and flew at full throttle for three or four minutes. Sgt. Senour, second gunner, heard an explosion and saw the port wing and engine a mass of flames. Both gunners baled out at around 600 feet, Senour's parachute miraculously opening in about seven seconds. He was picked up by the tank-landing craft *Prince Charles* after 25 minutes in the water. The pilot and observer were lost. Undaunted, 88 Squadron was off again at 07.33 sending six more aircraft to another battery, and again their bombs missed.

A desperate plea for more smoke came from the land forces at 07.00 hours but it was impossible to answer. It took forty minutes to load the aircraft. No gun batteries had been silenced but clearly they had suffered harassment. In the second smoke operation[1] four crews of 226 Squadron each taking four Small Bomb Containers and three 100-lb. smoke bombs left at 10.15 to lay smoke to blot out the aim of the *Hindenburg* battery. They attacked at 11.13, at the height of the army operation, leaving a good smoke screen which drifted seawards.

At 10.15 two other crews of 226 Squadron fitted with smoke-curtain gear left to place a screen over the Dieppe beach, trailing it from fifty feet for a mile or so. This was the most hazardous operation so far, as they found when speeding through cross fire from the enemy above on

---

[1] 13 and 614 Sqns. of Army Co-operation Command also participated in smoke laying. Six Blenheim IVs of 13 Sqn., Z6089: F, Z5811: P, V5380 (FTR), Z5882, Z6558 and Z3545: K, dropped 100-lb. phosphorus bombs on the landward side of anti-aircraft guns at dawn. V6002 Flt. Lt. P. Robarts of 614 Sqn. also participated. Flt. Lt. J. E. Scott in V5626 also of 614 Sqn. took-off to lay smoke. On approaching the target he was wounded in both arms and the left leg by light flak. He led his formation back to Britain and crashed near Friston. His smoke bombs had hung up and his aircraft burst into flames on touching the ground. Scott was badly burned, his gunner killed and a badly wounded observer died 36 hours later. Eight other aircraft of 614 Sqn. dropped smoke bombs around 10.50 hours.

the cliffs and from untrusting friends at sea. Of the smoke layers two crash-landed, one at Shoreham with a wounded gunner and Flt. Lt. MacWilliams killed by a cannon shot, and the other at Gatwick also carrying casualties.

The third wave of smoke aircraft comprised a crew of 88 Squadron and one of 226. They left at 10.58 to lay smoke across the harbour mouth. At 11.52 smoke belched forth as they belted over the east jetty at about seventy feet and flew to the cliffs a mile to the west. Laying was good but Bofors fire was intense and a Boston smashed into the sea. Losses were hardly surprising with the aircraft operating so low, sitting targets at a steady height and speed.

A pause in the bombing ended at 11.23 when Griffiths led a dozen Bostons for another attempt against the guns. This time the target, amid smoke, was straddled. At 11.30 107 Squadron fighter-escorted took off to attack the *Hindenburg* battery firing against land and sea targets, as clouds were now thickening. Too late the first box saw the guns through a cloud gap. They decided to chance an attack from 3,000 feet. Seven bombs fell in the sea, but seventeen hit the target area.

Shortly before one o'clock six Bostons of 88 and 107 were hastily scrambled to attack a small tank column reinforcement moving on the Rouen–Dieppe road. Clouds and poor visibility made them impossible to find. Four crews bombed the railway at Auville.

For the Boston squadrons the Dieppe operation had been their busiest so far. Bombs dropped were 201 500-lb. and 288 40-pounders. Ten aircrew were lost in the operations. Three aircraft in the bombing force failed to return, six had major flak damage and seven minor damage. Five more in the bombing force were damaged by enemy fighter interception. Their effort was divided as follows:
Bismarck battery (E. headland) 12 aircraft attacked from 3,000 feet. *Rommel* battery (behind the town) 18 aircraft attacked from 5,000 feet. *Hitler* battery (on high ground by the R. D'Arques) 13 aircraft attacked from 600 feet. *Goering* battery (S.W. of Dieppe) 1 aircraft attacked from 800 feet. *Hindenburg* battery (W. headland) 12 aircraft attacked from 7,000, 2,000, and 3,000 feet. Dieppe/Rouen road 6 aircraft could not locate target.

All agreed that smoke-laying operations had been extremely hazardous—and although the bombing was over, more smoke laying had to be accomplished to cover withdrawal of the raiding force.

Five crews of 226 Squadron escorted by 66 Squadron at low level across the sea, each with two SCIs (smoke curtain installations), took-off at 14.40 to place a screen in front of Dieppe. They made eleven runs, four laying smoke from in front of the east cliffs. Defensive fire was terrifying and one machine was brought down in the sea two miles N.W. of the town after its run. Only one returned to base, the others landing where they could, for the weather was deteriorating fast. 66 Squadron found it difficult to bring them home and four Fw 190s bore down on the

Spitfires shooting down AB514 and AB517. A Fw 190 was downed in the sea ten miles N. of Dieppe.

After this final stage of the operation the smoke laying results could be summarised: the entire efforts were highly satisfactory and gave the required protection to the invaders. Six aircraft were seriously damaged, seven had minor damage. Two SCI machines were lost. Three were damaged. One of the misfortunes was that the Bostons overflew our ships and they met fire from them also. There was one fight between a Boston and a Fw 190. The fighter had dived in from 1,000 yards and broke off when the Boston gunner was firing at a range of 300 yards. It came in again, firing from the starboard quarter, and fell to the bomber's defensive fire. During the fight the Boston's speed rose from 220 to 290 m.p.h.—quite an achievement.

For their courage the smoke layers of 226 Squadron were well decorated, as they deserved to be. Wg. Cdr. Surplice, D.F.C., received the D.S.O., Sqn. Ldr. J. S. Kennedy a bar to his D.F.C., Flg. Off. Askey, D.F.M., received the D.F.C., and D.F.C.s were awarded to Flg. Off. Caset, Flg. Off. Smith, Plt. Off. Longhurst and Plt. Off. Rutherford. Donald Smith had begun his run when, about half way along, a shell shattered his windscreen and pieces of perspex became embedded in his right eye. Nevertheless he pressed on to complete the task. On the return run his left eye became affected by powdered perspex, but he reached home despite his great discomfort. Wg. Cdr. Surplice and Plt. Off. Rutherford were pilot and navigator of the leading Boston detailed to drop the first smoke bombs. The safety of the entire operation initially depended upon their skill and courage. They defied an unhampered barrage to drop their smoke bombs—to quote their citation, 'a most vital and dangerous task'.

During August 2 Group managed 220 sorties, 177 by day during which ten aircraft were lost, and 43 by night. Little activity took place in the first ten days for the squadrons were engaged on Exercise *Dryshod* in northern England, a preparation for Dieppe. Targets for the month included Abbeville, the docks at Ostend and Flushing, industrial targets in Germany and power stations at Comines and Pont à Vendin.

Blenheims intruded upon Twente, Gilze Rijen, Hamstede, Deelen, Venlo, Eindhoven, Vechta, Leeuwarden, Ardorf, Juvincourt, St. Trond, Nordhorn and Borkum.

Since August 1940 night intruder sorties had been flown by Blenheims. On 17–18 August, 1942 they ended. Five days later 114 Squadron began to move to West Raynham. It then proceeded on leave prior to Blenheim V conversion. It had fallen to Sgt. Rounding in Z7295: WV-F of 18 Squadron whose target was Leeuwarden (which he could not locate and so had bombed Borkum instead) to bring to a close the Blenheim's operational service in Bomber Command. He touched down at 01.45 on 18 August. Blenheim V conversion followed, for the squadron like No. 114 was earmarked for Operation *Torch*.

What had been achieved by the night intruders? Probably not a lot, despite valiant attempts. Without special navigation and bombing aids accuracy could not be good. Targets were difficult to locate and the strength of attack insufficient to cripple the foe. But for the Blenheim, and those who flew it, there can be nothing but praise. Its ability to accept crippling punishment, yet fly on, was amazing. Despite limitations apparent from the very start of the war it served 2 Group well. Now it would fall entirely to more modern, mainly American, aircraft to maintain traditions set.

During August Bostons flew thirty sorties on *Circuses*, bombing from 8,000–9,000 feet reached after a steep climb from sea level. Present policy was to lose a little height on the bombing run, sometimes diving to sea level for the return sea crossing. Squealers were still a nuisance to the bombers and occasional operations were mounted against them. Six Bostons of 88 Squadron were despatched in pairs at two-minute intervals for a low-level raid on Comines power station. Z2260 was hit by flak at the coast and crashed in a wood at La Panne. Two others with flak damage returned from the enemy coast, whilst Flt. Sgt. Attenborough in Z2236 flew so low that it was damaged on hitting the sea. One of the two that attacked dived on the power station from 300 feet, but its bombs overshot.

Mosquitoes during their 45 sorties flew four types of operation—high level, low level, cloud cover and photo reconnaissance. At high level they attacked Hanover, Bremen, Cologne, Wiesbaden, Hamburg, Wilhelmshaven, Stuttgart, Mannheim and Münster. Three were lost and thirteen sorties abandoned. Usual policy was to fly at about 21,000 feet where the Mosquito's speed advantage over the Fw 190—about seven m.p.h.—was greatest.

One Mosquito crew was jumped upon by two Fw 190s at about 28,000 feet. Group asked A.F.D.U. Duxford for suggestions as to what should have been done. It was their considered opinion that the Mosquito should have made diving turns to 21,000 feet or corkscrewed down at high speed giving the fighters a difficult target. But of one thing all were sure—the Mosquito had proved itself a very effective machine, and the enemy, too, was certain of this. He was clearly confused, too, for he had now introduced two types of air raid warning note to the population. One was for raiders presumed to be reconnaissance aircraft and one for bombers—but since Mosquitoes flew both types of operation his confusion was great.

Two Mosquitoes made a low-level attack on the Pont à Vendin power station. They crossed in at Mardyck. After avoiding flak at Hazebrouck they attacked the target from fifty feet. Then they turned right to leave the coast near Le Touquet. Four minutes out they spotted twelve Fw 190s two miles ahead above them. The '190s raced in, both aircraft were hit and badly damaged. One limped into Lympne with port engine and hydraulics out of action. The other ditched nine miles from

Dungeness the pilot being killed. His seriously wounded navigator was rescued by the A.S.R. organisation.

An important event was the appearance in the Group of two new types of American aircraft, the Lockheed Vega Ventura and the North American Mitchell.

The Ventura had been proposed by Lockheed late in 1939, a bomber based upon the Lodestar air liner. In February 1940, a small initial order was placed by Britain. Development was centred on the Burbank plant of the subsidiary company Vega. On 31 July 1941, the prototype AE658 was flown.

The first two production Venturas to reach Britain were AE662 and AE680 which arrived at Liverpool aboard the S.S. *Ocean Vespers* on 10 April 1942. A further ten were brought by the S.S. *Heranger* docked at Liverpool on 16 April 1942. All were erected at Speke and test-flown.

21 Squadron's overseas detachment disbanded on 4 March 1942 at Luqa, Malta. On the same day 21 Squadron completely reformed at Bodney taking over Blenheims left behind by 82 Squadron in February. It was planned that 21 Squadron would reform in 2 Group and Wg. Cdr. P. F. Webster, D.S.O., D.F.C., arrived on 1 April to command. Training on Blenheims for night-intruder work took place throughout April at the end of which the squadron supported the Army in Exercise *Sapper*. Between 20 and 24 April another exercise was flown, this time from Abbotsinch.

Next day a servicing training party arrived at Bodney to instruct on the Ventura, with which it had been decided to equip the squadron. Its first two Venturas, AE685 and AE681, joined the Bodney circuit on 31 May. Earlier that day five of the Blenheims made the first operation, an air-sea rescue search for crews who had ditched after the first 'Thousand Plan' raid.

A third Ventura, AE660, arrived from Speke on 9 June by which time the squadron had been given a chance to consider the type initially. Boscombe Down was meanwhile examining AE748 which reached Speke on 15 April and Boscombe on 27 May. AE762 had crossed the Atlantic by air, touching down at Prestwick 17 April. Boulton Paul at Wolverhampton examined its armament system then passed it to Boscombe.

The Ventura, which looked like an overgrown Hudson, a type used by Coastal Command since the start of the war, was hardly a glittering performer although preferable to the Albemarle. (See Appendix 4.) 'What can the Ventura do that the Hudson can't?' The question was often asked, and the regular answer was 'Consume more petrol!'

Only three 2 Group squadrons eventually equipped with Venturas, and for a brief period, and there was a rapid workthrough of 134 aircraft in the squadrons. A desperate need existed to replace remaining Blenheims and squadrons recently lost to overseas commands, but no replacement aircraft type was really available. The Boston had attributes of its own but was in short supply. The Mosquito did not fit the role, the Buckingham was far from ready—something had to be done. The Ventura was therefore selected as the Blenheim night intruder replacement.

On 10 June the first Ventura 'operational' sortie was prematurely flown when one machine joined Blenheims of 21 Squadron on an A.S.R. mission over the North Sea. During June flying training and ground handling were practised, in part using a dual-control Hudson.

Technically the Ventura was different from anything 2 Group had so far operated. Various teething troubles were encountered with the American equipment. Fuel tanks were found to leak, vacuum pumps seized up and there was dissatisfaction with the navigation station which, it was agreed, Cunliffe Owen should alter on all aircraft. Venturas trickled into 21 Squadron in July—the fifth came on 14th. Then, like a bolt from the blue, another new type arrived at Bodney. It was the North American Mitchell II[2] the first of which (FL179) touched down on 16th.

The squadron was perplexed—surely it was not expected to work out snags on two American bombers at the same time? Initial appraisal of the Mitchell showed it to be a far more effective aeroplane, more suited to daylight operations over the Continent than the Ventura could ever be.

Discussions started, and it was decided that the Mitchells should pass to 114 Squadron as replacements for its Blenheims soon to be withdrawn from operational service. Thus on 7 August the three machines flew to West Raynham. Their story from this point continues later.

Night-flying training on the Venturas with a view to their use on night intruders was started by Wg. Cdr. Pritchard on 5 August. Generally the aircraft were considered good for this although some trouble was experienced with the instruments, and the view from the pilot's and navigator's seats was limited. The Venturas' capacious, largely unused, interior was put to use when they transported stores to Ford for the Dieppe operation.

By 31 August 1942, 136 Venturas had arrived in Britain, most of them via Greenland and Prestwick. There were sufficient to equip two more squadrons which consisted of large numbers of Commonwealth personnel. To one of these, No. 487 Squadron established at Feltwell on 15 August, No. 21 Squadron sent some of its crews, which delayed the latter's commencement of operations. Wg. Cdr. F. C. Seavill was posted in from 22 O.T.U. Wellesbourne to command, and on 20 August Sqn. Ldr. Trent whose whole war service had been with the Group arrived to take charge of 'B' Flight. Three Venturas came on squadron strength on 16 September by which time crews were arriving for conversion training from both Blenheim O.T.U.s.

No. 487 was a New Zealand squadron. The next was No. 464 with

---

[2] Mitchell Is were put in the O.T.U. at Nassau.

Australian personnel. It began to form at Feltwell on 1st September, the first Ventura arriving, on loan, on 8 September. By 8 October ten Venturas had reached 464 and 487 had nine.

No. 21 Squadron began night intruder training over Mildenhall on 2 September and during the month—in which its strength rose to 22 aircraft—night operational training was busily undertaken.

Not only was there now a profusion of operational aircraft types whereas in other Bomber Groups there usually was one, but 2 Group with only four operational squadrons and relatively few aeroplanes had a multitude of roles. This was partly the result of employing differing types of aircraft whose performances prevented them from operating in concert. The feeling abounded that 2 Group now had no particular part to play in the bomber offensive and morale must soon suffer. There were, then, two pressing problems—decide how to employ the aircraft and boost any flagging morale.

In September 1942, 133 sorties were flown, all by day for the first time that year. And for the first time since 1939 the Blenheim did not figure on the operations musters. There were still Blenheims in the Group, mainly Mk. Vs in squadrons working up for overseas, but none were operational. Re-equipment programmes cut operations. The few Mosquitoes available flew 62 sorties, in 44 of which bombs were dropped. A development of Mosquito tactics was the dusk attack from medium level by a group of aircraft using failing light for added protection. These tactics were tried against Münster, Osnabruck and Wiesbaden. But the outstanding operations of the month were the first Mosquito 'spectaculars' flown by 105 Squadron's crews against Oslo and Berlin. In retrospect they came to be seen as morale raisers which they were not intended to be, and they pointed to two great Mosquito facets. This little aeroplane could carry a very useful load a long way at low level, and it could hit a precision target. Many times it was destined to deal with the enemy in like manner cutting for itself a niche in R.A.F. history ever to be admired.

The Oslo raid was ordered to take place between 25 and 27 September when a rally of Hirdsmen (Norwegian fascists) and Quislings was taking place in Oslo, and celebrating the second anniversary of succession to power of the Quislings. Target was the Gestapo H.Q. which lay between the Town Hall, a red brick building with two rectangular towers, and the Royal Palace standing on a hill. The Gestapo building was recognisable by its unusually shaped roof. As a last-resort target, the four Mosquitoes of 105 Squadron were given the marshalling yards 900 yards S.W. of the primary.

Four Mosquitoes, each with four 500-lb. M.C. T.D. 11 sec. bombs, set out from Marham and flew, bombs aboard, to Leuchars where they came under the command of Wg. Cdr. Hughie Edwards, V.C. They set off on 25 September and their leader, Flt. Lt. George Parry, recently recalled the operation:

46. AE658, the prototype Ventura, during its manufacturer's trials

47. Ventura 1 AE774: YH-V at Methwold. It served with the squadron 18.11.42–21.2.43
48. Engines running, Venturas of 21 Squadron are ready for take-off

49. AE939: SB-G, a Ventura II which served with 464 Squadron from 1.12.42 to 3.11.43 and flew 19 operational sorties

50. Ventura I AE660 wears special markings applied for Exercise *Spartan* in March 1943. AE660 joined 21 Squadron 5.6.42 and passed to 487 Squadron 25.10.42 staying with it until 3.11.43

51. A box formation flown by Mitchell IIs of 180 Squadron

52. Mitchell IIs of 180 Squadron. FL684 (*nearest*) served with the squadron from 19.6.43 until 20.3.44. Close by Z: FL707 with five bomb sorties recorded on her nose: with the squadron from 3.10.42 and shot down 26.11.43 during a raid on Martinvast

'The raid on the Gestapo H.Q. was put on as a morale booster for the Norwegians in their occupied country. There were four of us detailed for the raid. We flew to Leuchars and prepared. The four of us took off early in the afternoon and set out to cross the North Sea at fifty feet. We were about two minutes late taking off, but we made up this time on the way across the North Sea. We managed to make a sighting on Heligoland and then flew through the Skaggerak. We saw nothing, really, until we approached the coast near Oslo Fiord where we ran across some fishing vessels. We then turned northwards up the eastern side of the fiord until we reached the radio station on the eastern side of Oslo. We then turned left across the city making our run for the Gestapo H.Q. which we were able to identify from photographs which had been taken by Norwegians and submitted to us. The main building consisted of three large domes with a flag flying from the centre one. As we made our run up we were attacked by Fw 190s who then followed us as we made our getaway. We broke then and just as we were leaving we realised Flt. Sgt. Carter had been shot down having seen him with one engine on fire just prior to that. We then came out across Norway flying over the mountains and glaciers and flew back to Sumburgh where I landed first, then Pete Rowlands and Bristow last.

'The first thing our C.O., Wg. Cdr. Edwards, wanted to know was, did we get there on time? We weren't expecting Fw 190s— it was unfortunate, we were hoping to have cloud cover and a clear run through as we were unarmed. But there was a clear sky and they had apparently brought in these 190s for the Quisling rally and they must have been alerted as we flew up the fiord.

'We had no great difficulty in identifying the target and we could see the Royal Palace. We were accused of damaging it but it was not us, it was the 190s firing at us and some of their bullets went into the Palace.'

At least four bombs had entered the Gestapo H.Q. One stayed inside but failed to explode, and three careered out the other side without exploding. To the Norwegians the raid brought great delight and was the morale booster they deserved.

The first daylight raid on Berlin had been laid on for 19 September. George Parry remembers it like this:

'There were six of us. The weather was pretty bad and we had thick cloud all the way there, consequently none of us found the target. I descended through cloud over Berlin but could not break through with sufficient height to bomb. I eventually turned north and came back along the north coast of Germany down to the Dutch coast. We saw fighters on several occasions on the way there and back but managed to keep clear of them. Finally coming out under the cloud over the Dutch coast I was attacked by two '190s but eventually managed to evade them after getting hit several times, and arrived back at Horsham with a number of bullet holes and a few gallons of petrol missing.'

Only one of the Mosquitoes claimed to bomb Berlin, doing so on dead reckoning and through dense cloud. Two others abandoned the raid on being intercepted. During the operation the Mosquitoes were intercepted five times, one aircraft being attacked three times, twice evading fighters by dashing into clouds and the third time, at 1,500 feet, turning into the attacker and increasing speed to 330 m.p.h. using 12 lb. boost. Sqn. Ldr. N. H. E. Messervy, D.F.C., was seen to be shot down by a Fw 190 which attacked him from below. The raid was disappointing as an operation—but it proved that Mosquitoes could reach Berlin, and in daylight.

Another notable September raid was by five Mosquitoes ordered to attack the chemical works at Wiesbaden. They approached high and at dusk, then made shallow dive attacks bombing from 2,500–4,000 feet which, with a strong following wind, raised their speed to 450 m.p.h. Flak was intense, but bombs from four hit the target. Eighteen Mosquito operations were mounted in September.

Boston IIIs notched up 71 sorties in September making four medium-level fighter-escorted raids. Various tactics were employed after bombing such as turning to one side, climbing then diving, even maintaining level flight, all to confuse the flak gunners.

Eighteen Bostons were sent on low-level attacks on power stations in Belgium and northern France. Only five found and attacked their primaries and three were lost. One had a bird collision and some found no cloud cover. Crews were carefully routed to avoid flak and radar stations, crossing the coast at varying places at the same time and depending on cloud cover. To confuse enemy plotters the return flights were dog-legged.

One interesting point of the month's operations was that on one occasion Mustang Is—useful on account of range and high speed at low level—gave close escort to the Bostons on an abortive raid on Den Helder. It was not yet realised that with the Mustang lay the means of closely escorting bombers on deep penetrations of Germany.

Around midday on 8 September six 88 Squadron Bostons flying *Ramrod 37* were escorted by Polish Wings comprising eleven of 306 Squadron, twelve of 315 Squadron, thirteen of 308 Squadron and twelve of 302 Squadron. Rendezvous was at Selsey below 500 feet, then they crossed the Channel. Too soon the bombers climbed. This alerted enemy fighters and fearing a hot reception 306 Squadron climbed to 17,000 feet when '190s were seen. The enemy kept his distance until Le Havre had been attacked, and then eight to ten '190s engaged 315 Squadron without any successes to either. This showed how disastrous a small error could become. Luck was with the bombers who scored two hits on 'M' class gunboats.

The most successful Boston operation of the month was the bombing of the *Solglint*, a 12,000-ton whale ship attacked in Bassin Napoléon Cherbourg on 15 September, by 107 Squadron. Subsequent reconnaissance showed the ship gutted by fire.

By the close of September Mosquitoes were operating in a wide assortment of roles. Revised battle orders were issued for them on 3 October. Their primary role was now the attack of industrial targets in Germany, not only to destroy factories but even more to affect the morale of the civilian population. Targets were listed more for their relation to built-up areas than for industrial importance. This suggests that the value of Mosquitoes for mass precision attacks was not yet realised at Bomber Command. The Mosquito was unsuited, and not intended, for area bombing.

The secondary role was attack by one or more aircraft against specific industries in Germany chosen for their importance and vulnerability to small-scale precision attack. Photo reconnaissance and weather reconnaissance were also still required. Both Mosquito squadrons moved into Marham at the end of September where the Station Commander chose bombing targets from a long list, giving H.Q. 2 Group three hours' notice of his choice. Conservation of his valuable machines was important, and if they met fighters they were to evade them and return at maximum speed dropping bombs on alternative targets, airfields in enemy territory or factories and military targets in Germany. Chosen routes still took the Mosquitoes away from RDF stations and heavily defended areas. Usual bomb loads were four 500-lb. M.C. T.D. 11 sec. delay bombs or two 250-lb. G.P. plus two S.B.C.s carrying 30-lb. incendiaries.

Mosquito orders were followed by a memorandum on 9 October explaining recent deliberations on employment of other aircraft now in the Group. Primary tasks for Bostons were *Circus* and *Ramrod* operations; alternatively they would provide army support including gas spray (only as a retaliatory measure) and smoke laying as at Dieppe. Twice in recent weeks Boston squadrons had been warned of possible combined operations to which they would be committed. The first was Operation *Crucible* in which the three squadrons would have intruded against three airfields whilst paratroops damaged enemy radar installations and took prisoners for interrogation. For another, Operation *Flame* planned but abandoned, Bostons were to lay smoke screens.

Boston squadrons had, in their secondary role, intruder operations in good weather, low-level attacks on enemy land targets in occupied territory and against shipping and harbours too.

Principal employment for Venturas would be short-range night intruder operations, low-level attacks and smoke support of the Army. Other tasks would be low-level attack on land targets in occupied territory under suitable cloud conditions, attacks on enemy shipping, *Circus* and *Ramrod* operations. Already there had been a shift in plans for the Ventura, dictated by a desire to increase operations and shortage of day-bomber aircraft.

At West Raynham on 12 September 98 Squadron formed under Wg. Cdr. L. A. Lewer. Next day 180 Squadron also formed there under Wg. Cdr. C. C. Hodder. Both received Mitchells a few days later, and began a slow work-up pending a move to the planned station, Foulsham as yet unready. No. 180 Squadron moved to Massingham to ease the strain on Raynham and in October both went to their operational station, but were far from ready to operate. Their tasks were set as *Circus* and *Ramrod* operations, also army support. Their secondary role was low-level attack on land targets in occupied territory, attacks on important shipping and short-range night bombing. In the light of these instructions it is interesting how often aircraft operated in secondary roles.

Unfavourable weather in October again interfered with operations. Ten *Circuses* were prepared but only twice did the Bostons reach their target, Le Havre. After the successful raid on the *Solglint* in September five fighter-escorted operations were directed against an armed raider of the *Neumark* type. In early October she left dry dock at Le Havre where, six months earlier, she had been damaged. Twice in October raids had to be abandoned, but on 15th twenty-three Bostons reached Le Havre. The raider had left her anchorage in time and so a 5,000-ton motor vessel in the Bassin de Marée took the brunt of the bombing. Photographs taken two hours later showed the ship beached in shallow water, five tugs in attendance. A week later she was in dry dock for repair.

On 31 October seventeen Bostons using cloud cover were detailed for low-level attacks on power stations at Pont à Vendin, Gosnay, Mazingarbe and Comines. Only three attacked them, seven going after alternatives and the rest abandoning due to absence of cloud cover.

Mosquitoes flew ninety sorties, more than ever before. This was because the second Mosquito squadron, No. 139, was now fully operational. It flew nineteen sorties compared with 105's 71. High-level raids were mounted on Essen, Bremen, Trier, Frankfurt, Hanover and Ruhr targets. Fighters shot down two Mosquitoes. One pilot had flown a sortie aimed at causing maximum disturbance, a round tour dropping a bomb at Nordhorn, Hengelo and Lingen. Over Ameland he was intercepted by two Fw 190s which chased him for fifteen minutes before he safely reached cloud cover. They were quite unable to catch the Mosquito.

Flying in formation did not give the unarmed Mosquitoes any protection. Instead it permitted concentrated attack in a matter of moments. Three times such tactics were used in October, for attacks on Hengelo delivered at dusk with return in darkness. Ten shallow dive attacks were made, six near Liège and four on Hengelo. The importance of making only one pass on these low-level raids became apparent. In failing light one Mosquito failed to identify its target in time, then made a second run—passing over the target just as the bombs from the first wave were bursting. The crew 150 feet above the target were severely shaken although the aircraft was undamaged. Poor light and shallow dive raids were useful means of gathering extra security, by making it difficult for the defenders.

Of six Mosquito photo-reconnaissance flights during this month the most noteworthy was that flown to Le Creusot to obtain photographs of the Lancaster day raid. On the route to and from the target the aircraft flew low. A Fw 190 dived, firing on the Mosquito. It turned into the attack, climbing safely into cloud, then went on to make four runs at 2,000 feet over the target. 2 Group had supported the Lancaster raid by sending six Bostons on a feint raid towards Le Havre flying a mock *Circus* to engage the enemy RDF.

One of several ships bent on running the Allied blockade between Europe and the Far East was the 5,000-ton *Elsa Essberger*. Six Mosquitoes of 105 Squadron were despatched to attack her and her heavily defended *Sperrbracher* 'A.T.' (i.e. 'barrage breaker') in the mouth of the Gironde on 7 November. Three aircraft attacked each ship, Wg. Cdr. J. R. G. Ralston, D.S.O., D.F.C., leading the force. They went in very low achieving complete surprise, but soon the guns were fiercely firing and DK328: V was shot down. Hits were scored on both ships which subsequently limped into Bordeaux.

On 9 November the *Neumark* class ship in Le Havre was seen to have suffered a direct hit. She was carefully taken to Flushing for repairs only to receive more hits from two Mosquitoes. Kept out of service for eight months by the Bostons, she now needed further repairs.

Venturas were busily working up for operations. Two boxes of six aircraft were presently being flown in *Circus* practices, the night intruder role being discarded. At low level over the sea they were flying at 190 m.p.h. I.A.S., climbed at 165–170 m.p.h. and cruised at 170 A.S.I. at 8,000 feet. These speeds were agreed for coming operations although they were much slower than achieved with the Boston, and came at a time when the new faster Spitfire IX was appearing in increasing numbers on *Circuses*. It meant a Spitfire V escort, the version easily outshone by the Fw 190. Ventura *Circus* training had been initiated in September and continued in October by which time plans for operational introduction of Venturas had been decided upon. They were to commence their offensive with low-level attacks under Group Operations Order No. 24 formulated as long ago as March 1941, and covering cloud-cover attacks on occupied territory.

On 3 November three Venturas of 21 Squadron led by Wg. Cdr. Pritchard were ordered to open Ventura raids with a low-level attack on Hengelo. They took-off at 14.34, Pritchard (in YH: Z) placing his bombs on the railway line and blowing a gap in the northern track. It was hard for them to keep together in misty conditions. Flt. Lt. Dennis bombed the railway line between Apeldoorn and Amersfoort straddling the main line. A misunderstanding had arisen when the leader did not attack the chosen target. The third aircraft which did not bomb had to make an emergency landing in a field near Tollesbury.

Four Venturas of 21 Squadron set out on 6th. Again it was misty and this time they wrongly pinpointed their position at the Dutch coast.

They had intended to attack shipping at Maasluis but the leader, Wg. Cdr. Werfield, settled for a ship in Rotterdam. One bombed barges at Maasluis, one abandoned the mission and YH-X disappeared.

Six others were despatched in pairs to Roosendaal, Ijmuiden and Den Helder. Only Flg. Off. Hicks bombed, again due to bad visibility. YH: V and YH: L both failed to return, probably flak victims.

Next day pairs set out for Ghent and Terneuzen. Orders were for a low-level approach to the enemy coast then for attacks at low or medium altitudes. Flt. Sgt. Hoggarty bombed Flushing airfield, Sqn. Ldr. Ray Chance attacked a large ship in the Scheldt Estuary scoring near misses, and AE734-YH: P (W. Off. V. R. Henry) failed to return. After this three squadrons co-operated in training, making more *Circus* trials. The Ventura was far too slow and clumsy for lone forays, but it might still be useful for *Circuses*.

This was indeed proved so on 23 December. Six Venturas of 21 Squadron attacked the torpedo workshops and naval barracks at Den Helder. Thirty-six out of 42 bomb bursts were in a single close group across the target. No fighters were met, there was little flak and the bombers came home undamaged. No work was possible in the work-shops at Den Helder for over a month, supply stock, warehouses and equipment were damaged, buildings of the 34 M.S. Flottille were heavily damaged and so was a harbour guardship. A tug and ferry boat were sunk and three cranes damaged. The same day Bostons scored hits in the dock area at St. Malo where a large explosion followed.

By this time 2 Group had undertaken its most memorable raid of the war. Operation *Oyster* had been mounted.

Chapter 15
Operation Oyster

'Group Captain Denis Barnett, Station Commander at Swanton Morley, summoned me from Oulton,' recalls Wg. Cdr. Pelly-Fry. 'There's to be a big show soon, Pelly, and it needs a lot of practice. It's to be a low-level affair, but I don't know where the target is. The big problem will be getting a large group of aircraft to arrive at very precise times, and we shall be using different types of aircraft of varying speeds. You'll all need a lot of practice.'

In great secrecy Bomber Command had, on 9 November 1942, authorised planning to begin on the most ambitious raid 2 Group was ever called upon to perform, the destruction of the Philips radio and valve works at Eindhoven in a built-up area of Holland which meant a daylight precision raid. Eindhoven lay within the enemy fighter zone, which precluded a Lancaster day raid, and it was only fifty miles from the Ruhr. This was the largest valve factory in Europe fully harnessed to German needs, producing over one-third of the German supply of valves and certain radar gear. It was also engaged upon experimental work connected with radio counter-measures. Although decentralisation of Philips had taken place in 1929, and plants were established abroad, the Eindhoven works remained the largest of their kind. Since March 1942 an attack had been envisaged and now it was passed to the planners of 2 Group to devise a devastating raid.

Estimated Group strength available for the operation was 36 Venturas, twelve Mitchells, 36 Bostons and twelve Mosquitoes. The only fighter protection possible would be withdrawal cover from the Dutch coast extending perhaps fifteen to twenty miles inland. Suitable diversions in the Ostend area by 11 Group might confuse the defenders, and a further distraction would be a raid by American B-17s on Lille.

Had the Group been equipped with only one type of aircraft planning would have been straightforward. Instead Group was being asked to commit almost its entire strength to one operation, using four types.

Speed, range and manoeuvrability were at a maximum in the Mosquito IV, a minimum with the Ventura. Between lay the sturdy Mitchell yet to prove itself, and the very tough, reliable Boston. This was a pilot's aeroplane, a lovely machine in which to sit. 'Extremely comfortable,' in Pelly-Fry's opinion, 'and beautiful to fly. It bred self

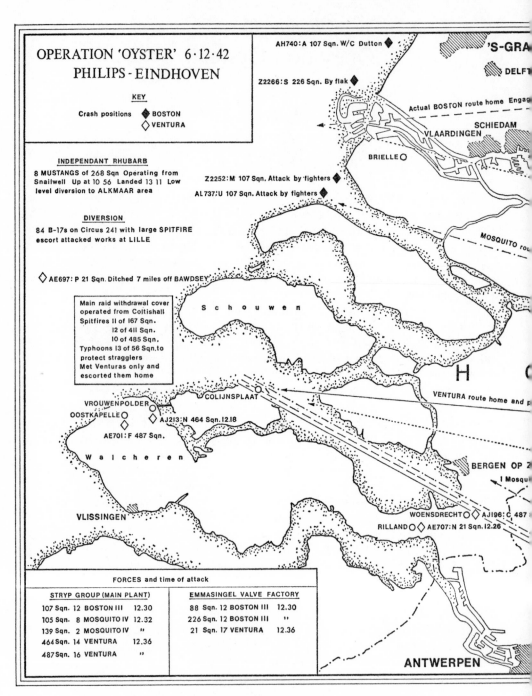

OPERATION 'OYSTER' 6·12·42
PHILIPS - EINDHOVEN

KEY

Crash positions ◆ BOSTON
                 ◇ VENTURA

INDEPENDANT RHUBARB

8 MUSTANGS of 268 Sqn Operating from
Snailwell Up at 10 56 Landed 13 11 Low
level diversion to ALKMAAR area

DIVERSION

84 B-17s on Circus 241 with large SPITFIRE
escort attacked works at LILLE

◇ AE697: P 21 Sqn. Ditched 7 miles off BAWDSEY

Main raid withdrawal cover
operated from Coltishall
Spitfires II of 167 Sqn.
          12 of 411 Sqn.
          10 of 485 Sqn.
Typhoons 13 of 56 Sqn.to
protect stragglers
Met Venturas only and
escorted them home

VROUWENPOLDER
OOSTKAPELLE ○ ◇ AJ213:N 464 Sqn. 12.18
         ◇
      AE701: F 487 Sqn.

W a l c h e r e n

VLISSINGEN

AH740:A 107 Sqn. W/C Dutton ◆
Z2266:S 226 Sqn. By flak ◆

'S-GRA
DELFT

Actual BOSTON route home Engage

SCHIEDAM
VLAARDINGEN

BRIELLE ○

Z2252:M 107 Sqn. Attack by 'fighters ◆
AL737:U 107 Sqn. Attack by fighters ◆

MOSQUITO rou

S c h o u w e n

VENTURA route home and p

COLIJNSPLAAT

H   C

BERGEN OP Z

I Mosqui

WOENSDRECHT ○○ ◇ AJ196: C 487
RILLAND ○ ◇ AE707:N 21 Sqn. 12.26

ANTWERPEN

FORCES and time of attack

STRYP GROUP (MAIN PLANT)				EMMASINGEL VALVE FACTORY			
107 Sqn.	12	BOSTON III	12.30	88 Sqn.	12	BOSTON III	12.30
105 Sqn.	8	MOSQUITO IV	12.32	226 Sqn.	12	BOSTON III	''
139 Sqn.	2	MOSQUITO IV	''	21 Sqn.	17	VENTURA	12.36
464 Sqn.	14	VENTURA	12.36				
487 Sqn.	16	VENTURA	''				

MAP 13. *See Appendix 12, pages 504/5 for notes*

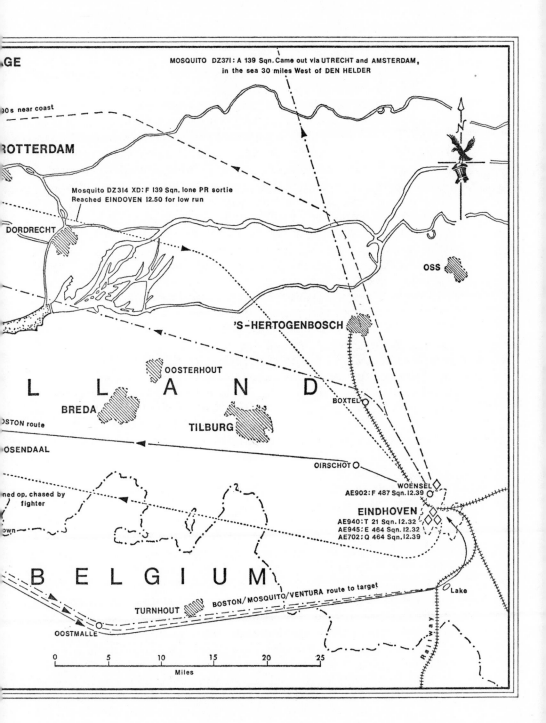

MOSQUITO DZ371: A 139 Sqn. Came out via UTRECHT and AMSTERDAM,
in the sea 30 miles West of DEN HELDER

GE

...00s near coast

ROTTERDAM

Mosquito DZ314 XD:F 139 Sqn. lone PR sortie
Reached EINDOVEN 12.50 for low run

DORDRECHT

OSS

'S-HERTOGENBOSCH

OOSTERHOUT

L   L   A   N   D

BREDA

BOXTEL

...OSTON route

TILBURG

...OSENDAAL

OIRSCHOT

WOENSEL
AE902:F 487 Sqn.12.39

...ned op. chased by
fighter

EINDHOVEN
AE940:T 21 Sqn.12.32
AE945:E 464 Sqn.12.32
AE702:Q 464 Sqn.12.39

...own

B E L G I U M

Lake

TURNHOUT

BOSTON/MOSQUITO/VENTURA route to target

Railway

OOSTMALLE

0   5   10   15   20   25

Miles

12

confidence and you could fly it as easily as a Tiger Moth. Its cockpit layout was neat and tidy, everything was where you wanted it. For low level work the view was extremely good, with the two engines and propellers nicely out of the way. And perhaps most important of all for a twin engined bomber it was extremely manoeuvrable.'

These, and the qualities of the Mosquito, were somewhat nullified by those of the Ventura whose range was short and manoeuvrability poor. To a large extent its performance appeared to dictate routes to and from the target. In any case these needed to be restricted to achieve a maximum strike in minimum time. To achieve this and curtail difficulties of timing and restrict possible navigation errors, the whole force soon became governed by the qualities of the Ventura. Bearing in mind the problems, a rough operational plan was drawn up at Headquarters taking account of the fact that each Ventura was to carry three 250-lb. $\frac{1}{2}$ hour delay G.P. bombs and four containers each of eight 30-lb. incendiary bombs. These aircraft were to act as fire raisers. The next problem was one of bomb fusing, important since many aircraft would be making low-level attacks. So often bombs with the usual 11-second delay skidded and so nullified their effectiveness by bouncing along the ground and exploding beyond the target. If the attack was at all lengthened by use of instantaneous fusing the risk of fighter interception was increased for aircraft attacking in later stages of the raid. The final decision, one which affected the whole success of the operation more than anything except, perhaps, the interference of flak at the target, was that all high-explosive bombs would be fused T.D. 025 seconds, and that the bombing height for most aircraft would be from 1,000 to 1,500 feet. Only the Venturas with their incendiaries and long-delay bombs would go in at low level.

The following plan was decided upon. Venturas would attack at Zero Hour, Mitchells two minutes later, Bostons a further two minutes later and Mosquitoes six minutes after Zero. Twenty-four Venturas would take the Stryp Group main plant and twelve the Emmasingell valve and lamp factory, a smaller separate part some distance south-east. Twelve Mitchells and 24 Bostons would aim for the large target, whilst a further twelve and the Mosquitoes would go for the small works. With this basic plan in mind 2 Group officers went to 12 Group on 9 November to discuss arrangements for fighter withdrawal cover. On 13th they visited 11 Group to discuss elaborate diversions.

Operations Order 82 detailing the plan was sent to 2 Group stations on 17 November. The main plant was now to be bombed by 24 Venturas at Zero Hour, twelve Mitchells at zero plus two minutes and twelve Mosquitoes at Zero plus six. The valve and lamp factory would be hit by twelve Venturas at Zero Hour, 36 Bostons at Zero plus four. All aircraft were to fly in pairs in company echelon to starboard, no formation exceeding six aircraft. Route from base to target was to be flown at very low level, all aircraft except Venturas climbing to release bombs from 1,000–1,500 feet, after which they would dive to low level as fast as possible. In order not to alert enemy RDF until the last possible moment it was stressed that all aircraft should remain below fifty feet on the sea crossing. Route was set as Base–Orfordness–Colijnsplaat–Turnhout–target–Oirschot–Colijnsplaat–Orfordness–Base. The importance of adhering to route, indicated air speeds and timings was stressed. To ensure accurate ground speed the distance between the railway line running S.S.W. from Norwich to Stowmarket and Orfordness was to be used as a check. Suitable weather for the operation was a cloud base of not less than 1,500 feet.

Some degree of inexperience existed in the Group at this time because two squadrons would be making their first operational sorties although there would be experienced squadron and flight commanders in them and a few second tour crews. It was realised that much training would be needed to acquire the necessary skill at low flying, accurate timing, methods of approach, delivering the load and getting away.

Ventura squadrons had been working up for some weeks practising bombing and formation flying for *Circuses*, but the Mitchell squadrons were only just getting under way. The nature of the target, the complexity caused by operating differing types of aircraft and the need to operate in daylight prescribed that a lot of practice flying was needed. First this was to be done by small numbers, growing in size to the stage when close on a hundred were thundering at tree-top height all over Norfolk, Essex, Cambridgeshire, Hertfordshire and Bedfordshire—and finally Huntingdonshire where the practice target lay, St. Neots power station. Many mistakes were made—in navigation, accurate timing, run-up techniques, evasive action and, by the Bostons, in working out their 'formation', in pairs in a close-knit stream. Assembling a hundred aircraft into a crocodile that would quickly pass over the estimated weakest spot in enemy flak defences on the Dutch coast was no mean task. A point was indeed reached when the crews were getting over-trained, over-anxious and argumentative.

On 17 November the first large-scale practice was flown, on a route simulating that to be taken. Squadrons took-off from their bases and after getting into pre-arranged formations made their way to Spalding–Goole–Flamborough (which had represented the route to our own coast), from Flamborough to Cromer (the sea crossing); Cromer–Newmarket (the run over enemy territory); Newmarket/Little Barford power station near St. Neots, with this as the small target and St. Neots town the large target. Then the homeward run was simulated by the route Kimbolton–Digby–bases. The suddenness with which the exercise was mounted, unfavourable weather and the presence of North Sea convoys which called for re-routing, prevented it from being as successful as it might have been.

Many basic lessons were learnt, and witnesses at the 'target' were able to comment helpfully. Just what was involved with the timing and routing became apparent, and also the need for excellent station keeping since a straggler could upset the entire operation. It was realised that bombing practice on the climb was required, for the target could be crossed only once. It lay in occupied Allied territory and the minimum of civilian lives should be at risk. Timing would be such that few people would be in the factory.

Violent evasive action near the target would possibly be needed but it was laid down that the actual bombing run should be steady, regardless of opposition until 'bombs gone'. Pilot-aimed low-level bombing reduced the steady period to a minimum. The Bostons at 1,000–1,500 feet relied upon bombsights even though the pilots were tracking over the target and a few 'left, left' and 'rights' were given. In the Venturas the pilots had no bomb button on the control column and the release was judged by the navigator using the American style 'Mickey Mouse' and immediately punching the jettison button in case of a hang-up. The 'Mickey Mouse' released a stick of bombs.

In the practice some aircraft began their climb too near the target, some too far away. Others failed to dive away quickly enough. The risk of bird strike was realised although eye witnesses claimed that birds seemed to dive away when aircraft approached. But it was a serious hazard as Reggie Goode discovered. 'It was clearly illustrated to the crew of which I was a member very early in our training, although it was not then regarded as of any significance. This was the action of pigeons smashing through the window of our Ventura which, apart from covering the pilot's face with pigeon's blood, necessitated the navigator reporting to the M.O. upon landing to have small pieces of perspex removed from his face.'

To assemble the formation, early take-off was essential and everyone needed to understand clearly which target he was to attack—one aircraft taking the wrong target could spoil the entire operation. Targets must be attacked at maximum speed, particularly by the slow Venturas.

The first practice immediately showed up the inadequacies of the Mitchell formation. These aircraft needed clear vision panels and Sutton seat harnesses before they could operate, and clearly they were an untrained force. On this first practice fighters were absent and so it was decided to mount another with 12 Group intercepting at intervals, the bombers' safety clearly resting in good formation keeping.

After the exercise the formation was replanned to obviate the slipstream effects whilst maintaining aircraft in pairs grouped in sixes.

On 18 November Venturas alone carried out a simulated attack on the same training route, for theirs had been the main errors. Only thirty were flown and a vast improvement was noticed. Zero Hour was set at 15.15 and fourteen 'attacked' the power station at 15.13 and the remainder the town exactly on time, although two aircraft passed between the two targets and would have failed to attack.

A practice for all crews was held on 20th, routes as previously. This time the Ventura assault on the power station was excellent, that on the town rather scattered. Boston attacks were good, climb-away fine, timing good—like the approach—but the time taken to attack too long. Four Mitchells climbed near the power station, off track—and they were not going all-out. Nine minutes later two Mitchells recrossed the power station—quite unforgivable. The first Mosquitoes arrived nine minutes later. Five attacked in a scattered manner and only one descended to low level after the attack. Generally, though, the timing was better and stragglers fewer. Clearly, a lot was being demanded of the crews and much practice was still needed. Group planners took a look at orders covering the recent Lancaster daylight raids by 5 Group, but these did not help much.

But now, like a bolt from the blue, came the realisation of a major flaw in planning, that the operation in its present form would be chaotic. It had been previously decided that the slow Venturas would bomb first. If they did the smoke from their fires would obliterate the target for aircraft with H.E. loads. So it seemed that the fire raisers must be placed last. This threw up another unpleasant prospect. Previously the least manoeuvrable aircraft had been given a straight run-in with the element of surprise. More lively machines were reckoned better able to contend with any stirred-up hornet's nest. It was no mean crisis to reverse the plan, but clearly this was inevitable.

Two alternatives presented themselves—put the Venturas first with H.E.s and 30-lb. incendiaries which would produce less smoke, or employ them last with full incendiary load. If the first was adopted surprise was still achieved with the slowest aircraft, but they would climb more slowly than the other types and start doing so further from the target. If employed last their Small Bomb Container capacity and substantial load could be put to good use, and they could attack at low level although there would be difficulties with timing and safety.

Representatives went from Group to the Ventura stations to discuss the problem. Finally it was decided to adopt the second proposal looking again at routing and timing. At this stage it was decided to withdraw the Mitchell squadron since its aircraft and crews could never be operational in time. Planning then went ahead with an attack on the main plant using twelve Bostons, twelve Mosquitoes and 24 Venturas, leaving 24 Bostons and twelve Venturas to cope with the smaller works.

Grp. Capt. Barnett, Station Commander at Swanton Morley, again called Wg. Cdr. Pelly-Fry from 88's base at Oulton close to Blickling Hall where the squadron lived in feudal style. As 88's C.O. Pelly-Fry had a splendid room overlooking the park and the lake, the bedroom once occupied by Anne Boleyn. Denis Barnett told him that he was to lead the Bostons, and as the Bostons were to lead the whole 'Balbo' it meant that he would lead the operation. Pelly-Fry took a deep breath, tried to smile convincingly and went back to Oulton very much aware that he had quite a task to carry out. He knew it would be a dicey operation, and estimated losses could be up to 30%.

Originally all aircraft were to use the same route, faster gaining on the slower so that a short time over target was achieved, and withdrawal made in one large group providing an extremely formidable force against enemy fighters expected to be busy. Now the plan was for the same result by different routing. From the enemy coast inland Bostons and Venturas would fly the route already agreed after making landfall in quick succession. Mosquitoes were to fly a longer track before swinging behind the Bostons. On the return the latter would withdraw long before the Venturas, so now they were to fly a longer route reaching the coast only seven minutes ahead of the Venturas, leaving the Mosquitoes to find their own way home at high speed.

It proved most difficult to fit into the timetable over a given distance, Mosquitoes flying at 260 m.p.h. I.A.S. and Venturas at 220 m.p.h. I.A.S. But the Mosquitoes veering north would serve as an additional diversion to the main effort, and help overwhelm the ground reporting system. So much amended was the original plan that a new Operations Order code name *Oyster* was issued on 23 November.

This laid the plan as follows: main factory—twelve Bostons at Zero Hour, twelve Mosquitoes at Zero plus two minutes and thirty Venturas at Zero plus six; valve and lamp factory—24 Bostons at Zero and twelve Venturas at Zero plus six minutes. The Ventura route was now base–Southwold–Colijnsplaat–Oustemaal–target–Oirschot–Colijnsplaat–Southwold–base. Bostons would take the same route as before except that, from the target, they would fly to Boxtel instead of Oirschot. The Mosquito track lay via Orfordness–Colijnsplaat–Turnhout–target—and back by their own devices. Speeds were carefully set for each stage of the route. To reduce time interval to the coast on return Venturas had to increase their speed to 220 m.p.h. I.A.S. after bombing. Minor speed adjustments were later made.

For testing the new arrangements a large-scale practice at operational speeds was organised. Targets were changed to Godmanchester and Huntingdon. This trial again revealed improvements, and interceptions by 12 Group fighters showed that beam and three-quarter attacks would probably have been ineffective. This was encouraging since the bombers needed to rely upon their own defences for survival. A new ploy intended to divert the defenders' attention was for the first three Bostons on each target to drop 11-second delay bombs and attack at very low level leaving the remainder to climb before attack.

In the time between major exercises squadrons intensively practised low flying over East Anglia, incredibly low flying which meant lifting a wing over a clump of trees, climbing over telephone wires, avoiding following roads and keeping 'hull down'. Over the continent power lines would have to be watched and on the sea crossing the wave tops which aircraft sometimes clipped with their propeller tips. Pelly-Fry and crew took-off on 2 December and practiced low-level run-ups to the Oulton control tower, his deputy leader and one other doing likewise. All was ready for Operation *Oyster*.

With the stage finally set unfavourable weather intervened causing daily postponements. Crews realised something big was afoot, but the target for the morrow was not revealed until 20.30 hours on 2 December when the initial briefing was made, after which all personnel were confined to camp. 3 December broke fine but misty. At 11.05, as aircrews were going out to their aircraft, postponement again came through, and aircraft were unloaded. Fighters could not get off from their bases. No flying took place at the bomber stations; no one wanted to risk unserviceability or to miss the show. Confinement continued and next day postponement came at 10.00 hours. Tension was now high, each postponement bringing another sleepless night. Pelly-Fry telephoned Grp. Capt. Barnett on the scrambler and told him that everyone was getting distinctly fidgety—he himself perhaps not least—and that if, as he suspected, the same thing was happening on other squadrons then the best thing was to recommend Group to postpone the operation, at least temporarily. That way they might get a night's sleep, relax a bit, eat their food better.

Shortly afterwards that was done and the squadrons briefed accordingly. Pelly-Fry added, 'We always—or it seems always—do the tougher operations on Sundays. I am again betting on Sunday, and so should you.' They could all unwind, at least for 48 hours. Low cloud and heavy rain on Saturday 5th precluded operations, but behind the scenes there was feverish activity.

The morning of Sunday 6th was mainly cloudy with slight rain, but over the target better weather was forecast. The word was flashed: '*Oyster* is on.'

Raid planning had been conducted with great secrecy and care. For example, the Ventura formation navigation leader, Flt. Lt. E. F. 'Hawker' Hart, D.F.C., had acquainted himself with route details during a number of sessions with an epidiascope and strip map of the track. He was able to see photographs of the route recently filmed from a Mosquito, which showed useful landmarks. He later reported, 'I had a complete picture in my mind's eye of the whole trip.'

Briefing was particularly good and thorough. Each navigation leader took a strip map, to one side of which was attached the navigation and observation column and log sheet prepared by the station navigation officer. This would save valuable moments so essential in low flying. A silhouette of the enemy coastline ten miles to either side of the projected landfall was supplied from data obtained in *The North Sea Pilot*. It enabled the coast to be easily identified some six to eight miles out.

Crews of Nos. 105, 107, 139, 464 and 487 Squadrons were detailed to attack the Stryp Group main plant leaving Nos. 88, 226 and 21 Squadrons to deal with the Emmasingel valve factory. Bostons, led by Wg. Cdr. J. E. Pelly-Fry in Z2236 of 88 Squadron, would open the attack. To all participants the vital need to adhere to precise levels, times and routes was stressed.

The first two Bostons were to be armed with 250-lb. bombs fused for 11-second delay and make a low-level attack. The remainder would climb just short of the target, bomb from 900–1,200 feet, then descend to deck level. Pelly-Fry the leader had with him Flt. Lt. 'Jock' Cairns, D.F.C., D.F.M., as navigator and Flg. Off. 'Buster' Evans, D.F.C., D.F.M., an ex-Cornish policeman of vast proportions and utterly unflappable as gunner. 'One point that Jock and I agreed upon,' says Pelly-Fry, 'was to modify the route from the dog-leg turning point to the run-up to the target. The area between Turnhout and Eindhoven was as flat as a billiard table, with little or no visual check points, especially at a height the equivalent to riding on the top of a double-decker bus. It was vital not so much to find Eindhoven as to approach the target (in the centre of the town) on precisely the correct line; thus the target would be square-on and not end-on. To this end, we added another dog-leg, aiming slightly south of the direct track approximately East North East, and this would give us a chance to pick up—but not to cross—the railway line running into Eindhoven from a southerly direction. Crossing the railway line would be fatal, as this would entail the whole crocodile swinging off to the right in ever increasing momentum and thus ruin, as a golfer would say, the correct lie to the green and the pin. We reckoned that we should see the railway line converging on us, so to speak, and by starting our gentle turn to port we would sidle up to the railway line at around 250 m.p.h., settle down nicely on the correct lie, open our bomb doors, take aim, push buttons, close bomb doors, and get the Hell out of it, still in our respective station-keeping positions.'

Bomber crews of the U.S. VIIIth Air Force were meanwhile being briefed for their part in *Circus 241*. Eighty-four American Fortresses strongly escorted by Spitfires would bomb the Fives-Lille locomotive works. At Coltishall, Digby, Ludham and Matlask four fighter squadrons scheduled to give withdrawal cover to 2 Group were briefed. Nos. 167, 411 and 485 Squadrons would assemble at noon at Coltishall and fly to an area west of Schouwen Island to await the returning Bostons and Venturas. No. 56 Squadron would act as a mopping-up force in the same area protecting stragglers from enemy fighters.

Operating independently, No. 268 Squadron's Mustangs flew a low-level Rhubarb diversion over northern Holland, mainly around Alkmaar. They first attacked coastal flak defences then toured via Enkhuisen–Urk–Stavoren–Makkum and between Vlieland and Terschelling, led by Sqn. Ldr. W. E. Malins. Railway engines, lock gates, tug boats, five small ships, barges and infantry were fired upon. Up at 10.56, the eight aircraft touched down at 13.11.

At the 2 Group bases detailed plans were revealed and Ventura crews told they would bomb from 200 feet, and use maximum machine-gun fire to silence enemy defences which would surely be aroused by the time they sped across the factories. After the attack the force, again in three groups, would fly home at low level.

Parachutes were slung, navigators grabbed their wallets and over 300 men, all talented volunteers, made their ways to the crew wagons. Around 11.00 hours they bumped their ways to the aircraft. The numbers of these had again changed, for the Ventura force had been increased to make up for the lost Mitchells. Serviceability was high, and 47 Venturas, 36 Bostons and nine Mosquitoes roared into life leaving one to zoom across Eindhoven after the assault to take pictures for damage assessment purposes.

Take-off was around 11.20 for the Bostons and Venturas. Right from the start the numerous exercises allowed the raid to get off to a good beginning. Despite the large number of Venturas which had to get airborne from Feltwell there was precision from the start. Soon the bombers had formed up into sections and were boxed. When they had achieved this all 47 Venturas led by Wg. Cdr. R. H. Young, A.F.C., O.C. of 464 Squadron, roared low over Feltwell, an impressive sight for the ground crews, as they set course south-east. Wg. Cdr. Young's aircraft had the tail cone painted yellow and the tail light was switched on to make it plain who was the leader of this unusual formation. No. 21 Squadron kept station close behind in a similar but smaller formation.

Mixed were the feelings aboard the aircraft. 'The target which had emerged at the briefing was exciting enough but Eindhoven seemed to be quite a long way into enemy territory, and although we were going to fly at nought feet I, for one, would have been happier with the extra speed of a Mosquito or Boston, especially since the Venturas were going to be last into the target,' Reggie Goode remembers thinking. 'But as we formed up and then crossed the English coast one could not fail to be thrilled by the close formation with which we were surrounded.'

Sqn. Ldr. A. F. Carlisle, D.F.C., was at the back helping to peg the formation and prevent bunching or straggling. 'During practice,' he wrote, 'we had evolved our own formation based on a vic of three in echelon starboard so that the leader had one aircraft to port and four to starboard in a shallow echelon almost line abreast. Four or five similar lines followed but the second and fourth were staggered half a space to port. The formation was designed to fit the width of the target, to get over it quickly without the slipstream problem being severe and to permit a turn to port after bombing. Those long practices had meant flying for hours in the slipstream of all the aircraft in front, and at low level you couldn't step up or down a few feet to avoid it. Venturas were known as "pregnant pigs", the 2,000 h.p. engines driving paddle-blade propellers gave shocking turbulence. Controls were spongy, heavy and slow to take effect. They were pigs to fly in conditions such as described, and they left us tired, sweaty and bad tempered.'

Denis Barnett went to Oulton to see 88 Squadron off, said that all was well and everyone on top line. The Boston crews climbed into their aeroplanes with maps, pencils, knee-pads, anti-flak tin hats, parachutes, escape gear, money, Mae Wests, photographs of wife or girl friend (but no personal wallet), tins of glucose and chewing gum; and a rabbit's foot if you were that kind of fellow.

Taxiing out behind Pelly-Fry as his number two, who would take over if anything befell him, was that remarkable chap Flt. Lt. 'Jock' Campbell. Tall, good-looking, every inch a Scot, the crooner in Joe Loss's band before the war, he was a superb pilot who flew so accurately that he was just about his leader's shadow—always there, always in the same position, and always precisely one wing span away. These two crews were to make the opening low-level attack. No. 88 was also to be the camera squadron. Flg. Off. 'Skeets' Kelly and Flt. Lt. 'Charlie' Peace had gone to great pains to ensure a photo record of the operation. Their end product, spoiled though it was by a processing accident, was to be emblazoned across the movie screens of the Kingdom.

The 36 Bostons in sets of six were soon formed up and were heading out low level for the Essex coast. Wind was lighter than forecast, consequently speed had to be increased in order to reach the targets on E.T.A. and meet the fighters on withdrawal. By the time the coast had been reached Z/88 Squadron had turned back with an engine cutting. P/107 Squadron had hatch trouble and she also aborted.

The Mosquitoes were taking a more northerly course. Cloud base was only 200 feet, and everyone was flying really low. Some way before the enemy coast a Ventura had engine trouble and plunged into the sea. 'We were all low over the water as the Dutch coast showed as a smudge on the horizon, and we wondered whether it would be sufficient to avoid the flak which was hurled at us from gun positions on the Dutch coast,' says Goode. 'Heavy coastal defences—naval type guns I suppose —started firing at our solid formation when we were still some miles out,' recalls Tony Carlisle. 'We could see the various flashes at surprisingly frequent intervals and just had to wait for the splashes!' At the coast the whole formation began an undulating evasive action. Flg. Off. R. A. North was flying in one of 487's aircraft. 'As we crossed the salt marshes by the shore,' he recounts, 'hundreds of frightened ducks wheeled up ahead of us and many soon collided with aircraft. We felt two bumps and later discovered two holes in the leading edge of the wing, and the remains of a duck which had bent petrol pipes from the wing tank into a semi-circle. Others had been less fortunate having birds through windscreens and blood and feathers over the cockpit, unpleasant and highly dangerous. We were relieved to reach cultivated land.'

Ahead the Bostons had made an excellent landfall thanks to Jock

Cairns. They had encountered flak as they crossed over the Oosterschelde, being fired upon by heavy flak on the south side of Schouwen although the bursts luckily fell short. 'Those gunners should have been in church,' thought Pelly-Fry. In return the Bostons machine-gunned several barges being towed by tugs. It was 12.11 when Flg. Off. Freddie Deeks, navigator to Sqn. Ldr. John Reeve leading the second box of six aircraft of 88 Squadron in AL693, recorded that they were crossing Colijnsplaat dead on track. Four minutes later they crossed the coast about four miles south of Bergen op Zoom where the Boston force met a mixture of accurate light and heavy flak which caused the squadron to take violent action, weaving and corkscrewing.

As soon as gunfire from pits in the sand had been passed, course was altered to the first turning point inland. Quite suddenly the bombers found themselves in the midst of flocks of birds through which it seemed impossible to fly without collisions. Indeed, many aircraft were hit and this was the first operation when bird strike was seen to be a very serious hazard.

The crocodile which had traversed the cold, inhospitable North Sea was closing. Visibility was good—some eight to twelve miles—and from the crossing points course was maintained without difficulty, the bombers just clearing hedges and trees as they raced over the countryside, roads, railways and spotlessly clean little Dutch hamlets, and Jock Cairns, Pelly-Fry's navigator, map-reading all the way and giving small course corrections. His pilot had little time to look at his strip map but just looked out of his window, occasionally at his watch, spoke very little—and wondered why his flying gloves felt so damp. From the Bostons a Fw 190 was seen taking-off from Woensdrecht which lay on their starboard bow. It curved into the attack but was soon left behind. The slightly more southerly track of the Venturas had taken them directly over Woensdrecht which was well defended. Flg. Off. North was about 100 yards from his leader and remembers how 'the relief from the ducks lasted only a few moments as we suddenly found ourselves under fire from cannon and machine gun posts on the perimeter of the airfield. We felt very naked over this flat open ground, and returned the fire. Wg. Cdr. Seavill was in front on our left and we were formating on him. Suddenly his plane dipped ten feet, hit the ground and exploded instantly. A second or two later we were clear of the aerodrome, trees and houses making us feel less exposed.'

Other aircraft had been hit, Sqn. Ldr. Carlisle's aircraft getting a 20 mm. shell in the starboard engine. Sgt. Smock, a Canadian flying with 464 Squadron, suffered a mighty blow which blew off all the built-in slots and over five feet of the wing down to the flap brackets at the trailing edge, an amazing sight. He abandoned the sortie and landed back flaps down at 160 m.p.h. Some brick dust was found in the wing which suggested he may have hit a chimney, or that his jettisoned load may have blasted a gun post sky high. Another of 464's aircraft hit in an engine completed the sortie. Onwards the Venturas roared without any more interference.

Both Mosquito squadrons had an eventful trip as they sped over Holland led by Wg. Cdr. Hughie Edwards, V.C., D.F.C. Sqn. Ldr. D. A. G. Parry, D.S.O., D.F.C., recalled the operation recently: 'This was the only mixed operation of this type we ever had in 2 Group. We rendezvoused over the North Sea to approach the Scheldt and took position behind the Bostons. We slowed down as we crossed the Estuary and caught up with the Boston formation as planned. As we were passing Woensdrecht '190s were taking off alongside us. I had already arranged with my Flight that if any fighters attacked us the last man, Flt. Lt. Bill Blessing, would break away attempting to take the fighters with him. This occurred twice and was successful. My number two was Flt. Lt. Patterson, who had an Air Ministry photographer with him, and when fighters came in he went forward into the front formation and I turned away to take the fighters with me. I was able to shake them off and rejoin my formation. Mosquitoes were certainly operating at a disadvantage. We had to fly at the speed of the Bostons, which was very much below our normal cruising speed. In fact we were down to 20–30 m.p.h. above stalling speed at one time. When a Mosquito with a '190 in hot pursuit roared past the Venturas on a reciprocal course many of the crews were seeing the only fighter they observed during the entire operation.'

At 12.23 the Bostons flew over Turnhout and altered course to the turning point five miles south of the target. Tension in the lead Boston was at fever pitch. 'As we neared Eindhoven,' says Pelly-Fry, 'we looked desperately in the distance for that important railway line. We could see what should be Eindhoven, but it might have been another town. We were getting damn close to our ETA, and we had the spectre of not knowing precisely where we were since the last known position. No railway! Surely they could not have pulled it up—perhaps to use the metal for another purpose? Suppose we did not find that goddam railway, what then? Nothing to it but to press on and hope.'

'It's a minute before we should see the railway,' said Cairns, and then a good turn would be needed to swing the Boston formation on to the final track. 'We just mustn't cross the line, we must turn gently on to it. I still can't see it . . . I can't see it . . . it must be ahead,' said Pelly-Fry. By now he was starting to get gently irate—and at tree-top height. He stared searching desperately, then 'My God, smoke.' 'It's from a railway engine,' called Cairns, 'this must be it.'

They had been saved by a thin plume of smoke, moving smoke. A most co-operative small train was chugging happily along in the direction of Eindhoven. Pelly-Fry began a very gentle turn to port and was soon flying close alongside the track. They were going to make it. Better still, they were now determined to make it really good. The job was in the bag.

At 12.29 the formation reached the run-in position. One minute to go and John Reeve's formation was well in place, climbing from fifty feet to 2,000 and just below cloud level.

Jock Campbell, as previously planned, fell behind his leader to follow him in. The factory, now that they could identify it for sure, seemed every bit as big as the photographs showed at the briefing. One could not really miss it at low level—and it was square on their line of flight. They climbed slightly, half a mile away, then roared in to hurl their bombs through the windows of the lamp factory drawing slight flak, for the gunners were watching the attack upon the main plant where Sqn. Ldr. R. J. N. Maclachlan of 107 Squadron was leading another section at deck level. His bombs hurtled into the far side of the bakelite factory and main buildings. In a moment the second building on the left of the radio-erecting shop disintegrated in an orange eruption. A stalwart gunner had been seen to duck just before the bombs burst. The remaining aircraft reported hits galore, on the machine shop, paper and cardboard stores and radio-erecting shop where the largest tower crumbled into smoke. Against the flak the packed formation was most effective, quite overwhelming the gunners.

But disaster was ever close and moments after Pelly-Fry's 11-second delay bombs were released his aircraft swerved violently. One wing instantly dipped and he was soon doing a steep right bank. Indeed the aeroplane tried to roll. 'I put on full opposite aileron to level her, but she wouldn't respond properly,' he recalls. 'We were on the easier target but the aircraft had been hit and careered to the right over the factory roof. Chaps playing football alongside ran for their lives, whilst my pre-occupation was in keeping my aircraft flying. I struggled, kept on full opposite aileron, some left rudder and all the trim I could muster, and nursed her from her course now too far right, edging her round very slowly. A shell had hit the wing at about maximum camber tearing up some skinning about the size of half a dinner plate. My hydraulic pressure had fallen from 1,200 to 100 lb. which boded badly for landing. I handed the lead to Jock Campbell, and with 107 Squadron tagging behind 88 we came out making a wide sweep around the back of Rotterdam whereas the planned route had been via Boxtel, westward of Tilburg and Breda and back to Colijnsplaat to meet our own fighters.'

Meanwhile the south section of the works had been severely hit, smoke billowing to 300 feet. One enormous explosion rocked the northern part and there were many smaller explosions in the western section. By the time 88 Squadron had finished its attack the target was blazing. All twelve of 226 Squadron led by Sqn. Ldr. J. S. Kennedy and Sqn. Ldr. G. R. 'Digger' Magill dropped their bombs in the face of mainly inaccurate flak. By the time their attack was over—in much less than a minute—the target with its delicate irreplaceable equipment had taken a tremendous hammering. Now the Bostons on their unwanted course were beating it for home, many in the rear not aware of what trouble the leader had encountered but guessing.

The Mosquitoes dive-bombed the northern works releasing their loads on to the blazing factory. DZ371 of 139 Squadron was hit by the aroused flak defences and made her getaway streaming smoke, making her way out via Utrecht and Amsterdam. But she never made home, and fell in the sea thirty miles off Den Helder. Another Mosquito somehow joined the Bostons, sitting there for some time for safety.

Last in, the Venturas arrived six minutes after the Boston attack. Eindhoven aerodrome was close by as they ran in and by the time the Venturas were passing it was firing everything it had in the direction of Philips's. Tony Carlisle remembers it as 'lots of spectacular streams of red berries from our left. As we came up on the factory some of the gunners on the roofs of remaining buildings were still firing, and many of our upper gunners who got a horribly good view could see them banging away amid smoke and burning incendiaries. Hopelessly trapped they were still firing at point blank range with 20 mm. cannon and probably some 40 mm. guns.'

To Flg. Off. Rupert North the town had hove into view, then 'the target, a large oblong building square on to us about five or six storeys high and over one hundred yards wide with lower sheds in front. We were under fire from light anti-aircraft guns. Our aircraft was aimed at the centre of the main works. On our right and slightly above a plane was on fire. The main building was now spattered with rosettes of fire from incendiaries, and a pall of smoke towered from it. Everything went black for a moment as we went through the smoke—and I prayed that no chimney was in the way. Suddenly we could see again the houses, one or two in ruins, a wrecked plane and, most urgent, a power line to avoid.

'Now we began to pick up formation again. In the mêlée I noticed one of our aircraft converging upon us, very near and slightly lower. As I shouted to the pilot to pull up and let him under, the other plane rose sharply and swept overhead. Soon after, my pilot called to say that we had touched the other machine.'

To Reggie Goode, attacking the smaller factory, 'on the run up there seemed to be an awful lot of flak around; that over the target a blazing Ventura was formating on our port side; that as we dropped our bombs the smoke from the burning buildings made it impossible to see ahead; that a German gunner manning what would appear to be a machine gun was firing in the middle of the chaos; that very clearly as the bombs were dropped one heard on the intercom a sudden shout of anguish—and then the bombs were gone and one was through the smoke. Ahead were power lines which it seemed impossible to avoid, but which one did because my pilot decided that flying under them was better than flying over them.

'A hurried turn and the target was behind us, the flames appeared to be higher and the smoke thicker. The only worry left was to avoid further enemy action and get the Hell out of Holland. There were far fewer aircraft in the formation now and I hoped that the crews were safe. Now and again desultory flak was aimed at us and the birds were still flying up in clouds and the German gunners still appeared to think they might get some sort of revenge. But they were unsuccessful.'

For the Venturas the route home started from a point north of the prescribed track as they reformed. This was soon rectified as it was necessary to avoid a heavily defended town reached in Grand National style, just over tree tops and using the same evasive tactics as over the coast, and facing a spot of inaccurate fire from the coastal defences on the banks of the Scheldt Estuary. There was a moment of excitement aboard one aircraft when flak hit three Very cartridges igniting them. Hasty action with an extinguisher righted things.

At 12.45 hours a lone Mosquito of 139 Squadron was approaching Eindhoven from the N.W., its aim to secure damage assessment photographs. At 2,000 feet and just below cloud base two Bf 109s were spotted astern at about 880 yards. They made three attempts to close but could not obtain correct deflection—they just were not fast enough to catch the Mossie. Ninety seconds later the bomber raced into cloud and soon after zoomed low over the Philips works, by now a mass of flames and smoke.

Meanwhile the Bostons were making their wide sweep across Holland, getting slightly strung out and recrossing the Dutch coast about five miles S.W. of Brielle at 12.53, having passed between Dordrecht and Rotterdam. At this point Sqn. Ldr. John Reeve poured some shots into coastal guns to frighten the gunners. Further flak followed the Bostons for about five miles out to sea, and there were fighters in the area.

What of Wg. Cdr. Pelly-Fry nursing his damaged machine home? A second problem had arisen. The starboard engine—it had to be that one with the starboard wing already in trouble—began playing up with pops, bangs and black smoke and it rattled in its mounting. He throttled back the port engine to compensate for swing and found the starboard engine would run well enough at fast idling which was better than no power at all. He decided to leave well alone.

By now most of the other aircraft had overtaken him as he grumbled his way back to the enemy coast. Then suddenly it was the turn of 'Buster' Evans, the Cornish gunner, calmly saying 'Two '190s astern, seven o'clock, 600 yards, closing. Stand by to corkscrew. Corkscrew!' All Pelly-Fry could do was to fly up and down, with an engine coughing, just as if he were on a scenic railway. But it worked about half a dozen times. By then they were out to sea and the '190 still following them gave up the chase. It was now back to England, any old bit of England, at about 800 feet flying at about 180 m.p.h.

No. 226 Squadron had withdrawn across the Hook meeting flak up to five miles to sea. Having missed their fighter escort they had to fight their way home. A straggler flying on one engine was caught by a '190 just off the coast near Rennesse. 'A' of 107 Squadron flown by Wg. Cdr. Dutton came down in the sea after a fight, 'U' of 107 Squadron was shot down by several fighters and 'M' was last seen ablaze. Two Bostons were believed to come down in the Schmedi Estuary off Krammervolkerak.

For the Ventura force their rendezvous with the fighters was as planned, and uneventful, and the fighters had no engagements with the enemy. Long-range Spitfires escorted a damaged Ventura home. Another, 'P' of 21 Squadron, had a petrol pipe shot through and flew across the North Sea on one engine until, seven miles from Bawdsey, it was ditched. The crew escaped via the astro hatch and were rescued by an A.S.R. launch from Felixstowe. Two other aircraft landed on one engine. Only three of 21's aircraft escaped flak damage, and all were damaged by bird strike. In the reckoning 34 Bostons, nine Mosquitoes and 44 Venturas flew effective sorties.

Twenty-three aircraft were damaged in bird collisions during the operation, many as the force swept in over the Dutch coast. This had been expected. A seagull came through the observer's perspex of a 107 Squadron Boston over Colijnsplaat, the inrush of air blowing all his maps away. He worked the course by memory. On the way home his aircraft was attacked over Oostersch by a Bf 109. It made four passes, scored no hits and was damaged by return fire. One Ventura's observer was hit in the face by a large duck which burst through the windscreen. During the return journey he held his tin hat against the gaping hole. Six Bostons, sixteen Venturas and a Mosquito suffered bird damage.

It was 13.25 when the Bostons crossed the English coast at Lowestoft, the uneventful stages of the crossing requiring drift checks. Landfall by the Venturas was so accurate that arrival at the British coast was for them only half a minute late! Ventura flying time was 2 hours 45 minutes and Wg. Cdr. Young was later awarded the D.S.O. Flg. Off. Gordon-Park of 487 Squadron crash-landed in the Fens, an engine out of action, but the only other damage to the aircraft was a broken tail oleo leg. The Bostons, some damaged by fighter attacks, were in rather worse state. Sergeant Taylor of 88 Squadron in the veteran Boston Z2211, flak-damaged, had to force-land in a field near Lowestoft. Flt. Sgt. Nichol of 107 Squadron crashed at base and Sgt. Burns also of 107 landed at Ipswich his wing leading edge riddled with flak fragments.

Wg. Cdr. Pelly-Fry was still making his way home at what seemed an abysmally low speed. 'Jock kept telling me it was 35 minutes to the English coast,' he recalls, 'when he knew damn well how slow we were going. Later he admitted he cooked the books but did so to keep us happy. The so-called good port engine coughed and faded out three or four times, and down we went to some 100 feet above the wave tops before it picked up again.

'Once the Suffolk coast had been crossed, and the armed forces below had not shot at us, as they sometimes did, I decided that Blickling Hall had a certain charm, and that we would head for base. But I gave the crew the opportunity of baling out if they wished to do so. No, they wanted to get—or try to get—back to Oulton too.

'We arrived overhead, called the tower, said that the Boston was in poor shape—and told them to get ready to pick up the pieces. Due to hydraulic failure we had no working undercarriage, and no flaps. I left the former "up" (better that way with so little power available) and put the flap lever to "down" which meant that at least the flaps dropped. Fine pitch, cockpit cover ready to jettison, everyone strapped in and low over the hedge on to the grass we came at a little matter of 180 m.p.h.—just in case we lost what little control we had. A bit of a bump from the belly of G-George, a slide across the grass and then blissful silence. We were home.

'We left the Boston looking a bit ragged with bent propellers, holes here and there, that small remaining bit of starboard aileron still hanging on, the cockpit canopy on the ground, and walked to the control tower. "Buster", that robust Cornishman, forgot himself so much that even he muttered "Very dicey do, very dicey indeed." We lit our cigarettes and went to join the rest of the boys in the briefing room. Denis Barnett, bless him, was waiting to see us as well. Then we tried to sort out what had happened, who was back, who wasn't, who saw what, who thought they had hit what, and the usual animated gossip and stories followed. Eggs and bacon at Blickling Hall never tasted so good.' Pelly-Fry was awarded the D.S.O. for his part in the operation. Eight D.F.C.s and two D.F.M.s were also awarded.

The inevitable amusing situations arose. Hughie Edwards's navigator, 'Tubby' Cairns (brother of Jock), telephoned not so much to ask if he was back safely as to tell him that he was a lousy navigator—he was five minutes late on target. During the animated conversation from Horsham, where the Mosquitoes lived, the Photographic Section produced the rush prints of the target. In one of them was the Town Hall clock. It said 12.30—and that was precisely what it was planned to be!

'Jock and I got out the boat and went pike fishing on Blickling Lake. All was so utterly peaceful, and we caught a couple of fish, not that it mattered. The following day Jock's room mate said that he was sleeping badly. Whilst out with shot guns after pheasant in the nearby field I tackled him. "It's nothing," he said, "stiffness in the back after that belly landing." I asked "Did you have your cushion or your parachute to sit on when we hit the grass?" No, he did not. I had previously experienced this one with a French crew who made an inadvertent "touch down" when low flying. Like them off went Jock to Norwich hospital; the same result—cracked vertebrae. Three months in a plaster waistcoat followed, and we all put our signatures on it, usually rather illegibly by night!

'One thing I was sure of, the Boston was just about the nicest, toughest, safest, fastest and most pleasing operational aeroplane that ever happened. Later on, let it be whispered ever so softly, I kind of got to have a passion for the aeroplane to beat all aeroplanes; its name was that magic word "Mosquito".'

Meanwhile the Germans were assessing the damage to Philips's. In their report they wrote 'Damage was caused to nearly all the work buildings.' Warehouses and supplies for a great part of the works were destroyed, but there was relatively light damage to machinery, which was often the case after raids on factories. Work was halted, particularly by the disruption of electricity, water and gas supplies. Extensive damage was also caused to the rail network halting traffic for some days. Until they had dealt with unexploded bombs, of which there were many, the Germans were unable to assess the damage. But there was something on the debit side for the Allies: a considerable number of Dutch homes had been destroyed or damaged.

The raid gave a fillip to Dutch patriots around Eindhoven and on the route over which the large formation had flown. The loss of fourteen crews whilst heavy enough was not as high as expected—indeed when one remembers how close the target lay to the heavily defended Ruhr it is somewhat surprising.

Aircraft losses amounted to four Bostons, three of which certainly fell to fighters, one Mosquito and nine Venturas. One of these fell to flak en route, two were ditched and the others probably fell around the target, some perhaps set on fire by phosphorus splash. Minor flak damage was caused to eighteen aircraft (three Bostons and fifteen Venturas) and heavy damage incurred by a Boston and a Ventura. Fire from fighters damaged a Mosquito and a Boston while another Boston was damaged when it clipped a branch from a tree.

Time passed, the scars of war healed and one day Pelly-Fry was visiting the Royal Netherlands Air Force at Eindhoven airfield as part of his NATO assignment. The Dutch Colonel commanding, by way of chatting about simple things, asked him if he had ever been to Eindhoven before. He admits he had to chuckle, and said that he had put a dent in the Philips factory one Sunday morning, and that he was being followed by about a hundred other aeroplanes about to do the same thing.

Unintelligible Dutch followed from the Colonel to one of his officers, who walked away. A few minutes later when he was doing his best with another Bols the officer returned; more Dutch and the Colonel said 'Mr. Otten, the Chairman of Philips's, would like a word with you. Can you call on your way to Paris?'

The events which followed can best be recalled only in Pelly-Fry's own words: 'The Philips works seemed bigger than ever. Storeys, one above the other, climbed up and up. What a Helluva lot of electric light bulbs they must make, I thought, as the impressive commissionaire met me on the front steps and took me into the lift and up somewhere to where the Management offices were. The Chairman's office was impressive and simply arranged. Mr. Otten, boss over 30,000 people at Eindhoven alone, was smiling as he held out his hand.

' "I've come," I said, for want of anything better to say, "to apologise for knocking down your factory." He smiled again. "As you can see, we've got a much better one now!"'

'His fellow Directors came in, and we had a most interesting talk. Otten himself was not in the office at the time of the raid, others were. One was just leaving and had time to lie down in the road for what protection he could get. His worm's eye view was more than somewhat! Another saw one of the German flak posts on the roof lifted by bomb blast and drop to the ground like a giant bird's nest, German gunners aboard. Another said that one bomb only probably did more structural damage than all the rest put together. It fell down a lift shaft and exploded at the bottom. All the floors were lifted up by inches and the whole place had to be rebuilt.

'I asked, very tentatively, about civilian losses. Otten said that our coming on a Sunday morning could not have been better timed, that the factory was virtually empty. The losses to life, according to my new-found Dutch industrial friends, was about 25 people. Frankly I was staggered at such a low figure. We must have been better than we thought we were at bombing accuracy. Philips's was contributing so much to the German economy that it had to be destroyed—or at least put out of action for as long as possible. Yet the factory complex was in the middle of the town. It was essential to hit it but at the same time bring the minimum loss of life to our Dutch Allies.

'We had achieved both aims.'

Chapter 16
Mosquitoes to Berlin, Venturas to the Continent

Ten squadrons situated at seven stations were operating four types of aircraft in January 1943. Directives called for *Circuses* and *Ramrods* against shipping and airfields. Mosquitoes were to make low-level raids, particularly against rail targets in failing light or under cloudy conditions as well as photo-reconnaissance/met. sorties. Bostons were billed for low-level raids on power stations. Ventura squadrons were ready for *Circuses*, but Mitchell squadrons were still training.

Mosquitoes opened operations for the 1943 campaign, attacking rail installations at Amiens, Mons and Tergnier. During January they flew 41 sorties. Attacks were sometimes delivered from shallow dives or runs at 50–100 feet or 1,000–1,200 feet with bomb fuses set at 11 or .025 seconds. Sea crossing on the run-in was often as low as twenty feet—tricky if the sea was very still or it was misty—to escape radar detection. Once over the shore, target course would usually be set at about 270 I.A.S., with dusk attacks giving good withdrawal cover. Generally the Mosquitoes operated in pairs, the leader doing the navigating and the rear man keeping a watch for fighters. Flak, often accurate for height, was usually well behind the fast-flying Mosquitoes.

On 20 January they attacked the Stork Works at Hengelo on their biggest raid yet, eight of 105 Squadron taking part at low level. Led by Sqn. Ldr. Roy Ralston they roared in low over the Dutch countryside, and one was hit by flak. It turned back, and another which lost formation bombed the docks at Lingen, leaving the remainder to deliver a telling attack.

Ventura medium-level *Circuses* began on 9 January. In fine weather twelve crews of 21 Squadron led by Wg. Cdr. Pritchard, D.F.C., attacked the steel works at Ijmuiden. Following a low-level sea crossing the formation climbed at 600–700 f.p.m. at 165 m.p.h. I.A.S. as ordered. After a gentle descent for evasive purposes they bombed from 8,000 feet scoring hits on the coking ovens, benzole plant, engine house, a gas holder and the rolling mill, facing only slight flak.

Using diverse aircraft types posed problems. Welding them into one force was difficult as the Eindhoven raid proved. But it did permit tactical flexibility, albeit at the expense of might. This was evident on 13 January when six Mosquitoes of 105 Squadron bombed rail sheds at Aulnoye, Laon and Tergnier, 226's Bostons raided Port Rouge airfield and eighteen Venturas of 21 and 464 Squadrons attacked Fw 190 dispersal areas at Abbeville/Drucat from 7,000 feet. Enemy fighters rose to engage but the escorting eight Spitfire squadrons waded in destroying three and damaging two.

Bostons had another go at that old adversary, the *Solglimt*, in Cherbourg docks on 15th, and 20th was the busiest day yet. 88 Squadron led by Wg. Cdr. J. E. Pelly-Fry bombed the dry dock inner haven at Flushing securing hits on the bow of a ship, the docks and a slipway. 226 Squadron flew to Cherbourg where clouds interfered with the bombing and 107 Squadron found the same trouble. Meanwhile a dozen Venturas raided Caen.

The most eventful Ventura raid of the month, a three-phase operation, came on 22nd when eighteen aircraft drawn from 21, 464 and 487 Squadrons went to raid dispersal points at Cherbourg/Maupertuis airfield. Wg. Cdr. Pritchard was again leading, and rendezvous with the 10 Group escort was made over Ibsley. For an unknown reason Sgt. Powell of 464 Squadron was seen to fly into the Channel, he and the crew being seen no more. Fifteen minutes from the target rapid climb was made to 9,000 feet for concentrated bombing on the south-east dispersals by the three boxes. Flak, intense and accurate for height, damaged four aircraft in the second box. As the third box came into range flak was deadly and 487 Squadron suffered. Flg. Off. Perryman ditched twenty miles off the Isle of Wight. He and his navigator were rescued but Flg. Off. Jones subsequently died. Of 487's three crews only Wg. Cdr. Grindall made base. Sgt. Baker landed at White Waltham, his engines in deplorable state.

Training on the Mitchell squadrons had now reached feverish pitch, but technical troubles with the aircraft continued. Guns had been jamming after firing about twelve rounds, but by January the troubles seemed largely cured. The Mitchell had a good performance and carried a goodly load, and on trial Wg. Cdr. Lewer of 98 Squadron reached 25,000 feet in a fully loaded aircraft. Weather in January was variable, the Mitchell base at Foulsham a sea of mud, and a suitable time to start operations was awaited.

On 21 January orders reached both Mitchell squadrons. They should next day each despatch six aircraft to target Z.885 comprising the Perfine oil tanks and the Sinclair oil refinery alongside the Ghent–Terneuzen canal. Somewhat surprisingly a low-level operation was ordered, with a climb to safe bombing height, although the aircraft was a medium-level bomber. At the briefing the route was revealed—base–Southwold– Koningsplatt–Hulst–target–Cadzand–base. Take-off came shortly before 14.00 hours on 22 January, 98 Squadron leading with Wg. Cdr. Lewer heading the raid. In six pairs[1] they flew the prescribed track. A seagull crashed through the perspex of FL210 and Sqn. Ldr. Slocomb's face was badly cut—he had to turn for home. Near the targets the Mitchells climbed to 1,500 feet and flak was soon intense and accurate. Plt. Off. Wood's aircraft received a direct hit, disintegrated and fell as a shower of fragments. Hits were obtained on the targets and black smoke whirled up. But Wg. Cdr. C. C. Hodder, A.F.C., leader of 180 Squadron, had run into murderous fire before bombing and his starboard engine was soon burning. On its way out the aircraft was set upon by Fw 190s. They shot it into the sea, also Plt. Off. Cappleman's machine. Soon after, the remainder came under the protection of 169 Squadron's Mustangs.[2] These drove off the enemy after '190s had made six damaging attacks on FL672. Bomb load of the Mitchells had been two 1,000-lb. M.C. and four 500-lb. M.C.—an appreciable load for a 2 Group force.

Fourteen *Circuses* were despatched in January, but not all of them were effective. The enemy was inconvenienced and sometimes rose to engage although clouds prevented much bombing. This was the case on 29 January when 21 Squadron set out for the coking ovens at Zeebrugge, closely escorted by 118 Squadron with 167 Squadron (also long-range Spitfires) slightly above. The Venturas flew ten miles inland planning to attack on the way out, but 9/10 cloud covered the target and only two aircraft bombed. Since there was only a small escort German fighters rose to the bait, and forty-six '190s were seen breaking cloud before the bombing. They waded into 118 Squadron before they could turn to engage. A fierce battle evolved and Sgt. L. M. Lack of 118 Squadron was shot into the sea and two Spitfires damaged, but a '190 was claimed. The same day twelve Bostons of 226 Squadron led by Flt. Lt. D. T. Smith aimed at Morlaix railway viaduct. Flak met them on the way in and bombing was scattered. About six miles from the French coast about ten '109s and '190s attacked the second box, and there was a ten-minute fight. Flg. Off. C. S. Thomas's aircraft, AL278-Y, was hit and the starboard engine set on fire. He tried to ditch but there were no survivors. Nine Spitfires of 310 Squadron, the close escort, engaged the enemy, Flt. Sgt. V. Popelka destroying one. Fifteen miles from France a dozen

---

[1] Aircraft used: *98 Sqn.:* R: FL186 (Wg. Cdr. Lewer), U: FL674 (Plt. Off. McDonald), FL210: P (Sqn. Ldr. Slocomb), FL683: L (Sqn. Ldr. Pitcairn), FL693: O (Plt. Off. Woods), FL176: B (Flt. Sgt. Calder). *180 Sqn.:* FR212: A (Wg. Cdr. Hodder), FL217: H (Sgt. A. H. Rue), FL678: J (Plt. Off. W. H. Cappleman, D.F.M.), FL672: B (Sgt. T. S. Martin), FL218: W (Plt. Off. W. E. Dawes), FL205: G (Sgt. Fooks).

[2] Mustangs of *169 Sqn.* used were: AP187 (Sqn. Ldr. L. T. Wallace—shot down), AP257, AP246, AL989, AG649, AM231, AP189, AL990 (Flg. Off. Preston—shot down). They encountered moderate flak from Walcheren, and intense flak from an armed trawler, and escorted the bombers on return journey. Take-off was at 13.55 hours, landing at 16.00 hours.

'190s dived singly firing at the tails of the bombers. Again the Spitfires of 310 raced into battle and Sqn. Ldr. E. Foit (AR498) and Flt. Lt. Hrbacek (EP287) shot down two and damaged one. One Spitfire was lost.

The most spectacular raids of the month were by Mosquitoes. Nine drawn from 105 and 139 Squadrons and led by Wg. Cdr. H. E. Edwards, V.C., made a dusk raid on the Burmeister Wain Diesel works in Copenhagen after a long sea crossing dog-legged to disguise the destination. Bombs fell on the works but the flak was intense and the lead aircraft damaged. So low did the Mosquitoes fly in this attack that one damaged itself on high-tension cables.[3]

The previous September plans had been carefully laid for a daylight Mosquito raid on Berlin. Bad weather ruined that operation. Careful Mosquito range measurements had now been made showing that even a dog-legged track could take the small wooden unarmed bombers to Berlin and back and leave them with a reasonable fuel margin. So, for 30 January, the day Goering and Goebbels were to boast of Nazi might at massed rallies in Berlin, 2 Group laid plans to address the meetings too, and make the sirens wail over a large part of Germany. Only the Mosquito, only 2 Group, were able to make this unique contribution—and twice in one day.

Order AA97 reached Marham in the very early hours of 30 January. It was deep night when three crews of 105 Squadron tumbled from their beds. At 05.30 they were briefed, their surprise great when the target was revealed as Berlin and their delight considerable when they realised that they were to broadcast their mission on German radio as a background sound to a speech by Goering!

Route out was detailed as follows: Base to 53° 20′ N/04° 20′ E (Position A)–53° 05′ N/05° 22′ E (B)–52° 54′ N/08° 12′ E (C)–52° 42′ N/ 09° 13′ E (D)–Berlin 54° 05′/09° 00′ E (E)–54° 30′ N/06° 00′ E (F) giving a total DR distance of 1,145 miles. From base to Position D they were ordered to fly at zero feet to avoid radar detection. Then they were to climb to 25,000 feet for the attack. Two plans for the return flight were detailed. Either they were to descend to 20,000 feet using cloud expected at this height to give them effective cover, fly to Position F then descend on the last leg to base or, if cloud was lacking, they were to fly home all the way at zero feet. Thus, for the return, alternative flight plans were carried. All major pinpoints on the way were carefully studied. So careful had the planners been that by working out the tidal state on the Dutch coast they discovered that mud or sandbanks might be a useful visible pinpoint near Vlieland.

First away, at 08.47, were Sqn. Ldr. R. W. Reynolds and his navigator Plt. Off. E. B. Sismore. The three aircraft formed up setting course two minutes later in open formation echelon starboard for Position A. They crossed the English coast at 09.00. It was bumpy over the rough sea

---

[3] See *Mosquito*, p. 198.

with continuous rain. By 09.20 they were eleven minutes from Position A and found the forecast wind velocity was correct. They turned for Position B, Makkum, northernmost tip of the causeway across the Ijsselmeer. Intended landfall was the southern tip of Vlieland but they actually crossed the island two miles south of track at Eierland on the north tip of Texel at 09.36. Position B, where they set course for C, was passed at 09.41. Three minutes later they left the town of Sneek about a mile to port and were low enough to see the Dutch flag flapping above the Town Hall. Map reading was difficult due to rain, but they were considerably helped by pinpointing church spires which seemed everywhere to sprout through the murk.

It was 09.59 when they crossed the Dutch/German frontier conspicuously marked by red and white striped posts and sentry boxes. From now on the weather improved. German roads were almost clear of traffic although they spotted a large single-deck red bus, and numerous cyclists. They roared over a field where ploughing was in progress. Both horses reared violently and, to the amusement of the crews, overturned plough and driver! Some moments later a farm labourer was seen to fall to his knees in the middle of a field, pull his hat right down over his ears and pray. They avoided towns and villages, to miss possible flak defences.

Position C was reached at 10.11 and they set course for D, by which time the rain had stopped. Just north of Nienburg they began their battle climb to 25,000 feet, visibility improving and the formation climbing at 1,500 f.p.m. in the initial stage. Soon the Steinhuider Lake and Hanover passed to starboard, then they entered cloud at 6,000 feet which they did not clear until 13,500 feet. At 10.46 and 25,000 feet they levelled out, exactly as planned, for the final 77 miles to the Big City. A careful lookout had to be kept for Fw 190s since nearest cloud was 14,000 feet below. A large cloud gap appeared at 10.55 and they started gentle evasive action. The first thing to be seen was steam and smoke from a train, then a vast built-up area with a lake near Kopenick to starboard ahead. They had reached the capital of the Third Reich.

At precisely 11.00 bombs were dropped in long sticks on the city, at the exact moment that Goering was about to speak to a vast Nazi rally. The presence of the Mosquitoes was, however, known and there was confusion as the radio announced, to muffled banging noises, an hour's postponement of the speech.

The crews had expected a warm reception but nothing had happened until Sqn. Ldr. R. W. Reynolds in the lead aircraft turned away in a gentle dive heading for course of 300 degrees towards Position E. Several spontaneous bursts of flak were then seen to the north of the city, but the general impression was that the anti-aircraft gunners must have been stood down to hear the Nazi boaster. A few moments later Sismore spotted an unidentified aircraft flying a parallel course below and to starboard. Reynolds dived at about 310 I.A.S. to gain cloud cover but soon recognised the aircraft as another Mosquito.

3. Mitchell II EV-R: FL185 which served with 180 Squadron 28.6.43 until 27.3.44

4. Boston IIIAs of 342 Squadron on dispersal. BZ290: OA-S nearest, wearing 233645 on her fin, was with the squadron from 13.5.43 until 28.2.44

55. Cmdt. Henri de Racourt and crew discu an operation after r turning. Note revise nose contouring of t Boston IV, and t Lorraine motif. Th aircraft is OA-E : BZ4 used from 7.9.44 unt 5.4.45

56. Low-level attack on th naval stores at Rennes

7.   Low-level attack on the naval stores at Rennes

8.   Low-level attack on Denain steel works

59. Mitchell II FV916: EV-N being refuelled and rearmed at Dunsfold during operation *Starkey*. FV916 was used by 180 Squadron from 17.7.43 until written off in an accident on 23.4.44

60. 'T-Tommy' of 226 Squadron had 20 sorties to her credit when this was taken, and is possibly FV920. Note the individual letter on the fin and evidence of U.S.A.A.F. insignia

Cloud tops below were at about 10,000 feet and in a clear blue sky the crews headed for home at 20,000 feet leaving Hamburg about seven miles to port, far enough away to be safe from its heavy defences. Cloud ahead began to rise and they were soon flying through wisps. At 11.46 Reynolds set course for point F and with Heligoland behind began a descent to 300 feet at I.A.S. 250 m.p.h. reaching it at 12.12 at 15,000 feet. It was 13.06 when he crossed the British coast and 13.18 when he touched down. Apart from some fighters and flak which greeted Flt. Lt. Gordon near Bremen they had made their lengthy journey in the sort of immunity Geoffrey de Havilland and Charles Walker had forecast for the Mosquitoes.

Already three crews of 139 Squadron had taken off from Marham. They used a track which took them north of Heligoland to Lübeck, by which time they were at 20,000 feet, above cloud and heading for Schwarm. Shortly before 16.00 hours they ran up on Berlin which was clear of cloud and where Goebbels was about to speak. One can imagine the fury of the Nazi leaders who this time had arranged a welcome for the Mosquitoes. Two of them nevertheless escaped, thanks to their superior speed, but Sqn. Ldr. Darling was shot down.

The most important outcome of these Mosquito raids was yet to come, for very careful records of fuel consumption on the raid had been maintained. Results showed that the Mosquito could easily reach this distant target with full bomb load and fuel for a diversion course. From this proof eventually stemmed 8 Group's sustained operations against Berlin in the final months of the war. For the present, though, the operation was a resounding propaganda success, a grand morale booster, and it was an accolade for the Mosquito and all who believed in its concept.

By the end of January 366 sorties had been flown, but the total might have been much higher. Flushed with the success of the Eindhoven raid Group planned another, Operation *Tartar*, along similar lines. This time the target would be coking ovens at Tertre in Belgium. About 4½ million tons of metallurgical grade coke were being produced in Belgium for the Germans, and the Tertre plant was the most important. It also produced benzole, tar and gas for the grid system. Coke was a bottleneck item in steel production, and every effort was being made to increase its output. To seriously upset production all the Boston and Ventura squadrons were to be committed—with a dozen Mitchells, if they were ready, in place of Mosquitoes whose enforced speed reduction had caused them to operate with limitations on the Eindhoven raid. Venturas would open the attack with incendiaries whose smoke would drift away from the works before others attacked, for this time wind direction would be carefully studied. Tactics were otherwise similar to those employed previously—and care would be taken not to over-fly airfields. Some mass training flights were undertaken. But the Mitchell squadrons were not ready, the weather proved unco-operative and the operation was

K

abandoned. Had it been flown it would have been one of the most impressive of the war.

Bad weather punctuated February's operations. On thirteen days Group operated flying 390 sorties—297 of them on 27 raids for which 10, 11 or 12 Groups provided fighter escort. 115 sorties were abortive due to weather, and 92 were directed at low level against rail targets.

On 3rd with an escort of six 11 Group Spitfire squadrons twelve Venturas of 21 Squadron led by Wg. Cdr. King took-off to bomb Courtrai/Wevelghem airfield. There was confusion en route when the formation came across an unexpected British convoy, but luckily it did not open fire. Just short of the target cloud caused the attack to be abandoned but heavy flak and fighters were still met. Three times the latter pressed home their attacks over a twenty-minute period, by which time the beehive was five miles north of Calais. During the last attack delivered head-on Sgt. K. G. Moodey was shot down, two of his crew baling out. Aircraft flown by Flt. Sgt. Lear and Flt. Sgt. Hagerty were seriously damaged, one landing at Manston, the other crashing at Eythorne near Deal. Wg. Cdr. King's gunner claimed a '190.

Caen marshalling yards were bombed by 487 Squadron on 10 February. Spitfires of 485 Squadron flanked the bombers. Cloud was 10/10 at 9,000 feet making 610 Squadron's task of top cover impossible. Suddenly Fw 190s bounced the squadron being led by Wg. Cdr. J. E. Johnson. A fight developed and three '190s were shot down. Intense flak was met over Caen and Sgt. Liskowski of 610 Squadron flying EE747 : A was not seen again. Two more Spitfires, EE724 : T and EE767 : N, were ditched. Flg. Off. Smith attacked two '190s then his engine was hit, his tail broke off and he baled out. Plt. Off. Wright of 610 Squadron was attacked from astern but escaped. Two more '190s then attacked him from below. He was soon inverted and in cloud wherein he recovered control then rejoined his squadron 10 miles west of Scilly. No. 165 Squadron also claimed a Fw 190.

No. 226 Squadron managed an attack on a large motor ship at Boulogne on 13th, busiest day of the month, when five raids were despatched. 107 Squadron tried for the lock gates at St. Malo but missed, getting hits on the docks instead. If cloud did not favour *Circuses* and *Ramrods* it was useful as cover for the low-level raids mounted by 107 Squadron on 11th. In pairs the Boston hit an assortment of targets— the steel works at Caen Mandeville, a factory at Serquex and adjacent railway lines. Flg. Off. Turner and Sgt. Burns attacked the marshalling yards at Roosendaal. Heavy flak set Burns's starboard engine on fire and he was last seen entering cloud. Wg. Cdr. Carver and Flt. Sgt. Harrop aimed for the marshalling yards at Alkmaar. Avoiding shipping off Holland they found themselves making wrong landfall. Heavy flak met them at Alkmaar airfield and two of Carver's crew were wounded. Battered by ground fire both abandoned their sorties with Carver's Boston, Z2256 : A, suffering from a damaged starboard engine.

An unusual feature of 226's February operations was the use of Airspeed Oxford trainers[4] of 1515 Blind Approach Training Flight for a sea search on 2nd when overturned dinghies were sighted. These were among the few operational sorties by Oxfords. Others, flown by a 2 Group B.A.T. Flight followed the Cologne 1,000 bomber raid.

It was now that a change came in equipment of the Boston squadrons. Blenheim V losses in North Africa had been heavy so their Mk. IIIs were ordered to the M.U. at Burtonwood there to be prepared for reinforcing squadrons in North Africa. Thus the Group received a body blow just as 1943's offensive was getting under way. For Bomber Command, obsessed by a night offensive conducted in great strength, it seemed to matter little that an organisation so spirited should be deplenished. All that was left to fight with were three Ventura squadrons and the Mosquitoes. Ironically it was the 2 Group Mosquitoes of all bombers, minute in comparison with the multi-engined might of Bomber Command, that really captured the public imagination and caused considerable annoyance and worry to the enemy. 107 Squadron flew its last Boston III raids on 11th. 88 and 226 Squadrons were the last to operate Boston IIIs on bombing operations.[5]

Ventura raids continued. On the morning of 13th Wg. Cdr. King led 21 Squadron to attack coking ovens at Ijmuiden steel works. Bombing was not good but it was possible to see damage caused by earlier raids. In mid afternoon the attack was repeated with better results. '109s and '190s came up for a seven-minute fight. Eight '190s made a frontal attack on the Venturas running up to the target, four closing to the bombers. Two sections of 118 Squadron engaged and drove them away. As the bombers dived away more German fighters dived on the bombers out of the sun damaging six of them, but a Ventura claimed a probable. Above, 167 Squadron engaged a dozen Fw 190s and a dogfight without claims followed.

In the second half of February Venturas were eight times despatched. Torpedo boats and facilities at Den Helder and an unarmed raider in Dunkirk, a 5,000-ton motor vessel, were targets. After the attack on Dunkirk 124 Squadron flying Spitfire VIs climbed to 18,000 feet and, turning for home over St. Omer, where they had been blown by a gale, were intercepted by about forty enemy aircraft. An intense battle developed, four Spitfires being shot down. During the afternoon of 26th all of 464's machines suffered flak damage. Sqn. Ldr. Dale and his

---

[4] Oxfords used: V4060-A, V4062-C, V4063-D, V4064-E, AT777-F, V4138-J.
[5] The target was twice a large ship in Dunkirk. Aircraft used: 88 Sqn.: W8293, W8365, W8320, Z2233, AL740, Z2216, AL289, AL751, Z2292, Z2267, AL748 operated during the morning on *Circus 265*. In the afternoon a repeat attack (*Circus 267*) was made by 226 Sqn. using: Z2281-B, Z2258-G, Z2284-C, AL670-D, AL285-L, W8337-H, Z2234-X, AL678-R, AL750-Z, W8287-F, AL676-U, Z2166-V.

navigator, Flg. Off. Robson, D.F.C., D.F.M., were both blinded by perspex splinters but were able to crash-land AE847 at base, its hydraulics damaged and two bombs still aboard. After bombing, Appledore control informed 331 Squadron that twenty to thirty bandits were in their area. The Spitfires bounced them and 2/Lt. Bjornstad shot down one whilst Capt. R. Lunst and 2/Lt. Sogness (in BS531-A) each claimed a probable.

Next day three Ventura squadrons set out to raid the ship in Dunkirk only to find it had sailed up-Channel. Another one in its place was bombed, and again the flak was fierce. Flt. Sgt. Heagerty of 21 Squadron had to belly-land at base with hydraulics shot away and controls seriously damaged.

Eleven Mosquito operations were mounted in February. The armament works at Liège was attacked on 12th by 139 Squadron, Tours engine sheds in two big attacks again by 139 Squadron, and twenty Mosquitoes were despatched against Rennes on 26th. Sqn. Ldr. Bagguley was leading 139 and Wg. Cdr. Longfield No. 105. A sharp turn to avoid an airfield en route caused two of 105's low-level formation to collide and the force was late at the target, arriving as 139's shallow-divers were roaring down. Nevertheless the attack was extremely successful, an ammunition store exploding. But it cost 105 Squadron its leader whose place was taken by the late Wg. Cdr. John Wooldridge.

Throughout March Mosquitoes of both squadrons continued their offensive, accurately navigating over long distances to precise targets. On 3rd came the first outstanding attack, ten crews of 139 Squadron attacking the molybdenum mine at Knaben, considered Norway's most important economic target. A very high standard of navigation involved a low-level sea crossing of 375 miles followed by the difficulty of making correct landfall on the Norwegian coast. Shore crossing was within a mile of the appointed spot, then the force climbed over snow-capped mountains. Six shallow-divers pulled away leaving four to deliver the initial low-level assault. Brown and white smoke rose from the target where the flotation plant received direct hits and other buildings were damaged or destroyed. Course was set for the coast then '190s intercepted, but the Mosquitoes rapidly drew away although one of their number was destroyed after a fifty-mile chase.

Another noteworthy operation was a deep penetration to Paderborn engine sheds in Germany on 16 March by six low-level raiders led by Flt. Lt. W. C. S. Blessing and ten shallow-divers of 139 Squadron led by Sqn. Ldr. Berggren. All went well until over the Zuyder Zee the formation crashed into low-flying ducks, ever a hazard at this point. Three burst into Sgt. Cummins's aircraft, a frightening experience producing an awful mess. He was forced to turn for home. Flying very low the formation pressed on over Holland and north-west Germany until the time came for the shallow-dive force to climb. It was hazy, but the attack was carefully delivered. Flak was a little late opening up, but it claimed a Mosquito which crashed on Texel; another crash-landed near Marham.

All through March the Mosquito force continued its campaign against railway repair shops, locomotives and the rail system of the occupied countries. Le Mans, Nantes, Aulnoye, Lingen—all figured on the target lists. Intercepted R/T suggested that the enemy was unable to get help from the RDF chain on low-level raids and relied upon the observer corps, the speed of whose reports meant that the raiders were twenty to thirty miles ahead of supposed positions.

So far two versions of the Douglas Boston III had been used by the squadrons, the DB-7B and the A-20C which appeared in 1941. A-20Cs supplied to the R.A.F. had combat range increased from 800 miles in the D-7B to 1,050 miles at 16,000 feet on 66% power. The A-20C could carry self-sealing bomb bay tanks of 140 gallons' capacity. It had different radio and compass equipment. Continuous feed was provided to the twin .30 in. upper guns from hard plywood feed boxes. Trouble had been experienced with the nose-wheel locking device so this was improved and modifications made to the nose-wheel strut.

Another improvement concerned the exhaust system. In place of the collector ring assembly Douglas had designed ejector-type exhaust stacks on each cylinder. This modification was incorporated on A-20Cs in the AL263–502 range only. Others, AL668–907, built by Boeing, were unmodified. The change increased top speed by about 15 m.p.h., and better engine performance was achieved by improved cooling. Another result of the modification was that the heating system changed from steam to electrical. Troubles, however, ensued for many months with the new exhaust system.

A-20C Boston IIIs operated in the squadrons alongside older machines[6] until early 1943 when another version appeared, the Mk. IIIA. These aircraft were built by Boeing, and all had the new ejector exhaust system. Lower engine cylinders on each engine had individual short stack exhaust pipes emerging into cowled louvres. Upper cylinders exhausted into a collection manifold with two short exit pipes which emerged at the rear of the engine cowling immediately below the nacelle/wing fillets.

The first two Mk. IIIAs, BZ196 and BZ203, flew into Britain on 13 October 1942. BZ201 reached Boscombe Down on 28 November 1942, where it stayed for lengthy tests. In December level-speed measurements showed its top speed faster than a trial Boston III W8269 fitted with collector ring and single flame damped exhaust pipes. BZ201's maximum level speed in M.S. gear proved to be 309 m.p.h. T.A.S. at 1,800 feet, 320 T.A.S. at 10,500 feet in F.S. gear. All the

---

[6] 118 Boston IIIs were used by the squadrons, 25 'W' serialled aircraft, 43 'Z' aircraft, 17 in the first 'AL' series and 33 in the second.

Mk. IIIAs had air cleaners ahead of the air intakes on top of the cowling, a modification made to tropicalised Mk. IIIs and which extended the air scoop on top of the cowling to the latter's leading edge.

By the end of January four IIIAs were in service, BZ211 (to 226 Squadron 8.1.43), BZ318 (to 107 Squadron 30.1.43), BZ320 and BZ324 (both to 107 Squadron 31.1.43). They trickled into 88 and 226 Squadrons in February by the end of which thirteen were in squadron hands. Equipment took place mainly in March and April, 107 Squadron having fifteen of the 74 which had arrived by air by the end of March. From February to May the Boston squadrons were training on the IIIAs mainly because new crews had been posted in to replace those who went overseas.

Ventura squadrons had been taken off operations on 27 February for Exercise *Spartan*, the most important tactical exercise held during the war. 2 Group H.Q. was assigned a special role. No. 124 Mobile Airfield had to be formed around 88 and 226 Squadrons (at reduced strength) and the paperwork involved constituted a major feature of the exercise which was testing plans being made for the eventual invasion of France. 2 Group also formed 'X Group' which had to prepare imaginary airfields for fourteen mobile squadrons under its command flying light bombers, fighter-bombers, fighters and tactical fighters, and move them as the advance across 'France' took place. Feltwell operated three Ventura squadrons on the 'Allied' side joined by 98 Squadron. They made many 'attacks' on troops in southern and central England. Sorties were flown by Bostons simulating gas spray attacks and the exercise continued at high pressure until mid March.

A 12 Group *Circus* for twenty-four Venturas had Wilton's shipyards at Rotterdam as target on 28 March. Nos. 464 and 487 Squadrons damaged six ships and scored direct hits on three including a 470-foot spevrbrekker and an Aberkirk-class motor vessel. Bombs also fell on the Nieuw Waterweg shipyards and on floating pontoons. A large fire was started in the dock area on the east side of the Balkengatt.

Flushed with success Ventura squadrons made two more *Circus* operations on Rotterdam next day. On 28th flak had damaged seven machines and on 29th four more in the front box were hit and one in the second. Take-off for the twenty-four aircraft from the three squadrons was around 09.00 hours and Wg. Cdr. King led. Rotterdam was cloud-clad, bombs from the lead box overshooting to the west. The second box was unable to run up to the target due to the first turning on to finals too late. Instead the second 21 Squadron box bombed a barge concentration at Dordrecht twelve miles east of the aiming point. 464 and 487 Squadrons attacked railway installations nearby.

At midday 464 and 487 Squadrons, with Wg. Cdr. Sugden leading, attempted to bomb marshalling yards at Abbeville, but strong wind caused all the bombs to go astray. Excitement revolving around enemy action then caused London's balloon barrage to be flying at 6,000 feet on the return route of the bombers. The balloons had to be hauled down quickly to prevent a catastrophe.

It was decided to repeat the none-too-successful Rotterdam raid, twenty-four Venturas taking off at lunchtime. Over the target it was cloudless with fifteen to twenty miles' visibility. This time the bombs fell at Wilton's shipyards between Schiedam and Vlaardingen (where some had fallen in the morning) and around the Joost Pot factory. After the attack eight Fw 190s pounced upon 317 Squadron giving rear support with 302 Squadron, but fled when 118 Squadron closed to help. Venturas flew 66 sorties that day, their busiest so far.

Behind the scenes various moves were afoot. Expansion of No. 8 (P.F.F.) Group caused this formation to take over Graveley, a 3 Group station. Feltwell would now have to return to 3 Group to house displaced units which would temporarily cause Venturas to be based at Methwold. Provisional arrangements were made to form a new Polish Mosquito squadron, No. 305, to be located at Marham. A Free French Boston squadron, No. 342, was to form in the West Raynham clutch, and No. 320 Squadron, Royal Netherlands Navy, was to transfer from Coastal Command to 2 Group. It arrived at Methwold on 15 March from Bircham Newton, and moved to Attlebridge on 30th to work up on Mitchells closely allied to Foulsham. Accordingly a string of squadron moves was occasioned at the end of March.

Most of 2 Group's airfields had grass surfaces but labour now became available for laying hard runways at six stations. Group decided to request two runways for West Raynham—which meant it would be out of use for some months.

The Mitchell squadrons were still not fully operational because of armament troubles. They had, however, flown a lot of air-sea rescue sorties—useful for training—which 98 and 180 Squadrons inaugurated on 3 February. That month 98 Squadron flew 24 and 180 made 47. In March 180 flew 32 and in April both logged 16 each. But it was mainly training, practice *Circuses* and modification programmes that occupied these squadrons. The chief trouble arose with the mid upper turret, but a new fuel-tank feed designed at Foulsham had also to be fitted. No. 320 flew its first Mitchell training flight from Foulsham on 9 March, receiving its first aircraft, FL143 and FL149, on 17 March. Money for these and others operated by the Dutch was provided by their Government.

Nos. 464 and 487 Squadrons moved into Methwold in early April.

Although there were still communication difficulties, 464 and 487 Squadrons began operations on 4th sending 24 machines for a noon attack on Caen/Carpiquet airfield. Later another 24 escorted by Spitfires of 118, 167, 302, 316, 317 Squadrons and Typhoons of 56 Squadron left on a *Circus* against Rotterdam. Heavy accurate flak was met and twenty Venturas were holed. Sgt. Lush's aircraft of 464 Squadron was also hit. He flew on until about forty miles off the Dutch coast by which time he had fallen behind losing height. Fw 190s pestered the bomber and completed the kill then destroyed another lagging machine. Four of 487's aircraft each flew back on one engine.

No. 21 Squadron at the same time was flying under the protection of 10 Group's Spitfires, attacking Brest and St. Brieuc. Flt. Lt. Dennis led 21 Squadron on *Ramrod 53* with the Ibsley Wing as close escort and Perranporth Wing (65 and 602 Squadrons) as escort cover in sections of eight aircraft, with an oil tanker in Brest as target. Heavy explosions followed the bombing, bursts being seen alongside the ship. Before and after the bombing about fifteen Fw 190s swept in shooting down a Ventura in the first box before the target was reached, despite the active escort. Another was downed on leaving the target by which time close escort had fallen back to engage. A third, badly damaged by flak and fighters, ditched forty miles from the Lizard and a fourth near Portreath, from which fishermen rescued the crew twenty minutes later. It was a cloudless day, flak and fighters having ideal conditions. Two more raids, both led by Wg. Cdr. King, were directed against the whale oil ship *Solglimt* still in Cherbourg's dry dock and the coking ovens at Zeebrugge.

After the heavy Ventura losses on 5th five Bostons of 88 and 226 Squadrons carried out an unsuccessful sea search. This was noteworthy inasmuch as it was the last time Boston IIIs operated, AL285: MQ-L being flown by Flg. Off. W. J. O'Connell and AL678: MQ-R by Flg. Off. W. R. Grey.

Eleven Venturas of 487 Squadron set off on 13 April on *Circus 288* with a close escort of Spitfire Vs and with 331 and 332 Norwegian Squadrons as escort cover. Soon after bombing, S.W. of Caen two '190s attacked 332 Squadron whose Blue 1 shot down a fighter in a wood five miles from the town. A formation of '190s trying to bounce the close escort was then attacked by 331 Squadron. Fifteen miles out, eight '190s swept in to attack the rear of the bombers and 332 Squadron dealt with this. Sgt. Bedtker in BS249 engaged one and was promptly set upon by eight others, but he escaped to Ford. The bombers were safeguarded and 331 Squadron claimed a '190.

On 16th 464 Squadron had as its target the chemical works at Ostend and again the Norwegian fighter boys were involved, orbiting Walcheren as the Venturas did their stuff. '190s were about and when 331 Squadron spotted three they dived upon them and shot all down for the loss of a Spitfire. The Wing reformed at 24,000 feet, then 332 Squadron spotted fifteen enemy aircraft above coming from the Sas van Ghent area. In the mêlée Major F. Thorsager in BS507 claimed one.

The same afternoon 487 Squadron was detailed for the marshalling yards at Haarlem. The operation had a sticky start for, as the first box was taking off from Methwold, one machine swung badly. Its port oleo leg collapsed, preventing the second box getting away. All were recalled. The *Circus* was repeated with disastrous results for the townsfolk of

Haarlem where 85 houses were destroyed and 1,479 slightly damaged, 85 people were killed and 160 injured and the famous Town Hall was hit by incendiaries. Repairs cost 1,000,000 guilders. As the Venturas were landing one of them burst into flames. Considerable interest had been aroused at Methwold by the first arrival of Horsa gliders whose steep descent was long a talking point. They were to be stored here until needed for the invasion of France, as indeed many others were on East Anglian airfields.

487 Squadron on 20th attacked the Catreau marshalling yards at Boulogne, boxes being led by Wg. Cdr. G. J. Grindell and Flt. Lt. A. V. Duffill. Flak was intense but bombs fell in the target area and on adjoining steel works. Duffill in AE884 made a brakeless-flapless landing on one wheel, a beautiful landing which little damaged the aircraft. Sgt. Whitewell, seriously wounded over the target, landed his machine single-handed at Lympne an engine blazing at the time. It was later found that he had a compound fracture of the left arm.

Next day it was 21 Squadron's turn for an air battle. Led by Flt. Lt. Dennis, and covered by 11 Group squadrons, they made for their target the marshalling yards at Abbeville. During none too accurate bombing the eleven Venturas were intercepted by fifteen '190s whilst others took on the escorting fighters. They made determined head-on, under and quarter attacks simultaneously, breaking through the fighter screen to within fifty yards of the bombers. Flg. Off. Hicks in AE913 was downed near Abbeville and Sgt. Wells's aircraft banked away, flames pouring from the port motor. A third bomber was soon after destroyed. Losses were due to the courage and strength of the fighter interception.

Despite the limited number of aircraft available for operations due to Boston re-equipment and Mitchell snags, 342 sorties were despatched in April—254 by Venturas on *Circuses* and 88 by Mosquitoes whose employment showed a new face. *Circuses* were limited by fighter availability on days when such operations were possible. On eighteen days and four nights operations were flown. There were eighteen Ventura *Circuses* (six against shipping, eight against rail targets, one on an assembly plant and two on industrial plants, one on an airfield).

Both Mosquito squadrons were still short of aircraft but low-level operations continued with railway installations as usual targets. Lingen, Paderborn, Trier, Ehrang, Namur, Julich, Tergnier, Tours—all were raided. Tactics were as before, success was sustained, but twice Mosquitoes were intercepted. The enemy reporting system was much improved. On 3 April both aircraft detailed to bomb the rail sheds at Aulnoye were interrupted. One chased by fighters was not seen again; intercepted R/T showed plotters to have been fast and accurate. Four Mosquitoes were detailed to attack the Stork works at Hengelo and four, Malines. The former were intercepted south of Bentheim by two formations of Fw 190s, all the bombers being attacked and one shot down. On the second raid the Mosquito force crossed the coast at Blankenburg, and saw a Ju 88 on a parallel course ¾ mile away. Suspicion was that it was reporting their progress, like Flushing radio. Ten minutes later two Fw 190s intercepted the force near Echloe concentrating on the last aircraft in the formation, and shooting it down. In each instance evasive action consisted of turning into the attack and making violent corkscrew motions between 250 feet and ground level. After these interceptions, which caused some concern, it was decided to widen attack techniques, alter timings and introduce night operations.

This was a major breakaway having a most important effect on all Mosquito bomber operations. In April 27 such sorties were flown at heights between 18,000 and 25,000 feet. The A.O.C., Air Marshal d'Albiac, had in mind simultaneous high and low level Mosquito raids, the high-level force (a new 305 Squadron) being equipped with Mosquitoes powered by supercharged Merlins, but activation of such plans remained months away because of aircraft availability. Instead, the A.O.C. committed his Mosquito force to night raids, sometimes in support of the main effort of Bomber Command, sometimes to create diversions, sometimes as a raid in its own right. Night raids were begun by 105 Squadron early on 14th when six sorties were flown, two each against Hamburg, Wilhelmshaven and Bremen independent of other operations. Bomber Command now appreciated the interesting potential of the Mosquito bomber. Three hours after a concentrated raid on Duisburg on 26th–27th four Mosquitoes made a nuisance raid on the city from 20–25,000 feet, making their homeward run at roof-top height. It was moonlight with clouds topping 10,000 feet over the target. Even so, no enemy aircraft intercepted them and flak was only slight. When a large force of heavies attacked Rostock and Stettin on 20th–21st eleven Mosquitoes were ordered to make the first high-level nuisance/diversion raid on Berlin. They were led in on almost the same route as the heavies and timed to attack fifteen minutes ahead of them. Defenders were successfully deceived into thinking the capital was the target and, in moonlight and clear weather, Mosquitoes bombed it from 16,000–23,000 feet. This time height was maintained until after the enemy coast was behind. Enemy fighters were active, one finding the Mosquito flown by Wg. Cdr. Peter Shand who was shot down in the Zuyder Zee area. It was a grievous loss to 139 Squadron for he had been leader on many famous Mosquito raids.

Another night diversion followed on 28th–29th, six Mosquitoes raiding Wilhelmshaven whilst the large main force was minelaying. This time the Mosquitoes dropped flares to deceive the enemy and, flying the same course as the main force, were timed to be over their target as the first of the minelaying aircraft crossed the German coast.

On seven nights[7] in May Mosquitoes were despatched. On 13th twelve crews from the two squadrons were despatched to Berlin making a diversion raid on the city and placing bombs in the S.W. and N.E. quarters. Another crew bombed it on 15th. But during May both squadrons were being prepared for transfer to 8 (P.F.F.) Group as nuisance raiders and pathfinders, their spectacular work in 2 Group all but finished.

Before this happened both squadrons contributed one more month of low-level operations culminating in a deep, spectacular penetration into Germany. The month opened with six crews of 105 Squadron damaging the repaired Philips works at Eindhoven. Thionville railway workshops, the power station at The Hague, Tergnier engine sheds and railway shops at distant Nantes were targets. Mosquitoes had been operating for a year and, rounding off their campaign, the squadrons made their deepest-ever daylight penetration of Germany. This was an attack on the Schott glass works and Zeiss optical factory at Jena. Leading was Wg. Cdr. Reynolds, veteran Mosquito pilot, with Flt. Lt. Sismore, equally qualified, as his navigator. It was an evening raid at very low level, and highly successful. Wg. Cdr. Reynolds's colourful account appears in *Mosquito* (Faber and Faber).

In their twelve months of operations with 2 Group the two squadrons flew 726 sorties losing 48 aircraft, basically a loss of 96 crew members some of whom were P.O.W.s and some of whom escaped capture. Some very accurate bombing had been achieved. Proved was the concept of the fast unarmed bomber in a period when the armed bombers of 2 Group lost 78 of their number during 1541 sorties whilst attacking much easier targets and usually heavily escorted by fighters. To the people of the occupied countries the Mosquito brought hope in a world of despair, as its superb form flashed low over their countryside and usually beyond the reach of the foe. For a small investment Mosquitoes brought a rich reward, and had 2 Group been entirely equipped with them its story would have been much different, its contribution to victory so much greater.

---

[7] Night raids by 2 Group Mosquitoes at this time may be analysed as follows: *105 Sqn.:* April: 14th—6 sorties effective out of 6 flown, 20th—8/9 Berlin, 27th—2/3 Duisburg, 28th—5/5 (four with flares, one with bombs) Wilhelmshaven; May: 13th—5/7 Berlin, 15th—1/2 Berlin, 16th—6/6 two each to Cologne, Düsseldorf, Münster, 17th—3/3 two to Munich, one Mannheim, 21st—1 to Berlin. *139 Sqn.:* April: 20th—2/2 Berlin one FTR, 27th—1/2 Duisburg, 28th—1 Wilhelmshaven; May: 13th—4/5 Berlin one FTR, 16th—3/3 two to Berlin, one Kiel, 19th—Berlin, 21st—2/2 Berlin (139 Squadron).

Chapter 17
Mosquitoes to Liège

A Day in the Operations of
No. 2 Group Mosquito Bomber
Wing 1943, by Squadron Leader
John Bergrren

'I was, at the time, Officer Commanding "B" Flight 139 Squadron which, with 105 Squadron, comprised the only Wing of daylight bomber Mosquitoes in Bomber Command. Daylight raids proved so costly in the early days of the war that Bomber Command had now almost entirely turned its hand to night operations. The exception was 2 Group who considered themselves a race apart. In 2 Group, then operating from East Anglia, were ten squadrons. The Mosquito Wing had far and away the fastest aircraft in the Group and were rather inclined to go our own way. 105 Squadron had started the ball rolling being equipped with the Mosquito first, and 139 were now operating with much success. The squadron was commanded by Wg. Cdr. Peter Shand, an expert navigator, whilst 105 was captained by Wg. Cdr. Hughie Edwards, V.C. The station was commanded by a tough little "Digger", Grp. Capt. Kyle, an exceedingly forceful personality around whom the station revolved. There were also excellent backers up on the Admin. Staff, amongst them Sqn. Ldr. Harley our Admin. Officer and all those others who did more than their fair share to make the outfit successful. There was also our small W.A.A.F. contingent among whom was Cynthia, No. 139's attractive W.A.A.F. driver. Her pretty face was more often than not the first thing we saw when clambering from our aircraft after a long sortie.

'Because we were completely different from the rest of Bomber Command, more often than not our targets differed too, and indeed differed throughout 2 Group because of its variety of aircraft equipment. Our aircraft were Mosquito IVs with a top speed of 350–380 m.p.h. They carried a crew of two, a pilot and observer, and a bomb load of 2,000 lb. Their duration was about 5½–6 hours and during the first six months of 1943 they were used almost exclusively on low level daylight operations over N.W. Europe. Because the aircraft were totally unarmed our only defence was through surprise and high speed. Our cruising speed on these operations ranged 260–300 m.p.h. When I mention low level I really *do* mean low level, when 100 feet was considered way up. I flew hundreds of miles across Europe on many occasions only climbing to avoid power cables, and I once inadvertently flew through them.

'The list of selected small targets difficult to get at was given to "Digger" Kyle by Bomber Command, to attack as opportunity offered. Usual procedure was that "Digger", after consultation with his two Squadron Commanders or the four Flight Commanders, made a selection of a target at a conference after breakfast each morning. The choice as to which target to attack took only a few minutes and the two C.O.s thereafter left for their units to put the squadron machinery into motion.

'Next step was normally a unit conference with the C.O. and Flight Commanders present, together with the Squadron Adjutant. At this meeting crews and aircraft states were discussed. The size of attack to be mounted depended to a large extent on size of target and its importance. Decisions were taken upon the number of aircraft to be used and which crews would take part. According to size and importance of attack, individual flights or squadrons would be led either by Flight or Squadron Commanders. The squadrons didn't necessarily operate as a unit, sometimes the entire wing would be used on one attack. In these cases I have known twenty or more aircraft and on one occasion a maximum effort called for fifteen aircraft from each squadron. Each squadron had approximately eighteen aircraft as its I.E. so that, allowing for unserviceability and casualties from enemy action, twelve to fifteen aircraft represented our maximum effort.

'We used two methods of attack and almost invariably took a bomb load of 4 × 500-lb. bombs fitted with instantaneous or 11 sec. delay mechanism. In the first instance the instantaneous bombs needed to be dropped from a height of not less than 1,200 feet and this necessitated a quick climb a few miles short of target to, say, 3,000–4,000 feet, from which a shallow dive fast attack was made to required altitude for bombing. In the second method the run-in to target was made directly along some well defined feature such as a canal or railway line, and bombs dropped from a low altitude. They more often than not bounced on to the target going off several seconds after departure of the aircraft. In a big Wing attack the two methods were used together, with the low level aircraft going into attack first and the others coming down with the dive bombing attack seconds after first bombs had burst. Formation throughout the long low level run-in to the target was held in echelon on the leader until the attack had taken place. This was normally planned for dusk or just before darkness, so that the aircraft could normally make their way back to base individually under the cover of half light or darkness.

'The operation I am about to describe took place on 12 March 1943, and was composed of twelve aircraft, six from 105 and six from 139 Squadrons. It was carried out against the John Cockerill Steel

Works in Liège, east Belgium. The attack had to be carried out as accurately as possible as the steel works were situated in the town. It was important to cause as little loss of life amongst our Allies as possible. In the event this is what happened and we were able to pick the target out of the centre of the town with as little fuss as possible and as little damage to the town as practicable.

'The day started with the usual Squadron and Flight Commander's conference at which the target was decided upon, number of aircraft to be used and method of attack. 105 were to go in low level and the echelon of 139 led by myself would do the dive attack coming on to the target run half a mile after the first six had gone across with 11 sec. delay bombs.

'When I got the news from Peter Shand, and we had picked the crews who were to fly, I went out to acquaint them with the news. Most of them were in our dispersal area, a quiet corner of the airfield, swinging some of the aircraft compasses. I drove out in my small Service pick-up to give them the necessary details. From some distance my crews saw the pick-up motoring along the peritrack and by the time I had reached the first aircraft they had all crowded round to hear what I had to say. There were simulated groans from several of them and they had all gathered round my window before I could get out, so I had to read the Battle Order out to them from my seat, giving brief details of who was to accompany me on the operation, the hour of the attack, the approximate time of take-off, then instructing them to finish swinging the compasses and get down to their respective messes for an early lunch. This was preparatory to attending briefing before take-off. Briefing had to be in the Station Operations Room as it was a combined squadron operation and we should not therefore be using our own briefing section as would be normal for a squadron operation.

'Morale was very high on the Mosquito Wing and competition to have a place on the various raids was always very keen, despite the fact that losses were fairly high and almost inevitably one or two aircraft failed to return from operations.

'In March dusk over N.W. Europe falls between 5 and 6 o'clock and as the route in with several dog-legs was likely to take between 2 and $2\frac{1}{2}$ hours take-off must be between 3 and 3.30.

'At briefing, attention was paid to the routes in and out, weather to be met, examination of target maps and a long talk from the Senior Intelligence Officer regarding flak positions on the route and information on the dispositions of enemy airfields and fighters. It would take a couple of hours and therefore not leave much of the day unfilled. The briefing for this raid took place at 12.15 and most of the details were gone through quite quickly. The weather was thought to be clear with cloud cover at about 5,000 feet and visibility in the target area was presumed to be some six miles or more. This would allow a clear run to the target, and we also had an exceedingly good lead-in directly along the River

Meuse. The Intelligence Officer stood to say his piece. This covered flak and fighters about which most of us were already aware. The next point of interest he raised was that two crack fighter squadrons of the Luftwaffe had recently been moved to Woensdrecht, south of Rotterdam, and that these had recently been equipped with Fw 190s. Our route took us to the north of Rotterdam, so this new information was of utmost interest. Our last act was to synchronise our watches.

'After briefing we loaded ourselves, together with our parachutes, flying helmets, Mae Wests, maps, briefing bags and flying paraphernalia on to the squadron pick-up, and were dropped at our aircraft dispersal points. We made every endeavour to keep our own individual aircraft. My particular machine, DZ478[1] V-for Vanguard, I had already flown on many operational flights. I heard later that this aircraft went on flying long after I had left the squadron after having completed my second tour of operations. Eventually it had to be taken off operational flying because it had suffered so much damage from enemy action that it had become slow. It was the aircraft I flew through the high tension cables when going to attack engine sheds at Malines.

'We always tried to allow half an hour out at dispersal before take-off so that we could complete an adequate inspection of our aircraft and get ourselves comfortably settled in the cockpit.

'Precisely at 3.30 from all around the dispersal areas the first twelve Merlin engines started as one. After ten minutes to warm up and allow slow starters to get moving, all twelve aircraft converged on the airfield where they formed up in a long line on the downwind side of the airfield. In those far off days Marham had no runways and was simply an enormous expanse of grass off which we could take the entire Wing in echelon formation. So getting a mere twelve off in one go was child's play. In next to no time the twelve of us were off the ground, wheels and flaps were up and we had reached our cruising speed of some 270 m.p.h.

'In a wide low level turn to the south we set our first course towards Dungeness. We had been briefed to leave England via Romney Marsh and Dungeness, then fly across the Channel to France and up over the cliffs just to the west of Cap Gris Nez, then on at nought feet over the heavily defended Pas de Calais. After this there were dog-legs across northern France, Belgium and our run-in to target along the river.

'Everything in the initial stages went according to plan and without further mishap, and seldom flying at more than 100 feet or so, we arrived in the target area. Here we split and the 105 formation with 11 second

---

[1] DZ478 joined 139 Squadron 11.2.43 and became XD-V. After DZ587 XD-C crashed at Hardwick on 5–6.11.43 DZ478 became XD-L. It passed to 692 Sqn. 1.2.44 becoming P3-L, making its first operation in new hands on 4.2.44 flying to Frankfurt and next night to Berlin. It returned to 139 Sqn. 13.3.44 and joined 627 Sqn. 21.4.44 where it was written off due to battle damage 7.5.44.

delays went straight in at low level. We, in our turn, started our hurried climb to 3,000 feet or so preparatory to diving on to the target. I had just reached this height, and was some 3 to 4 miles short of the factory when I saw the bombs from 105's effort already bursting and I and my entire force came down in a steep dive right on to the target. As our bombs instantaneously went off directly beneath us we were all shaken all over the sky with odd bits of debris, pieces of bricks and mortar flying up all over the place and through our formation. As we turned away to the north we could see a huge mushroom of smoke building up over the main target area.

'Intelligence reports later indicated that we had done an exceedingly good job and put the factory out of action for several months to come.

'After leaving the target area it was normal practice for the formation to break into individual aircraft, and we all raced for home in the gathering dusk. My own formation had once more come down to tree top height and we set course to leave Holland in the area of The Hague.

'Shortly after leaving the target I decided to take a short cut home and informed my observer, Peter Wright. Accordingly I told him that it was my intention to leave Holland between Antwerp and Dordrecht which would mean coming out over the coast 60 miles further south than the main formation, and would reduce the journey by at least half an hour. This was, of course, against orders, but I took the view that, as I had already completed nearly sixty operations and was of senior rank, it would be permissible. Peter, who was a most serious minded school-master in civilian life and a tower of strength in the air, muttered something uncomplimentary and we went on to work out an alternative course. For the next 20 minutes at a speed of 280 m.p.h. we flew along this new course.

'Dusk was gathering. The ground was getting quite dark although there was still quite a lot of light in the sky and we had to come up a couple of hundred feet or so to avoid flying through H.T. wires which criss-cross that part of the world. As we flew along our new course we could just faintly see the lights of Brussels to the left. We passed Antwerp 6 or 7 miles away then we turned slightly more to the west to come out over the low lying islands of the Scheldt Estuary. It was here that our bit of trouble started.

'On the way from the target I had noticed another Mosquito flying along in a similar direction to ourselves for some miles. It was now a few miles in front of me and as we had been holding the same course and speed I kept him in sight almost from the time of leaving the target. We both reached the Antwerp area towards the end of the dusk period and by now, although there was still some light in the western sky, the ground was dark. I had glanced up every so often and could still make out my companion, when suddenly I saw long streams of tracer open up on him. When anything like this happened it was standard practice in the Mosquito Wing to get as low as possible, and go as fast as possible too. To do this the RPM control was pushed into the fully forward position, the throttle was then opened fully and the "panic valve" was also pulled. This was merely a lever which, when pulled, gave full supercharger pressure on both engines. The three operations could be done almost simultaneously, and I took this action now. For all I knew we might be running into all sorts of trouble ahead. I had a fairly good view of the other Mosquito[2] silhouetted against the Western sky, and he appeared to be caught in a cone of fire from several light flak guns which were firing from a heavily defended airfield. This turned out to be Woensdrecht where the Fw 190 wing was based, and the place we had been trying to avoid. There was nothing for it now but to go straight on as low as possible right through the defended zone. The Mosquito ahead not flying as low as mine seemed to be in difficulties. As I glanced up I saw a flicker of flame from his port engine which rapidly blossomed into a streaming, fiercely flaming fire, as the tanks in the port engine caught alight also. In dreadful fascination I watched him gradually take fire all over until, in a long stream of bright light, he crashed on the runway of the airfield. On impact the aircraft broke up entirely and the whole thing left a stream of burning debris along the runway.

'Meanwhile I wasn't doing so well myself for, as I looked up once again to scan the sky, I was badly shaken to see the silhouettes of Fw 190s entering their circuit. I first counted two pairs, then others until the whole sky seemed almost full of them. Eventually I counted twelve pairs of '190s all now orbiting in the circuit. This was quite obviously no place for me and I took the only action I could by trying to get away as fast as possible. I was already going flat out and although flying very low felt I could get down even lower but with the risk that I might hit something on the ground if I was too low. By this time I took the view that if I was going to get clobbered it wouldn't matter which way we went out. I flashed across that airfield literally at nought feet like a scalded cat, with all the light flak guns which could be brought to bear shooting at us. I think those that hadn't guns were throwing stones at us, and anything they could lay their hands on.

'All this time twenty-four '190s were circling above us, presumably asking for landing instructions and wondering what the Hell was going on. Luck was indeed on our side. After hurtling over a block of buildings which appeared to be an administrative part of the camp we got clear away without one little hole. Soon after we were lost in the gloom and out of range of the guns. I must admit I didn't return the "panic valve" to its normal position for several minutes. By this time I think my Mosquito was going faster than it had ever done before. I didn't really relax until we were half way across the North Sea. The rest of the journey home was fairly uneventful, but I had one more bad moment. We flew across one of our own coastal convoys heavily escorted by

---

[2] This aircraft was DZ373-XD: B.

naval vessels. These, in their usual gayest abandon, opened up with everything they had. We nevertheless made base without mishap. We landed and taxied to the temporary parking area from which the aircraft would be moved to their dispersals next morning. The crews were picked up by our little W.A.A.F., Cynthia, and were taken to de-briefing to relate personal accounts of the raid.

'One particularly interesting aspect of this operation came to light through the "Y" Service participation. The "Y" Service, in short, used a powerful listening device which was tuned in to the German fighter VHF and W/T frequencies, all of which we monitored and recorded for future information. It appeared that the German tracking arrangements had worked very well during this operation. For example, their radar had picked up our formation of Mosquitoes very shortly after it left the coast at Dungeness despite our low flying. We'd been tracked across the Channel to Cap Gris Nez. In the short time available to them some guns on Gris Nez had opened up on us. This they had done by dropping shots into the water ahead of our aircraft making huge spouts of water in the hope of bringing us down. In fact some aircraft flew through these spouts, and one of my pilots had a bad moment when his engine faltered through taking too much water into the air intake.

'After this had come the very rapid climb to clear the cliffs. Very soon after we'd crossed the coast various Luftwaffe Sector Stations had been alerted and, once our track was ascertained, fighter units had been directed for the kill. The reporting stations had only fallen down in one aspect, this was our cruising speed. We'd been plotted on our way in at about 250 m.p.h. whereas we had been flying at 280 m.p.h. So the intercepting arrangements had been hopelessly out.

'We had penetrated through the fighter defences and arrived at our target unscathed, with several Luftwaffe fighter wings vectored across our track but always after we had passed, and this included the Woensdrecht Wing who had lost us on the way in. It had been ordered to split into two formations the first to patrol the coast north of Dunkirk, the second between Ostend and Flushing in the hope that we would make our exit somewhere along this line and they would catch the rat on the way back to his hole. As night fell the two '190 formations were called to base. They arrived there at the same time as I did and probably hadn't enough fuel to chase me.

'There was nothing special about that raid, and there was never a dull moment on the Wing. Once I was leading the last box of six on a deep penetration over west France to the St. Joseph locomotive works at Nantes. We were spaced 2–3 miles apart and on our track there was one of the many small Luftwaffe reporting stations sprinkled throughout enemy territory. These were generally triangular in plan with a barbed wire perimeter, several wireless masts, buildings and the "privy" at one end—on its own on this occasion. It must have been occupied and the occupant must have been decommoded by the large number of aircraft very low overhead. As I came up I saw the door flash open and a large fat German in field grey with his trousers still around his knees fell out on his way to take cover.

'A little later on the same flight, when flying over some open fields being harrowed, I happened to come upon an elderly French countryman whose startled horse had bolted with the harrow. The Frenchman was so livid that as I came up he took his beret from his head, threw it to the ground and then seized an enormous clod of earth and hurled it at me as I passed.

'These were memorable, exciting days. I don't think that any member of the Wing—be they air or ground crew—would have traded his place for any other job in the Royal Air Force at that time.'

Chapter 18
Amsterdam Adversity

Since March 1943, the Boston squadrons had been re-equipping, training, flying sea searches; but only 107 Squadron was yet ready for operations. They resumed action on 1 May when boxes led by Wg. Cdr. England and Sqn. Ldr. Spencer attempted a raid on cloud-clad Caen; it proved abortive but the flak was heavy.[1]

Next day 107 Squadron attacked the steel works at Ijmuiden but scored only overshoots into docks and barges. '190s were about and 331 Squadron shot down three. It was 28 June before 88 Squadron rejoined the fray and 226 Squadron had barely begun to re-equip before it was decided it should arm with Mitchells which kept it out of the fighting for many months.

The Royal Dutch Steel Works at Ijmuiden was a tempting fringe target which Venturas of 464 Squadron also tried for on 2 May. They flew their customary low-level sea crossing making a battle climb to bombing height. Moderate flak greeted them and on their return they were intercepted forty miles out by Fw 190s which scored hits on the third aircraft in the second box and one in the first causing thigh wounds to Sgt. Carruthers in AE688. The escort included 118 Squadron which claimed two of the enemy. The raid had caused damage to the coke factory, sulphate plant, benzole unit and the compressor and store houses. Three ships were hit, two of them sinking. But the steel works escaped damage. Another raid was decided upon.

This time two boxes each of three Bostons[2] were ordered to make a low-level attack. The operation was to be carried out in conjunction with a diversionary *Circus* by Venturas of 487 Squadron, directed against Amsterdam power station. Both formations set out from Coltishall and the Bostons headed out low level across the North Sea. Then, from nought feet, the first vic scored good hits on the switch and transformer stations at the factory but again missed the steel works despite a good run-in from an incredibly low level.

---

[1] Aircraft flown on this, the first raid by Boston IIIAs, were BZ230 (Wg. Cdr. England), BZ223, '241, '280, '227, '203, '253, '259, '351, '303, '226, '260.

[2] Aircraft used: BZ230 (England), BZ223 (Nichols), BZ241 (Healey); BZ351 (Simpson), BZ220 (Dunn), BZ227 (Harrop).

Shortly after leaving the Dutch coast they were set upon by '109s and '190s, and by carrying out evasive action the formation escaped. The second vic scored direct hits on the factory and met much light flak. On turning out they ran into the fighters. Flt. Sgt. F. S. Harrop's aircraft crashed on fire into the sea. Nichols and Simpson drew away but on their route home they saw a Ventura plunge into the sea without any survivors evident. They had witnessed part of a shattering tragedy.

Fourteen crews of 487 Squadron had earlier been briefed to attack the Amsterdam target, to encourage the Dutch Resistance and aid Dutch workers in organising strikes against the Germans. Twelve aircraft were ordered to rendezvous with their escort, Nos. 118, 167 and 504 Squadrons, over Coltishall at 17.00 hours below 1,000 feet, fly for 33 minutes low level at 190 m.p.h. I.A.S., climb at 165 I.A.S. to bombing height and run in. The target was known to be well defended, but the order was to press home the attack regardless. Unbeknown to Group a convention of fighter pilots was taking place at Schiphol, into which many of the best pilots in the West had flown. This assembly was then held on alert during a visit of the German Governor of Holland to the town of Haarlem—which lay on the Venturas' route to Amsterdam.

At 16.43 the twelve Venturas of 487 Squadron became airborne. Five minutes later Q-Queenie flown by Sgt. Barker turned back; she had lost an escape hatch. The others formated, met the Spitfire V escort and set off over the water. Leading the bombers was Sqn. Ldr. Leonard Trent with Flt. Lt. A. V. Duffill as his deputy.

Ahead of them was a formation of Spitfires of 11 Group flying *Rodeo 212*, a diversion to the Flushing area. There had been an error in timing, and this group of fighters appeared thirty minutes too soon near Flushing. It had the effect of putting the enemy radar and fighters on to a high-alert state. Could the British be going to attack Haarlem? No chances were taken. The main bomber force began its climb at 17.35 and was soon at 12,000 feet, in good weather by the time the Dutch coast was reached. Meanwhile some seventy enemy fighters were assembling in four formations, Fw 190s to deal with the Spitfires and Bf 109s the bombers. The Venturas pressed on oblivious to what was to unfold. They had entered the ambush.

As soon as Trent saw the enemy fighters he told his squadron to close into one formation for maximum protection. Meanwhile at the coast twenty plus enemy aircraft swept down upon 118 and 167 Squadrons which formed the close escort, as thirty other fighters went after 487 Squadron. No. 504 Squadron was some three miles behind when the action began and the entire beehive was still making its climb. The '190s raced in ahead of the fighters effectively cutting them off from the bombers. Wg. Cdr. 'Cowboy' Blatchford, the fighter leader, desperately tried to recall the Venturas but within seconds they were completely hemmed in by fighters. A tremendous battle ensued, '190s repeatedly diving on 167 Squadron. No. 504 Squadron in the rear did a 360° turn

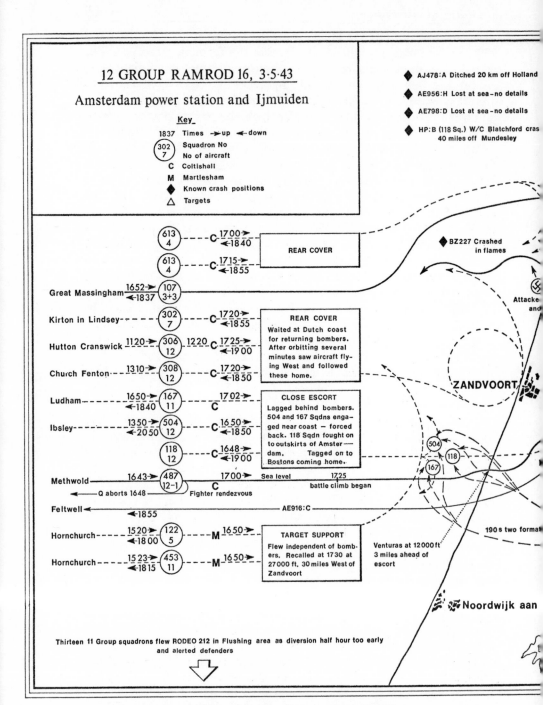

12 GROUP RAMROD 16, 3·5·43

Amsterdam power station and Ijmuinden

Key

1837	Times →up ←down
(302/7)	Squadron No / No of aircraft
C	Coltishall
M	Martlesham
◆	Known crash positions
△	Targets

◆ AJ478:A Ditched 20 km off Holland

◆ AE956:H Lost at sea – no details

◆ AE798:D Lost at sea – no details

◆ HP:B (118 Sq.) W/C Blatchford cras
40 miles off Mundesley

◆ BZ227 Crashed in flames

(613/4) —C 1700→ ←1840   **REAR COVER**

(613/4) —C 1715→ ←1855

Great Massingham 1652→ ←1837 (107/3+3)

Kirton in Lindsey --- (302/7) --- C 1720→ ←1855   **REAR COVER**
Waited at Dutch coast for returning bombers. After orbitting several minutes saw aircraft flying West and followed these home.

Hutton Cranswick 1120→ (306/12) 1220 C 1725→ ←1900

Church Fenton --- 1310→ (308/12) --- C 1720→ ←1850

Ludham --- 1650→ ←1840 (167/11) 1702→ C   **CLOSE ESCORT**
Lagged behind bombers. 504 and 167 Sqdns engaged near coast — forced back. 118 Sqdn fought on to outskirts of Amster—dam.   Tagged on to Bostons coming home.

Ibsley --- 1350→ ←2050 (504/12) — C 1650→ ←1850

(118/12) — C 1648→ ←1900

Methwold --- 1643→ (487/12-1) 1700→ Sea level   1725 battle climb began
← Q aborts 1648   C Fighter rendezvous

Feltwell ← ←1855   AE916:C

Hornchurch --- 1520→ ←1800 (122/5) — M 1650→   **TARGET SUPPORT**
Flew independent of bombers. Recalled at 1730 at 27000 ft, 30 miles West of Zandvoort

Hornchurch --- 1523→ ←1815 (453/11) — M 1650→

ZANDVOORT

(504) (118) (167)

Venturas at 12000ft 3 miles ahead of escort

190 s two format

Noordwijk aan

Thirteen 11 Group squadrons flew RODEO 212 in Flushing area as diversion half hour too early and alerted defenders

MAP 14. *See Appendix 12, pages 505/6 for notes*

Castricum

H O L L A N D

Edam

Beverwijk

1753 Sea level

IJMUIDEN POWER STATION & ROYAL DUTCH STEEL WORKS

Noordzee Kanaal

Tagged onto Bostons

ZAANDAM

Hernbrug
AE713:T Crashed 1753

Kometen Polder
AJ209:V Crashed 1800
△ POWER STATION

HAARLEM

118
Bornstrasse
AE780:S Shot down 1750

AE716:U Crashed in Polder 1800

AE731:O Emergency landing 1745

AMSTERDAM

Vijthuizen   AJ200:G Shot down

C hit, abandons op.

AE684:B Shot down 1745

Amsterdam Rijn Kanaal

SCHIPHOL

109 s two formations

Aalsmeer

Sixty-seventy Bf109 & Fw190
alerted and waiting for attack.
One force contains fighters &
one force attacks bombers

Miles
0   5   10
0   5   10   15   20
Kilometres

attempting to attract the '190s, but the ruse did not work. With the fighter force overwhelmed the Venturas had to go it alone. Sgt. R. J. Flight of 118 Squadron destroyed two '190s and 167 another. Blatchford's Spitfire was badly shot up and he came down in the sea forty miles off Mundesley.

Pestered and pursued, 487 Squadron proceeded and one of the first Venturas hit was Duffill's. Its hydraulics were put out of action and both engines set on fire. Both gunners were seriously wounded after one had claimed a fighter. With his aircraft in a terrible state Duffill was forced to try for home. His was the only aircraft to return.

As Duffill turned back two of his section followed him but were soon shot down. Presumably the enemy considered Duffill's chances of getting home nil, and transferred their attention elsewhere. His navigator managed to get the bomb doors open and to release three bombs. After a time the fires died out and the chance of getting home was greater. Eventually Duffill made Methwold and on arrival each member of the crew was immediately decorated although two of them were rushed to Ely hospital.

Over Holland the Venturas were being picked off one by one until there were only five left to begin the bomb run. Still the fighters kept swooping upon the Venturas until only Trent's aircraft was left. Two Venturas had blown up and fallen as a shower of fragments. Flg. Off. Foster had turned away and his badly damaged aircraft was ditched. Three of the crew were taken prisoners. A German fighter shot across Trent's bow so he opened fire—the fighter curled away burning.

Trent, now on his own, was determined to bomb the target. He tried, but his load overshot and caused only blast damage to the target.

Now he had to face the journey home, an impossible journey. Hardly had he bombed when the fighters waded in ignoring the flak. All his controls were shot away and AJ209 began a dive which was to end in Kometon Polder. Trent and his navigator were hurled from the wreck at 7,000 feet and ultimately captured, but the other two were trapped in the shattered aircraft. It was not until the war had ended that the story could be pieced together. Sqn. Ldr. L. H. Trent was awarded the Victoria Cross, a salute to him and indeed all who had taken part in a disastrous operation.

Trent's adventures did not end this day for he was one of those who participated in the great escape from Stalag Luft III in March 1944. He had helped dispose of the sand from the tunnel and, as No. 79 to leave, was about to break cover when the guards fired.

Some men had died in their aircraft, others in crashes; and survivors were few. There were many courageous deeds: Flg. Off. McGowan and Flg. Off. Thornber dragged their gunner from his turret, put on his parachute and pushed him out to safety. They were killed soon after. Sgt. Stannard had an incredible escape. Trapped in the tail of a burning aircraft he saw no means of escape; death seemed certain. Suddenly there was an explosion and the tail portion broke away and, by good fortune, began gliding down. Eventually it hit a tree and Stannard was knocked unconscious. When he came-to he was in a Dutch mansion taking wine in the drawing room—with a Gestapo officer and a Luftwaffe official ready to take him into custody. One of the survivors was Flg. Off. Rupert North whose memory of the operation is still very vivid:

'We made rendezvous with our close escort who took up stations on our flanks and made an uneventful crossing of the Channel. No sooner had we crossed the Dutch coast than all Hell broke loose. Tracer bullets were whizzing around, enemy fighters were flashing past and our planes were going down in pieces or flames. It was plain we would soon be hit and the tension and suspense were paralysing. Sqn. Ldr. Trent's trio was still ahead, the escorting fighters were bobbing up and down to avoid cannon fire. Then a series of bangs and the plane juddered. I looked back from my position in the nose, past the pilot into the doorway leading to the back of the plane where the rear gunner and upper turret were stationed. There were flames. I negotiated the narrow passage to the pilot's compartment and saw him reaching up to release the escape hatch above his head. There was a fire extinguisher on the wall beside the entrance to the rear of the plane and I reached out to grasp it, although the fire seemed too fierce to be combated. I was met by a surge of flames probably drawn forward when the escape hatch blew off.

'I felt no pain at the time, more as if I had been struck a heavy blow. The pilot seemed ready to go and my clothes were on fire. I grabbed my parachute pack and, without clipping it on, stepped on to the seat and leaped through the roof hatch. There was a moment or two when things went blank and then I found myself in the air without any feeling of falling but nevertheless was most anxious to fit the parachute pack, still clutched in my hands, to the harness. A sudden draught seemed to have extinguished my burning clothes so I set about fixing the pack. It seemed more difficult than usual and when it finally snapped on I found that the right hand ring was on the left clip and I would have to take it off again or risk being supported by one catch. Time, I argued, must be short, and in undoing the clip I might lose the pack so I pulled the release and hoped for the best. It worked all right and the descent seemed to take ages. Everything was quiet and peaceful with Holland like a map below and not seeming to come any nearer, and then approached more and more rapidly as the time to brace myself for impact approached.

'I made a perfect landing in a soft field of tulips. I sank to my ankles in soft soil but didn't fall over. Quite proud of my first parachute jump, I watched the silk gracefully fall to the ground; then it billowed out like a spinnaker and whisked me off my feet to plough a lonely furrow through the flowers for about fifty yards before I could release myself.

'I was soon picked up by a German motor-cycle patrol which took me to a military post. I went thence by lorry (in which I was overjoyed to find my rear gunner) to hospital in Amsterdam, where the electric power was still operating.'

Gloom hovered over Methwold. Catastrophes such as this were less common at this stage of the war. This was the fourth time that an entire squadron had been virtually wiped out in one operation. In this instance it hit hard a squadron many of whose crews came from the Dominions.

The day after the raid hope was that at least some of the crews had baled out. Indeed, the fighter boys claimed to see seven parachutes. At the roll call on 6 May the squadron could muster only six crews and eight aeroplanes so, for the next couple of weeks, the task was to rebuild 487.

Morale had taken a hefty blow, on 464 Squadron too, for there were so many faces suddenly no longer around. It was a sobering thought, too, that the toss of a coin between Sqn. Ldr. Meakin and Leonard Trent had decided which squadron should make the raid. 487 recorded in its diary: 'It's a very bleak day with the loss of crews like Sqn. Ldr. Trent's, Flg. Off. Perryman's, Andy Coutts's, Tom Baynton's, Foster's, McGowan's, Terry Taylor, Len Richbell, Stanley Coshall, Rupert North and so many others. A better set of boys couldn't be found in thirty years. Everyone is dazed by the news.' In May Sqn. Ldr. A. G. Wilson arrived to command, and build-up to 21 crews followed.

On 23 May 487 Squadron resumed operations with an attack on coking ovens at Zeebrugge meeting little opposition. News spread that an important visitor would be arriving at Methwold on 26th. When he did so he came with his wife. It was H.M. King George VI who, ever sensitive to the suffering of his people, came to pay his respects to the gallant crews there and as token of his regard for the fallen. Fourteen crews from each squadron greeted him, others lined the route to cheer their popular monarch. A few days later Sir Archibald Sinclair came to see how the rebuilding of the squadron was progressing. That day 464 Squadron bombed Caen/Carpiquet.

No. 107 was the only Boston squadron to operate in May 1943 for other than sea searches. Its five operations following the Ijmuiden raid were all *Circuses*, directed against Abbeville, Cherbourg and Poix. Most eventful was that of 15th. After a false start two boxes led by Wg. Cdr. England and Sqn. Ldr. North scored hits on the runway and dispersals at Drucat. Between Poix and Le Touquet they were subjected to repeated attacks by '109s and '190s. Fighters claimed two Messerschmitts and Flt. Sgt. Kindle, England's gunner, damaged two. His fuel tank holed, Flt. Sgt. Noble put down at Detling and Flt. Sgt. Truxler had to force-land in a Kent hopfield near East Peckham.

Mitchell offensive operations were resumed, by 180 Squadron, on 11 May with Boulogne marshalling yards as the target. Seven more Mitchell raids were mounted this month. On 25th 180 Squadron was detailed to bomb Abbeville airfield. Heavy flak in the target area scored a direct hit on Hanafy's aircraft, FL175, leading on the run-in. Pieces fell away and damaged Plt. Off. Martin's aircraft forcing him to dive for safety. Sgt. L. F. Paterson's Mitchell, FL211, was shot down.

The principal Mitchell raid was on Flushing when 98 and 180 each sent six aircraft. Flak was again heavy and forced Sgt. A. L. H. Dobbie to ditch FL198 off Clacton. An obvious advantage of the Mitchell was its ability to carry 1,000-lb. bombs, but it lacked the manoeuvrability of the Boston.

News had by now spread through the Group that a major change was afoot. It was to leave Bomber Command. The fervour was greater when it was known that there was to be a new Commander, none other than Air Vice-Marshal Basil Embry, dynamic leader of 107 Squadron early in the war. He arrived at Group at the end of May, his Command taking effect on 1 June when the Group passed under Fighter Command in a holding operation whilst the 2nd Tactical Air Force was established. Thus it was that 31 May witnessed the end of an era: 2 Group, ever the Cinderella of Bomber Command, was coming under entirely new revitalising management.

On the last day of May, all three Ventura squadrons operated, 487 to Cherbourg docks, 464 escorted by twelve fighter squadrons against Zeebrugge and 21 Squadron despatching twelve aircraft to Caen covered by the Exeter Wing and led by Wg. Cdr. King. Five Fw 190s tried for the bombers but 312 and 313 Czech squadrons drove them off.

At 18.30 hours the Venturas were home. Operations by 2 Group, Royal Air Force Bomber Command, had ceased. It would soon all be so very different.

What had been achieved? The Blenheim crews against superior odds and at terrible cost had done their best to impede the enemy in Norway and France, had interfered with his daily preparations during the Battle of Britain, intruded by day and night, carried out a fearful assault on shipping and almost cut Rommel's lifeline to the desert war. By 1941 2 Group's offensive was also waged mainly against fringe targets tempting the Luftwaffe to battle and acting as bait to its fighters—until the Mosquitoes wrote a page of Royal Air Force history quite unparalleled.

Now, with the war swinging in the Allies' favour and the American daylight offensive over Europe well into its stride, 2 Group was to prepare itself for the greatest event of the war, the return of the armies to France. Gone, almost, were the days of disaster. The offensive was to be truly productive of victory, only victory.

Chapter 19
Offensive Crescendo

Throughout the early years of the war home-based elements of the Royal Air Force remained structured to combat attacks upon Britain. By 1943 they had become mainly an offensive force, acting in concert with the U.S.A.A.F., attacking on a wide front. Ultimately overriding all else in 1943 was the planning of the invasion of France. To meet this challenge home-based Commands underwent a complete shake-up. Fighter Command was split into a 'homeguard' element, Air Defence of Great Britain, and a fighter offensive force, the 2nd Tactical Air Force, whose task was first to prepare the way into France for the Army and then to give it very close support.

From its inception 2 Group was basically an army support organisation, yet it had rarely operated along these lines although limited training for such a role spasmodically took place. To the Commander-in-Chief, Bomber Command, 2 Group seemed a misfit. The policy prescribing its operations was far different from that covering the rest of the Command. Thus, when it was decided that Fighter Command should split, 2 Group was logically placed in the Tactical Air Force. But by now Bomber Command had come to appreciate fully the potentialities of the Mosquito bomber so that, when 2 Group changed Commands, it did so without 105 and 139 Mosquito Squadrons. They did not like the idea at all, particularly when they learned that they would be making nuisance night raids and lose their very special niche in the bombing campaign carved by loss and hard labour. Shorn of its most spectacular performers 2 Group was transferred to Fighter Command (yet to split) on 1 June 1943. But in place of the Mosquitoes it had, on 27 May, retrieved something important. It was now commanded by Air Vice-Marshal Basil Embry.

His name is revered to this day by those who served under him in 2 Group, and many consider him the greatest Air Force figure of all time. Many will say 'To me Basil Embry was, and still is, 2 Group and all that it meant to me.' His immense courage, resourcefulness, persistence and brilliance made him a magnificent leader although these qualities did not always endear him to those outside his command. His own story in *Mission Completed* makes splendid reading, and one cannot but be deeply sorrowful that his magnificent qualities were not fully appreciated in the turbulent post-war world.

Air Vice-Marshal Embry's main task from the outset was to prepare the Group for Operation *Overlord*, the invasion of France, the greatest seaborne landing ever mounted. He conducted his share of the planning in Bylaugh Hall, a large country mansion seven miles from East Dereham, Norfolk, very much in 2 Group territory. His drive and efficiency were remembered of old and everyone in the Group was soon aware of a dynamic personality. He was quick to detect faults in the structure of the Group he inherited and was determined to delete them. To be fair to his predecessor the troubles pervading were not of his making. He had lost the Bostons when they were doing well, he was unable to get more Mosquitoes (which was the fault of the Air Ministry's lack of foresight) and his Group was operating, still, as bait for enemy fighters. He had been saddled with the Ventura, hardly the sort of aeroplane to wage an effective bombing campaign with. 'We were achieving very little and at some cost,' recalls one Group member. 'We felt that we were a nuisance more to Bomber Command than to the enemy, and until we were better equipped we could do little about it. When we even lost the Mosquitoes our morale sank lower—but we had Basil Embry. Things couldn't, nay wouldn't, stay like this for long. We had one of the greatest war-winning weapons—in person!'

When 2 Group was transferred it had an operational strength of only six squadrons, Nos. 21, 464 and 487 flying Venturas, 107 Squadron using Boston IIIAs and the two Mitchell squadrons barely operational. No. 88 Squadron was working up on Boston IIIAs, flying gas spray exercises on detachments in various parts of Britain and making occasional air-sea rescue sorties. It became operational on the Mk. IIIA on 28 June.

Also working up on Boston IIIAs was 226 Squadron. Then came an unexpected change of plan. Boston supplies were limited. It was therefore decided to re-arm the squadron with Mitchell IIs, the first of which, FL164 and FL203, joined it on 31 May. A new training programme had to be undertaken, and it was July before 226 was again operational.

Meanwhile a new squadron had entered the Group, No. 342 (Lorraine) Squadron manned by the Free French. Its origin lay in two French squadrons in the Middle East. In September 1942 their personnel were ordered to Britain. They arrived by January 1943—except for those in two ships which were sunk. Refresher courses for the airmen were held, then a new French squadron was formed at West Raynham on 7 April under Wg. Cdr. A. C. P. Carver with Wg. Cdr. Henri de Rancourt as French Commandant. It comprised two flights of Boston IIIAs, 'A' Flight known as Metz Flight and 'B' as Nancy, under Capts. Charbonneaux and Ezzano. Every man wore on his left shoulder the Fourragère de Croix de Guerre to mark the Squadron's fighting record. For training 342 Squadron was equipped with a mixture of Bostons, Havoc 1s and IIs, so hard to come by were the Boston IIIAs.

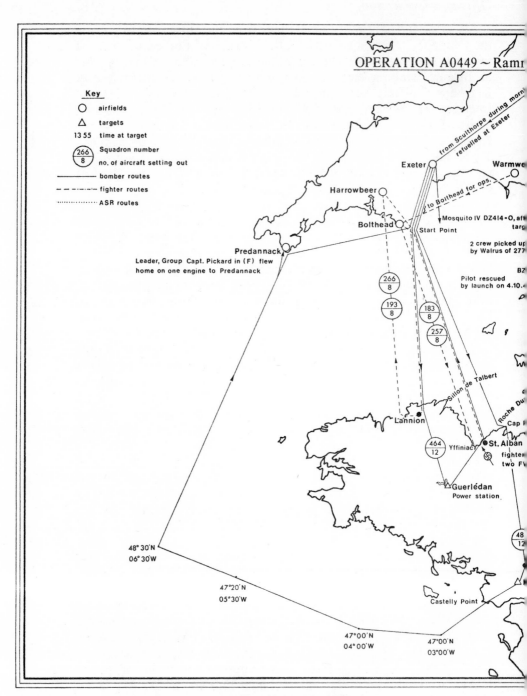

Key

○ airfields
△ targets
13 55 time at target
(266)
(8) Squadron number / no. of aircraft setting out
——— bomber routes
—·—·— fighter routes
·········· ASR routes

OPERATION A0449 ~ Ram

from Sculthorpe during morni
refuelled at Exeter

Exeter   Warmwe

Harrowbeer

to Bolthead for ops.

Bolthead   Mosquito IV DZ414-O, af
Start Point   targ

Predannack   2 crew picked up
Leader, Group Capt. Pickard in (F) flew   by Walrus of 277
home on one engine to Predannack

(266)
(8)   BZ
Pilot rescued
(193)   (183)   by launch on 4.10.
(8)   (8)
(257)
(8)

Sillon de Talbert
Roche Du
Cap
Lannion   St. Alban
(464)   Yffiniac   fighter
(12)   two F

Guerlédan
Power station

48° 30'N
06° 30'W   (48
(12

47°20'N
05°30'W   Castelly Point

47°00'N   47°00'N
04°00'W   03°00'W

MAP 15. *See Appendix 12, pages 506/7 for notes*

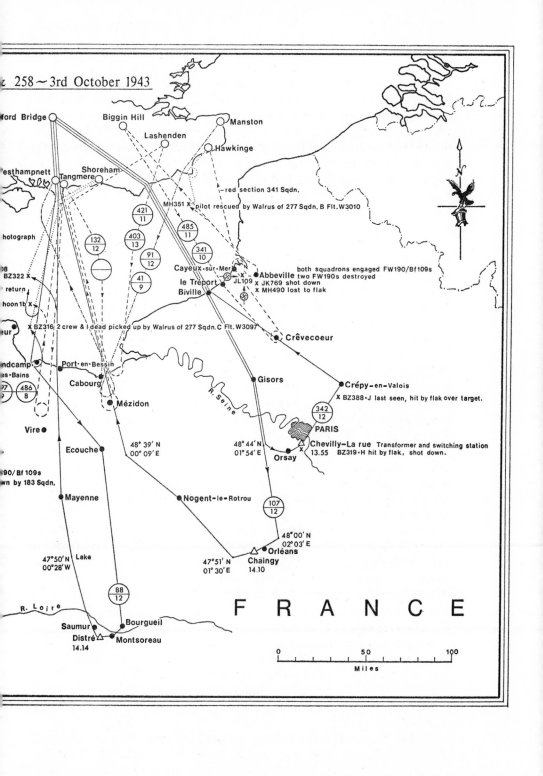

ford Bridge

Biggin Hill

Lashenden

Manston

Hawkinge

red section 341 Sqdn.

esthampnett
Tangmere
Shoreham

MH351 X pilot rescued by Walrus of 277 Sqdn. B Flt. W3010

hotograph

(421/11)

(485/11)

(132/12)

(403/13)

(341/10)

(91/12)

08
BZ322 X

(41/9)

Cayeux·sur·Mer
JL109

X
X JK769 shot down

both squadrons engaged FW190/Bf109s
Abbeville two FW190s destroyed

return

le Tréport

X MH490 lost to flak

hoon 1b X

Biville

X BZ316 2 crew & I dead picked up by Walrus of 277 Sqdn. C. Flt. W3097

Crêvecoeur

eur

ndcamp
es·Bains

Port·en·Bessin

Gisors

Crépy–en–Valois

X BZ388·J last seen, hit by flak over target.

97 (486/8)

Cabourg

R. Seine

(342/12)

Mézidon

PARIS

Vire

48° 39′ N
00° 09′ E

48° 44′ N
01° 54′ E

Chevilly-La rue Transformer and switching station
13.55 BZ319·H hit by flak, shot down.

Ecouche

Orsay

90/ Bf 109s
wn by 183 Sqdn.

Mayenne

Nogent-le-Rotrou

(107/12)

48° 00′ N
02° 03′ E

47° 50′ N
00° 28′ W

Lake

47° 51′ N
01° 30′ E

Orléans
Chaingy
14.10

(88/12)

R. Loire

Saumur
Distré
14.14

Bourgueil

Montsoreau

F R A N C E

0   50   100

Miles

In May the squadron moved to Sculthorpe to await the call for operations. The Dutch squadron, No. 320, was still in training.

It was therefore quite an international band that A.V.M. Embry inherited as well as a motley collection of operational aircraft. This was most unsatisfactory, and he made it quickly known that there was only one type of aeroplane he wanted—the Mosquito. Just coming along at this time was the Mk. VI fighter-bomber, but the small quantity likely to be available for many months was earmarked for the Middle East and Fighter Command. Embry had to settle—for the moment—for Bostons, Mitchells and Venturas, but he had the promise of Mosquito VIs, when they became available, to replace the Venturas and equip new squadrons joining the Group for the invasion.

The multiplicity of aircraft resulted in a very elaborate training programme providing crews for very specialised and widely differing aircraft types each of which needed a team to operate it—pilots, navigators, observers, gunners, radio operators—whereas the Mosquito needed only a pilot and navigator. Embry knew the Mosquito well from his days at Wittering, and was quick to see that the Boston with quite good qualities was slower—and it only carried a third of the load of the Mitchell, a sturdy aeroplane making for a good bombing platform. Mitchells and Mosquitoes he might settle for—and then the Air Ministry came up with a shocking decision. It proposed the re-equipment of the Group with Vultee Vengeance dive-bombers. Embry tried out the Vengeance and declared it slow, sluggish and under-manned—a glorified Fairey Battle quite unsuited to the campaign he envisaged waging, and utterly unsuitable for the war in Europe. He went to Leigh Mallory, who invited him to attend a meeting when Group re-equipment would be discussed. From personal experience he explained the failings of the Vengeance—and he came away with the firm promise that 2 Group would get Mosquito VIs.

There were other problems that concerned the new commander. It was obvious that for months past the Group had not been operating very profitably. It had carried out orders to act as bait to entice enemy fighters, in consequence of which the targets chosen seemed apparently of secondary importance. This was hardly likely to boost morale. There were many in the Group, too, for whom those months of shipping attacks were an indelible memory, so the past had not been good.

Repeated programmes of re-equipment and vacillation in operational planning had taken a toll of efficiency. Nevertheless Embry realised only too well that the formation he headed contained many people of very high calibre, to whom he was adding others who had proven themselves most able in his previous associations, although this move was not universally popular.

Embry suspected that bombing accuracy left something to be desired, and when he was told that it was 'excellent' he harboured doubts. A thorough check on bombing photographs revealed an average error

51. Mitchell FV914 of 98 Squadron, she served from 9.10.43 to 9.5.44 and first operated on 25.11.43. Photographed during a *Noball*

52. From left to right: W.O. Baker, Wg. Cdr. England, Sgt. Kendall and Sgt. Lennett at West Raynham in 1942. Behind is England's usual mount, 'England Expects'

63. The crew of a Mitchell 'P-Peter' (previously 'T-Tommy') stand before their aircraft which has completed 100 sorties

64. Distré power station under attack on 3.10.43
65. The model used for briefing for the Amiens Prison raid in February 1944

66. A dusk raid on the Aulnoye railway installation by Mosquitoes

67. Flt. Lt. Sugden lays to rest the head of a duck at Feltwell. It had collided with a Ventura during the Philips raid

of over 1,000 yards which was bad, and unacceptable if the Group was to pave the way for and then spearhead *Overlord*. He therefore toured the squadrons, met the crews, studied the records, flew the aircraft until he felt in a position to implement plans in keeping with the new task handed to him.

The change in command could have no immediate effect upon target selection, and Group operated on nine days in June, with Venturas, Bostons and Mitchells operating independently. Nine raids were attempted by the Ventura squadrons, the first by 21 Squadron being on coke ovens at Zeebrugge. Next day 487 Squadron raided Caen, and Gordon Brewer's aircraft (AE797: P) was seen on fire as he dived away. 'Q' Queenie landed at Tangmere with a badly wounded navigator who died in hospital. Opposition was such that 487 Squadron was again put out of action for a few days.

At 06.00 on 13th 464 Squadron was briefed to attack St. Brieuc viaduct. They took off at 07.35 led by Wg. Cdr. Meakin in AJ466 for rendezvous with five fighter squadrons. Approaching Guernsey the rear box of 464 Squadron was attacked from above and behind by four '190s and Flt. Sgt. Kane-Maguire flying AE937 was shot down. Spitfires of the Exeter Wing jettisoned their long-range tanks but were too slow to catch the enemy. No. 129 Squadron, however, quickly climbed, succeeded in attracting the '190s, and drove them off. Rapidly the weather deteriorated so the beehive turned for home. Moments later a Fw 190 nipped in and shot up another Ventura. A third crash-landed with a burst tyre.

Heavy guns near Abbeville/Drucat were billed for attack by 21 Squadron on 22nd, twelve aircraft being despatched led by Wg. Cdr. R. H. S. King who had Grp. Capt. W. V. Spendlove, Station Commander at Swanton Morley, as his passenger. It was now policy for Station Commanders to fly on operations to see for themselves what was going on. Heavy flak was encountered at the target and King's aircraft received a direct hit and fluttered to earth.

Before the month ended Venturas attacked Yainville power station, airframe and assembly shops at Flushing and the Maupertuis airfield. On 30 June Flg. Off. W. D. Parsons was awarded the D.F.C., and his gunner Flt. Sgt. B. McConnell the D.F.M., for their part in the action on 13th. Their machine AE908 was badly shot up and lost five feet off its mainplane. Although the turret had been put out of action and McConnell blown out of it, he climbed back in to give his pilot evasion instructions.

The first Mitchell operation of June was an abortive attempt to bomb a power station near Ghent. In the heavy flak Flt. Sgt. Grindley's aircraft was hit and fell away, its port engine burning. Flg. Off. Fee's aircraft was forced to land at Manston. No. 180 Squadron lost another during a raid on Flushing on 13 June when they combined with 98 Squadron. During the bombing 416 Spitfire Squadron engaged about

L

thirty Bf 109s. Apart from the Mitchell which blew up in the target area two others were severely damaged, and Sqn. Ldr. McNair of 416 Squadron escorted one back through a swarm of darting enemy fighters which were evaded. Both squadrons bombed Wilton's shipyards at Rotterdam and Guipavas airfield before the month was out, teaming up for operations as they were to do very many times in months ahead.

The first combined raid by Nos. 107 and 342 Squadrons came on 12 June when Rouen was successfully bombed. Eight crews of 342 Squadron were in the second vic of the front box, Wg. Cdr. de Rancourt in BZ208: A, Sqn. Ldr. Ezzano flying BZ270: N and Plt. Off. Pineau BZ322: C. Next day an airfield near Lille was bombed by 107 Squadron the flak being so heavy that every machine was holed. On the evening of 23rd two boxes of six Bostons led by Wg. Cdr. England and Sqn. Ldr. Spencer with three crews of 342 Squadron made a diversionary raid, for a large B-17 operation, on an aircraft factory at Meaulte close to Albert, in Belgium. Near Abbeville six fighters tried to attack the Bostons but Spitfires stopped them, 118 and 416 Squadrons engaging in combat whilst 402 Squadron kept close to the bombers. The fighters then tried head-on attacks, from Doullens to the coast, but the escort intercepted these shooting down a '190 near Rue.

On eighteen days in July 2 Group operated, 107 Squadron opening the month's activity with pairs of low-flying Bostons attacking rail targets in France. Wg. Cdr. England and Flg. Off. Attenborough went to the Lille area, Flt. Lt. Evans and Flg. Off. McCormack to Courtrai, Turner and Shaw to Ghent, and they used their guns to shoot up locomotives, their sheds and stations, and gasometers. In the words of 107's diary, it was 'a brilliantly planned day's work proving what a fine machine the Boston is for low-level operations'.

Next day 107 Squadron, joined by two of 342's crews, made similar attacks although low cloud present yesterday was missing today. Nevertheless Wg. Cdr. England and Sgt. Lang pressed on to Pont à Vendin power station. After a climb to the French coast they dived to deck level, and despite light flak England placed a bomb neatly on the target, and three more after a vigorous turn. After Lang made his pass he was engaged by a Fw 190 which he evaded by corkscrewing into cloud. The pair from 342 Squadron, briefed for Langerbrugge in Belgium, found little cloud. One turned back but of Plt. Off. Pineau no more was heard.

On 11th 107 Squadron had another twelve aircraft on low-level operations, to power stations at Mazingarbe, Choques and Bouvray. But such raids could be mounted only in ideal conditions and when 88 Squadron set off on 12th only two crews risked carrying on and Flt. Sgt. R. L. Davies never returned. The other crew bombed a factory near Tournai and brought their aircraft home badly peppered.

Bostons also continued their *Circus* operations, making forays to Abbeville, Poix, Amsterdam, Yainville and Schiphol. The latter raid was flown on 25th six crews each from 107 and 342 Squadrons operating in a clear sky. Bombing was very accurate, hits being scored on dispersals, runways and billets. Next day the target was Courtrai/Wevelghem airfield, and things went badly wrong. The bombing was poor then the formation turned to port and started heading south-east. At 11.17 with Courtrai 140° six miles east, 'Butch' Evans in Pelly-Fry's aircraft reported fighters and a Fw 190 suddenly appeared alongside Sqn. Ldr. Reeve's Boston. Closing to about fifty yards it shot across No. 2 in the formation, did a flick roll and dived away pursued by a Spitfire. From then onwards things became chaotic for the formation continued to head south-east. Attempts were made to draw the leader's attention to this but they could not contact him since his R/T was on transmit for the gunnery leader to have control. The formation and escort continued to be attacked and corkscrew evasive action was taken with occasional moments of steady flight to enable gunners to take aim. In the St. Amand area Flg. Off. Wilson (No. 2 in the first box) broke formation and as he descended jettisoned his top hatch so that he and his crew (Plt. Off. MacDonald navigator, Flt. Lt. Partridge gunner and Sgt. Hunt of the R.A.F. Film Unit) could bale out. Eventually the fighter escort became so alarmed that they tried hard and succeeded in turning the formation. Had they not done so all the Bostons would have run out of fuel!

It was quite an eventful operation for the fighters. Nos. 66 and 504 Squadrons were providing escort cover and just after bombing they saw fifteen to twenty '109s and '190s dive past them after the Bostons. 504 broke and raced into action, Flt. Sgt. Wright getting a '190. But the engagement cost them their 'B' Flight Commander, Flt. Lt. McCarthy-Jones, in BM145. The Polish squadrons giving withdrawal cover were called into the battle and over Lille 316 Squadron tried to attack about ten enemy aircraft. They found they were quickly overshooting, and that they could not identify them. Quite suddenly the enemy—which they thought to be Koolhoven FK 58s—flicked over and away. Their camouflage foxed the squadron; it was curious, 'like that of Italian aircraft operated under German control'. Noses and tails were yellow.

No. 317 Squadron had met the Bostons over Clacton with 302 Squadron, and then climbed to 11,000 feet. An English squadron joined them mid Channel. They kept with the bombers and between Tournai and Lille were attacked by '190s. Four latched on to Wg. Cdr. Zak, then a free-for-all developed during which Zak sustained hits in his tailplane and radio. Flt. Lt. Wroblewski managed a long burst at a '190 attacking the Bostons and saw it explode. When they reformed Flg. Off. Felk and Flt. Sgt. Bartys were missing.

Mitchells made eight raids in July. Targets ranged through Amiens/Longeau marshalling yards, St. Omer rail installations, the Fokker works at Amsterdam, and airfields at Brest/Guipavas, Merville, Tricqueville and Fort Rouge. *Ramrod 124* of 4 July proved the most eventful. Fighters from Ibsley, Kenley and 83 Group picked up the bombers over Rye and after bombing the beehive turned to port. Ten miles east of Abbeville four Fw 190s were seen so Red Section of 222 Squadron providing high cover swooped to engage. Then a mixed gaggle of '109s and '190s—about thirty—appeared, and was soon firing at the bombers from all directions. More of 222 Squadron dived to take on the enemy and Wg. Cdr. Ratton fired a successful nine-second burst into a '190. Flt. Lt. Tripe singled out another and sent it spinning down and yet another was damaged before the fighters re-assembled and the beehive came home.

Current plans called for an additional three Mitchell squadrons in the Group. No. 320 was still working-up at Attlebridge and 226 busily training, having relinquished its last Boston on 1 July. If there were to be so many Mitchells it seemed desirable to find the best method of operating them in the face of fighter attack. Therefore, 226 Squadron was sent to Drem to work out tactics with the aid of the French 340 Spitfire squadron.

It was reckoned that under escort the top speed of the Mitchell would be about 210 m.p.h. Corkscrewing proved of no use with this heavier aeroplane, the fighters finding they could easily follow it. Turning into the attack was satisfactory since all the Mitchell's guns could be brought to bear. Any undulation by boxes required the second vic to be stepped down to provide sufficient room. It was decided that the first gunner to spot an enemy aircraft should tell the leader its position, then the first gunner could give the order to undulate as a slight turn was made to meet the attack. The gunner would then tell the pilot what action to take, bearing in mind that the best defensive fire would come from a steady aircraft. Several mock attacks were tried from below. In order to nullify their effectiveness it was decided to keep a gunner in the uncomfortable tail cupola of the leading aircraft.

Meanwhile No. 98 Squadron was engaged on a very different venture and came off operations on 15 July. Intelligence sources indicated the strong possibility of a German attack on Portugal. If this happened it was proposed to send to the aid of our Ally a task force comprising Spitfires, Beaufighters and 98 Squadron. It formed at Honiley where, for the next two weeks, fuel consumption tests were carried out. Then it appeared the venture was unlikely to be needed and the task force disbanded leaving 98 Squadron to return to Foulsham at the end of the month.

Between them the three Ventura squadrons flew only three operations in July. Embry considered the Ventura 'thoroughly bad, being slow, heavy, unmanoeuvrable and lacking in good defensive armament'. He probably wanted to rid himself of this encumbrance at the earliest opportunity. Four times 487 Squadron was alerted for operations which were called off. Then, apart from a sea search on 15 July, it ceased operations. One of the other squadrons, No. 21, was earmarked for Mitchells with whom it had a brief flirtation in June until these were passed to 464 Squadron to also become acquainted with them. It was at this time that the firm decision for the Group to get Mosquitoes was given and so it was decided to keep two Ventura squadrons operational until Mosquitoes arrived in the late summer. Before July ended 21 Squadron (under Wg. Cdr. North) had made a very successful raid on the benzole plant at Zeebrugge, and bombed Yainville power station.

On 10 July 464 Squadron was briefed early, fourteen Venturas led by Wg. Cdr. Jack Meakin getting away at 07.16. They met seven Spitfire squadrons over Sandwich. In good weather hits were scored on aircraft assembly sheds at St. Omer. Enemy fighters were encountered and flak damaged a Ventura.

Two days later Air Vice-Marshal Embry visited Methwold and to Grp. Capt. Young broke the news that 464 and 487 Squadrons were to receive Mosquitoes, and that the move to Dunsfold planned for that day was off. Mosquitoes, he said, would operate as night intruders, and each pilot was to fly an intensive course of conversion. Re-equipment of the squadrons would be complete in six weeks.

Everyone received the news with utter glee—except the W. Op./A.G.s who realised they would be redundant. Methwold was unsuitable for night Mosquito operations, and at first there was talk of using Feltwell again, but 3 Group wanted it. Embry considered that invasion support would be far better if the squadrons were placed in southern England, but bases there had yet to become available to him. Things moved fast and 342 Squadron was pushed into Massingham, which left Sculthorpe in Norfolk free for the Mosquitoes. The clouds hung low over Methwold on 21 July, but this did not daunt 464 from leaving. Within a month both squadrons had received Mosquito VIs, and work-up was intense.

Meanwhile 21 Squadron soldiered on with 'pigs' so as not to reduce operational pressure too much. A successful raid was flown on 16 August, Tricqueville being the target. In perfect, cloudless conditions, two boxes led by Sqn. Ldr. Dennis met their escort over Selsey Bill, two squadrons of Spitfire Vs close, the two Mk. XII squadrons as escort cover and two Mk. IX squadrons as top cover. There was some flak but fighters did not challenge them. Bombing was good, fires being visible when fifty miles away. Two days later 21 Squadron moved south, to Hartford Bridge (now known as Blackbushe) along with 88 and 107 Squadrons moving for special operations.

As soon as three Boston squadrons were available Group considered that they should be employed now in concert, and in a low-level role wherein their strength and effectiveness best lay. Once again St. Neots power station was chosen as focal point for one of 1943's outstanding raids. Maximum effort was ordered, amounting, it was hoped, to some forty aircraft.

At the briefing the target was revealed as the naval stores at Rennes already bombed by 2 Group Mosquitoes. The Bostons would spectacularly rendezvous low over the roof of Group H.Q. at Bylaugh Hall from where the impressive force would set course for Start Point, cross to Puren then run into target. The Bostons would be unescorted, but 10 Group would provide a fighter diversion, and 11 Group would fly two others.

In mid afternoon on 8 August the Bostons set forth, fourteen from 107 Squadron and twelve each from Nos. 88 and 342 Squadrons with Wg. Cdr. England leading the show. They took off in pairs each carrying 500-pounders and flew in sixes roughly line abreast, with 107 leading followed by 342 then 88. At 250 feet they raced across England and out to sea so low that their slipstream stirred the water. At the enemy coast they met no reception. Visibility was good but Flg. Off. Baker navigating the lead aircraft found it difficult to pinpoint any objects on the planned run-in started fifteen miles from the target. There were no major roads, rivers or railways, just open countryside—far from ideal for the enterprise. But by eventually identifying a minor railway, and twisting and turning to hold it, they found the target which showed up on the skyline four or five miles away. They were bang on course. As they swept across the stores at deck level to drop their 11 sec. delay bombs the leading six of 107 Squadron blazed away with their guns. Behind them, some four miles out, the remainder climbed to 1,500 feet to avoid any bombs skidding and take good aim after the flak silencers had done their best. Then they were to dive low to follow the leaders out via Mont St. Michel.

Despite considerable flak the naval stores were well and truly plastered, bombs on the main section causing a dull red fire and smoke rising to 1,000 feet. There was no sign of fighters but later they learnt the enemy had been up in strength but about forty miles behind.

In the lead machine was the famous cameraman Skeets Kelly who recently shot the flying sequences for the Battle of Britain film and who was tragically killed soon after. As the flak burst around him he continued obliviously to film the operation. Then to Dicky England's astonishment Kelly fell asleep . . . he had, he later told the crew, run out of film and what else was there to do?

Shortly after leaving the target Plt. Off. Angus of 88 Squadron was seen to break away, his starboard engine burning. Flak ripped the port wing off W. Off. Roberts's machine. Flg. Off. Roberts of 107 Squadron had his arm seriously injured when a 40 mm. shell burst in the nose of Sqn. Ldr. Spencer's aircraft which had to force-land at Hurn with its A.S.I. useless and half the port elevator shot away. Flg. Off. Allison had flown so low near the target that he left behind his pitot tube hanging, he felt sure, on a high-tension cable. But the intrepid Dicky England went in so low that he came home with five yards of cable trapped in his bomb doors. Later he was heard to mutter something about 'always wanting a tow rope for my car . . .'.

The operation had been extremely successful, the right aeroplane had been employed in its best role. It was decided to repeat the style, with the armament and steel works at Denain, France, as target, one not previously attacked. Again Wg. Cdr. England would lead, thirteen crews of 107 Squadron heading the force with twelve each from 342 and 88.

Take-off was in the late afternoon of 16 August. Flying in loose units six abreast they made their way low level to Pevensey Bay in gorgeous sunshine and headed for France where squadrons of Typhoons joined them and then escorted them fifty miles inland. A good landfall had been made at Pont Haut-Blanc and no opposition met. A few moments later Sqn. Ldr. Evans of 107 Squadron had to turn about with engine trouble and Flg. Off. Rankin took over the lead box. A little while later the force roared over an airfield guns blazing. Flt. Sgt. Lawrence was so low that his wing tip grazed the grass, but he pressed on.

From Doullens the formation headed to Posiers then turned north-east for the bomb run. Still the weather was ideal, the visibility so far excellent—and flak en route was only slight. Among the slag heaps England picked out the target and led his six aircraft in at deck level guns blazing away, whilst the remainder clambered to 2,000 feet, then dived to bomb from 1,500 feet after the first six had pulled away. There was little flak but one of the low-levellers was seen to be on fire and soon crashed. Bombs were on the target which erupted with a red explosion, and some overshoots were seen on the railway. A few minutes later Flt. Lt. Patterson nipped in for a photo pass having recorded the attack from the veteran Mosquito DZ414.

Elated, they rebunched and headed for home. But soon trouble struck. Countless small flies were smudged over the windscreens and, far worse, the whole formation was now flying into the sun at very low level. Near Douai there were many H.T. cables and an aircraft collided with one, reared steeply then spun in. Around Arras the flak was intense. Typhoons arrived to meet the Bostons just as enemy fighters opened an attack on 88 and 342 Squadrons. By now the bombers were in very loose formation, ideal for interception. The outcome of these few moments was the loss of four aircraft of 88 Squadron, all piloted by experienced people. One was Sqn. Ldr. R. S. Gunning, a Flight Commander of high standing and affection who was taken prisoner. Another was Sqn. Ldr. 'Ace' Hawkins who had flown many missions. There was also Flg. Off. A. B. Smith and Flt. Lt. A. H. 'Rufus' Riseley. It was a grievous blow to the squadron involving popular members of long standing. Months later the survivors all had memorable stories to relate, but none was more astonishing than that of Flt. Lt. Riseley.

His Boston came down in a field and he quickly vacated it to get help for his wounded crew, after disguising himself by wearing his uniform inside out. After seeing to his crew's needs he set off to try and reach England. On the hazardous way he heard that in one village the local Gestapo chief had turned traitor. He met this man whose name, he learned, was Weiler. The traitor, backed by his authority, was able to show Riseley the enemy defences in the Arras area and Riseley recorded what he saw. But how could he pass this useful learning to his friends? Through the French Resistance he was able to send his hoard by carrier pigeon to Britain. Then he heard about secret preparations in a heavily guarded wood near St. Pol. He determined to discover what was afoot so, disguised as a French workman, he joined a lorry crew and was able to enter the site. It was one being prepared for the launching of flying bombs, although he did not discover this at the time. He decided he must learn more about the goings-on, and made a second fearful journey into the secret area. Afterwards he drew what he had seen and decided he must now escape to Britain with his precious findings. He put the papers inside a stale loaf and was put aboard a fishing boat, which safely brought him to England. His papers he at once passed to Intelligence, a very useful item at a vital time. In a matter of weeks 2 Group was bombing such installations, and Riseley was decorated by the King for his exploits.

During the remainder of August the Boston squadrons prepared for Operation *Starkey*. Nos. 88 and 107 Squadrons moved to Hartford Bridge coming under 11 Group. They attempted two *Circuses* on Beaumont-le-Roger and on the afternoon of 27th 107 Squadron despatched six aircraft for a low-level attack on Gosnay power station. Two attacked before the third was hit by flak and collided with another and both of them crashed. On the way in and out Fw 190s had attacked them destroying another Boston.

Mitchells of 98 and 180 Squadrons made nine combined raids in August, targets including marshalling yards at St. Omer, Bernais St. Martin, Monchy Breton and the Forêt d'Eperlecque. Both squadrons moved to Dunsfold on 18 August.

No. 226 Squadron became operational on Mitchells at the end of July. Flg. Off. R. M. Christie with three Bostons of 88 Squadron on an A.S.R. search flew to a dinghy emitting signals and circled it. Suddenly eight enemy aircraft arrived, some of them Me 210s. Christie headed for home as fast as he could but the enemy caught up with him. Their first attack was thwarted. Sgt. Norburn managed some good shooting but the enemy closed and soon both engines were burning and Norburn was dead. FV932: X ditched at over 200 m.p.h., bounced and broke up. Christie could not get out but Eynton-Jones surfaced after some minutes via the astro dome. Two other crew members, trapped, initially by radio gear on their feet, managed to get free and clambered aboard a dinghy. They circled the wreck finding a first-aid kit and releasing three 'K' Type dinghies to make their plight more conspicuous. With a few emergency tablets and no water they waited hopefully. Two Hudson crews had seen X-ray ditch before fighters drove them away. During the day other aircraft circled them and next day an airborne lifeboat was dropped. They clambered aboard, changed into dry clothes and soon had the engine started. It petered out after three hours. Then they used the sail and steered a course flashed to them by an A.S.R. Hudson. Each day aircraft appeared and on 3 August Beaufighters came guiding Royal Navy launches which picked them up and at once dispensed sweet tea which, they said, 'was the best they had ever tasted'. Their subsequent sleep was disturbed by three enemy aircraft which to everyone's relief never attacked. They reached Grimsby on 4 August after six memorable days.

On 17 August armourers of 226 Squadron went to their bomb dump to dust the cobwebs from the bombs so long untouched. They put them into six aircraft which set off for Dunkirk. Luck was out for the leader's aircraft would not climb. On 18th they tried for Flushing but bad weather halted the operation. It was September before they operated again.

The Dutch squadron, No. 320, had also been busy training. On 17 August they flew their first real operation following sea searches. With van Waartp leading in FR141: B they took off at 10.58, met their escort over Ashford, and facing inaccurate flak bombed Calais marshalling yards. An uneventful *Ramrod* took them to Poix next day. Now they were operating from Foulsham. On 20th they attacked the Dornier works at Flushing; near there heavy flak hit FR147: C and, with smoke pouring from her starboard engine, she was soon lost from sight. Capt. Nienhuish warned his crew that he would be ditching, after which they all climbed into a dinghy and drifted until 17.10. Two Mustangs came upon the scene soon replaced by Spitfires. Shortly after they saw to their great joy a Walrus which alighted, picked them up and took them to Coltishall. The raid had been very successful, the aircraft assembly shed at Scheld receiving heavy damage which halted all work— in direct contrast to the U.S.A.A.F. attack of the previous day when a vast tonnage had left the factory unscathed. The Dutch squadron flew no more sorties in August and moved to Lasham for *Starkey*.

There was only one Ventura squadron, No. 21, operational in August. It managed one raid against Tricqueville before it too moved south. Before August was out 21 Squadron had flown two more raids, on Forêt d'Eperlecque and the Forêt de Hesdin—preliminaries to a great deception.

Operation *Starkey* had a twofold purpose. It was a vast combined operation designed to bring the Luftwaffe to large-scale battle and force it to bring forces back from Italy. This was done by a simulated invasion scheme made convincing, first, by a heavy onslaught on airfields and military targets, and then by assembling large troop concentrations, transports and assault craft.

The prelude to the feint opened early in September and reached its climax on 9th, the final day. In the work-up period Mitchells raided ammunition dumps in the Forêt de Hesdin, Forêt d'Eperlecque, rail targets at St. Omer and Abbeville, docks and shipping at Boulogne, Vitry airfield and the Fort de la Creche near Boulogne. No. 21 Squadron participated against similar targets.

Bostons were employed in a different manner. Their task was smoke laying over our shipping in the Channel. On 1 September 88 Squadron began smoke laying and next day were joined by 107 Squadron smoke laying over minesweepers eight miles off Boulogne, making six paired sorties for an hour. On 6, 7, 8 September they resumed their role, and also bombed Woensdrecht, rail yards at Amiens and, on the afternoon of 4th, preceded by 21 Squadron, E-boats in Boulogne.

On 8 September Venturas during *Circus S.1* bombed Abbeville marshalling yards. About a dozen Fw 190s were seen below and 222 Squadron dived to bounce them but they had been warned and fled. Nos. 402, 416 and 118 Squadrons were escorting eighteen Mitchells to Vitry on *Ramrod S.41* and seven Bf 109s were seen after the bombing. 421 Squadron maintained top cover and spotted fifteen '190s about to bounce them. In the fight 402 claimed a '109 and 403 another. But generally the operations were disappointing. Outnumbered, the Luftwaffe kept on the ground.

Starkey reached its climax on 9th. Assault and landing craft sailed from ports between Dungeness and Dover, escorted by naval craft, and sailed towards Boulogne. The day's air operations were opened by six Mitchells of 98 Squadron airborne at 06.41 to attack Boulogne followed by six more soon after. Before they were home the Bostons were operating. The task for 88 Squadron was to cover the H.Q. ship in smoke for heavy guns had been firing that week from France. A huge fighter screen was flown, and it was hoped the enemy would play his hand on the ground. The first call on 88 Squadron came early with take-off set for 08.00. Six pairs were to get airborne at five-minute intervals to trail smoke from SCI, but before the last pair got away threatening heavy mist had covered their airfield cutting visibility so that the final pair could not take-off. Over the sea visibility was better and smoke was laid as planned. 107 Squadron stood by but was not called. Instead the crews joined 342 Squadron in an afternoon *Circus* on Monchy Breton. Eighteen Mitchells of 98 and 180 Squadrons bombed Bryas Sud when the only enemy fighters seen were two '190s diving away in the Béthune area. After nine Venturas had bombed Merville 129 and 222 Squadrons were bounced by a dozen '190s which they chased off without success. Two '190s tried to formate on 416 Squadron escorting Mitchells attacking Bryas Sud, but by and large the enemy reaction was slight.

Results from *Starkey* were extremely disappointing and 2 Group's share was limited. Spitfires flew 786 sorties and nearly 300 Allied light-bomber sorties had been directed at the Boulogne area. Thirteen airfields were attacked by nearly 340 heavy and 85 light bombers and fighter-bombers supported by 550 more fighters. About 150 enemy aircraft came up to fight but only two were destroyed on 9th, one a high flier shot down by 124 Squadron off the Isle of Wight. Clearly the enemy had not been tricked.

For 21 Squadron *Starkey* marked the close of an era. It carried out two raids on 9 September, against Boulogne's heavy guns and Merville airfield, the latter being the last time when Venturas operated in 2 Group. In October 21 Squadron then at Sculthorpe equipped with Mosquitoes.

Once *Starkey* was over a more usual round of operations was resumed. Mitchells of 98 and 180 operated as a Wing raiding Serquex, Lens, Rouen/Sotteville, Amiens, Brest/Guipavas and Lannion/Poulmiac during largely uneventful operations. On 19th 421 Squadron was giving top cover for a Lens raid when 21 '190s came up from the Lille area and tried to bounce the high fliers. The squadron engaged them and Flt. Lt. R. A. Buckam in MA226 shot down a fighter before he was shot down. Spitfire cover for *Ramrods* was now vast, and it was customary now for these operations to take place in parts, with Spitfires making forward sweeps over a large area thereby providing great depth of cover. On 21st, when Plt. Off. Cooke-Smith was taking his turn in leading 98 Squadron, '190s did break through to the Mitchells. FL674 was hit by cannon fire in the hydraulic system and FV944 damaged over Hesdin force-landed in the sea about ten miles off Berck. Her crew were rescued by a Dover launch. FL683's crew were all killed when their aircraft dived into the ground near Hesdin. Spitfires of 331 Squadron had fought the enemy, Capt. Gran in MA225: S shooting down a fighter while Capt. Heglund claimed a probable. On 24th 98 Squadron running up on Brest met heavy flak, '928 being hit and '701, with her port engine damaged, landing at Predannack. On the run-up 8 Fw 190s seen coming from the east passed below the bombers as nine Bf 110s came in from below astern. Nos. 310 and 313 Squadrons promptly engaged them, Flt. Lt. Chocrin in AR335 getting one before they fled after shooting down a Spitfire of 310 Squadron.

The Dutch Mitchells flew five more raids in September. No. 226 Squadron had a busier time than of late making eight raids. Frequently the pilots of 2 Group still flew wearing tin hats and the value of these was apparent, for instance, on 19th when Flt. Sgt. Suttle was on the Lens raid. So accurate was some flak that a piece penetrated his steel helmet. Flak was a nuisance to the close boxes now being flown, but often it was inaccurate. Evasive action and stepped formations usually defeated its effectiveness.

Throughout September 464 and 487 Squadrons were busy learning how to use the Mosquito. Remembering those days Wg. Cdr. H. J. Meakin recalls: 'Almost overnight we were re-equipped with Mosquitoes and many of the most highly decorated officers joined us: Grp. Capt. Pickard, "Pick", Bob Braham, "Attie" Atkinson, "Laddie" Lucas, Donaldson and a host of others. The tempo changed, as did our role. We became low level precision pin-point daylight bombers and night intruders. Pickard became the Station Commander and determined to fly with us as Wing Leader. Busy on the scene, too, was David Atcherly, one of the R.A.F.'s most colourful characters whom Basil Embry had chosen as his S.A.S.O. Between them these three planned a vigorous pattern for operations. Sculthorpe, almost on the Wash, Pickard took one look at, and declared he wasn't satisfied with the accommodation. He commandeered "The White House", a fine Georgian mansion, and he took the three Squadron Commanders—Willie Wilson, "Daddy" Dale and myself—and moved in. We trained hard both by day and night but when the weather was foul we played hard too.' On 2 October the first two squadrons became ready for action.

An impressive five-pronged operation plan was drawn up for 3 October, opening time for the Mosquito squadrons which were to operate at the same time as the Bostons. Soon after midday 88 Squadron led by Wg. Cdr. I. J. Spencer set off for Distre transformer station, one of a group chosen in an attempt to deprive much of the French rail network of electric power. Luck was out for the leader and his number two who had to abort due to engine trouble. The remainder pressed on under Plt. Off. R. Linguard in BZ212 and made a very successful attack on their target. On the return sea crossing Flt. Sgt. W. D. D. Davies ditched and Sqn. Ldr. G. C. Knowles circled the spot until his fuel ran low. Davies, and Flt. Sgt. G. K. K. Grey who had aborted early, were rescued, Grey by a Walrus.

Part II of the operation was another low-level raid, on a transformer station at Orleans, by 107 Squadron Dicky England leading. From Pevensey Bay they crossed the Channel making landfall at Biville-sur-Mer where, in line abreast, they opened up with their front guns to silence flak. Making use of all possible cover they reached Gisors and altered course for the target. Two high-wing aircraft seen at St. Leger were too far away to be engaged, and at Toury two He 111s made off fast. The six low-level aircraft went in at fifty feet, the remainder bombing Orleans from 1,500 feet. As they were about to bomb the load from the leader blew up and smoke belched forth to 3,000 feet. Flt. Sgt. Hiegg's aircraft, G-George, was hit in the tail by flak, but he kept station. There was some flak back at the coast but they made Bognor Regis safely.

The French Squadron, 342, carried out Part III of the operation, eleven Bostons led by Henri de Rancourt bombing Chevilly transformer station near Paris, four from low level, the rest from between 1,500 and 1,800 feet. Attacks were very successful with much smoke and flame issuing and numerous electrical flashes. Moderate flak greeted the force and BZ319 dived away towards a river. BZ388 left the formation with her port engine stopped, but the rest made base safely. Withdrawal cover for the Bostons had been arranged at the coast, but strong tailwinds brought the bombers out ahead of rendezvous times.

Damage assessment showed very good results from the raids. 'Two reports from reliable sources,' it stated, 'indicate that the attack on the transformer station serving the P.O. Midi main line from Paris to Tours was remarkably successful. Station at Chaingy was completely destroyed, that at Chevilly 90% destroyed. Six transformers were completely destroyed and another put out of action for a long time. Steam traction has had to be introduced between Paris and Tours and steam locomotives transferred from region Sud Est. It shows the effect of simultaneous attacks if these are successful.'

Although the raids were highly effective all eyes at Group were on the Mosquitoes. Early in the day the two Squadrons taking two reserves left for Exeter there to refuel. A cameraman of the R.A.F. Film Unit photographed the scene unknown to some of those taking part. When his results were screened there was much amusing comment for there stood Grp. Capt. Pickard beneath his Mosquito—which was fully armed and refuelled—happily puffing at a cigarette. Then the camera turned on 'Wg. Cdr. Smith' whom everyone knew was really Air Vice-Marshal Embry who had with him his S.A.S.O. David Atcherley valiantly about to take part with his arm in plaster. As the film reeled on it showed that the Group Commander was trying to get the S.A.S.O.'s Mae West correctly fitted. Atcherley seemed to tell him to give up the task—and climbed aboard without it! Just before 13.00 hours the Mosquitoes set off, Pickard leading 487 Squadron and Jack Meakin No. 464. 'I had the honour of leading Basil Embry,' recalls Meakin, 'who flew rear end Charlie in the formation. My navigator, Basil Kennet, pinpointed all the turning points on the long course and brought us directly over target where all bombs were dropped.' They, too, had as their targets power stations—464's was at Mur de Bretagne and 487's at Pont Château, which took 487 on a very long course flown back over the sea. At the target they employed low-level and shallow-dive attacks in the manner of Mosquitoes months before. Along with them went the veterans, Flt. Lt. Patterson and DZ414, to photograph the results of the attacks.

That the Group Commander was on the raid cannot but have been wonderful for the morale of all who took part. It gave him a fine opportunity to see the results of the planning first hand. He felt that not enough attention had been paid to studying landmarks en route, and on the run-in, and that approach speeds needed careful attention. The target must be crossed before any bombs exploded. He ruled that the last aircraft must be at least 300 yards from the target area before the first bombs exploded and that the leader and last man must not be more than 1,000 yards apart.

Air Vice-Marshal Embry brought back an impressive bonus item, a large duck which hit and badly damaged his Mosquito. There was nothing new in this, but it brought home strikingly an ever-present hazard in low flying. He soon had Peter Scott suggesting where the most likely bird collisions would take place so that routing could embrace this aspect.

The Mosquito raids were fully analysed. Careful routing, a high standard of navigation and accurate bomb runs were clearly needed for such raids. Accurate low flying was essential and so the crews were told to work avidly for an improvement. Another idea followed up was the use of models for briefing purposes.

The finale of the raids on 3 October had been a special medium-level *Ramrod* by Mitchells of 320 Squadron escorted by four Spitfire squadrons, with the Grand Quevilly power station at Rouen as target. Nos. 403 and 421 Squadrons flew a diversion in the Roye area where a bitter fight evolved. Seven enemy fighters were seen to crash, shot down by Plt. Off. Hicks (MA579), Plt. Off. H. F. Packard (MA592), Plt. Off. K. R. Linton (MA713) and by Flg. Off. W. F. Cook (BS522) who was subsequently shot down. All of these pilots were from 421 Squadron. Flt. Lt. A. C. Coles of 403 Squadron claimed two other enemy aircraft.

On 9 October came the second Mosquito raid. Meakin remembers: 'I led 24 aircraft with Kennet, with the engine works at Woippy as the target. It was a hazy day and soon after leaving the coast we came across the British Navy. We had to alter course to avoid flying over them and in consequence crossed the coast a little off course and received a warm reception, and one aircraft was shot down. We continued to the target only to find that it was covered by cloud and we could not see to bomb. It was therefore rather an abortive operation and we lost four aircraft.' Wg. Cdr. Wilson leading 487 Squadron had also pressed on to the Messerschmitt engine works, bombed, then had to find his own way home since his navigator had died of flak wounds. Trouble hit others over Holland and Belgium, particularly when two apparently inadvertently mistook the bomb-release button for the intercom button, and their bombs blew them up. Further training was certainly needed.

After heavy rain overnight on 21–22 October the weather improved sufficiently for the next major low-level raid. Group ordered operations for the Bostons at 09.45 and crews of the three squadrons were briefed for a major raid on the aircraft factory at Courcelles, Belgium. Wg. Cdr. England was to lead, taking Flg. Off. Anderson as his navigator. Henri de Rancourt would head No. 342 and Wg. Cdr. Ian Spencer No. 88.

Take-off was shortly before 14.00 hours, then the aircraft set course for the Dutch coast by way of Harpenden and Stowmarket setting course at Orfordness for Colijnsplatt. Soon it was clear that something was wrong in the lead aircraft. Possibly the compass was giving a five-degree error—although it had been checked four days previously. Inconceivably it seemed England was well off track. He pressed on probably oblivious and led the formation to make landfall two miles south-west of Domburg some eight to ten miles off correct track, and light flak was met. They pressed on over Walcheren to Veere, by which time the lead formation was strung out in line abreast and sitting targets for the coastal gunners as they crossed the dunes. In a flash England's aircraft was hit and crashed in flames on the shore. Moments later Flt. Lt. McCulloch's Boston was down followed by two more of 107 Squadron piloted by Flg. Off. J. R. Bryce and Flt. Lt. Hoog. One of them disappeared in a huge fire ball which plunged into the sea. The guns also brought down Flg. Off. Stoloff whose starboard engine caught fire. He hit a hedge whilst trying to land in a field. It all happened in a few seconds.

The two remaining crews of 107 Squadron's 'A' Flight joined up with 'B' Flight having, like the remainder of the formation, poured all the fire at their command into the flak positions. After the confusion it was found that Flt. Sgt. I. J. Chappeles's aircraft was also missing.

This grievous loss of six aircraft and such experienced men understandably upset the entire formation, but Flt. Lt. John Reeve soared into the lead. He steered 165° and pinpointed himself first at the Scheldt, then by a lake near Holst. From this point the formation was on track passing two miles west of Howl. About eight miles from the target over a wood the new leader climbed 1,000 feet, as Wg. Cdr. England said he would at briefing, in order to locate the target before descending to low level for the attack. His navigator, Freddie Deeks, was surprised to see a large industrial area ahead with slag heaps and railway lines which were not what he had been led to expect at briefing. It made pinpointing difficult, and he could not locate the target. Actually the target lay $3\frac{1}{2}$ miles to the east and some crews saw it too late to turn and bomb. The formation accordingly set course for home on the ordered route, experiencing much light flak at Ecloe where Flt. Lt. Vickers of 107 Squadron had an engine put out of action. At the target area Flg. Off. Pateroux, Wg. Cdr. Rancourt's navigator, was wounded and he was unable to pass any bombing instructions. None of the aircraft released their bombs. Navigation on the homeward run was fairly accurate and they met the Typhoon withdrawal cover at the planned rendezvous. Failure to locate the target had been due to smoke and haze and a wrong mental picture of the target which was not at all easy to pick out.

Such losses as were encountered that day seemed unbelievable, particularly that of Wg. Cdr. Richard Geoffrey England. Ironic it was that next day news came through that England had been awarded the D.S.O. His citation read: 'This officer has taken part in a very large number of sorties including attacks on important targets in northern France. In August 1943 he led the formation of aircraft in an attack on Rennes. Bad weather was encountered on the outward flight but Wg. Cdr. England unerringly led his force to the precise target which was successfully bombed from a low level. Some days later this officer led a bomber force in an attack on a works at Denain. In spite of poor visibility and in the face of intense flak the objective was bombed accurately. Much of the success of the operation was attributed to Wg. Cdr. England's inspiring leadership, great courage and exceptional skill.' Of England Embry wrote 'His loss is a severe blow to the whole Group. He was a great leader who commanded universal respect and admiration.'

Three days later it was the Mitchells which encountered a heavy blow.

Twenty-four aircraft of 98 and 320 Squadrons were despatched to bomb the Brest/Lanvioc Poulmic airfield. All went well until 320 began to lead them in on the bomb run. To the surprise of 98's leader the Dutchmen were flying straight and level despite the flak which was soon accurate. There was suddenly a tremendous flash as Sgt. C. J. Bank's machine received a direct hit. Then another, as Cdr. Bakker's Mitchell disintegrated in a welter of fragments and flame. Roosenburg found that his hydraulics were out of action, instruments too, and that oil was streaming from his starboard engine. Worse, he had an arm wound. He managed to hold the aircraft level long enough for the bombs to be dropped. Soon after he found he had lost 3,000 feet, wrestled to regain control and steered for home alone. He skidded to a belly landing at Portreath.

The tremendous force of the explosions had thrown the aircraft of the leader, J. H. Maas, on to its back, then it too received a direct hit between the radio operator's position and the dorsal turret. At once the machine went into a dive from which recovery was miraculously made since the controls were badly damaged. The air gunner had been seriously wounded and was given immediate first aid. Then all movable gear was taken to the rear of the Mitchell until trim was adjusted. Crippled, it staggered back to Exeter for an excellent landing despite two tyres punctured and extensive structural damage.

There was a major enquiry into what had gone wrong. It was the considered opinion of the survivors that the leader might have sooner begun evasive action, and that the second box was too close to the first. Nevertheless the raid was not a failure, for 98 Squadron had scored accurate bombing on ammunition stores, hangars and dispersals.

On 28th the target for 320 Squadron was shipping at Cherbourg. Bombs fell on the Colonial Artillery barracks and the power station. Once more flak was accurate, and Loeff's Mitchell was hit. The bomb-release gear was damaged, but he managed to jettison his load. He kept formation and during the run-up the aircraft was hit again, in the observer's compartment and rear fuselage. Smoke and flames were soon streaming from the starboard engine, much oil was being lost and the propeller could not be feathered. More flames spewed from the propeller reduction gear and vibration became excessive. Loeff threaded his way home, made landfall near Bournemouth and put down at Tarrant Rushton. Immediately he found he had no brake pressure, and overran the field.

Behind the scenes a new campaign was being worked out with a sense of urgency which was to alter much of the remaining period of 2 Group's war. The losses of the last few days can be seen to coincide with a turning point. No longer was 2 Group mere bait for the enemy, it was now to fight a struggle vital to the winning of the war. It was to help pave the way for *Overlord*, and at the same time fight another vicious face of the enemy.

Chapter 20
Crossbow and the Preparations
for *Overlord*

Towards the end of October 1943, Air Vice-Marshal Basil Embry was called into conference with Air Chief Marshal Sir Trafford Leigh Mallory, C.-in-C. Fighter Command. Threat of attack on southern England by pilotless aircraft, rockets and long-range guns was rapidly developing. Throughout 1943 German developments had been watched. Recent reconnaissance over northern France indicated that the enemy was preparing sites from which to attack Britain and the invasion build-up. By late October 88 launching sites for pilotless aircraft had been located. Evidence suggested about fifty more existed. Photographs showed the completed ones to appear, from the air, shaped like a ski. A concrete platform about twelve feet wide and thirty feet long seemed in each case orientated towards London. At each site there was a square control building and two rectangular ones. Many sites were in the Pas de Calais. Others elsewhere were directed towards Bristol and Portsmouth, one of the main collection zones for ships needed to effect a landing in France. These might come under attack—and quite soon.

Leigh Mallory explained all this to Embry. If the likely scale of attack could not be curtailed it might demand the evacuation of London and, more important, upset the invasion plans. He asked Air Vice-Marshal Embry if 2 Group, now skilled in precision attacks, could bomb accurately enough to destroy these small sites in occupied territory. Embry said he thought it could.

Almost immediately orders were given to halt current Boston and Mitchell operations and switch to these new targets. From November 1943 until May 1944, destruction of flying-bomb sites and associated targets attracted 4,710 sorties, an effort as great as the whole for 1943. Massive contributions to the campaign were made by Fortresses and Liberators of the U.S. 8th Air Force, by B-26s and A-20s of the U.S. 9th Air Force and by Typhoon and Spitfire fighter-bombers of the 2nd Tactical Air Force, sometimes operating in conjunction with 2 Group.

On 5 November the assault opened with raids by B-26s and 2 Group Bostons and Mitchells. A large formation of 24 Bostons of 88 and

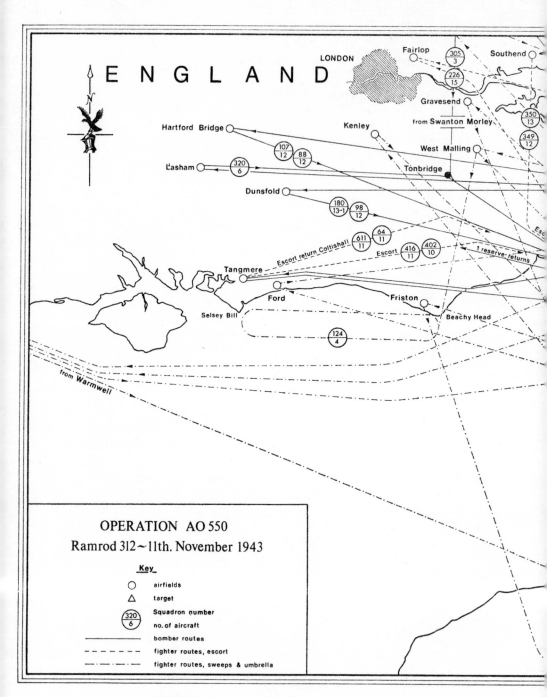

E N G L A N D

LONDON

Fairlop ○ ⓪305/3

Southend ○

⓪226/15

Gravesend ○

from Swanton Morley

⓪350/13

⓪349/12

Hartford Bridge ○

Kenley ○

West Malling ○

⓪107/12 ⓪88/12

Tonbridge ●

L'asham ○ ⓪320/6

Dunsfold ○

⓪180/13-1 ⓪98/12

⓪611/11 ⓪64/11

Escort return Coltishall

⓪416/11 ⓪402/10

1 reserve-returns

Esc

Tangmere ○

Escort

Ford ○

Friston ○

Selsey Bill

Beachy Head

⓪124/4

from Warmwell

OPERATION AO 550
Ramrod 312 ~ 11th. November 1943

Key

○ airfields

△ target

⓪320/6 Squadron number
        no. of aircraft

——— bomber routes

- - - - fighter routes, escort

—·—·— fighter routes, sweeps & umbrella

MAP 16. *See Appendix 12, pages 507–509 for notes*

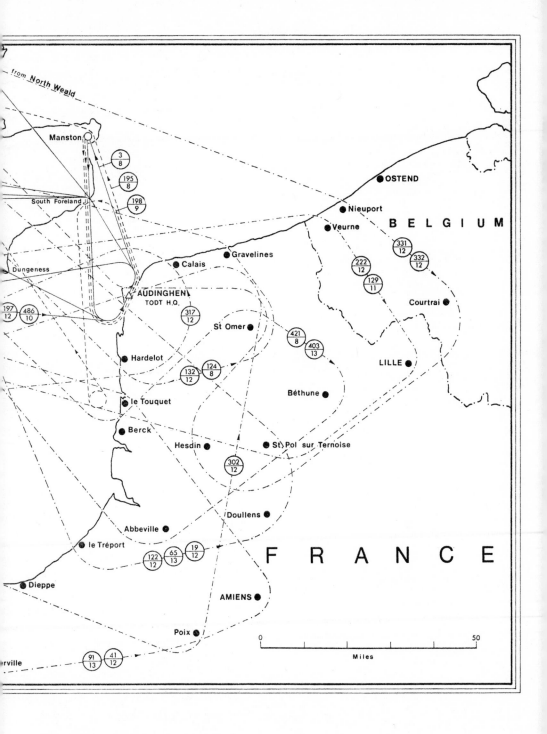

from North Weald

Manston

$\frac{3}{8}$
$\frac{195}{8}$
$\frac{198}{9}$

South Foreland

Dungeness

$\frac{197}{12}$ $\frac{486}{10}$

Calais

Gravelines

AUDINGHEN
TODT H.Q.

$\frac{317}{12}$

St Omer

$\frac{421}{8}$
$\frac{403}{13}$

Hardelot

$\frac{132}{12}$ $\frac{124}{8}$

le Touquet

Béthune

Berck

Hesdin

St Pol sur Ternoise

$\frac{302}{12}$

Doullens

Abbeville

le Tréport

$\frac{122}{12}$ $\frac{65}{13}$ $\frac{19}{12}$

Dieppe

AMIENS

Poix

erville

$\frac{91}{13}$ $\frac{41}{12}$

OSTEND

Nieuport

Veurne

BELGIUM

$\frac{331}{12}$
$\frac{332}{12}$

$\frac{222}{12}$

$\frac{129}{11}$

Courtrai

LILLE

FRANCE

0   50

Miles

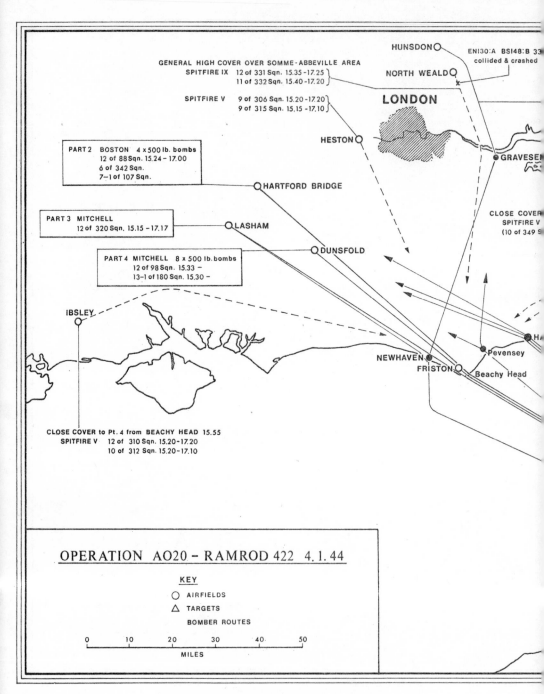

GENERAL HIGH COVER OVER SOMME-ABBEVILLE AREA
SPITFIRE IX 12 of 331 Sqn. 15.35-17.25
           11 of 332 Sqn. 15.40-17.20

SPITFIRE V 9 of 306 Sqn. 15.20-17.20
           9 of 315 Sqn. 15.15-17.10

HUNSDON

ENI30:A BSI48:B 33
collided & crashed

NORTH WEALD

LONDON

HESTON

GRAVESEN

PART 2 BOSTON 4 x 500 lb. bombs
       12 of 88 Sqn. 15.24 - 17.00
       6 of 342 Sqn.
       7-1 of 107 Sqn.

HARTFORD BRIDGE

CLOSE COVER
SPITFIRE V
(10 of 349 S

PART 3 MITCHELL
       12 of 320 Sqn. 15.15 - 17.17

LASHAM

DUNSFOLD

PART 4 MITCHELL 8 x 500 lb. bombs
       12 of 98 Sqn. 15.33 -
       13-1 of 180 Sqn. 15.30 -

IBSLEY

NEWHAVEN

Pevensey

HA

FRISTON

Beachy Head

CLOSE COVER to Pt. 4 from BEACHY HEAD 15.55
SPITFIRE V 12 of 310 Sqn. 15.20-17.20
          10 of 312 Sqn. 15.20-17.10

OPERATION AO20 – RAMROD 422 4.1.44

KEY

○ AIRFIELDS
△ TARGETS
BOMBER ROUTES

0   10   20   30   40   50
MILES

MAP 17. *See Appendix 12, pages 510/1 for notes*

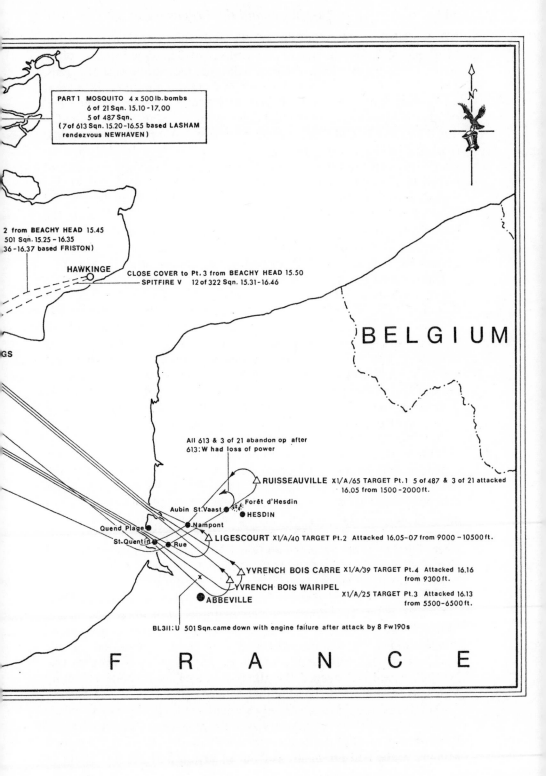

PART 1 MOSQUITO 4 x 500 lb. bombs
6 of 21 Sqn. 15.10 - 17.00
5 of 487 Sqn.
(7 of 613 Sqn. 15.20 - 16.55 based LASHAM
rendezvous NEWHAVEN)

2 from BEACHY HEAD 15.45
501 Sqn. 15.25 - 16.35
.36 - 16.37 based FRISTON)

HAWKINGE   CLOSE COVER to Pt. 3 from BEACHY HEAD 15.50
           SPITFIRE V   12 of 322 Sqn. 15.31 - 16.46

GS

BELGIUM

All 613 & 3 of 21 abandon op after
613: W had loss of power

△ RUISSEAUVILLE XI/A/65 TARGET Pt.1 5 of 487 & 3 of 21 attacked
                                       16.05 from 1500 - 2000 ft.

Aubin St: Vaast   Forêt d'Hesdin
                  ● HESDIN
Quend Plage ● ● Nampont
St.Quentin ● ● Rue   △ LIGESCOURT XI/A/40 TARGET Pt.2 Attacked 16.05-07 from 9000 - 10500 ft.

                     △ YVRENCH BOIS CARRE XI/A/39 TARGET Pt.4 Attacked 16.16
                                                                from 9300 ft.
           x   △
             ▲ YVRENCH BOIS WAIRIPEL
         ● ABBEVILLE   XI/A/25 TARGET Pt.3 Attacked 16.13
                                                        from 5500 - 6500 ft.

BL3II: U 501 Sqn. came down with engine failure after attack by 8 Fw 190s

F   R   A   N   C   E

107 Squadrons, 24 Mitchells of 98 and 180 Squadrons, fourteen Mitchells of 226 with four of 305 and six of 320 Squadrons set off to attack workings at a huge site near Mimoyecques south-west of Calais. The nature of the target was kept secret from the air crews; to them it was merely 'enemy excavations and installations'. Heavy mist and bad weather in recent days which had delayed the opening of the campaign was lifting and in mid afternoon the bombers took-off. The Bostons had reached Guildford when Wg. Cdr. Spencer, leading, decided that the weather was still too poor for them to operate without special aids and turned his wave for home. The Mitchells relying on *Gee*, and in two waves each of 24 aircraft, proceeded. Sqn. Ldr. R. K. F. Bell-Irving led Nos. 98 and 180 Squadrons and Wg. Cdr. C. E. R. Tait, D.S.O., the second group comprising 226, 305 and 320 Squadrons. Spitfire Vs took station as close escort and soon there were eighteen squadrons of Spitfire Vs, VIIs, IXs and XIIs providing fighter cover over France.

Flak opened up in the Desvres area and as the Mitchells ran up on the mysterious target more was encountered, some bursts unusual in that they released showers of small metal discs. It was immediately obvious to the crews that the target must have special significance. To the Germans the assault proved that the Allies were aware something important was afoot. The first formation placed 187 500-lb. H.E.s across No. 8 excavation, but bombs from the second wave fell 400 yards N.E. of the aiming point. These targets, in the face of determined flak, were not going to be easy ones. In an attempt to offer explanation and encouragement to the French, who were going to have to face up to some unpleasant raids, leaflets were dropped by many aircraft.

With so many bombers operating against one target, a valuable one at that, enemy fighters might have been expected to interfere. This did not prove to be the case. Indeed, throughout the entire *Crossbow* campaign they hardly ever appeared. Defence instead consisted of a vast array of anti-aircraft guns of varying calibre, giving the raiders a hot reception and upsetting their aim. Nevertheless no chances were taken where fighters were concerned and on 7 November 24 Bostons bombed aircraft dispersals and station H.Q. at Bernay. In this *Circus* operation, designed to attract enemy fighters, none appeared.

It was soon realised that the Mimoyecques raid barely marked this important target. Therefore on 8th crews drawn from all the Boston and Mitchell squadrons had a rude awakening, early breakfast, rapid briefing whilst the weather held, and were soon on their way to the workings of what was already known as 'happy valley'. This time two Mitchell squadrons opened the attack followed by Bostons and more Mitchells in what was to be a familiar pattern.

They found the defences already strengthened. All the way from the coast to the target enemy gunners were banging away—and accurately. Bostons took most of the damage but Wg. Cdr. Tait heading the second Mitchell wave had an engine cut out of action and Flt. Lt. Smith in

R: FV927 of 226 Squadron was shot down over the target. Despite some cloud, hits were scored on Nos. 5 and 8 workings, but the general consensus of opinion was that flak had upset the aim, considerable evasive action being demanded. Tait, whose Mitchell had suffered badly, headed for Manston, could not make it and crashed in a nearby field. No one was hurt but FV939: B was a write-off.

There was no doubt Mimoyecques was a vital target, and so next day 24 Bostons drawn from the three squadrons flying with 24 Mitchells were to make yet another attack. The Mitchells were to precede the Bostons by ten minutes allowing smoke to clear for the second wave. But just as the crews were climbing into the aircraft the raid was called off. Attacks on targets in occupied territory were carried out only in suitable weather, and 2 Group always adhered to this maxim.

Attacks on V-weapon sites were first priority, but the question was posed, where else might effective attacks be made to halt the building progress? Surely no better place than the headquarters from where the work was controlled. Intelligence sources disclosed that the Todt organisation was master-minded from the village of Audinghen. 2 Group supported by Typhoon bomber squadrons was ordered to obliterate it. Five heavy raids were mounted over the next few weeks.

The first was abandoned by the Bostons since 10/10 cloud was met at the French coast, but the leading Mitchells of 98 and 180 Squadrons navigated by *Gee* and led respectively by Wg. Cdr. Phillips and Wg. Cdr. J. F. Castle pressed on, bombing through cloud on estimated positions and getting a good spread of bombs over the target area. The second Mitchell wave was lucky, for it found a cloud break over Audinghen. The village was small and only a goodly concentration of bombs would delete it. Another raid was needed.

On the following afternoon three groups of bombers set out, preceded by two formations of Typhoons totalling 47 aircraft (mainly dive-bombers) whose role was principally to soften the target and its anti-aircraft defences. *Ramrod 312* was a major operation, as Map No. 16 shows. Six Spitfire V Squadrons closely protected the bombers whilst overhead flew Spitfire VIIs and IXs of six more squadrons. Five Spitfire diversion sweeps were flown in a radial pattern around the target, to prevent any fighter interference none of which was met. Bostons of 88 and 107 Squadrons, Sqn. Ldr. A. F. Carlisle leading, dropped 92 500-lb. bombs getting hits on the village outskirts and some buildings in the N.E. section. Mitchells claimed limited success. Flak, moderate this time was not very accurate.

Typical November weather now set in, and there was no possibility of continuing the attacks. Not until 23rd were they resumed, opened once more by Typhoon fighter-bombers. It was cloudy and hazy, but bursts were seen in the centre of the village with over and undershoots. Flak was expected to have increased, but this was not the case.

On 24th the V-site at La Glacerie came under attack for the first time and, also for the first time, some Fw 190s tried to interfere but dived away before interception could take place.

There was still a need to place an effective load on Audinghen. On 25th, the first possible day, it was decided to deliver really crippling blows. Two raids were mounted, the first by 72 aircraft and the second by 66, with Typhoons again opening the assault. This was the busiest day since *Starkey*. Bombing was very good, particularly by Nos. 88, 180 and 320 Squadrons. Formations were again protected by Spitfire V squadrons whilst hordes of other Spitfires flew overhead or swept to the east and west for enemy fighters which never appeared. This time the flak was really intense and in the morning raid fourteen Bostons suffered damage as well as Mitchells. Bostons put their bombs into the village centre, to the W.S.W., N.W. and in fields around. Leading Mitchells on the morning raid dropped theirs right in the village centre, and to the south. Flg. Off. R. F. H. Martin of 98 Squadron had his aircraft seriously damaged by flak but managed a safe landing after the under-carriage was pumped down by hand. As the Mitchells went in during the afternoon heavy flak again met 98 Squadron and every one was damaged. By the end of the raid very few buildings were still standing and many were burning.

Bostons had suffered particularly from flak in the morning raid. Plt. Off. D. J. N. Gibson of 88 Squadron put up a good show by somehow getting his peppered aircraft back to Hawkinge. Wounded in the left collar bone, he also had facial injuries. For a while he felt that he had lost control of BZ217 which went into a dive. He ordered the crew to bale out, but recovery came in time and they all made home safely.

By the time the third wave had left in the afternoon raid the village was a burning mess. Nevertheless the U.S. 9th Air Force made sure of its destruction with a morning raid next day.

During *Ramrod 333*, the afternoon attack, some enemy fighters had been encountered by the sweeping Spitfires. Over Béthune No. 122 Squadron led by Sqn. Ldr. P. R. W. Wickham at some 19,000 feet was astonished to see two Bf 109s join up with them in error. They soon broke away, one firing at extreme range. Plt. Off. Gilbert flying BS192 fired but his cannon jammed after only six rounds. Then he used up his machine-gun ammunition as a result of which pieces fell off the elevator of one of the enemy claimed as damaged. Flt. Sgt. D. Bostock in MA764 called up to say he had high glycol temperature, fell away to 10,000 feet and was lost. Meanwhile No. 332 Norwegian Spitfire Squadron had been bounced by six enemy fighters fifteen miles S.E. of Lille. In the ensuing fight 2nd Lt. Aanjersen shot down a Bf 109 and to the delight of the squadron the enemy fighters destroyed one of their own Fw 190s and a Bf 109; 332 could never have done this, most of the guns were iced up!

On 26 November 2 Group's bombers struck again, this time at Martinvast. A large-scale morning raid was despatched but recalled because of the weather. In the afternoon an attack was delivered by three waves flying ten minutes apart and at around 12,000 feet, the usual height. Seven squadrons were involved, elements of the entire medium-level force at Embry's command. Flak was again heavy and 180 Squadron, leading, lost three Mitchells. Cloud interfered with the Bostons' run-up and seven crews quickly chose to attack an alternative ski site in a not particularly successful operation. Top cover, three squadrons of Typhoons and two Spitfire squadrons over the leading formation, met a few enemy fighters destroying a Fw 190. During the day 119 sorties had been despatched against Martinvast.

Weather conditions for these relatively complicated operations had to be good, and always the fighter needs met. On 29th 320 Squadron was despatched to the S.N.C.A.N. factory at Albert. Originally 24 Mitchells had been detailed. Then the met. forecast suggested a 70 m.p.h. wind at 15,000 feet. Although 320 Squadron set out, fighter support was impossible. The raid was abandoned.

Throughout November the Mosquito force was being built up and busy. On 5th six crews of 487 Squadron made a low-level raid on the electrical works at Hengelo, a familiar Mosquito target. No. 464 Squadron was detached to Bradwell Bay on 10th, a base for intruder operations. The A.O.C. had always wanted to wage a day and night campaign, such as was to pay enormous dividends in 1944. The present contribution was to resume night intruders on airfields, which would be helpful to the bomber offensive and at the same time offer useful night training to Mosquito crews. These Mosquitoes would be helping the newly formed No. 100 (Bomber Support) Group. By the end of November 464 Squadron had flown nineteen intruder sorties, against airfields at Florennes, Juvincourt, Coulommiers and Laon/Couvrant.

All through December flying-bomb sites were principal targets for Bostons and Mitchells, but the weather was extremely bad from 3rd until 19th and no operations were possible at this crucial time. Raids were resumed on 20th and flown on six more days in December. Names soon to be familiar to the crews came through on the teleprinter operations orders, names of tiny villages where small V-sites were skilfully hidden, like Heuringham, Drionville, Puchervin, St. Pierre des Jonquières, Le Mesnil Alard, Pommeréval, La Glacerie, Bois de Capelle, Crécy, Yvrenche, Ligescourt. Almost all were very small targets difficult to locate in fine weather, almost impossible to find on dull days. Their defences varied. Sometimes flak was intense at medium levels, and within weeks the enemy surrounded the most vulnerable sites with barrages. Enemy fighters almost absent from the scene showed up on the morning of 21st, Nos. 132 and 602 Squadrons being bounced by about forty Fw 190s just north-east of Cambrai. Hopelessly outnumbered the Spitfires were forced to withdraw, but not before 602 Squadron had destroyed two 190s and lost Flt. Sgt. A. H. Morgan.

For the most part these raids were relatively uneventful—until the flak was really turned on—and almost exclusively they were carried out at medium levels. This approach made between light and medium flak levels allowed a fair chance of getting bombs in the target area, but to hit a small building was difficult and sometimes it needed several attacks, maybe in the face of very stiff flak which often holed many aircraft. As soon as the Germans realised the squadrons were really after a particular site they strengthened its anti-aircraft defences.

An unusual and spectacular attack was made by a force of 36 Bostons on 23 December. This was an experimental low-level operation on Le Mesnil Alard led by Wg. Cdr. Henri de Rancourt of 342 Squadron. The force formed up, set course from Odiham and crossed out at Hastings. Soon after they flew into a flock of birds at Brévil; formation keeping was bad and there was soon chaos. Weaving and erratic courses led to 107 Squadron being quite unable to find the target so instead they bombed Serquex marshalling yards then made for home, except for Turner and his crew who chanced upon the site at Puchervin. After circling it at 2,000 feet for identification they made their attack. de Rancourt led his force to the original target area and was forced to make several low runs until he located and bombed it, the only one to do so. The plan had been for two leading crews of 342 Squadron to mark the target from 500 feet with the others following in at 1,500 feet. Over the target, one pilot recorded, 'it was a fantastic sight with Bostons on all sides.' Flak was fierce and Flg. Off. Pettit's starboard engine was soon out of action. Another aircraft came down in a wood. No. 88 Squadron had found great difficulty in locating the target, too, and most of the formation bombed Serquex. Flak damaged ten of its aircraft. No more low-level raids of this nature were attempted by the Boston squadrons, which were untrained for such work.

Employment of the Mosquito squadrons had been quite different. Their speed and range began to be put to good use late in November when 21 Squadron started *Day Ranger* flights. By the end of November, 21 Squadron had visited the transformer stations at Vannes, Lingen and La Roche, but the most noteworthy attack of the period came on 1 December.

A 475-foot blockade runner, the *Pietro Orseleo*, was found creeping along the west coast of France, and Sqn. Ldr. Cussens, Plt. Off. Sparkes with Plt. Off. Darrell—all from 487 Squadron—were ordered to leave Sculthorpe on 30 November, fly to Predannack, and attack her from there. The ship, defended by six anti-aircraft guns, quickly became a high priority target. Even so, the aircraft under short notice did not reach Predannack until 15.30 hours at which time they should have been taking-off for their rendezvous with escorting Typhoons. Accordingly the raid was postponed until next day when two of the Mosquitoes were declared unserviceable. Cussens took-off alone to meet his fighter escort which took him to the target vessel.

Watched by 10 Group escort he steered a magnificent course and off the Ile de Groix pressed home his attack single-handed, and in the face of fearful enemy fire, placing his bombs within twenty feet of the side of the ship. He was then shot down and the Typhoon pilots flew home to tell a tale of great courage. Rumours quickly circulated that he was to be awarded a posthumous Victoria Cross, but nothing came of them. Other information indicated that, when the ship put into harbour, her damage was found to be quite serious and she could not put to sea again.

At this time the second 2 Group Mosquito Wing was forming at Lasham and 613 Squadron, part of it, flew its first sortie (a weather reconnaissance) on 19 December. No. 464 Squadron was still flying intruder patrols known as *Flowers*.

Bad weather had interrupted Mosquito operations as much as other raids. It had now been decided that the Mosquito force must join the attacks on flying-bomb sites. On account of their higher speed and nimbleness the Mosquitoes would concentrate on what had been their traditional role, low-level attack. On 21 December the Sculthorpe Wing attempted their first assault on a flying-bomb site. It was cloudy and attack was impossible, but next day Nos. 21 and 487 Squadrons managed to reach St. Agathe, the original target. Next day a pack of Mosquitoes made a low-level attack on Pommereval. On the last day of the year the largest force of Mosquitoes yet employed, 35 including seven of 613 Squadron, on that unit's first bombing raid, were sent to Le Ploy. It was an unusual operation because the Sculthorpe-based squadrons were making it whilst en route to their new base at Hunsdon, nearer to the scene of current action.

Just how the Mosquitoes should be employed provoked considerable thought. At first it was decided they should cross the Channel at low level and continue the run-in at that height. They were soon suffering badly from anti-aircraft fire at the coast, particularly light flak. It was then decided they would climb to about 4,000 feet some four miles out. Once inland they would dive to low level, sometimes to deliver dive attacks from 1,500 feet. When flying very low the pilot would come upon the target suddenly and therefore it was important to take a good route in, and for the crews to be conversant with the general layout of a site. To give them practice a mock site was built on a bombing range.

During December trials were made with the run-in at about 11,000 feet to allow for site detection, with bombing from a dive to about 6,000 feet. Such an attack would be possible only in good weather such as rarely existed at this time, and even then target identification was still difficult. The average bombing error appeared to be about 150 yards after the long dive, but only wing-mounted bombs could be dropped from a diving Mosquito. Therefore this tactic was dropped in favour of the low-level approach. Whatever the tactics the V-weapon sites were difficult targets.

Apart from a few night intruders the end of 1943 found 2 Group entirely concentrating on the V-weapon campaign. Much in Embry's mind, however, was the constant thought of how he should apply his forces in support of the invasion, for they were to have a most important part in the operations of the 2nd Tactical Air Force of which they were now a part. The flying-bomb sites must be quickly destroyed since 2 Group was required to help pave the way for *Overlord*, planning of which was now very advanced. 2 Group was operating four Mosquito VI squadrons, three flying Boston IIIAs and four with Mitchells. The Polish squadron, No. 305, had recently given up its Mitchells after only five operations and was now working-up on Mosquitoes using a handful of Mk. IIIs and VIs at Lasham.

Plans to make the Group more efficient were now revealed. It was to be streamlined to secure maximum mobility and flexibility for, in a few months, it seemed likely that squadrons would advance into Europe behind the army. Four Wing Headquarters were formed, each embracing three squadrons, controlling operations and aircraft servicing. A reduction in establishment of ground personnel was made possible, those released being posted into special Servicing Echelons for each squadron; and centralised under, and controlled by, Wing Airfield H.Q. Wings established in December were No. 137 Hartford Bridge, No. 138 Lasham, No. 139 Dunsfold and 140 Sculthorpe later at Hunsdon. Servicing Echelons were numbered from 13 to 21 and 31 to 32, one for each 2 Group squadron. Early in 1944 in preparation for the invasion of France Group H.Q. moved to Mongewell Park, Berkshire. Wings moved to forward airfields and were billeted under canvas.

Despite the poor seasonal weather attacks on *Crossbow* targets had to continue in January, large-scale *Ramrods* being possible only on six occasions. Mosquitoes were able to operate when other bomber formations could not rendezvous or fighter cover was impossible, and concentrated upon low-level attacks. Sometimes they operated in pairs in small formations, at other times in large packs. On 2 January, for instance, there were seven boxes of Mosquitoes raiding Neufchâtel. Sqn. Ldr. Newman nursed home LR271 on one engine because of flak damage, still plentiful at low heights. Flt. Lt. Leven's aircraft had been hit by flak at the coast on the way in, which burst his port tyre and damaged the undercarriage and a fuel pipe. He carried on but over base found it difficult to lower the wheels. When they were down he faced the prospect of landing on a flat tyre—not easy in a Mosquito. For him it was an eventful sixtieth trip.

Each formation of Bostons and Mitchells at this time usually had a close escort of two Spitfire V squadrons, some fitted with cropped blowers more suited to low-level operations. The faster VIIs, IXs and XIIs found slow-flying bombers hard to keep with and instead were now either providing a fighter umbrella high over the entire area of any *Ramrods* taking place or flying fan-shaped fighter sweeps. Often Mosquitoes would be participating in the same *Ramrod* with their own fighter cover, usually given by the two Spitfire Mk. XII squadrons and sometimes by Typhoons. These flew about ten minutes ahead of the

Mosquitoes and gave target and withdrawal cover. On 6 January when 41 Squadron's Spitfire Mk. XIIs were part of the high fighter umbrella, enemy fighters were reported coming from the Paris area as the bombers swept in. The Spitfires went to head them off—none were then seen, although an enemy fighter shadowed a Mosquito home and 65 Squadron scrambled to intercept without success.

The enemy was constantly moving and increasing his flak defences around flying-bomb sites. On 7 January Wg. Cdr. Newman and Flg. Off. Hester both had their Mosquitoes hit on crossing into France. Newman saw the gun whose shots hit him and made a point of silencing it on the way home. Three days later Hester crash-landed LR366, its rudder cables severed by flak. Plt. Off. Cobley was unable to control his damaged Mosquito after landing on 14 January and it tipped on to its nose; Flt. Lt. Oliver hit by flak on the same operation did not return.

Mosquitoes of 464 Squadron continued night intruder operations throughout January, operating on eight nights to targets in Belgium, France and Holland including Twente, Venlo, Melsbroek, St. Trond, Leeuwarden, Gilze Rijen. On 21 January, when the Luftwaffe began its 'Baby Blitz' on London, 464 Squadron operated against Reims, Alkmaar, Deelen, Twente and Venlo. HJ774 penetrated to Münster/Handorf, a base from which some bombers operated against England. Over the next few weeks the Mosquito campaign was extended to bomber bases in order to catch enemy aircraft coming home from raids. But in the main Mosquito operations were still by day against *Crossbow* sites. Airfields were difficult targets to find unless the lights were on, and many sorties proved fruitless.

Two daylight *Ramrods* were flown on 4 January, and one is depicted in map form. A relatively simple operation, it can be seen to be quite complex when compared with a *Circus* earlier in the war. During the morning whilst a large force of American Marauders, covered as usual by an armada of Spitfires, raided Woensdrecht, 25 Bostons and 36 Mitchells had attacked three *Noball* targets. A quick turn round followed and, making the best of fair weather, a second *Ramrod* was flown in which the Mosquitoes took part. Sometimes a *Ramrod* was divided into three or four parts and directed against differing targets, each part having a close fighter escort; an alternative was to space the parts by about ten minutes and direct them to the same target over which a fighter umbrella was placed. Diversionary sweeps were flown too.

On 7 January 24 Mitchells of 226 and 320 Squadrons, which between them were so far credited with the destruction of five V-1 sites, delivered an outstanding attack. No. 226 Squadron went in relatively low at around 4,800 feet and No. 320 at 7,800. They scored a direct hit and two near misses on a control building, a direct hit on another hut, a near miss on a large rectangular building, and saw another fall to bomb blast. Other buildings were damaged, all at Campneuseville. At this time

320 Squadron was getting outstanding bombing results. Usually the Mitchells and Bostons flew in boxes stepped up from 11,000 to 14,000 feet, and this meant they could take only limited evasive action once the flak started. If the weather was poor at base there was always the risk of trouble should the aircraft be damaged. Two crews of 98 and 180 Squadrons in such circumstances collided on one occasion, and all the personnel in the aircraft were killed.

On 14 January the Bostons were busy. Targets were small but 88 Squadron led by Sqn. Ldr. J. F. Castle managed hits on Gorenflos although as so often some bombs overshot. Twelve crews of 107 and 342 Squadrons led by Flt. Lt. Langer in U-BZ261 had to take evasive action against the flak and eight of the twelve aircraft were damaged. They soon found themselves off course. Quickly Langer chose an alternative target, Flixicourt-Domart where some bombs probably hit the ski site. 'L' of 342 flown by Flg. Off. F. Iozoy was so badly damaged that it had to put down at Pevensey Bay and the crew entered hospital.

The weather was clear, and after a quick lunch the Boston crews were off again, with Flottmanville Hague I as target. Flak was again intense, particularly from Alderney and Cherbourg. C/342 lost engine power and aborted, then S/88 was hit in an engine. Despite the defences a fair attack was delivered.

Between 1 December and 20 January 1,362 sorties had been despatched against flying-bomb sites, 820 successfully. Fickle weather brought about 408 abortive sorties, mechanical troubles another 99. Alternative targets had received another 28 sorties, three aircraft were missing and two crashed during operations. Such was the priority of *Noball* targets that operations were often laid on when the weather might prove quite unsuitable, and the gamble often did not come off. *Noball* attacks brought a threefold problem: guessing the weather—usually the night before—finding a small target and accurate bombing. The first part was a headache for the Group Met. Officer, Mr. Poulter, but he did surprisingly well.

Some comparison of raids was already possible. So far the Americans had been credited with the destruction of 27 sites, and 2 Group for far less effort twelve, which put them well ahead of the Marauders of the 9th Air Force.

Abortive sorties had been high but the situation improved later in the month by which time twelve targets had been suspended. Six had fallen to the Mitchells, three each to the Bostons and Mosquitoes.

Flak damage to low-flying Mosquitoes continued to be serious despite the high-low operations profile. Ritchie of 21 Squadron had to abort on 21st, his tail peppered with bullet holes. During an attack on St. Pierre on the evening of 26th light flak damaged all of 21's aircraft in one box and Flg. Off. Pennil was hit twice in the leg. Wheeler had to land at Ford after his starboard engine was hit. Flg. Off. Smith with a badly holed rudder landed at Manston. Tuck, badly shot up three days later, nursed MM406 into Ford—and Flt. Lt. Morgan flew into a flock of birds, an ever-present hazard.

On 21 January during *Ramrod 468* the target for 226 and 320 Squadrons was La Guisemont. Sqn. Ldr. A. B. Wheeler, D.F.C., was leading 226 and Lt. Mulder No. 320. They had 310 and 312 Spitfire V Squadrons as close escort, with two Mk. IX squadrons and Nos. 41 and 91 with XIIs flying top cover. Through a navigation error they failed to bomb, and then a few Fw 190s broke through the fighter screen concentrating their fire on FV919-M, number five in the second box. Two of the crew were wounded and so too was Flt. Sgt. E. D. Moon in the gunner's compartment. Flt. Sgt. K. C. Brown, number four aircraft's gunner, quickly opened fire from about 100 yards managing a hit on a fighter.

The Spitfires had been stung to action against six fighters diving past their rear in the target area. Plt. Off. Liskuten of 312 Squadron fired at one without success. It was 12.00 hours when 41 and 91 Squadrons came across eight '109s and '190s coming out of the sun near St. Pol. They dived after them and it seems probable that the enemy was forced to dive through the bombers' close escort which at first did not see them. No. 91 Squadron split chasing individual Huns. One was forced to ground level and after five minutes' chase it drew away spewing black smoke. Red one chased it as far as Amiens but made no claim. Red four chased another without success. This was the only contact 2 Group had with enemy fighters during January.

Throughout February the main effort continued to be against flying-bomb sites, with 487 Squadron replacing 464 Squadron on night intruders. It began these on 7–8 February. Mosquitoes were delivering mixed day raids, either completely low level or employing the hi-lo profile, and usually flew in pairs. At the close of the month 305 Squadron commenced operations on a limited scale with Mosquitoes.

Perhaps the most portentous item now was the introduction of the excellent blind-bombing aid *Gee-H* believed to have been first taken into action by 98 Squadron on 3 February during an attack on the construction works at Auffay. Wg. Cdr. Phillips was leading, but the gear gave trouble and most bombs were brought back.

A second *Gee-H* raid was planned for 5th against the airfield at Beauvais, but abandoned when the Spitfire escort failed to show up. It was during a raid on Livossart village that *Gee-H* was first used successfully for bombing with Flt. Lt. E. Chandler operating it in the lead aircraft FV977-M. But against such small targets even this sophisticated aid was only of limited use and the best results were still achieved by visual bombing, through a cloud gap. In the afternoon Wg. Cdr. Phillips took Flt. Sgt. Pollard as his *Gee-H* operator, targets at Fenycourt and Wattleblery being hit with the use of the new aid. *Gee-H* was to prove invaluable against larger targets when clouds were 10/10.

On 5 February, when again the Spitfires did not show up, the Boston squadrons elected to press on alone to Beauvais Tille's dispersal areas attacking the only non-*Noball* target for many weeks. A small patch of cloud drifted into the leading bomb aimer's sight just as the target came into view. Hits were nevertheless scored on the runway intersection and dispersals. 320 and 226 Mitchell squadrons had also proceeded, covered by four Spitfire IX squadrons. Their bombs overshot into the nearby town.

Whilst these squadrons were operating 24 Mosquitoes of Nos. 21, 464 and 613 Squadrons attacked *Noball* target XI/A/114, the V-site at Boismeigle. For them it was a bumpy ride in hazy weather. There was slight flak over France and two of 464's aircraft were hit on the run-in. Flg. Off. Foster soon had a damaged engine to worry about. As his squadron sped homewards they had varying troubles to contend with. Flg. Off. Binnie's windscreen had been shattered. One of Sqn. Ldr. McRitchie's hydraulic pipes had been smashed and Bob Iredale's starboard mainplane and tailplane had been damaged when LR334 hit a tree. But the Mosquito was strong and battleworthy, and all the damaged machines reached home.

Next day the target for Mosquitoes of 613 Squadron was Airaines. As usual on these low-level strikes, the flak was intense, and Flg. Off. Pigg's aircraft LR353 was hit in the fuselage shearing some of the cables therein. Further hits rendered the gun-firing mechanism useless. All the aircraft crossed the coast homewards then glycol was seen to pour from Grp. Capt. Bower's machine. Sqn. Ldr. Newman, and Flg. Off. Pigg in his damaged machine, latched on to the leader escorting him across the Channel. He could not make base and force-landed. Although the aircraft was wrecked he and his navigator managed to get clear.

Behind the scene plans for the invasion of France were occupying vast numbers of people. 2 Group's share had been agreed months ago. After night interdictor work by Mosquitoes, smoke laying by two Boston squadrons would screen the landing craft. Periodically Boston crews now undertook smoke-laying training. From 11 to 13 February 88 and 342 Squadrons practised during Exercise *Savy*. Half the formations would carry SCI gear, the remainder drop 60-lb. smoke bombs in the Poole area. Plans were set for the smoke to trail on 12th. Crews were to operate from Beaulieu, but just before take-off the wind changed and the SCI layers were cancelled. A few moments later it was clear the cloud base was too low. As the Bostons turned for their dispersals three ran off the perimeter into mud and it took hours to dig them out. One was so deep it had to be left to be worked upon some other time! Then to cap it all the Luftwaffe next day arrived in the vicinity . . . the Bostons might have to operate without practice!

As part of the D-Day planning it had been decided to take 107 Squadron off operations as soon as 305 Squadron became operational, equipping it with Mosquitoes to form the third squadron of No. 138

8. The Gestapo office in The Hague under attack by 613 Squadron
9. 'Bombs gone!' from the Bostons of 88 Squadron during the Audinghen raid of 11.11.43

70. The flying bomb site at Mesnil Allard, one of the original 'ski sites' being bombed by 88 Squadron

71. Audinghen village being bombed on 23.11.43. Bombs are bursting in the village, but large cloud patches nearly obscured the target at the moment of aiming

2. Ligescourt V-1 site during the raid on 4.1.44. The site, as often, was carefully concealed in a wood

3. In the snowy winter of 1944–5 Mitchell II FR199: NO-M being swept clear. She had flown 27 sorties. By her side another Mk. II, FR181: NO-R, shot down on 15.1.45. In the lines some Mk. IIIs distinguishable by their forward-placed turrets

74. Mitchells of 180 Squadron taxi out for operations, and wear various styles of A.E.A.F. white and black stripes. Leading is a Mk. II srs. ii

75. The Mitchell II srs. ii was an interim version with the dorsal turret still aft, yet fitted with the rear position of the Mk. III but without provision for tail guns. The machine depicted is MQ-F: FW153

Airfield. The opportunity was taken at this time to slightly re-arrange the Mitchell force by positioning 320 Squadron in 139 Airfield at Dunsfold and place 226 Squadron in 137 Airfield as its third squadron, useful since the Bostons had no radar bombing aids whereas the Mitchells had *Gee-H*.

Quite often the Spitfire 'close' escort was some way from the bombers. Probably the Mitchell crews attacking X/1A/31 on 15 February would have been amazed to find that 501 Squadron escorting them had in its midst a Spitfire that had seen service during the Battle of Britain! X4272 had joined 19 Squadron in September 1940, then passed to A.F.D.U. Northolt. Between 22 January 1941 and 24 March 1942, it was used after conversion to a Mk. VB by 92 Squadron, and passed via 154, 313, 222 and 317 Squadrons to 501 Squadron on 22 October 1943. This unit used it for bomber escort until 17 August 1944, when it was withdrawn to survive the war as 5522M at Cosford. It was one of the longest-service Spitfires.

Meanwhile 88 and 342 Squadrons were busy bombing. Wg. Cdr. A. B. Wheeler led six crews of 88 Squadron to Flottmanville Hague and six of 342 Squadron attacked the alternative target Martinvast. Heavy flak greeted 88 Squadron from the Franmanville area south of their target and from Cherbourg as they returned to the coast. All the aircraft were hit and just after bombing Flg. Off. Baron's machine BZ254: G received a direct hit in the starboard engine. It burst into flames, a wing folded up, the aircraft spun down and hit the ground near Hemmeville. 342 Squadron fared little better, two aircraft being hit and a third, BZ333-H, crashing near Swanage.

During January 1944, information reached London that over 100 French patriots were awaiting execution in Amiens jail. Could the R.A.F. puncture the prison and its walls to allow the prisoners to escape? The only hope was that Mosquitoes of 2 Group might achieve this.

The raid was planned with the aid of a model of the target. Attack was planned for noon when many of the guards would be at lunch in the centre of the building. Six aircraft of 21 Squadron, seven of 487 and five of 464 Squadrons were chosen along with DZ414, the Mosquito IV of the F.P.U. Grp. Capt. Charles Pickard was to lead the raid, although the Group Commander had hoped to do this himself until forbidden to do so.

Briefing was conducted in great secrecy using a model which clearly showed the prison walls, twenty feet high and three feet thick. The first wave, 487 Squadron, was to breach the north and east walls and aim bombs at the base of the main building to shake open locks on the cell doors. The second wave would open walls at either end of the courtyard and bomb the quarters occupied by the Germans. A third wave would be available to complete any task not accomplished already, and the French Resistance would be informed of the time of attack.

M

Shortly before 11.00 hours on 18 February the Mosquitoes left Hunsdon in swirling snow, and headed to meet their Typhoon escort at Littlehampton. So bad were the conditions that two crews of 21 and 464 Squadrons became lost and abandoned the operation. Only eight Typhoons were able to attach themselves at the fighter rendezvous.

Weather improved over snow-drenched France and the formation swept round north of Amiens to run in along the Albert road. Leading 487 Squadron was Wg. Cdr. I. S. Smith, whose bombs pierced the prison's outer wall. Others were equally successful, and the prison doors were shaken free. Quickly 464 Squadron attacked the garrison billets, so successfully that 21 Squadron was told not to attack. Meanwhile the F.P.MU. osquito, which had been orbiting, swept across to take a cine film of the event. Grp. Capt. Pickard also circled, to watch the results of the attack—by which time Typhoons were engaging some Fw 190s. Sqn. Ldr. McRitchie's Mosquito was shot down and moments later Fw 190s apparently finished off Pickard's Mosquito HX922. He and his navigator were buried next day alongside the prison.[1]

Two hundred and fifty-eight prisoners out of 700 escaped including half of those awaiting execution, but many others were shot by the Germans as they fled from the scene of action.

Bad weather then interfered with operations until 24th when the medium bomber squadrons went into action, against flying-bomb sites. During the afternoon the Mitchells had a Typhoon close escort, unusual since some of the Typhoons were carrying bombs. These latter raced ahead, made an attack on the targets, then reinforced the close escort.

Another phase in the build-up for D-Day was initiated for, during the evening, Bostons of 88 Squadron began night flying training. They must be available to operate by night and day in support of the invasion.

Typhoon bombers again formed part of the close escort on 28th. Nos. 226 and 320 Squadrons were briefed to bomb Moyenneville as part of the large *Ramrod 598*. The target for 226 lay near Abbeville. Three Mitchells in the first box dropped 500-pounders—the usual load, although on some targets 1,000-lb. bombs were dropped—on the eastern part of the target. Three in the second box also believed they scored hits, by which time flak was heavy and accurate. They turned, enveloped in bursts. Soon Lt. Hendry U.S.A.A.F. was lagging behind and last seen five miles inland. Flg. Off. Burrows in G: FV910 managed to get his aircraft out of France but had to ditch. Two of the crew, Symons and Crick, were later picked up by a Walrus and the body of Plt. Off. Latress was retrieved next day; of Burrows no trace was found. FV940: C flown by Flt. Sgt. A. B. Mills was badly shot up and caught fire. The navigator, W. Off. Morgan, tackled the fire in the bomb bay and was badly burned.

---

[1] Mosquitoes used in the attack were: *464 Squadron:* F: LR334, U: MM410, V: MM403, A: MM402, T: MM404; *487 Squadron:* R: LR333, T: HX982, H: HX856, Q: HX855, C: HX909, J: HX974, F: HX922 (Pickard).

On one engine Mills nursed the bomber home, to a crash landing at Friston. If the flak was on target—and mercifully this was often not the case—the bombers stood little chance of escape. They could only 'jink' to a small degree when in formation. Fortunately fighters which might then close in as they did in 1940 were absent—and the huge fighter escort was ever at hand.

Throughout March the offensive against flying-bomb sites occupied most of the Group's effort. By night Mosquitoes of Nos. 21, 464, 487 and 613 Squadrons were busily engaged on bomber support *Flower* operations. No. 107 Squadron worked-up on Mosquitoes during the first half of the month, and 305 Squadron remained restricted to daylight operations.

Despite the use of radar aids V-1 sites were still very difficult to destroy, so the very accurate radio aid *Oboe* was brought to bear. On 1 March an experimental raid led by two Mosquitoes of No. 109 Squadron of the Pathfinder Force led half a dozen crews of 21 Squadron in an attack. It was cloudy so the bombing had to be on sky markers. When this method of target marking was next employed, on 6 March, the Forêt des Halles was the target.

The month's operations got boldly under way on 2 March with a four-pronged afternoon *Ramrod*. At 17.48 eighteen Mitchells escorted by a squadron of Spitfire IXs bombed target X/1A/53. Eight minutes later twelve Bostons of 88 and 342 Squadrons ran up on Bois de la Justice. It was cloudy but the flak was nevertheless heavy and accurate. Just after bombing V: BZ308 of 342 Squadron was hit in the starboard engine and dived away on fire, the crew of three baling out. At 18.00 hours eighteen Mitchells of 226 and 320 Squadrons (226 leading) bombed Maisoncelle. Overhead flew a fighter umbrella of two Spitfire IX squadrons. In the final phase came eighteen Mosquitoes flying very low and each carrying four 500-lb. M.C. Mk. IV bombs. Target cover was given by three squadrons of Typhoons two of which were carrying bombs; these they aimed at X/1A/64, and immediately reformed, and continued to give the Mosquitoes fighter support whilst 140 Wing bombed X/1A/101 and 138 Wing X/1A/107.

A complete breakaway from the usual style of operations came on 5 March when Wg. Cdr. Bob Braham (then at Group H.Q.), with the consent of the A.O.C., took a Mosquito of 613 Squadron for an afternoon *Ranger* flight to central France. He flew by way of Fleurs–Florent–Bourges–Avord and at Châteaudun came across a Heinkel 177 at which he fired. It turned into a spin and exploded in a field. Braham flew another *Ranger* on 12th but saw no activity. His most successful exploit came on 24 March when he flew to Denmark. In the vicinity of Aalborg he came across a low-flying Ju 52 with a Bf 109 escort. The enemy fighter pilot lowered his undercarriage to join the Aalborg circuit as Braham roared in to attack from astern. His adversary was soon on fire and blew up on hitting the ground. Braham then chased the

Ju 52 catching it fifteen miles south of Aalborg. He gave it a burst from 1,000 feet and saw pieces fall away in a shower of sparks, then the transport began a gentle spiralling dive. Two more beam attacks were made before the Junkers crashed, inverted, in a marsh and was burnt out. Braham raked the scene for good measure.

A busy period of *Ramrods* came to an end on 6 March, for from 7th to 14th the weather was extremely bad with fog and low cloud over the Continent. In any case much of the Group was about to begin intensive training with the Army, and bombing practice.

Sir Archibald Sinclair, the Air Minister, visited Hartford Bridge on 11th to meet crews of 137 Airfield. Whilst there he decorated four French officers with well-deserved D.F.C.s. These were Wg. Cdr. H. M. de Rancourt who led the August 1943 raid on Rennes naval stores, his navigator Flt. Lt. Pateureau who had been the leading navigator of the very successful raid on Chevilly power station on 3 October when it was completely destroyed, Plt. Off. Roussellat veteran of many of 342's attacks, and Plt. Off. Iozoy.

The period of poor weather marked a useful point at which to review the recent activity. Between 20 December and 12 March the Group had flown 3,357 sorties during 208 attacks and dropped 2,605 tons of bombs. Poor winter weather had caused 787 sorties to be abortive. Another 316 were abandoned when it was impossible to pinpoint targets, whereas only 114 abandonments were due to mechanical failure. Even so $29\frac{1}{2}$ of the V-weapon targets were suspended due to 2 Group attacks, and they shared five more. Although enemy fighters had been almost entirely absent during these raids 25 aircraft and crews had been lost, ten to flak, the others from unknown causes. During 679/997 of their sorties Mosquitoes had attacked dropping 530 tons and causing sixteen targets to be suspended for a loss of thirteen aircraft. A further 104 were damaged, 86 by flak. This gave the low loss rate of 1·3%. Mosquitoes had been extremely successful, one target being suspended for every sixty-two sorties.

Mitchells and Bostons had made 2,363 sorties, 1,200 of which were successful, during which 2,075 tons were dropped. For the loss of twelve aircraft and 198 damaged (all except one by flak) $13\frac{1}{2}$ targets were suspended, one for every 175 sorties. This gave a loss rate of 0·5%. Of the aircraft despatched 8·4% were damaged.

To date 64 V-weapon targets had been suspended, nearly half of them credited to 2 Group, a very notable performance for they were so difficult to hit. Of these, 25% were totally destroyed representing 43% of the total suspension. Air Vice-Marshal Embry in his summing-up wrote, 'This is an achievement of which the Group may well be proud.'

Additionally Mosquitoes had been very active making night intrusions whenever weather permitted. There had been some creditable successes; Flg. Off. Cowen, for instance, bombing an airfield in France then making three more strafing attacks before leaving it. Airfield flak defences were hazardous to the low-flying Mosquitoes as, for instance, when Flt. Lt. Hole of 464 Squadron was attacking a flare-path. His aircraft was hit and after returning on one engine he had to put down on the south coast.

Even if enemy fighters were missing there was still plenty of drama on operations. To find himself hanging out of a Mitchell at 8,000 feet was the hair-raising experience of Flg. Off. Pitchforth, a navigator in 180 Squadron. His formation had just made rendezvous and was crossing the Channel when, the sun being strong, it was decided to dispense with the heating system. Pitchforth turned it off and when returning to his usual position placed his full weight on the escape hatch. He was reaching for the stopcock when the hatch opened. He immediately grabbed a projection and held on. Luck was in, the slipstream trying to close the door. He was able to drag himself in again. A faulty catch had brought him a close shave.

The weather improved and daylight operations were resumed on 15 March with 21 Squadron making another *Highball* attack. It also saw the resumption of operations by 107 Squadron now equipped with Mosquitoes which, led by Wg. Cdr. Pollard, attacked X1/A/42. By the end of the month 107 Squadron had made seven *Noball* attacks and lost only one aircraft, NS856: T which was shot down by a U.S.A.A.F. P-51 over France on 28th.

The next low-level Mosquito precision attack on a target other than a V-weapon site came on 18th. The target was the Hazemeyer electrical equipment factory at Hengelo. Nos. 21, 464 and 487 Squadrons each despatched four Mosquitoes which were accompanied by a Mk. IV of the F.P.U. They took-off mid afternoon but D/487 soon encountered engine trouble and abandoned the operation S.W. of Lowestoft its place taken by a reserve. A low-level attack at 16.35 from heights ranging from 15 to 300 feet in two boxes was made, one coming from the north the other from N.E. Their 46 M.C. Mk. IV 11-sec. delay bombs soon started a large fire in the main building and two columns of smoke from the centre building towered to over 1,000 feet. There was considerable tracer directed at the leading box and guns firing almost horizontally engaged them as they turned away after attack. More firing came from the roof of one of the buildings. Coloured tracer curled upwards, red from fields to the N.W. and yellow from a truck on the railway to the north. As they flew off the raiders fired their cannon into barges in the Gorr area. Two aircraft were damaged by flak and Sqn. Ldr. Sugden's aircraft, hit in an engine, was shot down.

A planned Mustang escort had been late so the Mosquitoes proceeded without it. The first box led by Wg. Cdr. Iredale achieved only limited success but the second box, leader Sqn. Ldr. Ritchie, did extremely well. Despite heavy haze over Holland navigation was extremely good. The attack was well concentrated in the centre of the Hazemeyer Works and there was widespread destruction of major buildings. A fire in the impregnating shops spread. Much of the metal-working shop was gutted, the nickelling shop was burnt out and the main gear-grinding shop badly damaged. Two stock rooms containing signalling equipment were destroyed, the main machine shop half wiped out and the main metal-working shop hit. The nearby Ven Brega Stork works was also hit. Wg. Cdr. Reynolds flying the F.P.U. Mosquito obtained some good photos. Among those taking part was Flg. Off. Monihan who was on his fourth visit to Hengelo in a Mosquito.

Earlier in the day a new venture had been tried. The weather did not look too good but, led by Wg. Cdr. J. F. Castle, 180 Squadron headed for Pevensey to formate. Here three crews could not locate the formation, but the other nine proceeded without any fighter escort, relying on two Spitfire IX squadrons for top cover over the target Domart en Ponthieu. Despite the absence of close escort no enemy fighters appeared and there was little flak. But the target was very small, and despite the excellent conditions the bombs fell in a line error to port.

In the afternoon 320 Squadron led by J. N. Mulder set off for Gorenflos. After dropping 64 500-lb. bombs in a good concentration eight aircraft were damaged by flak. H: FR180 flown by Sgt. J. H. Ot was shot down, also N: FR159, pilot Lt. Voorspij. Ditching a Mitchell successfully for the crew to escape was quite feasible if the crew knew their dinghy drills. Both these crews did and were helped by rapid assistance given by the A.S.R. squadron at Hawkinge. Ot ditched a few miles from France yet a Sea Otter landed and picked up the whole crew. With so many aboard it could not take-off so had to taxi for four hours across the Channel until it met an A.S.R. launch which took them to Dover. Ot's Mitchell had been in a bad way with the nose perspex broken, a two-foot-square hole on the starboard side of the bomb aimer's compartment, the port engine on fire extinguished after the propeller was feathered, the starboard engine out of action, only five degrees of elevator left, ailerons put out of order and the instrument panel smashed. Ot's performance was outstanding. Two of the crew were wounded and Ot was at 9,000 feet. Unlike some crews this one braved up to realising they could not make home and so prepared for ditching. It was often fatal to do dinghy drill at the last moment, but here was a disciplined crew taking early and wise action. With flaps out of order and little elevator control, the Mitchell flattened out at the bottom of a glide, hit the water at about 160 knots—with quite a wallop— and suffered violent deceleration. Already the hatches were open and the crew quickly entered the dinghy released from outside by the pilot. The aircraft sank within two minutes, but by then they were safely away. They were two hours in the dinghy, but only after Spitfires began circling them did they open their escape and survival kits. Their experiences were somewhat heightened when an American B-17 jettisoned five large bombs about 500 yards away, lifting the frail little dinghy out of the water. Ot and crew had regularly done their dinghy drill, and were now thankful for it.

Voorspuy's aircraft had been in better state and he managed to get nearer home. He was at 13,000 feet when he decided to ditch. His aircraft had a large hole in the bomb aimer's compartment, he could not feather his troublesome starboard engine, his hydraulics had packed up, one wheel hung down and his flaps became stuck at 25 degrees. Try as he might he just could not move them. His aircraft hit the water at 98 m.p.h. It floated for five minutes and the crew again were able to get away. Within an hour they were picked up by a Walrus and safely taken to Hawkinge.

As well as operating by day the Mitchell squadrons began night flying, needed for their part in Operation *Overlord*. On 22 March the order was issued for Exercise *Night Light* 'to carry out experiments for the best means of night attacks on road convoys'. The order stated: 'Technique for trial involves dropping flares and other pyrotechnics from one force of aircraft to illuminate the target so that a synchronised attack can be carried out by a second force. For the purpose of the trial a formation of Mitchells of 98 Squadron will launch flares in the air and other illuminations will be fired statically on the ground, whilst a token force of Mosquitoes will represent the striking force.' The object of the trials was to compare lighting techniques, to assess the number of each type required to illuminate the road convoy and, if possible, formulate tactics for illuminators and strike force, ascertaining the merits of attack from medium and low levels.

Trials were set for a suitable night at the end of March. Before 98 Squadron moved to the Group Practice Camp (Swanton Morley), members of the squadron visited Ramsbury to obtain some information about night formation operations. They watched Dakotas towing off Horsas in darkness—if anyone could do *that* then 98 Squadron could fly night formations.

Just before trials took place a sudden urgent switch in Group activities was ordered. The Mitchell and Boston squadrons were thrown into an attack on Creil marshalling yards. The intention had been all along that 2 Group should participate in the pre-invasion assault on the French rail network. This had been interrupted by *Crossbow* which had taken most of the Group effort since November. Creil was 25 miles north-east of Paris, a deeper penetration of France than of late.

On the night of 29–30 March nine Mitchells of 98 Squadron carried out the planned night trials over the Potlington–Froghill road north of Thetford. The 'attack' was upon twenty vehicles, each aircraft dropping 24 4·5-inch flares. These they released from 9,000 feet and 'they seemed to light up the whole of Norfolk'. A few moments later Grp. Capt. Wykeham Barnes and Wg. Cdr. Braham made mock attacks to assess the effectiveness of such tactics. It all seemed very successful. A few moments later red target indicators were fired on the ground, and other colours were tried. The night's work was highly portentous, for the tactics resulting were to be employed night after night by Mosquito squadrons.

All the great names of 2 Group gathered at Group H.Q. on 31 March to hear about the trials. The A.O.C. spoke giving his opinion after the trials. He said, 'As far as I can see, attacks on roads probably fall into complementary phases—(1) attacks to interrupt enemy traffic, (2) single Mosquitoes on intruder patrol attacking small targets and making harassing attacks, (3) attacking large targets from intelligence sources, illuminated by flare-carrying force, with attacks from medium altitude by any type of aircraft and (4) follow-up attacks on any successes achieved.'

If the Mitchells were to operate by night they would need to keep their navigation lights on. It seemed desirable to enlarge the flare slings to carry five flares each. The O.C. 140 Wing considered the illumination sufficient for attacks from even as low as fifty feet, but he had difficulty in identifying the type of vehicle. He had been flying at 3,000 feet three miles away and by listening to the commentary could anticipate the moment of flare ignition. His only difficulty was, in his first attack, 'to line up his aircraft with the direction of the road'. Visibility under flares he likened to a misty afternoon in winter.

Throughout March the Mosquito squadrons had continued their low-level and shallow-dive attacks on V-weapon sites. These were often extremely hazardous for the crews flew exceedingly low facing intense light flak. At such low levels target identification was difficult even if bombing accuracy was good. On 24 March 487 Squadron ventured to bomb Freval. 'C' Charlie was so low it hit telegraph wires near Belleville and had to turn for home. The other two went into the attack but after circling found they had bombed Bois Robert. Flt. Lt. J. H. W. Yeats then received flak damage which ripped away a large piece of the aircraft tail, but he managed to get home safely.

The next large-scale attack on a target other than a *Noball* came on 26 March. The change of targets brought no regrets, since these taxing raids had an element of monotony. It was considered that by late March the offensive had appreciably cut back the building of these sites. What in January seemed an immediate threat was now a forcibly postponed one. A limited number of sites was being re-established, but it was considered that pre-invasion operations were now more important.

E-boat pens were being rapidly completed at the Dutch port of Ijmuiden. Once complete they would afford shelter to many E-boats that could take a considerable toll of our shipping. So important seemed the threat that this time most of the medium force of 2 Group was to join in a forty minutes' four-wave attack with an armada of 378 B-26 Marauders of the U.S. 9th Air Force.

Take-off was shortly after midday. The bombers met their fighter escort over Yarmouth then flew straight to the target. Leading was

Wg. Cdr. Lynn at the head of three Mitchell squadrons. (226 did not take part, being at this time at A.P.C. Swanton Morley.) Heading the two Boston squadrons was Wg. Cdr. Maher of 88 Squadron. The formation was spotted by the enemy when out to sea and in the opinion of 180 Squadron 'the gunners of Ijmuiden literally rubbed their hands in joyful anticipation. What a reception they gave our aircraft, seven of which were damaged.' The attack went in at 13.32 hours at 11,000 feet, the first bombs overshooting the target. Others fell to the N.E. and on wharfs. 320 Squadron, with Burgerhout at the head, claimed a few hits with 1,000-pounders on the E-boat pens.

Three minutes later the Bostons attacked with 500-pounders but again most bombs fell wide, some in Heering and the nearby harbour. A third of the aircraft were damaged.

March ended with one of the large-scale exercises training crews for the forthcoming landings in France. These extended into late April under the general title Exercise *Smash*, the principal purpose of which was to practise and develop fire support against a defended coast in support of the Army and Navy.

For the first seven days of April the weather was so bad that no daylight operations were possible, and when a Mitchell attack on Hirson was billed for 8th it had to be abandoned. This operation however set the scene for the first series in April, for marshalling yards at Monceau sur Sambre and Charleroi were attacked by Mitchells and Bostons. The Monceau raid was particularly effective, many 500-pounders falling on loco sheds and railway yards.

On 11 April Mosquitoes of 613 Squadron, led by Wg. Cdr. R. N. Bateson in a low-level attack, destroyed the Dutch Population Central Registry in Scheveningsche Wegg, near the Peace Palace in The Hague. German records of the Dutch Resistance were kept in a five-storey house some 95 feet high. On to it were hurled 500-lb. delayed action H.E.s and incendiaries. Operating from Swanton Morley, the Mosquitoes flew in a lo-hi-lo profile. The first pair of aircraft dropped 30-second-delay bombs then the next two went in with incendiaries. Such was the smoke that only one could locate. The fifth dropped a mixed load, but the sixth had to abandon the operation. All that was left of the building was a heap of smouldering debris. Not one Dutch civilian outside the building was killed, and only one window smashed in the Peace Palace.

It was now accepted policy that the Mitchells and Bostons would support the landings in France with night operations. An intensive night training scheme needed to be run—and with crews operating daily this posed considerable problems. Some experience of night operations before D-Day was desirable and on 11–12 April 226 Squadron flew the first Mitchell night intruder sorties. Sqn. Ldr. Cooper raided Gail airfield bombing on his fourth run, but the other two aircraft had to abandon their attempts.

Much of the Mosquito effort was currently at night in support of

M2

Bomber Command Main Force operations, Nos. 21, 305, 487 and 613 Squadrons concentrating on *Flowers*. Occasionally, when the clouds were low, *Day Rangers* by pairs of Mosquitoes were flown, and on 7 April on one of these Sqn. Ldr. Bodien and Flt. Lt. Taylor of 21 Squadron hunting in the Bayeux-Châteauroux area came across three staff cars which they strafed. Their principal target was the Panzer divisional H.Q. at Laval which they could not locate; instead they shot up covered wagons, a large army camp and flak cars.

12 April saw the next Mosquito special operation. Two targets had been chosen, both important locomotive repair centres. 107 Squadron led by Wg. Cdr. Pollard was to attack Hirson. 487 Squadron's target was at Haine St. Pierre in Belgium. Rendezvous was, as often, made over Littlehampton where two Typhoon escort squadrons (197 for 107 Squadron and 609 for 487 Squadron) were picked up. The entire formation, sixteen Mosquitoes, set course in pairs and their escort crossed the Channel at fifty feet soaring to 5,000 at the enemy coast at Toqueville. Over enemy territory both Mosquito squadrons kept together until close to their targets, when they descended to 3,000 feet. The attack on Hirson proved the more fruitful. The target was sighted in excellent weather at 13.57 hours and there was no opposition. Both leading aircraft dived to 400 feet peppering the target's roof with cannon fire, and placing 500-lb. 11-sec. delay bombs on four buildings. The remainder waded in (and only 'L' Love had any hang-ups), as a result of which the target was obliterated. After bombing they made a low-level getaway and Nos. 1 and 2 started a leisurely climb for home to allow the formation to close. Flak had opened up seriously damaging the aircraft leading the second pair but the performance of the excellent machine was unimpaired.

The attack by 487 Squadron was less successful since the target was difficult to locate, being set amongst numerous slag heaps. Four aircraft bombed the target area on a low-level pass, two sighted it too late and two others dropped their bombs on an airfield near Furnes.

There were many crews who would have liked to take part in a Mosquito *Ranger*, but this was barely 2 Group's job although from time to time experienced crews obtained the official go-ahead. One inveterate intruder was Wg. Cdr. Bob Braham; another was Flt. Lt. Gregory. The two of them obtained the go-ahead for a *Ranger* on 13th. They crept into the north of Denmark and soon found an ancient He 111 orbiting a G.C.I. beacon near Esberg; it exploded as it hit the sea. Later they came across a Fw 58 but as they closed to fire two Bf 109s appeared. They shot down the '58, but tracer from the fighters was soon whipping past. They quickly took cloud cover. Commenting on the episode in one of his periodical reviews of operations, the A.O.C. said, 'Ranging is not a normal 2 Group job, it is only undertaken at odd times by experienced crews. Intending applicants therefore relax!'

It was 464 Squadron's turn on 15th for a low-level attack, on a rail installation at St. Ghislain, near Mons. It was quite an effective operation carried out low level throughout. Goods depots and wagon repair shops were hit by bombs from four aircraft, although the leader and his No. 2 abandoned the raid taking the wrong course over enemy territory. Next day the three squadrons of 140 Wing (Nos. 21, 464 and 487) began their move to Gravesend to be better placed for operations.

With the invasion nearing, the Supreme Allied Commander, General Dwight Eisenhower, visited Hartford Bridge on 18th. He congratulated the crews of 88, 342 and 226 Squadrons on their recent operations and explained what future operations would entail. Afterwards he went to Dunsfold to talk to more Mitchell crews. Whilst he was there Sqn. Ldr. Knowles and Flt. Lt. Bance of 88 Squadron gave him a smoke-laying demonstration showing their skill at what would be one of their D-Day tasks.

After lunch all the medium bomber squadrons stood by for operations. There had been a foggy spell but now the weather was clearer. Six squadrons were once more directed on to flying bomb sites. These had not of late figured in the target manifestos. But there had been no abatement in building and repairing the V-1 sites. For the next eight days a hefty series of attacks was delivered in an attempt to destroy them. It was 98's turn the following night to attempt night operations for the first time and by way of an experiment Mosquitoes dropped flares on a *Noball* target for two Mitchells to bomb.

No. 305 Polish Squadron that evening had despatched six pairs of Mosquitoes to the heavy artillery position in the Ourville-la-Rivière area. They met very intense light flak in the target area and Flt. Lt. Rayski's aircraft hit on the way in had to be put down at Friston. The leader, Wg. Cdr. K. Konopasek, with his navigator Sqn. Ldr. J. Lagowski, whose aircraft had been hit when crossing the coast, continued to lead the operation. He had heard a loud detonation, but detected no fault in the aircraft. When recrossing the coast his Mosquito Z/824 was again hit and heavily damaged, but it still brought him safely home.

Whilst Mitchells and Bostons hit the V-1 sites by day Mosquitoes operated against airfields by night. No. 107 Squadron was taken off operations on 20th for a week's intensive training at Swanton Morley, the Group A.P.C. Here the aim was to train crews for attacks on road and railway targets using the expertise they had acquired during night intruder sorties. The latter were never without moments of excitement and when Flg. Off. D. Bell Irving crossed the south coast NS837's wing tip hit a barrage balloon cable. The effectiveness of this form of defence as regards the number of enemy aircraft it brought down was poor; it claimed far more friendly aircraft. Bell Irving, like many others, was able to control the aircraft after the collision so well that he went on to score a hit on his target!

It was now 487's turn for a spell under canvas for night interdictor training with the Army from Swanton Morley. Meanwhile 107 Squadron took part in three more special daylight operations. The first was a cloud-cover operation against locomotive repair and maintenance sheds at Mantes, a small town on the Seine fifteen miles west of Paris. Four pairs were detailed to dive-bomb the target and by the time that the last pair was attacking the flak was heavy. Flying low over an enemy airfield on the way back Sqn. Ldr. Brittain's aircraft was hit on a spinner and he had to return on one engine. As Flt. Sgt. Smith touched down in OM-G: NS836 his starboard tyre burst, the oleo collapsed and the aircraft was badly damaged although repairable. 107's next day raid was an attack on Heudière near Le Torp-Mesnil, and led by Sqn. Ldr. Wallington. *Gee* failed in the lead aircraft and the coast was crossed ten miles from the intended point. After course alterations had been made the target was found. No. 5 was just turning on to target when he saw Flg. Off. Hadley, who was diving very low, catch his leader's slipstream and crash into the ground at very high speed. Bombing results were generally poor, so next day the raid was repeated and many hits were scored on the site.

The following night, during the course of night flying practice near the North Foreland, a crew saw an aircraft without recognition lights flying away from the London area and taking evasive action. As a raid was in progress, and German marker flares were in evidence, they flew to investigate. Believing it to be a Do 217 the pilot opened fire . . . and soon a Mitchell of 320 Squadron was making a forced landing. Its navigator baled out and the rest of the crew were safe but for a severe shock. 107 Squadron began night intruder operations at the end of April.

Between 26 and 29 April marshalling yards were again the principal 2 Group targets although some sorties were again directed at heavy gun batteries. The main novelty was the *Highball* operation in which Mosquitoes of No. 8 P.F.F. Group led Mosquitoes of 140 Wing in high-level attacks, from around 20,000 feet, on Abancourt and Serquex marshalling yards, under the watchful eyes of Spitfires of 11 Group. It was of only limited success.

Of much more import was Exercise *Nightlight II* held on the night of 25–26 April to test to the full the pattern of events to be undertaken at night once the invasion had been mounted. Mitchells of 98 Squadron were ordered to drop flares over two large areas of East Anglia and in the Warminster–Salisbury region, each Mitchell unloading 24 5-inch flares. On seeing any movement by the land forces involved, a Mitchell had to call up a Mosquito of 138 or 140 Wing which then made a dummy attack. The results were highly successful and permitted final formulation of the pattern of attack to be adopted in the subsequent night campaign.

A Special Flight was at this time added to 226 Squadron. Its Mitchells—six in number—were specially fitted out at Hornchurch and Cranfield and bristled with additional aerials. They were to operate, following the landings in France, over central France dropping leaflets by night and occasionally by day, and making radio contact with special agents and the French underground, picking up useful intelligence material on troop movements. Their crews needed to fly very accurately for up to three-hour sorties.

May started with a swing, with the Mitchell squadrons penetrating deep into Belgium to attack marshalling yards then turning their attention to Serquex for a *Gee-H* led raid. By night the Mosquito intruders were busy. Flt. Lt. K. Rach of 305 had Le Culot as his target, could not find it so instead attacked another airfield where the defences scored on his Mosquito 929-V. With the port engine badly damaged and glycol streaming he was lucky to make Bradwell where he was forced to belly-land.

Next day the Mitchells made another deep penetration to Namur marshalling yards and, except for two occasions when gun positions were attacked and when *Noballs* were bombed, the Mitchell and Boston squadrons carried out an intensive offensive against railway targets until 15 May, targets including Cambrai carriage and wagon works, engine sheds at Monceau sur Sambre, marshalling yards at Abancourt, Tourcoing and Douai.

On 5 May during a raid on the locomotive sheds at Cambrai it fell to Flt. Lt. Bance of 88 Squadron to introduce a Boston IV BZ449: RH-P into operations. Eight Mk. IVs arrived during March, BZ402 the first of 49 for 2 Group reaching Britain on 16 March 1944. The first Mk. IVs were allotted to the two Boston squadrons on 25 April 1944. BZ449 went on 1 May to 88 Squadron where Wg. Cdr. Maher did familiarisation and trials flying. 342 Squadron accepted BZ422.

It was immediately apparent that the new version with its re-contoured nose from which framing had been eliminated, and the long-awaited dorsal Glen Martin turret carrying two M.2 0·5 in. machine guns, was a quite different aeroplane to the much admired Mk. III and IIIA. General flying characteristics had deteriorated noticeably, especially manoeuvres controlled by the rudder and elevators. The Mk. IV lacked good longitudinal and directional stability, and gone was the favoured excellent control response. Fortunately the attrition rate of the Mk. IIIA was fairly low and so the Mk. IV trickled into the two squadrons at a slow rate, although by the end of the year Mk. IVs outnumbered the IIIAs on operations.

Mosquito *Rangers* periodically continued, Flt. Lt. W. J. Bodington flying LR366: L of 613 Squadron to the Châteaudun–Orleans area on 16 May. He shot up three flak positions very effectively near Châteaudun. On 19th the same squadron managed two *Rhubarb* operations against the navigation beam stations at Lanmeur and Sortosville. Flak was heavy during the second operation and Flt. Lt. M. R. Muir in LR370-Y had to ditch his aircraft which was burning from flak hits. Other Mosquito crews of 21 and 487 Squadrons were meanwhile doing a high-level raid led by 8 Group on the *Noball* target at Yvrenche Conteville.

After taking part in Exercise *Fabian* 88 Squadron withdrew to Swanton

Morley on 6 May for army support training and to practise smoke laying. The culmination of this training came on 28 May when an army demonstration was given on Salisbury Plain during which the Army fired smoke marker shells and many 2 Group aircraft flew overhead to observe this style of indication to be used when the Army wanted very close support and marked targets a few yards ahead of its front line in France.

On two more days Mitchells hammered away at gun positions some of which could interfere with the invasion. With these damaged, and the railway network in France severely battered by the Allied Air Forces, 2 Group next turned its attention to airfields from which the enemy might interfere with the invasion soon to come, while Mosquitoes continued to attack coastal gun positions. By night they carried on their offensive against enemy airfields.

Three days of airfield bombing by Mitchells and Bostons took place from 23 to 25 May, targets being at Dinant/Pluertit, Evreux, Lille/Vendeville and Chièvres. During the latter raid 226 Squadron carried out a very effective raid on the Officers' Mess at Châteaux Bauffe. Flak was heavy and the fighter escort took a caning. Five squadrons of Spitfire Vs gave close escort whilst two of Mk. IXs wheeled overhead during the five-minute raid. The pattern of the raid consisted of 24 Bostons of 137 Wing leading, followed by 24 Mitchells of 139 Wing and twelve from 137 Wing flying as two boxes of eighteen aircraft 139 Wing leading. The same day Nos. 21 and 487 Mosquito Squadrons carried out a high-level raid on guns at St. Cecily guided by *Gee-H*, after which the Mosquito squadrons flew almost entirely night interdictor or intruder missions and came off day raids.

27 May was a very busy day for the medium squadrons, as the offensive against guns and airfields approached its climax. Two large operations were flown in three phases, each formation being escorted by three squadrons of Spitfire Vs whilst above giving top cover were two of Mk. IXs. 98 Squadron was detailed to attack Courmeilles over which, for the first time, a squadron of Tempest Vs was supporting a 2 Group operation. 180's target was the fuel dump at Creil. Leading was Wg. Cdr. Ford who, despite being hit by flak in the port aileron, carried on his bomb run so that the squadron obtained a good bomb concentration on the aiming point and across the airfield. Heavy flak was encountered which continued to burst among the bombers on the way home damaging two more. Ford's aircraft, FW115, became increasingly difficult to manage and he was forced to put down at Friston. Later the squadrons operated against gun positions.

Further smoke practice was undertaken by 88 on 28 May, after which the two Boston squadrons aimed their bombs on heavy guns at Gravelines. 226 Squadron had twelve aircraft flying with six of 139 Wing with guns at Marck as its target. Just after bombing Sqn. Ldr. Cooper found himself almost colliding with another Mitchell and had to quickly take evasive action which began with a roll followed by a stall. Then he was spinning down. Two bombs were jettisoned safe in the sea before FW 130 could recover from the manoeuvre.

Next day the raids on the guns continued with the Bostons bombing Quand as well as the marshalling yards at Monceau.

The weather was fine and warm and the Mitchells were sent, on 30th, to a small but vital target, a bridge at Courcelles sur Seine. It was difficult to locate, let alone hit, and the bombs overshot into a large nearby building which burnt for many hours. The attackers tried again in the afternoon when the lead navigator mistook the lock gates and dam at Notre Dame Garenn. This time the load undershot causing great havoc in a factory and destroying a petrol store. This finished the Group's preparation work for *Overlord* and the squadrons all withdrew for intensive night flying training. For the ground crews the task was now to prepare the aircraft for maximum effort with 100% serviceability.

Between 21 December 1943 and 31 May 1944, 2 Group flew 4,710 sorties against *Noball* targets losing 41 aircraft. Another 419 were variously damaged by flak. About one-fifth of the attacks were delivered at low level which called for careful routing. Targets were allocated depending upon the likely anti-aircraft fire. Out of a total of 103 targets suspended, 2 Group was credited with 32 whilst the U.S.A.A.F. B-17s and B-24s destroyed 35—the only people to do better, but for far more effort. The American A-20s and B-26s were credited with 28 and fighter-bombers 8. But of all these the achievement of the 2 Group Mosquitoes was quite exceptional. They needed only 39·8 tons of bombs per target suspended whereas the Bostons used on average 344·3 tons, Mitchells 224·5 tons, B-26s 223·5 tons, B-17s 195 tons and B-24s 401 tons. In the course of about the same number of sorties as 2 Group the fighter-bombers lost 27 aircraft and suspended only five targets.

During May, when the weight of attack fell mainly on pre-invasion targets, 2 Group's mediums made 23 attacks on rail centres, nine on airfields, two on a bridge and only eleven on V-1 sites. Mosquitoes eight times raided radio beam stations, five times rail targets, four times gun positions and three times V-sites. During the course of five *Ranger* operations they claimed two enemy aircraft. But the Mosquito effort was mainly by night when 244 sorties were directed against 59 airfield targets supporting Bomber Command Main Force operations.

All was now set for the greatest invasion of all time. Air Vice-Marshal Basil Embry had his Mosquitoes specially trained for night interdiction work and indeed the whole of 2 Group could operate by night and day. Tactical training had prepared it to closely support the Army in the way the A.O.C. wished. The smoke layers were prepared to screen the assault on the enemy shore. All was ready; only the weather might interfere—and interfere it did.

Chapter 21
Unlocking the Gates of Europe

Months of planning 2 Group's contribution to *Overlord* were explained in Operations Order No. 3 of 3 June 1944. It outlined plans agreed by T.A.F. and A.E.A.F. in these words:

'Intention: To cause maximum delay to the movement by road and rail by enemy forces at night in the area prescribed. General plan: All Mitchell and Mosquito squadrons in the Group will be used, throughout the hours of darkness, to delay enemy road movements in the following inclusive areas: Lessay–Caen–Lisieux–Argentan–Domfont–Fougères–Avranches. Any movement is to be attacked whenever seen in the area, but particular attention is to be concentrated on the following roads: Avranches–Coutances–Lessay; Fougères–Vire–St. Lo; Domfont–Flers–Caen; Argentan–Falaise–Caen; Evreux–Lisieux–Caen.

'*Mitchells* will be employed to attack static targets decided upon as a result of tactical information received from various sources. Attacks will be carried out by one or other of the following methods:

i. Aircraft fitted with *Gee-H* to bomb or as pathfinders to illuminate the target by means of flares or TIs for attack by non-*Gee-H* fitted aircraft.

ii. Aircraft not fitted with *Gee-H* to make individual but closely co-ordinated attacks on static targets visually by the light of flares or TIs dropped by pathfinders.

iii. In suitable weather, and moon conditions, flying independently to attack selected targets by visual means.

'*Mosquitoes:* The primary role of these squadrons is to attack all road movements as detailed, particularly that of thin skinned vehicles as distinct from AFVs. It remains to be seen whether the differentiation between the types of vehicles will be possible. These attacks will be carried out by one of the following methods depending on conditions of moon, weather and visibility:

i. By low flying attack with cannon, machine gun and bombs using the cat's eye method against enemy vehicles, convoys and roads.

ii. Similar attacks but against targets marked or illuminated by pathfinders as in *Nightlight*.

'*Bostons:* As these aircraft have no radar navigation aids it is intended only to operate them in good weather, moonlight and good visibility.

In these circumstances it is probable their efforts will be directed to supplement that of the Mosquitoes. As these maintain visual bombing of not easily identifiable targets it necessitates flying at lower than the normal medium altitude to avoid damage by their own bombs. Attacks will, however, have to be made at altitudes of not less than 1,000 feet. These conditions may well restrict the number of occasions upon which Bostons can be used.'

The two Mosquito Wings 138 and 140 were to be allotted 'tennis courts' in approximately equal proportions for each night's operations. They were to maintain, if possible, continuous patrols by single aircraft over each 'tennis court' throughout the hours of darkness. In addition each Wing was to maintain an airborne reserve of two additional aircraft whilst resources permitted. Length of each sortie in the 'tennis court' area was reckoned as about thirty minutes. If at the end of this time no attack on enemy movement had been made the aircraft would bomb a given static point, then return to base for re-arming. The airborne reinforcement aircraft were to spend an hour over the area and if not called upon to attack would then raid a static target. It was estimated that the effort of any one squadron would be to maintain patrol over a complete Wing area of five 'tennis courts' for one hour, i.e. two sorties of thirty minutes each in each of five tennis courts plus two held in the airborne reserve. Remaining aircraft in any squadron—approximately six—would be held at readiness to fill any gaps in the programme caused by short patrol times due to frequency of attacks. The operations rooms would have to feed the Mosquitoes into 'tennis courts' or waiting areas.

With so many aircraft operating almost individually at night careful flight planning was demanded. Two corridors to the scene of action were laid down: one from Bridport–Alderney–Cap de la Lague and entry via the west coast of the Cherbourg Peninsula south of point 49° 10′ N, the other the easterly route from Bexhill to between St. Valéry en Caux–Verlets–Yvetot and Montford.

During the morning of 5 June crews of the two Boston squadrons practised smoke laying. At 14.00 hours they assembled in the crew rooms and their squadron commanders informed them that they were confined to camp, and that all outgoing mail would be censored. It was obvious something special was afoot. It could only be the invasion.

They stood by in Messes and tented sites until late evening, by which time their aircraft had been loaded with SCI gear and smoke canisters and were now gaily decorated with black and white 'invasion stripes' after the manner ordered at 14.30 hours. At 20.00 hours the battle order was drawn up and the squadrons informed that they would be called for breakfast at 01.30 on 6th and their navigators briefed at 02.00, and that there would be a main briefing at 02.30. Operations would be at first light, and of utmost importance.

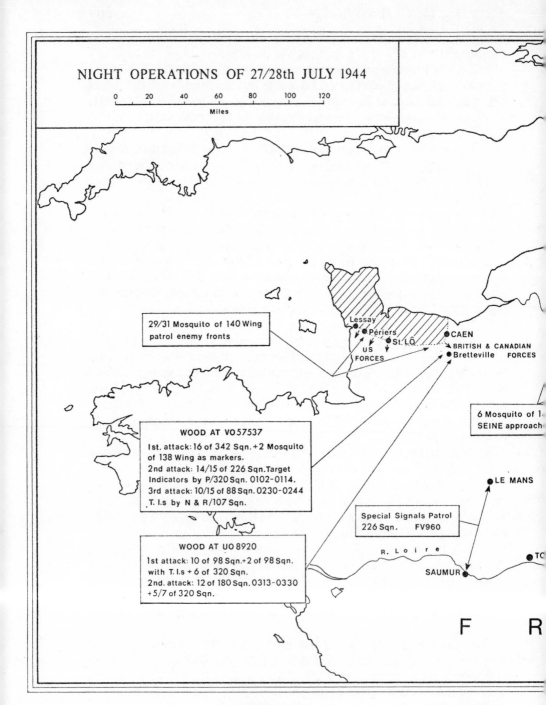

NIGHT OPERATIONS OF 27/28th JULY 1944

0   20   40   60   80   100   120
Miles

29/31 Mosquito of 140 Wing
patrol enemy fronts

Lessay
Périers
St. LÔ
US
FORCES
CAEN
BRITISH & CANADIAN
Bretteville   FORCES

6 Mosquito of 1
SEINE approach

WOOD AT VO 57537
1st. attack: 16 of 342 Sqn. + 2 Mosquito
of 138 Wing as markers.
2nd attack: 14/15 of 226 Sqn. Target
Indicators by P/320 Sqn. 0102-0114.
3rd attack: 10/15 of 88 Sqn. 0230-0244
T. I.s by N & R/107 Sqn.

WOOD AT UO 8920
1st attack: 10 of 98 Sqn. + 2 of 98 Sqn.
with T. I.s + 6 of 320 Sqn.
2nd. attack: 12 of 180 Sqn. 0313-0330
+ 5/7 of 320 Sqn.

Special Signals Patrol
226 Sqn.   FV960

LE MANS

R. Loire

SAUMUR

TO

F   R

MAP 18. *See Appendix 12, page 511 for notes*

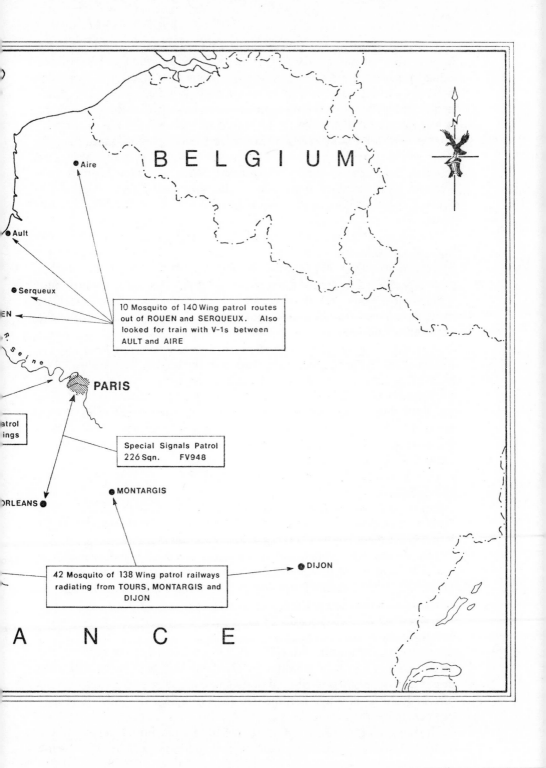

BELGIUM

● Aire

● Ault

● Serqueux

EN

R. Seine

PARIS

10 Mosquito of 140 Wing patrol routes
out of ROUEN and SERQUEUX. Also
looked for train with V-1s between
AULT and AIRE

atrol
ings

Special Signals Patrol
226 Sqn.   FV948

● MONTARGIS

ORLEANS ●

● DIJON

42 Mosquito of 138 Wing patrol railways
radiating from TOURS, MONTARGIS and
DIJON

A   N   C   E

The plan revealed was that 88 Squadron would screen with smoke a huge seaborne landing force from attack by guns at Le Havre. 342 Squadron would provide smoke to screen the landing force from defences on the eastern side of the Cherbourg Peninsula. The latter demanded a 10,000 yard long screen as soon as possible after dawn when it was thought that the sea forces would be visible from the shore. The 10,000 yard long smokescreen was twice the maximum length one aircraft could provide, and so 342's crews operated in pairs every ten minutes, the second aircraft beginning when the first aircraft had released from its third container. Fully briefed the crews waited for take-off shortly before dawn. Meanwhile the Mosquito force was already busy.

The great campaign to be waged almost nightly against enemy road and rail movement ahead of the Allied armies opened at 22.00 hours on 5 June with the take-off of the first Mosquitoes. Ninety-eight Mosquitoes were that night despatched from six squadrons, ninety of them bombing villages and road and rail junctions in Normandy. There was little movement since the operation had been kept highly secret. Mitchells attacked specific points.

Wg. Cdr. Maher was the first of the Boston force to take-off. He headed straight for the planned position of the mighty fleet, approached at 300 feet, descended to sea level and began his smoke run at exactly 05.00 hours off Cap Barfleur. The warships were a little further east than had been intended, and so when the aircraft turned left after smoke laying it came within range of shore-based flak batteries which were to fire at several aircraft. Some were also fired upon by six E-boats which came out of Le Havre. In the ensuing confusion one of 88's eighteen aircraft was fired upon by our ships and W. Off. Boyle's aircraft fell to enemy flak.

But the task was well done, and the first detail was then reloaded for a further operation which was not called for. All day they stood at forty minutes' readiness until 23.00 hours and stand-down.

The smoke runs were soon being made from 1½ miles east of the monitor *Robert*, third warship from the north end of the Fleet facing Le Havre, other aircraft following at ten minutes interval although the smoke drifted fast due to the high surface wind.

Ten crews of 342 Squadron completed the operation as planned, although one aircraft hit the water half way along its run and abandoned the sortie, whilst another inexplicably plunged into the sea north of the laying area. The first casualties in *Overlord* had been sustained. 'No doubt the operation contributed in no small measure to the total success of that historic landing,' commented the Group Commander in a later message to the Group.

During daylight hours 2 Group rested. In the initial stages of the landing it had an exclusively night role. It was expected that by evening the enemy response would be considerable and that to avoid our fighter-bombers he would bring forward troops in reserve and transport under darkness. Immediately ahead of the slender footholt in France Mosquitoes roved in over roads in the area Bayeux–Carentan–Granville–Avranches–Bayeux. To the east over the Caen–Lisieux–Evreux–Dreux–Alençon–Caen area flew more Mosquitoes and a third force scoured in a wide arc from Argentan to Pontorson. Thus the battle zone was sealed from night reinforcement. 122/129 Mosquitoes attacked using 486 500-lb. bombs. Numerous vehicles were shot up including a convoy a mile long. Sixty Mitchells from the four squadrons operated, 49 of them dropping 204 1,000-lb. bombs on the villages of Villers Bocage and Falaise, on a bridge at Dives and in a defile through Thury Harcourt, a village that was to be repeatedly attacked. Of twelve Bostons briefed to bomb Mézidon only two attacked, four going to the secondary, Lisieux, and three to targets of opportunity.

The order for night operations held and on 7–8 June some tempting railway targets became available. Mitchells were despatched to troop-detraining points at Villedieu, Vire and Flers whilst Bostons dropped 20-lb. anti-personnel bombs at Folligny. Fifty-three Mosquitoes of 21, 464 and 487 Squadrons sought out M.E.T. (mechanised enemy transport) and troops in a disc centred roughly on Argentan and extending to Domfort and Lisieux, whilst another seventy from 107, 305 and 613 Squadrons operated to the west, sealing approaches to the battle zone. Other Mitchells and Bostons bombed Mézidon.

By now the enemy was well aware of the risk of night movement, and he won respite only when it rained on 8–9 June. The main effort then was against nine Normandy railway stations whilst thirty Mosquitoes patrolled roads in the Caen–Vire–St. Remy–Falaise area. The bad weather meant that the Mosquitoes had to fly low over dangerous terrain. Their crews needed to develop 'cat's eyes' to detect slight movement of troops, vehicles and trains. Next night only 37 Mosquito sorties were possible.

Beneath the protecting clouds the enemy had brought along tank reinforcements, and now 2 Group swung partly over to its other role of close army support. A tank concentration had been discovered at the Château de La Caine, Panzer H.Q. for the Panzer Group West. An operation was laid on for 14.00 hours on 10 June, but thick cloud still covered Normandy. It was postponed in the hope cloud would clear. Eventually it took place late in the evening, 71 Mitchells being despatched with Spitfire escort. Ahead of them flew four squadrons of Typhoons, forty aircraft of Nos. 181, 182, 245 and 247 Squadrons to fire rocket projectiles into the AFVs and to open the attack which was undertaken using *Gee-H*. From 21.19 to 21.21 hours 436 500-lb. M.C. bombs rained down blanketing the target area in a very successful attack that left volumes of flame and smoke. News soon filtered back that much damage had been caused to buildings and vehicles, but more important the

German Chief of Staff, General von Dawans, and also his entire Staff, had perished.[1]

It was around 22.15 hours when the force landed back and at once a turn round was ordered for different night missions to the beachhead area. 98 Squadron's sixteen aircraft dropped flares and bombed St. Sauvent and Le Haye, and seventeen crews of 226 Squadron joined in these raids and did flare-dropping patrols. Mosquitoes too were active again, fifteen of them joining in the attacks on St. Sauvent detraining point and also Le Vicomte, bombing by the light of flares dropped at fifteen-minute intervals from 02.30 to 04.00 hours by 140 Wing. Another fifty patrolled the area Mortain–Avranches–St. Lo–Vire relying upon the light of the flares of 139 Wing's Mitchells, and dropping 216 500-lb. M.C. bombs on road and rail communications. In this they were joined by the heavies of Bomber Command.

A good example of quick service tactical bombing was provided by Mosquitoes on 11 June when, merely two hours after receiving a target, they were bombing petrol tankers in the rail yard at Châtellerault at the Army's request. Nos. 464 and 487 Squadrons each provided three aircraft and No. 107 six. Wg. Cdr. Iredale and Wg. Cdr. I. S. Smith led their sections. Told the target at 19.45 hours, crews were by their aircraft fifteen minutes later, helping the bombing-up. Engines were started at 20.15 hours, then the force was held for last-minute instructions. Smith's trio was to be first away. As they had no flight plan they drew a straight line from the easterly entrance route to the battle area and the target, measuring distance and direction. Just as they were about to take-off the leader was handed a slightly different route so that they could avoid flak. So as not to delay the raid they planned to measure this in the air. During these last few moments a target map had been passed from the

---

[1] Aircraft used: *98 Sqn.* (led by Sqn. Ldr. Eager): FW189: A, FW102: X, FW215: V, FL675: N, FV969, FW168: U, FW256: W, FW115: K, FW201: C, FW253: F, FV976: L, FV931: H, FW184: D, FW102: M, FL186: G, FL182: J; *180 Sqn.* (17/18 attacked, led by Wg. Cdr. Lynn): FW124, FW135, FW161, FV998, FW113, FW240, FW191, FW158, FL217, FW101, FW206, FL679, FL210, FV967, FW207, FW269, FW118, FW125; *226 Sqn.* (17/18 attacked, led by Wg. Cdr. A. D. Mitchell): FW116: X, FW134: P, FV989: J, FW181: Z, FW160: E, FW105: C, FW144: B, FV936: G, FW111: T, FW163: Y, FW152: V, FW130: A, FW112: U, FV958: D, FW210: S, FV919: M, FW153: F, FW128: H; *320 Sqn.:* FR202: G, FR188: H, FR185: Z, FR192: M, FR207: U, FR205: O, FR200: Q, FR151: C, FR204: S, FR167: V, FR189: F, FR191: A, FR190: E, FR160: J, FR176: P, FR156: Y, FR149: N. Typhoons used on the operation were *181 Sqn.:* JR513, MN714, JP800, JP923, MN756, JP916, MN607, MN690, MN199, JP506, which also attacked Martigny. *182 Sqn.:* JR513, MN771, JP934, MN575, JR300, MN768, JR220, JR255, MN714, MN472. *245 Sqn.:* No details known of aircraft used. *247 Sqn.:* MN373, MN599, MN809, MN430, MN591, MM575, MN799, MN241, MN317, JR300, DN260.

Intelligence Officer for position details of the target—when they were airborne they discovered they had left it behind. Nevertheless they pressed on regardless. Let Wg. Cdr. Smith take up the story:

'We set course in cloud in formation at 1,000 feet and made the whole trip between six and eight thousand feet using *Gee* as the only navigation aid. We broke cloud forty miles from Le Mans and then flew along the base of the cloud until we went off our map. We then went down on the deck and flew two courses which my navigator had been able to scribble on a piece of paper. On the run-up to target I flew 7 degrees further north across the main double track railway leading south from Tours. I intended to find the line and fly along it to the first big town, then find the marshalling yards. This would have been Châtellerault. Twenty miles from target No. 3 got a definite pin point and took over the lead. He then flew a course only 2 degrees different to the one we were steering and attacked from 100–150 feet. I bombed the northern end. No. 2, Flt. Lt. J. B. Ellacombe, bombed the south end and Flt. Lt. W. J. Runciman the centre. We then flew out on a reciprocal, climbed to 7,000–8,000 feet and returned in cloud. North of Bernay my No. 2 warned me of the presence of a "snapper" who made a tentative attack from port beam about 1,000 yards away. He then disappeared. Iredale's formation went into cloud for two minutes to evade him then continued course to the target at ground level.'

'We reached the target,' Iredale said, 'and attacked from the south. I saw 487's successful attack and I cannoned a goods train at the south end of the rail junction and bombed trains in the station, but I could not identify whether they were petrol tankers. After bombing I decided to reconnoitre this very long railway line at low level until it was too dark to do so. Between the target and Châteaudun many trains were attacked, mostly troop trains stationary in small sidings.'

When Wg. Cdr. Collard and 107 Squadron arrived at 22.44 hours they found a fire burning in an area 300 × 170 yards, with smoke rising to 4,000 feet. 107 Squadron did an excellent job both in the speed with which they got away and in their navigation, for they were above cloud for half the journey there. Interpretation after tactical reconnaissance on 13th revealed much damage to the south end of the station with the platform roof knocked down and several wagons damaged. Nearby buildings had been demolished and platforms damaged.

Attacks on 11–12 June on detraining points at Le Haye and Sauveur showed the Bostons and Mitchells getting into their stride at night, and the Mosquitoes improving their technique. Le Haye was a small town with a railway junction, sited west of Carentan on the main rail route running along the west side of the Cherbourg peninsula with a branch line connecting with the main line from Carentan. Fifty aircraft of Nos. 88, 98, 107, 180, 226 and 320 Squadrons were involved. Damage assessment showed the main road north and south of the village choked with debris, and five hits on the railway and on a cutting. Twenty-three aircraft of Nos. 88, 98, 180, 320 and 487 Squadrons attacked Sauveur on the railway from Le Haye to Cherbourg. Three hits were scored on the line and trucks were hit. The main east to west street was choked with debris, and hits were scored on storage tanks, a factory and an old château.

During 12 June all the Boston and Mitchell squadrons prepared for their biggest daylight operation since D-Day, mounted against the 21st Panzer Division dispersed in the Forêt de Grimbecq. Ninety aircraft were despatched in the evening. It was a highly effective, spectacular attack and included a concentrated raid on a servicing echelon. Flak was quite heavy. 'N' of 320 Squadron fell away on fire and 'A' of 320 Squadron crashed into the Channel, the crew being picked up by an M.T.B.

'An immediate turn round was ordered,' 98 Squadron's diary recorded. 'All crews hurried back for briefing. It's Total warfare with a capital T now. Ground crews are magnificent. Sqn. Ldr. Dring, the CTO, and Flt. Lt. Ballet, Armaments Officer, are at their very best with the men. The war goes well and the spirits are high. Tonight four aircraft detailed to bomb Mézidon marshalling yards using *Gee-H*. Flt. Lt. Dawes and crew failed to return on their second tour—some of us knew them on 180 at Foulsham and prior to that on 18 at Raynham.'

The Mitchells were sent in two forces flare dropping for Mosquitoes, 24 of which from 140 Wing scoured the area Mézidon–Lisieux–Argentan–Domfront–Mortain and another thirty from 138 Wing operated over the area Lessay–Mortain–Avranches–Granville–Lessay. Six of the nine Mitchells deployed dropped flares but FR205-O flown by J. C. Sillevis of 320 Squadron was missing, bringing the squadron's loss for the day to three machines. Another Mitchell was chased by a Ju 88, and FV989 (98 Squadron) was also lost. Five Mitchells bombed Mézidon, and another 23 Mosquitoes operating mainly in pairs bombed Le Mesnil-Mauger rail centre.

Reserve enemy aircraft flew to France after the invasion and some 675 day-fighters and 465 night-fighters were assembled by now within reach of the battle area. Although it was six months since 2 Group had met enemy fighters reaction in strength was expected now, particularly against lone aircraft or stragglers.

On the evening of 13 June 24 bombers plastered units of the 21st Panzer Division at Le Bas de Bréville south-east of the Orne Estuary.

Already 2 Group Support Unit was a valuable asset readily supplying crews replacing all forms of wastage. Its organisation had been undertaken long before D-Day, for a good reserve was essential to continued success. No. 13 O.T.U. had been completely reorganised before the end of 1943. This entailed replacement of Blenheims on the unit which, with 17 O.T.U., had for years supplied the Group with crews at a fast rate. Boston and Mitchell Flights had been built up on a larger scale without interfering with unit output. It was decided at the same time that

No. 60 O.T.U. should train Mosquito crews for the Group and by June 1944 both 13 and 60 O.T.U.s were training Mosquito crews to a very high standard. Both Units were controlled by another Group and with wastage unpredictable it was not always possible for the O.T.U.s to have crews immediately ready. Hence the establishment of this 'buffer unit', No. 2 G.S.U., which was planned to hold five crews per squadron in addition to five Wing Commanders and thirteen Squadron Leaders as reserve flight and squadron commanders. The G.S.U. was designed to be transportable to follow the Group at all times.

On 13–14 June 42 Mosquitoes of 107, 305, 464 and 613 Squadrons strafed and bombed enemy movements between Evreux and Lisieux, Dreux and Falaise, Tours and Alençon and Angers-Vire. The medium bombers' crews were meanwhile resting for the next evening's effort by sixty aircraft against a POL (petrol, oil and lubricant) dump at Condé sur Vire. The night saw a continuation of attacks on this target. Sqn. Ldr. Eager and Flt. Lt. Brown of 98 Squadron dropped flares so that a dozen of 320 Squadron could again bomb it whilst 138 Wing's Mosquitoes roamed the Le Haye–St. Lo–Le Mans–Avranches region and 140 Wing operated south from Lisieux, and on the west side of Paris. During the night stationary vehicles were attacked in the light of 180 Squadron's flares and 140 Wing had a successful night against a variety of targets including 24 goods wagons in a siding.

Another large-scale Mitchell and Boston raid was mounted on 15th on a Panzer Division dispersed in a wood at Posilion north of Condé. Spitfires escorted the force being led by 36 Mitchells in two boxes of eighteen in close company, which were followed along the Selsey–Isigny route by 24 Bostons escorted by a Spitfire IX Squadron with one of Spitfire XIVs as high cover.

At night poor weather limited operations. On 17th the rail installation at Mézidon was raided by Mitchells and Bostons and on the following night 68 Mosquitoes operated against activity near the front line with 98 Squadron providing the flare-dropping force.

The Forêt de Bourse again attracted the Bostons and Mitchells on 18th then at night 75 Mitchell/Mosquito sorties were flown against road/rail activity close to the battlefield between Avranches and Le Mans. Two of the Mitchell flare force from 226 Squadron were missing and it was presumed night-fighters were now operating in the area. Weather was again poor and little movement was seen, but there was a sighting of some flying bombs one of which was inconclusively attacked by a Mosquito. In the event this was portentous.

On 14 June the enemy had launched the first flying bombs against London. By now attacks on southern England were such that the medium bombers had to be withdrawn from tactical support to hammer the V-1 sites once more. This decision was reluctantly taken and aroused Group protests to no avail.

Fifty-three Mitchells of 98, 180, 226 and 320 Squadrons were detailed for *Noball* operations against Ecalles-sur-Buchy, Bois Coquerel and Motorgenil on 19 June. It was a cloudy day and these small targets had to be attacked using *Gee-H*. Next day Moyenville, Grand Parc and Hambures sites—the latter in full operation—were the targets. The threat was so serious that much of A.D.G.B. was being marshalled to meet it, but the weight of bombs 2 Group could direct now was deemed insufficient to make much difference. Therefore strongly escorted heavy bombers were brought into action releasing 2 Group for army support operations. Commenting in Operations Digest No. 7 Air Vice-Marshal Embry wrote: 'It is unfortunate that we have had to switch part of our attention to *Noball* targets. We had hoped to direct the whole of our energy to support of the Army in the field. But as the safety of our country is again at stake, it is only right and proper we should be called upon to help settle this nuisance once and for all. I regard this as an additional item to our principal role.'

Very little progress had yet been made by the land forces which were still held before Caen. One enemy strong point was in the Mondeville steel works south of Caen, a target already known to 2 Group. The Army asked that it should be heavily bombed. Forty-eight Mitchells of 98, 226 and 320 Squadrons with 24 Bostons following flew in over St. Aubin to attack the factory—some 1,500 yards ahead of our troops—with a mixed load of 284 500-lb. and 48 1,000-lb. bombs and made an attack which brought from the 51st Highland Division a signal of congratulation.

The enemy now anticipated a southern advance by our forces and on 22–23 June a Panzer Division was reported moving west through the battle zone. Sixty-one Mosquitoes were despatched to attack four areas and for several nights these operations continued. Two infantry divisions coming from north of the Loire were also attacked and Mitchells were sent to the rail junction at Marigny, dumps and movement in the Forêt d'Anglais and the rail centre at Verneuil.

Such was the menacing tone of the V-1 offensive against London that 2 Group was again brought into the campaign against it, bombing three châteaux from which the operations were controlled, at Merlimont, de Frohen and d'Ansenne. These three were again bombed in daylight on 25 June.

On 27–28th 79 Mosquitoes and 16 Mitchells harassed the enemy in the area adjacent to the 2nd Army front during Montgomery's attempt to forge ahead from Caen. The extent of the effort can be gauged from the ammunition expended: 236 500-lb. M.C. bombs, 16,950 rounds of 20 mm. cannon and 26,900 rounds of .303 in. bullets.

No further day raids were made in June, but on 29th/30th 77 Mosquitoes and eleven Mitchells supported the battle west of Caen, first by halting movement through Villers Bocage and Thury Harcourt and then by harassing all movement from St. Lo to Evreux. Consistent bad weather had been met through June and the Mosquitoes had to fly very low to find their targets in the rolling country and *bocage*. Sharp eyes were needed to see the foe but soon crews became skilled at spotting trains some miles away by their smoke. Countless attacks had already been made upon the rail network in France, journeys now being painfully slow. The Mosquitoes made them well-nigh impossible at night and such reinforcements as the enemy advanced had torturous and hazardous journeys. By day the fighter-bombers of 2nd T.A.F. saw to it that movement was equally difficult.

The end of June 1944 found the Allied armies firmly entrenched in Normandy with bad weather holding up their supplies. The inadequacy of the Luftwaffe prevented the Wehrmacht being effectively supplied, but it was stubbornly holding on. Bomber Command and the Americans were therefore called upon to make devastating raids to clear a path for the soldiers. Even so it took a number of raids to blast a way ahead.

Mitchell operations had been at a high intensity, well shown by the fact that in seven hours on one night the three Dunsfold squadrons managed 102 sorties. One crew did a turn round in 21 minutes including interrogation, a quick meal, briefing, preparation, refuelling, re-arming and checks—a fine show.

Originally it had been decided that the Bostons and Mitchells would be a reserve for night operations in moonlight and suitable weather, but in fact they operated regardless of such limitations. By the end of June it could be seen how well night intruder operations by Mosquitoes earlier in the year were paying off. The aim now was for 100 nightly Mosquito sorties.

Their effectiveness was brought home when $\frac{2}{3}$ of a batch of P.O.W.s admitted they had surrendered 'because they were terrified by the bombing and harassing attacks against them at night'. A report stated: 'There is no doubt that night attacks are infinitely more damaging on the nerves than those by day. Loss of sleep alone causes lowering of the fighting value of troops, and some have even gone so far as to say that night bombing should be forbidden as it is unfair to subject troops who have been through Hell all day to any discomfort at night!'

Fortunate it was that on most nights in July the Group was able to operate. In June–July 4,172 sorties were flown—getting on for as many as in the whole of 1941. At night 11,000 500-lb. bombs were dropped and 400,000 rounds of ammunition fired. But it was difficult to assess results even by the light of flares although it was reckoned that 212 trains were hit. Sixteen lengths of track were shot up, over 120 road convoys strafed and at least 118 vehicles left blazing. Twenty-eight bridges were variously damaged for the total loss of 33 aircraft over two months. Nightly the Mosquito harassment continued with penetrations from the battlefront to the Loire and beyond in search of rail movement. Operations were flown around Paris, Amiens and Abbeville in search of trains, and attention began to be given to the Seine crossing points.

The effectiveness of these operations was well experienced by a prisoner from a Panzer Regiment which took three nights to move from Versailles to Argentan, moving from wood to wood for fear of attack. Another showed an order reading: 'The ever-growing danger of air attack necessitates the strictest observation of orders concerning black-out . . . under no circumstances will lights—even tail lights—be allowed. No dashboard lights will be allowed, and care is to be taken in lighting cigarettes. All machine-guns will remain in position and fire will be opened only against direct attack.'

The first 'big night' in July came on 3rd–4th when 102 Mosquito and 36 Boston sorties were flown to prevent reinforcements being brought up to combat the American offensive. No. 140 Wing alone shot up thirteen trains and destroyed four lengths of track. These operations followed a large-scale *Ramrod* on Argentan POL dump. Next day Mitchells went for the V-1 H.Q. at Château d'Ansenne and Bostons that at Hélicourt, but the bombing was none too good. It was, however, night operations that were mainly now occupying the Group, 342 Squadron operating on five nights up to 9th–10th and again at the end of the month. Whereas the Mitchells and Mosquitoes could carry *Gee* the Bostons depended upon other aircraft for target selection and flares; this limited their usefulness.

Principal day targets were POL depots at Alençon, Chartres, St. Malo, Bois de Morleans and Livarot. The aim was to starve the enemy of these essentials. Attack effectiveness depended upon cloud conditions and flak reception. Bombing was often by *Gee-H* through cloud gaps, repeat raids often being required. The only enemy fighter reaction came at midday on 6 July.

Forty-two Mitchells of Nos. 98, 180 and 320 Squadrons closely escorted by three Spitfire V squadrons, with No. 132 Wing (Nos. 66, 331 and 332 Squadrons) as top cover, were briefed for an afternoon raid on the Chartres POL dump. Bombing was good then ten miles from Chartres about twenty '109s and '190s dived upon the close escort. The top cover wheeled down in hot pursuit of the Huns who descended to deck level, spreading in all directions chased by Spitfires. Sqn. Ldr. W. Foster of 66 Squadron and three others raced after the foe at tree-top height, Foster getting cannon hits on a Bf 109 which then climbed steeply before the pilot baled out. A minute later he saw a dozen enemy fighters 2,000 feet above, pulled up and scored a kill before his cannon jammed. Flg. Off. J. Pattison in NH150 had scored another success, but W. Off. A. McKibben had been hit and was last seen crossing the Allied lines. The Norwegians, too, had a field day. Two '190s fell to Capt. Bjorstad leading 331 Squadron and 2/Lt. Gundeson, Major Gran and Lt. L'Abee-Lund each claimed a '109. Another was shot down by Wg. Cdr. Berg.

On 10–11 July night operations had high priority. They were attracted by railway activities in the Lille–Amiens–Hirson area, and increased activity at the Seine crossings, as well as rail traffic from La Roche and

Vitry towards the battlefield, and as far back as Laval and Le Mans. But again the weather clamped and the 74 Mosquitoes had to settle for battle area targets. Next night another attempt was made to reach the specified areas and this was more effective. The Seine crossings were becoming more important and on 14th–15th flare-dropping Wellingtons of 34 Wing were called in to light the targets for the Mosquitoes. On 17–18 July Flt. Lt. Rippon and Flt. Sgt. Ridout of 107 Squadron were patrolling over the Seine when, by flare light, they picked out a ferry boat near Montreauville. They roared in bombing and gunning it, then made a second run. By now the flak was intense. It damaged the rudder and put the pitot head out of action. But of the ship there was no sign— 2 Group had sunk a ship, something it had not done for many months.

Sqn. Ldr. Eager flying FV985: S of 98 Squadron made his hundredth sortie during a raid on Alençon on 17 July. Wg. Cdr. L. A. Lynn, 139 Wing Leader with more than 150 sorties to his credit, considered the reception given to the Mitchells by German gunners on the evening of 24 July one of the hottest he had ever known. Some 88 mm. tank guns were being used as air defence weapons. It had been planned to bomb on *Gee-H* but signals failed on the run-in and then there was not time for Lynn's navigator to switch to visual bombing. He made a second run and this time there were friendly aircraft below. One of the crew said that the flak was so intense he could not see the target, in a wood at La Hogue. It was a collection of about sixteen mobile guns and 1,800 troops massing for a counter attack. Their flak positions were under mortar fire from the 2nd Army, but this did not deter the tough opponent. The sixty-Mitchell attack was so disorganised that only a third of the force bombed. Early next day the bombers were back and, in fine weather, plastered the target.

Within 24 hours Mitchells flew three large raids. For 98 Squadron the most eventful was that of 23 July. Fifteen crews led by Grp. Capt. J. G. C. Paul with Sqn. Ldr. Paynter and Flt. Lt. Brown leading the other two boxes made a *Gee-H* raid on the rail yard at Glos Montfort. At the moment of bombing there was a tremendous explosion, then a flaming mass. Paynter's aircraft, FV985 S-Sugar, had exploded. The wreckage cascaded on to FW122, the aircraft of Flt. Lt. Weekes, which dived away aflame into the clouds. Flg. Off. Berry's machine was in a bad way and he decided he would never be able to cross the Channel. With his gunners Flg. Off. Morin and Sgt. Berwick both wounded, he needed all his skill to make a landing. When he brought FL186 down the squadron lost their veteran Mitchell in the crash, an aircraft with nearly 100 sorties to her credit.

Wounded in the leg and in great pain, Flt. Sgt. Harnden in Flg. Off. Harris's Mitchell made sure the bomb doors were closed before he dragged himself from the nose compartment through the eighteen-inch tunnel to the centre of the aircraft. Reaching the first-aid kit he gave himself a shot of morphia. Meanwhile with both engines damaged, instruments knocked out and hydraulics out of use. Harris struggled to get the aircraft across the Channel. He called the tail gunner forward to assist him, but W. Off. Glazer could not get out since the bulkhead door to his position was jammed. Flt. Sgt. Williams, the dorsal gunner, gave first aid to Harnden, applied a tourniquet to his leg and made him comfortable staying by his side for the inevitable crash landing. Desperately Glazer hammered on his turret door with the butt of his revolver. The undercarriage would not lower and 'chutes were brought to the ready. They were not needed. With commendable skill Harris brought H-Harry into a safe landing. It was a splendid show by the whole crew.

This period of intense operational activity built up to a climax on the evening of 26 July when Mitchells made their longest trip so far, to the Fontainebleau POL dump. Some 226 bombs straddled the target and large explosions erupted at its west end pushing smoke nearly a mile high. Accurate flak rose from Dreux airfield and the Spitfire escort was heavily engaged by enemy fighters. It claimed five successes and four probables without loss to itself. Heavy flak on the run-in from Chartres forced FR161 to turn back, but the only loss was van Leeuweng in FL185: Z of 320 Squadron.

The busiest night of the offensive so far came on 27–28 July. Maximum effort was ordered and the weather was excellent. Each Wing had targets in front of the battle area and on its approaches. Total effort amounted to 180 aircraft including 31 Bostons. Forty-two Mosquitoes attacked rail movements south of Paris, 31 movement in front of both Allied armies, six attended to movement across the Seine and ten went for more road and rail movements around Rouen and Serquex and searched for a V-weapon train between Ault and Aire. In all 143 aircraft attacked, Mosquitoes very successfully south of Paris. Details of the night's operations may be found on Map No. 18. Next night 95 Mosquitoes gave forward support to the advancing Americans.

Ever-increasing attention was being given to the Seine crossing points. Bridges had been brought down by heavy bombing and extensive use was beginning to be made of pontoon bridges over which the enemy was going to and fro. The A.E.A.F. therefore decided to seal his exits.

News was flashed to Group on the morning of 1 August that the barracks at Poitiers were filling with German troops being deployed to quell the Maquis in that area. It was decided to mount a Mosquito low-level precision raid that evening in the belief that then, or early in the morning, the troops would be in their quarters. That evening they would probably be concentrated anyway in view of the unsettled conditions in the area. There was insufficient time to build the customary model for briefing, but the barracks were large and a prominent feature on the side of the town. Twenty-four Mosquitoes of 140 Wing were detailed, to attack in waves of six with 32 11-sec. delay bombs and fifty set to explode instantaneously, dropped in shallow dives from 2,000 feet.

The attack took place as planned and reconnaissance pictures showed a very clean attack, and that only three bombs fell outside the target area. Of the three large barrack blocks one was nearly destroyed, the others flattened. A serious fire had gutted the western part, seven other buildings were destroyed or gutted and forty to fifty vehicles battered.

Two similar operations were mounted next day, in one case on a château south of Châtellerault to which SS troops concerned in atrocities to P.O.W.s and civilians had moved after being attacked by Mosquitoes at Bonneuil Matours on 15 July when 150 were killed. Eighteen Mosquitoes of 138 Wing were to take part because the château was of solid construction and it was decided to scatter the attacks to the fringe of a surrounding wood in which the enemy was also camping. At least 28 bombs hit the building, cine shots confirming success. A further eight Mosquitoes of 138 Wing attacked a château north of Le Mans known to house a saboteurs' school. Results were unseen because of the smoke, but the raid was highly successful.

Sorties flown in August went two-thirds of the way to beating the combined totals for June and July. There was a greater number of day raids in support of the army. Nearly 4,000 tons of bombs were dropped and 662,385 rounds fired. Over 10,000 flares were dropped and 2,000 vehicles attacked. The Army rushed forward from Normandy, the enemy retreated in rout. At least 1,150 vehicles were left burning at night and 125 trains were attacked. By day 36 attacks were carried out on POL dumps, strong points, H.Q. and special targets for a loss of 35 aircraft. The busiest period was the 72 hours ending 07.00 hours on 29th during which 770 sorties were flown. Among these were five attacks by Mitchell and Boston squadrons; the targets included two POL dumps and there were three attacks on transport attempting to cross the Seine at Rouen as a result of which 2 Group received the highest possible commendation. During an evening attack there over 800 out of 1,400 vehicles were destroyed or damaged beyond repair. It was estimated that 3,000 were lost to the enemy in three raids. By night 900 M.E.T. were attacked for the loss of three Mosquitoes.

The month opened with attacks on ammunition dumps, a heavy raid being mounted by 48 Mitchells and thirty Bostons on a munitions factory at Montreuil Belfry near Anger. This was a deep penetration for the day-bombers and they could see just how confused the ground situation had become in the American sector. In the evening of 2nd Mosquitoes of 107 and 305 Squadrons attacked two châteaux, Maulny, the saboteur school, and Château de Fer, an SS police H.Q. south of Châtellerault where 28 hits were scored on the main evening.

Close support to the Army came on 4th when 47 Mitchells and thirty Bostons attacked a strong point east of Caen marked by red smoke shells after the manner practised before D-Day. Such attacks demanded great care with our own troops close at hand. When fuel tankers were attacked on 15 August using the same method the Germans fired red smoke shells into our lines . . . one had to be careful.

The first busy night of the month—the weather had cut early efforts—was 4th–5th when 88 Mosquito, 28 Boston and two Mitchell sorties were flown in a three-stage operation embracing operations in eight areas. Attacks were made by 109 Mosquitoes. Six Bostons were lost from causes that did not apparently come to light. Possibly they were downed by flak during low-level attacks, although night-fighters did operate over the beachhead area.

Following two day raids on ammunition dumps on 7th a strong night offensive was mounted by 74 Mosquitoes which attacked twelve trains and 23 lines of trucks. A warehouse was fired and exploded.

On 9th 48 Mitchells and 18 Bostons set off for another ammunition dump, in the Forêt de Lyons. It was known that the operation would take them through a heavily gun-defended area and to 98 Squadron at the briefing Dunsfold's station commander, Grp. Capt. Dunlap, made it clear that it was the crews' duty to reach the target. Wg. Cdr. Paul led the first three boxes, Wg. Cdr. Lynn the second three. They crossed into France at Beville meeting heavy flak en route. Bombing was very good, but on the way back they again encountered heavy accurate flak. Two of 180's aircraft fell west of Senarpont and a third was hit. MQ-R, Flt. Lt. J. M. Bett's aircraft, had to land in France and FR143 'S' of 320 Squadron was ditched. 'B' of 320 Squadron landed at Friston with a badly injured wireless operator who died in hospital. Four other aircraft from the squadron were damaged.

On the evening of 12th–13th reports were flooding into Group H.Q. to the effect that the enemy was now retreating fast towards the Seine, and that American forces in the south were racing east to close his escape route. Maximum effort was therefore called for from all Wings, to impede retreat from the battle front throughout the night. In Part 1 of the operations 138 Wing would attack movement from the front and watch crossing points over the River Orne, also patrol all routes radiating from Amiens. Tasks for 140 Wing were: movement in the Paris–Orleans–Chartres–Rouen area; movement on railways from Paris to the battle area; additionally 38 of the Wing to attack all movement in the battle area. Forty-six Mosquitoes of the two wings were detailed to make a second sortie. Meanwhile Mitchells of 98 and 180 Squadrons with Bostons were also to attack battle area targets and light an Orne bridge with flares for Mosquito attack. Mitchells of 98, 180 and 320 Squadrons attempted to create road choke points and two Mitchells of 226 Squadron flew special dropping missions. The official survey of the night's operations compiled by H.Q. 2 Group reads: 'General results: 224 aircraft of Group detailed, 212 attacked 11 aborted and 1 of 88 Squadron missing. 603 × 500 lb. and 570 × 40 lb. bombs dropped, 1,143 flares, 36,150 rounds cannon, 53,418 rounds machine gun used. Group effort involved a turn round of 45 Mosquitoes (38 from one

Wing). 141 Mosquito sorties flown and 83 Mitchell-Boston sorties. Bostons bombing under flares had unobserved results owing to low cloud and haze. Considerable activity seen by Mosquitoes over battle-front area and on roads leading to Paris. It was on these roads that most attacks took place, where greatest effort was concentrated. There was little movement in other areas except on railways leading to Paris. . . . Estimated at least 19 convoys including one of 100 MT were attacked and 27 set on fire or destroyed in addition.'

On the three following nights a tremendous effort was made. On 13th–14th 197 Mosquitoes were detailed (79 flying second sorties) and six aircraft of 613 Squadron managed three sorties each. 539 500-lb. bombs were dropped, 74,470 rounds fired although haze and 8/10 low stratus interfered with the operations. Next day the day-bombers attacked enemy troops, then at night 114 Mosquito sorties were flown to harass all movement by road and rail west of St. Pierre sur Dives, N.E. and S. of Paris as far as Lens, Givers and Moulins. On 15th–16th 95 Mosquitoes set out to harass movement from the Seine to west of Mézidon and from Paris as far as Dieppe, Shermont and Montluçon.

During 17th 36 Mitchells set off for the POL dump at La Mailleraye-sur-Seine. As 320 Squadron bombed a 500-pounder fell through the star-board rudder of FR186: B from Steengracht von Moyland's Mitchell. The aircraft made base safely, despite a heavy dose of flak from Caudebec.

At night maximum effort was again demanded from the three Wings. Ninety-six Mosquitoes of 140 Wing were to harass all movement in the Trouville area along the Seine to Vernon, Conches, Aubecq and Lisieux and to specially watch crossing points over the Risle. They were to patrol the rail routes Aulnoye to Creil, Hirson to Le Bourget, Dijon to Gretes. Four Mosquitoes of 140 Wing were ordered by H.Q. 2nd T.A.F. to drop flares over the gap between Trouen and Argentan, with Bostons and Mitchells making attacks in strips on battle area country-side. Of the 186 aircraft detailed 175 attacked dropping 698 500-pounders, 800 fragmentation bombs and 384 flares, and firing 12,970 cannon and 19,480 machine-gun rounds. Eight aircraft aborted and one was lost.

News came to hand of another Gestapo H.Q., this time at a school in Egletons. Fourteen Mosquitoes of 613 Squadron were despatched to destroy it with Air Vice-Marshal Embry flying in PZ222. The attack was made between 18.02 and 18.18 hours, from between fifty and 1,500 feet, and a load of twelve 500 M.C. and eighteen 500 M.C. T.D. 11-sec. was dropped. At least twenty hits were scored, the rear and front walls being demolished. The whole target quickly became enveloped in smoke into which the Mosquitoes poured their fire. There was just time to see six men run into the building carrying a red warning flag which did nothing to save them. The F.P.U. aircraft accompanied them obtaining good photographs on its three cameras.

When darkness fell the Mosquitoes were off again, 142 sorties being

N

flown and nineteen by Mitchells three of which were missing. Fifty-eight of the Mosquitoes were flying second sorties. It turned out to be the most successful night's operations since D-Day, very effectively dealing with barge traffic across the Seine. In the battle area much MT was found and slaughtered, forests were set ablaze and roads hit. The enemy was in full flight along the Lisieux road, and between Aubecq and Bernay motor transport was three deep. Throughout the night flares from Mitchells lit the Falaise gap for Mosquitoes where during the day Typhoons had exacted a heavy killing. The task now was for the Mosquitoes to attack the Seine crossing points at Duclair, Quillerboeuf, Elboeuf and the roads leading to these places.

Nightly attacks along the Seine followed and on 25 August Mitchells and Bostons were ordered to make a day raid on Duclair. Hardly were they airborne when a signal was flashed to them changing their target to MT massing on the south bank of the Seine at Rouen. News of troops massing there too soon poured in and an all-out raid was ordered on the afternoon of 26th. Smoke from fires in the MT park rose to 5,000 feet. Moderate heavy flak defended Rouen, Mitchell FW196 being brought down and four Bostons damaged one of which crashed at Hook on return.

Five hours later Bostons and Mitchells started a night hammering of the same target. Some 130 Mosquitoes, 21 Bostons and 44 Mitchells were detailed. The plan was for a Mosquito of 613 Squadron to light the south bank at Rouen, with two more dropping green target indicators for the bombing of the marshalling yards near the southern bridge. The second task of Part 1 of the night's operations was for 31 Mosquitoes of 107 Squadron to attack all movement at Duclair, Caudebec and Le Malleray. From 305 Squadron 29 sorties were to strafe road traffic in the Rouen–Neuchâtel–Beauvais–Gisors area, and from 03.00 hours 613 Squadron was ordered to maintain the offensive at Rouen. In Part 2 of the night's work 140 Wing attacked a Seine bridge and rail routes. All their Mosquitoes managed a second sortie and one a third. Main activity was on the roads from Rouen where there were up to 400 vehicles, many soon blazing.

During the evening of 28th, to round off a period of intensive activity, Bostons and Mitchells delivered a knock-out blow on the Duclair ferry point. Woods surrounding it were soon blazing, but the flak was accurate and claimed Sqn. Ldr. Campbell's Mitchell.

This highly successful operation rounded off the first stage of the invasion campaign. How different it all was from 1940. Not once did the flak entirely break up the formations, rarely did the Luftwaffe attempt to interfere—massive fighter support ensured this. To those who had flown in the early war days the campaign in support of the Allied Expeditionary Force seemed 'quite a piece of cake'. Just how effective some of the operations had become is well shown by the following report on a Mosquito daylight raid.

6. Mitchell IIIs of 342 Squadron wearing French roundels and rudder stripes. OA-B: KJ645 nearest and OA-L: KJ683 evident. Behind, an escort of Tempest Vs

7. After a raid Mitchell IIIs of 180 Squadron taxi in

78. FW166, diverted with her squadron to Lille/Vendeville after a raid on Vielsham
made a heavy landing, and her nosewheel collapsed. Note the ventral turret an
the dorsal turret as fitted to the Mk. II

79. 88 Squadron had, as its 1942–3 home, Blickling Hall in Norfolk

80. Headquarters and Wing Officers at Brussels shortly after VE-Day. Left to right: *front row:* Wg. Cdr. Collins, Grp. Capt. Leslie Bower, Grp. Capt. Colbeck-Welch, Grp. Capt. R. N. Bateson, Air Cdr. David Atcherley, Air Vice-Marshal Basil Embry, Grp. Capt. Kippenburger, Grp. Capt. M. Ely, Grp. Capt. T. Horgan, Grp. Capt. J. G. C. Paul, Grp. Capt. R. Edwards; *second row:* Wg. Cdr. R. Iredale, Wg. Cdr. Maher, Cdr. Witholt, Wg. Cdr. 'Robbie' Robinson, —?—, Wg. Cdr. W. Wilson, Wg. Cdr. P. Thomas, Wg. Cdr. P. Corkey; *third row:* O.C. 342 Sqn., —?—, Wg. Cdr. J. Wallace, Sqn. Ldr. Angus Horn, Wg. Cdr. E. Frayn, —?—, —?—, Wg. Cdr. J. Meakin, Wg. Cdr. C. Newman; *top trio:* —?—, —?—, Wg. Cdr. D. Newton

81. Mosquito NS840 of 487 Squadron at Holme-on-Spalding Moor. The pilot is Grp. Capt. Wykeham-Barnes. NS840 served as 'X' and 'B' of 487 Squadron, and was destroyed in a flying accident on 20.7.45 when with 2 Group Communications Flight

82. A Mosquito VI of 613 Squadron climbs away on an operational sortie
83. MM401 joined 464 Squadron as 'SB-J' on 29.1.44. She was very badly shot up during a raid on the Pas de Calais on 21.2.44 and subsequently written off 31.3.44

'During the late afternoon of 31 August several hundred SS troops learned in a way that left no room for argument how thoroughly our Mossies handle special daylight targets allotted them. The unlucky Huns were having their tea, or at least thinking about it, when six Mosquitoes of 487 Squadron led by Flt. Lt. Hanafin with Flg. Off. Rudgrove as navigator were humming along the deck towards their barracks on the outskirts of Vincey. These barracks were two large buildings in which French schoolchildren once learnt the art of peace before the SS arrived. They were brightly decorated buildings easily distinguishable from the air, as the Mosquito crews discovered as they pulled up over a hill and prepared for the bombing run.'

Flt. Lt. Askew, a navigator, described what happened: 'Four rows of cottages pointed directly towards the school, and we pulled up to bombing height just before reaching the target. As soon as the bombs went in the Gerries began to pour out. About fifty of them dressed in some sort of blue uniforms came out of the front doors on the west side of one building. A number of them were heading for slit trenches in front of the school, but a lot didn't reach cover. This run was at 1,500 feet and by the time we'd turned again for a low level strafe, smoke was obscuring parts of the target. We made second and third attacks with guns then I was able to see that the back of the larger building had been wiped out and the front of the other was in ruins.'

All the available evidence indicates that 2 Group's contribution to the success of *Overlord* was considerable. Particularly was this true of its night interdictor role, and repeatedly captured soldiers added their testimony in support of its effectiveness. Now the Armies were racing across France and the enemy was in full retreat. The task was to see that this was maintained.

Chapter 22
Storming the Bastion

The Army advance was indeed rapid. Verdun fell on 1 September and Brussels on 3rd. There a victory parade was about to take place to fête Field Marshal Montgomery, certain hero of the people. His outriders formated upon a large staff car and, failing to recognise the occupant as a very senior officer of 2 Group with a marked sense of fun, escorted it along the parade route. The Field Marshal was not amused. But by now there was very close liaison between the Army and Group, working together well as had been envisaged long ago, and all was soon forgiven.

Rapid advance imposed increasing difficulty on Group's operations, as 98 Squadron recorded in its diary on 5 September: 'Spectacular advance of our armies in France is imposing a new difficulty on the squadron. That is of catching the Hun long enough in one place to bomb him. No ops today.' Indeed between 2 and 8 September no operations were possible by day.

The U.S. 9th A.A.F. was now operating a new type of medium bomber, the Douglas A-26 Invader. Its predecessor, the Boston, had been popular. Group decided to look into the possibilities of using its successor. It had high appeal since, although it was able to carry a heavier load than the Boston, it weighed little more. Reported flight characteristics were similar. One great advantage was that there was a small communicating passage from the pilot's cockpit to the navigator's station amidships in whose compartment there was ample room for radar and radio gear. The crew comprised a pilot, a navigator and one gunner who, using periscopic sighting, controlled remotely the guns sited in dorsal and ventral barbettes.

Examples being used as formation leaders had transparent noses in which the bomb aimers sat, and this allowed a navigator to concentrate on his basic task. Bomb load could reach 4,000 lb. Only six 500-lb. bombs could be carried internally, although there was a chance this might rise to eight. A U.S.A.A.F. squadron at Dunmow had managed a 6,000-lb. load by carrying four 1,000-lb. bombs internally and four 500-lb. on wing racks. The Group Commander decided to borrow an A-26 from the Americans. Its loan ended disastrously.

Invader 41–39158 was obtained in August 1944, an early example featuring a solid nose fitted with fixed guns. Trials were brief. On

4 September the dorsal gun cupola suddenly came adrift and embedded itself in the fin. The aircraft was at 4,000 feet when it happened, and suddenly the elevator and rudder controls were blanked out. The aircraft became unmanageable. With great skill Wg. Cdr. Mitchell, D.F.C., A.F.C., brought her in for a remarkable landing. Suddenly control was wrenched from him and the aircraft careered across the airfield and hurtled into some Nissen huts. Sqn. Ldr. Wilson was killed, Flt. Lt. E. Chandler pinned beneath a nacelle. The aeroplane was completely smashed like the high hopes held. 'The very thought of remotely controlled guns is likely to make the gunners' union wag their heads—"not practical". This set-up however really has something,' an official comment had read. The loss of the aircraft brought a sudden end to any suggestion that 2 Group at this late date in the war should convert on to this new type.

The Allies were still racing across Europe, but they left behind pockets of resistance in the French Channel ports. Progressively Bomber Command reduced them to submission and 2 Group contributed on 8 and 9 September by attacking Boulogne.

Bad weather was again cutting the Mosquito offensive, but the advance caused them quickly to become the night scourge of new regions. Now they were raking trains and roads in Germany. On 5–6 September, for instance, 62 were detailed to operate, 28 in the area Eindhoven–Roermond–Liège–Hoy and 28 to attend to rail movement in the areas Düsseldorf–Kempen–Goch–Hertogenbosch–Kempen–Venlo–Eindhoven, Cologne–Rheydt–Roermond–Sittard, Cologne–Düren–Aachen–Maastrict–Kassel. A further dozen searched for shipping on the Maas–Rhine and Scheldt Estuary. The latter area quickly assumed more importance.

Antwerp was captured on 4 September, but garrisons on Walcheren in South Beveland prohibited use of the deep-water harbour by dominating the Scheldt Estuary. Enemy forces were retreating on the Breskens–Flushing route and so on 11 September a heavy attack was mounted on the Breskens ferry pier and a vehicle park close by. At night 98 Squadron illuminated the area for twenty Mosquitoes of 305 and 613 Squadrons. For several nights these raids continued and on 12 September the Brabant–Beveland causeway was the mediums' target and later the Walcheren–South Beveland bridge. Bostons attacked the ferry stages at Ternuezen, a ship being fired and a large ferry left burning. Still the vehicles were crossing the routes to the island and when the medium bombers attacked on 13th they breached the causeway in three places.

Meanwhile it had been decided that Boulogne must be overrun. A 2 Group raid was mounted on 14th against La Trescrie strong point, a small village to the north-east of the town marked by the Army with red smoke then taken by the Canadians who congratulated the bombing force. Boulogne was a hard nut to crack and on 16th another raid was

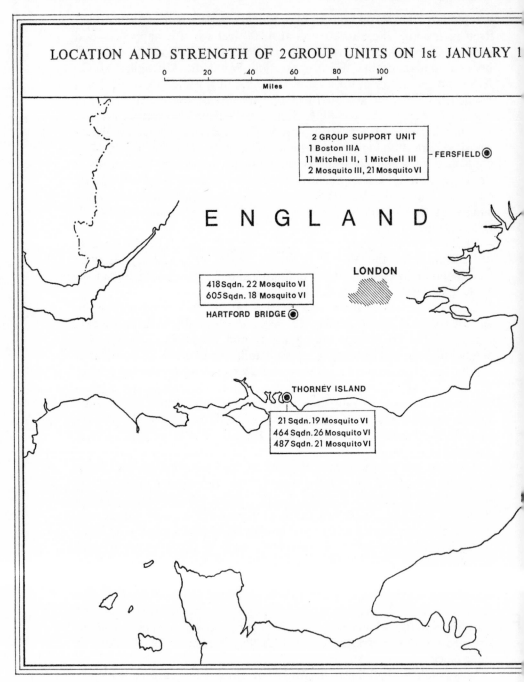

LOCATION AND STRENGTH OF 2 GROUP UNITS ON 1st JANUARY 1

0   20   40   60   80   100

Miles

2 GROUP SUPPORT UNIT
1 Boston IIIA
11 Mitchell II, 1 Mitchell III
2 Mosquito III, 21 Mosquito VI

FERSFIELD ◉

E N G L A N D

418 Sqdn. 22 Mosquito VI
605 Sqdn. 18 Mosquito VI

LONDON

HARTFORD BRIDGE ◉

THORNEY ISLAND ◉

21 Sqdn. 19 Mosquito VI
464 Sqdn. 26 Mosquito VI
487 Sqdn. 21 Mosquito VI

MAP 19. *See Appendix 12, pages 512–514 for notes*

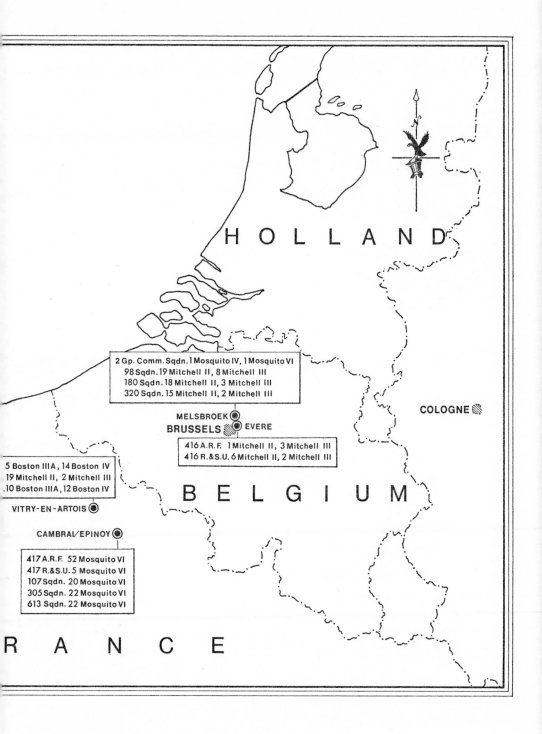

H O L L A N D

COLOGNE ◈

2 Gp. Comm. Sqdn. 1 Mosquito IV, 1 Mosquito VI
98 Sqdn. 19 Mitchell II, 8 Mitchell III
180 Sqdn. 18 Mitchell II, 3 Mitchell III
320 Sqdn. 15 Mitchell II, 2 Mitchell III

MELSBROEK ◉
BRUSSELS ◉◉ EVERE

416 A.R.F. 1 Mitchell II, 3 Mitchell III
416 R.&S.U. 6 Mitchell II, 2 Mitchell III

5 Boston III A, 14 Boston IV
19 Mitchell II, 2 Mitchell III
10 Boston III A, 12 Boston IV

VITRY-EN-ARTOIS ◉

B E L G I U M

CAMBRAI/EPINOY ◉

417 A.R.F. 52 Mosquito VI
417 R.&S.U. 5 Mosquito VI
107 Sqdn. 20 Mosquito VI
305 Sqdn. 22 Mosquito VI
613 Sqdn. 22 Mosquito VI

R A N C E

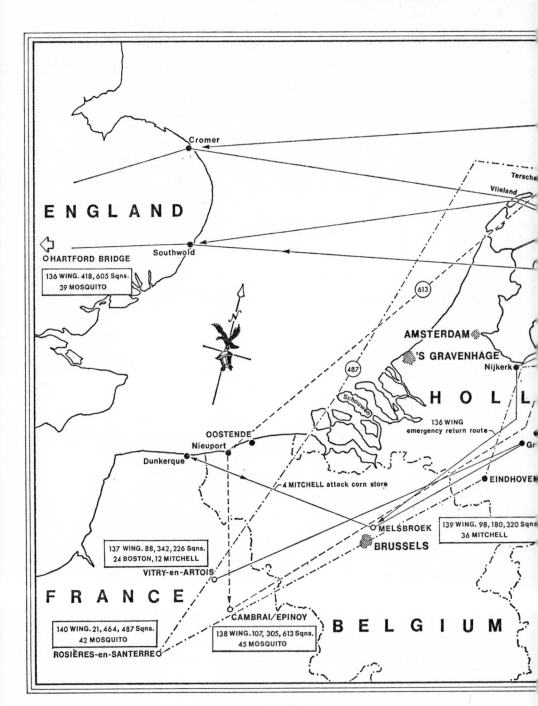

ENGLAND

O HARTFORD BRIDGE

136 WING. 418, 605 Sqns.
39 MOSQUITO

Cromer

Southwold

Terschel

Vlieland

613

AMSTERDAM

'S GRAVENHAGE

Nijkerk

487

Schouwen

HOLL

136 WING
emergency return route

Gr

OOSTENDE

Nieuport

Dunkerque

4 MITCHELL attack corn store

EINDHOVE

139 WING. 98, 180, 320 Sqns.
36 MITCHELL

MELSBROEK

BRUSSELS

137 WING. 88, 342, 226 Sqns.
24 BOSTON, 12 MITCHELL

VITRY-en-ARTOIS

FRANCE

CAMBRAI/EPINOY

BELGIUM

140 WING. 21, 464, 487 Sqns.
42 MOSQUITO

ROSIÈRES-en-SANTERRE

138 WING. 107, 305, 613 Sqns.
45 MOSQUITO

MAP 20.

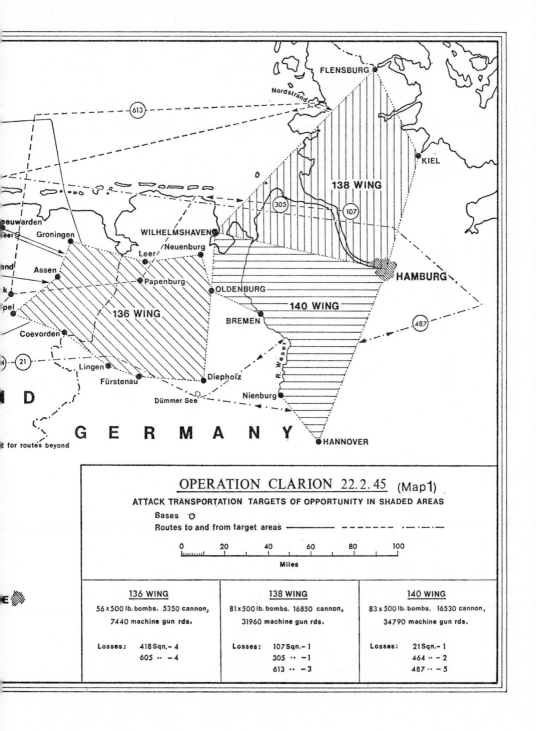

OPERATION CLARION 22.2.45 (Map1)

ATTACK TRANSPORTATION TARGETS OF OPPORTUNITY IN SHADED AREAS

Bases O

Routes to and from target areas ——— — — — — · — · —

0   20   40   60   80   100

Miles

136 WING	138 WING	140 WING
56 x 500 lb. bombs. 5350 cannon, 7440 machine gun rds.	81 x 500 lb. bombs. 16850 cannon, 31960 machine gun rds.	83 x 500 lb. bombs. 16530 cannon, 34790 machine gun rds.
Losses: 418 Sqn.– 4 605 ·· – 4	Losses: 107 Sqn.– 1 305 ·· – 1 613 ·· – 3	Losses: 21 Sqn.– 1 464 ·· – 2 487 ·· – 5

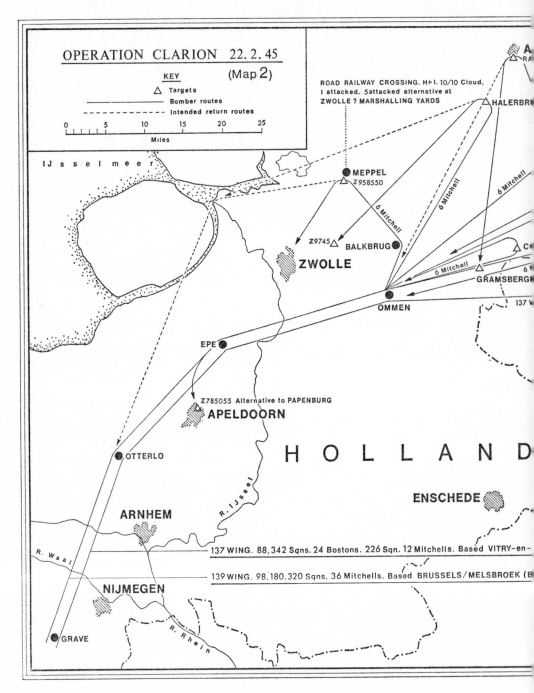

OPERATION CLARION 22.2.45

KEY   (Map 2)
△ Targets
——— Bomber routes
- - - Intended return routes

0   5   10   15   20   25
                Miles

ROAD RAILWAY CROSSING. H+l. 10/10 Cloud.
1 attacked. 5 attacked alternative at
ZWOLLE? MARSHALLING YARDS

IJ s s e l m e e r

HALERBR⌐

MEPPEL
△ Z958550

6 Mitchell   6 Mitchell   6 Mitchell

Z9745 △ BALKBRUG

ZWOLLE
                                  6 Mitchell
                                                          △ C
                        6 Mitchell △
                                          GRAMSBERG⌐
OMMEN   6
                                          137 W

EPE ●

Z785055 Alternative to PAPENBURG
APELDOORN

H O L L A N D

● OTTERLO   ENSCHEDE

ARNHEM
R. IJssel

R. Waal   137 WING. 88,342 Sqns. 24 Bostons. 226 Sqn. 12 Mitchells. Based VITRY-en-

                  139 WING. 98,180,320 Sqns. 36 Mitchells. Based BRUSSELS/MELSBROEK (B

NIJMEGEN
                  R. Rhein
● GRAVE

MAP 21.

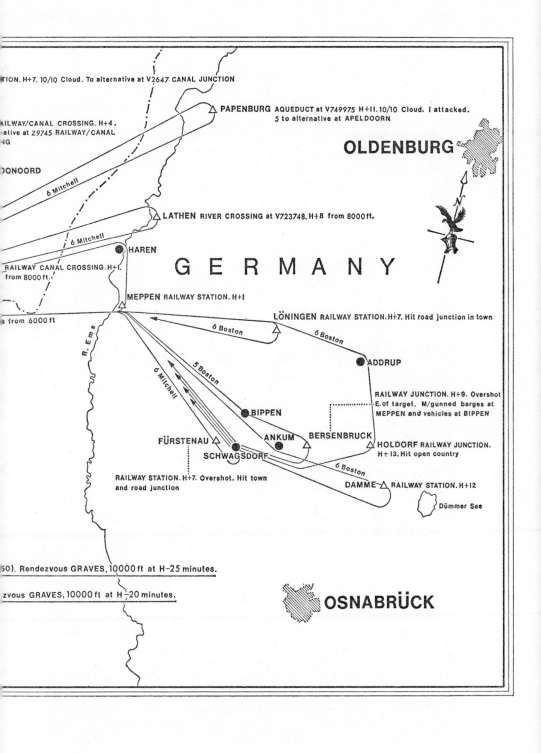

TION. H+7. 10/10 Cloud. To alternative at V2647 CANAL JUNCTION

△ PAPENBURG AQUEDUCT at V749975 H+11. 10/10 Cloud. I attacked.
5 to alternative at APELDOORN

AILWAY/CANAL CROSSING. H+4.
ative at Z9745 RAILWAY/CANAL
NG

OLDENBURG

ONOORD

6 Mitchell

△ LATHEN RIVER CROSSING at V723748. H+8 from 8000ft.

6 Mitchell

● HAREN

G E R M A N Y

RAILWAY CANAL CROSSING. H+I.
from 8000ft.

MEPPEN RAILWAY STATION. H+I

s from 6000 ft

LÖNINGEN RAILWAY STATION. H+7. Hit road junction in town

6 Boston

6 Boston

● ADDRUP

5 Boston

6 Mitchell

RAILWAY JUNCTION. H+9. Overshot
E. of target. M/gunned barges at
MEPPEN and vehicles at BIPPEN

● BIPPEN

ANKUM △   BERSENBRUCK

FÜRSTENAU △

△ HOLDORF RAILWAY JUNCTION.
H+13. Hit open country

SCHWAGSDORF

6 Boston

RAILWAY STATION. H+7. Overshot. Hit town
and road junction

DAMME △ RAILWAY STATION. H+12

Dümmer See

R. Ems

50). Rendezvous GRAVES, 10000 ft at H-25 minutes.

zvous GRAVES, 10000 ft at H-20 minutes.

OSNABRÜCK

made, this time against Fort de la Crèche which guarded the town from the north.

Perhaps no episode in the Second World War dragged from participants more courage than was expended—largely fruitlessly—during the airborne landings around Arnhem. All the tactical elements of 2 T.A.F. were involved but hand to hand fighting limited 2 Group's contribution.

Shortly before 13.00 hours on 17 September all the Boston and Mitchell squadrons were despatched against the Ede barracks, 137 Wing leading to support the landings. Weather was so poor that some crews did not bomb and many bombs fell wide. Operating at low level Mosquito crews were more successful. They had five targets and hits were claimed on all. The official summary of the daylight operations on this day read as follows:

'2 Group Opsum No. 299 Dawn–Dusk 17.9.44: (i) 42 Mosquitoes of 138 and 140 Wings, 24 Bostons of 137 Wing and 48 Mitchells of 137 and 139 Wings attacked barracks at Nijmegen, Arnhem and Ede. 82 attacked dropping 425 × 500 lb. bombs. Of the five Mosquito targets, hits were reported on all with excellent results in at least one attack. Weather conditions 6–8/10 at 6,000–9,000 feet hampered medium attacks, but one barrack block was hit and set on fire. Some boxes made three runs over target in order to obtain a visual. 3 Mosquitoes lost to flak, 14 other aircraft hit. (ii) 16 Mosquitoes 140 Wing detailed barracks near Nijmegen. 5 attacked at 12.22–12.30 hours from 50–500 feet. Some hits generally unseen. 3 attacked alternative target—barrack square at Cleve inside Germany. 7 abortive, 1 damaged by bird strike on run up, 5 couldn't locate, 1 abandoned, 1 missing hit by flak over target, 4 damaged by flak two by birds. (iii) 34 Mosquitoes 139 Wing attacked targets at Arnhem—4 aiming points. (a) 8 attacked, bursts on south side of archives building. (b) 8 attacked, bursts in east part near water tower. (c) 9 attacked large square building, straddled with hits in N.E. corner. (d) 9 attacked, 1 hit on target area, buildings on south side left burning.'

Poor weather at night cut any further Mosquito support but rail routes leading to Arnhem and Walcheren were attacked on 19th–20th. On 21st Calais and Boulogne were raided then the Army followed up by capturing Fort de la Creche.

Close support to the Arnhem landing was almost impossible and poor visibility made it dangerous. On 25 September mortar and gun positions were raided but in the target area eight Fw 190s broke through the fighter screen and destroyed two Mitchells of 98 Squadron. This was the last occasion during the war when they achieved such success. The bombers had no close escort, relying upon area cover by three Mustang squadrons.

For many of the crews 26 September was, indeed, a red-letter day. The Boston and Mitchell squadrons made their first raid on Germany and bombed a road/rail bridge at Cleve. Direct hits were achieved by 226 Squadron. The flight was long, tiring, visibility was bad and navigation difficult. A swarm of Spitfires and U.S.A.A.F. Thunderbolts escorted them. German targets increasingly figured in battle orders and by the end of the month Goch, Geldern and Emmerich had all come under attack. Nightly, Mosquitoes were roaming West Germany harassing routes leading to Arnhem, Walcheren and the railways supplying the Wehrmacht.

October's weather proved bad, cutting Group effort and preventing operations on thirteen days and eleven nights. On 2nd a strong point at Huissen ahead of the Canadian push towards Walcheren was raided, close army support continuing until 13th with raids in the Arnhem, Ardenburg and Cadzand areas, after which the enemy was quickly driven from the latter. Well behind the front the POL dump at Amersfoort was attended to. At night Mosquitoes maintained their *Ranger* flights over the western rail network linking the fronts.

On 8 October the general order for the Mitchell and Boston squadrons to move to the Continent was given, but it was 21 October before they were all operating from the European mainland. First to go were Nos. 98, 180 and 320 Squadrons which began to move on 9 October. The Boston squadrons were more mobile and did not leave until 16th with 226 Squadron, whose present task was to lead them into action using its blind bombing gear.

A new phase in operations began on 14 October when Nos. 88, 226 and 342 Squadrons began a lengthy series of operations against important bridges leading to the 2nd Army front, mainly rail bridges over the Maas and Ijssel at Zutphen and Deventer. Once all the squadrons were at their new bases they directed their attention almost daily to bridges at Hedel, Roermond, Venlo and Deventer. They were small targets, hard to destroy. Persistent raids frequently undid repair work, but the flak around them was intense and often as much as a third of the bomber force would return holed.

On 31 October the Gestapo Headquarters in Jutland, housed in two buildings of Aarhus University, was destroyed by 24 Mosquitoes drawn from Nos. 21, 464 and 487 Squadrons and led by the veterans Reynolds and Sismore. Crews were briefed, using a model, for this raid to destroy Gestapo records. Four sections each of six aircraft including a Mosquito of the Film Production Unit comprised the formation, and 11 second delay bombs were carried in the bellies of the aircraft to achieve greater accuracy. Timing had to be excellent to permit a concentrated attack by waves each avoiding bursting bombs.

The surprise attack in misty weather was made from a very low level, and bombs were extremely well placed. The round trip totalled 1,235 miles. Later a letter was captured from an SS officer who had been at the receiving end. He wrote 'Last Tuesday a terrible disaster happened in Aarhus which has made a great impression on us. The whole of our H.Q. was shot up by English airmen. 22 of our men are dead and many are wounded and missing. Some soldiers were also killed. The Head of

Security Services, SS Obersturn Fuehrer Lonechun, was also killed. The attack took place about 12 midday and was concentrated on the university where our H.Q. was situated. Our local H.Q. is very isolated but could easily be hit by deep diving bombers without much damage to the civilian population.' Air Vice-Marshal Embry and his navigator Peter Clapham were flying on the raid, the former under the usual disguise of 'Wg. Cdr. Smith'. To find a Group Commander flying on operations was unusual, but so typical of Embry. He was never the sort of person who would ask others to do what he was unprepared to do himself.

Plans had been laid for Operation *Infatuation* on 28 October. The 2nd Canadian Army was approaching to clear the enemy from Walcheren, the entire centre of which had been flooded. The Wehrmacht was concentrated on a coastal strip to the north and north-west of the island. It was planned that Boston IIIAs with SCI gear would screen a landing force at Westkapelle from observation. Next day they would screen a landing in the Zooterlande area. Bostons would trail smoke over a 3¾ mile stretch for 45 minutes, flying singly at five-minute intervals. Next day twelve Bostons would repeat the style for one hour. Crews stood by on 1 November, their aircraft loaded with smoke. Visibility was very poor and the operation was postponed, but bad weather again caused the raid to be cancelled.

November's weather proved worse than October's. On seventeen days and thirteen nights it was impossible to operate, but if the weather was likely to offer the slightest chance of success operations went ahead. Of 1,199 sorties despatched by day 557 were abortive due to the weather. During the month the Mosquito force was exclusively employed at night, usually in a strength of about forty aircraft for the harassment of enemy troops from the bomb line to about thirty miles behind, and for the continuous harassment of rail, road and water communications used by the enemy to supply his forces. 217 trains, 94 barges and four small ships were attacked. The main task for the mediums was again the destruction of bridges particularly those at Venlo, Deventer and Zwolle, a dozen raids being directed at four vital bridges with limited success. It was reported on 7 November that the Venlo bridge had been hit and that the spans were down, but the enemy quickly repaired it. Rail centres at Oldenzaal, Kempen, Viersen and Rheydt were bombed and some damage resulted. Cross roads at Randerath, Brachelen and Harderath were bombed to aid the Army. Poor weather and heavy flak brought none too good results, over 30% of the attacking aircraft being damaged. Absence of fighter reaction meant that only small cover was needed, given by 83 and 84 Groups and usually amounting to three Spitfire squadrons.

In the six days 3–8 November six attacks were despatched against the Venlo and Roermond bridges before bad weather again set in. In the circuit over base, back from Roermond, the weather was poor.

FW228 of 180 Squadron collided with an aircraft of 98. All of '228's crew were killed and FW201: C of 98 Squadron landed badly damaged. No. 226 Squadron's second box had dropped its load straddling the target and getting at least two hits.

After a week of inactivity bombing was resumed on 18th with raids on Venlo and Kempen. On the Venlo raid of 19th the lead aircraft of 226 Squadron flown by Sqn. Ldr. G. Campbell received a direct hit in the wing outboard of the nacelle. The wing immediately folded up and the aircraft fell to its doom taking its experienced crew.

Another spectacular loss was of HD336: T of 226 Squadron flown by Plt. Off. S. Moore. Six squadrons were raiding Rheydt marshalling yards when it was decided, because of cloud, to attack München-Gladbach instead. Flak was extremely heavy and '336 received a direct hit in the port engine. Enveloped in flames it dived away and exploded on hitting the ground. Seven other aircraft were also damaged. It was an unlucky period for 226 Squadron since they lost another aircraft during the Deventer raid of 26th. At the time of bombing FW230: B, Flg. Off. Twining's aircraft was hit amidships and broke in two just below the waist gun positions, and all were lost. To some extent the loss was avenged when a box of 88 Squadron scored a direct hit on the bridge and some very near misses on the afternoon of 29th. The same day 98 and 180 Squadrons scored very near misses on the central span of the Zwolle bridge.

For Wg. Cdr. Hamer and crew the latter raid was certainly eventful. Soon after setting course Hamer's gunner reported fighters, but they made no attack. Shortly before the target a V-2 rocket shot up in front of them then, seconds later, the aircraft's aileron balance and control cable were put out of action by flak. Hamer managed to hold on for bombing and the bomb aimer reckoned their bombs hit the target. Then the pilot managed to get the machine fully under control by applying coarse rudder and opening up one engine to get more lift. As they crossed the Allied lines near Arnhem they were hit again. The aircraft started to slide about and had to leave the formation. Both engines were behaving beautifully so Hamer flew on, escorted by another Mitchell. Near base he decided to try a belly landing and ordered the crew out, although the navigator opted to stay with him. For an hour they stooged around the airfield awaiting a clearance. They were beginning their landing run when a V-1 flying bomb shot past and once more they were in the vicinity of flak—their own! It was getting dusk and possibly the excited airfield defenders could not see the Mitchell. Eventually Hamer came in to land and to his horror saw a five-ton lorry in his path. Luckily it managed to get out of his way and FW192: Y made a good landing. Both gunners, who had safely baled out, stood at the ready to greet their skipper. The navigator, Flg. Off. Pulman, was on the first sortie of his second tour.

December's weather proved the worst of an already bad three months.

On sixteen days and fifteen nights operations were impossible. The day-bomber squadrons managed only 22 operations and had often to attack secondary targets. At night Mosquitoes sometimes operated when visibility at bases was less than 800 yards. The last eight days of December saw the Group operating at maximum effort to support the Army in repelling the Ardennes offensive. During the month the Mosquitoes shot up 74 trains and attacked over 1,000 wagons. On three occasions they made night-long attacks on villages housing German troops. During one night 140 Wing managed a complete turn round operating ninety of the 140 sorties despatched during which 75 M.E.T. were destroyed in the Ardennes.

Main targets for the mediums were choke points. They raided four rail junctions too, two bridges and Dunkirk. The latter, still in German hands far behind the lines, was being partly used for practice bombing and twice the Group Support Unit took part in the raids. Most of the targets for the medium force lay on the fringe of the Ruhr where they met very heavy flak. Much of the land was snow-clad and, with poor visibility, target identification was difficult. The best results were achieved at Geldern on 3rd, Gemünd choke point on 24th and Recht road junction. Bridges at Deventer and Zwolle suffered more superficial damage.

On 3 December 180 Squadron set off for choke points at Kaldenkirchen and Straelen. FW209, Flg. Off. L. H. Iddon's aircraft, was hit and he ordered the crew out as the machine fell out of control. Flt. Sgt. E. L. Woolf baled out but the navigator was injured and decided not to jump. The W. op./air gunner, Flt. Sgt. F. Tomkins, went forward to assist and succeeded in landing the battered Mitchell at Eindhoven. For his splendid achievement he was awarded the Conspicuous Gallantry Medal.

The busiest night for the Mosquitoes for some time was 6–7 December. They made the most of fair weather for snow was about to fall. No. 140 Wing detailed 51 aircraft, 34 harassing rail movement in Holland and 14 rail movement in western Germany as well as canal traffic and activity on the Ijssel Dam. Three more were ordered for a special task, destruction of a rail bridge near Haarlem or the blocking of the railway there. The attack was carried out, the train was seen, but results could not be assessed. Of 51 detailed, 44 aircraft made attacks and one of 487 Squadron was missing.

Meanwhile 48 Mosquitoes of 138 Wing were detailed, 43 to harass and attack throughout the night enemy troops billeting in Oberbruch and five others troops in Wassenburg. All attacked with H.E. and incendiary loads in the continuous light of flares and poured 10,870 rounds of cannon fire and 13,820 of machine-gun ammunition into Oberbruch. The village was soon burning, then the weather began to deteriorate and torrential rain interfered with the raid. Later the weather improved and more fire was added to the inferno. On 11th–12th three other villages received similar treatment and the following night 140 Wing raided Leiden railway station where V-2 rockets were being unloaded. There the weather was so poor that the attack had to be halted.

Over the Continental bases thick fog and very cold conditions set in during the middle of the month, conditions for which the enemy was waiting. Despite the intensive campaign against the enemy transport routes von Rundstedt, the German commander, had been skilfully withdrawing armoured divisions during October and November, resting and re-equipping them. Then he secretly moved fourteen infantry and ten armoured divisions towards the Ardennes Sector of the First American Army. Hitler had set his heart on a massive counter attack which should cut the Allies in two, would thrust its way through the gap over which 2 Group had fought so bitterly in 1940 and perhaps bring a second Dunkirk. If the Wehrmacht could stabilise a line along its western front, German troops could be released to stem the surge from the east. What was needed was a period of very bad weather which would ground the Allied air forces.

It came in mid December and in the thick fog of 16th the Sixth Panzer Army attacked near Monschu, the Fifth Panzer in the middle of the front between Olzheim and Bitburg and the Seventh Army on the left flank near Echternach. It was a complete surprise to the Allies who were thrown into confusion momentarily. Eisenhower read the situation aright and ordered large American reinforcements to the area from the north and from the south where a thrust had been directed towards the Saar. St. Vith and Bastogne were tenaciously held and the enemy forced on to muddy side roads which slowed his hoped-for advance to the Meuse.

For almost a week dense fog covered the battle area and many Allied air bases. Low cloud, rain, snow and fog did what the Luftwaffe could never now achieve: they denied air support to our armies. All that could be done was to send in the heavy bombers under radar control to attack communications and fuel dumps and such targets to the rear of the fighting zone.

On 18th–19th 24 Mosquitoes of 138 Wing had been sent to the fighting area and ordered to attack any movement seen on roads leading to the Ardennes and in the Düsseldorf, Trier and Koblenz areas. A further 49 of 140 Wing were despatched to the same areas in the second part of the night. They all found very poor weather and by the time 140 Wing was there the 10/10 cloud was down to 1,500 feet and in places a mere 300 feet. They managed to bomb 14 road/railway junctions, 8 small towns and various roads. No operations were possible on the next three nights and it was 22nd–23rd before Mosquitoes again operated.

There was a slight improvement in the weather on 22 December. Three Mitchell squadrons attempted a *Gee-H* attack on troop concentrations at Hinebach, but they found 10/10 cloud and results were unseen.

On 23rd a high-pressure system which had been slowly moving westwards reached the battle area. It brought five days of fine weather— and the Tactical Air Force went into action. 2 Group first delivered heavy assaults on troop concentrations at Darscheid and Schmidtheim. But the fluidity of the battle now made bomber support difficult and planned operations had twice to be postponed. As 342 Squadron flew over the target area they noted that 'the Ardennes are white with snow, the rivers are frozen and target identification is extremely difficult'.

Twenty-six Mosquitoes operated on 22nd–23rd, some making two sorties which brought the total to 37. They left an ammunition train ablaze from end to end, and other trains were attacked. After nightfall on 23rd, in better weather, a grand effort was staged. Fifty Mosquitoes of 138 Wing were despatched to the Koblenz–Cologne–Düren–Stadtkyll area in search of trade. Thirty-seven fired over 10,000 rounds and 40,000 machine-gun rounds at five large road convoys, eight trains and 45 vehicles. By the time their patrol time was up the weather had clamped and thirteen more had to land away at Manston and Tangmere. A further 54 of 140 Wing operated in the same area, along seven rail routes leading to the battlefield and over three main roads. Between them, the thirteen diverted and 140 Wing's aircraft had fired 13,430 cannon and 15,630 machine-gun rounds so that the total for the night was 23,560 rounds machine gun and 56,890 cannon, the greatest in any night so far. Attacks had been particularly directed against Blankenheim, Mayen, Bitersborn, and Prum where the 5th Panzer Army's H.Q. was left on fire.

Two day raids followed on 24th, Mitchells being directed to Kall and Bostons and Mitchells to Gemünd. Near the latter Bf 109s which had been active over the front tried to ward off the bombers. They were intercepted by the 84 Group escort but broke through to 88 Squadron one of whose Bostons was shot down. In the hazy conditions of mid-winter the railway target at Gemünd was not identified and rail sidings north of the village were bombed instead. Later, six medium-bomber squadrons bombed rail installations at Recht in Belgium. They caught sight of an Me 262 jet fighter, but it did not close.

Whilst the weather was excellent it was decided to mount a supreme night effort on 24th–25th. No. 138 Wing operating from Cambrai managed a complete turn round and 81–91 sorties were effective. Targets were again mainly close to the fighting, woods at Neuerburg and Vianden, the Forêt de Boulange, Prum village and detraining points at St. Vith, Neuiberg and Euskirchen. A total of 221 500-lb. bombs was dropped and rounds fired were cannon 27,660 and machine gun 33,150. Ammunition dumps, large M.E.T. convoys and the rail station at Geroldstein were left on fire. The 2 Group Rear Force, 140 Wing, managed 48 sorties forming the second wave to the same area. They used 130 500-lb. bombs, 16,300 rounds cannon and 22,100 of machine gun. They had considerable success at Meurenbruch where an ammunition train was attacked and disappeared in a gigantic explosion. From another the fragments hurtled 4,000 feet high.

The weather was not so good on Christmas Day, but the mediums were ordered to bomb Tondorf and Stadtkyll. No. 342 Squadron was called at 05.30 but there was ice in the aircraft and only seven crews got away. One minute before the target they and 226 Squadron were recalled. Bad weather had prevented the fighter escort getting away. This did not seem so to the crews who said 'We never saw so many Allied fighters in the air!' The weather at base was very bad and the landing of the aircraft took a long time. Once that was complete, the customary Christmas dinner was served, officers waiting on the airmen. There had been some flak during the morning raids, in one of which Flt. Sgt. Nichol of 98 Squadron had back injuries and died before base was reached. The Mitchells had been attacking Stadtkyll where about 250 trucks were hit.

Once home a hectic day ensued for all with much dining, wining and inebriation. For 226 Squadron the evening meal was memorable as their French cook did his best and the Group Captain, showing Christmas spirit, announced to the delight of all that Flg. Off. Lind serving a sentence of enforced abstinence for an earlier indiscretion was formally released.

The weather was deteriorating again although Mosquitoes operated on 25–26 December. Soon they had to be recalled; mist was rising over their bases. Fog, too, came down on the medium-bomber bases and stayed until 29th when Vielshalm close to our forward troops was bombed. Conditions were still poor next day but 137 Wing managed a repeat attack on the previous day's target. Mosquito harassment continued and on 31 December–1 January 71 sorties were flown and two V-1s were downed in addition to the usual interdictor work.

By this time the German offensive had spent itself far from the Meuse. Another attempt yet to be made, against the U.S. Seventh Army, was to be equally fruitless. Hitler was very dissatisfied and ordered this other thrust to be made beginning 3 January against Bastogne. Before that date the Luftwaffe mounted a desperate operation to eliminate much of the Tactical Air Force with 'der Grosse Schlag', Operation *Hermann*, on New Year's Day.

The composition of 2 Group then was No. 137 Wing (88 and 342 Squadrons—Bostons, and 226 Squadron—Mitchells based at Vitry-en-Artois), No. 138 Wing (107, 305 and 613 Mosquito squadrons based at Epinoy) and 139 Wing (Nos. 98, 180 and 320 Squadrons flying Mitchells based at Melsbroek) forming 2 Group (Continental). No. 136 Wing (418 and 605 Squadrons flying Mosquitoes based at Hartford Bridge) and No. 140 Wing (21, 464 and 487 Squadrons flying Mosquitoes based at Thorney Island) formed 2 Group (Rear).

Operation *Hermann* had been planned as a prelude to the Ardennes offensive but the weather was so poor that it had to be postponed and the essential veil of secrecy maintained, which was difficult. As many possible fighters and fighter-bombers as could be spared were mustered for a tree-top assault on Allied airfields in Belgium and Holland. Great care was taken in planning so that each group of fighters was allotted two Ju 88 night-fighters to lead the formation accurately. Nearly 800 aircraft were mustered for the operation launched shortly after 08.00 hours on 1 January against sixteen airfields. Briefing of the enemy crews was not good, and some formations became disorganised and appeared to lose their way. The precise manner of attack was not apparently laid down and the whole operation was, by Allied standards, chaotic. This was fortunate because some of the airfields attacked were ice-bound and ground defences were far below the desirable.

Meanwhile, on some of the 2 Group stations, activity was considerable too. At 05.15 hours No. 88 Squadron was brought to readiness, also 226 and 342 Squadrons comprising the Wing. Further east at Melsbroek the crews of 139 Wing tumbled early from their beds. Briefing, too, was fortunately early, for Domburg communications centre in the Ardennes. Thirty-six Mitchells of 139 Wing were to lead, meeting their two Spitfire escort squadrons of 84 Group six miles south of Arlon at 12,000 feet. Then they would head for the target and return via Neufchâtel with 137 Wing's twelve Mitchells and 24 Bostons tagging along behind.

Take-off time was 08.30. Twelve crews of 98 and nine of 180 Squadron, with eleven of 320 Squadron, made up the lead group. On reaching the fighter rendezvous, they circled for ten minutes, but the Spitfires did not show up. They could not: the German intruders were already at work. The bomber leader decided to risk going on without the escort and 137 Wing followed suit.

At 09.25 a swarm of Bf 109s and Fw 190s roared across Melsbroek at roof-top height firing indiscriminately and inaccurately. Fortunately 98 Squadron's remaining Mitchells were well dispersed, but cannon and machine-gun fire tore into HD351 and HD353; FV982 was so badly damaged that it became a write-off. Two of 320's machines suffered superficial damage but none of the personnel of the two squadrons was injured. No. 180 Squadron had six Mitchells on dispersals all of which were damaged and three of which—FV903, FV945 and FW199—were write-offs. Additionally two Mitchells in the hands of 416 A.R.F. and a Boston IV BZ444 were destroyed in the half-hour attack. There were other aircraft on the field. Those which suffered included five veteran Harrow transports of 271 Squadron.

The inadequacy of the enemy was patently obvious when a count of his losses was made, which concluded that 137 aircraft had come down in the British zone and 5 in the American. Post-war research never fully discovered the enemy loss figure. Some sources now put it as high as 300 aircraft. Remains of 96 were found in the British Sector and 115 in the American. In any case the losses were the highest ever sustained in one attack during the whole of air warfare. Some enemy aircraft came down in German territory and a number are known to have fallen in the Ijsselmeer. British losses were considerable, 144 aircraft destroyed and 84 seriously damaged, but the attack did not put the 2nd T.A.F. out of action.

While the attacks were being made the 2 Group force tried for Domburg. They found the small target was difficult and finally they settled for a nearby village upon which they rained their loads.

The assault on Melsbroek brought great confusion and 139 Wing diverted most of its aircraft to Epinoy. Other squadrons flew to their own base which had escaped attack, did a rapid turn round and bombed Zaltbommel rail bridge where 226 Squadron scored two direct hits. It had been a hectic day and at night the Mosquitoes were ordered to make a maximum effort against the enemy building up around Bastogne. Unfortunately the weather clamped and operations were impossible.

The weather in January could only be described as appalling. Operations were impossible on 22 days and twelve nights, and on many other occasions were possible only from Britain or the Continent. Nevertheless, 733 day sorties were attempted and thirteen attacks made, mostly against the villages of Houffalize, St. Vith, Wegburg and Wassenburg. At night Mosquitoes attempted 989 sorties, a commendable effort in poor conditions. On every possible occasion troops in the Ardennes area were relentlessly assaulted. Some 75 trains and 2,000 trucks were beaten up and over 600 M.E.T. attacked; night operations costing in all twelve crews and two more by day.

The Ardennes offensive was over by 16 January when Allied troops closed in towards Houffalize from north and south, then drove the enemy eastwards. The von Rundstedt offensive had delayed the Allied advance about six weeks, but now plans for the advance to the Rhine and the taking of Germany could but succeed.

Chapter 23
To the Rhine, the Elbe and Victory

Once the 'Battle of the Bulge' was over the Allied Armies regrouped. Three tasks were tabled: (1) destruction of the Wehrmacht west of the Rhine, (2) crossing the Rhine, and (3) liquidation of remaining enemy forces by thrusts across Germany. It was decided to leave the Ruhr and encircle it with advances to the north and south. Chosen Rhine crossing points lay between Mainz and Karlsruhe, and Rheinburg and Rees in the north. It was over the latter region, and especially around Wesel, that 2 Group operated. The Canadian 2nd Corps was to hold the line of the Rhine and Maas from Emmerich to the sea and could turn to 2 Group for tactical support.

The Rhine, notorious on account of its width and strong currents, had to be crossed before melting Alpine snow brought flood conditions. Two operations were therefore planned, *Veritable* in which British and Canadian troops were to advance to the line Xanten–Cleve, and *Grenade* in which the U.S. Ninth Army would advance from the Julich–Roermond line to the river. During these operations as much of the enemy army west of the Rhine was to be destroyed as was possible, whilst the Tactical Air Force was to attack routes leading to the river from the east.

Wegburg communications centre was under attack by 320 Squadron on 23 January. Just before bombing flak splinters hit Sgt. Holleman, fracturing a bone in the left arm where a main nerve was severed causing paralysis of the wrist and hand. Despite the pain he made no mention of his trouble until after the bombing, when the Belgian navigator, Flg. Off. Verhulsel, bound the arm whilst Sgt. Slater helped fly FR200: Q and brought it in to a good landing. Holleman had refused morphia—he thought it might impair his senses, which was only true on a long mission.

Blind bombing using *Gee-H* was now reaching a peak of effectiveness, and bombing accuracy further improved when Mobile Radar Control Posts were established near the forward positions. Fighter interception was now almost nil, but flak remained a menace. On 6 February, for instance, when Deventer was the target, 27 aircraft of 137 and 139 Wings received flak damage. Nevertheless 139 Wing operated later against oil stores at Emmerich.

Veritable was launched on 8 February. During the previous night

90 Mosquitoes set out to kill as many enemy soldiers as possible in towns, billets and on roads ahead of the assault areas, as well as to harass roads and railways as far away as Hamm and Munster. Already their night offensive had taken them to distant Magdeburg and Brunswick. Additionally on 7th–8th 95 Stirling IVs and Halifaxes of 38 Group co-operated with 2 Group by bombing three towns west of the Rhine.

After the army attack was launched Bostons and Mitchells hit Kranenburg, bombing about 1,000 yards ahead of advancing Canadians, bombs from the first box running straight through the town which was captured soon after. Next night 63 Mosquito sorties were despatched. No. 140 Wing operated in the area Kempen–Geldern–Rheinburg–Essen, 138 Wing ahead of the bomb line in the zone Nijmegen–Rhine–Cologne–Nijmegen leaving 16 other Mosquitoes to roam the railways in the area Deventer–Arnhem–Wesel–Unna–Paderborn–Osnabruck–Almelo–Deventer.

By day Bostons and Mitchells attacked communications centres at Rheinburg, Geldern, Xanten, Sonsbeck, Kevelaer, Udem and Weeze. On 10th–11th 100 Mosquito sorties were flown over the battle area, and on routes Apeldoorn–Hamm and west of the line Roermond–Neuss. Cleve fell on 12 February and despite bad weather a footing on the Rhine bank was secured on 14 February.

A feature on many nights at this period was the use of Halifax IIIs and Stirling IVs of 38 Group for bombing principal towns, mainly in the path of the advance to come under Operation *Grenade*. Operating under 2 Group control, they rained some heavy loads upon Grevenbroich, Erkelenz, Wegburg, Nederkrutchen, Udem and Marienbaum. The use of Stirlings as bombers long after the type had been withdrawn from Bomber Command was far from uneventful. On 21–22 February Rees across the Rhine on the British front was the target for 196 Squadron. Wg. Cdr. M. W. L. Baker in LJ894 was shot down by heavy flak. Then, at 22.30 hours, as Flt. Lt. D. R. Campbell was bringing LK126 in to land at Shepherds Grove he was fired upon by an intruder—possibly an Me 410. Although the Stirling was set on fire he managed to land the aircraft from which all except the rear gunner escaped.

At 13.00 hours on 22 February a massive operation was unleashed against road and rail facilities throughout Germany. Some 9,000 aircraft took part operating over the area Emden–Berlin–Dresden–Vienna–Mulhouse. The aim of the operation was destruction of all communications facilities—marshalling yards, rail facilities and crossings, garages, canal locks and road junctions—in short, any destruction which could cause interference with the communications system. It had been concluded that such attacks if on a wide scale might cause more inconvenience than massed attacks on larger targets.

Group detailed 215 sorties for this, Operation *Clarion*. From the Continent 176 sorties were flown and the rest by 136 Wing from Britain.

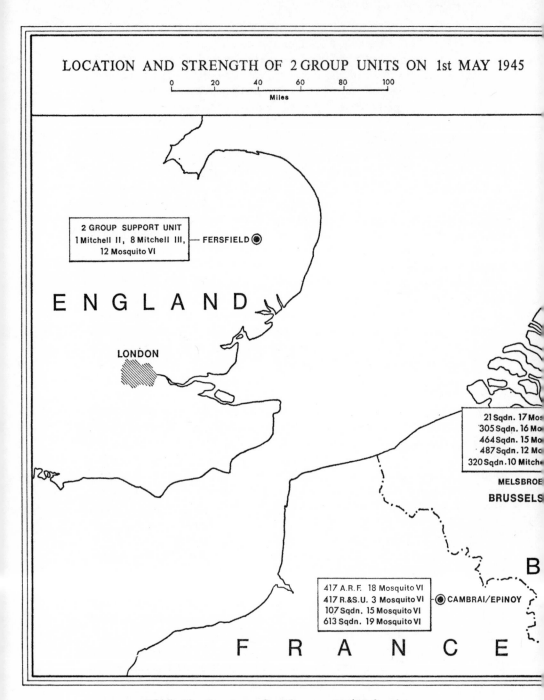

LOCATION AND STRENGTH OF 2 GROUP UNITS ON 1st MAY 1945

0   20   40   60   80   100
Miles

2 GROUP SUPPORT UNIT
1 Mitchell II, 8 Mitchell III,
12 Mosquito VI
— FERSFIELD ◉

E N G L A N D

LONDON

21 Sqdn. 17 Mos
305 Sqdn. 16 Mo
464 Sqdn. 15 Mo
487 Sqdn. 12 Mo
320 Sqdn. 10 Mitch

MELSBROE

BRUSSELS

B

417 A.R.F. 18 Mosquito VI
417 R.&S.U. 3 Mosquito VI
107 Sqdn. 15 Mosquito VI
613 Sqdn. 19 Mosquito VI
◉ CAMBRAI/EPINOY

F   R   A   N   C   E

MAP 22. *See Appendix 12, pages 514/15 for notes*

98 Sqdn. 4 Mitchell II, 18 Mitchell III
180 Sqdn. 3 Mitchell II, 19 Mitchell III

⊙ ACHMER

OSNABRÜCK

OLLAND

⊙ VOLKEL

418 Sqdn. 19 Mosquito VI
605 Sqdn. 20 Mosquito VI

⊙ GILZE-RIJEN

226 Sqdn. 2 Mitchell II, 20 Mitchell III
342 Sqdn. 2 Mitchell II, 15 Mitchell III

G E R M A N Y

COLOGNE

Mitchell III

ERE

A.R.F. 31 Mitchell III
R.&S.U. 5 Mitchell II, 9 Mitchell III

L G I U M

The area of operations and the targets are depicted on Map 21. Attacks were made by 191 aircraft dropping 696 bombs and firing 38,730 cannon and 74,190 machine-gun rounds. Attacks on twelve specific small rail targets in Holland were made by 71 Bostons and Mitchells, the most successful being those on Coervorden, Lathen, Mappen and Dedensvaart. Claims from 120 Mosquitoes which delivered attacks as far east as Hanover and Hamburg and as far north as Kiel and Flensburg were: two M.E.T. destroyed 31 damaged, twenty trains damaged, 41 T.R.G. destroyed 629 damaged, seven locomotives destroyed 47 damaged, fourteen T.R.P. destroyed sixty damaged, one H.D.T. destroyed six damaged, four barges sunk 24 damaged, five tugs damaged, three signal boxes destroyed fourteen damaged, four bridges destroyed, two motor vessels shot up, seven small vessels damaged, three rail cuts made and a gasometer damaged. Additionally, railway stations, marshalling yards, factories, barracks and villages were attacked with good results. The total loss was 21 Mosquitoes—eight of them from 136 Wing—and forty were damaged, which was a heavy loss rate. Operation of Mosquitoes in this manner was never repeated.

Next day the U.S. Ninth Army launched Operation *Grenade*, advancing from the line Julich–Roermond. 2 Group supported by bombing Niersbroich and the rail bridge at Schweinheim. Now the day effort was divided between the two fronts, against Rheinburg aiding *Veritable* and against Udem and Rees to assist the Americans. Twelve raids were delivered by the end of the month by which time the Americans had taken Venlo, München-Gladbach and Roermond. On 4 March the Allies joined at Geldern and by the 11th the enemy was cleared from the west of the Rhine in these sectors.

During the first three weeks of March the task was to prepare Operation *Plunder*, the crossing of the last major obstacle to the armies, the River Rhine. Meanwhile Mosquitoes continued their night offensive harassing enemy routes leading to the river and attacking the Wehrmacht's last ferry points. Rail centres and choke points were the principal daylight targets; 23 attacks were made between 1 and 20 March in the region north of the Ruhr. Kevelaer, Wesel, Dorsten, Ahaus, Lingerich, Bocholt, Borken, Dulmen, Isselburg and Raesfeld—all figured in battle orders, as well as the approaches to the bridges at Deventer and Zwolle.

A very significant operation had been that of 26 February when boxes, each of six aircraft drawn from five squadrons, were directed under the guidance of the first Mobile Radar Control Post on to gun batteries near Udem. Receiving equipment in the lead aircraft picked up signals on the bomb run and the release order came from the control post. Against short-range targets the M.R.C.P. system had great possibilities and was used for the second time on 2 March when Mitchells of 137 Wing delivered a very accurate attack on the rail yards at Kevelaer.

Since September 1944 Britain had been bombarded by V-2 rockets.

So far 2 Group had taken little part in the operations to halt the attack. Launching sites were small, often located in built-up areas and woodland. Halting the attack would be most successfully done by overrunning the sites, but they were some way ahead of the Allied line in Holland, and particularly placed in and around The Hague. On 3 March 2 Group made its first and only raid on the launching pads. Three Mitchell squadrons and 342 Boston Squadron participated. Results were disastrous. The raid was against a V-2 store on the outskirts of The Hague. Orders were for a *Gee-H* attack, but at the last moment some of the box leaders switched to visual target identity only to find they could not locate the target. Some boxes bombed what they thought was the store, others went round for a second run. Too late it was realised they were aiming some 500 yards off the true aiming point. Five-hundred-pounders smashed into a residential area with heavy casualties. No more medium-bomber raids were directed against the V-2 sites.

Between 5 and 9 March the battle situation west of the Rhine was too fluid for daylight operations, but Mosquito night raids were now spread over large areas of Germany to prevent movement of troops to and from the Ruhr, and harass the front-line troops. A typical night of the period was 8–9 March, when the effort comprised 65 sorties. Nos. 138 and 140 Wings attacked transport moving in the region south of Hamm–Dorsten and the area bounded by Koblenz–Limburg–Hanau–Hamm. Eighteen of 136 Wing harassed in the area north of the line Hamm–Dorsten as far north as the line Utrecht–Leeuwarden–Oldenburg. For the next five nights bad weather reduced the effort.

Bridges had proved tough targets and even with M.R.C.P. control that at Wesel escaped damage on 9 March. In an effort to cut wastage of sorties due to weather it was now customary to despatch an escorted Mitchell on a wind direction and cloud assessment sortie ahead of any raid. This was the case on 12 March when raids were directed against a rail bridge at Dülmen and rolling stock in the same area. Some of the crews saw rocket weapons fired against them from ground defences, for the Germans already had deployed primitive guided weapons. Next day's operations were even more eventful, as the Squadron Diary of 226 Squadron shows:

'Another early call. Early fog soon cleared and take-off was not delayed. Sqn. Ldr. W. Lyle, D.F.C. and Bar, led the Squadron and Flt. Lt. Parsons the second box against Lingerich, one of the Squadron's deepest penetrations for a long time. The target was 12 miles south-west of Osnabrück. As the first wave approached the bomb line at 14,000 feet a thin layer of alto-cumulus cloud was seen spreading inland at 15,000 feet. The leader decided to climb above it and take evasive action. There were a few accurate flak bursts just after the bomb line. Both boxes were over enemy territory about fifty minutes doing gentle weaving, and they bombed visually. For the first time for a long while 137 Wing led the attack and No. 139 Wing followed. It was timely, for 139 Wing was jumped by Bf 109s east of Wesel losing HD307 of 180 Squadron. One escorting Spitfire was also shot down. Despite the long trip the squadron did a turn round, four aircraft (the only ones serviceable in 'A' Flight) bombing marshalling yards at Borken.'

Low-level daylight Mosquito precision raids captured the imagination as much as any wartime operations. One of the most exciting took place on 21 March. It was Operation *Carthage*, the raid on the Gestapo Headquarters in the Shell House, Copenhagen. The distant target required a long accurate sea crossing and Sqn. Ldr. Sismore did the route planning. Wg. Cdr. R. N. Bateson was chosen to lead the raid and Air Vice-Marshal Embry flew also in the first box.

To avoid crossing Germany elements of Nos. 21, 464 and 487 Squadrons were positioned at Fersfield from where the Mustang escort from Nos. 64 and 126 Squadrons also operated. The first wave included 21 Squadron and a Film Production Unit Mosquito IV. Next came 464 Squadron led by Wg. Cdr. Iredale, followed by six from 487 Squadron led by Wg. Cdr. F. H. Denton who had another F.P.U. Mosquito IV for company.

They made their sea crossing at very low level at 250 m.p.h. I.A.S. and climbed to 200 feet over land at 275 m.p.h. The attack was carried out in three waves, the second and third increasing their time interval behind the leaders to one minute by circling Lake Tisso after entering Jutland through a gap in the coastal defences.

Attack was planned for 11.15 hours when the maximum number of Gestapo members would be in the building. It was known that interrogation of patriots was undertaken on the upper floors of the building, and so orders were to aim at its base.

Bombs from the leading wave rammed into the lower storeys at 11.14, but as he ran over the town No. 4, Wg. Cdr. Kleboe, struck a tall pole in Dybbolsbro Station yard with his wing tip. He flew on, his starboard engine smoking, but his aircraft with its tail badly damaged fell on to a garage and burst into flames. The second and third waves were apparently misled by the smoke. The leader of the second wave missed the primary target on the run-in but after an orbit dropped his bombs on the north-east corner of the Gestapo H.Q. Two other aircraft became separated from the second wave and photographs showed them bombing the crashed aircraft. Another aircraft out of position due to the orbit brought its bombs back, and two machines of 464 Squadron failed to return.

There was soon an inferno in Frederiksburg where Kleboe had crashed, on to which four crews of 487 Squadron rained their loads. Some of the bombs also fell on the Jeanne d'Arc School killing and maiming some of the children, despite the meticulous planning of the operation. One crew identified the correct target blazing and with some of its frontage missing, but they found it too late and jettisoned their load in the sea. One of 487's aircraft failed to return. The two cine

Mosquitoes ran in as planned, but bumpy conditions made it hard to hold the cameras for filming. In all sixteen 500-lb. 11 sec. delay bombs and sixteen 500-lb. 30 sec. delay bombs and four M.76 incendiaries were dropped between 11.14 and 11.20, and the force made base around 14.30 hours after a $5\frac{1}{2}$ hour trip.

Flak positions detailed to be silenced by the Mustangs were not in use or tarpaulin-covered. One was strafed and the Mustang pilots reported Shell House blazing. They also told of a Mosquito of 487 Squadron (Flt. Lt. Patterson) heading for Sweden and that one of 464's with a feathered engine ditched at 56° 02′ N 11° 42′ E and that another went into the sea at 56° 02′ N 12° E. Two Mustangs were lost and other Mosquitoes (one of which belly-landed) were damaged by flak. The flak hadn't opened up until the Mosquitoes were on the way home, and the only opposition had been from ships in the harbour. The leading navigator did his job so well that the aircraft landed back only two minutes later than scheduled.

The Germans put out a rumour that most Gestapo officials were out at a funeral at the time of attack, but the Danish Underground sent a message suggesting that 150 Gestapo men were killed, and that 30 patriots imprisoned in the building had escaped. The cruiser *Leipzig* was in the harbour and rapidly got under way, the crew apparently thinking that the Mosquitoes were after this remnant of the German Navy.

As soon as the war ended Air Vice-Marshal Embry, Sismore, Clapham and others visited Copenhagen to meet some of the patriots who had escaped from the building which had been reduced to a burnt-out shell. They also went to see some of the children injured in the raid and still in hospital, which they said was a deeply moving experience. But modern war is total and civilian casualties can now never be avoided completely.

Between 20 and 23 March the Tactical Air Force gave the enemy along the bomb line sheer Hell. On 21 March 2 Group attacked seventeen towns close to the river in a maximum softening-up effort. Final targets before the launching of the river crossing were enemy camps and barracks, twenty of which were attacked in three days. Between 21 and 24 March the whole of the Allied Air Forces in Europe flew over 42,000 sorties against Germany, a fantastic effort.

On the afternoon of 23 March the crossing of the Rhine really began when Bomber Command bombed Wesel and later that day repeated the dose as the first Commando forces set out to cross the river. A vast array of gliders and paratroops would be dropped next day but beforehand 2 Group took on a task vital to this operation. Its job was to silence anti-aircraft guns in the area.

During the night of 23rd–24th 96 Mosquito sorties were directed to three principal tasks. The first, by 36 aircraft of 140 Wing, was the harassment of transport in the area Emmerich–Groenlo–Coesfeld–Dülmen–Dinslaken along the bomb line to Emmerich. Secondly, 24 of

136 Wing operated against military targets in the built-up areas of Isselburg and Anholt under the control of No. 1 M.R.C.P. Thirdly, 36 Mosquitoes of 138 Wing sought out military targets in Drevenach, Peddenburg and Raesfeld directed by No. 2 M.R.C.P. Ninety-three Mosquitoes attacked using 337 500-lb. bombs, ten M.76 incendiaries, 16,440 rounds cannon and 50,380 machine-gun ammunition. It was a very effective night's work.

Bombing of anti-aircraft positions by the day-bomber force took place as planned, but none of the guns was hit although there were many near misses. No. 88 Squadron recorded its participation as follows: 'Earlier call than usual—we learnt that all possible aircraft were to operate in support of the British and Canadian Armies' thrust across the Rhine. In the morning twelve crews of 88 led by Wg. Cdr. Evans, D.F.C., were detailed to attack artillery areas under No. 2 M.R.C.P. Reception was too loud and both boxes had to switch to visual on the last few seconds of the run up, which upset accuracy. All took-off 07.52, bombed at 08.53, an hour before the landing. Both boxes undershot the first by 1,000 yards, second by 500 yards. Perfect weather but ground haze and smoke made identification difficult. No opposition, all landed by 09.45. In the afternoon two separate attacks with six Bostons each were ordered. Sqn. Ldr. Betts led the first wave, took-off 13.40 and attacked guns under No. 1 M.R.C.P. at 14.53. 336 × 20 lb. fragmentation bombs fell 500 yds. N.W. of A.P. 2nd wave led by W. Off. Altschweger took-off 13.49 and attacked gun positions from 13,000 feet under 1 M.R.C.P. with 336 × 20 lb. fragmentation bombs. Fell across aiming point. Control by 1 M.R.C.P. left nothing to be desired.'

Throughout the day 2nd T.A.F. was at hand to give close support and silence enemy artillery shelling the crossing point. Very successful blind-bombing attacks under M.R.C.P. were carried out on two successive days, particularly against two positions west of Isselburg which had been harassing the bridging sites on XXX Corps front. Medium bombers for the first time employed a 'cab rank' system, for five hours. Six bombers were given a target every thirty minutes and on these two days only two out of forty guns were able to fire.

On the night of 24th–25th 96 Mosquito sorties were despatched over Holland and routes leading to the Rhine and against six gun positions near Isselburg which were again bombed under M.R.C.P. control.

On two further days before March closed, gun positions were targets for daylight raids; then on 31 March came the end of the participation in the war by the Douglas Bostons of 88 and 342 Squadrons. Targets were yet again artillery positions with 226 Mitchell Squadron leading twelve crews of 88 Squadron (leader Wg. Cdr. D. Evans in BZ250: Z) and twelve from 342 Squadron (leader Cmdt. G. Mentre in BZ544: Z). Last man home was S/C R. Argot in BZ290: S of 342 Squadron. Very popular but aging, the Boston was having spares problems. No. 88 Squadron which had served in the Group so valiantly disbanded on

6 April. By then 342 Squadron had nearly converted to Mitchells with which it first operated on 8 April the target being Sogel.

For 88 Squadron March had been without parallel. Some 400 sorties were flown, over 1,000 hours of operational flying. Efficiency had never been so high. 'We feel the squadron's record in this war,' comments the Diary, 'has maintained the traditions set in the last. We leave our colours flying.' Victory was now assured and 88 had ceased to exist before the peace it had fought so hard to achieve. Its link with 2 Group was to be resumed in peacetime when, as a Canberra squadron, it formed part of the post-war 2 Group.

By 1 April 1945, the Ruhr was encircled and the German forces therein trapped. Resistance slowly crumbled. Meanwhile the Americans and British parted company with Montgomery's Army heading for the Weser, Bremen, the Elbe and the Baltic coast. The night of 31 March/ 1 April was particularly productive for the Mosquitoes which attacked nineteen trains, 300 M.E.T. and eighteen barges and caused five rail cuts.

Two-thirds of the daylight bombing in March had been undertaken relying on *Gee-H* or M.R.C.P. control. The results of radar bombing were studied, but the use of fragmentation bombs made the results difficult to decipher. It was concluded that about 65% of the bombs dropped by *Gee-H* control fell within 500 yards of the target, but the average error under M.R.C.P. was only forty yards. Little wonder, then, that increasing use was made of the latter.

Excellent weather during much of April made it a busy period. Only on four days and nights were operations limited or impossible. Rapid advances brought fewer targets until 8th when calls began to be made for the medium bombers to silence gun positions, to bomb strong points, choke points and rail centres mainly ahead of the First Canadian Army. Their task was to clear the enemy from Holland and 2 Group raided gun positions and choke points especially when the Lower Rhine was crossed at Arnhem. Thirty-two raids were launched in April against 23 targets. One of the more successful was against guns at Zutphen on 4th, a quick reply to an army request. An Auster A.O.P. flying near by observed two tremendous explosions after the bombing. Another very successful operation reduced the barracks at Oldenburg to rubble, and on 26th Potriu marshalling yards were hit by bombs from seven out of eight boxes of Mitchells.

Soon the enemy had either to capitulate or move his H.Q. and troops to a safer area. It had been assumed the High Command would vacate Berlin for Bavaria where mountainous terrain might afford some protection. Instead, in the third week of April the High Command left for Flensburg and clearly the plan was to fight on from northern Germany and Scandinavia. The Second British Army therefore took Bremen, a likely pocket of resistance, then crossed the Elbe heading north-east.

From 14 April the Army headed towards the Weser with intense support from the Tactical Air Force until 22nd, when 2 Group began concentrated attacks on strong points around Bremen. It made six concentrated attacks on the gun positions, usually in boxes of six, M.R.C.P.-controlled from information radioed by the Army. On 25 April No. 2 Division XXX Corps entered Bremen and next day the town capitulated. The moral effect of this reduced German resistance and the Elbe was crossed more easily than expected on 29 April.

On nearly every night immediately leading to this date Mosquitoes had operated over the parts of Germany still in enemy hands. The extent of these operations is indicated by Operations Order AO135 of 1–2 April 1945:

'The 9th and 1st U.S. Armies have joined east of the Ruhr and the 3rd U.S. Army is advancing east on Wismar. 21st Army Group is advancing north and north-east against lessening opposition. There is still movement out of Holland. Task I: Harass road/rail movements in the area Hanover–Sieson–Göttingen–Hamm–Münden—bomb line— Deventer – Zwolle – Meppen – Quackenbruck – Nienburg – Hanover. Task II: Transport targets in the following areas/routes: Oldenburg– Meppen – Quackenbruck, Bremen, – Diepholtz – Nürnberg – Hanover, Velzen–Celle, Lehrta–Hildesheim, Stendaal–Hanover, Magdeburg– Brunswick – Hanover, Magdeburg – Oschersleben – Ringenhelm – Hildesheim – Harmen – Lohne, Halberstad – Galsheim, Göttingen – Hanover, Northem–Nordhausen–Blankenheim. 136 Wing 24 sorties Tasks I and II dusk—23.30 hours. 138 Wing 36 sorties Tasks I and II 22.30–02.00 hours. 140 Wing 36 sorties Tasks I and II from 02.00 to dawn.' 136 Wing had moved from Hartford to Coxyde in Belgium on 15 March and so it was now customary to divide the night into three periods for Mosquito operations. Between 1 and 9 April, the nightly effort exceeded ninety sorties.

One of the most auspicious nights was 6–7 April when transport targets were attacked in the area Emden–Lübeck–Berlin–Halle– Hildesheim–Mureimburg–Latham–Emden. For the first time since May 1943, Berlin figured in the Battle Orders. Ninety-three aircraft attacked in the given region dropping 105 500-lb. bombs and 264 flares, and fired 23,000 cannon and 33,400 machine-gun rounds. Twenty-one trains were attacked and forty M.E.T. destroyed.

During April more trains were seen than in any month since D-Day. Over 300 were attacked, forty on one night. Thirty-six locomotives and 975 trucks in sidings, were destroyed. One of the most outstanding individual results came during an assault on the Fritzwalk rail centre where the raid by one Mosquito left a crater 200 feet across and sixty feet deep. An ammunition train had exploded causing widespread damage. All rail tracks were cut or blocked, many buildings were destroyed together with two other trains. On another occasion a small arms dump erupted producing 24 more fires.

For the third time in recent months Mosquitoes of 2 Group made a

84. These two illustrations show the A.O.C.s of 2 Group at the most critical periods. Left is Air Vice-Marshal Robb, A.O.C. in May 1940

85. Air Vice-Marshal Embry planning a low-level Mosquito raid with, to his right, the late David Atcherley. To his left, Grp. Capt. Peter Wykeham-Barnes and Pat Shallard

86. Wg. Cdr. A. F. Carlisle and Rex Ingram fly their Mosquito low over France practising before the raid on Shellhaus in Copenhagen

87. Three Mosquitoes of 21 Squadron doing high-level formation practice near Rosières-en-Santerre before the Copenhagen raid

8. A Mosquito of 464 Squadron flies low over Copenhagen during the raid of 21.3.45

89. A Mosquito curves away from Shellhaus during the Copenhagen low-level attack
90. Boston IV's of 88 Squadron bombing in support of the British Army advance into Europe

low-level raid on Denmark. On this occasion the target was a school building on the outskirts of Odense which the Danes called 'Torture Castle'. The Gestapo used it to keep the island of Fyn under subjection and inflicted some fearful tortures here. At the request of the Underground six Mosquitoes of 140 Wing, led by Grp. Capt. R. N. Bateson with Sqn. Ldr. Sismore as his navigator, set off to destroy the building and its occupants on 17 April. They operated from Belgium taking the normal load of 4 500-lb. bombs, crossed out over north Holland, flew to Heligoland Bight then crossed to Fyn. Navigation was excellent, as before. But the target building was so well camouflaged that bombing was impossible until the fourth run. Indeed, the film Mosquito flown by Flt. Lt. Greenwood made a fifth run. To the attackers it was quite a sight watching six Mosquitoes in the circuit with escorting anti-flak Mustangs milling around. Only one Bofors gun needed attention and the only damage to the Mosquitoes came from bomb blast which hit Flt. Lt. McClelland's aircraft. He returned on one engine.

Two days later 16 Squadron flew a reconnaissance to the target and photographs showed two-thirds of the building destroyed and both wings gutted. Living quarters were almost completely destroyed, but again there was some civilian damage, five houses being destroyed.

The retreat of the enemy had quickly left the medium-bomber squadrons far to the rear of the battle and so, towards the end of April, the Wings advanced, 136 to Volkel, 137 to Gilze Rijen, 138 to Achmer and 140 to Melsbroek. After the Elbe was crossed on 29 April the Luftwaffe from bases close at hand was stung to desperate action. Part of the response was a radar-controlled raid on Lübeck/Blankensee airfield on 1 May. Next day rail yards at Itzehoe were bombed. A later raid for which 226 and 342 Squadrons were despatched was abandoned. With this the medium-bomber offensive ended.

Mosquitoes operated on one night in May, 2nd–3rd, harassing transport in the area Emden–Westerland–Flensburg–exclusive of Lübeck–Hamburg–along the bomb line to Emden. Forty-two aircraft attacked using 78 500-lb. bombs, 143 flares, 6,020 cannon and 5,040 machine-gun rounds. Six vehicles were destroyed, 31 damaged and nine trains attacked one of which violently exploded. Seven towns were attacked and in Itzeheide two fires burned. Leck airfield was strafed. The final Mosquito sortie was a meteorological reconnaissance flight by an aircraft of 136 Wing on 3–4 May as a result of which other operations were cancelled. The end had come, inauspiciously. The European war was won, the ceasefire being effective at 08.00 hours on 8 May.

o

Chapter 24
Conclusions

No. 2 Group was unique, the only formation in the Royal Air Force in action from the beginning of hostilities in Europe to their cessation. In five and a half years it flew 57,581 sorties at a cost of 2,679 personnel killed or missing in action, and 396 seriously wounded. Aircraft losses totalled 910—282 to flak, 118 to fighters, 62 to battle accidents, 448 to unknown causes. Set against the total loss of 70,253 aircrew killed or missing during the war, 2 Group's loss may seem small. But it was always the smallest Group in Bomber Command and 2nd T.A.F., and its loss rate in the first 28 months of the war was exceedingly high. Between 10 May and 17 June 1940, during the hopeless struggle to save France, the Blenheim crews flew 1,546 sorties losing eighty aircraft in 38 days. Personnel losses in this period were 246 missing or killed, compared with Fighter Command's loss of 520 in four months during the Battle of Britain. By any reckoning 2 Group's loss rate in 1940–1 was grievous. No other formation in the Royal Air Force had squadrons so repeatedly decimated during individual operations.

Its costly contribution to the battle for France was nothing short of heroic: every man who participated was a hero. In the face of swarms of Messerschmitts and persistent flak he had little option. Feeling in the Group was strong when many members who baled out came back with stories of weak defence put up by French ground forces, a sore which never healed. In direct contrast in later years there were those of the Free French, albeit small in number when compared with contingents from smaller Allies, who fought as well as any.

Following the grim fight over France 2 Group was ordered to undertake a difficult daylight campaign to tempt enemy fighters to do battle and encourage the enemy to maintain his fighter defences on a wide front. Bomber Command had switched mainly to night operations—except for 2 Group. Well into 1943 its role was maintained, although from 1941 it did have the comfort of strong fighter cover. Looking back to the days of the Blenheims many 2 Group aircrew readily admit that their experiences were exceedingly frightening, and it says much for them that morale remained high.

Choice of targets was limited, both by the range of the indispensable escorting fighters and the capability of the bomber aircraft. The idea that *Circus* operations against small and relatively unimportant targets could draw off sufficient fighters to open a way into Germany for the heavies to make daylight forays must have included some element of wishful thinking.

Added to this there was the shipping campaign, memories of which remain very vivid to this day in the minds of those who took part. Despite a magnificent show of courage, it seems from post-war research, little was achieved. Certainly the enemy needed to take additional precautions to safeguard his shipping, but the German returns of shipping losses show them to have been light. In the Mediterranean theatre success was rather higher, and Axis shipping sailing to North Africa was seriously interfered with.

No doubt can remain that an error was made by the Air Staff in not ordering the Mosquito bomber sooner. One can appreciate their dilemma: here was another scheme for a bomber faster than opposing fighters which must have evoked memories of the Blenheim which was outclassed in such a role long before the war. Official disbelief in the de Havilland forecasts of what their machine would achieve was, to say the least, unfortunate. Yet to have committed themselves to going ahead with an unarmed small bomber, for which its inventors claimed astonishing performance figures, would have demanded considerable nerve. In any case the die had already been cast: the Air Force was to rely upon heavily armed bombers. This, and the requirements for the fighter force, put great demands upon Rolls-Royce Merlin production, and there were no possibilities of engines being available for the Mosquito without interfering with other production lines. Nevertheless, in 2 Group hands this supreme performer could have transformed the bomber offensive by day and night—and it even struck deep into Germany in daylight with a low loss rate, something the heavies were never able to do until very late in the war. Had the 'larger Mosquito project' proceeded the entire bomber offensive would have been altered, and crew losses would undoubtedly have been lower. Yet by the time the Mosquito was showing its worth the powerful night offensive was under way and the Mosquito was then removed from 2 Group, its value only too well appreciated now by many who had earlier failed to realise its potential.

The Group was really kept intact for such time as it could support the Army's return to the Continent. Between 1940 and 1943 Bomber Command seems to have regarded it as something of an anomaly, a formation whose employment was unsuited to area bombing. No blame for its employment in an assortment of roles can be attached to the Group. Policy decisions that led to its making considerable sacrifices for little return were made at the highest of levels, and they had to be taken with consideration of the limitations of 2 Group's equipment.

As soon as Basil Embry took command things rapidly changed. He pressed for Mosquito fighter-bombers and, using them by day and night, was able to employ the Group very effectively and for some time as an intruder force supporting Main Force bomber operations. His force could, in current jargon, 'take out' the smallest of targets in a manner difficult to better even with today's sophisticated equipment. It is always easy to be wise after the event, but there can be little question that, equipped with Mosquito bombers fitted with *Oboe* and a re-organisation of the bombing campaign, a very effective war could have been waged against the western industrial areas of Germany and at comparatively little cost.

Contributions by the Boston must not be overlooked. It was an excellent aeroplane, tried and found ideal for low-level assault, but it lacked the all-round excellent Mosquito performance. In the Mitchell, 2 Group had a fine, stable bombing platform, a tough aeroplane which could accept considerable punishment.

By 1944, with the invasion of Europe near, it was indeed unfortunate for the Allies that the enemy was able to install his V-weapon sites under the nose of the Allied air forces. Once again the ideal counter weapon was the Mosquito in 2 Group's hands and, in the Group's opinion, it was by far the most successful used in the destruction of the flying-bomb launching sites. As soon as *Overlord* was under way 2 Group proved it a useful weapon with which to delay enemy movement by night; passage was already made well nigh impossible during daylight by the Tactical Air Forces.

It is worth noting that many members of the Group, by any means open to them, contrived to stay with it from the start to the finish of the war. Talking of it now they repeatedly make this point and reveal an astonishing loyalty. This may have been due in part to the fact that the Group was particularly well endowed with able group, wing and station commanders—to say nothing of many exceedingly popular squadron commanders.

It is impossible to estimate what contributions many of the fallen of this and indeed other elements of the Royal Air Force might have made to post-war Britain. Certain it is that these lost men, all of high mental capability, would have made considerable impact in positions of authority, and their loss was one the nation could ill afford.

Within the Services many of the survivors have risen to high positions. Those who served with him watched with pride Lord Elworthy rise to become Chief of the Air Staff and then Chief of the Defence Staff. Marshal of the Royal Air Force Sir Dermot Boyle who served in 2 Group before the war also held the coveted position of Chief of the Air Staff. Abroad Henri de Rancourt who flew with 342 Squadron became Commander-in-Chief of the French Air Force, and G. van der Wolf who flew many sorties with 320 Squadron reached a similar status in the Royal Netherlands Air Force. The first Commander-in-Chief, R.A.F. Strike Command, Sir Wallace Kyle, was Station Commander at Marham during the spectacular Mosquito days. Air Chief Marshal

Sir Basil Embry is soon mentioned wherever 2 Group men gather. They will say 'To me he symbolised all that 2 Group meant.' In the post-war world he became Commander-in-Chief Fighter Command and, later, Commander, Allied Air Forces Central Europe. The late Air Chief Marshal Sir James Robb was also one-time Commander-in-Chief of Fighter Command. He it was who had to shoulder the decisions during the 1940 French campaign. Air Chief Marshal Sir Hugh Pughe Lloyd left 2 Group to command Malta during the worst of the island's ordeal, and later became Commander-in-Chief of Bomber Command. Air Chief Marshal Sir Denis Barnett became Air Officer Commanding-in-Chief of Transport Command.

Many members of 2 Group reached the rank of Air Marshal, including Sir Peter Wykeham who retired as Deputy Chief of the Air Staff, and Sir Leslie Bower, a famous name in Mosquito days. Among Air Vice-Marshals were G. R. 'Digger' Magill who served long in the Group, G. T. B. Clayton, 'Bull' Cannon, Ian Spencer, R. N. Bateson, Sir Laurence Sinclair and E. Colbeck-Welch. No mention of those who reached high command could possibly be made without including the late Air Marshal David Atcherley, whose boundless sense of humour and tremendous vitality made him such a tremendously popular person.

With these let us pay tribute to the many whose names were never to become household words. There was that veritable army of Sergeants who formed the core of the force at the worst of times; the armourers who, sweating and exhausted, lifted the bombs aboard the Blenheims in the grimmest weeks of the war; the w. op/air-gunners proud that they were not just air-gunners, sometimes L.A.C.s and largely forgotten in the final analysis. Without these and the untiring efforts of the groundcrew—men and women—operations would have been impossible.

The end of the war did not bring an end to 2 Group. First it formed part of the British Air Forces of Occupation, flying Mosquito VIs. It disbanded in May 1947, but reformed on 1 December 1948, as the Cold War settled upon Europe. New stations in Germany were opened, before the Group again disbanded in May 1958. Its squadrons flew Meteors, Vampires, Sabres, Hunters, Venoms and Canberras, all so far removed in every way from types with which it had fought the war. A change to high professionalism had set in when *Overlord* was being planned so that even by the end of the war the Royal Air Force had changed beyond recognition from the force that faced the enemy in September 1939.

The exploits of the Royal Air Force during the Second World War are something which every British man, woman and child needs to remember—with gratitude and admiration.

Appendix 1

Noteworthy Aircraft
Used Operationally by 2 Group

A combination of chance, pilot skill and sheer luck caused some aircraft to have longer, more exciting lives than others. Individual sortie records were noted by squadrons in their Operational Record Books. Regrettably, these contain anomalies and omissions. Bearing this in mind the following surveys of aircraft types (based on Forms 78, 540 and 541 listing) indicate which aircraft had outstanding careers. Necessary abbreviations are listed on page 15.

(i) Bristol Blenheim (U.K. service)

Four 2 Group Blenheims each flew sixty sorties or more. No sortie records apparently exist for 2 Group Blenheims operated from Malta, but here their lives were usually brief. 2 Group worked through 1,012 Blenheim IVs between 1939 and 1942, the last being withdrawn from a squadron (No. 18) in October 1942. Official records are contradictory, but it appears that 403 Blenheims failed to return from operational flights, a further 86 were damaged beyond repair as a result of operations and 96 were destroyed in flying accidents. The most successful machines appear to have been the following:

R3772. Flew the largest number of sorties, 64. Delivered to 9 M.U. 21.5.40, to 110 Sqn. 25.5.40. Left behind when the squadron proceeded to Malta 29.6.41, it passed to 17 O.T.U. Upwood on 28.7.41 where it was written off, after a crash on 30 March 1942, on 3.4.42. R3772's first sortie came on 27 May 1940. Piloted by Wg. Cdr. Sinclair it left Wattisham at 16.25 hrs. to attack a troop concentration near St. Omer. By the fall of France it had flown eleven sorties sometimes in the hands of Flt. Lt. Peter Simmons. Its first cloud-cover sortie came on 18 June, again with Wg. Cdr. Sinclair as pilot. By the end of June it was being overhauled after fourteen sorties. Operations were resumed 9.7.40 reconnoitring Zwolle, and it flew some damage assessment flights. The first night operation was flown against Caen 22.7.40, followed by day raids on airfields and on 30 August on Emden when Plt. Off. Powell was the pilot. A few raids on barges followed and the aircraft often participated in night raids on Germany. During December it made attacks on airfields and on 10th, flown by Flt. Lt. Beaman, the Focke Wulf factory at Bremen. Then the aircraft was off operations until 12–13 March when night operations were resumed. Its first anti-shipping raid off Holland came on 12 April. On 24 May it was one of ten aircraft attacking a convoy off Norderney. Its final operation was against shipping in the Weser–Ems Canal on 11 June 1941.

P4839 and *R3684* each flew 61 sorties. The former was delivered 22.8.39 to 82 Sqn. whom it served awhile coded UX-L. It went to 90 Sqn. 16.6.41, to 17 O.T.U. 25.10.41 and to the Telecommunications Flying Unit early 1942. On 23 May P4839 rejoined 17 O.T.U. It passed to 13 O.T.U. Bicester 23.4.43 where it was involved in a flying accident on 13 June, was categorised E on 9 August and S.O.C. 10.8.43. Its first sortie came on 26.12.39 when it flew a North Sea sweep. On 19.3.40 it attacked flak ships. It was on the Breda raid of 14 May, flown by Plt. Off. Toft, and flew eight sorties during the French campaign. On 19 June it led an evening raid on St. Omer airfield, and was sent towards Germany for the first time on 21 June when it made an abortive sortie. It attacked airfields and its first 1941 sortie, on 4 February, took it to Nieuport harbour. Shipping raids off Holland followed, and a few to Norwegian waters. Its final sortie, from Portreath on 13 May 1941, was to St. Nazaire. The squadron went overseas leaving it behind.

R3684 was delivered to 8 M.U. 16.4.40, 110 Sqn. 26.5.40 and was damaged in battle 16 April 1941. It went to Cunliffe Owen Aircraft for repair 20.4.41, then to 15 M.U. 12.7.42. No. 17 O.T.U. received it 26.8.42 and 13 O.T.U. on 29.8.42. Here it ended its days on 7.3.44 when it was S.O.C. during a major inspection. Its first sortie was flown on 30 May 1940, against Furnes. It was involved in the Vignacourt operation of 30 June, when Bf 109s attacked the formation. It took part in an abortive raid on Aalborg on 6 August. After overhaul it operated against the Channel ports and some airfields. Night raids followed against Germany and, on 13 April 1941, the first shipping raid, which proved abortive. On 16 April when taking off for Heligoland, it crashed but her crew were safe. No more operations were flown.

L9390 flew 60 sorties. Initially delivered 13.2.40 it passed to 4 M.U. 12.8.40, 21 M.U. 31.8.40 and to 18 Squadron 5.9.40. No. 139 Sqn. received it 15.10.41, 82 Sqn. on 28.1.42, 21 Sqn. 18.3.42. It was involved in a flying accident 8.6.42 and left 21 Sqn. for 27 M.U. Shawbury 9.11.42. Here it was stored then passed to the Royal Navy on 22.2.44. It was S.O.C. 9.6.45. Its first sortie was against Dunkirk on 14.9.40. Its five September raids against Channel ports were followed by more on airfields, during which its bombs fell on Cormeille's flare-path on 14 November. It flew no operations in January, but by February was 'U' of 18 Sqn. Its first shipping Beat was flown 9.4.41 and on 24th it attacked a 1,000-tonner from 50 feet. Its first *Circus* raid (on 21 May) was abandoned. During a convoy attack on 2 June a fighter chased it into cloud. Shipping Beats, fringe raids, an attack on the Kiel Canal on 30 July, squealer Beats and *Circuses* followed. Its last sortie came on 18 September when a 1,000-ton ship was bombed off Holland. No. 18 Squadron went overseas leaving L9390 behind and it passed among squadrons flying only training sorties.

Despite their hazardous employment 97 Blenheims managed thirty or more sorties. Details of them follow.

Aircraft	Sortie total	Notes on aircraft
T1795	59	To 139 Sqn. 12.6.40, FTR 8.6.41(?)
R3875	57	To 21 Sqn. 13.6.40, 17 O.T.U. 19.8.41, burnt out 7.9.41
R3681	56	To 110 Sqn. 26.5.40 until 2.8.41. Later with 5 A.O.S. and 1 A.A.S.
R3816	55	Became J/107 Sqn. 3.6.40, crashed 7.8.41
T1828	54	To 40 Sqn. 29.6.40, 82 Sqn. 29.6.40, 21 Sqn. 18.3.42, 105 Sqn. 28.3.42, Cat. E FA 1.4.42
L9240	53	A.A.S.F. France 18.5.40, 10 M.U. 26.5.40, G/18 Sqn. 30.5.40, seriously damaged 25.5.41, in the sea on Kiel Canal raid 30.7.41
R3814	52	To 40 Sqn. 11.6.40, 110 Sqn. 11.6.40, 17 O.T.U. 25.7.41, missing on trng. flight 17.9.41
L9029	49	H/21 Sqn. 24.2.40, 13 O.T.U. 19.6.41, 54 O.T.U. 23.9.41, RIW 18.6.42, 27 M.U. 25.11.42, S.O.C. 15.8.44
T1832	49	139 Sqn. 9.7.40, FTR 16.6.41, shot down on Beat 9
R2791	48	XV Sqn. 1.9.40, 139 Sqn. 7.11.40, FTR 25.5.41, shot down on Beat 9
R3600	48	A.A.S.F., P.D.U. Heston 22–24.5.40, 110 Sqn. 26.5.40, FTR 6.5.41, shot down on Beat 7
R3740	48	107 Sqn. 19.5.40, FTR 18.4.41, in the sea off Norway
R3873	46	107 Sqn. 10.6.40, FTR 18.8.41(?)
T1853	45	107 Sqn. 1.7.40, 88 Sqn. 29.9.41, 105 Sqn. 15.10.41, lost en route Middle East 4.11.41
V6431	44	N/18 Sqn. 28.5.41, M/114 Sqn. 25.10.41 to 30.12.42
L9192	43	Q/18 Sqn. 12.2.40, FTR 2.6.41 from ops. over N.W. Germany
L9379	43	105 Sqn. 14.12.40, 88 Sqn. 17.8.41, FTR 28.8.41 from an attack on Rotterdam
R3737	43	107 Sqn. 19.5.40, written off in accident 15.11.40
L8864	42	18 Sqn. 12.3.40, 15 M.U. 20.5.40, 53 Sqn. 27.5.40, W/18 Sqn. 30.5.40, S.O.C. 31.5.41 (last op. 23.5.41)
N6191	42	107 Sqn. 21.6.39, crashed on take-off for night raid on Calais 30.9.40 and burnt out

N3568	41	107 Sqn. 13.8.40, FTR 1.8.41 from attack on ship off Nieuport
P4860	41	110 Sqn. 15.9.39, 139 Sqn. 23.11.40, FTR 7.5.41 from shipping sweep off Delfziji
R3741	41	110 Sqn. 19.5.40, X/18 Sqn. 26.8.40, FTR 7.5.41, shot down in the sea on Beat 15
L8787	40	110 Sqn. 24.6.40, total wreck crashed St. Eval returning from Brest 28.3.41
N3584	40	21 Sqn. 9.7.40, 13 O.T.U. 3.7.41, Cat. E on major inspection 27.2.44
T2234	40	H/101 Sqn. 12.9.40, FTR 3.5.41, in the sea off Boulogne on shipping strike
R3874	40	110 Sqn. 11.6.40, 13 O.T.U. 25.6.41, Cat. E FA 6.11.42
R3803	39	101 Sqn. 4.8.40, N/82 Sqn. 10.5.41, FTR 30.7.41
T1931	39	105 Sqn. 13.7.40, 17 O.T.U. 24.4.41, Cat. E FA 11.10.42
R3903	38	139 Sqn. 12.6.40, FTR 4.6.41 from De Kooy airfield
L9421	37	101 Sqn. 3.5.40, 90 Sqn. 12.7.41, 1653 C.U. 23.2.42, flying accident 19.5.42; S.O.C. 1.44
R3765	37	82 Sqn. 10.6.40, FTR, in the sea 11.11.40
T1800	37	110 Sqn. 31.7.40 to 16.5.41; 1 A.G.S. 19.3.42, became 4124M at 6 S.T.T. 7.9.43, S.O.C. 6.1.47
T2122	37	82 Sqn. 10.10.40, 21 Sqn. 18.3.42, 105 Sqn. 28.3.42, 1482 Flt. 28.5.42, flying accident 1.7.42, to 15 M.U.
V6510	37	A/226 Sqn. 27.5.41, to 18 Sqn. 12.11.41, became H/114 Sqn. 17.1.42, to 18 Sqn. 31.7.42 to 1.10.42
L8777	36	107 Sqn. 16.10.39, 54 M.U. 11.2.41
N6190	36	107 Sqn. 20.6.39, crash-landed 2.6.40 after attack on enemy guns in France
T2033	36	82 Sqn. 14.8.40, 21 Sqn. 18.3.42, 105 Sqn. 28.3.42, 1482 Flt. 15.7.42, RIW 22.1.43, 9 M.U., S.O.C. 18.8.44
L8788	35	105 Sqn. 4.7.40, 88 Sqn. 17.8.41, in the sea 26.8.41
R3666	35	57 Sqn. 3.6.40 to 9.7.40; 218 Sqn. 12.9.40, K/18 Sqn. 10.11.40, FTR 24.7.41, shot down off Ijmuiden by Bf 110
R3871	35	107 Sqn. 10.6.40, to Air Service Training 17.2.41
L9413	34	XV Sqn. 15.9.40 to 10.9.40; 139 Sqn. 13.11.40— burnt out in flying accident 18.5.41
P6953	34	101 Sqn. 14.5.40, FTR 16.12.40 after a raid on Mannheim, missing near St. Quentin
R3843	34	F/18 Sqn. 17.6.40, FTR 20.9.41, in the sea off Heligoland
L8800	32	114 Sqn. 18.11.39, XV Sqn. 9.12.39, 114 Sqn. 12.11.40 Cat. E FB 5.6.42, crashed just after take-off
L9040	32	18 Sqn. 30.5.40 to 19.5.41 and subsequently stored in M.U.s
L9040	32	18 Sqn. 30.5.40 to 19.5.41, 27 and 15 M.U.s, Speke, 4.6.44, fate unknown

O2

R3708	32	D/82 Sqn. 19.5.40, 21 Sqn. 20.8.40, 57 Sqn. 27.8.40 to 5.12.40; to Middle East 1.6.41
R3766	32	XV Sqn. 24.5.40, 114 Sqn. 10.11.40 to 21.11.42; 1 A.G.S. 28.2.43, Cat E FA 21.8.43, S.O.C. 25.8.43
R3801	32	18 Sqn. 17.8.40, 101 Sqn. 18.8.40, 107 Sqn. 14.5.41, FTR 30.6.41 from attack on Sylt
T1826	32	105 Sqn. 5.7.40, Cat E FA 24.5.41
T1921	32	107 Sqn. 11.7.40, FTR 7.6.41, in the sea off Ijmuiden
R3611	31?	40 Sqn. 24.5.40, 139 Sqn. 8.11.40 to 6.5.41; 17 O.T.U. 28.10.41, Cat. E FA 17.6.42
T1936	31	105 Sqn. 13.7.40, 13 O.T.U. 28.6.41 to 9.8.41
N6182	30	107 Sqn. 1.6.39 to 30.9.39; 35 Sqn. 11.2.40, 101 Sqn. 15.3.40 to 23.1.41; 139 Sqn. 10.3.41, 101 Sqn. 16.3.41 to 11.6.41; 17 O.T.U. 20.9.41, 13 O.T.U. 31.3.43, Cat. E. on major inspection 7.3.44
R3758	30	82 Sqn. 23.5.40, 21 Sqn. 28.5.40, 614 Sqn. 1.8.41, Cat. E FA 29.8.42
R3773	30	110 Sqn. 25.5.40, crashed at Offton, nr. Wattisham, returning from a night raid on Emden 31.8.40
R3831	30	107 Sqn. 13.6.40, 110 Sqn. 13.6.40, burnt out in flying accident 11.11.40
T1932	30	105 Sqn. 13.7.40, 17 O.T.U. 24.4.41, FA 16.6.41

Abbreviations:

Cat. E FA—Written off due to a flying accident
FTR—Failed to return
O.T.U.—Operational Training Unit
S.O.C.—Struck off charge
A.G.S.—Air Gunnery School
O.A.P.U.—Overseas Air Preparation Unit
Cat. E FB—Written off as a result of battle damage, or during operations
A.O.S.—Air Observer School
A.A.S.—Air Armament School

(ii) The Boston III

Three squadrons, Nos. 88, 107 and 226, used 132 Boston IIIs. First assigned to a squadron was W8295 on 23.7.41. Last withdrawn was Z2262 on 16.8.43. Thirty were lost on operations, eight were written off through battle damage and ten after flying accidents.

The first Boston IIIs delivered were mainly modified into intruders for 418 and 605 Squadrons of Fighter Command. W8286, which reached Britain 8.6.41, was the first bomber to come, W8285 the first bomber earmarked for a squadron. It arrived 28.6.41.

After service with 2 Group 49 Boston IIIs were passed to the R.A.F. in North Africa where many continued their operational careers. *Z2216* flew the greatest number of operational sorties with 2 Group. It arrived in Britain 8.9.41 joining 88 Squadron 12.11.41 after preparation at Speke. Coded RH-A, it first operated in the hands of Wg. Cdr. Harris during the second Boston III operation of 13.2.42. Three days later it was on an anti-shipping raid. It operated against Comines on 8.3.42. During a raid on St. Omer railway sheds on 4.4.42 when 88 Squadron was intercepted by fighters, it was hit in the bomb bay by an explosive shell. Again, it was being flown by Wg. Cdr. Harris. At this time it was often leading the squadron on operations. On 25–26.6.42 in support of the Bremen 1,000-bomber raid '2216 flown by Sqn. Ldr. R. G. England was ordered to attack Gilze Rijen but failed in its task. Z2216's place as leader was now often taken by Z2229. It flew three sorties during the Dieppe raid of 19.8.42. At 10.58 flown by Sgt. Savage it laid smoke from SCIs westwards across the scene of battle, and later provided smoke for the withdrawal of land forces. It also bombed enemy guns at midday. It was by this time RH-F.

It was flown by Sgt. W. P. Angus on the December Eindhoven raid. Its first 1943 operation came on 15.1.43, the target being the *Solglimt* in Cherbourg. Its last operation with 88 Squadron came on 15.2.43 with No. 5 dry dock, Dunkirk, as target. Z2216 left 88 Squadron on 16.3.43 with 34 sorties to its credit. Subsequently it served in North Africa.

Z2211 flew 32 sorties with 2 Group. It joined 88 Squadron 27.11.42 and flew on the first Boston operation, 12.2.42. As RH-L it bombed the Matford works at Poissy on 8.3.42. It was frequently flown by Sqn. Ldr. D. R. Griffiths on operations at this time, for example against Calais 1.5.42, Dieppe 7.5.42, Dieppe 2.6.42 and Morlaix 5.6.42. On the night of 25–26.6.42 it attacked Volkel airfield. In the hands of Sqn. Ldr. Griffiths it took part in the low-level operations against power stations. Griffiths took it on its one operation during the Dieppe raid, an early attack on a gun battery. Z2211 took the lead against the *Neumark* in Le Havre dry dock on 16.10.42. As RH-N Sgt. Tyler flew it on its final sortie, against the Philips works at Eindhoven 6.12.42. It was seriously damaged by flak and had to be force-landed near Lowestoft at 13.35 hours and was subsequently written off.

AL740 also flew 32 sorties with 88 Squadron which it joined 27.1.42 having reached the U.K. 25.10.41. As RH-J it first operated abortively on the Paris raid of 8.3.42. It was busily engaged on *Circus* raids and made one sortie, still as RH-J, in the Dieppe raid. Eleven of its sorties had been made by the end of April 1942, and it flew six sorties in 1943 before leaving the squadron on 16.3.43 for tropical modifications at Burtonwood. In April 1943, AL740 became 'R' of 114 Squadron and took part in that unit's first operation with Bostons in the Middle East on 21.4.43. That year it operated from Tunisia, Sicily and Italy and was still in front-line use at the end of 1943.

Boston IIIs which flew fifteen or more sorties on 2 Group operations:

Aircraft	Sortie total	Historical notes (sortie totals in brackets)
AL693	31	88 Sqn. 23.3.42–13.9.42, 4.10.42–3.1.43; to N. Africa
Z2258	29	88 Sqn. (7) 1.12.41–226 Sqn. (22) 4.5.42–11.7.42; 107 Sqn. 12.3.43–22.3.43
Z2234	28	226 Sqn. 15.12.41–16.3.43; to N. Africa
AL289	28	88 Sqn. 4.1.42–12.4.43; to N. Africa
Z2236	27	88 Sqn. 26.11.41–342 Sqn. 23.5.43–28.6.43; to N. Africa
W8287	25	107 Sqn. (9) 16.1.42–19.8.42; F/226 Sqn. (16) 31.8.42–18.3.43; to N. Africa
Z2224	25	88 Sqn. 29.3.42—Cat. E 1.11.42
W8373	24	107 Sqn. (24) 28.1.42–13.9.42, 11.10.42–30.3.43; to 114 Sqn. in N. Africa
Z2267	24	88 Sqn. 6.12.41–28.2.43; to N. Africa
Z2281	24	226 Sqn. 8.12.41–2.6.42; 107 Sqn. 20.7.42–226 Sqn. (7) 31.12.42–18.3.43; to 114 Sqn. in N. Africa
Z2292	24	88 Sqn. (24) 1.12.41–18.9.42; 4.10.42–28.2.43; 342 Sqn. 17.3.43–?
AL676	24	226 Sqn. 9.12.41–1.6.42; 15.6.42–26.2.43; to N. Africa
Z2295	23	226 Sqn. 9.12.41—Cat. E FA 1.2.43
Z2297	23	226 Sqn. (16) 1.4.42–27.7.42; 107 Sqn. 17.8.42–88 Sqn. (7) 17.8.42–17.3.43
AL278	23	226 Sqn. 22.1.42–25.8.42; 29.8.42—missing from raid on Morlaix 29.1.43
AL750	23	226 Sqn. 8.6.42–4.7.42; 31.12.42–18.3.43
AL748	22	107 Sqn. (9) 5.5.42–28.8.42; 226 Sqn (1) 13.9.42–342 Sqn. 23.5.43–9.6.43. Also flew 12 sorties on loan to 88 Sqn. To Middle East 22.5.44
Z2229	21	88 Sqn. 18.11.41—Cat. B FA 16.12.42; to N. Africa
AL755	21	107 Sqn. 30.4.42–2.3.43; flew one sortie on loan to 88 Sqn. To N. Africa, Cat. E FB on 114 Sqn. 15.7.43
Z2286	20	107 Sqn. (20) 13.4.42–27.8.42; 12.10.42–342 Sqn. 25.5.43–21.6.43; to N. Africa
AL678	20	226 Sqn. 17.12.41–1.6.42; 107 Sqn. 19.7.42–226 Sqn. 31.12.42–342 Sqn. 12.5.43–4.7.43; to N. Africa
Z2166	19	226 Sqn. 14.5.42–18.3.43; to N. Africa
Z2260	19	88 Sqn. 27.11.41—officially recorded as Cat. E FB on 226 Sqn. 29.8.42
Z2264	19	226 Sqn. 25.11.41—Cat. B FA 19.8.42. Flew 8 sorties with 107 Sqn. and 11 on 226 Sqn.
AL285	19	107 Sqn. (5) 20.1.42–17.8.42; 226 Sqn. (14) 28.8.42–342 Sqn.–?—Cat. E FA 22.5.43
AL296	19	107 Sqn. 14.1.42–21.8.42; 226 Sqn. 4.9.42–107 Sqn. 5.9.42–2.3.43; to N. Africa

Aircraft	Sortie total	Historical notes (sortie totals in brackets)
AL670	19	226 Sqn. no dates recorded. Interned in Spain en route to Middle East 28.5.43
AL721	19	226 Sqn. 1.4.42–88 Sqn. (19) 5.4.42—Cat. B FA 28.1.43, later Cat. E.
AL738	19	88 Sqn. (2) 29.3.42–107 Sqn. (17) 10.6.42–2.3.43; to N. Africa
AL753	19	107 Sqn. 8.1.42–2.3.43; to N. Africa
AL708	18	226 Sqn. 13.2.42–28.8.42; 11.9.42–18.3.43; to N. Africa
AL719	18	107 Sqn. 2.7.42–2.3.43; to N. Africa
AL747	18	107 Sqn. 27.4.42–2.3.43; to N. Africa
AL677	17	226 Sqn. 8.12.41—missing from De Kooy 4.7.42
AL692	17	88 Sqn. 8.12.41—missing, in the sea off Dieppe 19.8.42
Z2285	16	88 Sqn. (15) 17.2.42—E FA 28.9.42, crash landing; flew one more sortie with 226 Sqn. on loan
AL690	16	88 Sqn. 8.12.41—missing, in the sea off Ijmuiden 28.7.42
Z2208	15	88 Sqn. 29.3.42–7.4.43; to N. Africa
Z2231	15	88 Sqn. 26.11.41—missing from Lille/Lomme 19.7.42
AL688	15	226 Sqn. 23.1.42—Cat. B FB 19.8.42; to N. Africa
AL752	15	107 Sqn. (15) 30.4.42–13.9.42; 29.9.42–88 Sqn. 23.3.43–342 Sqn. 13.5.43–21.6.43; to N. Africa

In addition the following aircraft gave long service:

W8295 88 Sqn. 23.7.41–3.4.42; 342 Sqn. 22.4.43–23.6.43 (no sorties)
Z2262 arrived U.K. 6.10.41–88 Sqn. 26.11.41–107 Sqn. (1 sortie) 19.4.42–27.6.42; 4.9.42–342 Sqn. 12.4.43–16.8.43; thence to 13 O.T.U. and S.O.C. 20.4.45, became 4058M
Z2268 88 Sqn. (4 sorties) 8.12.41–226 Sqn. 3.7.42–27.6.43

(iii) Lockheed Vega Ventura I and II

Three squadrons, Nos. 21, 464 and 487, and No. 1482 Flight, used 136 Ventura Is and IIs of which the Gunnery Flight used a total of seven aircraft. First assigned to a squadron, on 31 May 1942, was Mk. I AE681. Last to be withdrawn was AE873 which left 487 Squadron 21 March 1944, although this squadron had fully equipped with Mosquitoes by October 1943. Many Venturas were, strictly speaking, in squadron hands till late 1943, although they were picketed out for months at Sculthorpe awaiting disposal. No. 1482 Flight gave up its last aircraft, AE821, on 24 February 1944.

Thirty-one Venturas were lost on operations, nine written off because of battle damage and eight destroyed in flying accidents while serving 2 Group.

Delivery of the Ventura began with the docking of the S.S. *Heranger* on 6.4.42. All ordered by Britain had arrived by mid October 1942, delivery of both marks taking place simultaneously. Sixty-five Mk. Is were supplied to 2 Group. First of the 71 Mk. IIs to join a squadron was AE852 which reached 21 Squadron at Bodney 14.9.42 and was lost on 5 April when it crashed in the sea off Plaubenau on its eleventh sortie. AE848, the second, joined 21 Squadron 25.9.42 and was lost on the first Ventura raid of 6.11.42. AE853, '54 and '55 joined 464 Squadron in autumn 1942.

Sortie listing in Squadron Operations Record Books of the Ventura squadrons is far from complete except in the case of 464 Squadron. 487 Squadron merely recorded the aircraft letter, and 21 Squadron's sortie records cease at 30 August, although the last Ventura operation by 21 Squadron took place 9.9.43 against Merville airfield during Operation *Starkey*.

On evidence obtained it would seem that AE699: YH-J which made 39 operational sorties gained the highest total. It was operational throughout the period of raids by this type making its first sortie on 6.11.42 and last early on 9.9.43 against Boulogne. It had joined 21 Squadron 9.9.42 and passed to 1482 Flight 6.10.43 with which it served until 24.1.44 when it went into storage at 29 M.U. and then was S.O.C. 25.4.46.

AJ178: YH-L joined 21 Squadron 17.11.42 remaining until 9.10.43. After overhaul and storage at 29 and 83 M.U.s it was used by No. 60 O.T.U. (11.12.44 to 13.5.45) and eventually disposed of to Air Spares Ringway on 21.6.45. This aircraft first operated 17.2.43. Its last operation came on 9.9.43 when it flew with AE699.

AE776: YH-T joined 21 Squadron 11.12.42, flew 27 sorties and was lost in action 2.9.43 during a raid on Forêt d'Eperlecque. AE856: YH-Z joined 21 Squadron 14.10.42, flew 24 sorties and was destroyed in a flying accident on 6.6.43.

The other Ventura squadrons did not operate over so long a period as No. 21; accordingly their aircraft flew fewer sorties. AE880: SB-C, AE939: SB-G and AJ174: SB-F all of 464 Squadron each flew 19 sorties, the highest by any aircraft of that squadron. The top scorer of 487 Squadron was EG-P: AE797, shot down in flames near Caen 12.6.43. It, too, flew 19 sorties, but no others on 487 equalled it, mainly because of the slaughter of 3.5.43. AE916: EG-C managed 14 and AJ468: EG-A flew 12.

Following service with 2 Group Ventura Is and IIs mainly retired to M.U.s, but 299 Squadron operated quite a number between 11.43 and 3.44. Other operators were Nos. 5 and 60 O.T.U.s, No. 140 Squadron, No. 519 Squadron and No. 1407 Met. Flight.

(iv) North American Mitchell

Four squadrons—Nos. 98, 180, 226 and 320—1482 Gunnery Flight and the 2 Group Reconnaissance Flight used 323 Mitchell IIs. The first,

FL164, arrived in Britain on 15 June 1942, followed three days later by FL171, '185 and '188. Twenty-one arrived in Britain in June, 59 in July and four in August. Delivery continued until May 1944.

The first to reach squadron hands were FL169 and FL179 posted into 21 Squadron for trials on 16 July 1942. FL183 and FL189 went to Handling Squadron, Boscombe Down. Tactical trials were conducted at A.F.D.U. using FL203.

Turret and gun-firing trials and some engine modifications delayed the Mitchell's operational career. Initial operational squadron deliveries were made on 13 September 1942, to 98 Squadron West Raynham, which accepted FL169, FL178 and '179. By 28 September FL165, '166, '176, '186, '192, '201, '204, '205, '206, '207, '210 and '213 were among the 22 on squadron strength. The second Mitchell squadron, No. 180, received its first aircraft, FL166, on 29 September and FL675 next day. The Mk. II finally withdrew from service on 29 October 1945, with the withdrawal of FW229 from 98 Squadron.

During operations 85 Mitchells were missing, 26 were written off as a result of battle damage and 22 after flying accidents.

Some of the later Mitchell IIs were of the series ii type with square windows set in the side of the aft fuselage and rear gunner's position similar to that of the Mitchell III. No record of which machines were series ii appears to have been kept.

Sortie listing of individual aircraft in relevant Squadron Operations Books contains quite a lot of errors. Records suggest that *FL176* flew the greatest number of bombing sorties—125 and three on A.S.R. patrols. FL176 arrived by air at Scottish Aviation late June 1942, and passed to 20 M.U. 27.6.42. It joined 98 Squadron 21.9.42 and became 'B'. It participated on the first Mitchell raid on 22.1.43 then made A.S.R. flights during operational stand-by. It resumed bombing operations on 10.6.43 when attacking Ghent power station. Thereafter it was busily engaged until 11.8.44 when it flew its final sortie, against Ouilly-le-Tesson supporting Army operations. It was replaced by HD329. On 5.9.44 it passed to Reid & Sigrist, Desford, for intended overhaul but instead was stored at 49 M.U., then moved to 12 M.U., where it was scrapped 17.12.46.

According to the squadron O.R.B. the indications are that *FL186: G* of 98 Squadron flew the second largest number of sorties, 122 and five A.S.R. patrols. However, in his Group Newsletter of October 1944 Air Vice-Marshal Embry commented that 'when Flg. Off. Berry crash landed his Mitchell [on 23.7.44] the squadron lost their veteran aircraft and the race for 100 operational sorties was ended. "G" [i.e. FL186] had given the longest service to the squadron, 93 successful trips, and her ground crew had serviced it from the beginning of her battle career. They felt confident it would do 100 before "B", three in arrears. "B" has 92 sorties and a clear lead over competitors in the squadron.' (See also page 381.) FL186 reached Britain 23.7.42 and went to 20 M.U. Her first sortie was an A.S.R. mission on 12.2.43. She flew her first bombing mission alongside her competitor on 10 June. Originally she was R-Roger, becoming 'G' late June 1943.

The third most successful Mitchell appears to have been *FV928*. She reached Britain 25.6.43 and joined 2 Group Recce Flight 15.8.43, passing to 98 Sqn. 13.9.43. On 15.6.44 she was transferred to 180 Sqn. With 98 she had flown 47 sorties and made 43 with 180 Sqn.

Other Mitchells with distinguished careers were: (1) FL679: U of 180 Sqn. (on strength 28.6.43 to 15.8.44) with 84 bombing sorties; first operated 4.9.43 against Rouen/Sotteville, last operated 6.8.44 against Livarot. (2) FV938: W of 98 Sqn. (21.8.43–30.5.44). Flew 82 sorties, badly damaged in a belly landing 29.5.44. Hit by flak after bombing gun positions near Dieppe, then Flt. Sgt. Dodd crash-landed and the undercarriage folded up. (3) FL217 reached Britain 27.7.42, joined 180 Sqn. 11.10.42 and remained on strength until 11.7.44. As 'H' it was on the first Mitchell raid. Flew 35 sorties in 1943, and 44 in 1944 in addition to five A.S.R. sorties. On 20.6.44 when attacking *Noball* target X/1A/60 it was hit by intense flak. Its hydraulics were put out of action and it crash-landed at base. (4) FV916 served 180 Sqn. 28.6.43–8.6.44, 98 Sqn. 8.6.44–10.8.44, 226 Sqn. 10.8.44–5.4.45, and spent a short time with 342 Sqn. Its listed operational sorties were flown when on 98 Sqn., nineteen in 1943 and 58 in 1944. No record of its sorties appears in records kept by 226 Sqn. (5) FL695 with 180 Sqn. 15.3.43–8.6.44 flew 73 sorties. (6) FL168: H of 98 Sqn. 2.12.42–1.4.44 is recorded as making 70 sorties, and so also is FW191 of 180 Sqn. (8.6.44–damaged by enemy air attack 1.1.45).

North American Mitchell III

The Mitchell III began to arrive in Britain in May 1944. Heavier and less responsive to control, it was also less popular with the crews. Early squadron deliveries were: HD371 98 Sqn. (9.11.44–12.4.45), HD375 98 Sqn. (16.11.44–8.12.44), HD376 98 Sqn. (23.11.44–20.3.45), HD365 98 Sqn. (23.11.44–FTR 10.2.45 as 'C', from attack on Xanten), HD363 98 Sqn. (23.11.44–Cat. E. after enemy air attack 1.1.45), HD360 180 Sqn. (30.11.44–15.2.45), HD392 320 Sqn. (30.11.44–15.2.45), HD354 226 Sqn. (30.11.44–11.1.45), HD346 320 Sqn. (12.12.44–5.10.45), HD348 226 Sqn. (13.12.44–11.1.45) and HD351 98 Sqn. (14.12.44–20.9.45).

Six Mk. IIIs were lost on operations: HD307 (V/180 Sqn. 13.3.45 raiding Lingerich), HD365, HD380 (Y/98 Sqn. 6.2.45 raiding Deventer), HD390 (U/98 Sqn. 25.2.45 raiding Rees), HD397 (180 Sqn. 15.3.45 raiding Dorsten) and KJ563 (180 Sqn. 21.3.45 raiding Bocholt). Four Mk. IIIs were written off because of battle damage and three destroyed in flying accidents.

(v) The de Havilland Mosquito P.R. Mk. 1 (Bomber Conversion), Mk. III, Mk. IV and Mk. VI

The first Mosquito to join 2 Group was the P.R. Mk. 1 (Bomber Conversion) W4064 which reached 105 Squadron at Horsham on 15 November 1941, and failed to return on 31 May 1942. No. 105 Squadron received seven such aircraft: W4065 (GB-N: 27.2.42–missing 19.8.42), W4066 (GB-A: 17.11.41–14.1.43), W4068 (GB-B: 25.11.41– missing 1.6.42), W4069 (GB-M: 14.1.42–missing 16.7.42), W4070 (GB-C: 5.12.41–missing 27.8.42), W4071 (GB-L: 15.12.41–missing 17.9.42) and W4072 (GB-D: 27.2.42–1.10.42).

On 16.5.42 DK288, the first Mk. IV series ii for 105 Squadron, was delivered to Horsham and subsequently this mark took over and also equipped 139 Squadron from the end of 1942.

Using the number of sorties recorded in the relevant squadron Operations Record Books as the measure of success, DZ408: GB-F with 26 sorties and two abortives would seem to have been the most successful of the day-bombers. It continued to serve 105 Squadron for night operations until written off on account of battle damage on 21.1.44, by which time it had flown 26 night sorties. DK338: GB-O, between 12.9.42 and 1.5.43, flew 23 sorties and aborted on two more. DK302: GB-D, between 11.7.42 and 13.5.43, made 21 successful and nine abortive sorties with 105 Squadron and '4 plus 1' with 139 Squadron.

The first F.B. Mk. VIs reached 2 Group on 21 August 1943, Nos. 464 and 487 Squadrons each receiving one. Records maintained by the fighter-bomber squadrons are incomplete, particularly when aircraft flew more than one sortie in a night. Mk. VIs with long service included: HP927 (SY-B of 613 Sqn. 14.2.44–1.1.45), HX917 (EG-E of 487 Sqn. 7.9.43–FTR 5.7.44), HX919 (464 Sqn. 9.9.43, to 305 Sqn. 8.2.44, to 464 Sqn. 19.3.44–14.9.44), HX920 (464 Sqn. 9.9.43–FTR 22.2.45), HX921 (464 Sqn. 24.10.43, to 21 Sqn. 29.10.43, to 464 Sqn. 28.12.43, to 107 Sqn. 14.2.44–FTR 25.8.44), LR262 (613 Sqn. 18.11.43, to 305 Sqn. 2.2.44–Cat. E FA 24.9.44), LR264 (613 Sqn. 12.11.43, to OM-H/107 Sqn. 4.3.44–24.8.44, 107 Sqn. 7.9.44–17.9.44, to 613 Sqn. 8.3.45–9.8.45), LR302 (SY-S of 613 Sqn. 26.11.43–Cat. E FB 17.1.45), LR303 (613 Sqn. 2.12.43, to 305 Sqn. 8.6.44–8.3.45), MM403 (464 Sqn. 23.1.44–7.9.44, 464 Sqn. 19.10.44–FTR 18.1.45), MM407 (464 Sqn. 25.1.44–?.45) and MM408 (613 Sqn. 26.2.44–?.45).

Only a handful of Mk. III trainers entered 2 Group, among them HJ855 (139 Sqn. 1.8.42–6.1.43), HJ967 (487 Sqn. 27.9.43–12.7.44), HJ969 (464 Sqn. 29.9.43–19.4.44), HJ981 (613 Sqn. 16.10.43 to date unknown) and LR518 (305 Sqn. 20.2.44–20.6.44). See also under Appendix 3.

Appendix 2

Bristol Blenheim Mk. IV Aircraft Used by 2 Group Squadrons between 10 May 1940 and 16 June 1940 for the French Campaign
Dates of service given in brackets

L4893	101 Sqn. (14.4.39–20.9.40)
L4896	101 Sqn. (18.4.39–10.5.40)
L4899	101 Sqn. (18.4.39– ?)
L8732	S/21 Sqn. (11.9.39–17.6.40)
L8733	107 Sqn. (26.4.40–FTR 12.5.40)
L8734	21 Sqn. (12.9.39–FTR 25.5.40)
L8735	C/21 Sqn. (16.9.39–FTR 5.40)
L8736	110 Sqn. (10.5.40–S.O.C. 27.5.40)
L8737	F/21 Sqn. (16.9.39–11.11.40) FAO3
L8738	21 Sqn. (16.9.39–FTR 14.5.40)
L8739	21 Sqn. (17.9.39–FTR 12.5.40)
L8742	21 Sqn. (17.9.39–FTR 31.5.40)
L8743	21 Sqn. (17.9.39–FTR 11.6.40)
L8744	21 Sqn. (17.9.39–FTR 28.5.40)
L8745	21 Sqn. (17.9.39–1.11.40)
L8746	21 Sqn. (22.9.39–FTR 11.6.40)
L8748	107 Sqn. (? –FTR 12.5.40)
L8749	110 Sqn. (18.11.39–11.6.40)
L8751	110 Sqn. (18.11.39–23.11.40)
L8754	110 Sqn. (18.11.39–FTR 23.6.40)
L8755	110 Sqn. (1.4.40–25.6.41)
L8758	B/21 Sqn. (6.11.39–FTR 3.5.41)
L8761	110 Sqn. (21.3.40–FTR 22.5.40)
L8776	40 Sqn. (3.12.39–FTR 10.5.40)
L8777	107 Sqn. (16.10.39–11.2.41)
L8778	110 Sqn. (16.10.39–S.O.C. 22.5.40)
L8780	110 Sqn. (16.10.39–FBO3 2.8.40)
L8796	40 Sqn. (14.6.40–FBO 9.40)
L8800	XV Sqn. (9.12.39–12.11.40)
L8827	40 Sqn. (3.12.39–FTR 6.6.40)
L8828	40 Sqn. (3.12.39–FTR 10.5.40)
L8829	82 Sqn. (18.10.39–FBOE 13.6.40)
L8830	82 Sqn. (18.10.39–FTR L7.5.40)
L8831	40 Sqn. (3.12.39–FTR 10.5.40)
L8833	40 Sqn. (3.12.39–21.5.40)
L8834	40 Sqn. (3.12.39–FTR 24.5.40)
L8836	40 Sqn. (3.12.39–FTR 9.7.40)
L8847	XV Sqn. (10.12.39–FTR 12.5.40)
L8848	XV Sqn. (10.12.39–26.8.40)
L8849	XV Sqn. (10.12.39–FTR 12.5.40)
L8850	XV Sqn. (10.12.39–16.12.40)
L8851	XV Sqn. (10.12.39–FTR 11.6.40)
L8852	XV Sqn. (10.12.39–FTR 18.5.40)
L8853	XV Sqn. (16.12.39–FTR 18.5.40)
L8855	XV Sqn. (16.12.39–FAO3 6.7.40)
L8856	XV Sqn. (10.12.39–FTR 24.5.40)
L8858	W/82 Sqn. (4.4.40–FBOE 17.5.40)
L8870	101 Sqn. (11.4.40–FBO3 26.8.40)
L8872	M/21 Sqn. (1.4.40–FTR 9.7.40)
L8876	40 Sqn. (3.12.39–FAB 22.7.41)
L9023	21 Sqn. (11.1.40–FTR 8.6.40)
L9024	XV Sqn. (11.4.40–FTR 11.6.40)
L9029	H/21 Sqn. (24.2.40–19.6.41)
L9030	XV Sqn. (9.12.39–FBO3 20.5.40)
L9170	107 Sqn. (17.1.40–18.7.40)
L9175	110 Sqn. (21.12.39–FTR 11.5.40)
L9204	XV Sqn. (23.2.40–24.5.40)
L9208	XV Sqn. (13.6.40–28.6.40)
L9210	U/82 Sqn. (18.1.40–FTR 17.5.40)
L9213	M/82 Sqn. (9.4.40–FTR 17.5.40)
L9214	110 Sqn. (26.1.40–FTR 14.5.40)
L9217	110 Sqn. (1.4.40–FTR 14.5.40)
L9241	110 Sqn. (18.1.40–FTR 18.5.40)
L9258	101 Sqn. (15.3.40–FBO3 12.6.40)
L9269	21 Sqn. (11.4.40–FTR 13.6.40)
L9270	40 Sqn. (27.5.40–12.8.40)
L9306	107 Sqn. (19.4.40–24.7.40)
L9323	107 Sqn. (1.4.40–FTR 9.6.40)
L9326	40 Sqn. (30.5.40–FAO3 30.8.40)
L9391	107 Sqn. (10.5.40–FTR 27.5.40)
L9402	40 Sqn. (27.5.40–8.11.40)
L9403	XV Sqn. (7.5.40–FTR 23.5.40)
L9410	40 Sqn. (19.5.40–FTR 6.6.40)
L9413	XV Sqn. (19.5.40–10.9.40)
L9419	101 Sqn. (23.4.40–FTR 20.8.40)
L9420	101 Sqn. (23.4.40–20.12.40)
L9421	101 Sqn. (3.5.40–12.7.41)
L9467	107 Sqn. (25.5.40–FTR 30.6.40)
L9468	82 Sqn. (10.5.40–FTR 10.7.40)
L9469	XV Sqn. (13.6.40–FTR 25–26.7.40)
N3545	101 Sqn. (13.5.40–3.1.41)
N3552	40 Sqn. (13.5.40–2.7.40)
N3591	40 Sqn. (14.6.40–10.9.40)
N3592	C/40 Sqn. (7.6.40–FTR 14.6.40)
N3593	107 Sqn. (3.6.40–FTR 23.6.40)
N3594	F/82 Sqn. (11.6.40–7.10.40)
N3616	101 Sqn. (14.6.40–21.12.40)
N3618	21 Sqn. (14.6.40–4.3.41)
N3619	K/21 Sqn. (14.6.40–FTR 19.7.40)
N3620	107 Sqn. (15.6.40–FTR 30.8.40)
N3621	82 Sqn. (15.6.40–2.7.40)

N6140	101 Sqn. (24.4.39–FTR 5.7.40)	P6912	XV Sqn. (14.2.40–FTR 24.5.40)
N6141	101 Sqn. (27.4.39–30.6.41)	P6913	XV Sqn. (20.3.40–FTR 25.5.40)
N6143	101 Sqn. (2.5.39–18.6.41)	P6914	XV Sqn. (16.12.39–FTR 12.5.40)
N6151	XV Sqn. (20.3.40–FTR 12.5.40)	P6915	A/82 Sqn. (10.1.40–FBO 7.6.40)
N6174	101 Sqn. (9.4.40–FTR 25.7.40)	P6917	XV Sqn. (16.12.39–FTR 18.5.40)
N6176	101 Sqn. (9.3.40–FBO3 9.7.40)	P6924	101 Sqn. (30.11.39–FTR 18.7.40)
N6177	101 Sqn. (5.10.39 to XV Sqn. 16.5.40–14.6.40)	P6925	110 Sqn. (4.5.40 to 82 Sqn. 11.5.40–S.O.C. 6.42)
N6181	101 Sqn. (29.3.40–13.9.40)	P6953	101 Sqn. (14.5.40–FTR 16.12.40)
N6182	101 Sqn. (15.3.40–23.1.41)	P6954	21 Sqn. (18.1.41–FAE 28.7.41)
N6183	107 Sqn. (23.3.40–4.8.40)	P6955	101 Sqn. (4.3.40–FTR 8.9.40)
N6190	107 Sqn. (20.6.39–FBO 4.6.40)	R3600	110 Sqn. (26.5.40–FTR 6.5.41)
N6191	107 Sqn. (21.6.39–FTR 30.9.40)	R3603	XV Sqn. (23.5.40–FBO 18.7.40)
N6192	107 Sqn. (21.6.39–FTR 27.5.40)	R3604	XV Sqn. (23.5.40–20.11.40)
N6207	110 Sqn. (7.7.39–FTR 22.5.40)	R3606	107 Sqn. (29.5.40–FTR 10.7.40)
N6208	110 Sqn. (30.11.39–FTR 18.5.40)	R3609	40 Sqn. (24.5.40–FBO3 16.8.40)
N6210	110 Sqn. (10.7.39–FTR 18.5.40)	R3610	107 Sqn. (3.6.40–14.6.40)
N6217	40 Sqn. (2.12.39–FTR 10.40)	R3611	40 Sqn. (24.5.40–8.11.40)
N6236	40 Sqn. (—?—)	R3612	V/40 Sqn. (7.6.40–FTR 9.9.40)
N6237	107 Sqn. (11.8.39–11.9.40)	R3614	XV Sqn. (20.5.40–FBO 24.5.40)
N6238	101 Sqn. (26.7.39–FTR 24.11.40)	R3615	107 Sqn. (3.6.40–15.11.40)
P4828	K/82 Sqn. (11.8.39–FTR 22.5.40)	R3616	107 Sqn. (25.4.40–FTR 13.6.40)
P4838	R/82 Sqn. (18.8.39–FTR 17.5.40)	R3617	101 Sqn. (11.4.40–9.2.41)
P4839	82 Sqn. (22.8.39–16.6.41)	R3618	101 Sqn. (11.4.40 to 82 Sqn. 18.5.40–FTR 8.6.40)
P4843	82 Sqn. (22.8.39–FTR 7.7.40)		
P4851	82 Sqn. (26.8.39–FTR 17.5.40)	R3619	101 Sqn (11.4.40 to t/82 Sqn. 18.5.40–FTR 29.7.40)
P4852	O/82 Sqn. (26.8.39–FTR 17.5.40)		
P4853	D/82 Sqn. (26.8.39–FTR 17.5.40)	R3670	82 Sqn. (23.5.40 to 110 Sqn. 23.5.40 missing 8.6.40)
P4854	F/82 Sqn. (26.8.39–FTR 17.5.40)		
P4855	82 Sqn. (30.8.39–S.O.C. 15.5.40)	R3674	21 Sqn. (27.5.40–FBO 11.6.40)
P4856	107 Sqn. (5.3.40–28.8.40)	R3675	A/21 Sqn. (27.5.40–14.8.41)
P4857	107 Sqn. (8.9.39– ?)	R3676	21 Sqn. (31.5.40–FBO 12.6.40)
P4858	110 Sqn. (14.9.39–12.8.40)	R3681	110 Sqn. (26.5.40–2.8.41)
P4860	110 Sqn. (15.9.39–23.11.40)	R3682	40 Sqn. (25.5.40–15.7.40)
P4898	Y/82 Sqn. (3.11.39–FTR 17.5.40)	R3683	107 Sqn. (25.5.40–FBO 2.6.40)
P4903	U/82 Sqn. (9.9.39–FTR 17.5.40)	R3684	110 Sqn. (26.5.40–24.3.41)
P4904	B/82 Sqn. (15.9.39–FTR 17.5.40)	R3685	107 Sqn. (25.5.40–FTR 8.6.40)
P4905	40 Sqn. (3.12.39–FTR 12.5.40)	R3686	107 Sqn. (2.6.40–FTR 7.6.40)
P4908	40 Sqn. (13.2.40–FBO3 6.8.40)	R3687	N/21 Sqn. (2.6.40–burnt out 16.11.40)
P4909	40 Sqn. (6.12.39–FTR 24.5.40)		
P4912	101 Sqn. (2.3.40–FAO 6.6.40)	R3688	107 Sqn. (29.5.40–FTR 23.6.40)
P4913	40 Sqn. (3.12.39–FTR 15.5.40)	R3689	40 Sqn. (24.5.40–22.7.40)
P4914	107 Sqn. (30.11.39–FTR 12.5.40)	R3690	82 Sqn. (10.6.40–FTR 11.7.40)
P4917	40 Sqn. (3.12.39–FTR 6.6.40)	R3692	40 Sqn. (24.5.40–FTR 6.6.40)
P4918	40 Sqn. (6.12.39–6.10.40)	R3693	40 Sqn. (24.5.40–FTR 14.6.40)
P4919	107 Sqn. (20.9.39–FBO 2.6.40)	R3710	R/82 Sqn. (24.5.40–FTR 13.7.40)
P4920	40 Sqn. (3.12.39–FTR 25.5.40)	R3704	XV Sqn. (19.5.40–13.11.40)
P4925	107 Sqn. (3.11.39–FTR 22.5.40)	R3706	XV Sqn. (20.5.40–FBO 21.5.40)
P4927	40 Sqn. (3.12.39–FBO 6.6.40)	R3707	O/82 Sqn. (19.5.40–12.9.40)
P6886	21 Sqn. (16.10.39–FBO 29.5.40)	R3708	D/82 Sqn. (19.5.40–20.8.40)
P6889	110 Sqn. (8.3.40–FTR 14.5.40)	R3709	F/82 Sqn. (? –FTR 8.6.40)
P6890	21 Sqn. (16.10.39–27.5.40 S.O.C.)	R3730	U/82 Sqn. (19.5.40–FTR 8.9.40)
P6893	82 Sqn. (18.10.39– ?)	R3731	Y/82 Sqn. (19.5.40–FTR 27.6.40)
P6894	107 Sqn. (26.4.40–FTR 2.7.40)	R3732	82 Sqn. (23.5.40 to L/21 Sqn. 26.5.40–FTR 9.7.40)
P6895	82 Sqn. (18.10.39–FTR 2.7.40)		
P6901	40 Sqn. (3.12.39–S.O.C. 10.10.40)	R3735	107 Sqn.
P6905	101 Sqn. (2.4.40–FBO3 25.9.40)	R3736	110 Sqn. (19.5.40–FAO3 4.9.40)
P6906	101 Sqn. (2.3.40–5.6.41)	R3737	107 Sqn. (19.5.40–FAO3 15.11.40)
P6908	101 Sqn. (18.4.40–23.6.41)	R3738	110 Sqn. (19.5.40–FTR 25.7.40)
P6910	X/82 Sqn. (10.1.40–FTR 13.6.40)	R3739	82 Sqn. (19.5.40–FTR 8.6.40)
P6911	XV Sqn. (14.2.40–12.5.40)	R3740	107 Sqn. (19.5.40–FTR 18.4.41)

R3741	110 Sqn. (19.5.40–X/18 Sqn. 26.8.40)	R3812	82 Sqn. (7.6.40–FAO 4.3.41)
R3742	21 Sqn. (8.6.40–FTR 14.6.40)	R3814	110 Sqn. (11.6.40–25.7.41)
R3743	40 Sqn. (8.6.40–28.7.40)	R3815	T/107 Sqn. (3.6.40–FTR 10.7.40)
R3744	40 Sqn. (23.5.40–FBO 11.6.40)	R3816	J/107 Sqn. (3.6.40–24.6.41)
R3745	S/40 Sqn. (7.6.40–24.7.40)	R3820	J/21 Sqn. (9.6.40–FAE 23.7.40)
R3746	110 Sqn. (26.5.40 to 15 Sqn. FTR 12.6.40)	R3821	R/82 Sqn. (9.6.40–FTR 3.8.40)
R3747	110 Sqn. (26.5.40 to 15 Sqn. FTR 12.6.40)	R3822	O/82 Sqn. (13.6.40–in sea 9.7.40)
		R3823	107 Sqn. (13.6.40–FTR 30.6.40)
R3748	110 Sqn. (26.5.40–FTR 24.7.40)	R3829	82 Sqn. (9.6.40–S.O.C. 6.40)
R3749	110 Sqn. (26.4.40–E FB 29.10.40)	R3831	107 Sqn. (13.6.40–FAO3 11.11.40)
R3754	82 Sqn. (23.5.40–FBO 8.6.40)	R3845	101 Sqn. (12.6.40–4.1.41)
R3755	82 Sqn. (23.5.40 to 21 Sqn. 25.5.40–FBO3 5.9.40)	R3846	101 Sqn. (13.6.40–FTR 19.3.41)
		R3870	107 Sqn. (10.6.40–30.6.40)
R3756	C/82 Sqn. (23.5.40–FTR 13.7.40)	R3871	107 Sqn. (10.6.40–17.2.41)
R3758	82 Sqn. (23.5.40 to U/21 Sqn. 28.5.40–5.7.41)	R3872	21 Sqn. (13.6.40–29.7.40)
		R3873	107 Sqn. (10.6.40–FTR 18.8.41)
R3759	82 Sqn. (23.5.40–FAO 9.7.40)	R3874	110 Sqn. (11.6.40–25.6.41)
R3760	R/21 Sqn. (13.6.40–8.11.40)	R3875	21 Sqn. (13.6.40–19.8.41)
R3761	82 Sqn. (23.5.40 to P/21 Sqn. 25.5.40–3.7.41)	R3876	Q/21 Sqn. (13.6.40–FTR 9.7.40)
		R3893	40 Sqn. (7.6.40–FTR 12.6.40)
R3763	40 Sqn. (7.6.40–FTR 26.7.40)	R3894	XV Sqn. (12.6.40–21.11.40)
R3764	XV Sqn. (24.5.40–FTR 30.7.40)	R3896	XV Sqn. (12.6.40–FTR 1.7.40)
R3765	K/82 Sqn. (10.6.40–FTR 11.11.40)	R3900	G/21 Sqn. (14.6.40–FTR 31.3.41)
R3766	XV Sqn. (24.5.40–10.11.40)	R3904	XV Sqn. (14.6.40–28.6.40)
R3767	XV Sqn. (24.5.40–20.11.40)	R3905	XV Sqn. (14.6.40–12.11.40)
R3768	XV Sqn. (24.5.40–FTR 13.8.40)	R3910	82 Sqn. (15.6.40–FTR 10.8.40)
R3769	XV Sqn. (24.5.40–FAO3 4.9.40)	R3913	82 Sqn. (15.6.40–FTR 13.8.40)
R3770	XV Sqn. (24.5.40–FTR 15.8.40)	R3914	82 Sqn. (15.6.40–FTR 26.11.40)
R3771	XV Sqn. (24.5.40–FAO3, S.O.C. 9.8.40)	R3915	82 Sqn. (15.6.40–FTR 8.9.40)
		R3916	107 Sqn. (16.6.40–FTR 16.7.40)
R3772	110 Sqn. (25.5.40–28.7.41)		
R3773	110 Sqn. (25.5.40–FBO3 31.8.40)		
R3774	110 Sqn. (25.5.40– ?)		
R3775	110 Sqn. (25.5.40–FTR 10.8.40)		
R3776	110 Sqn. (25.5.40–FTR 26.6.40)		
R3777	XV Sqn. (29.5.40–27.11.40)		
R3778	40 Sqn. (29.5.40–FTR 27.6.40)		
R3810	107 Sqn. (3.6.40–FTR 12.6.40)		
R3811	40 Sqn. (3.6.40–FTR 26.8.40)		

Abbreviations: FAE—Flying accident. Category E—write-off.

FAO3—Flying accident on operations. Category 3—write-off.

FBO3, FBOE—Flying battle accident on operations. Category 3—write-off.

FTR—Failed to return.

Sqn.—Squadron.

S.O.C.—Struck off charge.

Appendix 3

Miscellaneous Types of Aircraft
Used by 2 Group

Avro Anson Is and Xs were used by the Group Communications Flight which, by 1945, had attained Squadron status, and was operating Anson XIIs including NL176 (24.4.45–19.6.46), NL180 (28.4.45–17.12.45), PH528 (3.5.45–11.4.46), PH529 (12.5.45–31.5.45) and PH563 (3.5.45–17.5.45).

Avro Tutor—see 1482 Flt., Appendix 11.

Airspeed Oxford—used by the Comm. Flt., as squadron transports and also B.A.T. Flights (which see Appendix 11).

Boeing Fortress I used by 90 Squadron, aircraft on strength: AN518 (9.8.41–to Middle East 11.41, later 220 Sqn. 3.2.42–1.7.42), AN519 (4.6.41–20.8.41; later at R.A.E., and on 206 Sqn., 59 Sqn., 1(C) O.T.U., and 1674 H.C.U.), AN520 (1.11.41–1.4.42, later used by 220 Sqn., 206 and 214 Sqns.), AN521 (28.4.41–11.41), AN522 (4.6.41–S.O.C. after flying accident), AN523 (20.5.41–burnt out 16.8.41), AN525 (21.8.41–FTR 8.9.41), AN526 (4.6.41–10.12.41, 13.2.42–25.2.42), AN527 (25.5.41–1.8.41, 22.10.41–12.2.42, to 220 Sqn.), AN528 (11.6.41–S.O.C. 10.7.41), AN529 (11.5.41–21.8.41, 20.9.41–16.10.41), AN530 (11.7.41–12.2.42, later to 220 and 206 Sqns.), AN531 (2.11.41–12.2.42, later to 220 and 206 Sqns.), AN532 (22.7.41–11.41).

Boulton Paul Defiant—see 1482 Flt.

Bristol Blenheim I. Apart from extensive pre-war use served variously on non-operational duties, for example: L1162 (107 Sqn. 12.12.40 to Horsham 21.11.41, to Watton 1.1.42, to 17 O.T.U. 21.2.42), L1313 (101 Sqn. 30.11.39–Grp. Trng. Flt. 12.9.40, 101 Sqn. 25.2.41–12.5.41), L1329 (101 Sqn. 30.11.39–23.3.40), L1342 (88 Sqn. 14.5.41–FAE burnt 28.7.41), L1344 (88 Sqn. 4.2.41–22.5.41), L1348 (88 Sqn. 26.3.41–4.5.41), L6693 (110 Sqn. 29.11.40–12.2.41, 110 Sqn. 7.4.41 to 18 Sqn. 13.3.42–7.6.43), L6796 (139 Sqn. 22.7.40, to Watton 1.1.42, to 105 Sqn 18.1.42–26.5.42) and L6812 (105 Sqn. 10.8.40–16.8.41, also 15.10.41–3.6.42).

Bristol Blenheim VD. Equipped three squadrons prior to their going overseas or in the case of 139 Sqn. and 1655 M.T.U. before equipment with Mosquito IV. 18 Sqn. used BA725, 735, 736, 738, 740 (to 1482 Flt. 25.11.42), BA780, 781, 792, 794, 795, 797, 801, 802, 803, 805, 811, 815, 818, 819, 820, 821, 870. Equipped 9.42.

114 Sqn.: BA690, 721, 727, 729, 742, 744, 746, 750, 754, 782, 792, 795, 798, 799, 804, 812, 822, 824, 826, 828. Used from 9.42.

139 Sqn.: AZ883, 890, 893, 894, 902, 922, 946, 947, 950, 952, 953, 955, 957, 961, 965, 966, 967, 969, 970, 985, 986, 987, 948. Used 6.42.–343.

1655 M.T.U.: AZ883, 922, 947, 948, 950, 952, 955, 957, 961, 969, 985. Used 5.9.42–1.5.43.

Curtiss Tomahawk—see 1482 Flt. notes.

de Havilland Mosquito T.III. Used by units for training, e.g. HJ855 (139 Sqn. 1.8.42–6.1.43), HJ858 (105 Sqn. 5.9.42–9.42), HJ868 (1655 M.T.U.), HJ875 (1655 M.T.U.), HJ888 (13 O.T.U. 15.3.45; this unit held a number on strength), LR518 (305 Sqn. 20.2.44–31.5.44–20.6.44), LR535 (464 Sqn. 8.5.44 to 2 G.S.U. 6.7.44–E FA 15.10.44), LR556 (305 Sqn. 5.5.44–to 2 G.S.U. 31.8.44–1.2.45).

Douglas Boston I used for trials and training: AE458 (88 Sqn. 12.1.41–18.2.42), AE465 (226 Sqn. 20.5.41–31.5.41, 139 Sqn. 31.5.41–13.7.41, 88 Sqn. 13.7.41–6.4.42), AE467 (88 Sqn. 30.3.41–28.6.41), AW399 (88 Sqn. 12.1.41–18.2.42), AW401 (226 Sqn. 24.12.40–14.4.41), AW406 (226 Sqn. 24.12.40–14.4.41).

Douglas Havoc I used for trials and training: AE464 (226 Sqn. 14.4.41–20.6.41, 107 Sqn. 5.3.43–13.4.43, 342 Sqn. 13.4.43–destroyed in flying accident 18.4.43), AE470 (88 Sqn. 10.4.41–22.6.41), AE472 (226 Sqn. 15.4.41–20.6.41), AW393 (110 Sqn. 28.11.40–5.4.41), AW400 (88 Sqn. 24.12.41–14.4.41), BD113 (342 Sqn.), BJ463 (342 Sqn. 18.4.43–21.5.43), BJ497 (110 Sqn. 12.11.40–10.2.41), BT463 (342 Sqn. 24.4.43–11.12.43) and BV203 (342 Sqn.).

Douglas Havoc II used for trials and training: AH459 (226 Sqn. 30.4.43–12.5.43, 342 Sqn. 1.6.43–9.2.44), AH462 (226 Sqn. 23.3.43–12.5.43, 342 Sqn. 12.5.43–14.1.44), AH499 (82 Sqn. ?–23.9.42), AH501 (82 Sqn. ?–23.9.42), AH510 (226 Sqn. 24.4.43–12.5.43, 342 Sqn. 12.5.43–11.9.43), AH519 (82 Sqn. ?–23.9.42), AH529 (342 Sqn. 29.4.43–Cat E FA 6.6.43).

Fairey Battle—see 1482 Flt. notes.

Handley Page Hampden. With Group briefly when 'B' Flt. of 61 Sqn. was detached to Watton 13.4.41. Withdrawn 30.4.41 after unsuccessful cloud-cover raids. First operations flown 18.4.41 from Bodney. Target was Cherbourg, for AD806, AD732, AD727, AD804 (abandoned) and AD825 which crashed near Swindon as a result of flak damage. On 21.4.41 abandoned raids attempted by X3127 and X3140 on Antwerp and Rotterdam. On 23rd three crews were briefed for Borkum and three for Emmerich. Targets were changed to Antwerp and Rotterdam but cloudless skies brought abandonment. X3138 (Sgt. Harris) penetrated to Hulst before returning. On 27th pairs of aircraft were despatched to Cologne, Münster and Osnabrück. Cloud ran out and only two aircraft reached Germany. AD804 (Sgt. Glover) bombed De Kooy and X3120 (Sgt. Assen) Ijmuiden. Also despatched were AD727, AD826, X3140, X3138. On 28th X3120, X3140, AD727, AD804, AD806 and AD826 attempted raids on Germany and on 29th two abortive sorties were attempted against Emden by AD804 and AD826.

Handley Page Halifax III. Squadrons of 38 Group operated these aircraft under 2 Group early 1945 for night bombing raids.

Hawker Hurricane IV—see 1482 Flt. notes.

Lockheed Hudson III. 139 Squadron equipped with these aircraft in December 1941, before going overseas as a Far East reinforcement squadron in February 1942. Aircraft used: V9114, V9162, V9175, V9189, V9225, T9401, AE513, AE515, AE516, AE518, AE519, AE531, AE534, AE551, AE556, AE558, AE564, AE565, AE593, AE601. Many were passed to 1428 Flt. Oulton, which trained Hudson crews under 2 Group. Their aircraft were AE513, AE515, AE519, AE531, AE534, AE558, AE564, AE565, AE585 and AE594.

Miles Magister. Used for training and communications duties. Pre-war aircraft used were L5948 (Wyton 27.9.37 crashed 18.5.38), L5951 (Upwood), L6912 (Wyton 22.6.38–7.1.39), L8160 (Wyton 25.5.38, became post-war G-AJHD), L8269 (18.8.38, crashed 13.9.38), P2387 (Wyton), P6439 (Watton), P6444 (18 Sqn.), P6445 (57 Sqn.) and P6455 ((Wyton).

Miles Master I. Used for navigational training by 105 Sqn. in 1942. Examples included T8288 (9.5.42–30.3.43) and T8667 (9.5.42–29.4.43).

Miles Martinet—see 1482 Flt. notes.

Miles Mentor. L4420 used at Hucknall (30.1.39–30.11.39).

Percival Proctor I. Used by Group Communications Flt. P6182 (Wyton

30.5.40–to Swanton Morley 17.5.43–27.6.44), P6183 (Wyton 30.5.40–26.10.40).

Short Stirling IV. Squadrons of 38 Group operated these aircraft under 2 Group control early 1945 for night bombing raids.

Vickers-Armstrong Wellington Ic. These were received by 101 Squadron in April 1941. They participated in seven operations under 2 Group control, and flew 55 sorties: 11–12.6.41 Rotterdam (two aircraft); 17–18.6.41 Rotterdam (eight); 21–22.6.41 Cologne (six); Dunkirk (three), one abortive sortie; 25–26.6.41 Bremen (five), Rotterdam (eight); 27–28.6.41 Bremen (seven), Den Helder (one), one abortive sortie; 29.6.41 Bremen (nine), 1–2.7.41 Brest (nine). Aircraft used were R1088 (6.5.41–Cat. E FB 3.8.41), R1219: R (5.5.41–FTR 11.10.41), R1699 (21.5.41–FTR 11.9.41), R1700: X (20.4.41–6.3.42), R1701 (20.4.41–S.O.C. 30.11.41), R1702: F (21.5.41–FTR 24.7.41), R1703 (21.5.41–FTR 31.8.41), R1778: G (22.5.41–Cat. E FB 30.11.41), R1780: B (7.5.41–4.4.42), R1781: C (7.5.41–4.4.42), R1800 (22.5.41–FTR 3.8.41), R1801: U (22.5.41–8.3.42), R3295: P (5.5.41–E FB 30.11.41), W5715: N (3.5.41–10.5.41), W5716 (3.5.41–10.2.42), X3206 (22.5.41–24.8.41) and X9601: V (22.5.41–burnt out flying accident 18.11.41).

Westland Lysander—see 1482 Flt. notes.

Appendix 4

Dimensions, Weights and Performance Data Applicable to Principal Types of Aircraft Used by 2 Group

In any listing of weights and performance of military aircraft it is exceedingly difficult to equate the information available on each type. Loading and other conditions cause precise performance of individual aircraft to differ in any case, and the following notes, based mainly upon Service trials, indicate the performance achieved by certain examples of the aircraft. The notes are arranged in order of the types' entry to service.

Hawker Hind (1 × 607 h.p. Rolls-Royce Kestrel V). Wing span 37 ft. 3 in., length 29 ft. 3 in., height 10 ft. 7 in., wing area 348 sq. ft. Weight data (for K4636): empty 3260 lb., service load 1,254 lb., fuel (94½ gals.) 728 lb., oil (6 gals.) 54 lb., all-up weight 5,296 lb. Armament: 1 forward-firing Vickers III or V .303 in. machine gun on port side of nose with 600 rounds, and 1 Lewis gun in rear cockpit with 5 × 97-round magazines. Bomb load up to 510 lb. Performance (take-off weight 5,220 lb., fuel load 103 gals.): max. T.A.S. m.p.h. 154 at S.L., 159 at 2,000 ft., 179 at 10,000 ft., 188 at 15,000 ft., 180 at 20,000 ft. Service ceiling 26,400 ft. Range 575 miles at 15,000 ft. at 130 m.p.h. T.A.S. (endurance 4·4 hours).

Fairey Gordon (1 × 525 h.p. Armstrong Siddeley Panther IIA). Wing span 45 ft. 9 in., length 36 ft. 8⅝ in., height 14 ft. 2⅜ in., wing area 438½ sq. ft. Weight empty 3,500 lb., loaded 5,906 lb. Armament: 1 Vickers gun fixed firing forward, 1 Lewis gun in rear cockpit. Bomb load 460 lb. Performance (fully loaded): max. T.A.S. m.p.h. 145 at 3,000 ft., cruising 110. Service ceiling 22,000 ft. Range 600 miles.

Fairey Battle I (1 × 1,030 h.p. Rolls-Royce Merlin 1). Wing span 54 ft., length 52 ft. 1¾ in., height 15 ft. 6 in., wing area 422 sq. ft. Weight empty 6,647 lb., loaded 10,900 lb. Armament: 1 × .303 in. Browning gun in starboard wing, 1 × Vickers K gun aft. Bomb load 1,000 lb. Performance: max. T.A.S. m.p.h. 210 at S.L., 240 at 10,000 ft., 241 at 13,000 ft., 243 at 16,200 ft. Economical cruise 148 m.p.h. at 15,000 ft. Landing speed 60 m.p.h., climb rate 8·4 mins. to 10,000 ft. Service ceiling 23,500 ft. Range 1,050 miles with 1,000-lb. bomb load at 16,000 ft. at 200 m.p.h., 640 miles at 16,000 ft.

Vickers-Armstrong Wellesley (1×925 h.p. Bristol Pegasus XX driving a 13-ft. diameter D.H. propeller). Data applicable to K7754: Wing span 74 ft. 6 in., length 39 ft. 1 in., height over prop. 15 ft. 4 in., wing area 630 sq. ft., wheel track 15 ft. 7 in., wing loading 19 lb./sq. ft. Weight empty 6,812 lb., loaded 11,128 lb. (bomb nacelles on, bombs in). Max. fuel capacity: 414 gals. in seven wing tanks plus one of $12\frac{1}{2}$ gals. Normal fuel load 271 gals. and 10 gals. oil. Armament: $2 \times .303$ in. Browning guns, bomb load 1,377 lb. Full throttle speeds (K7729): 186 m.p.h. at S.L., 191 m.p.h. at 2,000 ft., 207 m.p.h. at 10,000 ft., 200 m.p.h. at 20,000 ft. Max. T.A.S. (K7754 at 11,128 lb.) 204 m.p.h. at 9,400 ft. Normal cruise 133 m.p.h. at 15,000 ft. Range (K7729 at 10,120 lb. a.u.w.) at 15,000 ft. and 179 m.p.h. was 1,340 miles (7·5 hours' duration), 160 m.p.h. 1,575 miles (9·85 hours' duration), 130 m.p.h. 1,745 miles (13·45 hours' duration). Rate of climb 5·5 mins. to 5,000 ft. T.A.S. 130 m.p.h., 17·8 mins. to 15,000 ft. T.A.S. 140 m.p.h.

Bristol Blenheim I (2×840 h.p. Bristol Mercury VIII). Wing span 56 ft. 4 in., length 39 ft. 9 in., height tail down 9 ft. 10 in., wing area 469 sq. ft. Weight empty 8,100 lb., loaded (278 gals. fuel) 12,500 lb. Fuel load 2×140 gal. tanks and $2 \times 9\frac{1}{2}$-gal. oil tanks. Armament: $1 \times .303$ in. gun in port wing, $1 \times$ Vickers K gun in dorsal turret. Bomb load 1,000 lb. (usually 4×250-lb. bombs) and provision for light series carrier under rear fuselage. Max. T.A.S. m.p.h.: 240 at S.L., 254 at 5,000 ft., 269 at 10,000 ft., 265 at 15,000 ft. Economical cruise 165 m.p.h. at 15,000 ft. Landing speed 50 m.p.h. Climb 3·7 mins. to 5,000 ft., 7·2 mins. to 10,000 ft., 11·5 mins. to 15,000 ft. Service ceiling 27,280 ft. Typical range (full war load) 1,125 miles at 220 m.p.h. T.A.S., 920 miles with 1,000-lb. bomb load.

Bristol Blenheim IV (2×920 h.p. Bristol Mercury XV). Based on M.A.P. data of July 1941: Wing span 56 ft. 4 in., length 42 ft. 9 in., height 12 ft. 10 in. (9 ft. 2 in. tail down), wing area 469 sq. ft. Weight empty 9,240 lb., weight light load 10,600 lb., mean weight 13,800 lb., maximum weight 14,500 lb. Max. fuel load (full bomb load) 466 gals. Armament: $1 \times .303$ in. Browning gun in port wing with 400 rounds, $2 \times .303$ in. belt-fed Browning guns in dorsal turret (1,000 rounds), 1 .303 in gun beneath nose (500 rounds). Bomb load 1,000 lb. Performance (take-off weight 14,500 lb.): maximum T.A.S. m.p.h. 250 at 20,000 ft., 263 at 15,000 ft., 266 at 11,800 ft. (full throttle height), 227 at S.L. Most economical cruise 180 m.p.h. at 15,000 ft. Maximum weak mixture speed 225 m.p.h., time to 15,000 ft. 15 mins. Take-off run to clear 50 ft. (full load) 940 yards, landing run over 50 ft. 850 yds. Service ceiling 22,500 ft. at max. weight, 25,500 ft. at mean weight. Range with 1,000-lb. bomb load 1,460 miles.

Douglas Boston III ($2 \times 1,600$ h.p. Wright Double-Row Cyclone

GR-2600-23). Wing span 61 ft. 4 in., length 48 ft., height 15 ft. 10 in., wing area 465 sq. ft. Mean weight 20,500 lb., maximum weight 23,000 lb., weight empty 15,650 lb. Armament: 4 × .303 in. guns fixed in nose, 2 × .303 in. dorsal guns hand operated, 1 × .303 in. ventral gun. Bomb load: 4 × 250 lb., or 2 × 500 and 2 × 250 lb. Performance: maximum speeds m.p.h. (warload): 308 at 3,000 ft., 318 at 10,500 ft., 304 at 13,000 ft. Economical cruise 200 m.p.h. at 15,000 ft. Take-off run 1,100 yds. at max. wt., landing run light 1,200 yds. Climb to 15,000 ft. 11 mins. Service ceiling 24,250 ft. Range states: 1,240 miles with 2,000-lb. load and 447 gals. fuel; 2,035 miles light with 689 gals.

Boeing Fortress I (4 × 1,200 h.p. Wright Cyclone R-1820-73). Wing span 104 ft., length 66 ft., height 15 ft. 5 in., wing area 1,420 sq. ft. Crew: 6. Weights: empty 30,670 lb., light 34,560 lb., mean 43,500 lb., max. 53,200 lb. Armament: 1 × .30 in. nose gun, 6 × .50 in. guns (2 in both dorsal and ventral position, 1 in each side position). Bomb load: 2 × 2,000 lb., or 4 × 1,100 lb., or 2 × 1,100 lb. plus 2 × 600 lb. Performance: max. speed 325 m.p.h. at mean weight at 28–30,000 ft.; economical cruise 230 m.p.h. at 30,000 ft., climb to 30,000 ft. 37·5 mins. Take-off run to 50 ft.: 1,150 yds. Service ceiling 34,000 ft. (take-off weight 49,400 lb.). Range: 1,850 miles with 7,400-lb. bomb load and 1,415 gals. fuel; 2,860 miles with 2,075 gals.

Douglas Boston IIIA (2 × 1,600 h.p. Wright Cyclone GR-2600-23). Wing span 61 ft. 4 in., length 47 ft. 4 in., height 16 ft. 1½ in. Tailplane dihedral 10°. Weight loaded 21,700 lb. (with 2,000-lb. bomb load, 400 gals. fuel). Max. fuel load 489 gals. and 38 gals. oil. Armament and bomb load: as for Mk. III. Performance (take-off weight 21,000 lb.): take-off speed 110–110 m.p.h., landing speed 115–110 m.p.h. Max. speed 307 m.p.h. T.A.S. (M.S. gear) at 10,000 ft., 309 m.p.h. T.A.S. (M.S.) at 1,800 ft., 323 m.p.h. T.A.S. (F.S. gear) at 10,500 ft., 280 m.p.h. T.A.S. (F.S.) at 12,000 ft., 270 m.p.h. T.A.S. (F.S.) at 14,000 ft. On average 18 m.p.h. faster than Mk. III with collector ring and single exhaust pipe. Range (21,700 lb.) 1,100 miles at 240 m.p.h. T.A.S.

Douglas Boston IV (2 × 1,700 h.p. Wright Cyclone R-2600-29). Main dimensions as for Mk. IIIA, length 48 ft. 4 in. Revised nose transparency, air intake on cowl extended aft over wing to house air cleaners. Max. permissible loaded weight 27,600 lb., normal loaded wt. 24,000 lb. Armament: 2 × M2 0.50 in. guns in dorsal Martin turret, 2 × 0.50 in. guns fixed in bomb aimer's section, 1 × 0.50 in. M2 flexible mounted lower station gun. Max. T.A.S. speeds 327 m.p.h. at 10,600 ft., 295 m.p.h. at 12,100 ft.

Lockheed Ventura 1/11 (2 × 2,000 h.p. Pratt & Whitney Double Wasp R-2800-31). Data applicable to Mk. 1 AE748: Wing span 65 ft. 6 in., length 52 ft. 7 in., height 14 ft. 3 in., wing area 551 sq. ft. Weight: empty 17,468 lb., service load 5,616 lb., fuel (471 gals.) 3,391 lb., oil (25 gals.) 225 lb., bomb load 4 × 250 lb. and 3 × 500 lb. bombs, all-up weight therefore 26,700 lb. Max. landing wt. 22,500 lb. Armament: 2 × .50 in. fixed guns (500 rounds) on top of nose, 2 × .303 in. guns in nose position on flexible mounting (1,500 rounds), 2 × .303 in. guns in Boulton Paul Type C Mk. IV dorsal turret (2,000 rounds). Tunnel gun position with 2 manually trained .303 in. guns (2,000 rounds). Performance: max. T.A.S. speed (F.S. gear) 289 m.p.h. at 16,000 ft., max. T.A.S. (M.S. and flame dampers) 268·5 m.p.h. at 9,500 ft., weak mixture cruising speed T.A.S. (F.S.) 212 m.p.h. at 11,000 ft., 238·5 m.p.h. at 16,000 ft., rate of climb (M.S.) 1,130 f.p.m. S.L. to 9,000 ft., in F.S. gear 770 f.p.m. at 15,500 ft. Time to 10,000 ft. 8·9 mins., to 20,000 ft. 22·8 mins. Service ceiling 24,800 ft. Range 925 miles (2,500-lb. load and 470 gals. fuel).

North American Mitchell II (2 × 1,700 h.p. Wright Cyclone GR-2600-13). Wing span 67 ft. 6¾ in., length 54 ft. 1 in., height 15 ft. 9¾ in., wing area 610 sq. ft. Weight empty 16,000 lb., loaded 26,000 lb. Mean operating weight 25,280 lb., max. take-off weight 30,000 lb. Fuel load 4,059 lb. Armament: 2 × .50 in. guns in upper Bendix turret, 2 × .50 in. guns in lower Bendix turret, 1 × .30 in. gun in one of four ball and socket mountings in nose. Bomb load 4 × 1,000 lb. Performance: take-off speed (23,000 lb.) 105 m.p.h. stalling speed (undercarriage up) 119 m.p.h. I.A.S. Max. T.A.S. 294 m.p.h. at 5,500 ft. (F.S.), 288 m.p.h. at 12,000 ft. (M.S.), 294 m.p.h. at 14,800 ft. (F.S.). Climb 3·7 mins. to 6,000 ft. and 10·8 mins. to 15,000 ft. with warload. Service ceiling 26,700 ft. Range at 15,000 ft. 1,230 miles (M.S. gear, cold intake), 1,135 miles (F.S. gear, cold intake). Range with 4,000-lb. bomb load and 4,050 gals. fuel (30,000 lb. wt.) 925 miles at 15,000 ft.

North American Mitchell III (2 × 1,700 h.p. Cyclone GR-2600-13). Dimensions as for Mk. II but length 53 ft. 5¾ in. All-up weight 32,000 lb., max. landing weight 32,000 lb. Max. take-off wt. 34,000 lb. Armament: 2 × .50 in. guns in tail turret, 2 × .50 in. waist guns poking from Perspex blister on sides of rear fuselage, 2 × .50 in. guns in forward turret, optional fitting of 2 × .50 in. guns in steel blister on both sides of nose. Max. speed 303 m.p.h. at 13,000 ft. cruising speed range 180–235 m.p.h. I.A.S., stalling speed 118 m.p.h. (86 m.p.h. with undercarriage and flaps down). Differed from Mk. II in having a tail turret, navigator/bomb aimer's station in nose instead of amidships. Had additional 125-gal. fuel tank over bomb bay.

de Havilland Mosquito B.IV (2 × 1,280 h.p. Rolls-Royce Merlin 21). Wing span 54 ft. 2 in., length 40 ft. 9½ in., height 12 ft. 3½ in., wing area 454 sq. ft. Weight lightly loaded 15,318 lb., mean wt. 18,390 lb., loaded 21,462 lb. Bomb load 2,000 lb. (no guns carried). Performance: max.

speed T.A.S./ft. 283 at S.L., 322 at 10,000, 341 at 20,000, 329 at 25,000, 380 at 14,000. Economical cruise 265 m.p.h. at 15,000 ft. Climb: 9 mins. to 15,000 ft. Service ceiling 33,000 ft. Range at econ. cruise 1,040 miles at S.L., 1,110 miles at 5,000 ft., 1,220 miles at 20,000 ft., 1,210 miles at 25,000 ft. Range at high-speed cruise (7 lb. boost) 805 miles at S.L., 860 miles at 5,000 ft., 990 miles at 20,000 ft.

de Havilland Mosquito FB.VI (2 × Rolls-Royce Merlin 21/22/23/25-variously fitted). Dimension as Mk. IV, but length 41 ft. 2 in. Weight empty 13,727 lb., service load 3,192 lb., fuel 2,962 lb., oil 293 lb.—flying weight 20,114 lb. Armament 4 × .303 in. nose guns and 4 × 20 mm. Hispano cannon. Bomb load 2 × 250 lb. in belly bay, 2 × 250 lb. on wing racks (2 × 500 lb. on srs. ii aircraft—the usual type used by 2 Group). Performance: max. speed (M.S.) 278 m.p.h. at S.L., 327 m.p.h. at 13,900 ft., 329 m.p.h. at 20,700 ft. (F.S.). At 19,000 lb. with Merlin 25s, manifold exhausts—top speed 378 m.p.h. T.A.S. at 13,000 ft. Range with 100-gal. drop tanks (650 gals. fuel load) 1,325 miles at S.L. economical cruise. (For fuller details of loadings etc., see *Mosquito*, Appendices 4, 5, 6, 7.)

Appendix 5

Aircraft on Group Strength—
1 June 1943

(*i*) *Squadrons operating Boston IIIA:*

No. 88   BZ205-R, BZ206, BZ212: L, BZ214, BZ217: Q, BZ224: B, BZ225: C, BZ248, BZ267, BZ299: O, BZ323: P.

No. 107 BZ202, BZ203: G, BZ220: U, BZ223: H, BZ226, BZ230: A BZ235: K, BZ237: S, BZ241: B, BZ253: C, BZ259: M, BZ262, BZ266: O, BZ275: K, BZ278, BZ279: T, BZ280: D, BZ281: P, BZ303, BZ308, BZ317, BZ321: L, BZ335.

No. 342 BZ208: A, BZ270: N, BZ290: B, BZ325, BZ313: B. Also on strength Boston IIIs W8295, Z2236, Z2262, Z2286, Z2292, AL678, AL748, AL752, Boston I BT463 and Havoc IIs AH459, AH462 AH510, AH529.

(*ii*) *Squadrons operating Ventura I and II:*

No. 21   AE697, AE699: J, AE730, AE736: W, AE762: K, AE776: T, AE787, AE790, AE856, AE918: X, AE927: V, AJ163, AJ178: L, AJ447: G, AJ452: O, AJ458: D.

No. 464 AE688: Q, AE732, AE753, AE785, AE792, AE798, AE853, AE854, AE855, AE880: C, AE884, AE920, AE937: E, AE939: G, AE947, AJ167: K, AJ174: F, AJ182, AJ231: D, AJ232, AJ453, AJ456, AJ466: H, AJ491: P.

No.487   AE660, AE661, AE679, AE681, AE691, AE706, AE723, AE733, AE788, AE797: P, AE819, AE821, AE822, AE833, AE846, AE894, AJ193, AJ446, AJ461.

(*iii*) *Squadrons operating Mitchell II:*

No. 98   FL166: A, FL167: F, FL168: H, FL174, FL176: B, FL186: R, FL192: M, FL201, FL202, FL204: C, FL210: P, FL213, FL674: U, FL682: N, FL683: L, FL698, FL704, FL700: J.

No. 180 FL170: L, FL173: J, FL188, FL198 (damaged in action 30.6.43), FL205: F, FL217: H, FL675: X, FL677: N, FL681: C, FL686: M, FL689: A, FL695: B, FL707: Z, FR396: K.

No. 320 FR142, FR143: A, FR144: C, FR147: C, FR149: D, FR168, FR170: G.

No. 226 Squadron was equipping with Mitchell II and had received FL164 FL196, FL203 and FL680 and still had two Bostons AL268 and BZ211.

No. 1482 Bombing & Gunnery Flight was using Venturas AE695, AE719, AE811 and AE842, also Mitchell IIs FL169 and FL178.

Appendix 6

Aircraft on Specified Operations

Aircraft and Crews which Operated 4.9.39

No. 107 Squadron

N6184 (FTR) Flt. Lt. W. F. Barton (K), Flg. Off. J. F. Rees, Cpl. J. R. Ricketts (K).

N6188 (FTR) Plt. Off. W. J. Murphy (K), Sgt. Maud, A.C. E. M. Pateman (K)

N6240 (FTR) Sgt. A. S. Prince (K), Sgt. G. F. Booth, A.C. L. G. Slattery.

N6189 (FTR) Flg. Off. H. B. Lightoller (K), Sgt. Hards, A.C.1 E. W. Lyon (K)

N6195 Plt. Off. W. J. Stephens, A.C. Innes-Jones, A.C. White.

No. 110 Squadron

N6204 Flt. Lt. K. C. Doran, Plt. Off. S. R. Henderson, Sgt. D. Pennington, A.C. J. Smith.

N6201 Plt. Off. G. O. Lings, Sgt. T. C. Hammond, A.C. W. Bingham.

N6198 Sgt. J. H. Hanne, Sgt. C. Beavis, A.C. B. Gray.

N6197 Sgt. R. Abbott, Sgt. L. Bancroft, A.C. J. Rosemond.

N6199 (FTR) Flg. Off. H. L. Emden (K), Sgt. Grossie, Sgt. S. G. McKotty (K), A.C. R. Evans (K).

(K): Killed in action

No. 139 Squadron

Aircraft used: N6216, N6217: XD-R, N6218, N6224: XD-F, N6225.

Notes on Aircraft used:

N6195 with 107 Sqn. 26.6.39–13.3.40. After storage in 8 M.U., with 53 Sqn. 12.9.40–9.2.43. Written off 13.5.44.

N6197 with 110 Sqn. 26.6.39–3.2.40, then used overseas.

N6198 with 110 Sqn. 29.6.39 until crashed and written off at Barking Tye Common.

N6201 with 110 Sqn. 29.6.39–S.O.C. 7.3.40.

N6204 with 110 Sqn. 29.6.39–S.O.C. 29.10.39.

N6216 with 139 Sqn. 13.7.39–missing 12.5.40.

N6217 with 139 Sqn. 29.8.39, to 40 Sqn. 2.12.39–FTR 10.40.

N6218 with 139 Sqn. 11.7.39–14.11.39. Prepared for 36 Sqn. in Far East; instead passed to 5 B.G.S. 8.12.40: in flying accident 8.8.41, S.O.C. 6.10.41.

N6224 and N6225 with 139 Sqn. 24.7.39, abandoned in France May 1940.

Aircraft used on 'Circus Operation No. 1', 10 January 1941

Forward Support:
242 Squadron (Hurricanes): V6913, P2982, P2961, P3718, P3207, V6985, R4115, V6740, V6675, V7203, V6984, V6578.
249 Squadron (Hurricanes): V6561, V7600, V7000, V6945, V6615, V7171, V6582, V7538, V6584, P3579, V6728, V6534.

Top Cover:
41 Squadron (Spitfires): P7738, P7666, P7284, P7299, P7302, P7558, P7508, P7371, P7610, P7590, P7816, P7612.
64 Squadron (Spitfires): P9555, R6975, N3108, R6977, R6732, X4481, X4647, N3059, N3122, P9556, X4611, R6972.
611 Squadron (Spitfires): R6914, X4662, X4817, X4253, X4547, X6759, R6765, N3225, X4317, X4060, X4609, X4017.

Close Escort:
56 Squadron (Hurricanes): V6880: V, P3055: P, V7509: S, V7315: L, V7508: N, P3855: O, V7611, V7179, V6944, P3784, V7505, V7105.

Bomber Box:
114 Squadron (Blenheim IV): V5494, T1849, T1838, R3743, Z5902, T2125.

Withdrawal Cover:
66 Squadron (Spitfires): P7669, P7670, P7500, P7568, P7660, P7668, P7602, P7540, P7625, P7571.
74 Squadron (Spitfires), P7537, P7310, P7352, P7506, P7559, P7561, P7542: P7359, P7740, P7502, P7623, P7741.
92 Squadron (Spitfires): R6833, X4419, X4479, X4561, X4616, X4606, X4484, X4412, one not known.

Aircraft involved in Ramrod 14 and Circus 112 on 8 March 1942

(a) *Ramrod 14*—target: Matford Works, Poissy, France
88 Squadron: Boston III Z2211: L, Z2260: N both bombed. Remainder—
AL740: J, AL268: T, Z2261: D, Z2230—jettisoned loads.
226 Squadron: Boston III Z2209: G (Wg. Cdr. Butler), AL278: G, Z2264: F, Z2294: A, AL275: Z, AL688: Y.

Withdrawal Cover: 41 Squadron (Spitfire V): W3654, BL248, W3383, BL405, BL415, AD477, BL595, W3719, W3852, BL477, BL674, —?—.
129 Squadron (Spitfire VB): 12 aircraft serial numbers unknown.

(b) *Circus 112A*—target: Comines Power Station
88 Squadron: Boston III Z2216: A, Z2229: B, Z2231: F.
226 Squadron: Boston III AL700: T, AL677: P, Z2234: H.

Close Escort: 121 Squadron (Spitfire VB): AD548, AD460, BL239, AA880, AA904, AD471, W3711, AA922, AD139, AD463 (FTR), AD501, AD373;
222 Squadron (Spitfire V): AD233, BL437, W3606, AD131, AD249, AB196,

AD133, P8780, BL768, P8755, W3769, —?— (FTR); 403 Squadron (Spitfire VC): C: BL707, D: W3425 (FTR), E: BL590, F: W3421, U: 364, M: 978, Z: 940 (early return), N: 871, T: AB865, V: AA835, B: 967, L: AD208 (early return).

Escort Cover: 303 Squadron (Spitfire V): BL656, AA908, AD116, AA882, AA940, BL375, AB824, AB383, BL672, W3506, AD138, W3765; 315 Squadron (Spitfire V): AB247, AD262, AB904, W3507, AB789, AD895, AA943, AD240, W3618, AD134, AB898, AB931, AB241; 316 Squadron (Spitfire V): BL646, W3748, AB180, W3798, AB735, AB809, AB920, BL631, W3825, P8606, AD130, W3510.

High Cover: 64 Squadron (Spitfire V): BL787, W3839, BL725, AD182, AD252, AD271, AB921, W3802, W3815, BL232, AB786, W3947; 313 Squadron (Spitfire V): AA869, AB916, AD390, BL769, AD197, AB276, BL480, BR581, W3969, AD380, AA765, P8531.

Rear Support Wing: 412 Squadron (Spitfire V): AD381, AA748, BL242, W3949, AD357, BL471, W3958, AD226 (and 4 more aircraft); 609 Squadron (Spitfire V): P8699, AD396, BL486, AD202, W3705, AA857, AD137, AA766, BL263, AB787, —?— (early return) and 'HT: U'.

(c) *Circus 112B*—target: Abbeville Marshalling Yard
107 Squadron: Boston III AL280: A, AL702: F, Z2179: O, W8287: U, AL296: S, W8373: W.

Close Escort: 72 Squadron (Spitfire V): BL318, AB283, AD183, AA945, AA867, BL773, BL338, W3321, AB252, BL721; 124 Squadron (Spitfire V): BL321, AA866, AB280, W3312, AB814, W3758, AA761, W3332; 401 Squadron (Spitfire V): AD234, BL598, BL708, BL685, AD418, AA973, R7336, AA926, P8783, AD421, W3440, AD917, BL538.

Escort Cover: 452 Squadron (Spitfire V): AB994, W3950, BL633, AB989, AB185, AA851, BL744, AA909, AB260, AD563, AA935, AB792; 485 Squadron (Spitfire V): AA732, W3528, BL385, BL346, AD114, AD248, W3577, W3640, W3747, BL513, AB851, W3407; 602 Squadron (Spitfire VB): 12 aircraft unknown.

High Cover: 302 Squadron (Spitfire V): BL549, W3831, W3637, P8742, AA861, AD297, W3902, W3309, W3906, AA856, AA850, AD428; 317 Squadron (Spitfire V): T: AD308, V: AA758, S: BL563, R: 279, P: 439, AD140, AD321, AD259, AD250, AD368, AD269, BL563.

(d) *Diversion 10 Group*—Cherbourg area
118 Squadron (Spitfire V): W3943, R7334, BL464, AD210, AD204, AA744, AA724, W3832, AA791, BL264, BL332, AA729; 234 Squadron (Spitfire V): W3936, AA946, AD227, W3935, AA981, W3937, BL241, BL668, BL889, AA938, AB725, BL623; 501 Squadron (Spitfire V): W3984, W3840, AB965, AA924, W3845, AB179, W3846, AD237, BL240, AD200, P8741, W3842.

P

Aircraft operated under 2 Group control on 30–31 May 1942

13 Squadron
Juvincourt: B: Z6357*, I: T2254*, K: N3545*, R: N3616 (FTR).
St. Trond: E: R3879*, F: Z6084*.
Venlo: T: Z5811*.

18 Squadron
Juvincourt: F: Z7492, G: V6317*, T: Z7304*, V: Z7344*, X: V5385*.
St. Trond: A: Z7351*, D: V5638 (early return), E: R3879*, F: Z6084*,
              H: Z7279, M: V5503*, P: Z7372*, R: V6371*.
Venlo: B: Z7283, C: T2331, L: Z7358, Q: Z7348, R: Z7284, Z6358.

114 Squadron
Bonn: F: Z7356*, G: V6262*, J: V5515*, K: Z6073*, M: V6431*,
              N: Z7284*, P: Z7319*, X: V6264*.
Twente: C: L8800*, D: V6337*.
Vechta: O: Z7761* (only one to attack), A: R3620, L: V5455,
              Q: V5635, R: V5645 (FTR), V: V6456, W: V6443, Z: Z6161
              (bombed Ardorf).

614 Squadron
Twente: A: N3536, E: V5752*, H: V5808*, J: V5626*, M: Z6173*,
              O: R3758, R: V5451*.
Vechta: L: Z5882 (bombed Norderney).

   * claimed to attack primary target. All Blenheims.

Aircraft operated under 2 Group control on 1–2 June 1942

13 Squadron
Juvincourt: B: Z6357, K: N3545.
St. Trond: E: R3879, F: Z6084.
Venlo: E: Z6186 (FTR), M: Z6358.

18 Squadron
Rheine: C: T2331, F: Z7492, T: Z7304, V: Z7344, X: V5385.
St. Trond: R: V6371, A: Z7351, D: Z7415, H: Z7279, M: V5503,
              P: Z7372.
Venlo: B: Z7283, L: Z7358, Q: Z7348, R: Z7285, Y: T2431,
              W: V6443.

114 Squadron
Ardorf: N: Z7284, M: V6431, P: Z7319, X: V6264.
Bonn: A: R3620 (FTR), L: V5455, Q: V5635†, U: V6443, Z: Z6161†.
Borkum: J: V5515 (secondary target).
Leeuwarden: G: V6262.
Twente: D: V6337 (FTR), C: L8800, V: V5456.
Vechta: F: Z7356†, K: Z6043†, O: Z7761.

614 Squadron
Bonn: L: Z5882.
Twente: A: N3536†, E: V5752†, H: V5808†, J: V5626†, M: Z6173,
            P: L1454 (Mk. I), R: V5451.

† known to have attacked primary target. All Blenheims.

Boston IIIAs Used on Low-Level Operations in 1943

(i) 8.8.43—Rennes:
107 Squadron: BZ230: A, BZ280: C, BZ253: C, BZ223: D, BZ203: G,
BZ371: S, BZ254: N, BZ226: T, BZ325: U (W. Off. Roberts—FTR),
BZ235: K, BZ260, BZ275: J, BZ220: B, BZ317: E.
88 Squadron: BZ242: E, BZ224: B, BZ225: C, BZ296: H (Plt. Off. W. P.
Angus—FTR), BZ278: G, BZ359: A, BZ205: R, BZ299: O, BZ212: L,
BZ217: Q, BZ351: Z, BZ289: N.
342 Squadron: BZ208: A, BZ360: J, BZ332: C, BZ319: H, BZ304: K,
BZ370: E, BZ376: T, —?—: P, BZ270: N, BZ268: G, BZ233: U, BZ276: Q.

(ii) 16.8.43—Denain:
107 Squadron: BZ230: A, BZ279: P, BZ259: M (Flg. Off. McCormack—
FTR), BZ260: L, BZ266: T, BZ275: J, BZ253: C, BZ371: S, BZ235: K,
BZ281: R, BZ290: B, BZ280: H, BZ317: E (Flt. Sgt. Turl—FTR).
88 Squadron: BZ242: E (Sqn. Ldr. R. S. Gunning—FTR), BZ359: A
(Flg. Off. A. H. Riseley—FTR), BZ225: C, BZ211: F, BZ316: J, BZ278: G,
BZ351: Z (Sqn. Ldr. C. E. Hawkins—FTR), BZ289: N (Flg. Off. A. B.
Smith—FTR), BZ299: O, BZ212: L, BZ323: P, BZ205: T.
342 Squadron: BZ313: S, BZ276: Q, BZ376: T, BZ349: V, BZ233: U,
BZ270, BZ332: C, BZ304: K, BZ344: F, BZ370: E, BZ305: L, BZ208: A.

(iii) 22.10.43—Courcelles:
107 Squadron: BZ230: A (Wg. Cdr. R. England—FTR), BZ223: D (Flg. Off.
J. R. Bryce—FTR), BZ275: J, BZ372: F, BZ234: K (Flt. Lt. McCulloch),
BZ203: G (Flt. Lt. Hoog—FTR), BZ323: Q, BZ253: C, BZ279: P, BZ303: V,
BZ281: R, BZ294: S, BZ308: T (reserve—no attack).
88 Squadron: BZ254, BZ398, BZ212: L, BZ205: R, BZ334, BZ217: Q,
BZ221, BZ389, BZ225: C, BZ312, BZ364, BZ307 (Flt. Sgt. I. J. Chappell
FTR).
342 Squadron: BZ208: A, BZ290: O, BZ376: T, BZ261: U, BZ270: N,
BZ301: S, BZ302: B, BZ304: K, BZ305: L, BZ318: G, BZ332: C, BZ344: F.

Aircraft and Units Engaged in Operations against Ijmuiden—26 March 1944

Fighter rendezvous: Great Yarmouth. Route flown: Direct to target, then
turn left and route retraced to Yarmouth then dispersal to bases.

2 Group effort:
(a) Mitchell IIs with Spitfires of 64 and 611 Squadrons:

98 Sqn.: FW107: X, FV913: O, FL176: B, FV938: W, FL186: G, FV914: A.
N.B. Effort cut due to Night Light trials.
180 Sqn.: FW142, FL185, FL685, FV915, FV967, FW118, FW113, FW110,
FV945, FR182.
320 Sqn.: FR142: F, FR188: H, FR202: G, FR151: C, FR184 (abandoned
sortie at Redhill) FR191: Y, FR186: B, FR143: A, FR182: R, FR176: B,
FR178: T.

(b) Bostons with Spitfire V escort of 402 Squadron:
88 Sqn.: BZ225, BZ274, BZ221, BZ286, BZ323, BZ264, BZ301, BZ374,
BZ357, BZ231, BZ285, BZ289.
342 Sqn.: BZ302: B, BZ270: N, BZ263: J, BZ281: R, BZ318: G, BZ208: A.
General high cover for one hour over target by 65 Squadron Mustangs.

U.S. 9th A.A.F. effort:
First wave: 322 B.G. (Andrews Field)   55 B-26
                 344 B.G. (Stansted)   52 B-26
                 387 B.G. (Dunmow)   47 B-26
Fighter cover: Spitfires of Nos. 66, 222, 331 and 349 Squadrons.

Second wave: 386 B.G. (Chipping Ongar)   47 B-26
              391 B.G. (Matching)   49 B-26
              323 B.G. (Earls Colne)   51 B-26
              394 B.G. (Boreham)   54 B-26
Fighter cover: Spitfires of Nos. 41, 132, 310, 312, 313, 453 and 602 Squadrons.
Reconnaissance: Two P-51s of 67th Group followed by another two made
weather recce to the target area prior to attack, operating from Middle
Wallop.
Target support: Mustang IIIs of Nos. 19, 65 and 122 Squadrons.

Appendix 7

Aircraft Serviceable and Available for Operations at 09.00 hours

Explanation and abbreviations:
Listed are the number of aircraft available, on the given date, for operations at 09.00 hours. Those marked * are additional aircraft in operational reserve only. To 24.7.41 all the aircraft listed are Blenheim Mk. IVs. Symbols used subsequently to indicate type/mark are as follows: F: Fortress I, H: Hudson, BS: Boston III, BS3A: Boston IIIA, BS4: Boston IV, M: Mosquito IV, MIII: Mosquito III, MVI: Mosquito VI, BV: Blenheim V, V: Ventura, VI: Ventura I, VII: Ventura II, MT: Mitchell II, MT3: Mitchell III.

‡ Return for 2 Group (Continental) only.

Equipment: Blenheim IV

Sqn.	21	107	114	101	82	110	139	15	40
Date									
22.9.39									
Range State I	7	5	16	16	—	—	—	—	—
Range State II	4	—	—	6	5	13	7	—	—
Range State III	4	5	—	—	10	3	9	—	—
3.11.39	17	13	13	15	11	14	10	—	—
15.12.39	15	10	—	10	10	13	—	—	—
31.1.40									
Range State I	—	—	—	?	—	—	—	—	—
Range State II	—	—	—	9	—	—	—	20	20
Range State III	21	20	—	—	20	21	—	—	—
1.3.40	15	10	—	11	13	13	—	—	—

The following pages contain the remainder of the table

Sqn. Date	21	107	114	101	82	110	139	15	40	18	57	105	218	226	90	88
26.4.40	16	14	—	17	13	15	—	12	15	—	—	—	—	—	—	—
7.6.40	12	13	—	14'	14	18	—	16	11	—	—	—	—	—	—	—
28.6.40	18	17	—	13	15	16	—	16	17	4	13	—	—	—	—	—
26.7.40	12	16	13	12	18	19	18	19	18	17	18	—	—	—	—	—
30.8.40	12	12	19	19	17	19	18	19	18	18	17	16	14	—	—	—
13.9.40	11	13	18	19	20	16	19	15	15	16	18	16	16	—	—	—
18.10.40	17	14	19	19	19	19	15	16	19	18	18	18	15	—	—	—
13.12.40	16	15	15	16	15'	16	17	—	—	15	—	9	—	—	—	—
3.1.41	18	20	15	17	12	18	14	—	—	20	—	15	—	—	—	—
7.2.41	19	20	18	16	17	18	11	—	—	17	—	16	—	—	—	—
7.3.41	17	—	7	17	15	16	16	—	—	15	—	15	—	—	—	—
4.4.41	10	—	—	13	12	17	14	—	—	17	—	16	—	—	—	—
26.6.41	15	14	—	12	15	16	16	—	—	12	—	19	—	11	—	—
24.7.41	17	10	—	15	16	18	16	—	—	16	—	16	—	12	—	—
21.8.41	15	8	12	—	12	13	12	—	—	17	—	—	—	13	3F	10
25.9.41	11	—	14	—	9	15	17	—	—	13	—	—	—	12	4F	9
23.10.41	10	—	13	—	12	14	16	—	—	—	—	16	—	J1	4F	5
20.11.41	15	—	15	—	17	18	19	—	—	—	—	6	—	—	7F	2
25.12.41	—	—	17	—	17	16	—	—	—	—	—	—	—	1	5F	16BS
1.1.42	—	—	14	—	16	13	15H	—	—	—	—	2M	—	1	—	12BS
22.1.42	—	3	6	—	16	17	13H	—	—	—	—	3M	—	14BS	—	—
12.2.42	—	—	13	—	21	18	—	—	—	—	—	2M	—	11BS	—	11BS
12.3.42	21	13BS	12	—	21	20	—	—	—	—	—	7M	—	14BS	—	12BS
2.4.42	8	10BS	13	—	—	—	—	—	—	12	—	5M	—	14BS	—	13BS
28.5.42	—	14BS	21	—	—	—	—	—	—	14	—	8M	—	18BS	—	17BS
2.7.42	—	17BS	13	—	—	—	—	—	—	11	—	4M	—	16BS	—	19BS
27.8.42	—	9BS	—	—	—	—	—	—	—	—	—	8M	—	6BS	—	16BS
24.9.42	1 12V	14BS	—	—	—	—	—	—	—	—	—	4M	—	11BS	—	7BS
22.10.42	11B	11BS	—	—	—	—	13BV	—	—	—	—	13M	—	14BS	—	10BS
5.11.42	17V	14BS	—	—	—	—	9BV	—	—	—	—	8M	—	14BS	—	12BS
31.12.42	18V	7BS	—	—	—	—	—	—	—	—	—	7M	—	17BS	—	11BS
28.1.43	16V	10BS	—	—	—	—	5M	—	—	—	—	12M	—	16BS	—	14BS
4.2.43	12V	13BS	—	—	—	—	5M	—	—	—	—	12M	—	12BS	—	13BS
25.2.43	15V	3BS 1BS3A	—	—	—	—	13M	—	—	—	—	13M	—	8BS3 8BS3A	—	—
2.3.43	10VI 6VII	1BS 1BS3A	—	—	—	—	15M	—	—	—	—	12M	—	12BS3A	—	10BS3A
25.3.43	9VI 7VII	4BS3A	—	—	—	—	11M	—	—	—	—	4M	—	1BS 2BS3A	—	—
1.4.43	12VI 7VII	—	—	—	—	—	10M	—	—	—	—	4M	—	2BS	3BS	3BS3A
6.5.43	8VI 7VII	12BS3A	—	—	—	—	3M	—	—	—	—	6M	—	4BS3A	2BS 5BS3A	—
3.6.43	6VI 6VII	16BS3A	—	—	—	—	—	—	—	—	—	—	—	4MT	10BS3A	10BS3A
1.7.43	8VI 1MT	14BS3A	—	—	—	—	—	—	—	—	—	—	—	7MT	—	14BS3A
5.8.43	7VI 6VII	14BS3A	—	—	—	—	—	—	—	—	—	—	—	0MT	—	10BS3A
26.8.43	1VI	14BS3A	—	—	—	—	—	—	—	—	—	—	—	13MT	—	10BS3A
30.9.43	11VI 8VII	13BS3A	—	—	—	—	—	—	—	—	—	—	—	15MT	—	16BS3A

98	180	320	1655 MTU	342	613	305	226 SF	416 ARF*	417 ARF*	418	605	2 GSU*
—	—	—	—	—	—	—	—	—	—	—	—	—
—	—	—	—	—	—	—	—	—	—	—	—	—
—	—	—	—	—	—	—	—	—	—	—	—	—
—	—	—	—	—	—	—	—	—	—	—	—	—
—	—	—	—	—	—	—	—	—	—	—	—	.
—	—	—	—	—	—	—	—	—	—	—	—	—
—	—	—	—	—	—	—	—	—	—	—	—	—
—	—	—	—	—	—	—	—	—	—	—	—	—
—	—	—	—	—	—	—	—	—	—	—	—	—
—	—	—	—	—	—	—	—	—	—	—	—	—
—	—	—	—	—	—	—	—	—	—	—	—	—
—	—	—	—	—	—	—	—	—	—	—	—	—
—	—	—	—	—	—	—	—	—	—	—	—	—
—	—	—	—	—	—	—	—	—	—	—	—	—
—	—	—	—	—	—	—	—	—	—	—	—	—
—	—	—	—	—	—	—	—	—	—	—	—	—
—	—	—	—	—	—	—	—	—	—	—	—	—
—	—	—	—	—	—	—	—	—	—	—	—	—
—	—	—	—	—	—	—	—	—	—	—	—	—
—	—	—	—	—	—	—	—	—	—	—	—	—
—	—	—	—	—	—	—	—	—	—	—	—	—
—	—	—	—	—	—	—	—	—	—	—	—	—
—	—	—	—	—	—	—	—	—	—	—	—	—
—	—	—	—	—	—	—	—	—	—	—	—	—
—	—	—	—	—	—	—	—	—	—	—	—	—
—	—	—	1M	—	—	—	—	—	—	—	—	—
13MT	14MT	—	—	—	—	—	—	—	—	—	—	—
11MT	16MT	—	1MIII 2MIV	—	—	—	—	—	—	—	—	—
10MT	13MT	—	4MIV 1MIII 1BV	—	—	—	—	—	—	—	—	—
15MT	14MT	—	3MIV 1MIII 2BV	—	—	—	—	—	—	—	—	—
5MT	—	—	5MIV 2MIII 5BV	—	—	—	—	—	—	—	—	—
—	—	—	3MIV 1MIII 2BV	—	—	—	—	—	—	—	—	—
16MT	15MT	—	3BIV 2MIII 4BV	—	—	—	—	—	—	—	—	—
12MT	15MT	—	4MIV 1MIII 2BV	—	—	—	—	—	—	—	—	—
10MT	13MT	4MT	—	—	—	—	—	—	—	—	—	—
7MT	6MT	8MT	—	—	—	—	—	—	—	—	—	—
10MT	12MT	8MT	—	11BS3A	—	—	—	—	—	—	—	—
16MT	15MT	6MT	—	11BS3A	—	—	—	—	—	—	—	—
15MT	15MT	12MT	—	12BS3A	—	2MT 1MIII	—	—	—	—	—	—
15MT	15MT	16MT	—	12BS3A	—	—	—	—	—	—	—	—

Sqn.	21	107	114	101	82	110	139	15	40	18	57	105	218	226	90	88	4
Date																	
28.10.43	7VI 4VII 11MVI	9BS3A	—	—	—	—	—	—	—	—	—	—	—	11MT	—	14BS3A	1C
11.11.43	1VI 4VII 11MVI	13BS3A	—	—	—	—	—	—	—	—	—	—	—	12MT	—	13BS3A	16
30.12.43	15MVI	16BS3A	—	—	—	—	—	—	—	—	—	—	—	15MT	—	10BS3A	1!
6.1.44	7MVI	11BS3A	—	—	—	—	—	—	—	—	—	—	—	13MT	—	10BS3A	8
17.2.44	8MVI	—	—	—	—	—	—	—	—	—	—	—	—	7MT	—	13BS3A	16
6.4.44	11MVI	8MVI	—	—	—	—	—	—	—	—	—	—	—	13MT	—	16BS3A	17
11.5.44	10MVI	12MVI	—	—	—	—	—	—	—	—	—	—	—	11MT	—	10BS3A	1
'7.6.44	19MVI	19MVI	—	—	—	—	—	—	—	—	—	—	—	18MT	—	17BS3A	1
6.7.44	13VI	17MVI	—	—	—	—	—	—	—	—	—	—	—	13MT	—	13BS3A 3BS4	1!
6.8.44	16MVI	14MVI	—	—	—	—	—	—	—	—	—	—	—	18MT	—	8BS3A 7BS4	1
5.10.44	16MVI	17MVI	—	—	—	—	—	—	—	—	—	—	—	13MT	—	5BS3A 6BS4	17
‡4.11.44	—	—	—	—	—	—	—	—	—	—	—	—	—	12MT	—	4BS3A 9BS4	—
2.12.44	20MVI	17MVI	—	—	—	—	—	—	—	—	—	—	—	12MT	—	6BS3A 10B4	1!
1.1.45	17MVI	16MVI	—	—	—	—	—	—	—	—	—	—	—	11MT 2MT3	—	2BS3A 10BS4	1
1.2.45	19MVI	16MVI	—	—	—	—	—	—	—	—	—	—	—	13MT 4MT3	—	4BS3A 14BS4	1
1.3.45	11MVI	16MVI	—	—	—	—	—	—	—	—	—	—	—	10MT 8MT3	—	3BS3A 11BS4	1
5.4.45	17MVI	15MVI	—	—	—	—	—	—	—	—	—	—	—	4MT 16MT3	—	3BS3A 16B4	1
3.5.45	16MVI	16MVI	—	—	—	—	—	—	—	—	—	—	—	1MT 14MT3	—	—	1

	98	180	320	1655 MTU	342	613	305	226 SF	416 ARF*	417 ARF*	418	605	2 GSU*
VI	10MT	14MT	5MT	—	13BS3A	—	7MT	—	—	—	—	—	—
VI	15MT	17MT	7MT	—	13BS3A	7MVI	5MT	—	—	—	—	—	—
VI	15MT	13MT	16MT	—	9BS3A	14MVI	2MT 1MIII 7MVI	—	—	—	—	—	—
VI	14MT	14MT	17MT	—	10BS3A	9MVI	1MT 7MVI	—	—	—	—	—	—
VI	14MT	10MT	12MT	—	14BS3A	10MVI	8MVI	—	—	—	—	—	—
VI	13MT	12MT	14MT	—	15BS3A	15MVI	14MVI	—	—	—	—	—	—
VI	11MT	11MT	12MT	—	13BS3A	12MVI	15MVI	—	—	—	—	—	—
VI	16MT	18MT	18MT	—	14BS3A	19MVI	23MVI	—	1BS 1MT	6MVI	—	—	—
VI	19MT	18MT	16MT	—	17BS3A 2B4	21MVI	20MVI	5MT	42MT 7BS3 15BS3A 9BS4	1BS3A 1BS4 7MT	—	—	—
VI	16MT	16MT	18MT	—	14BS3A 1B4	18MVI	18MVI	3MT	4MT	14MVI	—	—	—
VI	20MT	17MT	16MT	—	2BS3A 8B4	17MVI	19MVI	5MT	13BS 16MT	24MVI	—	—	9MT
	10MT	14MT	16MT	—	3B3A 7B4	—	—	—	4BS 9MT	—	—	—	—
VI	18MT	15MT	16MT	—	7B3A 6B4	16MVI	19MVI	—	5BS 4MT3	12MVI	19MVI	17MVI	—
VI	6MT 6MT3	11MT 2MT3	14MT 2MT3	—	4B3A 7B4	17MVI	19MVI	—	3BS	14MVI	17MVI	18MVI	—
VI	7MT 12MT3	10MT 7MT3	13MT 14MT3	—	7B3A 6B4	17MVI	19MVI	—	8BS 3MT 5MT3	—	17MVI	17MVI	—
VI	5MT	7MT 8MT3	11MT 6MT3	—	4B3A 9B4	14MVI	12MVI	—	10BS 1MT 8MT3	3MT 12MVI	12MVI	14MVI	—
VI	3MT 16MT3	3MT 13MT3	12MT 5MT3	—	4MT 15MT3	16MVI	19MVI	—	2BS 3MT 3MT3	15BS 3MT3 8MVI	19MVI	16MVI	—
VI	1MT 13MT3	1MT 17MT3	9MT 6MT3	—	1MT 13MT3	18MVI	19MVI	—	11BS4 3MT3	—	19MVI	14MVI	—

Appendix 8

Group Daily Strength and Sorties Flown
May to June 1940

Date	Aircraft serviceable for operations	Sorties flown
May		
10	80	39
11	61	29
12	59	42
13	64	Nil
14	56	34
15	57	24
16	63	Nil
17	59	12
18	62	12
19	58	Nil
20	56	71
21	63	55
22	73	59
23	60	27
24	58	69
25	56	42
26	64	36
27	63	48
28	63	48
29	79	51
30	74	67
31	87	91
June		
1	87	56
2	83	24
3	86	18
5	92	23
6	98	38
7	78	59
8	88	59
9	79	48
10	78	44
11	76	51
12	87	45
13	90	48
14	92	60
15	88	12
16	104	Nil

Appendix 9

Principal Operations flown by Boston Squadrons, 1942

Date	Operation	No. of aircraft/ squadron(s)	Target
March			
8	C-112A	3/88, 3/107	Comines power station
	C-112B	6/107	Abbeville m. yds.
	—	6/88, 6/226	Poissy/Matford
9	C-113	6/107	Gosnay power station
13	C-114	5/88, 3/107	Hazebrouck
14	C-115	6/226	Le Havre
15	—	6/226	Low-level shipping raid off N.W. France; abandoned
24	C-116	6/226	Abbeville m. yds.
		12/88	Comines power station
25	C-117	12/88	Sequedin; abandoned
	C-117	12/226	Lille
	C-117B	9/107	Le Trait
26	R-17	12/88, 12/107	Shipping—Le Havre
27	R-18	12/226	Ostend power station
29	C-118	12/88, 12/226	Lille power station; recalled
April			
1	R-19	12/107	Shipping—Boulogne
4	C-119	12/88	St. Omer rail sheds
12	C-122	9/107	Hazebrouck m. yds.
14	C-123	12/88	Caen/Mandeville power station
15	10 Grp. C-1	9/107	Cherbourg docks
16	R-20	12/226	Shipping—Le Havre
17	C-130	6/88	Rouen power station
	C-130	6/88	Rouen shipyards
17	10 Grp. 3-2	12/107	Shipping—Cherbourg
17	C-129	6/107	Calais silk factory
24	C-132	12/226	Flushing docks
24	C-133	6/88	Abbeville m. yds.
25	R-26	6/226	Dunkirk docks
25	R-28	12/88	Shipping—Le Havre
	10 Grp. C-3	6/226	Morlaix airfield; abortive
	10 Grp. C-4	6/107	Cherbourg
	C-137	6/107	Abbeville m. yds.

Date	Operation	No. of aircraft/ squadron(s)	Target
26	C-138	6/88	St. Omer railway station
	C-139	6/88	Hazebrouck m. yds.
27	C-141	12/107	Sequedin power station
28	C-144	6/88	St. Omer railway sheds
29	C-145	6/226	Dunkirk
30	C-146	6/107	Abbeville m. yds.
	R-31	6/88	Flushing docks
	C-148	6/226	Morlaix airfield
May			
1	C-149	6/88	Calais silk factory
	C-150	6/107	St. Omer railway station
3	C-154	6/107	Dunkirk dry dock
	C-145	6/107	Dunkirk (repeat of C-145)
4	C-153	6/88	Le Havre power station
5	C-156	6/226	Zeebrugge power station
	C-157	6/226	Lille power station
6	C-159	6/107	Caen power station
	C-160A	6/88	Boulogne
	C-160B	6/88	Calais silk factory
7	C-163	6/107	Zeebrugge power station
	C-164	6/226	Ostend power station
	C-165	6/88	Dieppe docks
8	C-166	—?—	Dieppe docks
9	C-168	6/226	Hazebrouck m. yds.
	C-170	6/88	Bruges oil tanks
17	R-33	12/226	Boulogne docks
June			
1	C-179	12/107	Flushing
2	C-182	6/88	Dieppe
3	10 Grp. C-6	6/226	Cherbourg dry dock
	C-184	6/107	Le Havre power station
4	C-185	6/88	Boulogne docks
	C-186	6/107	Dunkirk docks
5	C-188	6/226	Ostend power station
	C-188	6/107	Le Havre power station
	10 Grp. C-7	12/88	Morlaix
8	C-191	12/88	Bruges oil tanks
10	10 Grp. C-9	12/?	Lannion
20	C-193	11/88	Le Havre power station
21	R-34	12/226	Dunkirk dry dock
22	R-35	12/107	4,000-ton ship in Dunkirk
23	10 Grp. R-23	6/107	Morlaix
	R-36	10/88	Ship at Dunkirk
26	C-194	12/107	Le Havre power station
29	C-195	12/226	Hazebrouck m. yds.
July			
4	LL	12/226	Dutch airfields

Date	Operation	No. of aircraft/squadron(s)	Target
12	C-198	12/226	Abbeville
13	C-199	12/107	Boulogne m. yds.
19	LL	10/88	Power stations in France
		10/226	Power stations—Lille area
20	LL	2/226	Kuhlmann chemical works, Lille
22	LL	2/107, 2/107	Langerbrugge power station and Sluiskil chemical works
25	LL	6/226	Power stations—Lille area
30	C-200	6/107	Abbeville/Drucat airfield
31	C-201	12/107	,,
	10 Grp. R-24	12/88	St. Malo

August

1	C-202	6/107	Flushing docks
27	C-209	12/107	Abbeville airfield
29	C-212	4/226, 8/88	Fishing wharfs, Ostend
		6/88	Comines power station

September

6	C-215	12/107	Boulogne docks
8	10 Grp. R-37	6/88	Le Havre—whale-oil ship
	C-218	6/88	Cherbourg—whale-oil ship
15	10 Grp. C-10	12/107	Cherbourg
16	C-	9/88	Den Helder
22	LL	6/226, 6/107, 6/88	Power stations in northern France

October

15	C-227	9/226, 3/88, 11/107	*Neumark* in Le Havre
16	C-229	6/88	,,
17	—	6/88	Diversion on Le Havre for Lancaster raid
31	LL	6/226, 6/107	Power stations in northern France

November

1	C-233	6/88	St. Omer/Longuenesse airfield
7	—	9/107	Courtrai m. yds., Werlchuseck coke ovens, Swimmelden power station
8	C-236	9/107	—?—
10	C-237	9/88	*Neumark* in Le Havre
27	LL	2/107, 2/88	Steel works, Ijmuiden; oil refinery at Maasluis

December

23	10 Grp. R-41	6/88	Lock gates at St. Malo

Notes: All operations under 11 Group unless stated as 10 Group operations. 'C' operations—*Circus* operations; 'R' operations—*Ramrods*. 'LL' denotes low-level raids.

Principal Circus *and* Ramrod *Operations, 1943*

Date	Operation	No. of aircraft/ squadron(s)	Target
January			
1	C-247 Pt. I	12/226	*Solglimt* in Cherbourg, Operation abandoned
9	—?—	12/21	Ijmuiden steel works
13	C-249 Pt. I	12/226	St. Omer/Fort Rouge airfield
	C-249 Pt. II	9/21, 9/464	Abbeville/Drucat airfield
15	10 Grp. C-13	10/88	*Solglimt* in Cherbourg
18	C-251	6/21, 6/464	Caen/Carpiquet airfield
21	C-252 Pt. I	6/21, 6/464	Caen/Carpiquet airfield
	C-252 Pt. II	12/107	Triqueville
	10 Grp. R-47	12/226	Cherbourg docks
22	C-253 Pt. I	11/107	Abbeville
	C-253 Pt. II	12/88	St. Omer/Fort Rouge airfield
	10 Grp. C-14	6/21, 9/464, 3/487	Maupertuis airfield
25	C-255 Pt. I	12/226	Flushing docks
26	C-256 Pt. II	6/487	Bruges m. yds.
	10 Grp. R-49	12/21	Morlaix m. yds.
29	10 Grp. R-50	12/226	Morlaix rail viaduct
	12 Grp. C-8	12/21	Ijmuiden coke ovens
February			
2	C-257 Pt. II	12/487	Abbeville m. yds.
	C-257 Pt. III	12/21	St. Omer
3	C-258 Pt. I	12/21	Courtrai/Wevelghem airfield
	C-259	12/21	Abbeville m. yds.
10	C-261	12/487	Caen m. yds.
13	10 Grp. R-52	10/88	Lock gates at St. Malo
	C-262	12/226	Shipping at Boulogne
	C-264	9/464	Shipping at Boulogne
	12 Grp. C-9	12/21	Ijmuiden coke ovens
	12 Grp. C-10	12/21	Ijmuiden coke ovens
15	C-265	11/88	Ship at Dunkirk
	C-266	12/226	Ship at Dunkirk
17	C-269	12/21	Ship at Dunkirk
18	C-270	12/487	Ship at Dunkirk
19	12 Grp. C-11	12/21	Den Helder
22	12 Grp. C-12	12/487	Ghent
26	Roadstead	12/21, 6/464, 6/487	Shipping at Dunkirk
27	Roadstead	12/21, 6/464, 6/487	Shipping at Dunkirk
March			
3	—?—	12/21	Shipping at Brest
15	10 Grp. R-58	12/21	St. Brieuc airfield
18	12 Grp. R-1	12/464	Maasluis
22	12 Grp. R-2	12/487	Maasluis oil refinery

Date	Operation	No. of aircraft/ squadron(s)	Target
28	12 Grp. R-3	12/464, 12/487	Shipping at Rotterdam
29	12 Grp. R-4	12/21, 6/464, 12/487	Rotterdam docks
	C-277	6/464, 6/487	Abbeville m. yds.
	12 Grp. R-5	15/21, 6/464, 12/487	Rotterdam docks
April			
3	10 Grp. R-61	12/21	Shipping at Brest
4	—?—	12/487	Caen
	10 Grp. R-62	12/487	St. Brieuc m. yds.
	12 Grp. R-7	12/487	Rotterdam
5	10 Grp. R-63	12/21	Brest
13	C-281	12/464	Abbeville m. yds.
	10 Grp. C-23?	12/487	Caen m. yds.
15	C-282	12/21	*Solglimt* in Cherbourg
16	C-283	12/464	Chemical works at Ostend/ Zandvoorde
	12 Grp. R-8	12/487	Haarlem m. yds.
17	C-284	12/487	Abbeville m. yds.
	C-285	12/21	Zeebrugge coke ovens
	C-286	12/464	Caen m. yds.
18	C-287	12/487	Shipping at Dieppe
20	C-288	12/487	Boulogne/Outreau m. yds.
	C-289	12/21	Zeebrugge coke ovens
	10 Grp. C-25	12/464	Cherbourg docks
20	C-290	12/21	Abbeville m. yds.
27	10 Grp. C-27	13/487	St. Brieuc; abandoned
May			
1	C-293	12/107	Caen m. yds.
2	12 Grp. R-15	?/464	Ijmuiden steel works
	—?—	12/107	Rouen/Grand Quevilly power station
3	12 Grp. R-16	6/107, 12/487	Ijmuiden steel works and Amsterdam power station
4	C-294	12/464	Abbeville m. yds.
11	C-295	6/180	Boulogne/Outreau m. yds.
13	C-296	6/98	Boulogne m. yds.
	10 Grp. R-65	12/107	Cherbourg
15	C-297 Pt. I	6/98	Caen airfield
	C-297 Pt. II	12/107	Poix airfield
	C-297 Pt. III	6/180	Abbeville airfield; abandoned
16	C-298 Pt. I	6/180	Triqueville
	C-298 Pt. II	6/98	Caen airfield
17	C-299	13/21	Caen airfield
18	C-300	12/107	Abbeville
21	C-301	6/180	Abbeville airfield

Date	Operation	No. of aircraft/ squadron(s)	Target
23	C-302	11/487	Zeebrugge/Zandvoorde coke ovens
25	C-304	6/180	Abbeville/Drucat airfield
	10 Grp. C-33	12/107	Cherbourg; abandoned
29	C-305	12/21	Zeebrugge coke ovens
	C-306	12/Venturas	Maupertuis airfield
	10 Grp. R-67	12/464	Caen/Carpiquet airfield
31	10 Grp. C-34	12/107	Rouen/Grand Quevilly power station
	C-307	6/487	Cherbourg
	C-308	12/21	Caen/Carpiquet airfield
	C-309 Pt. I	6/180, 6/98	Flushing
	C-309 Pt. II	12/464	Zeebrugge coke ovens
June			
10	R-86	6/98	Langerbrugge power station
	R-87 Pt. I	12/21	Zeebrugge power station
	R-87 Pt. II	12/107	Gosnay power station
12	R-91	9/107, 3/342	Rouen
	R-91 (diversion)	12/487	Caen
13	R-93 Pt. I	6/98, 6/180	Flushing
	R-93 Pt. II	12/107	Lille/Seclin airfield and railway
	10 Grp. R-68	12/464	St. Brieuc airfield; abandoned
17	C-311	9/107, 3/342	Flushing
20	C-313	12/107	Poix
22	R-99	6/98, 6/180	Rotterdam shipyards, diversion for B-17 raids on Huls and Antwerp
	C-314	12/21	Abbeville/Drucat airfield
23	10 Grp. C-37	Venturas	Maupertuis
	10 Grp. C-38	6/98, 6/180	Brest/Guipavas
	R-100	9/107, 3/342	Meaulte; diversion for B-17 raid
24	R-102	12/464	Flushing
	R-103	12/107	St. Omer m. yds.
	R-106	12/487	Yainville power station
25	12 Grp. R-19	12/107	Amsterdam; abandoned
26	R-108 Pt. III	12/107	Abbeville/Drucat airfield
July			
3	C-?	6/98, 6/180	Triqueville
4	R-124	6/98, 6/180	Amiens m. yds.
9	R-127	12/180	St. Omer
10	R-129	12/464	St. Omer aircraft assembly sheds
13	10 Grp. C-44	12/180	Brest/Guipavas
14	R-134	12/107, 6/342	Abbeville/Drucat; diversion raid
15	R-142	12/107	Poix airfield
25	R-154	12/180	Amsterdam
	R-158	6/107, 6/342	Schiphol
26	R-159 Pt. II	9/88	Courtrai airfield
27	R-162	12/21	Zeebrugge coke ovens

Date	Operation	No. of aircraft/ squadron(s)	Target
27	12 Grp. R-20	12/180	Schiphol
29	R-171	6/107, 6/342	Yainville power station
30	R-174 Pt. III	12/180	Merville airfield
	12 Grp. R-23	12/107	Schiphol
31	R-180 Pt. I	12/180	St. Omer/Fort Rouge airfield
August			
5	—?—	12/98, 12/180	Forêt d'Eperlecque—ammo dump
8	10 Grp. R-73	12/88, 14/107, 14/342	Rennes
12	R-197 Pt. I	12/98, 12/180	Amiens/Longeau—rail targets
16	R-?	12/88, 12/342, 13/107	Denain LL raid
	R-203 Pt. III	12/21	Triqueville
17	R-206 Pt. III (b)	5/320	Calais m. yds.; abandoned
18	R-208 Pt. III	6/226	Flushing; abandoned
19	R-209 Pt. III	13/320	Poix airfield
20	R-210	11/342	Abbeville m. yds.
20	R-211 Pt. I	9/320	Flushing
23	R-214 Pt. I	12/98, 12/180	St. Omer m. yds.
25	R-S.2	12/88	Beaumont-le-Roger airfield
		6/98, 12/180	Bernay St. Martin airfield
26	10 Grp. R-78	12/342	Guerledon power station
27	R-S.7	6 Bostons	Gosnay power station
30	R-S.14 Pts. I & II	18/21, 12/98, 12/180	Watten
31	R-S.16 Pt. III	12/98	Monchy Breton airfield
	R-S.18	18/21, 12/98	Forêt de Hesdin
September			
1	R-S.21	10/342	Roosendaal m. yds.
2	R-S.24	21/21, 6/98, 12/180	Forêt d'Eperlecque
	R-S.25	10/342	Serquex
3	R-S.27	18/21, 12/98, 12/180	Forêt d'Eperlecque
4	R-S.29	18/21	Abbeville
		12/88, 12/107	Amiens m. yds.
		6/98, 12/180	Rouen/Sotteville m. yds.
4	R-S.30	12/88, 11/107, 18/21	E-boats at Boulogne
4	R-S.32	12/98, 6/180, 15/21	Boulogne
	R-S.32 Pt. III	5/98, 13/180	Boulogne
5	R-S.33 Pt. III	12/88, 12/107	Woensdrecht
6	R-S. 35 Pts. VI & VII	12/98, 12/180, 18/21	Boulogne docks
	R-S.36 Pt. III	6/98, 11/180	Abbeville m. yds.

Date	Operation	No. of aircraft/ squadron(s)	Target
7	R-S.38 Pt. III	12/98, 6/180	St. Omer
8	S-C.1	18/21	Abbeville m. yds.
	R-S.41 Pt. III	6/98, 12/180	Vitry-en-Artois airfield
	R-S.42 Pt. I (a)	12/98, 6/180	Fort de la Crèche, Boulogne (long-range guns)
9	Op. Starkey	12/21, 12/98, 11/320	Long-range guns at Boulogne
	Op. Starkey	12/88	Courtrai/Wevelghem airfield
	R-S.43 Pt. I	12/107, 11/342	Monchy Breton airfield
	Pt. II	6/98, 12/180	Bryas Sud airfield
	Pt. III	12/21	Merville airfield
11	R-216 Pt. III	12/320	Beaumont-le-Roger airfield
15	R-220	11/320	Bryas Sud airfield
16	R-223 Pt. IV	12/98, 6/180, 12/226	Serquex with 226 Sqn. to Rouen
18	R-228 Pt. I	5/320	Rouen m. yds.
19	R-233 Pt. I	15/226	Lievin ammonia works, Lens
21	R-235 Pt. IV	6/98	Lens synthetic paint works
22	R-236	12/180	Brest/Guipavas airfield
23	R-239	12/226	Rouen/Grand Quevilly power station
	R-240	13/98, 7/180	Brest/Lanvioc Poulmiac airfield
24	R-242 Pt. I	12/180	Amiens m. yds.
	R-243	12/226	St. Omer/Longuenesse airfield
	10 Grp. R-87	11/320, 12/98	Brest/Guipavas airfield
26	R-247	12/98, 6/180	Rouen/Sotteville; abortive
27	R-250	12/98, 6/180	Rouen/Sotteville
October			
3	R-258	12/107	Orleans power station
		11/342	Chevilly-la-Rue power station
		14/88	Distre power station
	10 Grp. R-90	12/464	Guerledon power station
		12/487	Pont Château power station
	R-259 Pt. II	12/320	Rouen/Grand Quevilly power station
8	10 Grp. R-91	12/88, 6/342	Brest/Lanvioc Poulmiac airfield
8	R-264 Pt. II	12/98, 12/180	St. Omer/Longuenesse airfield; abandoned
9	R-265	14/464, 12/487	Woippy
	10 Grp. R-92	12/180, 12/320	Brest/Guipavas airfield
22	R-282	12/226, 12/320	Rouen/Grand Quevilly power station
	R-281	12/88, 12/107, 13/342	Courcelles
24	R-284	12/226	Schiphol
	R-285	12/98, 12/320	*Münsterland* in Cherbourg
25	R-286	12/98, 12/320	Brest/Lanvioc Poulmiac airfield

Date	Operation	No. of aircraft/ squadron(s)	Target
26	R-287	12/98	Brest/Lanvioc Poulmiac airfield
28	R-288	6/320	Cherbourg docks
29	R-289	3/98	Brest
November			
5	R-292	6/320, 12/98, 12/180, 14/226, 4/305	Mimoyecques
6	R-?	7/487	Hengelo
7	R-297	12/88, 12/342	Bernay airfield
8	R-300	12/88, 12/98, 12/107, 12/180, 15/226, 3/305, 12/342, 6/320	Mimoyecques
9	R-?	12/107, 6/342, 6/88	Mimoyecques
10	R-308 Pt. IV	12/98, 12/180, 15/226, 3/305, 6/320	Audinghen
11	R-312	12/88, 12/107, 12/98, 12/180, 15/226, 3/305, 6/320	Audinghen
23	R-325 Pts. I, II, III	12/88, 13/107, 12/98, 12/180, 12/226, 12/320	Audinghen
25	R-330 Pts. I, II, III	12/88, 12/107, 12/98, 12/180, 12/226, 6/320	Audinghen
	R-333 Pts. I, II, III	6/88, 6/107, 6/342, 12/98, 12/180, 12/226, 11/320, 3/305	Audinghen
26	10 Grp. R-107	6/88, 7/107, 5/342, 12/98, 12/180, 8/226, 11/320, 3/305	Martinvast
December			
1	R-343	14/320	Albert/Otis aircraft works
2	10 Grp. R-111	11/88, 12/98, 13/107, 6/180	Martinvast
20	R-377 Pt. I	16/98	Audinghen
	Pt. II	12/226, 15/320, 3/305	Drionville
	Pt. III	11/88, 12/107, 14/342	Heringham
21	R-381	11/21, 9/487	St. Agathe

Date	*Operation*	*No. of aircraft/ squadron(s)*	*Target*
21	R-381	12/88, 12/107, 12/342	Mesnil Alard
		12/98, 12/180	St. Pierre des Jonquières
		14/320, 2/305	Puchervin
22	R-385	12/342, 12/88, 12/107	Mesnil Alard
		11/21	X/1A/46—V-1 site
		12/98, 12/180	St. Pierre des Jonquières
	R-387	8/21, 8/464, 10/487	St. Agathe
23	R-389	14/226, 12/320	Puchervin
		10/21, 10/464	Pommeréval
		12/88, 12/107, 12/342	Mesnil Alard
		15/98, 15/180	St. Pierre des Jonquières
24	R-393	12/226, 12/320	La Glacerie
		6/88, 11/107	La Glacerie
		12/98, 12/180	Mesnil la Bondonnerre
30	R-399	12/98, 12/180	Fouges Capelle
		6/88, 13/107, 7/342	Forêt de Hesdin
		12/226, 12/320	La Plouy
31	R-401 Pt. I	16/487, 13/464, 6/613	La Plouy
	II	12/320, 12/226	Bois de Waripel
	III	7/88, 12/107, 6/342	Ligescourt
	IV	12/226	Yvrenche
	V	12/98, 12/180	Gueschart-Crécy

Abbreviations: R—*Ramrod*
C—*Circus*
10 Grp.—10 Group, Fighter Command

Unless otherwise stated *Circus* and *Ramrod* operations were undertaken with 11 Group, Fighter Command. In the later months of 1943 these raids were often operated in parts, with the U.S.A.A.F., and also Typhoon fighter-bombers, frequently participating in some parts of the *Ramrod*. Deep penetrations over enemy territory by B-17s and B-24s of the U.S. 8th A.A.F. were also usually classified as *Ramrods*.

Appendix 10

Sorties Flown by 2 Group Squadrons, 1939–45

Sorties flown by 2 Group Squadrons, 1939–40

Months	1939				1940											
Sqn.	9	10	11	12	1	2	3	4	5	6	7	8	9	10	11	12
15	—	—	—	—	—	—	—	—	97	137	54	80	113	61	—	—
18	—	—	—	—	—	—	—	—	—	—	61	62	127	51	99	58
21	2	—	4	9	6	16	41	42	69	112	12	86	88	83	71	33
40	—	—	—	—	—	—	—	—	128	72	74	79	100	73	—	—
57	—	—	—	—	—	—	—	—	—	—	6	72	84	64	—	—
82	3	—	—	16	23	11	36	20	136	132	122	82	106	95	91	34
101	—	—	—	—	—	—	—	—	—	—	35	73	109	75	70	40
105	—	—	—	—	—	—	—	—	—	—	—	44	84	78	57	34
107	8	—	4	8	23	20	40	86	213	151	88	59	107	1	94	47
110	9	—	—	11	12	12	30	44	145	190	93	97	105	39	62	33
114	—	3	3	—	—	—	—	—	—	—	—	43	23	21	50	32
139	13	9	—	—	—	—	—	—	—	—	44	83	61	44	74	71
218	—	—	—	—	—	—	—	—	—	—	—	17	50	57	1	—
Monthly totals	35	12	11	44	64	59	147	192	788	794	589	877	1157	741	479	179

Total sorties flown: 1939—102; 1940—6,066.

Tabulation based on sortie records in Squadron Forms 540 and 541.

The Appendices to the 2 Group Form 540 give differing totals from the above, as follows:

1939 116 sorties: 4 aircraft lost to flak, 4 to fighters; 1 aircraft lost in a battle accident, 6 from unknown causes.

1940 6,350 sorties: 82 aircraft lost to flak, 41 to fighters; 14 aircraft lost in battle accidents, 64 from unknown causes.

Sorties flown by 2 Group over Northern Europe, 1941

Months / Sqn.	1	2	3	4	5	6	7	8	9	10	11	12	Total
21	42	35	88	97	69	85	93	61	15	29	13	—	627
18	29	40	33	91	80	116	91	60	68	M.E.	M.E.	M.E.	608
88	—	—	—	—	—	—	—	38	29	25	—	—	92
90	—	—	—	—	—	—	11	23	18	—	—	—	52
101	9	35	41	83	22	47[1]	9[1]	—	—	—	—	—	246
107	7	24	69	107	72	112	56	50	M.E.	M.E.	M.E.	M.E.	497
114	28	18	—	—	—	4	44	72	62	35	9	22	294
139	47	81	119	135	58	66	67	79	43	39	—	—	736
110	22	33	34	128	101	78	M.E.	26	24	34	—	11	474
82	63	45	89	159	73*	M.E.	9	—	26	24	22	21	532
105	14	52	54	55	94	26/ M.E.	M.E.	M.E.	M.E.	M.E.	—	—	385
Totals	261	363	527	855	569	642	484	484	318	213	44	54	4,900

[1] sorties flown using Wellington 1c.

M.E. squadron detached to the Middle East—no details on sortie totals available.

* Includes 38 sorties flown with Coastal Command.

Tabulation based on sortie records in Squadron Forms 540 and 541.

The Appendices to the 2 Group Form 540 give differing totals from the above, as follows:

Sortie total 4,490: 95 aircraft lost to flak, 39 to fighters; 16 aircraft lost in battle accidents, 61 from unknown causes.

Appendix 10   **471**

Sorties flown by 2 Group Squadrons, 1942

Type	Blenheim IV				Boston III			Mosquito		Ventura		
Sqn.	114	82	110	18	226	88	107	105	139	21	464	487
Month												
Jan.	22 (2)	22 (2)	25	—	—	—	—	—	—	—	—	—
Feb.	18 (1)	15	21 (1)	—	18	14	—	—	—	—	—	—
Mar.	48 (3)	—	—	—	39 (1)	46 (1)	39	—	—	—	—	—
April	52 (2)	—	—	17 (1)	66 (2)	66	78 (4)	—	—	—	—	—
May	18 (1)	—	—	31 (1)	41	40	24	4 (1)	1	—	—	—
June	67 (2)	—	—	73	54	69	81 (1)	17 (1)	2	—	—	—
July	48 (4)	—	—	57 (5)	60 (5)	40 (2)	66 (1)	54 (4)	2 (1)	—	—	—
Aug.	—	—	—	43	25 (2)	54 (1)	53 (2)	45 (4)	—	—	—	—
Sept.	—	—	—	—	6 (2)	31	34	62 (3)	—	—	—	—
Oct.	—	—	—	—	39	20	17 (1)	71 (5)	19 (1)	—	—	—
Nov.	—	—	—	—	26	17 (1)	11 (3)	19 (3)	—	19 (4)	—	—
Dec.	—	—	—	—	34 (1)	18	12 (3)	39 (2)	25 (2)	29 (2)	15 (3)	18 (3)
Totals	273 (15)	37 (2)	46 (1)	221 (7)	408 (13)	415 (5)	415 (15)	308 (23)	49 (4)	29 (2)	15 (3)	18 (3)

Monthly totals by type		Group total
Jan.	Blenheim 69	69(4)
Feb.	Blenheim 54, Boston 32	86(2)
Mar.	Blenheim 48, Boston 124	172(5)
April	Blenheim 69, Boston 210	279(9)
May	Blenheim 49, Boston 105, Mosquito 5	159(3)
June	Blenheim 140, Boston 204, Mosquito 19	363(4)
July	Blenheim 105, Boston 166, Mosquito 56	324(22)
Aug.	Blenheim 43, Boston 132, Mosquito 45	220(9)
Sept.	Boston 71, Mosquito 62	123(5)
Oct.	Boston 76, Mosquito 90	166(7)
Nov.	Boston 54, Mosquito 19, Ventura 19	92(11)
Dec.	Boston 64, Mosquito 64, Ventura 62	190(16)
Total	Blenheim sorties: 577(25)	
	Boston sorties: 1,238(33)	
	Mosquito sorties: 357(27)	
	Ventura sorties: 81(12)	

Tabulation based on records in 2 Group Appendices to Form 540. Numbers in brackets refer to aircraft lost on operations.

Sorties flown by 2 Group Squadrons, 1943

Months Type/Sqn.	1	2	3	4	5	6	7	8	9	10	11	12	Total
Ventura													
21	62	108	47	84	36	35	24	60	131	—	—	—	587
464	30	52	42	67	60	24	14	—	—	—	—	—	289
487	9	78	49	91	28	32	7	—	—	—	—	—	294
Boston													
88	49	23	—	3	15	22	61	49	108	39	79	81	529
107	47	16	—	—	94	107	104	40	103	25	73	98	707
226	48	36	—	3	4	—	—	—	—	—	—	—	91
342	—	—	—	—	—	9	38	63	31	30	55	50	276
Mitchell													
98	6	24	—	16	24	28	6	108	119	39	96	112	578
180	6	45	32	16	52	25	91	93	73	36	108	84	661
226	—	—	—	—	—	—	2	12	54	81	129	79	357
305	—	—	—	—	—	—	—	—	—	—	16	—	16
320	—	—	—	—	—	17	21	58	63	67	88	104	418
Mosquito IV													
105	41	33	56	49	61	—	—	—	—	—	—	—	240
139	9	42	76	26	18	—	—	—	—	—	—	—	171
Mosquito VI													
21	—	—	—	—	—	—	—	—	—	—	49	63	112
464	—	—	—	—	—	—	—	—	—	24	29	48	101
487	—	—	—	—	—	—	—	—	—	24	20	69	113
613	—	—	—	—	—	—	—	—	—	—	—	11	11
Totals	307	457	302	355	392	299	368	483	682	365	742	799	5,531

Tabulation based upon sortie records in Squadron Forms 540 and 541. Sortie in this instance is counted when aircraft crosses the British coast. The Appendices to 2 Group Form 540 give differing totals from the above and probably include some abortive sorties, as follows:

Total sorties 5,651; 18 aircraft lost to flak, 22 to fighters; 12 aircraft lost in battle accidents, 56 from unknown causes.

Sorties flown by 2 Group, and statistical breakdown for 1944

	TOTAL SORTIES	SUCCESSFUL SORTIES	ABORTIVE— WEATHER UNSUITABLE	ABORTIVE— OTHER CAUSES	LOSSES					DAMAGED		
					TO FLAK	TO FIGHTERS	NOT DUE TO ENEMY ACTION	UNKNOWN REASONS	TOTAL	BY FLAK	OTHER CAUSES	TOTAL
Day:												
Mitchell/Boston	14148	10647	2389	1295	23	2	2	21	53	1143	12	1155
Mosquito	1732	1320	122	281	17	1	3	11	32	122	24	146
Night:												
Mitchell/Boston	1243	988	1	254	2	—	2	21	25	2	—	2
Mosquito	9899	8877	226	806	4	—	1	73	78	50	—	50
Totals	27022	21832	2738	2636	46	3	13	126	188	1317	36	1353

Overall losses—0·69% sorties flown; damaged—5% sorties flown.
Mediums: losses by day—0·37% sorties flown; damaged—8·17%.
 losses by night—2·01% sorties flown; damaged—0·82%.
Mosquito: losses by day—1·84% sorties flown; damaged—8·43%.
 losses by night—0·78% sorties flown; damaged—0·50%.
In 33% of cases cause of damage not known, but 74% of these reckoned to be due to flak and 21% not due to enemy action.

Day operations, Mitchell and Boston, 1944

MONTH	NO. OF OPERATIONS	NO. OF SORTIES	SUCCESSFUL SORTIES	ABORTIVE— WEATHER UNSUITABLE	ABORTIVE— OTHER CAUSES	LOSSES					DAMAGED			TOTAL BOMBS DROPPED, ALL AIRCRAFT ALL OPERATIONS
						TO FLAK	TO FIGHTERS	NOT DUE TO ENEMY ACTION	UNKNOWN REASON	TOTALS LISTED	BY FLAK	OTHER CAUSES	TOTAL	
Jan.– Mar.	138	2638	1697	718	323	9	—	5	2	16	246	1	247	3202
April	50	1172	736	379	57	1	—	—	2	3	46	46	1199	2399
May	66	1654	1451	73	130	1	—	—	—	1	42	1	43	2240
June	30	1041	855	100	71	4	—	—	2	6	86	1	87	3388
July	29	1279	956	175	153	1	—	—	2	3	68	—	68	3159
Aug.	30	1506	1288	55	158	3	—	—	1	4	199	2	201	3878
Sept.	26	1633	1453	80	100	2	2	—	5	9	86	2	88	2318
Oct.	22	1088	1012	112	64	2	—	1	1	4	20	4	24	3546
Nov.	22	1199	942	557	—	—	—	1	4	5	212	—	212	1059
Dec.	15	938	557	140	239	—	—	—	2	2	138	1	139	944
Totals	428	14148	10647	2389	1295	23	2	7	21	53	1143	12	1155	25133

Day operations—Mosquitoes, 1944

MONTH	NO. OF OPERATIONS	NO. OF SORTIES	SUCCESSFUL SORTIES	ABORTIVE—WEATHER UNSUITABLE	ABORTIVE—OTHER CAUSES	LOSSES					DAMAGED		
						TO FLAK	TO FIGHTERS	NOT DUE TO ENEMY ACTION	UNKNOWN REASON	TOTALS LISTED	BY FLAK	OTHER CAUSES	TOTAL
Jan.–Mar.	126	1195	875	117	203	7	1	2	9	19	96	21	117
April	20	139	116	2	21	2	—	1	1	3	12	—	12
May	25	171	129	2	40	1	—	—	—	1	9	—	9
June	4	27	25	—	2	1	—	—	—	1	2	—	2
July	4	26	20	1	5	—	—	—	—	—	—	—	—
Aug.	8	90	89	—	1	4	—	—	—	4	3	—	3
Sept.	2	50	41	—	9	3	—	—	—	3	—	—	—
Oct.	1	25	25	—	—	—	—	—	—	—	2	3	5
Nov.–Dec.	—	—	—	—	—	—	—	—	—	—	—	—	—
Totals	190	1723	1320	122	281	17	1	3	11	32	122	24	146

Night operations—Mosquitoes, 1944

MONTH	NO. OF OPERATIONS	NO. OF SORTIES	SUCCESSFUL SORTIES	ABORTIVE—WEATHER UNSUITABLE	ABORTIVE—OTHER CAUSES	LOSSES					DAMAGED		
						TO FLAK	TO FIGHTERS	NOT DUE TO ENEMY ACTION	UNKNOWN REASON	TOTALS LISTED	BY FLAK	OTHER CAUSES	TOTAL
Jan.–Mar.	244	105	35	104	6	—	—	—	6	6	6	—	6
April	209	124	11	75	—	—	—	—	3	3	3	—	3
May	442	239	37	166	—	—	—	—	6	6	—	—	—
June	1706	1614	3	89	—	2	—	1	6	9	5	—	5
July	1786	1708	2	76	—	1	—	—	10	11	10	—	10
Aug.	2181	2090	22	69	—	1	—	—	12	13	11	—	11
Sept.	852	723	31	98	—	—	—	—	9	9	9	—	9
Oct.	789	726	21	41	—	—	—	—	3	3	4	—	4
Nov.	549	490	—	59	—	—	—	—	10	10	8	—	8
Dec.	1141	1057	64	37	—	—	—	—	8	8	—	—	—
Totals	9899	8877	226	806	—	4	—	1	73	78	50	—	50

Night operations—Mitchells and Bostons, 1944

MONTH	TOTAL SORTIES	SUCCESSFUL SORTIES	ABORTIVE—WEATHER UNSUITABLE	ABORTIVE—OTHER CAUSES	LOSSES					DAMAGED		
					TO FLAK	TO FIGHTERS	NOT DUE TO ENEMY ACTION	UNKNOWN REASONS	TOTAL	BY FLAK	OTHER CAUSES	TOTAL
June	513	405	—	108	—	—	2	5	7	—	—	—
July	352	268	—	84	—	—	—	6	6	1	—	1
Aug.	367	308	1	58	2	—	—	10	12	1	—	1
Sept.	11	7	—	4	—	—	—	—	—	—	—	—
Totals	1243	988	1	254	2	—	2	21	25	2	—	2

During 1944 missing crews totalled 22 with 23 P.O.W.s taken, and 34 aircraft returned with 75 crew members injured.

Types of targets attacked by day, 1944

Mediums: *Noballs* 201   Airfields 10   Railway 64
            A.S.R. searches 2   Guns 24   Bridges 28
            Strongpoints 45   P.O.L. dumps 33   Smoke laying 1
            Troops/guns at Calais, Boulogne, Dunkirk 11
            Choke points 16   Lock gates 2   E/R-boat pens 1
Mosquitoes: *Noballs* 124   *Ranger* flights 16 Special low levels 17
            Recce flights 2   A.S.R. search 1   Rail centres 12
            Guns 5   Beam stations 8   Petrol trains 3

Analysis of Mosquito Night Operations from June 1944

MONTH	TRAINS ATTACKED	LENGTHS OF TRACKS ATTACKED	MECHANISED ENEMY TRANSPORT DESTROYED	BARGES ATTACKED	BRIDGES ATTACKED	NO. OF BOMBS DROPPED	NO. OF FLARES DROPPED	NO. OF CANNON ROUNDS FIRED	NO. OF MACHINE-GUN ROUNDS FIRED
June	32	9	95	—	—	6050	298	164929	138912
July	180	51	91	40	28	7898	1223	239200	252589
Aug.	125	112	357	150	20	6123	9780	352390	463650
Sept.	96	8	50	200	2	725	3180	117083	167900
Oct.	169	15	35	263	2	895	1341	106000	169335
Nov.	218	4	51	94	4	1008	1116	102000	144000
Dec.	74	7	176	8	6	2430	1849	203000	261000
Totals	894	206	855	755	62	25139	18787	1284602	1597386

Miscellaneous over the period: 9 enemy aircraft destroyed, 42 vessels attacked, 11 factories attacked, 8 dumps, 1,000 trucks shot up, 4 V-1s shot down, 2 signal boxes destroyed.

Sorties flown by 2 Group, and statistical breakdown for 1945

	SORTIES				LOSSES					DAMAGED		
	TOTAL SORTIES	SUCCESSFUL SORTIES	ABORTIVE DUE TO WEATHER	ABORTIVE FOR OTHER REASONS	TO FLAK	TO FIGHTERS	ACCIDENTS	UNKNOWN	TOTAL	FLAK	OTHER CAUSES	TOTAL
Day:												
Mitchell/Boston	6072	5293	779	—	9	1	—	2	12	456	—	456
Mosquito	148	146	—	2	18	—	1	6	25	42	2	44
Night:												
Mosquito	6091	5561	530	—	2	—	2	45	49	31	—	31
Totals	12311	11000	1309	2	29	1	3	53	86	529	2	531

Overall losses—0·69% sorties flown; damaged—4·31% sorties flown.
Mediums: losses by day—0·197% sorties flown; damaged—7·509%.
Mosquitoes: losses by day—16·89% sorties flown; damaged 29·72%.
            losses by night—0·804% sorties flown; damaged 0·509%.
In 38·4% of cases cause of damage not known, but 33·75% reckoned to be
due to flak, 3·485% not due to enemy action.

Day Operations, Mitchell and Boston

	SORTIES				LOSSES					DAMAGED	
MONTH	NO. OF OPS.	SUCCESSFUL	ABORTIVE WEATHER	TOTAL	FLAK	FIGHTERS	ACCIDENTS	UNKNOWN CAUSES	TOTAL	FLAK	TOTAL
Jan.	13	498	235	733	—	—	—	2	2	145	145
Feb.	48	1380	205	1585	6	—	—	—	6	49	49
Mar.	66	2330	195	2525	3	1	—	—	4	247	247
April	60	992	117	1109	—	—	—	—	—	15	15
May	3	93	27	120	—	—	—	—	—	—	—
Totals	190	5293	779	6072	9	1	—	2	12	456	456

Day Operations, Mosquitoes

MONTH	SORTIES					LOSSES					DAMAGED		
	NO. OF OPS.	SUCCESSFUL	ABORTIVE WEATHER	ABORTIVE— OTHER REASONS	TOTAL	FLAK	FIGHTERS	ACCIDENTS	UNKNOWN CAUSES	TOTAL	FLAK	OTHER CAUSES	TOTAL
Jan.	—	—	—	—	—	—	—	—	—	—	—	—	—
Feb.	.1	120	—	2	122	15	—	—	6	21	40	—	40
Mar.	1	20	—	—	20	3	—	1	—	4	2	1	3
April	1	6	—	—	6	—	—	—	—	—	—	1	1
Totals	3	146	—	2	148	18	—	1	6	25	42	2	44

Night Operations, Mosquitoes

MONTH	SORTIES				LOSSES					DAMAGED	
	NO. OF OPS.	SUCCESSFUL	ABORTIVE WEATHER	TOTAL	FLAK	FIGHTERS	ACCIDENTS	UNKNOWN	TOTAL	FLAK	TOTAL
Jan.	21	732	237	969	—	—	2	8	10	10	10
Feb.	19	1319	106	1425	—	—	—	15	15	8	8
Mar.	28	1476	71	1547	—	—	—	10	10	5	5
April	26	1991	114	2105	2	—	—	12	14	8	8
May	2	43	2	45	—	—	—	—	—	—	—
Totals	96	5561	530	6091	2	—	2	45	49	31	31

Results achieved during Mosquito daylight operations, 1945

MONTH	TRAINS ATTACKED	TRUCKS DESTROYED/DAMAGED	M.T. DESTROYED	M.T. DAMAGED	BARGES SUNK/DAMAGED	BRIDGES ATTACKED	V-1 DESTROYED	V-1 DAMAGED	FACTORIES ATTACKED	RAILWAYS CUT	MISCELLANEOUS
Feb.	20	53/689	3	37	4/29	4	—	—	—	3	7 locos destroyed and 47 damaged, 3 signal boxes destroyed 14 damaged, 9 motor vessels damaged

Results achieved during Mosquito night operations, 1945

MONTH	TRAINS ATTACKED	TRUCKS DESTROYED DAMAGED	M.T. DESTROYED	M.T. DAMAGED	BARGES SUNK DAMAGED	BRIDGES ATTACKED	V-1 DESTROYED	V-1 DAMAGED	FACTORIES ATTACKED	RAILWAYS CUT	MISCELLANEOUS
Jan.	41	2030	157	603	33	2	4	8	12	4	3 locos destroyed, 31 lengths of track hit
Feb.	144	1640	136	596	65	1	2	1	22	10	1 ammo dump hit, 3 locos, 3 stations
Mar.	135	530	112	523	71	6	3	1	31	27	1 signal box destr. and 23 locos
April	305	975	304	962	23	4	—	—	44	29	36 locos destr., 6 small ships sunk
May	9	—	6	31	—	—	—	—	—	1	1 enemy ftr. shot down, 1 damaged
Totals	634	5175	715	2715	192	13	9	10	109	71	—

Rounds of ammunition fired: (Cannon/machine gun):
Jan. 192516/216212, Feb. 231518/229785, Mar. 174349/219487, Apr. 295477/405660, May 2110/6789. Grand total, 895970/1077933.
Number of 500-lb. bombs/flares dropped:
Jan. 2476/1332, Feb. 2489/3659, Mar. 3476/1592, Apr. 2617/4402, May 78/143. Grand total, 11136/11128.

Daylight operations: Types of Targets Attacked, 1945

January: Choke points 2, Railways/communications centres 7, guns 2, bridges 2, Dunkirk 3.

February: Choke points 22, communications centres 5 (and 12 by Mosquitoes), guns, 1, bridges 4, POL 3, Dunkirk 9. Mosquitoes flew 120 *Ranger* sorties.

March: Choke points 25, communications centres 27, guns 26, bridges 4, Dunkirk 3, V-sites 1.

April: Choke points 11, communications centres 6, guns 22, Dunkirk 8, barracks 4.

May: Communications centres 1.

During 1945 Mitchells and Bostons delivered 198 attacks and Mosquitoes 134 including the special low level raids on Copenhagen and Odense.

Total effort 1945: sorties 11,711, losses 29 to flak, 1 to fighters, 3 lost in accidents, 53 unknown—Total 86.

Total wartime sorties: 57,581. 910 aircraft failed to return.

Appendix 11

Squadrons and Units forming part of 2 Group, 1936–45

The unit bases are listed with the dates of occupation, and periods of service with 2 Group. Dates of movements are generally those of Main Party moves. Bracketed after the unit's title are its identity letters, applied from 1938 onwards.

No. 12 Squadron: Entered Group 6.10.36 at Andover, left 15.3.38.

No. 13 Squadron (OO): Based Odiham, loaned to Group from Army Co-operation Command for the Thousand Plan raids in 1942, detached to Wattisham 28.5.42–2.6.42 and again later 6.42.

No. 18 Squadron (GU pre-war, WV wartime): Entered Group 1.1.39 at Upper Heyford, left September 1939 when despatched to France. Re-entered Group at Watton 21.5.40. To West Raynham 12.6.40, operated from Great Massingham 9.9.40 et seq. To Oulton 3.4.41, to Horsham St. Faith 13.7.41, detached Manston 16.8.41, returned 27.8.41. Detachment left for Malta via Portreath 10.10.41. Meanwhile squadron moved to Oulton 5.11.41, returned to Horsham 5.12.41, to Wattisham 9.12.41 whilst detachment remained at Malta. Resumed operations in U.K. 26.4.42. To Ayr for training 13.5.42, returned 20.5.42. To West Raynham 24.8.42, left Group 10.42, proceeded to North Africa.

No. 21 Squadron (JP pre-war, YH wartime): Entered Group 1.8.36 at Abbotsinch, left Group 6.10.36. Mobilised in 2 Group 27.9.38 at Eastchurch, left again on resumption of normal peacetime establishment. Rejoined 1.1.39 at Eastchurch. To Watton 2.3.39. Scattered to Sealand 3.9.39, to Netheravon 18.9.39, to Bassingbourn 19.9.39, reassembled Watton 25.9.39. Dispersed to Bassingbourn 30.9.39, returned 2.10.39. Dispersed Bassingbourn 18.10.39, returned 20.10.39. Detached Horsham 11.12.39. Began operations from Bodney (satellite) 4.40. To Bodney 1.5.40. On 24.6.40 19 aircraft moved to Lossiemouth, returned Watton 29–30.10.40. Operated from there until 27.5.41 then began move again to Lossiemouth and began operations 30.5.41. Began return to Watton 14.6.41, resumed operations from there 16.6.41. Small detachment to Luqa 5.41. Detached Manston 17.7.41 to 25.7.41. On 5.9.41 began to move again to Lossiemouth, completed move 9.9.41. Returned Watton 20.9.41. Proceeded overseas to Luqa, arrived late 12.41. Left Malta for

SQUADRONS & AIRCRAFT OF No.2 (bomber) GROUP, AUGUST, 1936 TO SE

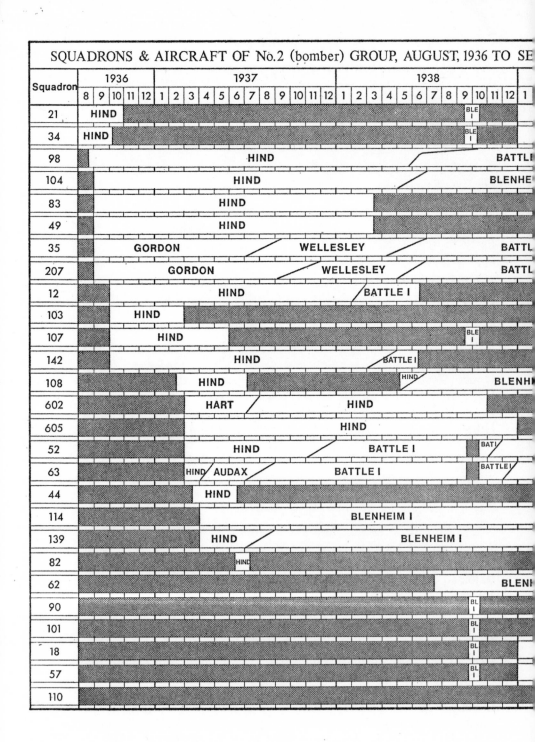

HEIM I

M I

EN I BLENHEIM IV

II

E II

BLENHEIM IV

BLENHM IV

BL
BLEN IV

BLENHEIM IV

BLENHEIM IV

EIM I

EIM I

BLEN I
BLENHEIM IV

Squadron	1939				1940												1941														
	9	10	11	12	1	2	3	4	5	6	7	8	9	10	11	12	1	2	3	4	5	6	7	8	9	10	11	12	1	2	3

15 — BLENHEIM IV

18 — BLENHEIM IV

21 — BLENHEIM IV

40 — BLENHEIM IV

57 — BLENHEIM IV

82 — BLENHEIM IV

88 — BLENHEIM IV — BOSTON I

90 — FORTRESS I

98 —

101 — BLENHEIM IV — WELLINGTON Ic

105 — BLENHEIM IV

107 — BLENHEIM IV

110 — BLENHEIM IV

114 — BLEN. IV — BLENHEIM IV — BLENHEIM IV

139 — BLEN. IV — BLENHEIM IV — BOSTON I — HUDSON

180 —

218 — BLEN. IV

226 — BOSTON I — BLENHEIM IV

305 —

320 —

342 —

418 —

464 —

487 —

605 —

613 —

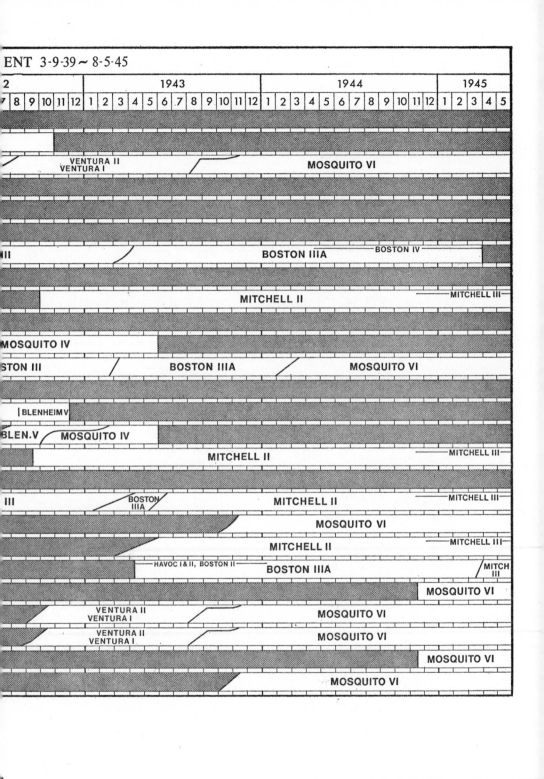

North African base 21.2.42, disbanded overseas 14.3.42. Reformed same day at Bodney. Detached Abbotsinch 20.5.42 until 25.5.42. To Methwold 30.9.42, completed move to Oulton 2.4.43. Detached Hartford Bridge for *Starkey* 18.8.43, returned 9.43. To Sculthorpe 9.43. On 17.11.43 became part of 140 Airfield. To Hunsdon 31.12.43, to Gravesend 23.4.44, to Dunsfold 16.6.44, to Thorney Island 23.6.44, to Rosières-en-Santerre 6.2.45, to Melsbroek 18.4.45, to Gutersloh 3.11.45, detached Sylt 10.11.45 to 30.11.45, to Münster/Handorf 27.6.46, to Wahn, to Gutersloh 25.9.46. Disbanded 7.11.47.

No. 34 Squadron (LB pre-war): Mobilised and entered 2 Group 9.38, back to 1 Group 8.10.38. Joined 2 Group at Upper Heyford 1.1.39. To Watton 22.2.39. On 22.7.39 given advance warning of move to reinforce Far East strength, sailed for Singapore 12.8.39.

No. 35 Squadron (WT pre-war): Entered Group 3.9.36 at Worthy Down. Detached Aldergrove 12.4.37 to 1.5.37, detached West Freugh 3.1.38 to 30.1.38. To Cottesmore 20.4.38, detached West Freugh 23.10.38 to 6.11.38. To Cranfield 25.5.39, left Group 2.9.39.

No. 40 Squadron (BL wartime): Entered Group at Wyton 3.12.39. 'B' Flight to Alconbury (satellite) 8.10.40. To 3 Group 1.11.40.

No. 44 Squadron: Entered Group at Andover 15.3.37, left 16.6.37.

No. 49 Squadron: Entered Group 3.9.36 at Worthy Down, left 14.3.38.

No. 52 Squadron (MB): Entered Group 1.3.37 at Upwood. 'A' Flight detached Northolt 7.38. Squadron detached Evanton 3.9.38 to 24.9.38. Partly dispersed to Alconbury 1.9.39. Joined 6 Group 2.9.39.

No.57 Squadron (EQ pre-war, DX wartime): Mobilised in 2 Group at Upper Heyford 28.9.38 to 8.10.38. Entered 2 Group 1.1.39 at Upper Heyford. Left 9.39 for France and Air Component. Rejoined 2 Group at Wyton 22.5.40, operated forward detachments first from Hawkinge then Gatwick. Completely based Wyton from 11.6.40. To Lossiemouth 24.6.40, also used Bog o' Mayne. Returned to Wyton 29.10.40. Passed to 3 Group 1.11.40.

No. 62 Squadron (JO pre-war): Transferred from 1 to 2 Group at Cranfield 15.7.38, left for Far East 23.8.39.

No. 63 Squadron (NE pre-war): Formed from 'B' Flight 12 Sqn. at Andover 15.2.37, to Upwood 3.3.37. Detached 24.10.37 to 4 A.T.S. West Freugh for three weeks, also 30.8.38 to 23.9.38. At 6 A.T.S. Warmwell 30.1.39 to 18.2.39. Transferred to 6 Group 2.9.39 move effective 9.9.39.

No. 82 Squadron (OZ pre-war, UX wartime): Reformed Andover 14.6.37 from 'B' Flight 142 Sqn. and entered Group. Transferred to 1 Group at Cranfield 8.7.37. To Watton 22.8.39 and re-entered 2 Group.

Scattered to Horsham St. Faith 1.9.39, to Netheravon 3.9.39. Dispersed to Bassingbourn 21.9.39 to 25.9.39 and again 3.10.39 to 6.10.39. Late October dispersed to Horsham and again to Bassingbourn. Consolidated Watton again by 1.11.39. Operated from Bodney from 19.3.40. On 1.5.40 aircraft returned from Bodney, place taken by 21 Sqn. Some operations from Bodney until squadron moved to Lossiemouth 17/18.4.41, returned to Bodney 3.5.41. Detachment to Luqa, Malta, 19.5.41, 4.6.41, 11.6.41, squadron base still Bodney. Six crews detached Lossiemouth 7.10.41, and small detachment then at Odiham. Returned to Bodney 5.11.41. Left Watton (main base) for Tangmere 25.1.42, returned 10.2.42. Left for Far East 21.3.42.

83 Squadron: Formed in Group at Turnhouse 4.8.36, to 3 Group Scampton 14.3.38.

No. 88 Squadron (RH wartime): Joined 2 Group at Swanton Morley 9.7.41. To Attlebridge 8.41, detachment to Manston 7.9.41, returned 30.9.41. Detachment to Long Kesh 12.1.42, returned 11.2.42. Detachments Abbotsinch 5.42. Detachment Ford 3–7.7.42, to Winfield 1–9.8.42, Ford 15.8.42 to 20.8.42. Moved to Oulton 30.9.42 (detachment Charmy Down in 9.42). Detachments Ford in 10.42, Hurn 1–12.3.43. Moved to Swanton Morley 31.3.43. Detachments Charmy Down 5–7.4.43, Dalcross 9–10.4.43, Charmy Down 24–29.4.43, Shobdon 7–11.7.43, Dalcross 7.43 for smoke demonstrations. Moved to Hartford Bridge 19.8.43, detachment Swanton Morley 8.43. To Vitry-en-Artois 16/17.10.44. Disbanded 6.4.45.

No. 90 Squadron (TW pre-war, WP wartime): Mobilised as part of 2 Group 27.9.38 to 8.10.38 at Eastchurch. Entered Group at West Raynham 10.5.39. Detached to 5 A.T.S. Penrhos 13.8.39, returned 27.8.39. Scattered to Weston-on-the-Green 2.9.39, to Brize Norton next day until 16.9.39 when squadron moved to Upwood. Left Group 18.9.39. Re-entered Group upon reforming at Watton 7.5.41. Operated from Bodney from 12.5.41. To West Raynham 15.5.41, aircraft flew from Gt. Massingham. Main party to Polebrook 26.8.41, detached Kinloss 5–8.9.41. Overseas detachment left U.K. for Middle East 28.10.41. Transferred to 8 Group 2.1.42. Disbanded 12.2.42.

No. 98 Squadron (QF pre-war, VO wartime): Entered Group at Hucknall 21.8.36. Transferred to 6 Group 2.9.39. Reformed West Raynham 12.9.42, to Foulsham 15.10.42, to Dunsfold 18.8.43 (detached Honiley 15.7.43–1.8.43). Detached Swanton Morley 26.3.44–11.4.44. To Melsbroek 9–18.10.44, to Achmer 28–30.4.45, to Fersfield for training 30.5.45, to Achmer 6.6.45, to Melsbroek 18.9.45 as first post-war base.

No. 101 Squadron (LU pre-war, SR wartime): Mobilised as part of 2 Group at Bicester 27.9.38, left 8.10.38. Entered Group at West

Raynham 9.5.39. Scattered to Brize Norton 3.9.39, returned Raynham a few days later and put on reserve basis as a training squadron 24.9.39. Returned to limited operational flying April 1940, full operational flying in July 1940. Detached Manston 4.41 to 4.5.41. Began intensive flying using Wellington 1C 1.6.41, moved to Oakington 6.7.41, transferred to 3 Group 7.7.41.

No. 103 Squadron: Entered Group at Andover 6.10.36, to 1 Group Usworth 4.3.37.

No. 104 Squadron (PO pre-war): Entered Group at Hucknall 21.8.36. Moved to Bassingbourn 2.5.38, transferred to 6 Group 2.9.39.

No. 105 Squadron (GB wartime): Entered Group at Honington 15.6.40, to Watton 10.7.40, operated from here and Bodney. To Swanton Morley 31.10.40, to Lossiemouth 5.5.41, to Swanton Morley 21.5.41. Twelve crews detached Malta 25.7.41; detached home by 11.10.41. To Horsham St. Faith 9.12.41, to Marham 29.9.42. Passed to 8 Group 1.6.43.

No. 107 Squadron (BZ pre-war, OM wartime): Entered Group Andover 6.10.36, transferred to 1 Group Harwell 14.6.37. Mobilised there in 2 Group 27.9.38 to 8.10.38. Re-entered Group 4.39 at Wattisham. Periodically used Ipswich as satellite early in the war. To Lossiemouth 14.4.40, returned Wattisham 3.5.40. Used Newmarket in 2.41 and Ipswich for operations, also Horsham. To Leuchars 3.3.41, to Great Massingham 11.5.41. Detached Manston 25.7.41 to 3.8.41. Some crews on detachment to Malta from 22.8.41, returned at end of the year. Detached to Ford 3.7.42 to 7.7.42 and again 17.8.42 to 20.8.42. To Hartford Bridge 20.8.43, to Lasham 2.44, to Hartford Bridge 23.10.44, to Epinoy 19.11.44, to Melsbroek 19.7.45.

No. 108 Squadron (MF pre-war): Entered 2 Group at Farnborough 16.2.37 as lodger unit. To Cranfield 7.7.37 to join 1 Group. Re-joined 2 Group at Bassingbourn 2.5.38, transferred to 6 Group 2.9.39.

No. 110 Squadron (AY pre-war, VE wartime): Entered Group 11.5.39 at Wattisham. Scattered to Ipswich 2.9.39, to Brize Norton 6.9.39. Using Martlesham for dispersal 10.39. Dispersed Ipswich 1–3.12.39, detachments at Ipswich 31.3.40. To Lossiemouth 14.4.40, returned Wattisham 2.5.40. Detached Manston 26.5.41 to June 1941. Seventeen crews detached under squadron to Malta 29.6.41, squadron base still Wattisham. Detached Lossiemouth 22.12.41 to 28.12.41. Squadron to Far East 17.3.42.

No. 114 Squadron (FD pre-war, RT wartime): Entered Group at Wyton 1.3.37. Scattered to Hullavington 1.9.39, to Alconbury 8.9.39, returned 9.9.39. Left for France and A.A.S.F. 7.12.39. Re-entered Group at Horsham 10.6.40. To Oulton 10.8.40. Detached Hornchurch 9–10.1.41. Loaned to 18 Group, Coastal Command, 2.3.41, returned to

Group at West Raynham 19.7.41 from Leuchars with 1420 Flight. Detached Lossiemouth 22.12.41 to 28.12.41. Detached Wigtown 2–9.8.42 for army co-operation duty. Became non-operational 24.8.42, training on Blenheim V. Left 2 Group 13.11.42 for Portreath and North Africa.

No. 139 Squadron (SY pre-war, XD wartime): Entered Group at Wyton 1.3.37, detached Aldergrove 28.10.37 to 19.11.37, and again in 12.38. Scattered to Hullavington 9.39 then to Alconbury, returned Wyton 19.9.39. Replaced 40 Sqn. in France from 1.12.39. Rejoined Group at West Raynham 30.5.40, to Horsham St. Faith 10.6.40. To Oulton 13.7.41, detached Manston 27.8.41, returned 7.9.41. Seven crews to Malta 5.41. To Horsham 7.9.41, to Oulton 9.12.41. Re-equipped with Hudsons for Far East reinforcement, left circa 5.2.42. Merged with 62 Sqn., then reformed Horsham St. Faith 8.6.42 and flying from Oulton using Blenheim Vs from 15.8.42. To Marham 29.9.42. Transferred to 8 Group 1.6.43.

No. 142 Squadron: Entered Group at Andover 6.10.36. Detachment to Leuchars 20.4.37 to 22.5.37. Left Group 6.38.

No. 180 Squadron (EV wartime): Entered Group upon forming at West Raynham 13.9.42, and also used Great Massingham. Began move to Foulsham 19.10.42, there by 1.11.42. To Dunsfold 19.8.43, moved to Melsbroek over period 8–18.10.44. To Achmer 30.4.45, detached Fersfield 7–14.6.45, to Melsbroek 17.9.45. Moved to Wahn 8–15.3.46. Disbanded 1.4.46.

No. 207 Squadron (WJ pre-war): Entered Group 29.8.36 at Worthy Down. To Cottesmore 20.4.38, to Cranfield 8.39. Transferred to 6 Group 2.9.39.

No. 218 Squadron (HA wartime): Entered Group at Mildenhall 14.6.40, to Oakington 19.7.40. Transferred to 3 Group 5.11.40.

No. 226 Squadron (MQ wartime): Entered Group at Wattisham 5.41. Detached Manston 3.8.41 to 16.8.41, detached Long Kesh 31.10.41 to 23.11.41 for army co-operation training. To Swanton Morley 9.12.41, detached Ouston 4–11.8.42 and to Thruxton 13.8.42 to 20.8.42. Detached Drem 19.7.43 to 29.7.43. To Hartford Bridge 14.2.44, to Vitry-en-Artois 17.10.44, to Gilze Rijen 22.4.45. Detached Fersfield 15.6.45 to 22.6.45. Disbanded 26.9.45.

No. 305 Squadron (SM wartime): Entered 2 Group at Swanton Morley 5.9.43, to Lasham 18.11.43, to Hartford Bridge 23.10.44, to Lasham 25.10.44, to Hartford Bridge 30.10.44, to Epinoy 20.11.44, to Volkel 30.7.45, to Gilze Rijen 7.9.45.

No. 320 Squadron (NO wartime): Entered Group at Methwold 15.3.43. To Attlebridge 30.3.43, to Lasham 2.9.43, to Dunsfold 18.2.44.

Detached Swanton Morley 5.5.44 to 18.5.44. To Melsbroek 18.10.44, to Achmer 1.5.45. Disbanded 2.8.45.

No. 342 Squadron (OA wartime): Entered Group at West Raynham 7.4.43. Moved to Sculthorpe 15.5.43, to Great Massingham 19.7.43, to Hartford Bridge 6.9.43, to Vitry-en-Artois 17.10.44, to Gilze Rijen 22.4.45. Transferred to French Air Force 2.12.45.

No. 418 Squadron (TH wartime): Entered Group at Hartford Bridge 21.11.44. To Coxyde 15.3.45, to Volkel 24.4.45. Disbanded 7.9.45.

No. 464 Squadron (SB wartime): Formed 1.9.42 at Feltwell. Moved to Methwold 3.4.43, to Sculthorpe 21.7.43, to Hunsdon 31.12.43. Detached Swanton Morley 25.3.44–9.4.44. To Gravesend 17.4.44, to Thorney Island 18.6.44, to Rosières-en-Santerre 7.2.45, to Melsbroek 18.4.45. Disbanded 25.9.45.

No. 487 Squadron (EG wartime): Formed 15.8.42 at Feltwell. Moved to Methwold 3.4.43, to Sculthorpe 20.7.43, to Hunsdon 31.12.43. Detached Swanton Morley 26.3.44 to 9.4.44. To Gravesend 18.4.44, to Thorney Island 18.6.44, to Rosières-en-Santerre 5.2.45, to Melsbroek 18.4.45, to Cambrai 7.45. Disbanded 20.9.45, re-numbered 16 Sqn.

No. 602 Squadron: Entered Group 14.2.37 at Abbotsinch transferring from 6 Group. Left 1.11.38, passed to 22 Group.

No. 605 Squadron (UP wartime): Entered Group 14.2.37 at Castle Bromwich transferring from 6 Group. Left 2 Group 1.1.39. Re-entered Group 21.11.44 at Hartford Bridge. Moved to Coxyde 15.3.45, to Volkel 25.4.45. Disbanded 31.8.45.

No. 613 Squadron (SY wartime): Entered Group at Lasham 12.10.43. Detached Swanton Morley 11–24.4.44. To Hartford Bridge 23.10.44, to Epinoy 20.11.44. Detached Fersfield 28.7.45 to 4.8.45. Re-numbered 69 Squadron 8.8.45.

No. 614 Squadron (LJ wartime): Based Macmerry, operated on loan from Army Co-operation Command for Thousand Plan raids in 1942, from West Raynham.

Squadrons detached for Service in Malta

No. 21 Squadron: First detachment left U.K. 26.4.41, returned May 1941.

No. 82 Squadron: First detachment left U.K. 19.5.41, second 11.6.41, squadron returned July 1941.

No. 110 Squadron: Left U.K. 30.6.41, took over commitment 4.7.41.

No. 105 Squadron: Left U.K. 28.7.41, remainder returned to U.K. October 1941.

No. 107 Squadron: Left U.K. 22.8.41, joined commitment 15.9.41. Remainder returned to U.K. January 1942.

18 Squadron: Left U.K. 12.10.41, joined commitment 10.41. Remainder to U.K. January 1942.

21 Squadron: Left U.K. late December 1941, took over commitment 1.42. Left for U.K. 4.3.42 on disbandment of detachment at Luqa.
Only the Blenheims flown to Malta in April 1941 returned to Britain. Others were transferred to the R.A.F. in the Middle East. They subsequently served in the desert war, in Iraq and in the Far East.

2 Group Training Flight/2 Group Target Towing Flight/ 1482 Bombing & Gunnery Flight/No. 2 Group Support Unit

On 22.2.40 2 Grp. T.T.Flt. formed at West Raynham to provide target towers for the Group Training Flight. The former equipped with Fairey Battle II target tugs: K9225 (Stn. Flt. W. Raynham 4.10.39 to 101 Sqn. 30.11.39 to 2 Grp. T.T.F. 22.2.40–9.1.41), K9253 (35 Sqn. then to 2 Grp. T.T.F. 15.3.40–9.1.41), K9275 (101 Sqn. 30.11.39 to 2 Grp. T.T.F. 22.2.40–9.1.41), K9312 (15 Sqn. to Stn. Flt. W. Raynham 4.10.39 to 101 Sqn. 30.11.39 to 2 Grp. T.T.F. 22.2.40–15.3.40), K9317 (Stn. Flt. W. Raynham 24.11.39 to 101 Sqn. 30.11.39 to 2 Grp. T.T.F. 22.2.40–5.3.41), K9358 (Stn. Flt. W. Raynham 4.10.39 to 101 Sqn. 30.11.39 to 2 Grp. T.T.F. 22.2.40–9.1.41), L5268 (2 Grp. T.T.F. 15.3.40–9.1.41). From this it can be seen that the new unit absorbed aircraft from 101 Sqn., previously the only Group operational training unit, and 101 was soon released for operations.

Also taken over from the Group Training Flight were Blenheims: L1100 (to Grp. Trng. Flt. 28.9.40—Cat. E 3.1.41), L1310 (from 101 Sqn. 9.2.41–15.3.41), L9257 (9.2.41–30.3.41), R3617 (9.2.41–19.3.41) and T1862 (5.12.41–16.1.42). An Avro Tutor K6087 (101 Sqn. 4.12.39–1.3.40) served with the unit 1.3.40 until S.O.C. 26.3.41.

In 1941 Lysander target tugs took over from the Battles and included R2010 (22.7.42–10.3.43), V9780 (12.9.41–2.3.43), V9781 (12.9.41–12.8.43) and V9782 (22.9.41–18.3.43).

On 1.1.42 the unit was renamed 1482 B & G Flt., and was still based at West Raynham. The first Boston III, W8354, came into use 15.3.42 to give realistic gunnery training. On 31.3.42 four BP Defiant target tugs came on to strength including N3332 (30.3.42–13.3.43), N3434 (1.4.42–17.2.43) and T4103 (30.3.42–14.4.43).

Blenheim IVs joined the unit in 1942: V5536 (13.5.42–22.1.43), Z7356 (7.9.42–21.11.42), V5456 (7.9.42–16.11.42), T2033 (18.3.42–28.3.42) and T2122 (28.5.42–5.11.42).

Four Miles Martinets came to replace the Defiants on 9.11.42: HN949 (written off in an accident 17.2.43), HN951 (used until 30.1.43), HN955 (used until 8.5.43), HN956 (Cat. E FA 27.6.43). HN950 was used 21.11.42–30.1.43.

The first Ventura joined the unit 22.11.42 and, in all, the following six were used: AE679 (23.2.43–8.5.43), AE683 (8.9.43–10.1.44), AE695 (8.2.43–31.12.43), AE719 (22.11.42–10.8.43), AE810 (4.12.43–10.1.44) and AE842 (1.6.43–24.1.44).

In November 1942 a Blenheim V flight formed using AZ876 (18.11.42–13.2.43), BA245 (18.11.42–8.1.43), BA740 (25.11.42–8.1.43) and BA789 (27.11.42–8.1.43).

The first Mitchell, FL178, came into use on 10.4.43 and served until 8.6.44.

On 19.5.43 all the aircraft were moved to Great Massingham, but the Martinet Flight returned to Raynham on 18.7.43. Its strength now included HP333 (14.2.43–4.12.44), HP355 (19.2.43—Cat. E FA 23.9.43), HP356 (19.2.43–?), HP357 (27.2.43–18.5.44), HP358 (28.2.43—Cat. E FA 19.7.43), HP410 (12.3.43–18.5.44) and HP411 (14.3.42–17.5.44).

Two Tomahawks including AK147 (4.8.43–3.10.43) joined the unit in August but were soon withdrawn. They offered fighter defence training.

All the twin-engined aircraft returned to Raynham on 17.9.43 and were joined by 2 Hurricane IVs in October. In November the establishment was 7 Mitchell IIs, i.e. FL178, FL215 (3.9.43–23.1.44), FV902 (3.1.44–21.3.44), FV956 (26.11.43–8.6.44), FV957 (4.12.43–24.3.44), FV962 (25.12.43–8.6.44) and FV968 (12.1.44–8.6.44), 12 Martinets and 2 Hurricanes.

A move was made to Swanton Morley on 1–2.12.43 and the Venturas left the strength in January 1944. On 13.3.44 a Mosquito T.III flight was attached, principally to convert Hampden crews posted in from 32 O.T.U. on to the Mosquito. On 1.4.44 the unit disbanded to form the nucleus of No. 2 Group Support Unit.

No. 2 G.S.U. formed at Swanton Morley 1.4.44 with an establishment of a Mosquito III, 5 Boston IIIAs, 7 Martinets and 3 Hurricanes. From May 1944 the unit held aircraft and crews to replace directly any lost by squadrons during the invasion period.

On 2.9.44 its establishment was increased to include the 6 Ansons of 2 Grp. Communications Flt. which also had Mitchell III KJ692 on strength 31.3.45–4.10.45.

The unit moved to Fersfield 14–17.12.44 where the holding of reserve aircraft and crews was maintained. A few operations were flown including one against Dunkirk's Fort Ouvrage Ouest on 27.12.44 by 9 Mitchells.

During May–July 1945, 2 Group squadrons were detached to the G.S.U. for intensive operational training until 1.8.45 when the unit was renamed 2 Group Disbandment Centre. To this unit came crews returning for demobilisation, and their aircraft passed through to the M.U.s, principally No. 12 at Kirkbride in the case of the Mitchells. A 2 Group Training Flight briefly existed before the unit at Fersfield disbanded 31.12.45.

Blind Approach Training Flights

Three Blind Approach Training (B.A.T.) Flights were lodged on 2 Group stations. They were as follows:

No. 1508 formed at Wattisham January 1941 and equipped with 4 Blenheims and known at the time as No. 8 B.A.T. Flt. Its aircraft were L1204 (20.2.41–19.2.42), L1294   L6646 (20.9.41–10.2.42) and L6774   . On 15.2.41 the unit moved to Ipswich, and to Horsham St. Faith 4.4.41 where it was renamed 1508 B.A.T. Flt. 1.1.42. It moved to Watton 20.12.41 and back to Horsham 19.1.42 where on 28.1.42 it received 4 Oxfords. During the general shake-up of 2 Group bases it moved to Attlebridge 4.4.43 and to Swanton Morley 29.8.43. Between 9.11.43 and 11.1.44 the Oxfords were detached to Lasham, then on 1.3.44 the unit became No. 1508 Flight giving *Gee* training to pupils from Dunsfold, Hunsdon, etc. It moved to Ouston 26.6.44 becoming 'C' Flt. of 62 O.T.U. and passed out of Group control. Its aircraft included Oxfords AT685 (26.1.42–25.2.43), AT723 (26.1.42–27.1.44), AT726 (26.1.42–5.5.43), DF289 (14.7.43–27.11.43), DF348 (14.4.42–25.7.44), DF431 (21.1.43–2.1.44, later used by 140 Wg., 139 Wg. 12.3.44, to 226 Sqn. 22.6.44, to 88 Sqn. 13.7.44–1945) and DF481 (31.7.42–11.9.42).

No. 1515 formed at Swanton Morley 20.9.41 and equipped with 8 Oxfords. In May 1942 it passed to 3(P) A.F.U. and out of the Group. Its aircraft included DF338 (3.4.42–13.9.43) and DF339 (2.4.42–27.8.43).

No. 1519 moved into Feltwell February 1942 and stayed there throughout the war, passing to 3 Group when the station changed hands in April 1943. Aircraft used included AT680 (26.1.42–30.11.42), AT681 (26.1.42–30.11.42), AT682 (17.1.42–17.10.43), AT683 (17.1.42–30.7.43), AT724 (26.1.42–4.6.42), AT725 (26.1.42–4.3.43), AT727 (26.1.42–27.9.43), DF297 (18.6.42–4.4.43), DF346 (20.12.42–16.5.42), DF428 (20.12.42–16.5.44), DF456 (20.12.42–16.5.44) and DF467 (14.11.42–16.5.44).

No. 13 Operational Training Unit

From its inception 13 O.T.U. like 17 O.T.U. was always looked upon as part of the Group although not under its control. On 1.3.45 No. 13 O.T.U. finally came under 2 Group in a general shake-up. It moved from Bicester to Harwell, Mosquitoes being based here and the Boston/Mitchell squadrons at Finmere. Hampstead Norris was also used. Then the unit re-sorted itself; Mosquito training was undertaken at Finmere and Hampstead Norris and night flying at Harwell. Remaining Venturas were replaced by Ansons. On 1.3.45 at Harwell 'A' Flt. had 10 Mitchells, 'B' Flt. 19 Mitchells and 'C' Flt. 10 Boston IIIAs. The 4 Ansons formed the radar training flight and for fighter affiliation there were 2 Spitfires and 4 Martinets. At Finmere the Initial Training Flt. had 14 Mosquitoes, the Intermediate Flt. 18 Mosquitoes and the Navigation Flt. 4 Ansons. At Hampstead Norris the Advanced Trng. Flt. had 18 Mosquitoes. The unit formed the basis of post-war Mosquito fighter-bomber training units.

No. 60 Operational Training Unit

This organisation had been training Mosquito intruder crews under 12 Group. On 13.3.45 it moved to Finmere and Hampstead Norris and amalgamated with 13 O.T.U. commencing flying 14.3.45. Its equipment on moving comprised 43 Mosquito II/VI, 8 Mosquito III, 3 Anson I, 6 Venturas, 1 Dominie and 4 Martinets.

No. 1655 Mosquito Training Unit

Formed at Horsham St. Faith 30.8.42 to train crews for the two Mosquito IV squadrons, it was forced by shortage of aircraft to equip initially with Blenheim VDs. Crew training began 8.9.42. On 29.9.42 the unit moved to Marham. Mosquito flying training began 30.9.42 under Sqn. Ldr. P. J. Channer, D.F.C., and consisted of dual, single, circuits, shallow-dive practice and cross-countries. On 18.10.42 the unit strength was 6 Blenheim Vs and 3 Mosquito IIIs (HJ857, HJ858, HJ863). Initially known as the Mosquito Conversion Unit, it was renamed 1655 M.T.U. on 18.10.42. Bisleys were now used for formation flying training. The seventh course began 21.3.43 and was the first to train exclusively on the Mosquito. On 23.3.43 5 Oxford IIs from Lindholme joined the unit. Lectures ceased when No. 8 course ended on 27.4.43. The unit disbanded 30.4.43, passing its aircraft to 13 O.T.U. It reformed 1.6.43 in 92 Group and later was under 8 Group. Aircraft used: Blenheim VD (which see); Mosquito B. IV srs. ii W4071 (17.9.42–12.4.43), W4072 (10.11.42–30.3.43), DK292 (3.10.42–1.5.43), DK333 (9.1.43–1.5.43), DZ347 (10.42–28.2.43 written off after flying accident), DZ348 (10.10.42–12.10.42), DZ346 (8.10.42—Cat. E FA 31.10.42), DZ345 (5.10.42–6.10.42) and DZ344 (5.10.42–5.3.43). Mosquito III HJ854 also used (26.1.43–1.5.43).

Appendix 12

Captions and Notes to Maps in Text

Map 1 *page 36.*
Aircraft on Group Strength 1 January 1937

Andover:	12 Squadron	15 Hawker Hinds K5547–48, K5550–55, K5560, K5394–96, K5399, K5501, K5526
	103 Squadron	7 Hinds K5519–24, K5557
	107 Squadron	5 Hinds K4653–55, K5543–44
	142 Squadron	16 Hinds K6654–69
Hucknall:	98 Squadron	19 Hinds K4641, K4647, K4648, K4651, K5368, K5379–81, K5444–45, K5514–15, K6613–19
	104 Squadron	8 Hinds K4641, K6620–26
Turnhouse:	83 Squadron	14 Hinds K5525, K5527–30, K5556, K6634–40
Worthy Down:	35 Squadron	17 Fairey Gordons: K1700, K2612, K2619, K2710, K2715, K2729, K2733, K2747–49, K2756, K2759–61, K2766, K2768, K2754
	49 Squadron	14 Hinds K4652, K5382–85, K5442–43, K6641–47
	207 Squadron	19 Gordons J9804, K2614, K2628, K2641, K2693, K2696, K2713–14, K2721, K2729, K2731, K2732, K2751–52, K2767, K2769

Group strength: 98 Hawker Hind, 36 Fairey Gordon

Map 2 *page 37.*
Aircraft on Group Strength 1 July 1937

Abbotsinch:	602 Squadron	11 Hinds K5500, K5502–11
Andover:	12 Squadron	10 Hinds K5547–55, K5560
	44 Squadron	5 Hinds K5417–21
	142 Squadron	14 Hinds K6656–69
Castle Bromwich:	605 Squadron	11 Hinds K5531–41
Farnborough:	108 Squadron	13 Hinds K6670–76, K6724, K6726–30
Hucknall:	98 Squadron	18 Hinds K4647, K5368, K5379–81, K6716–21, K6613–19
	104 Squadron	7 Hinds K6620–26

Turnhouse:	83 Squadron	7 Hinds K5556, K6635–40
		1 Audax K6754
Upwood:	52 Squadron	7 Hinds K5406–10, K5412, K5470
		6 Audax K6731–33, K6735–37
	63 Squadron	13 Hinds K5588–95, K7464–68
		5 Fairey Battles K7559, K7561–63, K7566
Worthy Down:	35 Squadron	16 Gordons K1700, K1762, K2612, K2733, K2747–49, K2754, K2759–61, K2766, K2768
		3 Vickers-Armstrong Wellesleys K7736, K7738, K7739
	207 Squadron	16 Gordons J9804, K2614, K2641, K2693, K2696, K2752, K2762, K2763, K2767, K2769, K2696, K2713, K2714, K2721, K2731, K2732
Wyton:	114 Squadron	12 Bristol Blenheim 1 K7035, K7037–46, K7057
	139 Squadron	3 Hinds K5375–76, K6683
		7 Audax K6710–15, K6734

Group strength: 119 Hinds, 14 Audaxes, 5 Battles, 32 Gordons, 3 Wellesleys, 12 Blenheims

Map 3 *page 38.*
Aircraft on Group Strength 1 January 1938

Hucknall:	98 Squadron	18 Hinds K4647, K5368, K5376, K5379, K5381, K5515, K6615–16, K6618–19, K6710, K6716–18, K6720–21, L7199, L7200
	104 Squadron	11 Hinds K6619–24, K6711–12, K6722–23, L7201
Turnhouse:	83 Squadron	10 Hinds K5556, K6635–37, K6639–40, K6754, K6840–41, L7198
Worthy Down:	49 Squadron	14 Hinds K5372, K5382, K5412, K5442–43, K6641–45, K6752–53, K6839, L7194
	35 Squadron	14 Wellesleys K7736, K7739, K7747, K7749–52, K7754–55, K7768, K7770, K8526, K8529, K8530
	207 Squadron	15 Wellesleys K7756–66, K7769, K8531–33
Andover:	12 Squadron	12 Hinds K5547–48, K5550–55, K5560, K6834, L7182–83
	142 Squadron	14 Hinds K6654–55, K6657–60, K6663–66, K6668, K6669, K6715, K6735
Abbotsinch:	602 Squadron	10 Hinds K5500, K5502–10
Castle Bromwich:	605 Squadron	11 Hinds K5531–41
Upwood:	52 Squadron	15 Fairey Battle 1 K7602–12, K7617–18, K7625–26
	63 Squadron	15 Battle 1 K7559–66, K7568–70, K7613–14, K7621, K7627

| Wyton: | 114 Squadron | 16 Blenheim 1 K7035, K7037, K7041–42, K7044–46, K7087–88, K7110–12, K7122–25 |
| | 139 Squadron | 12 Blenheim 1 K7060–65, K7074, K7089, K7115–18 |

Group strength: 100 Hinds, 30 Battle 1, 29 Wellesley 1, 28 Blenheim 1

Map 4 *page 39.*
Aircraft on Group Strength 28 September 1938

Upper Heyford:	18 Squadron	16 Blenheim 1 L1161–65, L1167–73, L1176–79
	34 Squadron	16 Blenheim 1 L1240–52, L1256–57, L1265
	57 Squadron	16 Blenheim 1 L1128–29, L1136–49, L1266. (L1143 SOC today as 1136M)
Bicester:	90 Squadron	22 Blenheim 1 K7050, K7058–59, K7068, K7091, K7113–14, K7126, L1151–52, L1197, L1237–38, L1238–89, L1335–36
	101 Squadron	15 Blenheim 1 K7048, L1223–36
Eastchurch:	21 Squadron	17 Blenheim 1 L1268–82, L1347, L1349
Harwell:	107 Squadron	14 Blenheim 1 L1290–1301, L1309, L1310
Cottesmore:	35 Squadron	14 Battle II K7695, K7705–12, K9176–77, K9180, K9182–83
	98 Squadron	16 Battle II K9199, K9201–06, K9209–13, K9215–18 and Hind K5432
	207 Squadron	17 Battle II K9181, K9185–9200
Abbotsinch:	602 Squadron	14 Hinds K4645, K5418, K5460, K5500, K5502–09, K5511, L7231
Castle Bromwich:	605 Squadron	18 Hinds K5531–41, K6672, K6674, K6676, K6710, K6716, L7203–04
Wyton:	114 Squadron	23 Blenheim 1 K7035, K7042, K7045, K7046, K7087–88, K7110–12, K7122–25, L1099, L1150, L1196, L1198, L1306–08, L1311–13
	139 Squadron	19 Blenheim 1 K7061–62, K7064, K7065, K7089, K7115–18, L1100, L1153, L1207–08, L1314–19
Cranfield:	62 Squadron	18 Blenheim 1 K7173–74, L1101, L1103–10, L1114–15, L1258–62
	82 Squadron	23 Blenheim 1 L1111–12, L1116–19, L1121–27, L1130–34, L1330–34
Bassingbourn:	104 Squadron	20 Blenheim 1 L1174–75, L1181–85, L1341–44
	108 Squadron	16 Blenheim 1 L1202–03, L1205, L1209–21

Group strength: 235 Blenheim 1, 47 Battle II, 33 Hinds

Map 5 *page 56.*

Squadron Aircraft 3.9.1939

18 Sqn. Blenheim 1 (Operational)
L1106, L1110, L1241, L1261, L1405, L1407, L1410, L1415, L1416, L1417, L1421, L1425, L1427, L1430, L1435, L1438, L1444, L1445, L1446, L6692, L6693, L6694, L8597, L8598, L8599.

21 Sqn. Blenheim 1 (Operational)
K7156, L1345, L1347, L1350, L1351, L1352, L1353, L1354, L1355, L1359, L1362, L1363, L1365, L1366, L1367, L1369, L1370, L1441, L1442, L8377, L8379, L8437, L8438, L8439.

57 Sqn. Blenheim 1 (Operational)
L1105, L1113, L1117, L1128, L1129, L1136, L1137, L1138, L1139, L1140, L1141, L1142, L1145, L1146, L1147, L1148, L1149, L1171, L1240, L1280, L1319, L1325, L1360, L1361.

82 Sqn. Blenheim 1 (Non-operational)
K7174, L1118, L1124, L1127, L1130, L1132, L1243, L1330, L1331.
    Blenheim IV (Operational, Long Range)
P4828, P4838, P4839, P4840, P4841, P4842, P4843, P4851, P4852, P4853, P4854, P4855.

90 Sqn. Blenheim IV (Non-operational)
L4865, L4866, L4867, L4868, L4869, L4870, L4871, L4872, L4873, L4874, L4875, L4876, L4877, L4878, L4879, L4880, L4881, L4882, L4883, L4884, L4885, L4886, L4887, L4888, L4889.

101 Sqn. Blenheim 1 (Non-operational)
L4891, L4892, L4893, L4894, L4895, L4896, L4897, L4898, L4899, L4900, L4901, L4902.
    Blenheim IV
N6141, N6142, N6165, N6238.

107 Sqn. Blenheim 1 (Non-operational)
L1274, L1276, L1309, L1310.
    Blenheim IV (Operational, Long Range)
N6166, N6174, N6176, N6177, N6178, N6180, N6181, N6182, N6183, N6184, N6185, N6186, N6187, N6188, N6189, N6190, N6191, N6192, N6193, N6194, B6195, N6196, N6237, N6240.

110 Sqn. Blenheim 1 (Non-operational)
L1204, L1263.
    Blenheim IV (Operational, Long Range)
N6197, N6198, N6199, N6200, N6201, N6202, N6203, N6204, N6205, N6206, N6207, N6208, N6210, N6211, N6212, N6213, N6214, N6242.

114 Sqn. Blenheim 1 (Non-operational)
K7088, K7122, K7123, K7124, L1196, L1313, L1326, L1329, L1340.
    Blenheim IV (Operational)
N6144, N6145, N6146, N6147, N6148, N6149, N6150, N6151, N6153, N6154, N6155, N6156, N6157, N6158, N6159, N6160, N6161, N6162, N6163.

139 Sqn. Blenheim 1 (Non-operational)
K7061, K7089, K7115, K7116, K7118, K7130, L1208, L1272, L1315, L1317, L1318.
    Blenheim IV (Operational, Long Range)
N6215, N6216, N6217, N6218, N6219, L6220, N6223, N6224, N6225, N6226, N6227, N6228, N6229, N6230, N6231, N6232, N6234, N6235, P4826, P4827.

Map 7 *page 112.*
Aircraft on Group Strength 30 August 1940

All squadrons were operating the Bristol Blenheim IV

Wattisham:	107 Squadron	22 Blenheims L8777, N3568, R3620, N3629, N6191, N6228, N6237, R3615, R3740, R3816, R3824, R3871, R3873, T1831, T1852, T1853, T1881, T1921, T1928 —?—, —?—, —?—.
	110 Squadron	15 Blenheims L8751, L9208, L9305, L9310, R3600, R3681, R3684, R3736, R3772, R3773, R3807, R3814, R3831, T1797, T1800
Horsham St. Faith:	114 Squadron	22 Blenheims L6811 (Mk. 1), L9267, L9303, L9375, L9383, N3542, N3612, N3613, N3617, N3626, N3628, R3672, R3753, R3805, R3806, R3809, R3813, R3884, R3891, R3897, T1793, T1861
	139 Squadron	21 Blenheims L9461 N3631, R3673, R3698, R3705, R3757, R3885, R3902, R3903, R3906, R3907, R3908, T1794–96, T1798, T1799, T1832, T1871, T1922
West Raynham:	18 Squadron	17 Blenheims L9170, L9240, L9247, L9378, L9387, N3552, P4858, P6934, R3619, R3734, R3741, R3841, R3843, T1814, T1829, T1862, T2004
	101 Squadron	32 Blenheims including four Mk. 1s —?— L1204, L1313, L1369 and Mk. IVs L8870, L9420, L9421, N3545, N3616, N3642, N6140, N6141, N6143, N6165, N6181, N6238, P6905, P6906, P6908, P6953, P6955, R2788, R3617, R3689, R3801, R3803, R3845, R3846, T1825, T1866, T2034, T2047
Lossiemouth:	21 Squadron	20 Blenheims L1441 (Mk. 1) L8737, L8745, L8758, L9029, N3564, N3538, N3584, N3618, P6954, R3636, R3675: A, R3687, R3755, R3758, R3760, R3761, R3875, R3900, T1878
	57 Squadron	12 Blenheims N3583, R3598, P4856, R3667, R3751, R3752, R3825, R3832, R3848, T1824, T2038 —?—

Watton and Bodney:	82 Squadron	21 Blenheims L8438, N3569, N3578, N3594, P4839: L, R2784, R3707, R3730, R3765, R3812, R3914, T1813, T1828, T2031, T2032, T2033, T2118, T2162, T2163, T2165 —?—
	105 Squadron	21 Blenheims L6812 (Mk. 1), L8788, L9209, R3838, T1826, T1884, T1885, T1886, T1887, T1890, T1891–96, T1897, T1930–32, T1936
Wyton:	15 Squadron	18 Blenheims L8800, L9413, N3588, N3627, R2786, R2791, R3594, R3604, R3704, R3766, R3767, R3769, R3777, R3905, T1859, T1860, T1924, T2002
	40 Squadron	23 Blenheims L1196 (Mk. 1) L8757, L8796, L8876, L9326, L9402, L9412, N3570, N3575, N3591, N6277, P4918, P6901, R2787, R3611, R3612, R3899, T1830, T1848, T1849, T1858, T1939, T1989
Oakington:	218 Squadron	21 Blenheims L1137 (Mk. 1), L8848, L9264, L9298, L9306, L9380, N3561, N3562, N3563, N3573, N3585, N3625, N6183, P6960, T1863, T1864, T1865, T1888, T1987, T1988, T1996

Map 9 *pages 166/7.*
Circus *and* Ramrod *Operations flown successfully in 1941*

Date	Operation	No. of aircraft/squadron(s)	Target
January			
10	C-1	6 of 114 Sqn.	Forêt de Guines
February			
2	C-2	6 of 139 Sqn.	Boulogne
5	C-3	6 of 114 Sqn., 6 of 139 Sqn.	St. Omer airfield
10	C-4	6 of 139 Sqn.	Dunkirk
26	C-5	12 of 139 Sqn.	Calais
March			
5	C-6	6 of 139 Sqn.	Boulogne
13	C-7	6 of 139 Sqn.	Calais/Marck airfield
April			
17	C-8	12 of 101 Sqn., 6 of 18 Sqn.	Cherbourg
May			
21	C-10	11 of 21 Sqn., 6 of 110 Sqn.	Gosnay power station. V6390 of 110 Sqn. FTR
June			
14	C-12	7/9 of 110 Sqn., 3 of 105 Sqn.	St. Omer/Fort Rouge airfield. 2 of 110 Sqn. **FTR**
17	C-13	7 of 18 Sqn., 5/6 of 107 Sqn., 6 of 110 Sqn., 5 of 139 Sqn.	Chocques chemical works
18	C-15	6 of 107 Sqn.	Bois de Licques

Date	Operation	No. of aircraft/squadron(s)	Target
June			
21	C-16	6 of 21 Sqn.	St. Omer/Longuenesse and Fort Rouge airfields
21	C-17	6 of 110 Sqn.	Desvres airfield
22	C-18	6 of 139 Sqn.	Hazebrouck
23	C-19	5/6 of 21 Sqn., 11 of 105 Sqn., 6 of 110 Sqn.	Etabs. Kuhlmann (chemical factory at Chocques)
23	C-20	5/6 of 107 Sqn.	Mardyck airfield. V5517 and V6195 FTR
24	C-21	7 of 18 Sqn., 5/6 of 107 Sqn., 5 of 139 Sqn.	Comines power station
25	C-22	6 of 21 Sqn., 6 of 110 Sqn.	Hazebrouck m. yds.
25	C-23	6 of 139 Sqn., 6 of 18 Sqn.	St. Omer/Longuenesse airfield. V6259: W of 18 Sqn. FTR
27	C-25	5/6 of 18 Sqn., 6 of 21 Sqn., 6 of 139 Sqn., 5/6 of 226 Sqn.	Fives-Lille factory
28	C-26	5/6 of 18 Sqn., 6 of 21 Sqn., 5 of 139 Sqn., 5/6 of 226 Sqn.	Therrick power station at Comines
30	C-27	10 of 18 Sqn., 7/8 of 139 Sqn.	Pont-à-Vendin power station
July			
2	C-29	6 of 21 Sqn., 6 of 226 Sqn.	Lille power station; Merville bombed instead. V5385 and Z7305 FTR.
3	C-30	6 of 139 Sqn.	Hazebrouck m. yds. V6452 FTR
3	C-31	6 of 18 Sqn.	Hazebrouck m. yds.
4	C-32	6 of 21 Sqn.	Chocques chemical works. (12 Blenheims of 16 Grp. bombed Abbeville)
10	—?—	9 of 21 Sqn., 3 of 107 Sqn.	Cherbourg docks. V6398: A of 21 Sqn. FTR
14	C-48	6 of 21 Sqn.	Hazebrouck m. yds.
22	C-57	6 of 114 Sqn.	Le Trait
23	C-59	6 of 114 Sqn.	Forêt d'Eperlecque
23	C-60	3/6 of 114 Sqn.	Mazingarbe oil refinery
August			
7	C-67	6 of 107 Sqn.	St. Omer
9	C-68	5 of 226 Sqn.	Gosnay power station. Gravelines bombed
12	C-71	5/6 of 226 Sqn.	Le Trait
14	C-72	6 of 107 Sqn., 5 of 114 Sqn.	Boulogne docks
16	C-74	6 of ? Sqn.	Marquise
16	C-75	6 of ? Sqn.	St. Omer/Longuenesse airfield
18	C-78	4 of 110 Sqn., 5 of 226 Sqn.	Lille
18	C-80	5/6 of 18 Sqn.	Marquise shell factory

Date	Operation	No. of aircraft/squadron(s)	Target
August			
19	C-81	6 of 18 Sqn.	Operation *Leg.* Gosnay power station, no attack
19	C-82	6 of 107 Sqn.	Hazebrouck m. yds.
21	C-83	6 of 18 Sqn., 6 of 88 Sqn.	Chocques chemical factory
26	C-87	6 of ? Sqn.	St. Omer/Longuenesse airfield
27	C-86	9 of 18 Sqn.	Lille power station; abortive
29	C-88	6 of 139 Sqn.	Hazebrouck
31	C-90	3 of 21 Sqn., 4 of 82 Sqn.	St. Omer/Longuenesse airfield. Railway at Calais bombed
31	C-91	6 of 18 Sqn., 5/6 of 114 Sqn.	Lille power station
31	C-92	6 of 139 Sqn.	Le Trait
September			
4	C-93	12 of 18 Sqn.	Mazingarbe chemical factory. Z7296: P FTR
17	C-94	5/6 of 226 Sqn.	Lens power station
17	C-95	5/6 of 82 Sqn., 12 of 114 Sqn.	Mazingarbe power station. V6086: X of 82 Sqn. FTR
18	C-99	1 of 18 Sqn., 10 of 139 Sqn.	Rouen/Grand Quevilly PS
20	C-100A	3 of 88 Sqn.	Hazebrouck m. yds.
	C-100C	6/9 of 82 Sqn., 3 of 114 Sqn.	Rouen shipyards
21	C-101	6 of 18 Sqn., 6 of 139 Sqn.	Béthune power station. 139 attacked Gosnay power station
27	C-103A	6 of 110 Sqn., 6 of 226 Sqn.	Amiens/Longeau m. yds.
	C-103B	12 of 114 Sqn.	Mazingarbe (La Bassée bombed)
October			
3	C-105	6 of 88 Sqn.	Ostend power station
12	C-107	6 of 21 Sqn., 12 of 110 Sqn., 6 of 226 Sqn.	Boulogne docks
13	C-108A	6 of 139 Sqn.	Arques ship-lift. Z7273: H FTR
	C-108B	12 of 114 Sqn., 6 of 139 Sqn.	Mazingarbe chemical works
15	10 Grp. R-12	1 of 110 Sqn., 11 of 226 Sqn.	Le Havre
23	10 Grp. R-13	6 of 114 Sqn.	Lannion
November			
1	10 Grp. R-15	3 of 82 Sqn., 9 of 114 Sqn.	Morlaix; Lannion airfield attacked in error
8	C-110	6 of 21 Sqn., 6 of 82 Sqn.	Lille railway shops; Gosnay bombed in error

Unless otherwise stated all operations were *Circuses* undertaken in conjunction with No. 11 (Fighter) Group which was responsible for the planning. Squadrons from 10 and 12 Groups sometimes participated.

Abbreviations: m. yd(s).—marshalling yard(s)

5/6 of 21 Sqn., etc.—five out of six aircraft proceeded on operation, one sortie abortive

Map 10 *page 169.*
   Aircraft on Group Strength 1 April 1941

All squadrons were operating the Bristol Blenheim IV

Wattisham:	110 Squadron	18 Blenheims L9305, R2787, R3600, R3681, R3684, R3743, R3772, R3874, R3905, R3906, T1800, T2227, V5385, V5426, V5620, V6071, V6072, Z5800
Ipswich:	1508 Flight— blind approach training	4 Blenheim Mk. 1 L1204, L1294, L6646, L6774
Horsham St. Faith:	139 Squadron	24 Blenheims (including Mk. 1 L6796 used for training), L9208, L9386, L9461, N3627, P4860, P6931, R2791, R3611, R3704, R3885, R3903, R3907, T1795, T1832, T1922, V5460, V5498, V5521, V5654, V5826, V5860, V5872
West Raynham:	101 Squadron	17 Blenheims (including Mk. 1 L1313 used for training), L9421, N3553, R3752, R3801, R3803, R3830, T1825, T2047, T2234, T2437, T2439, V5461, B5493, V5595, V5651, V6034
Swanton Morley:	105 Squadron	20 Blenheims L8788, L9244, L9379, P4918, R3707, R3838, T1826, T1885, T1887, T1931, T1932, T1936, T2141, V5384, V5502, V5823, V5828, V6028, V6032, V6039
Watton:	21 Squadron	22 Blenheims (including Mk. 1 L1441 used for training), L8758, N3538, N3584, P6954, R2784, R3599, R3758, R3761, R3875, T1814, T1878, V5580, V5825, V5853, V5874, V6025, V6029, V6031, V6073, V6075, Z5875
Bodney:	82 Squadron	22 Blenheims L4880, L9268, L9270, N3569, P6925, R3767, R3808, T1828, T2033, T2118, T2122, T2162, T2330, T2342, V5375, V5596, V5634, V5638, V5824, V6026, V6027, Z5818
Great Massingham:	18 Squadron	18 Blenheims L9040, L9192, L9240, L9247, L9390, R3607, R3666, R3741, R3841, R3843, T1829, T1862, T2004, T2232, V5681, V6038, Z5802, Z6161

Detached to Coastal Command, based at Leuchars:

	107 Squadron	22 Blenheims L4848, L4885, L9272, N3568, N3575, N3629, R3740, R3825, R3873, T1824, T1853, T1854, T1921, T2230, V5516, V5517, V5529, V5621, V5653, V6020, V6023, Z5795
	114 Squadron	21 Blenheims L8751, L8800, L9020, L9170, L9209, L9267, N3544, N3613,

R3766, R3805, R3806, R3891, T1830,
T1849, T2224, T2276, V5490, B5494,
V5650, V5875, Z5797

Map 11 *pages 172/3.*
Aircraft involved in Operation 77 *and associated* Circus,
12 August 1941

Force I—21 Squadron: X: V5580, C: V6020, P: V5874, R: V5525, A: Z7447,
D: Z7451 (FTR), N: Z7483, O: Z7452, —?—.
82 Squadron: D: V6226, E: V6445, A: V6534, C: V6146, B: V5856, Y: T2437,
V: V6435, R: R3767, —?—.
Force II—18 Squadron: U: V6497 (FTR), P: V6423 (FTR), C: V6437 (FTR),
R: V6262, F: R3843, H: V6038, A: V6425, Q: Z7495, W: V6436.
107 Squadron: V6433, V6395, Z7288, Z7492, Z7442, T1853; V6254 and L4885
operated with 114 Squadron.
114 Squadron: D: V6236, T: V5873, P: Z7281 (FTR), A: V5888, V: V6391,
H: V6179 (aborted), J: L9382, N: V6366, U: Z7347, Q: V5490.
139 Squadron: T: V6251, F: V5826, P: V6456, H: Z7497, A: Z7490, V5725
(FTR), Y: Z7448 (FTR), M: V6261 (FTR), —?— (FTR).
Fighter Leaders—226 Squadron both FTR: V5859, Z7352.
Fighter Withdrawal Cover—19 Squadron (Spitfire IIA), P7849, P6793 (FTR),
P8706, P7912, P8241, P7501, P7668, P7619, P8164, P8366, P7509, P7472.
65 Squadron (Spitfire IIA): P8132, P7287, P8235, P8174, P8147, P7894,
P8197, P8013, P7530, P7522, P8165, P8180, P7690.
266 Squadron (Spitfire IIA): P8515, P8471, P8608, P8190, P7686, P7676,
P8597, P8095, P8203, P8422, P7850, P8437.
66 Squadron (Spitfire IIA): P8278, P1831, P7757, P7821, P8435, P7363.
152 Squadron (Spitfire IIA): P7996, P8675, P8032, P8448, P7440, P7910,
P8388, P8444, P8378, P7680, P8446 (FTR), P8246.
234 Squadron (Spitfire IIA): P7995, P8583, P7907, P8083, P8260, P8659,
P8032, P8442, P8432, P7887, P8077, P8439.
High-altitude Attack—90 Squadron (Fortress I): AN523: D, AN529: C,
AN532: J, AN536: M.
Whirlwind Escort—263 Squadron: P7041, P7001, P7039, P7003, P7044,
P7002, P7009, P6991, P7013, P6999, P7042, P7004.
5 Group Circus *Diversions*—
(a) 106 Squadron—Gosnay Power Station—Hampdens AD799, AD760,
AE255, AE261, AE144, AD746.
Close Escort: 306 Squadron (Spitfire IIB) 12 aircraft unknown; 308 Squadron
(Spitfire IIA) P8310, P8576, P8317, P8318, P8179, P8311, P8647, P7527,
P8319, P8457, P8655, P8543; 315 Squadron (Spitfire IIB) P8344, P8545,
P8666, P8540, P8387, P8527, P8464, P7839, P7613, P7434, P8661, P8588.
Escort Cover: 72 Squadron (Spitfire VB) W3430, P8609, P8757, W3441,
AB854, R7228, W3321, W3431, W3513, W3367, W3429; 92 Squadron
(Spitfire VB) W3459, W3375, W3444, W3128, W3120, W3319, W3330,
W3245, W3562, P8784, W3314, W3319; 609 Squadron (Spitfire VB) W3574,
W3648, W3315, P8699, P8606, P8640, W3423, W3238, W3241, W3651.
Target Support: 41 Squadron (Spitfire VB) P8759, W3636, W3383, W3447,
W3565, R7213, W3634, R7210, W3561, R7307, P8782, W3564; 452 Squadron

(Spitfire IIA) P8148, P8379, P8381, P8073, P7567 (Mk. VB:) AB857, P8716, P8717, AB852, W3571, AB785, W3526; 485 Squadron (Spitfire II) P8593, P7926, P7788, P7970 (FTR), P7822, P7626, P7574, P7438, P8025, P7621, P7974, P7977; 602 Squadron (Spitfire VB) AB851, P8718, P8787, AB844 (FTR), AB862, P8793, W3641, P8751, W3638, P8799, W3640; 610 Squadron (Spitfire IIA) aircraft B, G, E, H, J, U, T, Q, N, Z, P; 616 Squadron (Spitfire VB) 12 aircraft unknown.
(b) 44 Squadron—Longuenesse aerodrome—Hampdens AD930, P4285, X3149, AD968, AD915, AD939.
Close Escort: 71 Squadron (Hurricane II) Z3345, Z3679, Z3494, Z3781, Z3828, Z3267, Z3182, Z3829, Z3170, Z3335, Z3677, Z3457; 111 Squadron (Spitfire VB) W3459, W3375, W3244, W3128, W3120, W3319, W3330, W3245, W3562, P8784, W3314, W3312.
High Cover: 54 Squadron (Spitfire IIA) P8380 (early return), P7744, P8425, P8090, P7442, P8373, P7917, P7756, P7352, (Mk. VB:) W3332; 222 Squadron (Spitfire II) P8644, P8649, P8316, P8232, P8541, P8244, P8593, P8332, P8234, P8517, P8692, P8575.
Target Support: 403 Squadron (Spitfire VB) V: W3446, C: P7256, L: W3502, B: P7301, G: W3438, F: P7220, E: P8740, X: W3436, Z: W3630, M: W3453, R: W3114, Y: P8792; 603 Squadron (Spitfire VA/B) P8729, W3138, W3569, W3379, W3629, W3632, W3631, W3118, R7333, R7226, W3130; 611 Squadron (Spitfire VB) W3522, W3242, W3647, W3653, W3515, P8798, AB756, W3567, P8780, W3650, W3318, W3445.

Map 12 *page 222.*
Order of Battle 12.2.42
Front Line Aircraft

18 Sqn. Blenheim IV
T2331, V5385, V5455, Z5806, Z6043, Z7283, Z7284, Z7348, Z7428, Z9677.

21 Sqn. Blenheim IV
V5503, V6028, V6178, Z7427, Z9812.

82 Sqn. Blenheim IV
L9303, T1828, T2033, T2122, T2430, V5515, V5536, V5635, V5638, V5856, V5864, V6025, V6138, V6147, V6424, V6433, V6454, Z7295, Z7297, Z7415, Z7491, Z7497.

88 Sqn. Boston III
W8295, Z2211, Z2216, Z2229, Z2230, Z2231, Z2234, Z2239, Z2258, Z2260, Z2261, Z2267, Z2292, AL268, AL279, AL289, AL680, AL690, AL692, AL718.

105 Sqn. Mosquito IV Ser. i
W4064, W4066, W4068, W4069, W4071.
　　Blenheim IV
L6812, Z9607.

107 Sqn. Boston III
W8273, W8287, W8320, W8337, W8355, W8373, W8387, AL264, AL266, AL280, AL285, AL286, AL288, AL290, AL291, AL296, AL737, AL744 AL753.

Blenheim IV
L4885, R3679, V5458, Z5876, Z5879.

110 Sqn. Blenheim IV
L6693, T2396, V5385, V5683, V6140, V6197, V6371, V6382, V6432, V6443, V6523, Z7279, Z7285, Z7304, Z7344, Z7358, Z7372, Z7422, Z7433, Z7436.

114 Sqn. Blenheim IV
L8800, N3613, R3620, R3716, T1922, V5456, V5458, V5645, V6032, V6510, Z6161, Z7276, Z7307, Z7319, Z7356, Z7770.

139 Sqn. Hudson
T9401, AE513, AE515, AE518, AE519, AE531, AE534, AE541, AE554, AE556, AE558, AE564, AE565, AE593.
Blenheim IV
V5691.

226 Sqn. Boston III
W8334, W8347, Z2209, Z2234, Z2235, Z2249, Z2264, Z2281, Z2284, Z2295, AL269, AL278, AL676, AL677, AL678, AL688, AL700, AL703, AL736.
Blenheim IV
V6511

Map 13 *pages 264/5.*
Aircraft which participated in Operation Oyster, *6 December 1942*

(i) Douglas Boston III
88 Squadron: Z2236: G (Wg. Cdr. Pelly Fry), Z2211: N, Z2233: K, Z2216: F, Z2197: C, Z2292: P, AL289: E, AL775: D, AL693: U, AL749: R, AL748: S, W8293: Z.
107 Squadron: AL738: Z (Sqn. Ldr. Maclachlan), AL752: G, W8330: E, W8320: V, W8302: J, W8373: F, AH740 (Wg. Cdr. Dutton—missing), Z2286: O, AL755: P, Z2252: M (shot down after attack, at sea), AL737: U (shot down after attack), AL754: D.
226 Squadron: Z2234: X, Z2261: W, AL678: R, AL750: Z, Z2266: S (shot down by flak off the Hook), Z2216: V, Z2295: A, W8287: F, W8337: H, Z2258: G, W8345: J, AL285: L.

(ii) de Havilland Mosquito IV
105 Squadron: DZ365: V, DK296: G, DK338: O, DZ372: C, DZ370: Z, DZ374: X, DK336: P, DZ367: J (abortive sortie).
139 Squadron: DZ373: B, DZ371: A (missing). Photo-reconnaissance sortie flown by DZ314: F.

(iii) Lockheed Ventura I/II
21 Squadron: AE856: Z, AE941: C, AE759: H, AE699: J, AE692: K, AJ221: F, AE839: A, AE744: G, AE892: B, AE717: O, AE774: V, AE852: S, AE821: U, AE910: Y, AE940: T (crashed at Eindhoven at 12.32), AE707: N (crashed at Rilland, Holland, at 12.26—three of crew P.O.W.s), AE697: P (ditched off Bawdsey).
464 Squadron: AJ466: H (Wg. Cdr. R. H. Young), AJ491: P, AE937: T, AE854: J, AE695: B (aborted), AJ169: A, AJ175: F, AJ224: C, AE751: M,

AE684: R, AE853: O, AE945: E (crashed Eindhoven 12.32—Sgt. B. M. Harvey, R.C.A.F., and crew killed), AE702: Q (crashed Eindhoven 12.39—Flg. Off. H. G. Moore and crew killed), AJ213: N (crashed in Vrouwenpolder 12.18—Sgt. S. C. Moss and crew killed).
487 Squadron: C: AJ196 (Wg. Cdr. Seavill, shot down at Woensdrecht), A: AJ468, G: AJ200, M: AE705, V: AJ209, O: —?—, S: AE780, P: —?—(abortive), U: AE716, E: —?—, B: —?—, L: —?—, H: —?—, Y: —?—, F: AE902 (crashed Woensal 12.39—all killed), F: AE701 (crashed off Ostkapelle 12.17—Sgt. Patterson and crew).

Aircraft engaged on Fighter Support Operations to Oyster, *6 December 1942*

(i) Diversion sweep by Mustang Is of 268 Squadron: AP232 (Sqn. Ldr. W. E. Malins), AP253, AP219, AM137, AP243, AP256, AP212, AM131.
(ii) Rear support squadrons:
56 Squadron (Typhoon IB) DN330, DN317, R8825, R8823, DN265, R8721, R7854, DN307: L, R7679: N, R8799: P, R7846: R, R7823: S, R8827: Z.
167 Squadron (11 Spitfire VBs) B, A, L, K, J, F, Z, P, Y, Q, N.
411 Squadron (Spitfire VB) EP178, BL464, BL981, BM583, W3951, BL992, BM652, EN908, BL981, BM535, AD292, AD847.
485 Squadron (Spitfire VB) BM147, BM238, BM233, BM513, BM412, BM354, BM509, BM200, BM208, EP387.

Map 14 *pages 310/1.*
Aircraft used on Ramrod 16 *3 May 1943*

Bomber force
487 Squadron:

Aircraft and Crews of 487 Squadron operating 3 May 1943

AJ209: V Sqn. Ldr. L. H. Trent (P.O.W.), Flt. Lt. V. Phillips (P.O.W.), Flg. Off. R. D. C. Thomas (K), Sgt. W. Trenery (K). Crashed in Kometen Polder, near Fokker Works, at 18.00.
AE916: C Flt. Lt. A. V. Duffill, Flg. Off. F. J. Starkie, Sgt. Turnbull, Sgt. L. Neill. Aircraft arrived back Feltwell 18.55.
AE731: O Plt. Off. T. L. B. Taylor (P.O.W.), Plt. Off. M. Shapiro (K), Sgt. L. Littlewood (K), Sgt. T. S. Tattam. Emergency landing 17.45 between Haarlem and Vijthuizen.
AE684: B Flg. Off. S. Coshall (K), Flg. Off. R. A. North (P.O.W.), Sgt. W. Stannard (P.O.W.), Sgt. D. H. Sparkes (P.O.W.). Shot down 17.45 at Bennebroek.
AJ200: G Flt. Sgt. J. D. Sharp (P.O.W.), Sgt. H. Gibson (K), Sgt. A. Stevens (K), Sgt. D. R. Rowland (K). Shot down at Vijthuizen.
AE780: S Flg. Off. S. McGowann (K), Flg. Off. E. B. Thornber (K), Sgt. C. R. Smith (K), Sgt. I. F. Urlick (P.O.W.). Shot down at Bornstrasse, Amsterdam.
AE716: U Flg. Off. T. L. Baynton (K), Flt. Sgt. P. B. Davies (K), Sgt. L. E. Price (K), Flt. Sgt. H. G. Lammercraft (K). Crashed in polder west of Amsterdam, at 18.00.

AE713: T Flg. Off. S. B. Peryman (K), Plt. Off. E. T. Williams (K), Sgt. G. E. Southam (K), Sgt. J. E. Allison (K). Crashed at Hernbrug at 17.53.
AJ478: A Flg. Off. A. E. Foster (P.O.W.), Flg. Off. T. A. Penn (P.O.W.), Sgt. R. W. Mann (P.O.W.), Sgt. T. W. J. Warner (K). Ditched 20 km off Holland.
AE956: H Flt. Sgt. A. E. Coutts, Flg. Off. L. E. Richball, Sgt. D. C. Robinson, Sgt. W. D. L. Goodfellow—all killed, lost at sea.
AE798: D Sgt. J. Low, Sgt. H. W. Toombes, Sgt. J. C. Lynas, Sgt. A. E. Downs—all killed, lost at sea.
Aircraft 'Q' (pilot Sgt. A. G. Barker) returned soon after take-off.

(K)—killed; (P.O.W.)—Prisoner of war.

107 Squadron:
Boston IIIA, BZ230, BZ223, BZ241, BZ351, BZ220, BZ227.
Close Escort: No. 118 Squadron (Spitfire V) AR447, AB403, EN966, AR453, EN959, EP413, EP515, EP124, P8753, BL303, EP126, 'HP-B'.
No. 167 Squadron (Spitfire VB) B (aborted), A, F, E, K, T, X, Z.
                    (Spitfire VC) D, H, P, W.
No. 504 Squadron (Spitfire VB) EP555, BM471, EN773; (Spitfire VC) EE624, EE620, AA968, EE619, AR503, EE621, EE603, AB254, EN953.
Rear Cover: No. 302 Squadron (Spitfire V) AR377, BL929, W3902, AB974, EN852, EN922, BM272.
No. 306 Squadron—12 Spitfire V.
No. 308 Squadron (Spitfire V) 674, 329, 494, BM594, 508, 940, AB875, W3774, AB275, 377, AB800.
No. 613 Squadron (Mustang 1) AM201, AM209, AM175, AP254, AG564, AG646, AP177, AP207.
Target Support: No. 122 Squadron (Spitfire IX) BR636 and four others.
No. 453 Squadron (Spitfire IX): C: BR600, J: BR140, '?': MA229, X: BS400, B: BR624, G: BF273, W: BS282, S: BR601, Y: BS315, V: BS280, T: BS441.

Map 15 *pages 318/9.*
Operation AO449—Ramrods 90 *and* 258—*3 October 1943*
Aircraft and units participating:

Ramrod 90 487 Squadron—aircraft W: HX832, T: HX831, Y: HX854, V —?—, S: HX908, C: HX909, E: HX864, H: HX856, F: HX922. 464 Squadron HX921, HX912, HJ774, HX949, HX910, HX913, HX914, HJ772, HP851, HX866, HX948.
Typhoon escort to French coast: 193 Squadron—8 Typhoon 1B. 266 Squadron JP846, JP906, EJ986, EJ998, JP512, EJ965, EK168, EJ990.
Return Escort: 183 Squadron Typhoon 1B JP402 (Flt. Lt. W. Dring shot down a Fw 190), JP427 (Flg. Off. J. E. Mitchell shot down a Fw 190), JP428, JP486, JP542, JP368, JP663, JP383. 257 Squadron Typhoon 1B JP898, JP510, JP494, JP491, JP597, JP490, JP742, EJ788. Photographic sortie by DZ414: O Mosquito IV, route unknown.

Ramrod 258 Part I—88 Squadron BZ254 (Wg. Cdr. I. J. Spencer—aborted), BZ212, BZ334, BZ243: N, BZ205, BZ255, BZ221, BZ389, BZ316 (ditched), BZ274, BZ312 (aborted), BZ322: K (ditched).
Return Escort: 197 Squadron Typhoon 1B JP546: D, EJ928: A, JP844: F,

DN548: H, JP787: K, JP504: Z, JP743: R, JP374: P, JP588: V. 486 Squadron Typhoon 1B R8843, JP683, JP845, JP688, JP495, EK272, JP901, JP667.

Part II—107 Squadron BZ281: R (Wg. Cdr. R. G. England), BZ203: G, BZ223: D, BZ372: F, BZ280: H, BZ394: S, BZ232: Q, BZ303: V, BZ279: P, BZ387: L, BZ308: T, BZ252: M.

Return Escort: 41 Squadron Spitfire XII MB843, MB857, MB847, MB834 (FTR), MB837, EN234. MB845, MB837, MB794, MB847, MB797 all returned early—long range tank troubles. 91 Squadron Spitfire XII MB849, EN654, EN621, MB841, MB831, EN651, MB803, MB842, EN626, MB833, EN619, EN623. 421 Squadron Spitfire IX MA226, MA794, MA592, BS200, BS129, MA713, MA582, MA591, MA579, MA849, LZ924. 403 Squadron Spitfire IX MA573, MH361, BS345, MA840, MH356, MA832, BS549, MA578, MA817, MA467, BS288, MH335, MA468. 132 Squadron Spitfire V BL755, AA850, BM257, AR377, W3518, BM522, BL925, BM272, BL965, BL335, BL445, BL479.

Part III—342 Squadron BZ332: C (Wg. Cdr. H. de Rancourt), BZ302: B, BZ388: J, BZ319: H (FTR), BZ390: N, BZ301: S, BZ376: T, BZ349: V, BZ305: L, BZ304: K, BZ299: P, BZ318: G.

Return Escort: 341 Squadron Spitfire IX MA312, EN628, JK795, MH374, MH381, MH478, JL373, EN579, JL109 (FTR). 485 Squadron Spitfire IX EN568, EN554, EN563, MH351, MH501, JK979, MH473, EN560, JK762, MH490 (FTR), JK769 (FTR).

Air-Sea Rescue Duty:

277 Squadron: Walrus W3097 (15.55–18.15 hrs.) picked up F/Sgt. Gray and crew (deceased) of 88 Squadron (Boston BZ316). Walrus HD908 picked up two crew from Boston BZ322. Spitfire IIC P8030 and P8096 located F/Sgt. Frehner of 485 Squadron, picked up by Walrus W3010 escorted by Spitfire IICs P8261 and P8375.

Air-sea rescue searches by 197 Squadron: 16.10–18.00 hrs. by Typhoons JP743: R, JP374: P, JP787: K, DN548: H, JP546: D; 17.00–19.00 hrs. by DN325: C, JP844: F, EJ928: A.

Map 16 *pages 338/9.*

Ramrod 312—*11 November 1943*
Target: Todt H.Q. Audinghen in the Pas de Calais

Bomber force:

Attack preceded by two attacks by groups of Typhoon dive-bombers.

Part I—24 Bostons (Hartford Bridge). Fighter rendezvous Dungeness at 15.30 (i.e. Zero hour). Escort—2 squadrons Spitfire V.

88 Sqn. leading: BZ389: E (Wg. Cdr. J. F. Castle), BZ264: B, BZ225: C, BZ274: D, BZ278:, BZ221: H, BZ217: Q, BZ334:, BZ212: R, BZ328: Z, BZ255: U, BZ398: A.

107 Sqn.: BZ218: B (Sqn. Ldr. W. C. Maher), BZ372: F, BZ370: E, BZ323: Q, BZ285: G, BZ480: H, BZ213: C, BZ252: M, BZ333: U, BZ350:O, BZ308: T, BZ387: L.

Part II—24 Mitchell II led by Wg. Cdr. Phillips of 98 Sqn. Fighter rendezvous at 15.40 Dungeness. Escort—2 squadrons Spitfire V.

98 Sqn. leading: FV938: W, FV949, FV931: V, FL701: A, FL166: Q, FL181: R, FL704: S, FL202: T, FL168: H, FV934, FL173, FL176.

180 Sqn.: FL205: G, FR396: K, FV904, FL217, FL188: D, FV945: L, FV915: O, FL173: J, FL218: W, FL707, FV912, FL679, FL685: V (one reserve aircraft left at fighter rendezvous).

Part III—24 Mitchell II, 320 Sqn. leading. Bomber rendezvous Tonbridge 12,000 feet. 320 Sqn. began orbit there at Z plus 6 minutes, set course at Z plus 11 minutes at which time the two Swanton Morley squadrons joined on behind. Fighter rendezvous Dungeness Z plus 20 minutes. Escort—2 squadrons Spitfire V.

320 Sqn.: FR170: G, FR146: O, FR142: F, FR165: S, FR159: N, FR157: X.

226 Sqn.: FV924: H, FV910: G, FV936: A, FV900: F, SM-O (305 Sqn.), FR673: C, FV919: M, FV947: X, FR397: V, FV930: W, FV920: T, FL680: Z, FL196: J, FV935: U, SM-L (305 Sqn.).

305 Sqn.: FL691, FV913, FV923.

Fighter-bomber force:

Part I—24 'Bomphoons' detailed, 22 participated, from Tangmere. Operated in three boxes of 8. Crossed into enemy territory over Audrescelles, dive bombed from 10,000 feet. (i) 486 Sqn.: R8843, EJ973, JR186, JP495, JP688, JP667, JP532, JP501, EK948, JP901. (ii) 197 Sqn.: JP504: Z, JP928: W, JP680: S, JP843: T, JP743: R, EK141: X, JR243: C, JP970: L, JP967: F, JP787: K, JR185: I, DN548: H.

Part II—8 'Bomphoons' and 17 Typhoons from Manston. 195 and 198 Squadrons escorting Typhoon dive-bombers of 3 Squadron. Dive attack from 11,000 to 5,000 feet. (i) 3 Sqn.: take-off 14.50 hrs. R8926, JP734, JP684, JP534, EK370, JP511, JP847, JP741. (ii) 195 Sqn.: JP607, JP407, JP222, JP437, JP139, JP935, JP149, JP408. (iii) 198 Sqn.: X, Z, M, V, P, D, G, J, K. After attack the squadron was vectored to 10 miles west of Le Touquet to engage enemy aircraft, four of which were seen diving away into France. No combats.

Fighter escort:

Boston close escort provided by 64 and 611 Squadrons operating Spitfire Vs from Bradwell Bay.

64 Sqn.: X4257, BL581, AD542, AB423, BL370, BM481, BM414, AR387, BM514, AA972, BL374.

611 Sqn.: (Mk. V LF/LR) EE622, AB467, AA858, EP300, AB210, AR373, AB512, AB170, BL263, AB964.

Mitchell close escort provided by 402 and 416 Squadrons operating from forward base Tangmere, and 349 with 350 Squadrons operating from Friston and Southend respectively. All units used Spitfire V.

349 Sqn.: AR432, EP354, EE745, AA765, AR437, EE660, W3262, AR283, W3373, EP660, AR292, EN781.

350 Sqn.: EE723, BM652, EN854, W3898, AR498, EP240, AD428, AR492, BM344, EP644, W3899, BM468, AB931.

402 Sqn.: EE686, BM535, AB897, EP637, BL547, EN767, AR493, EP120, AR604, W3454.

416 Sqn.: EN950, W3226, EP707, AR383, EE685, W3456, EE637, AD413, AR516, EP206, BM471.

Fighter umbrella:

Afforded by five Spitfire squadrons, four flying Mk. IXs and 124 Squadron flying Mk. VIIs.

124 Sqn.: MB761, MB820, MB826, MB806, MB825, MB827, EN497, EN505.
132 Sqn.: MH978, MH738, MH497, MH431, MH758, MH474, MH737, MH453, MH719, MH427, MH452, MH486.
302 Sqn.: MH313 (returned early), MH853, BS433, MJ219, MH327, BS486, MA843, MA235, BS336, MA791, BS462, LZ989.
317 Sqn.: MH717, MH723, MH854, MH528, MH712, MH847, MH761, MH731, MH727, MH713, MH725, MH846.
602 Sqn.: MH479, MH488, MH709, MH721, MH972, MH512, MH492, MH708.

Intruder defence:
124 Squadron provided four Spitfire VIIs to form an anti-intruder protection screen for bombers landing at bases in southern England, using BS121 MB822, EN285, EN310.

Protective fighter sweeps:
Five fighter sweeps were flown to protect the bomber operation, a customary feature of large scale day raids by 2 Group and the U.S. 9th Air Force at this period. Participating squadrons were: Sweep 1 Nos. 41 and 91; Sweep 2 Nos. 19, 65 and 122; Sweep 3 Nos. 403 and 421; Sweep 4 Nos. 129 and 222 and Sweep 5 Nos. 331 and 332. Aircraft used were as follows:
41 Sqn.: MB840, MB830, MB797, MB847, EN237, MB794, MB838, MB837, MB829, EN605, MB798.
91 Sqn.: MB876 (flown by Wg. Cdr. Harries leading the Wing), MB839, MB803, MB618, MB851, MB621, MB859, MB833, MB849, MB841, MB613, MB324, MB615.
19 Sqn.: MH355, MA795, MA806, MA837, MH352, MA842, MH316, CH354, BS409, MH319, BS512, MA818.
65 Sqn.: MA835 (flown by Wg. Cdr. H. Bird-Wilson leading the Wing) MH851, MH328, MH873, MH908, MH388, MH378, MH824, EN473, MA420, MA845, MA847.
122 Sqn.: MA836, MH382, MH368, BS147, MA764, MA875, MA805, MH369, MA875, BS272 (returned early), MH383, MH318.
403 Sqn.: MH831, BS129, MH840, MA840, MA578, MA642, MA573, MA832, MH835, MH844, MH842, MA844, BS533.
421 Sqn.: MH903, MH939, MH907, MA713, BS398, BS152, BS200, MA226, MH832, MH881, MA849, MA582, BS126 (spare aircraft, returned early—not needed).
129 Sqn.: MH495: G, MJ137: Y, MH386: A, MH441: X, MH879: D, MH414: V, MH487: H, MH425: T, MH418: S, MH480: U, MH445: K.
222 Sqn.: MH434, MH430, MH423, MH432, MJ150, MH476, MH439, MH499, MH428, MH496, MH491, MH753.
331 Sqn.: MJ120: B, MJ224: K, MA528: Y, LZ921: C, BS466: M, MH936: Z, MA601: N, MA225: S, MA755: W, MJ225: R, MA568: L.
332 Sqn.: MH830 (Major K. Birksted leading the Wing), MA422, MA228, MH839, BS254, MA621, BS131, MA301, MH870, MA871, MA229, EN177.

Map 17 *pages 340/1.*
Ramrod 422—*4 January 1944*

Zero Hour: 15.45.
Pattern of the operation:

Part I—Six Mosquito VI of 21 Sqn. (HX984, HX981, HX955, LR294, LR301, HX969) and six of 613 Sqn. (LR262, LR276, LR299, HX977, LR271, LR273) to attack target X/1A/65 (V-1 site Ruisseauville). Over Forêt de Hesdin Wg. Cdr. Blair leading 613 Sqn. had loss of engine power, turned back followed by his squadron and three aircraft of 21 Sqn. Remaining three attacked. Five Mosquitoes of 487 Sqn. (B, R, U, Q, A) attacked Ruisseauville.

Part II—Twenty-four Bostons to attack target X/1A/40 Ligescourt. Force comprised 88 Sqn. (BZ389, BZ264, BZ274, BZ225, BZ221, BZ254, BZ217, BZ212, BZ228, BZ226, BZ205, BZ334), 107 Sqn. (BZ252: M, BZ387: L, BZ280: H, BZ333: U, BZ394: S and BZ372: F with BZ350: O reserve aircraft which returned from the bomber rendezvous) and 342 Sqn. (BZ376: T, BZ344: R, BZ290: O, BZ349: E, BZ318: G, BZ305: L). Close escort provided by Spitfire Vs—349 Sqn.: U-AB175(VB), EE745: Z(VC), AR432: G(VC), AR292: T(VB), W3373: X(VB), EP660: Q(VB), BL334: F(VB), AA751: K(VB), AR437: J(VB), BL642: C(VB) and AR432: G(VC, flown by Sqn. Ldr. de Monceau leading). 501 Sqn. (Mk. VB): W3702: M (Sqn. Ldr. M. G. Barnett), BM385: W, W3817: O, BM304: T, BL311: U, AB186: P, W3931: F, EP570: A, EP244: C, EP757: B, W3605: L. (Two aircraft detailed to positions below and aft of squadron to take photographs of target, attacked by eight Fw 190s. Flt. Sgt. Knight force-landed 5 miles north of Abbeville in BL311: U.)

Part III—Twelve Mitchells of 320 Sqn. to attack target X/1A/25 Yvrench/ Bois Wairipel. One aircraft bombed wrong target. Aircraft used: FR143: A, FR181: K, FR184: U, FR180: H, FR177: M, FR170: G, FR185: Z, FR176: P, FR182: R, FR175: W, FR179: T, FR165: S (leading). Close escort provided by Spitfire VBs of 322 Sqn., J, B, F, C, H, A, R, T, V, Q, N, Y.

Part IV—Twenty-four Mitchells to attack target X/1A/39 Yvrench/Bois Carré. Attacked from 9,300 ft. Bursts in wood with overshoots to north and some to west in Bois Wairipel. Q/98 Sqn. had all bombs hang-up, S/180 load jettisoned live in target area. Force comprised 98 Sqn. (FV938, FL704, FL181, FL166, FL219, FL202, FL701, FL168, FV928, FV927, FL674, FL698) and 180 Sqn. (FV916, FL173, FL685, FL185, FL201, FL675, FL679, FL684, FL689, FL217, FV945, FV904, FL695).
Close escort provided by Spitfire Vs—310 Sqn.: EE631, AR499, BL258, W3180, AD419, EP250, EP129, BM402, AB925, BL259, AR514, AD249; 312 Sqn.: BM567, EP661, EN961, AR504, EE691, EP411, AD425, R6890, AR501, BP863.

General high cover in Somme–Abbeville area:
306 Sqn. (Spitfire V) Wg. Cdr. Zak leading the Wing, with A, L, E, M, K, T, V, U and two unknown aircraft.
315 Sqn. (Spitfire V) BM458, W3412, P8744, AB790, EP133, EE624, AB490, EP604.

331 Sqn. (Spitfire IX) MA828: Y (Major A. Austen leading the Wing) MA601: N, MA568: L, MH940: D, BS148: B, EN522: J, EN130: A, MA528: E, MH936: Z, BS125: M, LZ920: T, MJ225: R. (BS148 and EN130 collided soon after take-off.)

332 Sqn. (Spitfire IX) MA301, MH910, MA810, MH870, MH935, BS393, BS254, MH839, MA303, MA621, MJ220.

Map 18 *pages 370/1.*
Aircraft used on Operations on 27–28 July 1944

(i) Mosquito FB.VI:

21 Squadron: NT170, NT124, NS990, LR402, NS935, NT197, HX952, NS884, LR291, NS889, NT195, NS898, HR194, NS903.

464 Squadron: NS943, NT231, LR256, MM403, HX977, HR187, HR185, HR175, NT143, MM423, HX858, NT236, NT144, NT229.

487 Squadron: NS829: W, NS963: H, LR299: V, NS834: G, HX856: L, NT184: P, PZ164: K, NT171: F, HP924: T, HR144: J, HP933: U, NT144: A, NS937: E, LR333: R, HP933: B.

107 Squadron: NS910: T, LR257: F, NS908: N, NS958: R, HJ771: J, NS820: P, NS831: O, NS952: S, NS833: V, LR264: X, NT136: A, NS912: C, NT226: G, LR336: W, NS855: Q.

613 Squadron: NS848, LR369, LR302, HP828, LR354, LR366, HP927, NS898, HR199, NS877, NT124, NS977, LR374, NS859, NS899, MM408.

305 Squadron: A: LR303, D: LR295, Q: LR262, J: LR365, L: NS909, E: NT175, F: NT193, M: NS888, C: NS927, B: NS846, K: NS887, N: LR300, P: NS824, U: NT198, W: NS913.

(ii) Boston IIIA:

88 Squadron: BZ412: M, BZ210: A, BZ425: T, BZ301: J, BZ398: L, BZ239: K, BZ229: U, BZ357: X, BZ378: H, BZ411: R, BZ455: S, BZ236: G, BZ196: E, BZ382: C.

342 Squadron: BZ302: B, BZ352: V, BZ294: O, BZ285: Q, BZ338: P, BZ358: N, BZ372: R, BZ312: E, BZ252: J, BZ332: T, BZ208: A, BZ206: G, BZ261: L, BZ258: F, BZ334: H, BZ259: S.

(iii) Mitchell II:

98 Squadron: FW189: A, FW256: Y, FW211: F, FL182: J, FW173: G, FW275: F, FV976: L, FL176: B, FW168: U, FW256: W, FW264: S, FW203: T.

180 Squadron: FW135, FW161, —?—, FW228, FV928, FW158, FW172, FW170, FW125, FW269, FW206, FW199.

226 Squadron: FW111: T, FW146: P (aband.), FW130: A, FW105: C, FW196: E, FW171: G, FW174: M, FW216: S, FW195: Q, FW153: F, FW186: R, FW152: V, FW163: Y, FW160: U, FV919: H.

320 Squadron: FR189: F, FR196: T, FR190: E, FR188: H, FR160: J, FR143: S.

Map 19 *pages 390/1.*
    Aircraft on Group Strength 1 January 1945

2 Group Continental:

Vitry-en-Artois: (137 Wing)	88 Squadron	5 Boston IIIA BZ273, BZ326, BZ357, BZ378; 14 Boston IV BZ407, BZ408, BZ415, BZ428, BZ432, BZ433, BZ434, BZ442, BZ447, BZ448, BZ453, BZ454, BZ456, BZ458.
	226 Squadron	19 Mitchell II FV916, FV920, FV950, FW143, FW180, FW181, FW195, FW204, FW217, FW222, FW233, FW239, FW241, FW245, FW271, FW276, HD303, HD304, HD336; 2 Mitchell III HD348, HD354.
	342 Squadron	10 Boston IIIA BZ196, BZ206, BZ275, BZ284, BZ303, BZ352, BZ362, BZ370, BZ374, BZ381; 12 Boston IV BZ420, BZ424, BZ426, BZ429, BZ436, BZ440, BZ441, BZ443, BZ446, BZ450, BZ452, BZ457.
Cambrai/Epinoy: (138 Wing)	107 Squadron	20 Mosquito FB VI HR145, HR189, HR246, HR249, HR254, HR296, HR350, NS833, NS836, NS853, NS910, NS958, NT128, PZ222, PZ225, PZ232, PZ258, PZ336, PZ376, PZ392.
	305 Squadron	22 Mosquito FB VI HR191, HR253, HR360, HX980, LR303, LR365, NS844, NS887, NS927, NS909, NT193, NT227, NT233, NT234, PZ236, PZ299, PZ335, PZ357, PZ371, PZ374, PZ383, —?—.
	613 Squadron	22 Mosquito FB VI HJ666, HP927, HR199, HR207, HR247, HX828, LR302, LR338, LR351, LR353, MM408, NS827, NS828, NS848, NS859, NS899, NS977, NT230, PZ229, PZ289, PZ310, PZ375.
	417 A.R.F.	52 Mosquito FB VI HR181, HR184, HR188, HR242, LR356, NS884, NS999, NT234, PZ307, PZ349, PZ378, PZ380, PZ384, PZ389, PZ391, PZ399, PZ400, PZ401, PZ402, PZ403, PZ407, PZ409, PZ452, PZ454, PZ462, PZ484, RS522, RS526, RS528, RS529, RS530, RS532, RS533, RS534, RS551, RS553, RS557, RS558, RS559, RS560, RS563, RS567, RS569, RS570, RS573, RS599, RS600, RS603 and four unknown.
	416 R. & S.U.	5 Mosquito FB VI HR192, HR202, PZ273, PZ304, PZ404.

Melsbroek: (139 Wing)	2 Group Communica- tions Squadron	Mosquito IV DZ444, Mosquito FB VI NS840, Ansons, Proctors.
	98 Squadron	19 Mitchell II FL166, FV929, FV969, FV974, FV983, FV982, FW168, FW182, FW192, FW203, FW215, FW218, FW224, FW225, FW229, FW252, FW256, FW262, FW277; 8 Mitchell III HD350, HD351, HD363, HD365, HD371, HD376, HD380, HD390.
	180 Squadron	18 Mitchell II FV903, FV945, FV965, FW172, FW185, FW191, FW199, FW200, FW202, FW214, FW225, FW236, FW240, FW238, FW261, FW264, HD305, HD307; 3 Mitchell III HD360, HD375, KJ586.
	320 Squadron	15 Mitchell II FR161, FR168, FR181, FR183, FR188, FR193, FR198, FR199, FR200, FR202, FR207, FV970, FW178, FW227, HD306; 2 Mitchell III HD346, HD392.
Evere:	416 A.R.F.	1 Mitchell II FR145; 3 Mitchell III HD382, HD398, KJ587.
	416 R. & S.U.	6 Mitchell II FW206, FW208, FW212, FW213, FW255, FW275; 2 Mitchell III KJ592, KJ594.
2 Group Rear: Hartford Bridge: (136 Wing)	418 Squadron	22 Mosquito FB VI HJ821, HR148, HR151, HR195, HR343, HR351, HR358, MM426, NS823, NS830, NS849, NS857, NS930, NS991, NT115, NT152, PZ199, PZ235, PZ388, PZ396, PZ397, PZ458.
	605 Squadron	18 Mosquito FB VI HR152, HR203, HR205, HR206, HR338, HR349, MM415, NS826, NS914, NT153, NT155, PZ312, PZ343, PZ373, PZ377, PZ381, PZ390, PZ453.
Thorney Island: (138 Wing)	21 Squadron	19 Mosquito FB VI HR162, HR345, HR348, LR353, LR402, NS834, NS843, NS889, NS903, NS911, NS990, NT174, NT197, NT200, PZ297, PZ305, PZ306, PZ314, PZ316.
	464 Squadron	26 Mosquito FB VI HP924, HR175, HR186, HR352, HR353, HX920, MM398, MM403, MM407, MM427, NS890, NS896, NS994, NT131, NT144, NT177, NT231, NT236, PZ259, PZ309, PZ350, PZ353, PZ463, PZ464 and two more.
	487 Squadron	21 Mosquito FB VI HP933, HR177,

                                      HR182, HR337, HR339, HR340,
MM412, NS834, NS840, NS894, NS963,
NS964, NS981, NT123, NT171, PZ195,
PZ330, PZ331, PZ332, PZ339, PZ449.

Fersfield:	2 Group Support Unit	1 Boston IIIA BZ248; 11 Mitchell II FL182, FL183, FL673, FL680, FL699, FR157, FR208, FV962, FV979, FW157, FW242; 1 Mitchell III HD386; 2 Mosquito T. III HJ886, HJ778; 21 Mosquito FB VI HP925, HR178, HX833, HX919, HX969, LR284, LR294, LR298, LR372, MM416, NS832, NS833, NS854, NS883, NS891, NS904, NS926, NT133, RS519, RS601 and one more.

Map 22 *pages 408/9.*
Aircraft on Group Strength 1 May 1945

(i) Units equipped with Mosquito FB VI:

Volkel:	418 Squadron	HJ764, HR184, HR343, HR358, HX803, NS823, NS991, PZ219, RS531, RS560, RS594, RS613, SZ961, SZ962, SZ964, SZ965, SZ976, SZ991, TA374.
	605 Squadron	HR203, HR205, HR338, HR349, HX953, NS936, NT114, NT153, NT155, PZ312, PZ355, PZ373, PZ377, PZ453, RS557, SZ967, SZ980, SZ984, TA381, TA383.
Melsbroek:	21 Squadron	HR348, HR359, NS834, NS843, NT124, NT174, NT200, PZ297, PZ306, PZ307, PZ382, PZ471, RS551, RS573, RS599, SZ981, SZ996.
	305 Squadron	HR113, HR145, HR202, HR346, NS887, NT233, PZ335, PZ357, PZ383, PZ391, PZ401, RS528, RS559, SZ978, SZ982, TA378.
	464 Squadron	HP988, HR352, HR353, LR256, LR334, NS884, NS896, NS911, PZ353, PZ378, PZ473, RS617, SZ966, SZ968, SZ979.
	487 Squadron	HR340, HX856, NS894, NS999, PZ330, PZ331, PZ339, PZ392, PZ449, RS570, SZ985, SZ994.
Cambrai/Epinoy:	107 Squadron	HR181, HR189, HR246, HR354, HX832, NS958, PZ222, PZ241, PZ336, PZ376, PZ403, RS530, RS605, TA375, TA376.
	613 Squadron	HR207, HR220, HX828, LR264, NS898, PZ229, PZ273, PZ310, PZ393, PZ399, RS535, RS553, RS558, RS600, RS611, SZ970, SZ989, TA377, TA384.
	417 A.R.F.	HP924, HR337, PR295, PR362, NS903, NS914, NS994, NT144, NT152, PZ199,

		PZ221, PZ454, PZ463, PZ472, SZ993, TA379, TA380, TA388.
	417 R. & S.U.	MM412, NS853, TA373.

(ii) Units equipped with Mitchell II and III:

Achmer:	98 Squadron	4 Mitchell II FW192, FW201, FW218, FW229; 18 Mitchell III HD351, HD368, HD396, KJ564, KJ570, KJ576, KJ577, KJ591, KJ594, KJ621, KJ622, KJ624, KJ627, KJ633, KJ638, KJ644, KJ658, KJ674.
	180 Squadron	3 Mitchell II FV965, FW208, FW240; 19 Mitchell III HD374, KJ567, KJ573, KJ589, KJ592, KJ610, KJ612, KJ639, KJ649, KJ652, KJ656, KJ657, KJ665, KJ682, KJ684, KJ694, KJ705, KJ729, KJ736.
Melsbroek:	320 Squadron	10 Mitchell II FR145, FR157, FR159, FR161, FR163, FR183, FR198, FR199, FR200, FR207; 7 Mitchell III HD346, HD358, HD362, HD367, HD392, KJ596, KJ603.
Gilze-Rijen:	226 Squadron	2 Mitchell II FW213, FW245; 20 Mitchell III HD353, HD355, HD357, HD362, HD378, HD383, HD384, HD389, HD400, KJ561, KJ571, KJ572, KJ599, KJ608, KJ613, KJ616, KJ626, KJ635, KJ667, KJ672.
	342 Squadron	2 Mitchell II FW153, HD306; 15 Mitchell III HD379, KJ565, KJ568, KJ575, KJ585, KJ598, KJ609, KJ618, KJ630, KJ642, KJ645, KJ651, KJ666, KJ678, KJ687.
Evere:	416 A.R.F.	31 Mitchell III HD382, HD393, KJ566, KJ579, KJ593, KJ601, KJ606, KJ614, KJ620, KJ628, KJ640, KJ643, KJ653, KJ659, KJ660, KJ662, KJ679, KJ680, KJ681, KJ683, KJ689, KJ699, KJ701, KJ709, KJ732, KJ742, KJ746, KJ755, KJ763, KJ768.
	416 R. & S.U.	5 Mitchell II FW214, FW264, FW271, FW275, FW277; 9 Mitchell III HD375, HD377, KJ569, KJ574, KJ629, KJ631, KJ632, KJ691, KJ697.
Fersfield:	2 Group Support Unit	1 Mitchell II FV979; 8 Mitchell III HD369, HD395, HD399, KJ600, KJ605, KJ623, KJ677, KJ690,; 12 Mosquito VI HP925, HR190, HR347, HX833, HX980, LR298, LR365, MM416, NS832, NS903, PZ462, RS601.

Index